TANTRĀBHIDHĀNA

A Tantric Lexicon

TANTRĀBHIDHĀNA

A Tantric Lexicon

N.N. BHATTACHARYYA

MANOHAR
2002

First published 2002

ISBN 81-7304-439-2

Published by
Ajay Kumar Jain for
Manohar Publishers & Distributors
4753/23, Ansari Road, Daryaganj
New Delhi 110 002

Typeset by
P.K. Goel for
Aditya Prakashan
Delhi 110 002

Printed at
Lordson Publishers Pvt. Ltd.
Delhi 110 007

To the memory
of my Father
Late Bhupendra Nath Bhattacharyya

Contents

Preface

The title of the present work is self-explanatory. Though it is similar to Sir John Woodroffe's well-known work (comprising *Bījanighaṇṭu* and *Mudrānighaṇṭu*, published in *Tantrik Texts*, Vol. I, London and Calcutta, 1913), its scope is much wider and it is, unlike that of the aforesaid celebrated Tantric scholar, non-technical in nature, meant only for average persons interested in the Tantras. In my *History of Tantric Religion* (first published in 1982: Manohar, New Delhi), I incorporated a glossary of Tantric technical terms but those entries were selective, made only for a limited purpose. The present volume is comprehensive. Apart from dealing with the Tantric terms and concepts pertaining to the theoretical and practical aspects of all forms of Indian religious systems, it also contains entries on extra-religious contents of Tantrism such as chemical and medical sciences, philosophical speculations especially on metaphysics and epistemology, yoga and psychical exercises. Tantric deities are also dealt with—the hundreds of gods and goddesses who have no independent and real existence apart from the mind of the worshipper and the manner of worship. Tantric texts, with brief details of their content and publication, are given. All the important entries contain textual references which will prove useful for scholars and researchers. The present volume also contains a large and updated bibliography and a comprehensive introduction. Since it is not possible to list all the terms in the form of individual entries in this lexicon, a classified index dealing separately with terms and concepts, deities, texts, etc., has been given which will help the reader to find the reference even when it is not in the main body of the entries.

NARENDRA NATH BHATTACHARYYA

Joraghat
P.O. Chinsurah 712 101
W. Bengal

Introduction

The study of Tantrism has been handicapped and complicated by the preoccupations of the writers in this field which have given rise to various theoretical approaches, each claiming to explain all the intricacies of the subject in its own way. Among these, the traditional Indian viewpoint equates it with the totality of Hinduism and declares it to be the essence of the Vedas. Those who uphold this view justify their stand saying that Tantric ideas are so inextricably blended with different aspects of the Hindu way of life, and with doctrines of various religious sects and communities including those of the Buddhists as well, that it becomes difficult to separate the Tantric elements from the huge conglomeration of materials accrued in space and time. The more critical among writers on Tantrism are, however, aware of the fact that the Tantric texts in their present form are burdened with superimposed elements, that at different periods of Indian religious history though Tantric writers and commentators wanted to base their doctrines on the Vedas, the orthodox followers of the Vedic tradition denounced Tantrism stressing its anti-Vedic character.

Among the modern approaches, is the Western psychological approach which seeks to explore the obscure zone of the unconscious with the Tantric key. Such writers seek to find certain norms in Tantrism with a pragmatic anticipation of the peculiar mental, emotional and spiritual problems of our times. To these so-called obscure zones of the unconscious are attributed the problems of man's physiological, social, cultural and religious conditioning. This has eventually resulted in the study of the so-called sexual elements found in the Tantras which have been interpreted by the traditionalists as 'purely symbolical' and by the others as 'appliedly symbolical'. Anyone working on Tantrism cannot ignore the sexual elements, but the difficulty arises when the entire Tantric tradition is superimposed on these elements. This is due to the insistence on a 'misplaced reality' which even the most qualified scholars could not avoid.

Historically one has to admit that certain Tantric ideas and practices are evidently rooted in primitive sex rites based on fertility magic. One should remember that such primitive sex rites contributed everywhere to the development of religious ideas and, in a broad sense, to the evolution of human thought as a whole. The *dehavāda* (theory and practices related to the human body) and cosmogony of Tantrism are but elaborations of the corollaries of a most primitive belief, and Sāṅkhya philosophy is originally a development of the primitive proto-materialism which forms the substratum of Tantrism itself. The ancient empirical and analogical belief in the equation of earth and woman, of natural and human fertility, forms the infrastructure of numerous agricultural rites and reveals the mode of securing the material means of subsistence. It invariably connects the mystery of nature with that of the human body; from this equation it transpires that the birth of the universe is the result of a similar process as the birth of human beings.

Tantric sex rites have something to do with the Phrygian mysteries associated with the cult of Kubele or Cybele, the Eleusinian mysteries observed in Greece and in the Hellenistic colonies, those associated with the rituals of the Egyptian Osiris and Isis and the Chinese Taoist secret doctrines and practices. Ideas similar to primitive Tantric cosmogony may also be traced to the myths of the vegetative cycles current in Western Asia and in the Mediterranean and Aegean region which were clustered around a great goddess and her young subordinate male partner—the Devī and her Bhairava of the Tantric tradition. The psychophysical personality of the goddess was perhaps attributed to the woman of flesh and blood whose energy was thought to be transmitted to the psychic centres or planes of consciousness of the aspirant impersonating her male partner, thus calling forth a new orientation to the earlier formulation of Indian yoga. The concept of *yoni*, female organ or female womb, as the First Principle (cf. the list of cosmogonical theories in the *Śvetāśvatara Upaniṣad*) found its best theoretical expression in the Śāṅkhya concept of Prakṛti or Pradhāna, the material, as also the Female Principle of creation, the substratum of the earlier Tantras.

Many Tantric authors and commentators based their doctrines on the Vedas—not without reasons, as we shall presently see—and interpreted the contents of the Tantras in the Vedic perspective. The origins of the Tantras, however, are to be sought not in the Vedic tradition but in an alternative tradition as manifested in numerous non-Brahmanical and heterodox scientific and technological treatises; in regional, tribal and popular cults and their beliefs and practices; and on the broad background of the history of Indian thought in general. Tantra rejects the caste system and patriarchy as also all external formalities in regard to the spiritual quest, in virtual opposition to what is upheld in the Smārta-Paurāṇic tradition. From the earliest period to the end of the medieval age, Indian literature shows a set of ideas, and corresponding practices, different from the officially acknowledged norm. These have found expression in the beliefs and rituals of the Auls, Bauls, Sahajiyās, Kāpālikas, Nāthas, Lokāyatas and various other sects, all of which come within the purview of Tantra. They hold that the clue to the mysteries of the universe is to be sought in the Tantric maxim: That which is not in the body is not in the universe.

In accordance with the established norms followed by different schools of thought, the Tantras also speak about the problems of human bondage and suggest various means of liberation (*mokṣa, mukti, nirvāṇa*). But there are reasons to hold that in the Tantras originally the liberation of the soul was not conceived of as *puruṣārtha* or the aim of life. Rather we have the concept of *jīvan-mukti* or 'liberation within the span of life' in the form of the attainment of immortality which is found patronized in a good number of Tantric texts. The achievement of material immortality (cf. the Chinese Taoist concept of *hsien*) is possible by dietary techniques, heliotherapeutic techniques, gymnastic techniques (*haṭhayoga* and *kāyasādhana*) respiratory techniques (*prāṇāyāma*) and alchemical and pharmaceutical techniques (*rāsāyana*). The idea of rendering the human body deathless, by varied physio-chemical processes, and also the liberation of man by his monadic transformation is found. The use of mercurial drugs was one step in the process of overcoming death—it aimed at purifying and curing the cells, tissues and organs of the body. Later, the concept of a celestial substance, as against the material substance, forming the body was invented. This became the basis of a new theory of transmutation insisting on *divya-tanu* or divine and non-material body. The issue then came under the domain of subjective speculation.

In the pre-Vedic Harappa civilization, the Mother Goddess figurines, scenes on seals and ritual objects, and representations of the male and female organs in stone give glimpses of Tantric survivals of magic fertility rites that formed the basis of primitive Tantrism and of the deities arising out of them. In Tantra, as also in popular Hinduism, male and female organs stand for Śiva and Devī, and the prototype of the former is found in the posture of a yogin in several seals from Harappa and Mohenjodaro. The Vedic texts contain Tantric elements in profusion. The Vedic sacrifices of royal inauguration as well as the collective Satra-yāgas contain various types of sex rites. In the Vedic texts very often sexual union is identified with *yajña* or sacrifice. Numerous passages of the *Śatapatha Brāhmaṇa* stress the ritual efficacy of sexual union. The Vāmadevya Sāman of the *Chāndogya Upaniṣad* (II. 1) is the precursor of the Tantric *pañcatattva* (cf. ibid V. 8). The same may be said of the *Bṛhadāraṇyaka* (VI. 2; VI. 4). Besides the sex rites the Ṣaṭ-karmas of the Tantras, such as *māraṇa, vaśīkaraṇa*, etc., are mentioned in different parts of Vedic literature. Many of the Atharvanic practices of withchcraft are almost identical with similar practices of the Tantras. Traces of monosyllabic *mantras*, on the importance of which the Tantras lay so much emphasis, are also to be found in Vedic literature. The *Atharvaveda* is highly eulogized in the Tantric tradition. In fact, the supreme goddess is described as Atharvaveda-śākhinī.

The Jain texts refer to Tantric practices current among contemporary sects. Tantrism in the form of the Mother Goddess cult, magical rites like the Ṣaṭ-karmas, curative spells, incantations, efficacy of *mantra*, etc., are also met with in Jainism. Mahāvīra is said to have performed numerous miracles. Tantric elements in Jainism came about in the same way as in the case of Buddhism. It is quite possible that many followers or practitioners of Tantra were converted to Buddhism and that this class of people was responsible for introducing Tantric ideas and practices into the Buddhist order. Early Vaiṣṇavism was also influenced by Tantrism. Pāñcarātra Āgamas such as the *Lakṣmītantra* are regarded as authoritative even by the followers of the Śākta school.

According to the Pāñcarātra Āgamas, the Śakti or energy of Viṣṇu has the double aspect of *kriyā* and *bhūti*, answering to force and matter, and this effects the creation of the world. In the *Viṣṇu Purāṇa* the Female Principle is regarded as Mahālakṣmī. There are passages in the *Mārkaṇḍeya Purāṇa* which describe the goddess as Viṣṇumāyā, the *śakti* or energy of Viṣṇu, and Nārāyanī, the wife of Nārāyaṇa. The Mātṛkās have also been connected with early Vaiṣṇavism. It is to be noted in this connection that from the orthodox point of view both the Pāñcarātra and the Pāśupata systems are regarded as Vedabāhya, i.e. belonging outside the pale of the Vedas. The *caryās* or practices of the Pāśupata Śaivas, subdivided into *vrata* (vows) and *dvāra* (door), remind us of certain Tantric practices. With reference to the Pāśupatas Bhaṭṭa Utpala says that their scripture is known as *Vātula-tantra* which means 'the *tantra* of the lunatics'. In fact, there is actually a Śaiva Āgama of the same name.

Mahāyāna Buddhism was subdivided into two schools—Pāramitānaya and Mantranaya. The latter, also known as Mantrayāna, was the precursor of Vajrayāna and its offshoots—Kālacakrayāna and Sahajayāna. The Vajrayāna introduced the theory of five Dhyānī Buddhas as embodiments of the five *skandhas* or cosmic elements, formulated the theory of their *kulas* or families and also that of their emanations, the male and female deities. It also introduced the cult of Prajñā or Śakti. In Buddhist Tantras, the male and female principles are known as Karuṇā and Śūnyatā, or Upāya and Prajñā. The union of Prajñā and Upāya is *yuganaddha* or *samarasa*. The union of man and woman, symbolizing that of Upāya and Prajñā, produces *mahāsukha*, the greatest pleasure, the experience of perfect nonduality. Vajrayāna considers Śūnya, or void, as the ultimate reality and innumerable gods and goddesses as its manifestations. The gods have no real existence; they are born of the mind, issuing from the *bījamantras* uttered by the worshipper. Śūnya takes different forms according to different functions it has to discharge. The cosmic concept of Śūnya (or void) is equated with Bodhicitta which has been defined as the mind bent on attaining perfect enlightenment. Kālacakrayāna is an offshoot of Vajrayāna which came into vogue in the tenth century and also became popular in Tibet and China. It is a system of yoga in which, all its accessories of *maṇḍala* (magic circle) and all phenomenal objects are brought to be located within the body. The word Kālacakra means 'the wheel of time'. By *kāla* is denoted the ultimate immutable and unchanging reality in all the elements; and by *cakra* is meant the unity of the three kinds of existence. As such, Kālacakra is the same as the unity of Prajñā and Upāya. The Sahajayāna considers the human body itself as the seat of all human experience including that of *sahajamahāsukha* which is the peaceful, blissful, radiant and waveless experience of *sahaja*. In the matter of sexo-yogic practices, the Sahajiyā Buddhists go further than the Vajrayānists by laying greater emphasis on the imperative necessity of making the body sufficiently strong and fit before starting with yogic processes, and the conception of an internal female force in the *nirmāṇacakra* (the navel region) corresponding to that of the kulakuṇḍalinī Śakti of the non-Buddhist Tantras.

The concept of Śakti is found in the doctrines of various medieval Vaiṣṇava sects. The Śrīvaiṣṇava school of Rāmānuja holds that the relation between Viṣṇu and his Śakti is inseparable, such as the connection of substance and quality. According to the school of Nimbārka at the beginning of creation *brahman* manifests its *cit-śakti* (power of sentience) and *acit-śakti* (power of non-sentience) in the forms of Soul and Prakṛti, and from the latter there is a gradual evolution of the material world. Thus there is a slight difference between the cause and the effect despite their identity in principle. The concept of Śakti is also present in the dualistic school of Madhva and in the Śuddhādvaita school of Vallabha. According to the Acintyabhedābheda school of Śrī-Caitanya, there are three main *śaktis* of *brahman*: *svarūpa* or *cit* (sentient), *māyā* (non-sentient), and *jīva* (intermediate). The universe is created with the help of *māyā-śakti* which has two aspects, *guṇa-māya* and *jīva-māyā*. *Śakti* is conceived of by Rāmānuja and Madhva as Lakṣmī and by Nimbārka, Vallabha and Caitanya as Rādhā. The Parakīyā theory of Vaiṣṇavism evidently derives its main impulses from the Sahajayāna of the Buddhists. In Orissa, the Tanric goddess Ekānaṃśā was able to find her way into the Vaiṣṇava religion as the consort of Kṛṣṇa. The tribal god Jagannātha was taken into the fold of Vaiṣṇavism but Tantric rites associated with his cult continue to exist even today. According to the Śakta-Tantric tradition, the presiding deity of

Śrīkṣetra is the goddess Vimalā and Jagannātha is her consort or Bhairava. The increasing reciprocal relation between Tantrism and Vaiṣṇavism is attested to by the fact that the ten Avatāras of Viṣṇu have been correlated with the ten Mahāvidyā goddesses in the Tantric texts.

The three main schools of Śaivism are basically Tantric and their texts are regarded as authoritative by the followers of the Śākta Tantras as well. The Śaiva Siddhānta of south India explains the evolution of the world in terms of 36 principles or *tattvas* which are recognized by all other Śaiva and Śākta schools. A specific Tantric branch of the Śaiva Siddhānta is known as Āgamānta Śaivism. The Vīraśaivism of Karnataka is in fact a doctrine of Śakti which is why it is called Śakti-Viśiṣṭādvaitavāda. The Śākta-Tantrics claim Kashmir Śaivism to be their own system and its exponents such as Vasugupta, Somānanda, Abhinavagupta, Kṣemarāja, etc., are reputed names in the Tantric tradition. The Kāpālikas and Kālāmukhas were two Tantric offshoots of Pāśupata Śaivism. Together with the Aghorapanthīs and Kāruṇikasiddhāntis they were regarded as Atimārgikas (extremists) and were treated with contempt by their contemporary religious teachers and philosophers. In the absence of any literature of their own whatever is known about them comes from their opponents. The Mattamayūras of central India should also be mentioned in this connection. This sect held a liberal view regarding religious practices and insisted on yoga and social work. Their sacred texts form a significant part of Tantric literature. Among the six branches of the Gāṇapatyas the worshippers of Ucchiṣṭa Gaṇapati were followers of Tantrism.

Though most Indian religious systems were greatly influenced by Tantric ideas and practices, it was in Śāktism that Tantrism found a ground for its manifold development. From the Śākta point of view, Tantric aspirants belong to three categories—Paśu, Vīra and Divya—each representing a stage of *sādhanā*. Paśu denotes individual souls, average human beings. By moral efforts Paśu is transformed into Vīra, a qualitatively higher personality. Divya is a still higher stage which is achieved by an individual when his acquired qualities become an intrinsic part of himself. There are seven forms of Tantric *sādhanā*: Vedic, Vaiṣṇava, Śaiva, Dakṣiṇa, Vāma, Siddhānta and Kaula. The first three are meant for persons belonging to the Paśu category, fourth and fifth for persons who have reached the Vīra stage, and the sixth and seventh for those of the Divya rank. The aspirant should keep in mind that the Guru is no other than god; he has to receive initiation (*dīkṣā*) which is basically of three kinds—Śāmbhavī, Śāktī and Māntrī. The mantras have a very important place in Tantrism. The power of Mantra is two-fold—*vācaka* and *vācya*—the first revealing the nature of the second. Words constituting the Mantra are made of sound; the subtle state of sound is *bindu* and the subtler state *nāda*. The expression of sound is possible through letters, hence the letter is *bīja* (seed) of a Mantra. Just as a banyan tree remains in subtle form in the seed, so also the entire doctrine remains subtle in the *bīja* which is why the letter is also known as Mātṛkā. *Bindu* is the symbol of Śiva, *bija* of Śakti and *nāda* of their union.

Underlying Tantric cosmogony is the ancient belief that the body is the microcosm of the universe, therefore *kāmakalā* (the sexual process) is responsible for the creation of the world. The Tantric aspirants imitate this *kāmakalā* through symbolic or actual union with their female partners. The nature of creation is like a wheel continually revolving. Śakti, having issued from its source, completes a cycle of creation, preservation, destruction, and then returns to its source again. The process is imitated by the rite of the awakening of *kuṇḍalinī* and the *ṣaṭcakrabheda*. Śakti remains latent as the serpent power (*kuṇḍalinī*) in the *mūlādhāra-cakra* of the human body. This is to be awakened and sent to the *sahasrāra* (the highest cerebral region) through different *cakras* (nerve-cycles) (*svādhiṣṭhāna*, *maṇipura*, *anāhata*, *ājña* and *viśuddhi*) situated within the body. This is how Śakti meets its source. The *cakras* offer a bewildering variety of ideas. These appear to have been originally conceived in terms of a physiological viewpoint, representing the coccygeal, sacral, lumbar, dorsal and cervical plexuses. The Tantric theory regarding the *cakras* is concerned on the physiological side or the *bhogāyatana* aspect with the central spinal system, comprising the brain or encephalon contained within the skull, and the spinal cord contained within the vertebral column which itself is divided into the said five regions starting from the coccygeal and corresponding to the *cakras* starting from the *mūlādhāra*. At a subsequent stage, in conformity with the Tantric idea that the human body is the microcosm of the universe, worldly objects such as the sun, moon, mountains, rivers, etc., were connected with these *cakras*. Each *cakra* was thought to represent the gross and subtle elements. The latter again, as *tattvas*, are connected with the sense-organs. The Buddhist Tantras speak of three *cakras—dharma*, *sambhoga* and *nirmāṇa*—situated near the heart, neck and navel region. And also there is *uṣṇīṣakamala* in the cerebral region which corresponds to the Hindu *sahasrāra*. The female energy, known as *caṇḍālī*, which resides in the *nirmāṇa cakra* becomes accelerated like the *kuṇḍalinī*, kindles the *dharma* and *sambhoga cakras* and ultimately reaches the *uṣṇīṣakamala*.

In Tantrism Mantra denotes a power (*śakti*) in the form of sound (*śabda*) which is of four kinds. The first, *parā*, is the motionless causal sound conceived of as existing in the *kuṇḍalinī* in the *mūlādhāra-cakra* in the dreamless state of deep sleep (*suṣupti*). The second, *vaikharī*, is the gross sound, the uttered speech by which the ideas are expressed. The third and the fourth, *paśyantī* and *madhyamā*, are in between these two, the former representing a non-particularized motion (*sāmānya-spanda*) and the latter a cognitive aspect of mental movement. *Mantras* are not meant for propitiating gods; rather gods are produced from *mantras* according to the requirement of the aspirant. The unmanifested power of *śabda* (*avyakta-rava*) is the cause of manifested *śabda* (specialized in the forms of letters, words and sentences) and *artha* (meaning, object). There are a large number of short unetymological vocables or *bījas* such as *hrim, krim, huṃ, phat*, etc. These are abbreviations of the names of the deities and their functions, and are of three kinds—masculine, feminine and neuter. The proper intonation in the recitation of the *bījas* makes the meditation perfect and the deities are forced to appear before the aspirant. In the first stage it is known as Devatāsiddhi or god-attainment. The second stage is Jīvanasiddhi or the fulfilment of life which opens the door of direct knowledge.

The repetition of *mantras* is called *puraścaraṇa* in Tantric language. In a broader sense the rite consists of *dhyāna* or meditation, worship, *japa* or muttering of *mantra*, *homa* or fire-offering, *tarpana* (remembrance), etc. All the Tantric texts and digests have a chapter or section on *puraścaraṇa*. Another important method of Tantric worship is *nyāsa* which consists of feeling the god in different parts of the body. There are several kinds of *nyāsa* such as *haṃsa*, *praṇava*, *mātṛkā*, *mantra*, *kara*, *aṅga*, *pīṭha*, etc. Two other forms of Tantric worship are *maṇḍala* and *yantra*. *Maṇḍalas* for ordinary Tantric worships are geometrical diagrams to be drawn on the ground with powder of five colours. *Yantra* or *cakra* is also a geometrical diagram but it is engraved, drawn or painted on objects. While *maṇḍala* is employed in worship of deities in general, the *yantra* is for a particular deity and for a special purpose. One of the most popular forms of the *yantras* is *Śrīcakra*. There are nine *yonis* (female organs), five of which have their apex pointing downwards, and these represent Śakti.

While prescribing ways and means for the awakening of *kuṇḍalinī-śakti* the Tantras insist on yoga, the method by which the mental and intellectual feelings (*citta vṛtti*) are controlled and conditioned so that the aspirant is able to dissolve his own self into the absolute, the supreme reality as conceived by him. Yoga is generally classified into four categories. Among these, Mantra-yoga comprises all those forms of *sādhanā* in which the mind is controlled by means of its own object. Haṭha-yoga comprises those *sādhanās* which are concerned primarily with the control of gross or physical body for conditioning the subtle body. The word *haṭha* is composed of the syllables *ha* and *ṭha*, symbolizing the sun and the moon, the Prāṇa and Apāna *vāyus* respectively. The union of these two vital airs in the *susumnā* is called *prāṇāyāma*. The practice and exercises of Haṭha-yoga are divided into seven parts. The exercises of *Laya-yoga*, which is specially connected with the functioning of *kuṇḍalinī*, are required to revitalize the body on each side of the spinal column and to infuse into it the whole current of *prāṇa* (the life-force). *Prāṇa*, which exists in the form of vital air, generates heat which causes *kuṇḍalinī* to be aroused which then hisses and straightens itself and pierces the *cakras* to reach the *sahasrāra*. Rāja-yoga is the highest form of yoga through which *nirvikalpa-samādhi* is attained. It is conducive to the final liberation and is a purely mental exercise in which discrimination between the real and the unreal is possible.

The philosophy of the Tantras is deeply influenced by the non-dualistic and dualistic interpretation of the Vedānta, though other systems like the Sāṅkhya, etc., form its original basis. The Buddhist Tantras also speak of non-dualism. As in all idealistic systems the ultimate reality in Tantrism is pure consciousness, known as *saṃvit*, which is not limited by time, space and cause. In it the world is reflected just as an object is reflected in a clear mirror. The Tantric approach towards this *saṃvit* is not uniform. According to the purely non-dualistic approach as found in a few Tantras creation does not proceed from *saṃvit* or *brahman*, the so-called world of existence being false and illusory. In most Tantras, however, *saṃvit* is conceived of in terms of the functioning of Śakti in *prakāśa* (static) and *vimarśa* (dynamic) aspects. It is both immanent and transcendent. The former condition prevails when Śakti in its static state assumes the form of matter and the latter condition prevails when Śakti in its dynamic state assumes the form of consciousness. The first is known as *anaham* and the second as *aham*. At the time of the dissolution of the universe pure consciousness, or *saṃvit*, remains absolutely free from material contamination—it remains as pure *cit-śakti* or *parā-śakti*. But when the alternatives or material entities develop, Śakti manifests itself as Avidyā or material Prakṛti.

Thus the ultimate reality functions in its two aspects, as subject and also as object. Just as oil issues from oil-seed so also in the beginning of creation Śakti appears. This appearance causes an unmanifested sound called Para-Nāda that fills up the vaccum and eventually concentrates itself on a point or centre called Para-Bindu. The Tantras say that pure consciousness works through its Śakti or inherent power. This Śakti at first appears as Icchā-Śakti or will-power, the desire to be manifested. Subsequently it works in its two aspects—Vidyā-Śakti and Avidyā-Śakti or Māyā-Śakti. Both of these are conscious principles with the difference that while the former is illuminating consciousness, the latter is veiled consciousness, i.e. consciousness *appearing* as unconsciousness. This Māyā-Śakti is composed of three *guṇas*—*sattva*, *rajas* and *tamas*—and known as Triguṇa Śakti or Kāmakalā symbolized by the triangle. The process may be described using the analogy of a *caṇaka* or grain. A *caṇaka* has two seeds which are so close to each other that they seem one. They are surrounded by a single sheath. The seeds are Śiva and Śakti and the sheath is Māyā. When the sheath is peeled, Māyā Śakti operates, and the two seeds come apart. The sheath unrolls when the seeds again begin to germinate. It is like reawakening from dreamless slumber. In the dualistic Tantras, both Śiva and Śakti, the static (*prakāśa*) and kinetic (*vimarśa*) aspects of the same reality, are treated as individual conscious principles. Bindu is an eternal material entity which serves as the material cause of the world, while Śiva is the efficient cause and Śakti the instrumental. The evolution of the supreme being or supreme consciousness into the universe is described in a scheme of 36 *tattvas* divided into six groups; Śiva, Vidyā, Ātma, Śuddha, Śuddāśuddha and Aśudha Tattvas. The supreme being is not a personal god. The Tantric viewpoint holds that the supreme being is manifested in one of its aspects in an infinity of relations. And though involving all relations within itself, it is neither their sum total nor is it exhausted by them. Śakti, which is its functional aspect, works by negation, contraction and finitisation. As Mother-power she manifests herself as the world and again withdraws the world into herself.

A a

Ābhāsavāda: The theory of creation in Kashmir Śaivism which holds that the universe consists of appearance which are all real in the sense that they are aspects of the ultimate reality. Just as reflections in the mirror are inseparable from the mirror, yet they are distinct from one another and also from the mirror, so in the case of the universe which though void of distinction appears distinct from the perfectly pure vision of the supreme being. Diverse conditions are all parts of Śiva just as diverse products from the juice of sugarcane belong to the sugarcane itself. The manifestation of the universe is effected through the power (*śakti*) of Śiva which is not different from him. With the unfolding of Śakti, the universe appears and with her closing up, it disappears. Abhinavagupta's *Paramārthasāra* 12 ff.

Abhayākara Gupta: Author of *Niṣpannayogāvalī* (q.v.), a text on the *maṇḍalas* (q.v.). He lived during the reign of the Pāla King Rāmapala (AD 1084-1130). He was a teacher in the Vikramaśīla monastery and an exponent of the Kālacakra (q.v.) school which, according to the Tibetan texts, was developed outside India in a country called Sambhala and was introduced in Bengal in the Pāla period.

Abhaya-mudrā: An iconic *mudrā* depicting the gesture of protection. The hand showing this *mudrā* is slightly elevated and upturned, the palm facing outward, the fingers outstretched and raised.

Abhicāra: Rites for performing black deeds and causing harm to others. For example, *māraṇa* or killing, *vaśīkaraṇa* or hypnotizing, *stambhana* or arresting, *ucāṭana* or driving away, *vidveṣaṇa* or creating bad blood and so on. *Śāradātilaka* XXIII. 123-5, *Śaktisaṅgama*, Kālī, VIII. 102-5. Such acts should not be performed indiscriminately. *Tantrarāja* XIII. 94-5.

Abhijñā: Ten kinds of powers (*iddhi*, *ṛddhi*; cf. Aṣṭasiddhi q.v.) such as to project a mind-made image of oneself, to become invisible, to pass through solid things such as wall, to penetrate solid ground as if it were water, to walk on water, to fly through the air, to touch sun and moon, to ascend to the highest heavens, etc.

Abhinavagupta: A Kashmirian polymath. He was the son of Cukhela, grandson of Varāhagupta and elder brother of Manoratha, as he himself tells in his *parātriṃśikā-vivaraṇa*. In his *Locana* commentary on Ānandavardhana's *Dhvanyāloka* he refers to Bhaṭṭendurāja and Utpala as his *guru* and *paramaguru* respectively. Bhaṭṭa Tauta is also referred to in the same work as his guru while Laksmaṇagupta seems to have been his teacher in Śaiva philosophy. His literary activity seems to have extended from AD 990 to 1020, since we know that he composed his *Bhairavastotra* in AD 993 and his *Pratyabhijñāvimarśinī* in AD 1015. He has also given us two more works on the pratyabhijñā school of Kashmir Śaivism, namely, *Tantrāloka* and *Paramārthasāra*. His other works are *Bodhapañcadaśikā*, *Mālinivijaya-vārtika*, *Tantrasāra* and *Tantravaṭadhānika*.

***Abhidhānottara Tantra*:** Buddhist Tantra which furnishes considerable material for the study of Tantric Buddhist iconography. This Tantra is as yet unpublished.

Abhimukhī: A Tantric Buddhist goddess of the *bhūmi* (q.v.) category who is of golden colour and holds on a lotus the *prajñapāramitā* manuscript. Deities of the *bhūmi* category are the Vajrayanic deification of the traditional ten spiritual spheres through which a Bodhisattva moves in his quest for Buddhahood. *Niṣpanna* 55.

Abhiniveśa: One of the five *kleśas* or *kañcukas* of the Śaiva Siddhānta conception signifying evil qualities blackening the soul which is produced from *asuddhamāyā* (q.v.). This is concentration on false objects, others being *avidyā* (ignorance), *asmitā* (egoity), *rāga* (attachment) and *dveṣa* (aversion).

***Abhisamayālaṅkāra*:** A text attributed to Maitreya, of the Prajñāpāramitā doctrine which contains a great deal of Tantric elements. The Tibetan and Sanskrit versions of this text were edited by Stcherbatsky and Obermiller in 1929. Eng. trans. by E. Conze, SOR,

1954. The most helpful for the understanding of this text are Obermiller's *Doctrine of Prajñāpāramitā as Exposed in the Abhisamayālaṅkāra* and his incomplete *Analysis of the Abhisamayālaṅkāra*. The former was published in *Acta Orientalia* (1932-3) and the latter in three parts in Calcutta Oriental Series (1933-43). Of its numerous commentaries those of Vimuktasena, Buddhaśrījñāna, Dharmamitra, Ratnākaraśānti, Prajñākaramati and Jagaddalanivāsin are preserved in Tibetan. The Sanskrit edition of Haribhadra's commentary known as *Abhisamayālaṅkāraloka* was published by Tucci in 1932 and by Wogihara in 1932-5.

Abhiṣecikī: A form of consecration in which the teacher worships Śiva and Śakti in a vessel and then anoints the disciple with its water. Rāghava on *Śāradātilaka* V. 127-40.

Abhiṣeka: Consecration of the aspirant to be performed before or after initiation into any special aspect of human life, religious or secular. In the Tantric tradition *abhiṣeka* is of two kinds—Śākta or general and Pūrṇa or complete. Rāghavabhaṭṭa on *Śāradātilaka* II. 5; IV. 1. The former is done by sprinkling holy water on the aspirant while chanting *mantras* to propitiate different deities specially those effective for driving away evil spirits. *Puraścaryārṇava* V. 405 ff. The candidate for Pūrṇābhiṣeka or complete consecration has to pass through severe ordeals. This special form of consecration bestows upon the aspirant a divine nature. *Śaktisaṅgama*, Kālī, XI. 29.37. In certain cases the preceptor gives a new name to the disciple after the consecration. See Dīkṣā.

Abhūta-parikalpa: That which is devoid of all misconception or false mental construction, i.e. the substratum where there is the mere possibility of all subjectivity and objectivity, but in which duality has no reality. *Mahāyānasūtrālaṅkāra* XI. 31.

Abhyudaya: Progress or upliftment; it is the essence of Tantrism along with the other goal, *niḥśreyasa* (the highest good). It acts on the physical, vital and mental planes by which a centre of being can render itself an apparatus efficient for the purpose of encompassing the twofold end of *abhyudaya*.

Acala: A god of direction according to the Buddhist Tantras, the presiding deity of the Īśāna corner. He appears to be the same as Caṇḍaroṣaṇa. This six-armed god, also known as Vajrabhīṣaṇa and often identified with Trailokyovijaya, holds in two principal hands his *śakti* in embrace. Acala is also a deity of the *bhūmi* (q.v.) category, white in colour, with two arms and *vajra* on lotus as symbol. *Niṣpanna* 2, 52, *Sādhana* 172.

Acalaketu Lokeśvara: A form of Avalokiteśvara (q.v.) who is one-faced and two-armed and stands on a lotus. He displays the *abhaya-mudrā* with the right hand and holds the *piṇḍapātra* (bowl) in the left. A *chowrie* rests against his right shoulder.

Acala Vajrapāṇi: Name of Caṇḍaroṣaṇa (q.v.) who is yellow in colour, has one face and two arms. His face appears terrible, showing bare fangs. His symbol is a sword and he depicts the *tarjani-mudrā*. *Sādhana* 172.

Ācamana: Symbolic purification of the body by sipping water from the palm and sprinkling it on different parts of the body. It consists in the purification of the three forms of body, namely, the gross, subtle and causal. *Mahānirvāṇa* V. 39.

Ācāra: Means of spiritual attainment which varies from person to person according to competence. *Mahānirvāṇa* V. 39. It is generally of seven kinds—Veda, Vaiṣṇava, Śaiva, Dakṣiṇa, Vāma, Siddhānta and Kaula, categorized broadly as Dakṣiṇa and Vāma. Interpretations vary regarding the nature and grouping of the Ācāras. It is generally held that those who participate in the rituals of the five Ms (*pañcamakāra*, q.v.) belong to the category of Vāmācāra. *Kaulamārgarahasya* XI. According to a different tradition everyone is a follower of Dakṣiṇācāra by birth. It is only by initiation that one becomes a Vāmācarin. *Prāṇatosaṇī*, VII. 7.532. Some authorities are inclined to exclude Veda and Vaiṣṇava from the category of Tantric Ācāras. *Mātṛkābheda* 6. In a few works we come across a twofold division—Aghorācāra and Yogācāra.

Ācārya: The preceptor who has mastery over the scriptures, who understands the real significance of the rites and who is disciplined physically and mentally. *Kulārṇava* XVII.

Acchoda: A place sacred to the great goddess. It is modern Acchavat in Kashmir. The goddess is variously known as Śivakāriṇī, Śivadhāriṇī, Siddhidāyinī and Śaktidhāriṇī.

Matsya Purāṇa XIII. 26 ff; *Skanda* V. 3.98. 64 ff; *Padma*, Sṛṣṭi XVII. 184 ff; *Devībhāgavata* VII. 30.55 ff.

Acyutā: The *śāsanadevatā* of the Tīrthaṃkara Padmaprabha; also known by the name Śyāmā according to the Śvetāmbara tradition. Her vehicle is a man and she has four hands. She holds the *varada*, *vīṇā*, *dhanus* and (the fourth shows the) *abhaya* mudra. The name Acyutā or Śyāmā may have originated from Acyutā or Viṣṇu or Śyāma. The *vīṇā* symbol would qualify her as a Vidyādevī.

Adhaḥ-āmnāya: One of the six geographical regions of the Tantric cult presided over by goddesses such as Vāgīśvarī, Vajrayoginī, Paṇṇagī, Ṇairteśvarī, etc., of Buddhist and Jain affiliation. *Śaktisaṅgama*, Sundarī, III. 182-7; *Prānatoṣaṇī* I. 9, 64; *Puraścayārṇava* I. 13.

Ādhāra: Literally receptacle; the term is used in a variety of senses. The body, the nerve-plexuses, the ritualistic utensils and other ingredients of *sādhanā* including even *guru* and the holy texts are described as *ādhāra*. *Ādhāra-cakra* is supposed to exist at the lowest extremity of the spinal cord. The Kaula-worshippers consider the triangle of the *ādhāracakra* as the seat of the *bindu*.

Ādhāranī: Buddhist goddess, consort of Vajratīkṣṇa whose *mantra* is *oṃ vajrakoṣaguhya hum*. The name refers to the edge of a razor, *kṣurasya dhārā*, like *vajra-tīkṣṇa*. The word *koṣa* in the *mantra* means scabbard of a sword. *Sarvatathāgatatattvasaṃgraha* 34.

Adhikāra: Qualification and competence for Tantric worship. Only those who are free from all narrowness and are actively engaged in working for human welfare have this comptence. *Sarvahiṃsā vinirmuktaḥ sarvaprāṇīhiteratah, so' asmin śāstre adhikārī tadanyo brahmasādhaka*. *Gandharvatantra* II, 19. There are various types of Tantric *sādhanā* with a variety of purposes, hence the qualification for initiation varies from person to person according to the nature of *sādhanā* undertaken. Those who do not believe in the Vedic way are specially entitled to have Tantric initiation. *Kaulamārgarahasya* 91, 105.

Adhikārī-bheda: See Adhikāra.

Adhimukti: A vajrayanic goddess of the *bhūmi* (q.v.) category who is of the colour of a red lotus. Her right hand holds a *vajra* and the left a lotus. There is a goddess of the same name belonging to the *vaśitā* (q.v.) category; her colour is white and she holds the buds of *priyaṅgu* flower. *Niṣpanna* 55, 57.

Adhvan: The Tantric concept of six paths leading to the realization of the supreme being through the six centres of the body. These are *kalā* (attribute), *tattva* (category), *bhuvana* (region), *varṇa* (letters), *pada* (words) and *mantra* (q.v.).

Adhvaśodhana: The process of purifying the body. It consists of six *adhvas* technically known as *varṇa*, *pada*, *mantra*, *kalā*, *tattva* and *bhuvana*. Rāghavabhaṭṭa on *Śāradātilaka* V. 77.

Ādibuddha: Also known as Vajradhara, he is the supreme being in Vajrayāna and regarded as the embodiment of Śūnya to whom the Dhyānī Buddhas owe their origin. He is conceived in two forms, single and *yuganaddha*. In individual conception he is bedecked in jewels and ornaments, sitting in *vajrāsana*, carrying *vajra* in his right hand and *ghaṇṭā* in the left. In *yuganaddha* form he is locked in close embrace with his *śakti* who appears to be Prajñāpāramitā, representing karuṇā or compassion. *Niṣpanna* 8. Another alternative suggestion presupposes the existence of different cults according as one or another of the Dhyānī Buddhas is believed to be the principal Ādi Buddha. According to the *Kālacakra-tantra*, the cult was given the name Ādibuddhayāna or Ādiyāna.

***Ādikarmapradīpa*:** A text, including a commentary pertaining to Mantra-yāna which describes the ceremonies and religious acts which the Ādikarmika Bodhisattva has to perform. The work consists of a *Sūtra* text with a running commentary and contains precepts on the initiation ceremonies, the rules of rituals, the readings of the prajñāpāramitā, meditation and so forth. It was edited with introduction and analysis of contents by Vallee Poussin in *Mem. Acad. Belg* 1898, 177-232.

Ādinātha: The primal god in Nātha Siddha tradition. According to the Nātha cosmogony, before the beginning of creation when there was an all-encompassing darkness and void, the impulse of creation made a ripple in the void resulting in a bubble, an egg, from which emerged Ādinātha. From his sweat was born Ketakā, his spouse, who gave birth to Brahmā, Viṣṇu and Śiva. After a time

Ādinātha wanted to test his sons. He approached them in the form of a decomposed cadaver. Getting the putrid smell of the body, Brahmā made himself scarce and Viṣṇu waved it away. But Śiva recognized it to be their father's body. The three brothers then cremated the corpse and from his body were born the five Ādi Siddhas (q.v.) of the Nātha faith. The first of the nine Nātha *gurus* is also known as Ādinatha, the name evidently adopted after that of the primal god. Ādinatha of the Nātha tradition recalls the Jain Ādinātha, which is an appellation of the first Tīrthaṃkara, Ṛṣabhanātha.

Ādi Siddha: Five cardinal Saints of the Nātha faith who sprang from the body of Ādinātha (q.v.). Mīnanātha sprang from the navel; Gorakṣanātha came out of the skull; Hāḍi-pā originated from the bones; Kānu-pā was born from the ears; and Cauraṅgīnātha emerged from the feet.

Aditi: The Ṛgvedic goddess symbolizing 'infinity', 'boundlessness' and the eternal current of time consciousness, cf. *Ṛgveda* I. 89.10. Conceptually she is the precusor of the Tantric Kālī who is infinite, unlimited and the controller of eternal time, cf. I. 2. 209-10. In the *Kaṭha Upaniṣad* II. 1.7 Aditi is described thus: *Ya prāṇena sambhavati Aditirdevatāmayī, guhāṃ praviśya tiṣṭhantiṃ yā bhutibhirvyajāyate.* The same is spoken about Kuṇḍalinī in *Śāradātilaka* I. 55: *sarvadevamayī devī sarvamantramayī śivā.* In *Ṛgveda* X. 72.4 there is a reference to mutual interrelation between Aditi and Dakṣa in regard to origination. In later mythology Satī, the wife of Śiva, who had shown to the latter her Daśa Mahāvidyā form, is the daughter of Dakṣa. Though in the Tantras the Vedic Aditi is not mentioned but many of her attributes are common features of later Tantric goddesses.

Ādi Yāga: Sexual intercourse conceived of in terms of sacrifice. It is said that during copulation all wordly thoughts recede and various kinds of sounds are made by the participants. The articulation of such sounds in the forms of letters (*varṇa*) and row (*varga*) is brought in line with various forms of Śaktis especially those of will, knowledge and action as also with various nerve plexuses through which the *kuṇḍalinī* has her upward march. *Tantrāloka* III. 150 ff.

Advaita, Advaya: Non-dualism, as opposed to dualism (*dvaita*), which is one of the main features of the idealistic philosophical systems of India. In all forms of Indian religions, Tantrism included, this philosophical concept plays a significant role.The theistic sects conceive of the relation between *brahman* and the world in terms of identity, difference or identity-in-difference. The Śaiva-Śākta schools seek to establish the dogma of the static (*prakāśa*) and vibrating (*vimarśa*) aspects of *śakti* in terms either of transformation (*pariṇāma*) or transfiguration (*vivarta*) of *brahman*. In Tantric Buddhism *advaya* or non-duality stands for a psycho-physical process. The union of Prajñā (q.v.) and Upāya (q.v.), symbolizing respectively the female and male principles of creation, through the principles of Yuganaddha (q.v.) for the purpose of realization of non-dual state, symbolized by the physical union of the adept and his female partner, bring in succession *rāga* and *mahārāga* (emotion and more intense emotion, evidently transcendental, resulting from a genuine feeling of compassion), *samarasa* (oneness of emotion in which there is no cognition of Prajñā and Upāya) and finally *mahāsukha* or great bliss leading to Nirvāṇa. *Advayavajrasaṃgraha* 50.

Advaitabrahmasādhanā: Non-dualistic realization of *brahman* or Śakti which is emphasized in a few Tantric works which hold that at the first stage of spiritual exercise the sense of dualism prevails but at the final stage the aspirant finds no second entity apart from *ātman* or *brahman*: *atrātmavyatirekena dvitīyaṃ na vipaśyati*. The non-dualist aspirant should identify himself with the supreme goddess who is no other than *brahman* and thinks that he himself is the embodiment of *sat* (reality), *cit* (consciousness) and *ānanda* (bliss). *Kaulāvalinirṇaya* I, cf. *Devībhāgavata* VII. 34. 18-19; *Gandharvatantra* XIII. 3-4.

***Advayasiddhi*:** A Buddhist Tantric work composed by Lakṣmīṅkarā about AD 729. This work upholds the doctrine that one should offer worship to one's own body wherein all gods reside. It also says that in the three worlds there is none higher than the Ācarya (q.v.).

***Advayavajrasaṃgraha*:** A collection of 21 short works on Tantric Buddhist philosophy by Advayavajra of the eleventh century AD.

The origin of Tantric Buddhist deities and their gradual evolution from the germ syllable are given clearly. 'From the right perception of Śūnyatā (q.v.) proceeds the germ-syllable; from the germ-syllable proceeds the conception of an icon, and from the icon the external representations. The whole process therefore is one of dependent origination.' Iconic and conceptual description of the Dhyānī Buddhas (q.v.) and their consorts and Bodhisattvas are given in the *Advayavajrasaṃgraha*. It says that there are three yānas, namely Śrāvakayāna, Pratyekayāna and Mahāyāna. The first two are explained by the theories of the Vaibhāṣikas. The third, Mahāyāna, is of two kinds: Mantranaya and Pāramitānaya. Published with an extensive introduction by M.M. Haraprasad Sastri in GOS, 1927.

Ādyākālī: Same as Dakṣiṇākālī according to the *Mahākāla-saṃhitā*. But in the description, as given in the *Mahānirvāṇa* V. 141, it seems that there is some difference between the two. Ādyākālī represents the primordial energy.

Ādyānandana: Also known as Navamīsiṃha, he was the minister of Mahindra Malla or Bhupālendra Malla, king of Nepal (AD 1689-94) and author of *Tantracintāmaṇi* and *Kulamuktikallolinī*.

Ādyāśakti: Primordial energy conceived as the Female Principle of creation represented by the supreme goddess and her fragmentary forms. She is the ultimate reality and *parabrahma* in the form of pure consciousness and bliss. *Śaktisaṅgama*, Kālī I. 99. She is identical with Paraśiva beyond human comprehension, and is constituted of pure *sattva* with no tinge of *rajas* and *tamas* qualities. *Saubhāgyabhāskara* on *Lalitāsahasranāma* 4. This Ādyāśakti is conceived by the followers of Śrīkula (q.v.) in terms of Tripurā or Tripurasundarī or Śrīvidyā. *Nityaṣodaśikārṇava* IV. 4. The followers of Kālīkula identify her with *brahman* and project her as Kālī or Mahākālī, the creator of the gods. *Nirvāṇatantra* X. She is both with and without attributes. She is *saṃvit* (q.v.) having *prakāśa* (static) and *vimarśa* (vibrating) aspects, the latter being *cidrūpiṇī* (in the form of consciousness) in the subtle state and *viśvarūpiṇī* (in the form of the universe) in the gross state. The evolution of the Ādyāśakti into the universe is described in a scheme of thirty-six *tattvas*. This evolution is not a case of complete trans-formation because she is not exhausted; as a Mother power she unfolds herself into the world and again withdraws the world into herself.

Āgama: General term for denoting scriptures used by all religious sects of India. The term is specially used by the Śaiva and Tantric schools. The Jain texts are also known as Āgamas. The Chinese versions of the Buddhist Nikāyas are also mentioned as Āgamas. In the Tantric tradition it is said that the word is formed by the first letters of *āgata* (that which comes from Śiva), *gata* (that which goes to Pārvatī), and *mata* (that which is established). The terms *tantra, āgama* and *saṃhitā* are very often used interchangeably. According to *Piṅgalāmata* Āgama is that by which the objects around are known. According to the *Vārāhītantra*, as quoted in the *Śabdakalpadruma* under the title 'Tantra', Āgama deals with seven topics: cosmology, destruction, worship of god, *sādhanā*, *puraścaraṇa*, six forms of rites and four forms of meditation. It gives a list of twelve special Āgamas which are *Muktaka*, *Prapañca*, *Śāradā*, *Nārada*, *Mahārṇava*, *Kapila*, *Yoga*, *Kalpa*, *Kapiñjala*, *Amṛtaśuddhi*, *Vīra* and *Siddhasaṃvaraṇa*.

Āgamāntin: Śaivas who base their tenets on the Āgamas (28 in number) and enjoin that there are three principles—the Lord (Pati or Śiva), the individual soul (Paśu) and fetters (Pāśa) which bind the individual to his mundane existence. Like other Śaiva groups they also believe in *caryā* (means to achieve the end), *kriyā* (action), *yoga* (concentration) and *jñāna* (knowledge) as means of a well regulated religious life. Women, Śūdras and Pratilomas were allowed to participate in this system.

***Āgamasāra*:** A late-medieval Tantric compendium. Besides dealing with the usual Tantric topics, it interprets certain features of *pañcatattva* in terms of *divya-bhāva* and subtle esoterism not meant for the average person. It also insists on *vikalpa* or a substitute for the constituents of *pañcatattva* (q.v.) cf. *Yoginītantra* VI; *Kaulāvinirṇaya* V. 113-28.

***Āgamatattvavilāsa*:** Tantric treatise composed by Raghunātha Tarkavāgīśa in AD 1687 which deals with the process of creation, ritual with corpse, worship of different gods and goddesses, cult of Bhuvaneśvarī and other Mahāvidyā goddesses and usual Tantric topics. Ed. by P. Sastri, Calcutta 1985.

Agastyāśrama: A holy resort of the goddess Mahavidyā or Mattamedhā. It is one of the many places, especially in southern India, associated with Agastya's name. This place is probably Agastipuri near Nasik in Maharashtra. *Bṛhannīla-tantra* V. The goddess Mahāvidyā may have some conceptual relation with Agastyavidyā mentioned in the *Sammoha-tantra*.

Aghora: One of the five forms of Śiva. This is black in colour, terrible in nature, and is the presiding deity of the southern region. *Nirvāṇa-tantra* quoted in *Prāṇatoṣaṇī* I. 963-4. Aghora and its derivative Aghorī mean 'terrible' or 'fearful'. But the word *aghora* in itself means 'that which is not terrible' and in this sense the term is used as an appellation of Rudra in the *Vājasaneya Saṃhitā* XVI. 3. The worshippers of the Aghora form of Śiva formed a sect known as Aghorapanthīs. An *ācāra* named Aghorācāra is mentioned in some Tantric texts along with Yogācāra (not to be confused with the Buddhist Yogācāra or Vijñānavāda), apart from the seven traditional *ācāras* which are Veda, Vaiṣṇava, Śaiva, Dakṣiṇa, Vāma, Siddhānta and Kaula. This Aghorācāra is included within the broad category of Vāmācāra in *Śaktisaṅgama-tantra*, Tārā, I. 92-4.

Āgneya Kalā: Aspects of a particular state of cosmic evolution. These are connected with the element of fire symbolized by ten goddesses—Dhūmrārci, Umā, Jvālinī, Visphuliṅginī, Suśrī, Surūpā, Kapilā, Havyavahā and Kavyavahā. *Prapañcasāra* III. 18-9.

Āgneyakhaṇḍa: One of the three parts of the fifteen *kalās* mentioned in the commentary on *Saundaryalaharī* 32, Āgneyakhaṇḍa consists of *darśā*, *dṛṣṭā*, *darśatā*, *viśvarūpā*, and *apyāyamānā kalās*. Other *khaṇḍas* are Saura and Cāndra.

Āgneya-varṇa: Letters connected with the element of fire according to the Tantric tradition. There are *ya*, *ra*, *la*, *va*, *śa*, *ṣa*, *sa*, *ha* and *kṣa*. Rāghava's com. on *Śāradātilaka* II. 1-3.

Aham: The subjective aspect of the ultimate reality, known as Saṃvit (q.v.) or pure consciousness. Literally it means 'I-ness', as opposed to *idam* or 'it-ness'. The letters 'A' and 'Ha' constituting *ham* are suggestive of the *prakāśa* (q.v.) and *vimarśa* (q.v.) aspects of *saṃvit*, and they are symbolized by *bindu* (q.v.) and *visarga* (q.v.). The transcendent condition of Saṃvit which is caused by the conscious principle is called *aham*. Creation is the self expression of Supreme Being, the subject viewing itself as object, I (*aham*) as It (*idam*). I-ness and It-ness exist in a unitary state in Parā-Saṃvit (q.v.), in which Śiva represents the *prakāśa* (q.v.) and Śakti and *vimarśa* (q.v.) aspect. The latter contains the potentialities of the universe within it. It begins to function leaving the *prakāśa* standing alone as an 'I' without a 'This'. The purpose of this functioning is to make the subject experience itself as object. See Ahamātmikā, Anuttaralipi, Ahantā and Idam.

Ahamātmikā: A designation of the supreme goddess, the ultimate reality who is in the form of fifty letters and presides over the six *adhvans* (q.v.) or paths leading to absolute realization. She is known as Kāmakalā or Mahatripurasundarī and impersonates consciousness, bliss, will, knowledge and action. She is called Anuttaravimarśalipilakṣyavigrahā. By *anuttaralipi* (q.v.) is meant the letters 'A' and 'Ha', constituting *aham* (q.v.). The former is indicative of the *prakāśa* (q.v.) and the latter of the *vimarśa* (q.v.) aspects of *saṃvit*. 'A' is Śiva and 'Ha' is Śakti. These two letters do not belong to the gross *vaikharī* (q.v.) level but to the subtle *parā* level. 'Ha' is also called *visarga* (q.v.) or double *bindu* (q.v.). The single *bindu* is 'A'. These *bindus* or points are collectively called *tribindu*, *mahābindu*, *parabindu*, *kāraṇabindu*, etc., and they constitute the *trikoṇa* (q.v.) or triangle which is the same as Kāmakalā. *Cidvallī* on *Kāmakalāvilāsa* 6-7; *Varivasyā-rahasya* II. 67-9. Com. on *Nitya-ṣodaśikārṇava* IV. 10-11.

Ahaṃgrahopāsanā: Worship of one's own Self as the supreme deity which has been explained by Appaya Dikṣita in his commentary on the *Bhavanopaniṣad* as *taṃ vāhamasmi bhagavo devate'haṃ vai tvamasi*.

Ahaṃkāra: The principle of egoity; it is the second evolute of Prakṛti according to the Sāṅkhya. It determines one's attitude towards the objects of the world and is of three kinds. The first called *vaikārika* or *sāttvika* owing to its relation to the *sattva* element, gives rise to five *jñānendriyas* or organs of perception, five *karmendriyas* or organs of action and *manas* or mind. The second called *rājasa* serves as a link between the products of the first and those of the third, the *tāmasa* which generate the five *tanmātras* or the subtle elements. *Sāṅ. Kārikā* 25; *Sāṅ Pra. Bhāṣya* II. 18. In Tamil Saivite Tantras *ahaṃkāra* is produced from Buddhi or intellect and in turn produces *taijasa* (sense organs), *vaikṛta* (organs of action) and *tanmātra* (five subtle elements). *Mṛgendra Āgama* II. 3-7; III. 1. etc., *Pauṣkara* II. 17; III. 4; V. 9. Ahaṃkāra is brought in relation to *ājñācakra*, one of the six nerve-plexuses of the body. In Tantric Buddhism *ahaṃkāra* is the connection or identity of the worshipper with the deity. It is also the identity of the Bodhicitta (q.v.) with the deity, the manifestation of Śūnya or the ultimate reality. The identity is established with the *mantra*: 'I am the goddess and the goddess is in me.' The worshipper should conceive himself as the deity with the same complexion, form and limbs as described in the *sādhana* and should, instead of worshipping any external object, worship himself. *Guhyasamāja* XVIII.

Ahaṃpratyavamarśa: Same as the *vimarśa-śakti* or vibrating energy of Śiva. It is also known as *svatantra-śakti*. It is explained as *vastutaḥ punarapāhaṃpratyavamarśākhyā svātantrya-śaktirevāsyānti. Tantrāloka* I.108.

Ahantā: Subjecthood. The true subject has not the sense of distinction from anybody or anything. In the sphere of *māyā* (q.v.), which may be described as the region of the *idantā* or objecthood, any sense of *ahantā* or subjecthood is derived from the object or the *idam* (q.v.) which has separated itself from the true subject. The individuals under the influence of *māyā* are not genuine subjects. They represent *ahaṃkāra* and not *ahantā*, egoism and not real subjecthood. See Aham.

***Ahirbudhnya Saṃhitā*:** One of the most important Pāñcarātra Saṃhitās. It is a Kashmirian work in sixty chapters, believed to have been composed in fourth-fifth century AD. Though a Pāñcarātra text it contains some elements of Śaivism as well. It deals elaborately with the *vyūha* doctrine. It also enumerates thirty-nine Avatāras of Viṣṇu and deals with systems like the Sāṅkhya, Yoga, etc. It holds that Kapila's Sāṅkhya-tantra was originally divided into Prākṛta and Vaikṛta Maṇḍalas and these two had thirty-two and twenty-eight topics respectively and that Hiraṇyagarbha was the first to propound the two Yoga Saṃhitās, Nirodha-yoga and Karma-yoga. *Ahirbudhnya Saṃhitā* also lays down rules about the places where the *puraścaraṇa* of a *mantra* may be practised. Such places are river banks, caves, mountain tops, grounds near *tīrtha*, confluences of rivers, holy forests, peaks, etc. It deals elaborately with linguistic occultism, and holds that *mantras* have three senses and provides a procedure of Mahābhiṣeka as a remedy against diseases, for destroying all enemies, and for attainments of all desired objects. F.O. Schrader, *Introduction to the Pāñcarātra and Ahirbudhnya Saṃhitā*, Madras 1916. Eng. trans. by Nityasvarupananda, Calcutta 1964.

Aindri: See Indrāṇī. Aindrī is the name of a Vidyā, details of whose cult is given in the *Sammoha-tantra.*

Ajapā: A special form of effortless meditation. Rāghavabhaṭṭa on *Śāradātilaka* XIV. 91. The sounds *haṃ* and *saḥ* processed by the movements of breath themselves constitute the *mantra* and hence there is no need of muttering anything. The automatic constitution of the *haṃsa-mantra* takes place simultaneously in *mūlādhāra*, *anāhata* and *ājñā* cakras. *Gheraṇḍa* V. 85. Ajapā is twofold—secret and expressed. The latter is again divided into two categories, sound and light. See Haṃsa.

Ajitā, Ajitabalā: Śāsanadevatā of Ajitanātha, the second Jain Tīrthaṃkara. Her spirit is symbolized by an iron-seat (*lohāsana*) known for its hardness and metallic strength. The Śvetāmbara text *Ācara Dinakara* makes her vehicle a bull. Her other symbols are *varada mudrā*, noose, citron, and goad. In Digambara tradition she holds *varada*, *abhaya*, conch and disc.

Ājñacakra: One of the six nerve-plexuses of the Tantric tradition. It is situated between the eyebrows and looks like a two-petalled white lotus, symbolized by the letters *ha* and *kṣa*. It is regarded as the seat of mind. *Ṣaṭcakranirūpaṇa* XXXII. *Ājñā* denotes command, evidently of the *guru* who is supposed to reside symbolically within the nerve-cycle. *Saubhāgyabhāskara* on *Lalitā-sahasranāma* 90. Within the pericarp of the lotus resides the six-faced and white-complexioned goddess Hākinī.

Ajñāna: Ignorance, also known by the terms *avidyā* and *aviveka*, which is the basic cause of all misery and bondage according to all schools of Indian thought. In the Tantric tradition it is divided into two kinds, *pauruṣa* which concerns human nature, and *bauddha* which concerns intellect. The former is known as *ānava-mala* which is the root of wordly existence. *Tantrāloka* I. 55. *Vṛtti* on *paraśurāmakalpasūtra* I. 3.

Ākāśagarbha: Bodhisattva who is the essence of ether; also known as Khagarbha. He is green in complexion. He holds the *cintāmaṇi* jewel in one hand and exhibits the *varada* mudrā on the other. He is the bestower of jewels. *Niṣpanna* 58; *Sādhana* 49.

Ākāśatattva: The element of space (*vyoma* or *ākāśa*), one of the traditional five elements (*bhūtas*), conserved and crystallized as a state of spritual development and associated with the upward march of *kuṇḍalinī* to the *viśuddhi* region. *Śyāmārahasya*, Pari, I.

A-Ka-Tha: The *kuṇḍalinī* (q.v.) triangle constituted by three subdivisions of para-bindu (q.v.), namely, Apara-bindu, Bija and Apara-nāda (q.v.). The aforesaid triangle symbolized by Śiva (Apara-bindu), Śakti (Bija) and their equilibrium (Apara-nāda), is called A-Ka-Tha triangle, each of its lines comprised of sixteen letters.

Akhilāṇḍeśvarī: Presiding goddess of Jambu-keśvaram in south India. She represents the *ājñācakra*, the region between the eyebrows.

Akṣamālā: Same as *varṇamālā*. The chain of letters starting with *a* and ending in *kṣa*. *Ādikṣāntairakṣaraiḥ syādakṣamālā yatharthataḥ. Tantrarājatantra* I. 63. It also means a rosary or a string of beads for counting and uttering the name or seed-syllable of a deity. The beads consists of a kind of dried woody seed, called *rudrākṣa* (in Sanskrit). It may be made with other materials also, such as crystals, etc.

Akṣayajñānakaraṇḍā: Dhāriṇī goddess of Tantric Buddhism who is red in colour and holds in her left hand a basket full of jewels. *Niṣpanna* 57.

Akṣayamati: Bodhisattva 'of indestructible mind'. He is variously described as being golden or yellow, or white in colour. His most common symbol is a sword placed on a jar. *Niṣpanna* 50, 58.67.

Akṣayavaṭa: A sacred banyan tree, associated mostly with Śiva and Devī, located at many *tirthas*, notably at *Prayāga* or Allahabad in Uttar Pradesh and Gaya in Bihar. The presiding goddess is known as Akṣayā. *Bṛhannīlatantra* V; *Prāṇatoṣaṇī* 237-8. The *Kubjikātantra* VII mistakenly refers to it as Akṣayagrīva.

Akṣobhya: The second Dhyānī Buddha. He originates from the blue syllable *hum* which is placed on the orb of the sun. He is two-armed and one-faced, exhibits the earth-touching *mudrā* and sits in the *vajraparyaṅka* pose. He represents the primordial cosmic element of *vijñāna* or consciousness. He is the embodiment of the *vajra* family and represents the winter season, noon-time, pungent taste, faculty of hearing, the element of ether and sound and the *ca* (palatal) group of letters. *Advayavajrasaṃgraha* 40-1. Various other forms of *Akṣobhya* are found in Tantric works, some four-armed, some six-armed, some standing, some seated, some single and some in yab-yum. *Niṣpannayogāvalī* 3 ff. In Hindu Tantras, Akṣobhya is the consort or *bhairava* of Tārā. *Puraścaryārṇava* I, 13-4; *Tārātantra* 10.

Akula: The Śiva aspect of Śakti, *Akulasyāsya devasyakulaprathanaśālinī. Tantrāloka* III. 67. According to Abhinavagupta that which is manifested from Kula or Śakti is *akula* and is endowed with the element of Śiva.

Akuladhāma: The undecaying ever-blissful abode of Kālī or Mahākālī where the distinction between subject and object, of I-ness and It-ness, disappears and pure consciousness prevails. *Tantrāloka* IV. 183 ff.

Ali: Spiritous liquor used in Tantric worship.

Ālīḍha: A particular *āsana* or attitude of legs found in seated cult images. It resembles the attitude adopted in drawing the bow charged with an arrow: the right leg is outstretched while the left is slightly bent. When the position of the legs is reversed it is called *pratyālīḍha*.

Aliyantra: Vessel for drinking wine in which flower and scent are poured for concentration of mind on Ānandabhairava and Ānanda-bhairavī. *Mahānirvāṇa* VIII. 163.

Amākalā: A type of *kālā* (q.v.) or the active aspect of Śakti. It is equated with *ṣoḍaśikalā* in *Ṣaṭcakravivṛti* and described as eternal and creative containing nectar flowing from the union of Śiva and Śakti. See *Tantrik Texts* II.

130. It has also been brought in relation to the phases of the moon. It is said to reside within the triangle of the *sahasrāra* lotus.

Amarakaṇṭaka: The source of the Sone and Narmada in eartern Madhya Pradesh which is regarded as the holy resort of Caṇḍī or Amareśī. The place is variously called as Makarandaka and Marakantaka. *Matsya* XII. 42, *Devībhāgavata* VII. 30.71; *Bṛhannilatantra* V.

Amara Maitra: Nineteenth-century Tantric author who composed *Jñānadīpikā* (1831), *Amarasaṃgraha* (1843) and *Āmarīsaṃhitā* (1846).

Amareśa: Holy resort of the goddess Caṇḍī or Maheśvarī. It is on the south bank of the Narmadā, opposite Onkarnath and to the north west of Khandwa. *Bṛhannīlatantra* V.

Ambara: Holy resort of the goddess Viśvakāyā or Viśvakāmā. It is modern Amber in Jaipur, Rajasthan. *Matsya Purāṇa* XIII. 27; *Devībhāgavata* VII. 30.56.

Ambikā: Śāsanadevatā of Neminātha. According to Śvetambara tradition she rides a lion and bears a bunch of mangoes, noose, a child and a goad. In Digambara tradition she holds a bunch of mangoes in her two hands. Ambikā is mentioned as Rudra's sister in the *Vājasaneyi Saṃhitā* III. 57 and *Taittirīya Brāhmaṇa* I.6.10. She became Rudra's wife in *Taittiriya Āraṇyaka* X. 18.1. Later the name became common to all forms of Puranic goddesses. The name denotes 'mother'.

Ambikā: Holy resort of the goddess. It may be Ambikā-Kālnā in Burdwan district. The place is so named after the Jain goddess Ambikā. *Kubjikā* VII; *Bṛhannīla* V.

Ambikāśakti: A special dimension of Śakti. According to Bhāskara Rāya, Vāmā, Jyeṣṭhā and Raudrī emanating from the *prakāśa* or static form of Śiva-Śakti equilibrium are masculine in nature while *icchā* (will), *jñāna* (knowledge) and *kriyā* (action) represented by Bhāratī, Pṛthivī and Rudrāṇī emanate from the *vimarśa* aspect and are feminine in nature. They serve as wives of Brahmā, Viṣṇu and Rudra. The combination of the latter three energies is known as Ambikāśakti. Com. of *Varivasyārahasya* II. 64-5.

Amitābha: By far the most ancient among the Dhyānī Buddhas who is said to reside in the Sukhāvatī heaven. He presides over the *bhadrakalpa* cycle. Of the nature of the cosmic element of *saṃjñā* (name), he is an embodiment of attachment and belongs to the lotus family. His consort is Pāṇḍarā or Pāṇḍaravāsinī and Bodhisattva is Padmapāṇi or Avalokiteśvara. He exhibits *samādhi mudrā* in two hands. His colour is red, and vehicle the peacock. He presides over the group of letters beginning with *ṭa*, summer season, acid taste and evening twilight. *Advayavajrasaṃgraha* 41.

Amitaprabha: Bodhisattva whose name is also spelt as Amṛtaprabha. He is mentioned twice as white in colour and once as red. His recognition symbol is the jar of consecration. *Niṣpanna* 50, 59, 67.

***Amitayus Sūtra*:** Mahāyānic text which ushered in the conception of Amitābha (q.v.) and Avalokiteśvara (q.v.) for the first time in the Mahāyāna. It was translated into Chinese sometime between AD 148-70 and hence the time of its composition may be fixed at about AD 100.

Aṃkuśā: Śāsanadevatā of Anantanātha who is described in Śvetāmbara Jain tradition as seated on a lotus, and having four hands which hold a sword, noose, spear and goad. The name Aṃkuśā appears to have been derived from *aṃkuśa* or goad which this Yakṣiṇī carries.

Āmnāya: Zones in Tantric culture, five or six in number. *Kulārṇava* III. 7; *Śaktisaṅgama*, Sundarī V. 182-7. The Tantric texts speak of nine or six *āmnāyas* or regions—eastern, western, northern, southern, upper and lower—each containing its distinctive texts, cults and rituals. The *āmnāya* divisions are often brought under two general categories—Hādimata and Kādimata (q.v.)—in *Sammohatantra*, fifth Paṭala, which also refers to four geographical regions of the Tantras: Kerala prevailing in all countries from Aṅga to Mālava, Kāśmīra from Madra to Nepāla, Gauḍa from Śrīhaṭṭa to Sindhu and Vitasa in all countries.

Amoghadarśin: Name found in the list of sixteen Bodhisattvas headed by Maitreya. He is yellow in colour and holds a lotus in his right hand. *Niṣpanna* 66.

Amoghapāśa: A form of Lokeśvara. He is four-faced and eight-armed and stands on a lotus. He carries in his four right hands *vajra*, sword, goad and bow while the four left hands carry *ghaṇṭā*, *tridaṇḍī*, noose and arrow.

Amoghasiddhi: Dhyānī Buddha who has originated from the green syllable *kham* and hence his colour is green. His recognition symbol is *viśvavajra* (double thunderbolt). He exhibits *abhaya mudrā* and represents the cosmic element *saṃskāra* (conformation). He belongs to the *karma* family and presides over rainy season, bitter taste and labial group of letters beginning with *pa*. His vehicle is Garuḍa, consort Tārā and Bodhisattva Viśvapāṇi. *Advayavajrasaṃgraha* 41-2.

Amoghavajra: Disciple of Vajrabodha (q.v.) who went to China and propagated Tantric Buddhism. In AD 736 he returned to Śrīlaṅkā and went back to China in AD 746 with 500 manuscripts. Between AD 746 and 771, he translated 77 texts into Chinese including *Sarvatathāgatatattvasṃgraha*. He died in AD 774.

Amṛtadhāma: The abode of immortality symbolized by the letter *sa*, suggestive of the sound of screaming during *ādi-yāga* or primordial sacrifice performed through sexual union. In the higher spiritual level it is same as *anāhata-nāda* (q.v.). *Tantrāloka* III. 164-7.

Amṛtalakṣmī: Tantric goddess of western *āmanāya* (zone). *Bahuprabhedasaṃyuktā Kubjikā ca kulālika*; *mātaṅgāmṛta-lakṣmyādyāh paścimāmnāyadevatāḥ, Puraś-caryārṇava* I. 12.

Amṛtānanda: Author of *Dharmakośa-saṃgraha*. It is as yet unpublished. A manuscript of this work is in the Durbar Library of Nepal and a copy of the original is preserved in the Asiatic Society of Bengal.

Amṛtānandanātha: Author of *Yoginī-hṛdayadīpikā*, a commentary on the *Yoginī-hṛdaya*. He flourished in tenth-eleventh century AD and was a disciple of Puṇyā-nandanātha.

Amṛtaprabha: A form of Lokeśvara. He is one-faced and two-armed and sits in *vajraparyaṅka* attitude on a lotus. He holds a double *vajra* on his lap with his right hand, and a lotus on a water vessel in his left.

Amṛtīkaraṇa: Purification of the deity according to the Tantric rites. The aspirant should recite three times the *mūla-mantra*, the *dīpanī mantra* and the *mātṛkā*; then with letters and then with *dhenu-mudrā* he should sprinkle water on the head of the deity. *Puraścaryārṇava* V. 343.

Aṃśa, Aṃśāṃśa-mūrti: Concept or image of Śakti, the primordial energy, in fragments. A complete view consists of sixteen *kalās* or parts, each of which is known as *kalāmūrti*. *Aṃśa* and *aṃśāṃśa* are its further sub-divisions. *Garland of Letters* 194.

Anaham: That which is opposite of the principle of *aham* (q.v.) or 'I-ness'. It is the immanent form of *saṃvit* or pure consciousness which is the ultimate reality. This condition prevails when Śakti in its static state assumes the form of matter. In the sophisticated Tantras it is categorically stated that *anaham* is the so-called unmanifested material entity and it is caused by the conscious principle in three stages. The material entities develop owing to the self-contraction of *saṃvit* when Śakti manifests itself as *avidyā* or material *Prakṛti*. Thus the ultimate reality functions in its two aspects, as subject and as object.

Anāhata: One of the six nerve plexuses (*ṣaṭcakra*) situated in the heart region. It is conceived of as a twelve-petalled lotus and is the seat of the element of air. On the petals are the letters from *Ka* to *Tha* with the *bindu* above them, vermilion in colour. On the *bīja* of air is the three-eyed god Īśā who, like Haṃsa, extends two arms in the gesture of granting boons and dispelling fear. The goddess Kākinī is its presiding deity. Anāhata is also the name of a particular form of sound. *Ṣaṭcakra-nirūpaṇa* 22-3; *Nirvāṇatantra* VII. Anāhata-nāda is the eternal sound on which *Cidvallī* on *Kāmakalāvilāsa* 9 says: *eko nādātmako varṇaḥ sarvanādavibhāgavān, so' anastamitarūpatvādanāhata itīritaḥ*. The *Prānatoṣaṇī* I, 9 equates it with *Śabda-brahma*.

Anāhata-nāda: Undifferentiated sound which is eternally existing. It is not produced by friction. *Cidvallī* on *Kāmakalā-vilāsa* 9. This is same as *Śabdabrahma* (q.v.) and is symbolized by the *praṇava*, i.e. *Om*. *Prānatoṣaṇī* I. 1.9. But it is not that sound which is produced with the utterance of *Om*. Anāhata-nāda is a subtle sound not to be heard or felt by the sense organs. It is meant only for the Yogins.

Anākhya-śakti: One of the five forms of dynamic energy, others being *sṛṣṭi*, *sthiti*, *saṃhāra* and *bhāṣā* according to the Karma doctrine of Kashmir Śaivism.

Anala: Holy resort of the goddess Nārāyaṇī. It is the Nala lake near Ahmedabad, Gujarat. It is mentioned in the *Pīṭhanirṇaya*.

Ānandabhairava, Bhairavī: The chief male and female deities of the *bhairavīcakra* (q.v.). Meditation on them is necessary for the purification of wine. *Prāṇatoṣaṇī* VII. 2, 511. For the *mantras* used in meditation see *Mahānirvāṇa* VIII. 166-7.

Ānandādi Lokeśvara: A form of Lokeśvara. He stands in the *samabhaṅga* attitude, and carries a lotus held by the stem, in his right hand while the left displays the *varada* pose.

Ānandakanda: Name of the eight-petalled lotus in the *anāhata-cakra*.

Ānandalaharī: A celebrated hymn attributed to Śaṅkarācārya. There are many works of the title of *Ānandalaharī* and at least six hymns of the same name. The first part of *Saundarya-laharī* is also known as *Ānandalaharī*.

Ānandanātha: A name generally prefixed before the term *guru*. *Śaktisaṅgama*, Sundarī, I. 139-40.

Ānandaśakti: A concept of Śakti found in Kashmiri Śaivism. It is that form of energy which arises out of bliss (*ānanda*) in which instead of *idam* or *'It-ness' aham* or *'I-ness'* receives greater prominence. It reveals the *svātantrya* or distinctive aspects of Śiva. *Tasya ca svātantryaṃ ānandaśaktiḥ*. Abhinavagupta, *Tantrasāra* 6. In various places *svātantrya-śakti* is equated with *vimarśa-śakti* or vibrating energy of Śiva as opposed to *prakāśa* or static. Ānandaśakti which is both transcendent and immanent is symbolized by the letter A. *Tantrāloka* 81-2.

Anaṅgavajra: Author of *Prajñopāya-viniścayasiddhi* (q.v.) in which Śūnyatā has been defined as Prajñā and Karuṇā as Upāya (q.v.). It is asserted that the merging of these two, Prajñā and Upāya, is the *mahāsukha*, the creative principle of the universe from which innumerable Buddhas, Sambuddhas and Śrāvakas originate. Anaṅgavajra belonged to the seventh-eighth century AD. See B.T. Bhattacharyya, *Two Vajrayāna Works*, GOS, no. 44, Baroda 1929.

Anantamatī: Śāsanadevatā or Yakṣiṇī of Anantanātha in the Digambara Jain tradition. She is described as being carried by a swan, and she holds in three hands a bow, arrow, fruit while the fourth is in the *varada* pose. She is also a Vidyādevī like her Śvetāmbara counterpart Aṃkuśā (q.v.). Brahmā's wife Sarasvatī also has a swan as her vehicle.

Anantamukhī: The seventh goddess in the series of twelve Dhāriṇī deities of Tantric Buddhism. She is as green as *priyaṅgu* flower and holds in her left hand an inexhaustible jar full of treasure on the red lotus. In her right hand is the *viśvavajra*. *Niṣpanna* 57.

Āṇava-mala: One of the three kinds of ignorance according to the Trika system of Kashmir Śaivism, the two others being *kārma* and *māyīya*. Every being is enveloped by *kañcuka*—a coating of impurity. This coating is known as *āṇava-mala*. *Tantrāloka* I. 74; IX. 113, 144, 205-6. This *āṇava-mala* is also due to Śiva (see Aṇu); it is that by which individuals are fettered. The boundless and independent will-power of Śiva is beyond the comprehension of average individuals, it comes to them in a reduced, contracted form. Individuals with *āṇava-mala* have either a fettered condition but awareness of it, or an unfettered condition with lack of awareness of it. *Īśvarapratyabhijñā* III. 2.4; *Tantrāloka* IX. 62 ff; *Pratyabhijñāhṛdaya* 21.

Anavasthollāsa: The last state of spiritual progress according to some Tantric schools; where the mind of the aspirant becomes totally absorbed in the deity. The preceding stages are *ārambha*, *taruṇa*, *yauvana*, *praudha*, *tadanta* or *prauḍhānta* and *unmana*. According to the *Paraśurāmakalpasūtra* X. 68, the first four stages belong to the Samayācāra and the last three, *anavasthā* included, to Svairācāra.

Āṇavī-dīkṣā: One of the three forms of *dīkṣā* (q.v.), or initiation, mentioned in the *Rudrayāmala*. The other two forms are Śāktī and Śāmbhavī. It is an elaborate system of initiation in which *mantra*, *arcanā*, *āsana*, *nyāsa*, *dhyāna* and different *upacāras* or articles are required. *Prāṇatoṣaṇī* II. 4.117. It is of various types like *smārtī*, *mānasikī*, *yaugī*, *cākṣuṣī*, *spārsanī*, *vācikī*, *māntrikī*, *hotrī*, *śāstrī* and *abhiṣecakī*. Rāghava's com. on *Śāradātilaka*, V. 127-40.

Āṇavopāya: A means of spiritual attainment which is also known as *kriyā-upāya* in Tantrism. Though *kriyā* means action it is used here in the sense of knowledge. According to Abhinavagupta when knowledge is derived after the control of desires it is known as *kriyā*. *Tantrāloka*, I. 151. The knowledge by which *ānavopāya* or *kriyā-upāya* is characterized is, however, dualistic, and to some extent dependent on external objects. Ibid. I. 219-20.

Aṅganyāsa: Feeling of the deity in different

parts of the body. It is five-fold (*pañcāṅga*) or six-fold (*ṣaḍaṅga*). The centres are heart, head, protective *amulet*, eyes and intestines. Aṅganyāsa is illustrated as follows: *oṃ hṛdayāya namaḥ, oṃ śirase svāhā, śikhāyai vaṣaṭ, oṃ kavacāya huṃ, om netratrayāya vaṣaṭ, oṃ astrāya phaṭ. Jayākhya* XI; *Prapañcasāra* VI, *Kulārṇava* IV. 18 ff; *Śāradātilaka* IV. 29-41, V. 5-7; *Mahānirvāṇa* III. 41-3. V. 113-18.

Aṅgahāra: Thirty-two movements of the limbs, originally suggested in the *Nāṭyaśāstra* of Bharata, on which the Tantric *mudrās* (q.v.) are based. *Aṅgahāras* depended upon *karaṇas* or different arrangements of hands and feet.

Aṇimā: Superhuman power of becoming as small as an atom. It is one of the eight *siddhis*. The others are *laghimā* (levitation), *mahimā* (magnification), *garimā* (greatness), *prāpti* (power of getting anything), *prākāmya* (non-obstruction of desire), *vaśitva* (power of charming) and *īśitva* (sovereignty over all things). *Prapañcasāra* XIX. 62-3.

Aniruddha-Sarasvatī: Same as Dakṣiṇā-kālī, the primordial energy manifested in the form of twenty-two-lettered Vidyā. She is unlimited and without attributes. *Niruttara* II.

Añjali: Name of an iconic *mudrā* or gesture, also known as *sarvarājendra-mudrā* or the *sampuṭāñjali*. In this gesture the two hands are clasped against the chest, palm to palm, and extended upwards with all fingers erect or slightly bent.

Āṇji: Regarded as a *kalā* (q.v.) or evolute of Śakti, often described as the *vyāpikā-śakti* or all-pervading energy. Kālicaraṇa's com. on *Ṣaṭcakranirūpaṇa* XL. It is often described as an alphabetical symbol.

***Annadākalpa Tantra*:** A late Tantra in seventeen chapters dedicated to the *annapradā*, the food-giving form of the goddess conceived of in terms of *pāra, aparā* and *parāparā vidyās*. It deals with the qualifications of the *guru, mantra, dīkṣā, nyāsa, puraścaraṇa* and allied Tantric rites. One chapter deals with the methods of achieving material power, prosperity and happiness.

Annapūrṇā: Also known as Nityā, she is a goddess of the Bhairavī (q.v.) category. She is the distributor of food. She has Bhūmi and Śrī beside her. She wears a crescent on the head, a crown sparkling with the lustre of nine kinds of gems, and a waist band. *Puraścaryārṇava* IX. 809 ff.

Antaḥkaraṇa: The collective name for intellect (*buddhi*), egoity (*ahaṃkāra*) and mind (*manas*). *Tantrāloka* IX. 236, *Śāradātilaka* I. 36. Advaita treats *antaḥkarana* as being composed of four divisions, the fourth being *cit*, while the Mīmāṃsā treats it as composed of only one entity—*manas*.

Antaḥstha-varṇa: The letters *ya, ra, la* and *va*. These letters are suggestive of the power of will and expression and in undifferentiated relation with the self. *Tantrāloka* III. 159.

Āntarapūjā: Same as Antaryāga (q.v.). *Saṃvit* or pure consciousness is the real form of the great goddess who is without any attribute. Fixation of mind to this formless and unattached *saṃvit* is *āntarapūjā*. *Devībhāgavata* VII. 39.44. The goddess is to be invoked in the *anāhata-padma* which is situated in the heart region. Kālīcaraṇa on *Ṣaṭcakranirūpaṇa* 25.

Āntara-Mantrasnāna: Internal bathing with the flow of nectar when the *kuṇḍalini* rises from the *mūlādhāra* to *sahasrāra* (q.v.) by Yogic exercises. It is a symbolic bathing. *Gandharva-tantra* VII. 18-19; Rāghava on *Śāradātilaka* IV. 2.

Antardaśāra: The inner ground of the mystic Tantric diagram. According to the *Kāmakalāvilāsa* 30 it is the inner shade of the flames of the *cakras*, known as *bindu, trikoṇa* and *aṣṭakoṇa*, while in the *Nityaṣoḍaśikārṇava* VI. 15 it is the expressed ray of the *navatrikoṇa* or *navayonicakra*, i.e. the *cakra* consisting of nine triangles.

Antaramātṛkānyāsa: Feeling of the deity in the region around the neck where the existence of the Tantric *viśuddha-cakra* as a sixteen-petalled lotus is conceived. The letter or *mātṛka* symbolizing the essence of the deity supposed to exist in each petal is to be meditated upon and felt; *Jñānārṇava* quoted in *Tantrasāra* 68. See also *Puraścaryārṇava* V. 330.

Antartīrtha: Tīrthas or holy places supposed to exist within the human body. *Prāṇatoṣaṇī* III. 3.178.

Antaryāga: Internal worship meant for Tantric aspirants belonging to the higher grades. It is mental worship in which external formalities are redundant. *Mahānirvāṇa*-

tantra V. 143-9. Accroding to the *Devībhāgavata* VII. 39.44 pure consciousness is the absolute form of the goddess beyond all attributes and the complete merger of the self of the aspirant in this stream of consciousness is *antaryāga*. The *Gautamīya-tantra* IX says that *antaryāga* leads to salvation within the span of one's life. Its virtues are elaborately stated in the *Gandharva-tantra* XII. 24-7.

Aṇu: One of the three categories of the Trika philosophy of Kashmir Śaivism indicating *jīva* or individual, also known as *paśu*. This *jīva* or *paśu* is a fettered individual, and since in Trika philosophy *jīva* is equated with Śiva, this *aṇu* and the ignorance (*āṇava-mala*, q.v.) by which it is characterized are also due to Śiva. When Siva owing to his independence expresses himself in the contracted form of a fettered individual, he is called Aṇu. *Sa eva svātantryāt ātmānaṃ saṃkucitaṃ avabhāsayan aṇurīti ucyate.* Abhinavagupta's *Tantrasāra* 6. The term Aṇu is also used to denote a means (see Āṇavopāya) for spiritual attainment and has an element of dualism. It leads to *vikalpa* knowledge, i.e. knowledge based on an object, which is a means to an end but not the end itself. *Tantrāloka* I, 150-1, 219-21. According to Abhinavagupta that which is fettered by six false covering in the body is called Aṇu and as such the term is the synonym of *paśu*, *puruṣa* or *jīva*. Aṇu is also a term for *mantra*. As the external form of an individual is pure, so also the material body of a *mantra* constituted by sound appears to be pure. Though it is a mere combination of words and sound it is a conscious principle. Bhāskara Rāya's *Setubandha*, com. of *Nityaṣoḍaśikārṇava*.

Anukalpa: Substitutes, especially for the Tantric five Ms, such as garlic for meat, cococut-water for wine, etc. This substitution holds good also in the case of sacrifices. Each of the five Ms has several substitutes. For example wine alone has six substitutes such as powder-mixed water, coconut water, milk, whey, water mixed with jaggery and water mixed with sandalwood paste. Any edible which grows underground such as ginger, garlic, turnip, radish, etc., can be sustitute for flesh. Certain mixed preparations of cereals can themselves serve as substitutes for other brands in the case of *mudrā* while *maithuna* or sexual intercourse should be substituted by worship with sandalwood paste and paste made of a special kind of red powder, the former symbolizing semen and the latter female fluid. *Vṛtti* on *Paraśurāmakalpasūtra* X. 63; *Mahānirvāna* VIII. 172-3; *Śaktisaṅgama*, Tārā, XXXII. 25; *Kulārṇava* XVII. 64-9, *Prāṇatoṣaṇī* VII. 2.508.

Anupāya: Means for obtaining pure knowledge, by which the knower is merged in the knowable. This peaceful and blissful realization is possible only by the grace of *guru*. *Tantrāloka* I. 242.

Anusmṛti: Memory. In Tantric Buddhism it is the constant meditation on the object for which the psychic exercise is undertaken. By this *pratibhāsa* or revelation takes place, and the whole objective world appears as a contracted form to be meditated upon in the *bimba* or icon-circle. By this process, which should be continued at least for six months, transcendental knowledge is suddenly realized by the worshipper which is known as *samādhi* or visualization. *Guhyasamāja* XVIII.

Anuttara: That which is beyond comprehension. *Parātriṃśikā* 19. It is same as *brahman* or Śiva in Kashmir Śaivism. Ibid. 221. It is self-illuminating. Ibid. 39. It is symbolized by the first letter A of the Śāradā script symbolizing both the *prakāśa* (static) and *vimarśa* (vibrating) aspects of the supreme being. *Tantrāloka* III. 82. As *bindu* (q.v.) or dot it is *para-saṃvit* or pure consciouness, the all-pervading eternal reality. Ibid. III. 116-17.

Anuttaralipi: The letters 'A' and 'Ha', the former being suggestive of the *prakāśa* or static aspect of *saṃvit* (q.v.) and the latter of the *vimarśa* or dynamic aspect. These two letters together constitute *aham* (q.v.). Letters from 'A' to 'Ha' are the body of the supreme goddess known as Ahamātmikā (q.v.). She is also known as Anuttaravimarśalipilakṣyavigrahā in the form of fifty letters and in the capacity of being the producer of the universe and inner self of every being. *Cidvallī* on *Kāmakalāvilāsa* 6-7.

***Anuttarayoga-tantra*:** One of the four classes of Buddhist Tantras which deal with higher mysticism. This class is subdivided into three kinds. The *Guhyasamāja-tantra* (q.v.) is the ideal *Anuttarayoga-tantra* in which the term *vajra* is used to symbolize the ultimate reality in which there is absolute non-duality. It belongs to the Mahāyoga kind or category. The *Kālacakra* (q.v.) belongs to the Atiyoga category. The Yoginī-Anuttarayoga category includes *Cakrasaṃvara*, *Vajra-bhairava*, *Hevajra*, *Buddhakapāla*, *Dākārṇava*, etc.

Anuvyañjana: See Lakṣaṇa.

Apāna: One of the five vital airs which is complementary to *prāṇa*. The Tantras try to locate the visible universe within the human body. The time element has also been explained with reference to the course of the vital wind, viz., *prāṇa* and *apāna*. The implication seems to be that the human body represents the manifestations of the same energy which is at work in the vast cosmos. The important nerve on the right side, well known as *piṅgalā*, through which flows the *apāna* air is said to represent the principle of Śiva, while the left nerve, known as *iḍā*, through which flows the *prāṇa* air, is said to represent the principle of Śakti.

Aparājitā: Buddhist goddess, emanation of Ratnasambhava whose name also occurs in the *dhyāna* of Aṣṭabhujā Kurukullā. She tramples upon Gaṇeśa and one of her hands is raised in the attitude of dealing a slap while her parasol is held by important Brahmanical gods. She is yellow in complexion, two-armed and one-faced. *Sādhana* 403. Aparājitā is also the name of the Śāsanadevatā of Mallinātha according to the Digambara Jain tradition. She is described as riding a lion and bearing in three of her hands a citrus, sword, shield while the fourth is held in *varada mudrā*.

Apara-bindu: Bindu (q.v.) in a broad sense is the principle of *cit* or sentience and as such is not different from *brahman*, the Absolute in the form of pure consciousness. In a narrower sense it denotes the principle of producing the effect and as such is divided into *para* or *apara*, pertaining respectively to supra-mundane and mundane existence. Apara-bindu is a subdivision of para bindu (q.v.). In it the Śiva element dominates. Apara-bindu, together with Bīja and Apara-nāda (q.v.) constitute the Kuṇḍalinī or A-Ka-Tha triangle. *Śāradātilaka* I. 7 ff.

Apara-nāda: Nāda (q.v.) is the power of manifestation. As a creative principle it reveals an equilibrium of two complementary principles symbolized by Śiva and Śakti. The manifestations of the successive stages of creation are denoted by the term Apara-nāda. It is a subdivision of *para-bindu* (q.v.). While in the Apara-bindu the Śiva element dominates in Apara-nāda there is Śiva-Śakti equilibrium. Apara-nāda is also a constituent of the kuṇḍalinī triangle. *Śāradātilaka* I. 7 ff. See Nāda.

Āpyāyana: Processing of the *mantras* by various means *Tantrasāra* 54.

Ārambha-ullāsa: The first of the seven stages of spiritual attainment, the others being *taruṇa*, *yauvana*, *praudha*, *praudhānta*, or *tadanta*, *unmana* and *anavasthā*. According to *Paraśurāmakalpasūtra* X. 68 the first five of these stages require the aid of a preceptor. The *ārambha* stage is intended for persons belonging to the *paśu* or ordinary category. In this state the aspirant has only the desire for Tantric lessons. This stage, according to Rāmeśvara, the commentator on *Paraśurāma-kalpasūtra* belongs to the Samayācāra category.

Arapacana: A form of Mañjuśrī (q.v.). He is white or red in colour, seated in *vajrāsana* (q.v.) with four companions, his symbol being a book and sword. He has numerous sculptural representations. A few of his images have been found even in Indonesia. Arapacana is also the name of a mystic Buddhist script. See B.N. Mukherjee's paper in *Tantric Buddhism*, ed. by N.N. Bhatta-charyya, New Delhi 1999, 303-13.

Arbuda: Holy resort of the goddess Kātyāyanī mentioned in the *Jñanārnava-tantra*. It is Mount Abu in Sirohi district, Rajasthan.

Arcismatī: A *bhūmi* (q.v.) goddess of Tantric Buddhism who is of the colour of an emerald and holds in her left hand a blue lotus. *Niṣpanna* 55.

Ardhacandra-śakti: Symbolical half-moon as the repository of Śakti where the aspirant becomes all knowing. It has five *kalā* or functional aspects known as Jyotsnā, Jyotsnāvatī, Kānti, Suprabhā and Vimalā. *Ṣaṭcakraviveka* 126 ff.

Ardhakālī: A Śākta saint, daughter of Dvijadeva Ṭhākura of Panditbari in Mymen-singh district of Bengal who flourished in the seventeenth century. Her real name was Jayadurgā but she was called Ardhakālī because half of her body was dark. She was married to Rāghavarāma, a pupil of her father. She had acquired a very elevated spiritual status and was believed by people in general to be an incarnation of the divine mother.

Ardhanārīśvara, Īśvarī: Image or icon showing the combined form of Śiva and Śakti or their non-dual existence. It is a conception of the equilibrium of Śiva-Śakti in an artistic perspective. This state is called *sāmarasya* or *avinābhāva* (q.v.). *Saubhāgyabhāskara* on *Lalitāsahasranāma* 161; *Kaulamārga-rahasya* 45 n. It is said that Mahākāla (Śiva) and Mahākalī (Śakti) stay like a seed covered by a sheath. When the sheath is unpeeled one finds two equal parts of the seed in close union. The equilibrium of Śiva-Śakti is just like this: *Mahākālī mahākālaścaṇakākāra-rūpataḥ māyācchāditātmānaṃ tanmadhye samabhāgataḥ. Tantratattva* 109. The sheath is Māyā-Śakti (q.v.). *Ardhanārīśvarī* is also the name of a Vidyā (q.v.) details of whose cults are given in the *Sammoha-tantra.*

Ardhaparyaṅka: A particular *āsana* or posture of sitting. Both the legs are on the same pedestal, but one is bent with the knee remaining horizontal. It is also known as *mahārājalīlā.*

Arimantra: One of the four kinds of *mantras* according to a few Tantric texts like *Vārāhasaṃhitā* and *Piṅgalāmata*. While the Siddha, Sādhya and Susiddha *mantras* become efficacious to the spiritual aspirant, Arimantra destroys him. *Puraścaryārṇava* I. 59.

Artha: Meaning, denotation. It is the expressive aspect of *śabda* (q.v.), sound and word. Rāghavabhaṭṭa in his com. on *Śāradātilaka* I. 1 says that the Parāśakti at first introduces its *śabda* form as the denotative and *artha* form as the denoted. *Sarvasyāpyarthasya śabdaprakāsyatva-niyamāt jñeya*: every *artha* is to be understood as the expressed denotation of *śabda.* Ibid. *Artha* is of two kinds, subtle and gross. However, according to the Tantras there is no difference between *śabda* and *artha*. They stand in undifferentiated relation with each other, both being two aspects of the same reality. Com. on *Śaradātilaka* I. 1. But for practical reasons a subtle distinction is made and it is said the *śabda* originates from the Śakti or *vimarśa* (vibrating) aspect of *saṃvit* while *artha* is from its Śiva or *prakāśa* (static) aspect. *Kāmakalāvilāsa* 12; *Varivasyā-rahasya*, com. on verse 74. *Setubandha*, com. on *Nityaṣoḍaśikārṇava* VI. 10.11.

Artha: A goddess of Tantric Buddhism in the series of four pratisaṃvit deities. Her colour is green and she holds in her two hands a jewel and a noose. *Niṣpanna* 57.

Aruṇā: Name of the presiding Śakti of one of the eight corners of the Tantric *aṣṭakoṇa-cakra*. In the *Vāmakeśvara-tantra* she is regarded as the presiding deity of letters beginning with Ta. *Nityaṣoḍaśikārṇava* I. 191-2.

***Ārya-Mañjuśrīmūlakalpa*:** An extensive work of Tantric Buddhism written in *saṅgīti* style in prose and verse in mixed Sanskrit. It is included in the Tibetan Kanjur. It has now 55 chapters, but its Chinese translation of the 10th century has only 28 chapters. Endless *mantras, maṇḍalas* and *mudrās* are scattered here and there in the text, but without any systematization and correlation with the Vajrayāna pantheon. It does not refer specially to the doctrine of five Dhyānī Buddhas or even their names, *mudrās*, *mantras,* families, Śaktis, colour and directions. It gives a legendary biography of the Buddha and some historical information. It names and defines 108 *mudrās* and holds that the combination of *mantras* and *mudrās* bring success in all actions. One section is devoted to *paṭavidhāna*, i.e. directions for drawing pictures of different Buddhas, Boddhisattvas, Tārā and other goddesses and so forth. The drawing of *maṇḍalas* is another important feature of this work. Modes of painting abstract ideas are also described. The special expression 'Vajrayāna' is absent here. Instead, we find the term Mantrayāna which points to the fact that the text was originally composed when Tantric Buddhism was yet to be characterized by its most popular name. Ed. by T. Ganapati Sastri, Trivandrum Sanskrit Series, nos. XXVI, LXX, 1920-2.

Āsana: One of the eight disciplines of yoga. *Āsanas* or bodily postures are required for strength or firmness. There are numerous *āsanas*, of which eighty-four are common. The more important ones are *baddha-padmāsana, muktapadmāsana, muṇḍāsana, citāsana, śavāsana, siddhāsana, ugrāsana, svastikāsana, trikoṇāsana* and *bhujaṅgāsana*. *Śivasaṃhitā* III. 84-91; *Haṭhayogapradīpikā* I. 19 ff.

Āsana: A seat; attitude or posture of sitting found in cult images. The word *padmāsana* means the seat of lotus. Similarly *siṃhāsana* means lion-throne or the seat of a lion. The word *sukhāsana* means an easy attitude of sitting. When used in a technical sense āsana is of various kinds such as *paryaṅka*, *vajra-paryaṅka*, *lalita*, *ardhaparyaṅka*, *bhadra*, *ālīḍha*, *pratyālīḍha*, *nāṭya*, etc.

Āsanaśuddhi: Purification of seat (*āsana*) of the aspirant with *mantras* which is a pre-condition of Tantric worship: *Puraś-caryārṇava* III. 158-9, *Mahānirvāṇa* V. 81; Rāghava on *Śāradātilaka* XVII. 19.

Asaṅga: Buddhist scholar and philosopher. Sādhana no. 159 of the *Sādhanamālā* (q.v.) dedicated to the worship of Prajña-pāramita, is attributed to him. Whether Asaṅga himself had written Tantric works is doubtful, but on the basis of the statements of Lāmā Tāranātha the possibility cannot be ruled out. According to B.T. Bhattacharyya there seems to be a historical connection between the Yogācāra school and the rise of Vajrayāna. His view that the *Guhyasamāja* (q.v.) was composed by Asaṅga does not seem tenable. According to Lāmā Tāranātha Asaṅga introduced Tantrism in India. This view has also no genuine historical basis.

Āsava: A kind of wine used in Tantric rites.

Asmitā: Sense of personality which consists in the seen (the self) being held as if identical with the instruments of seeing such as mind and sense-organs. *Yogasūtra* II. 5.9.

Aśokā: Śāsanadevatā or the Yakṣiṇī of Śītalanātha according to the Śvestāmbara Jain tradition. She is described as seated upon a lotus in *varada* pose, and bearing in her hands, noose, fruit and goad. She has a dual character. In one aspect she is a Yakṣiṇī and in another a Vidyādevī.

Aśokakāntā: A form of the Tantric Buddhist goddess Mārīci (q.v.) when she holds the bough of an Aśoka tree in the left hand and exhibits the *varada mudrā* (q.v.) with the right. Her vehicle is a sow. *Sādhana* 306.

Āsphānaka-yoga: Yoga of psychic expansion which the Buddha himself practised. *Lalita-vistara*, R.L. Mitra's edn., 315.

Aṣṭadalapadma: Eight-petalled lotus, actual or imaginary used as universal Tantric symbol in the composition of the *cakras* within and without the human body and also in the diagrams. The petals are said to contain letters *ka*, *ca*, *ṭa*, *ta*, *pa*, *ya*, *sa* and *la*. *Kāmakalā-vilāsa* 33. The presiding goddesses are: Anaṅgakusumā, Anaṅgamekhalā, Anaṅga-madanā, Anaṅgamadanāturā, Anaṅgarekhā, Anaṅgaveginī, Anaṅgāṅkuśā and Anaṅga-mālinī. *Nityaṣoḍaśikārṇava* I. 177-8. They are known as Guptatarayoginī. The attainment is known as *mahimāsiddhi*, associated *mudrā* is *ākarṣiṇī*. *Gandharvatantra* V. 96; XVII. 42.

Aṣṭādaśa Vidyā: Eighteen subjects for enriching knowledge which are the four Vedas; six Vedāṅgas; Mīmāṃsā, Nyāya, Purāṇa, Dharmaśāstra (legal texts), Āyurveda (medical science), Dhanurveda (science of warfare), Gandharvaveda (music and fine arts) and Nītiśāstra (ethics). Rāmeśvara on *Paraśurāmakalpasūtra* I. 2).

Aṣṭaka: Eight groups of Tantric texts belonging to the category of Bhairava Āgamas. The *aṣṭakas* are Bhairava, Yāmala, Matākhya, Maṅgala, Cakra, Śikhā, Bahurūpa and Vāgīśa.

Aṣṭakoṇa-cakra: Octagonal diagram said to be the extension of *trikoṇa-cakra* or triangular diagram. *Kāmakalāvilāsa* 29. It is regarded both as the gross and as the subtle body of the goddess. *Cidvallī* com. on ibid. 40 ff. Each of the eight corners of this *cakra* is presided over by a goddess or Śakti known respectively as Vaśinī, Kāmeśī, Modinī, Vimalā, Aruṇā, Jayinī, Sarveśī and Kaulinī. *Nityaṣoḍa-śikārṇava* I. 191-2. The attainment resulting from this *cakra* worship is known as *bhukti-siddhi*. The presiding deities are collectively known as Rahasyayoginī and they are propitiated by exhibiting khecarī-mudrā. *Gandharva-tantra* XVII. 74-6.

Aṣṭa Mahābhaya Tārā: Tārā who saves her devotees from eight great fears. She sits in *ardhaparyaṅka* attitude and is surrounded by ten goddesses originating from the ten syllables of the Tārā-*mantra*: *Om Tāre Tuttāre Ture Svāhā*.

Aṣṭamaithunāṅga: Eight techniques required for sexual union. They are *smaraṇa* (evocative rememberance), *kīrtana* (uttering sweet words), *keli* (sport), *prekṣaṇa* (special looks), *guhyabhāṣana* (secret dialogue), *saṅkalpa* (determination), *adhyavāsāya* (patience and perseverence) and *kriyāniṣpatti* (completion of sexual intercourse). *Dakṣa-saṃhitā*. VII. 31-2.

Aṣṭamātṛkā: Eight *mātṛkā* goddesses—Brahmāṇī, Māheśvarī, Kaumārī, Vaiṣṇavī, Vārāhī, Aindrī, Cāmuṇḍā and Mahālakṣmī—supposed to reside in the *viṣṇurekhā* of the *bhūpura-yantra* in the Tantric tradition. *Nityaṣodaśikārṇava* I. 169-71.

Aṣṭāṅga-yoga: Eight kind steps of yoga (q.v.). These are *yama* (restraint), *niyama* (cultivation of good habits), *āsana* (sitting posture), *prāṇāyāma* (regulation of breath), *pratyāhāra* (withdrawal of senses from their respective external objects and keeping them under the control of mind), *dhāraṇa* (fixing the mind on the desired object), *dhyāna* (meditation) and *samādhi* (mind's perfect absorption in the object of contemplation).

Aṣṭanidhi: Eight treasures. They are *padma*, *mahāpadma*, *makara*, *kaccapa*, *mukunda*, *nīla*, *nanda*, and *śaṅkha* according to the *Mārkaṇḍeya Purana* list.

Aṣṭapāśa: Eight fetters leading to human bondage: *ghṛṇā* (hatred), *lajjā* (shame), *bhaya* (fear), *śaṅkā* (misgiving), *jugupsā* (upbraiding), *kula* (pedigree), *śīla* (manners) and *jāti* (birth or caste). *Paraśurāma-kalpasūtra* X. 70.

Aṣṭaprakṛti: Collective name of the first eight Sāṅkhya *tattvas*: Prakṛti, Mahat, Ahaṃkāra and the five Tanmātras.

Aṣṭaśakti: Eight presiding goddesses of *aṣṭakoṇacakra* (q.v.) known as Vaśinī, Kāmeśī, Modinī, or Mohinī, Vimalā, Aruṇā, Jayinī, Sarveśvarī or Sarveśī and Kaulinī. *Nityaṣoḍaśikārṇava* I. 191-2. Cold, heat, pleasure, pain, will and the three qualities of *sattva*, *rajas* and *tamas* are attributed to these goddesses. *Bhavanopaniṣat* 21. They are also known as Rahasyayoginīs. *Gandharva-tantra* XVII. 74.

Aṣṭasiddhi: Eight miraculous attainments which are: *animā* (atomization), *laghimā* (levitation), *mahimā* (magnification), *garimā* (greatness), *prāpti* (power of getting anything), *prākāmya* (non-obstruction of desire), *vaśitva* (power of charming) and *īśitva* (sovereignty over all things). *Prapañcasāra* XIX. 62-3. In some cases *kāmāvasayitva* (having perfect control over or suppression of all desires) has been substituted for *garimā*.

Aṣṭatārā: Eight forms of Tārā—*tārā cogrā mahogrā ca vajrā kālī sarasvatī; kāmeśvarī, bhadrakālī itaṣṭau tāriṇī smṛtā. Māyātantra* quoted in *Tantrasāra* 347. The group is thus composed of Tārā, Ugrā, Vajrā, Mahogrā, Kālī, Sarasvatī, Kāmeśvarī and Bhadrakālī. This group is also known by the name Aṣṭa-Tāriṇī.

Aṣṭāvaraṇa: Eightfold shields which, according to the Vira Śaivas, protect the devotee from the snare of nescience. These are *guru, liṅga, jaṅgama, pādodaka, prasāda, bhasma, rudrākṣa* and *mantra*.

Aṣṭayoginī: Eight special yoginīs who are described in the *Tantrasāra* which also quotes their *dhyānas* from the *Bhūtaḍāmara-tantra*. They are Kaṇakāvati, Kāmeśvarī, Nalinī, Padminī, Madhumatī, Manoharā, Ratisundarī and Surasundarī (q.v.).

Aśuddha-māyā: One of the two kinds of *māyā* (q.v.) according to the Śaiva Siddhānta. It is the material cause from which are produced *kāla* (time), *niyati* (destiny) and *kalā* (instrument). From *kalā* come *vidyā* (finite knowledge) and *prakṛti* (q.v.); from *vidyā* comes *rāga* (attachment) and from *prakṛti* come *citta* (mind) and *buddhi* (intellect) and from the latter *ahaṃkāra* (q.v.) and its evolutes. *Mṛgendra Āgama* II. 3-7; III.1; VII. 11; VIII. 1-5; IX. 2-4; *Pauṣkara Āgama* II. 17; III. 4; V. 9; *Śivajñānabodham* II. 5, XII. 3.

Aśvakrānta: The region extending from the Vindhya hills to the great sea. In the *Mahāsiddhasāra-tantra* the western boundary of *Aśvakrānta* has been located on the Karatoyā in the Dinajpur district and the eastern boundary in Yavadvīpa or Java. It is a Tantric region. Among the Tantras of this region the following may be noted. Bhūtaśuddhi, Guptadīkṣā, Bṛhatsāra, Tattvasāra Varṇasāra, Kriyāsāra, Guptatantra, Guptasāra, Bṛhattoḍala, Bṛhannirvāṇa, Bṛhatkaṅkālinī, Siddhatantra, Kālatantra, Śivatantra, Sārātsāra, Gaurītantra, Yogatantra, Dharmakatantra, Tattvacintāmaṇi, Bindutantra, Mahāyoginī, Bṛhadyoginī, Śivārcana, Sambara, Śūlinī, Mahāmālinī, Mokṣa, etc.

Aśvapradā: Holy resort of the goddess. It is probably the Aśvakrāntā hill near Gauhati in Assam. *Bṛhannīla* V.

Aśvatīrtha: Holy resort of the great goddess situated at the confluence of the Gaṅgā and the Kālīnadī near Kanauj. *Bṛhannīla* V.

Atimārgī(ka): Those who did not believe in the codified norms of spiritual realization. The Kāpalikas, Kālāmukhas, Aghorapanthīs, Kāruṇika-siddhāntins and other extremist sects of Śaiva-Śākta affiliation were known as Atimārgikas. These sects represented a special ritualistic trend, a tradition of hoary antiquity, containing many obscure elements. These sects had no literature of their own; whatever is known about them comes from the writings of their opponents. These sects were basically worshippers of the Female Principle. They had no faith in the authoritarian social values and the traditional social stratification as prescribed by the Smārta-Pauranic law-givers.

Atirahasyayoginī: Collective name of the three presiding goddesses of the three angles of the *trikoṇa* or mystic triangle. The goddess at the apex is known as Kāmeśvarī, on the right angle as Vajreśvarī and on the left angle as Bhagamālinī. *Gandharvatantra* V. 112-13.

Atiśūnya: The second stage of vacuity mentioned in the *Pañcakrama* which is said to be the manifestation of light (*alokābhāsa*) and the Upāya or the means. It is also said to be of the nature of constructive imagination (*parikalpita*) of the mind (*caitasika*), the solar-circle (*sūryamaṇḍala*) and the thunderbolt (*vajra*). There are forty momentary mental states of defilement associated with it.

Ātmasamarpaṇa: Self-surrender of the aspirant with all parts of his body after concluding his worship and rituals to his personal deity. *Śāradātilaka* VII, *Mahānirvāṇa* VI. 178-81; *Puraścaryārṇava* IV. 306.

Ātmaśuddhi: Purification of the self by various processes. *Kulārṇava* VI.

Ātmavali: Sacrifice of the self. Complete surrender of one's mental faculties like thinking, feeling and willing, to the supreme goddess. *Gāyatrī-tantra* V.

Aṭṭahāsa: A Śākta *pītha* or holy resort of the goddess Phullarā mentioned in the *Jñānārṇava-tantra*. It is near Labhpur in the Birbhum district, West Bengal. According to the *Bṛhannīla-tantra* V the presiding deity of this *pīṭha* is Bhīmākālī. A different version holds that the presiding deity of this *pīṭha* is Cāmuṇḍā or Mahānandā.

Audaka Snāna: One of the three kinds of bathing, others being *mantra* and *mānasa*. This is the most common form of bathing performed in river, lake, pond and the like. *Atha snānam; tacca trividham; audakamāntramānasabhedāt. Tārābhaktisudhārṇava* V. 127.

Avadhūta: A class of ascetics who are beyond all restrictions. According to the *Sannyāsopaniṣad* 13 they take food from persons belonging to all *varṇas*, except those who are charged with moral sins. They eat like an *ajagara*, i.e. while lying down and opening only the mouth, without any effort, and are solely absorbed in contemplation. According to the *Kulārṇava* XVII, an Avadhūta is the aspirant who commands universal reverence, who is free from prejudices and who has knowledge of his own. Avadhūtas are divided into two classes—householders and recluses. *Prānatoṣaṇī* VII. 4, 532. Avadhūtas belonging to the highest grade are known as Kulavadhūtas. *Mahānirvāṇa*, VII. 271-83.

Avadhutī: Tantric name of a nerve channel. It is same as *susumnā*.

Avaguṇṭhaṇa Mudrā: A hand pose formed by clasping all the fingers of the left hand with the thumb except the index finger which remains open and pendant.

Āvāhana: Invocation of the Supreme Being to be manifested through one's own personal or chosen deity, very often symbolized by image or other ritual articles. Theoretically *brahman* pervades the universe. Hence *āvāhana* is nothing more than having an experience of the great goddess by imagining a form and offering flowers, etc., for the satisfaction of mind. *Puraścaryārṇava* V. 345-6; *Kaulāvalinirṇaya* VII. 3-4.

Āvāhanī: Tantric *mudrā* or hand-pose. It is folding of both hands to make a hollow which can contain flower, etc. In this *mudrā* the thumbs touch the ring finger. *Tantrasāra* 567.

Avalokiteśvara: Most popular Bodhisattva in the Buddhist world. In the *Kāraṇḍavyūha* he is said to manifest himself in countless forms for the welfare of mankind. No less than 108 forms have been attributed to him and he is 'looked upon as a representative of the Buddha, the guardian of the Buddhist faith until Maitreya should appear on earth as Mānuṣī Buddha'. The *Sādhanamālā* 27 ff. gives 38 *sādhanas* which describe a variety of his forms. Among his numerous forms Padmapāṇi is the most common. He is the spiritual son of the Dhyānī Buddha Amitābha, generally one-faced and two-armed and represented as displaying the *varada* pose with the right hand and holding a lotus by the stem in the left. Among his more important forms mention may be made of Ṣaḍakṣarī Lokeśvara, Siṃhanāda, Khaṣarpaṇa, Lokanātha, Hālāhala, Padmanartteśvara, Harihariharivāhana, Trailokyavaśaṅkara, Raktalokeśvara, Māyājālakrama, Nīlakaṇṭha, Sugatisandarśana, Pretasantarpita, Sukhāvati Lokeśvara and Vajradharma (q.v.).

Avantī: Holy resort of the goddess, the same as Ujjayini. The goddess is Atipāvanī. *Bṛhannīla-tantra* V. In the *Śaktisaṅgama*, Sundarī VII. 32 the presiding goddess of this *pītha* is Kālikā. *'avantisaṃjñako deśaḥ kālikā tatra tiṣṭhati*. Atipāvanī may be an epithet of Kālikā.

Āvaraṇa-cakra: Another name of *navacakra* (q.v.). The nine *cakras* are Trailokyamohana, Sarvāśāparipuraka, Sarvasamkṣobhaka, Sarvasaubhāgyadāyaka, Sarvārthasādhaka, Sarvarakṣākara, Sarvarogahara, Sarvasiddhiprada and Sarvānandamaya. Each of these *cakras* is presided over by a Cakreśvarī and a yoginī or Āvaraṇadevatā. *Tantrarāja* V. 9-11.

Āvaraṇa-devatā: Nine yoginīs presiding over the *navacakra* or *āvaraṇacakra* (q.v.). Thus Prakaṭā presides over Trailokyamohana-cakra, Guptā over Sarvāśāparipuraka-cakra, Guptatarā over Sarvasamkṣobhaka-cakra, Sampradāyā over Sarvasaubhāgyadāyaka-cakra, Kulakaulā over Sarvārthasādhaka-cakra, Nigarbhā over Sarvarakṣākara-cakra, Rahasyā over Sarvarogahara-cakra, Atirahasyā or Parāpararahasyā over Sarvasiddhiprada-cakra and Parāparārahasyā or Parāparātirahasyā over Sarvānandamaya-cakra. *Setubandha* com. on *Nityaṣoḍaśikārṇava* I. 164-5; *Tantrarājatantra* V. 9-11.

Aveśa: A concept of Kashmiri Śaivism. In the Trika texts this term is used in the same sense of *upāya* or right knowledge which is the understanding that the individual self is not different from the cosmic self that is Śiva. Abhinavagupta interprets this concept as *asvatantrasya paratadrupatā nāmaveśaḥ iti, Tantrāloka* I, 209.

Avidyā, Avidyā-śakti: A term which pertains to all forms of Indian philosophy. Basically Avidyā denotes ignorance, false knowledge, misconception, appearance veiling reality and so forth. In Tantra Avidyā is equated with Māyā or the material principle of creation. According to Tantric cosmogony at the time of the dissolution of the universe pure consciousness or *saṃvit* (q.v.) remains absolutely free from material contaminations, but when the alternatives or material entities develop owing to the self-contraction of *saṃvit*, Śakti then manifests itself as Avidyā or material Prakṛti. Avidyā-śakti, also called Māyā-śakti, is veiled consciousness. This Śakti is composed of three *guṇas*—Sattva, Rajas and Tamas—and known as Triguṇa-śakti or Kāmakalā symbolized by the triangle. It is not unreal and it is the cause of the material world. *Tripurārahasya*, Jñānakhaṇḍa XIV. In the sense of ignorance or false knowledge the term Avidyā is also used in the Tantras. This ignorance is of five kinds which fetters the human beings. These are ascription of self where there is not; failure to recognize the cosmic self in individual self; making differentiation among beings; between God and self; and between sentience and self. *Kaulamārgarahasya* 68. See Māyā-śakti.

Avimukta: Holy resort of the goddess Viśālākṣi. It is the same as Vārāṇasī. *Bṛhanīlatantra* V.

Avinābhāva Sambandha: Relation of non-duality or identity which holds good in the case of Śiva and Śakti in the Tantras. This relation is same as what is known as *sāmarasya* in which Śiva and Śakti are both equal partners standing in undifferentiated relation. *Saubhāgyabhāskara* on *Lalitā-sahasranāma* 161; *Kaulamārgarahasya* 45 n. Avinābhāva is explained in a quotation from *Mātṛkācakraviveka* as *avirahaḥ śivayoḥ svabhāvaḥ*.

Avīra: Tantric aspirants belonging to the probationary stages of *ārambha*, *taruṇa*, *yauvana* and *prauḍha*. Rāmeśvara's *vṛtti* on *Paraśurāmakalpasūtra* X. 58. They are not sufficiently advanced in spiritual attainment to qualify as *Vīra*.

Avyakta: See Prakṛti. In *Saubhāgyabhāskara* 99 the term *avyakta* has been used to denote *kāraṇa-bindu* or the root cause manifested in effect. *Avyaktaṃ kārana yat tat triguṇa-prabhavā-pyayam. Síva Purāṇa* Vāyavīya, *pūrva* IV. 32.

Ayodhyā: Holy resort of the goddess Bhavānī or Annapūrṇā. In the *Kubjikātantra* VII and *Bṛhannīlatantra* V it is mentioned as a centre of Devī worship. The *Śiva Carita* mentions it as an Upa-pīṭha. It is modern Ayodhyā in the Fyzabad district, Uttar Pradesh.

Āyurvaśitā: Tantric Buddhist goddess of the Vaśitā (q.v.) category who is described as whitish red in colour holding in her left hand the image of the Buddha Amitāyus in *samādhi mudrā* on *padmarāga* jewel.

Bb

Badarī: Holy resort of the goddess Urvaśī or Śrīvidyā. Same as Badarikāśrama (Badrinath in Garhwal, Uttar Pradesh) in the Himalayas, *Kubjikā* VII; *Bṛhannīla* V; *Matsya Purāṇa* XIII. 26 ff; *Devībhāgavata* VII. 30.55 ff.; *Skanda* V. 3.98.64 ff.; *Padma*, Sṛṣṭi XVII. 184 ff.

Bahihrpūjā: See Bahiryāga.

Bahirdaśāra: The outer ground of mystic Tantric diagrams meant for the representation of the five elements like space, etc., and five *tanmātras* (q.v.) like sound, etc., symbolized by the ten letters beginning with *ka. Nityaṣodaśikārṇava* VI. 16. The ten triangles by which the theme is represented are presided over by ten goddesses (ibid. I. 184-6). They belong to the clan of *āvaraṇa-devatā* (q.v.) and are styled Kulakaula-yoginī. *Gandharvatantra* V. 102.

Bahirmātṛkānyāsa: Feeling the deity in three forms—creative, sustaining and destructive—in the outer parts of the body in terms of the symbolism of prescribed letters known as *mātṛkās*. It is to be done after performing the *antarmātṛkānyāsa* (q.v.). *Tantrasāra* 89.

Bahiryāga: External worship; counterpart of *antaryāga* (q.v.) or internal worship.

Bahudā: Holy resort of the goddess Anantā. Bahudā is the name of a small river which is identified with the Dhumela or Burha-Rapti, a tributary of the Rapti in the Ayodhya region. *Bṛhannīla* V

Bahulā: A Śākta Pīṭha where the left hand of Satī had fallen. It is mentioned in the *Pīṭhanirṇaya*. It is located at Ketugram near Katwa in Burdwan district, West Bengal. The *Śivacarita* calls it a *mahāpīṭha*.

Bahurūpāṣṭaka: A group of eight Bhairava Āgamas (q.v.) represented by *Andhaka, Rurubheda, Ajākhyā, Malasaṅgaka, Varṇakaṇṭha, Vibhaṅga, Jvālina* and *Mātṛrodana*.

Bahurūpiṇī: Śāsanadevatā of the Jain Tīrthaṃkara Munisuvrata. According to the Digambara tradition her vehicle is a black snake and she holds a shield, a fruit, a sword and shows the *varada mudrā*. Her other name is Naradattā. From the nature of her symbols and her Tīrthaṃkara's having a Śiva-like character she discloses herself in representation as a form of Durgā or a Brahmanic Śakti.

Bāhyamantrasnāna: Artificial bathing. If for the lack of water, or when for the shortage of time, or for any other valid reason bathing is not possible, one should purify one's body by uttering specific *mantras* and making *nyāsas* (q.v.) in different parts of the body. *Tārābhaktisudhārṇava* V. 131.

Bāhyapūjā: Same as Bahiryāga.

Bāhyasnāna: Bathing in river, lake, spring and tank and with water from well. Before bathing one should purify oneself by *malāpakarṣaṇa* or cleansing of the body with materials and *mantras*. *Bṛhannīla* I, *Śāradātilaka* IV, *Prāṇatoṣaṇī* III. 3.174.

Baindava-Bhuvana: Collective name of the five regions of the *tattvas* or principles of Śakti. The regions are Śāntyātīta, Śānti, Vidyā, Pratiṣṭhā and Nivṛtti.

Baindavacakra: A name of Sahasrāra or the highest cerebral region.

Baindava-śarīra: See Praṇava-tanu.

Balā: Also known as Acyutā she is the Śāsanadevatā of the Jain Tīrthaṃkara Kunthunātha. In the Śvetāmbara tradition she is described as riding a peacock and bearing in her four hands citron, spear, *bhuṣuṇḍi* and lotus.

Balabhadra: Brahmanical deity made head of a group in Tantric Buddhism. This group is described in the Dharmadhātuvāgīśvaramaṇḍala of the *Niṣpannayogāvalī* and includes Balabhadra, Jayakara, Madhukara and Vasanta. Balabhadra is described as riding an elephant and being white in complexion. He holds a sword and a plough. *Niṣpanna* 63.

Balapāramitā: Tantric Buddhist goddess of the Pāramitā (q.v.) group who is red in colour and holds the *Prajñāpāramitā* book in her left hand and *cintāmaṇi* banner in her right. *Niṣpanna* 60.

Bālā-Tripurasundarī: South Indian goddess associated with Skanda-Subrahmanya cult of Tamil Nadu. She seems to have been a combination of two Mahavidyā goddesses. She represents the wisdom aspect of the supreme being. She carries a rosary and a jar and shows the *cin-mudrā*.

Bali: Sacrifice. The Tantras allow substitutes for animal sacrifice. Various forms of vegetables such as pumpkin, sugar cane, cucumber, brinjal, etc., are used as subsititutes. *Puraścaryārṇava* XI. Sacrifices are of two kinds: gross and subtle. The greatest sacrifice is that of one's egoism. *Gāyatrī-tantra* 5.

Bālidaṅgā: A Śākta *pīṭha* where the right hand of Satī is said to have fallen. The goddess here is known as Rājeśvarī. This holy resort of the goddess is mentioned in the *Caṇḍīmaṅgala* and situated in the Hooghly district of West Bengal.

Balipura: Holy resort of the goddess. The place has been identified with Mahabalipura or Mamallapuram in Chingleput district, about 30 miles to the south of Chennai.

Bāṇaliṅga: Symbolic phallus of Śiva made of white stones found in rivers. It is believed that 14 crore *liṅgas* were established in various spots by Bāṇa, an Asura devotee of Śiva, and these came to be known as Bāṇaliṅgas. It is one of the three forms of *liṅga* (phallus), the others being *itara* and *svayambhū*. In the Tantric conception it is said to reside within the triangle of the *anāhata-cakra* (q.v.). *Ṣaṭcakranirūpaṇa* XXV.

Baṭuka Bhairava: Youthful (*baṭuka*) Śiva of the *bhairava* (q.v.) category. In iconic representations he is shown nude, terrible in appearance with protruding fangs, round rolling eyes, holding a sword and other weapons, often wearing wooden sandals and accompanied by a dog.

Beṇā: A river sacred to the goddess Amṛtā. It is same as the Beṇā, a tributary of the Krishna, the Benganga or the Wainganga. *Matsya Purāṇa* XIII. 41; *Devībhāgavata* VII. 30.70; *Skanda* V. 3.98.79.

Bhadrakali: That form of Kālī which bestows welfare upon her devotees. *Bhadraṃ kalyāṇaṃ kālayati bhaktān pratyānayati sā bhadrakālī.* Nīlakaṇṭa on *Mbh.* VI. 23.5. As destroyer of the sacrifice of Dakṣa she appeared with millions of Yoginīs. *Devī Bhāgavata* III. 27.9. Her *mantra* consists of twenty letters which satisfies the four aims of life in their benevolent aspects. *Tantrasāra* 325. While the *Tantrasāra* describes her as having an emaciated, dark, hungry and shabby figure with noose in hand the *Puraścaryārṇava* IX. 755-6 describes her as possessing a sharp, well-built and attractive body. Her colour is blue. She holds a trident. Flesh, blood and wine are her favourites. She is surrounded by the Piśācas with whom she dances and traverses the world. She emanates from the mouth of Śiva and is often surrounded by the Mātṛkās.

Bhadrakālī-Cintāmaṇi: A late-medieval text on the cult and conception of Bhadrakālī.

Bhadrakarṇa: Holy resort of the goddess Bhadrakarṇikā mentioned in the *Bṛhan-nīlatantra* V. It has been identified with Karṇapura or Karnali on the south bank of the Narmada.

Bhadrapāla: Bodhisattva whose name is found in the second list of sixteen Bodhi-sattvas headed by Maitreya. He is of red and white colour and holds a jewel in one of his hands. The other hand either shows *varada mudra* or rests on the hip. *Niṣpanna* 50, 67.

Bhadrāsana: A particular *āsana* (q.v.) or posture of sitting found in cult images in which both legs are pendant.

Bhadreśvara: Holy resort of the goddess Bhadrā or Bhadreśvarī. It is also known as Bhadra and Bhadrāśva, the latter being adopted from the name of a mythical division of Jambudvīpa. In the *Prānatoṣaṇī* the name of the goddess is given as Bhadrakarṇikā and Ramā. The place is possibly Bhadreswar in the Hooghly district of West Bengal. *Matsya* XIII. 31; *Devibhāgavata* VII. 30.60; *Bṛhannīla* V.

Bhagamālinī: One of the Āvaraṇadevatās (presiding deities) of the *Trikoṇacakra* (q.v.) also known as Atirahasyayoginī. The goddess Kāmeśvarī is in the top corner, Vajreśvarī in the right corner and Bhagamālinī in the left. *Gandharvatantra* V. 112-13. In *Tantrarāja* XXXV. 12-13, Bhagamālinī is associated with the Sāṅkhya category of Ahaṃkāra.

Bhāsāśakti: One of the five Śaktis according to the Krama theory expounded in texts like *Tantrāloka*, *Maharthamañjarī*, etc., others being Sṛṣṭi, Sthiti, Saṃhāra and Anākhya. It is also known as Pratibhā. *Bhāsā ca nāma pratibhā mahatī sarvagarbhiṇī.* This is the source of all, vibrating and is the power of consciousness. This Śakti transcends time and space and hence known as Kālasaṃkarṣiṇī.

Bhaga: Term for generative organ. The word

later came to mean different qualities of a human being. In a special sense it is applied to the six qualities or types of non-material wealth (*ṣaḍaiśvarya*)—fullness of sway, manliness or energy, glory, auspiciousness, knowledge and indifference to wordly objects.

Bhaga-liṅga Kriyā: Actions involving female and male genital organs in the cult of the female principle.

Bhagayāga: Pañcamakāra (q.v.) rituals with female partners. *Mahānirvāṇa* I. 52.

Bhairava: A human teacher who seems to have attained complete spiritual emancipation and become almost Śiva; their views are reflected in the Tantric yāmala literature. Eight yāmalas are said to have been communicated by the eight Bhairavas: Svacchanda, Krodha, Unmatta, Ugra, Kapālin, Jhaṅkāra, Śekhara and Vijaya. The term Bhairava also applies to Śiva, his emanations, incarnations and attendants and also to the consort-cum-priests of the Mother Goddesses of different Śākta Pīṭhas. Each goddess has a Bhairava of her own. For example, the Bhairava of Kālī is Mahākāla, of Tripurasundarī Laliteśvara, of Tārā Akṣobhya, of Chinnamastā Vikarālaka, of Bhuvaneśvarī Mahādeva, of Dhūmāvatī Kālabhairava, of Kamalā Nārāyaṇa, of Bhairavī Vaṭuka, of Mātaṅgi Sadāśiva and of Vagalā Mṛtyuñjaya. There is however, no uniformity in the Tantras regarding the names of the Bhairavas and their relation to the goddesses. The Tantric aspirant may also consider himself as a Bhairava.

Bhairava Āgamas: A set of sixty-four Āgamas classed under the category of eight Aṣṭakas (q.v.) known respectively as Bhairavāṣṭaka, Yāmalāṣṭaka, Matākhyāṣṭaka, Maṇgalāṣṭaka, Cakrāṣṭaka, Śikhāṣṭaka, Bahurūpāṣṭaka and Vāgīśāṣṭaka (q.v.). According to one tradition the southern face of Śiva represents the principle of non-duality and is called Yoginīvaktra. The remaining four faces represent four conditions—denotative, denoted, extinguishing and extinguished. The products from each of these combine to form the sixty-four Āgamas.

***Bhairavācāra Pārijāta*:** A medieval Tantric manual dealing with the details of the cults and rituals associated with various conceptualizations of Bhairava and also of Śiva. The name of its author is not precisely known but he refers to himself as a prince of the Vāghela dynasty.

Bhairavaikātmya: A Tantric form of *mokṣa* or *jivanmukti* (liberation). It is the unity of *Jīva* (individual) with *bhairava* (supreme being who is Śiva). Only those who are born of parents mentally approximating Śiva and Śakti are entitled to this form of liberation. *Parātṛmśikā* 234.

Bhairavaparvata: A holy resort of the goddess Avantī where the upper lip of Satī is said to have fallen. The *pīṭha* mentioned in the *Pīthaṇirnaya* is situated in West Malwa.

Bhairavāṣṭaka: A group of eight Tantric texts of the sixty-four Bhairava Āgamas comprising *Svacchanda*, *Bhairava*, *Caṇḍa*, *Krodha*, *Unmatta*, *Asitāṅga*, *Mahocchūṣma* and *Kaṅkāliśa*.

Bhairavī: Female partner of the Tantric aspirant who is supposed to impersonate Śakti or the Female Principle of creation, the supreme being of the Śākti-Tantric cults. Bhairavī is one of the Mahāvidyā goddesses who is the wife of Kālabhairava and is the creator, sustainer and destroyer of the universe. She has various forms such as Tripurabhairavī, Caitanyabhairavī, Siddhabhairavī, Kamaleśvarī-bhairavī, Kāmeśvara-bhairavī, Sampatpradā-bhairavī, Ṣaṭkuṭā-bhairavī, Rudrabhairavī, Annapūrṇā-bhairavī, etc. A Bhairavī is always associated with a Bhairava, often known as Vaṭuka. *Prāṇatoṣaṇī* V. 6, 374; com. on *Paraśurāma-kalpasūtra* I. 2; *Tantrasāra* 220-39.

Bhairavī-cakra: A Tantric *cakra* (q.v.) ritual in which the five Ms (see *Pañcatattva)* are used. The male and female aspirants sit together and perform the rites which include drinking of wine and sexual intercourse. For details see *Mahānirvāṇa* VIII, 54-206, *Kulārṇava* VIII, *Kaulāvalinirṇaya* VIII. There is a leader to conduct the affair and the participants sit in pairs or in two rows facing each other. There is no caste distinction in bhairavī-cakra. *Kulārṇava* VIII. 96-7. The participating males should consider themselves as gods and the females as goddesses. Bhairavī-cakra is not meant for the aspirants of the *paśu* (q.v.) category. It is for those who have reached the *vīra* stage. *Mahānirvāna* VIII. 177-8. It is said that the place where the bhairavī-cakra is performed is more efficacious than all the great *tīrthas* or places of pilgrimage. By performing this ritual one is expected to be free from all sins, lord of land and people, conquerer of death and receiver of *brahmanirvāṇa*. Ibid. VIII. 195 ff.

***Bhairavī Tantra*:** A late-medieval Tantric text. The Kālimāhātmya section of this text deals with the worship of Kālī. The work is devoted to Bhairavī, the traditional fifth Mahavidyā on whom two books are quite well known, viz., *Bhairavīrahasya* and *Bhairavīsaparyāvidhi*. There is also a *Bhairavī-yāmala*.

***Bhaiṣajyaguru*:** Name of a Mantrayāna Buddhist Sūtra, associated with the Dhāraṇi trend. Its central figure is Bhaiṣajyaguru, the Buddha of healing. It prescribes the use of incantations to avert various kind of evils. It has also a Tibetan version. Edited in *Gilgit Manuscripts*, Vol. I, Srinagar 1939.

Bhāṇḍabrahmāṇḍatattva: The theory that the body (*bhāṇḍa*) is the microcosm of the uinverse (*brahmāṇḍa*).

Bhāṇḍikera: A tantric sect mentioned in the *Śaktisaṅgama-tantra*.

Bhāskara: Tenth-century Kashmirian exponent of the Krama system who is also referred to in the Nātha Siddha tradition of that region. His commentary on the *Śiva-sūtras* is known as *Śivasūtravārtika*, ed. by J.C. Chatterjee, Kashmir Sanskrit Series, 1916.

Bhāskara Rāya: Also known as Bhāsurānandanātha, he was one of the leading Tantric interpreters of all times. Among his principal works we have the *Setubandha* commentary on the *Vāmakeśvaratantra* of which the *Nityaṣoḍaśikārṇava* is a part, the *Guptavatī* commentary on the *Devīmāhātmya* of the *Mārkaṇḍeya Purāṇa, Saubhāgyabhāskara* commentary on the *Lalitāsahasranāma* of the *Brahmāṇḍa Purāṇa*, and a Tantric digest *Varivasyārahasya* and its commentary *Varivasyāprakāśa*. He flourished in the eighteenth century.

Bhasma: Ashes. The inner intuition which reveals the self and dispells the illusion is thus called *bhasma* or the ashes. As an outer symbol of this, aspirants as ascetics of various religious communities, mostly of Śaiva-Śākta orientation enjoin *bhasmadhāraṇa*, i.e. besmearing the body with the holy ashes.

Bhaṭṭa Utpala: Tenth-century Kashmirian commentator whose *Spandapradīpikā* is a commentary on the *Spanda-Kārikā*. He has interpreted the Spanda and Yoga concepts in the light of Tantric Krama philosophy. He was also, known as Utpala Vaiṣṇava. *Spandapradīpikā*, ed. by V. Islampurkar, Bombay 1898.

Bhauma Snāna: Bathing by smearing the body with earth.

Bhāva: Dispositions according to which mankind is classified in Tantrism. These are *divya* or the man with a divine disposition, *vīra* or the man with a heroic disposition and *paśu* or a man with an animal disposition.

Bhāva-liṅga: One of the three forms of *liṅga* (q.v.) according to the Vīra Śaiva conception. It is associated with *yogāṅga* or the highest stage leading to perfection. *Bhāva-liṅga* is the infinite Divine which sees the truth in itself as the truth in its becoming as well as in its essence. It contains comprehensively and not separately all that emerges as ideas. *Bhāva-liṅga* and *yogāṅga* are concerned with *prajñājīva*, the condition of deep sleep symbolic of a transformation into a new state of consciousness.

Bhāvanā: Term for desire of the worshipper in Tantric Buddhism. It is of the nature of a psychic force that reacts on infinite energy giving rise to different manifestations according to the nature of the reaction. The nature of this reaction is of illimitable variety and thus the resultant deity also appears in an infinite variety of forms. *Guhyasamāja* XVIII.

Bhāvanāsiddhi: An aspect of *gauṇi-bhakti* which is meditation, muttering the name, worship and singing the greatness of *saguṇa-brahman* or personal god endowed with attributes. This is meant for spiritually backward classes of people.

***Bhavanopaniṣad*:** A late-medieval Tantric work dignified with the title 'Upaniṣad' as it deals with *bhāvanā* and summarizes the *vāsanāpaṭala* of *Tantrarājatantra*.

***Bhāvopahāra*:** A *Kramastotra* attributed to the eleventh-twelfth century author Cakrapāṇi. Its commentary known as *Vivaraṇa* is by Ramyadeva whose independent work *Akramakallolakārikā* appears to have been on the Krama system. Published in Kashmir Sanskrit Series, no. XIV. 1918.

Bhīmā: Holy resort of the goddess Bhīmā or Bhīmeśarī. It is Bhīmāsthāna of the *Mahābhārata* which is near Shahbazgarhi in Peshawar district. This *tīrtha* may also be connected with the Bhīmā, a tributary of the Krishna, *Bṛhannīla* V. In Tantric Buddhism it is one of the twenty-four *maṇḍala* goddesses associated with Buddhakapāla. She is described as a goddess of western direction and of green colour. The goddess Bhīma-darśanā belongs to the eastern direction of the outermost circle.

Bhoga: A pre-Christian Taoist immigrant from China. He is also known as Bogar. In his methods of tuning the body of impure matter through 'reverberation' and 'projection' to the pitch of practically cancelling demise, Bhoga sought to promulgate the lesser athanasic precepts of Lao-tze, since the vital objective of the *Tao-te-king* is the transfiguration of the immortalized ethereal body into a permanent garment of celestial virtue, in order to fit it to associate eternally with the Tao. There is another tradition that Bhoga taught the Śuddha-mārga of the Siddhas to both Śaivāgamics and Śāktāgamics of south India. He was apparently a contemporary of Mūla (Mūlar) or Śrīmūlanātha. He is also said to have brought with him a fellow countryman named Pulippāri. Another tradition places Bhoga as a junior contemporary of Agastya. The Śuddha-mārga orders founded by him, the Āgamic Siddhas, were influenced by Taoist esoterism. Tantric alchemy and medicine as well as the Rasa (q.v.) school owed much to him.

Bhogāṅga: The transformed *taijasa-jīva* (the soul in the dreaming condition) according to the Vīra Śaiva conception. The subtle body is the means through which the *taijasa-jīva* experience pleasure and pain by means of sensuous objects. The devotee having given up carnal objects, and taken to the realization of the self, takes delight only in what is conducive to spiritual growth. Hence he is called *bhogāṅgin*; for him *prāṇa-liṅga* (q.v.) becomes the object of worship.

Bhogapātra: Vessel for offering wine to the goddess; other vessels required for Tantric rituals are *devipātra, gurupātra, śaktipātra, yoginīpātra, vīrapātra, balipātra, pādyapātra* and *ācamanīyapātra*. *Kaulāvalinirṇaya* VI; *Kaulamārga-rahasya* 226.

Bhṛgu, Bhṛgupurī: Holy resort of the goddess Vajreśvarī mentioned in *Jñānārṇava* V. It is identified with Balia in Uttar Pradesh. Bhṛugupurī was also the name of Broach near Gujarat.

Bhṛkuṭi: An emanation of Amitābha, Bhṛkuṭi is four-armed, one-faced, three-eyed, yellow-coloured, with a very youthful appearance. She shows the *varada mudrā* and rosary in her two right hands and carries *tridaṇḍī* and *kamaṇḍalu* in the left hands. Bhṛkuṭi is also regarded as a form of Tārā (q.v.) and is often identified with Khadiravanī Tārā and Dhanada Tārā. *Sādhana* 341. In Jainism Bhṛkuṭi is the Śāsana devata of Candraprabha. Her vehicle is the swan and in her hands are a sword, a club, a spear and an axe.

Bhujaṅgama-mantra: A class of defective mantras. Rāghava or *Śāradātilaka* II. III.

Bhukti: Material comforts for which Tantric *sādhanā* is very often performed by the ordinary aspirants. *Bhukti* denotes the desire for a long life, a cure from diseases, energy, vigour, wealth, man-power, victory, prestige, fame, extermination of enemies, a happy next world, a place in heaven after death and so forth. The aim of Tantric *sādhanā* is liberation and not the enjoyment of material comforts. But the Tantras are permissive in this matter and do not consider the desire for worldly happiness as detrimental to the path of liberation. The Tantras put forward the concept of *bhukti-mukti* according to which both material happiness and spiritual salvation may be achieved at the same time by performing *sādhanā*. *Mahānirvāṇa* II. 20. *Śāradātilaka* III.

Bhuktisiddhi: An attainment consisting of material and spiritual success; it is to be achieved through the rituals of *aṣṭakoṇa-cakra*. *Gandharvatantra*. XVIII. 75.

Bhūmikās: Seven planes of knowledge described in the *Yoga-vāśiṣtha*. These correspond to the seven Tantric Ācāras (q.v.). The Bhūmikās are known as *vividiṣā* or *śubhecchā, vicāraṇā, tanumānasā, sattvā-patti, asaṃsakti, padārthabhāvini* and *turīyā*.

Bhūmis: Twelve Vajrayāna goddesses representing the different spiritual spheres through which a Bodhisattva moves in his quest for Buddhahood and omniscience. They are Abhimukti, Pramuditā, Vimalā, Prabhā-karī, Arciṣmati, Sudurjayā, Adhimukti, Duraṅgamā, Acalā, Sādhumati, Dharma-megha and Samantaprabhā.

Bhūmīndrakanyā: One of the eleven classes of women belonging to the lower order of society acting as the female companion of the aspirant and impersonating the *śakti* or Female Principle of creation. The classes comprise Naṭī, Kāpālikā, Veśyā, Rajakī,

Nāpitāṅganā, Yoginī, Śvapacī, Śauṇḍī, Bhūmindrakanyā, Gopinī and Mālikā. They are also known as Ramya Śakti. *Niruttara-tantra* XIV.

Bhūmisparśa: Also known as Bhūsparśa. It is the name of a *mudrā* in which the right hand has the palm turned inward and the fingers outstretched, with the tips touching the ground.

Bhupura: A Tantric quadrangle with four doors and a triangle inside the lines of which are known as Brahmā, Viṣṇu and Śiva. On the Brahmā line are situated ten *siddhis* (q.v.), on the Viṣṇu line eight *mātṛkās* (q.v.) and on the Śiva line ten *mudrā-śaktis*. *Gandharvatantra* V. 76; *Nityaṣoḍaśikārṇava* I. 166 ff.

Bhūriṇī: A Tantric Buddhist goddess associated with the Padmanartteśvara form of Avalokiteśvara. She represents the western petal of his lotus seat, is yellow in complexion and carries a *cakra* and a blue lotus.

Bhūtaḍāmara: Principal deity of the Bhūtadāmaramaṇḍala of *Niṣpanyayogāvalī*. He is an emanation of Akṣobhya with terrible appearance, colour as black as collyrium and four hands. His three *dhyānas* are found in *Sādhana* 521.

***Bhūtaḍāmara Tantra*:** A late Tantra designated after Bhūtaḍāmara, name of Unmatta Bhairava. Bhūtaḍāmara is also the name of a *maṇḍala* in the *Niṣpannayogāvalī* and is also that of an emanation of Akṣobhya (q.v.). The present text deals with the black arts, various *mantras* and *sādhanās* with women.

Bhūtalipi: The script of letters which has the characteristic of being pronounced through efforts. *Cidvallī* on *Kāmakalāvilāsa* 27. Apart from the long vowels other letters of the Sanskrit alphabet are known as *bhūtalipi*. Com. on *Śāradātilaka* VII. 2-3.

Bhūtāpasaraṇa: Chasing away evil spirits and disturbances with the help of *mantras*. During sacrifice it is done by sprinkling white mustard seeds around the altar. *Tantrasāra* 616; *Puraścaryārṇava* III. 154, Rāghava on *Śāradātilaka*. IV. 10.

Bhūtaśuddhi: Purification of the five elements—earth, water, fire, air and space—of which the body is constituted. It is done with *mantras* and rites and also with the help of yogic exercises. *Tantrasāra* 85-7. *Prāṇatoṣaṇī* III. 5, 202; *Puraścaryārṇava* III. 6, 166-8, *Tārābhaktisudhārṇava* V. 153-7. The aspirant should meditate on his *guru*, *iṣṭadevatā* and Gaṇeśa to protect himself from the influx of impurities from the ten directions by clapping his hands and uttering *phaṭ*. Then he must draw a line of water around himself and think of it as the outer wall and purify himself mentally. He should touch the different parts of his body and identify them with the twenty-four *tattvas* of Sāṅkhya-yoga. He has then to practice yoga with various kinds of breath control and to identify the *mātṛkāvarṇas* (q.v.) within himself. By fixing his mind on the *mūlādhāracakra* (q.v.) and uttering *haṃsa-mantra* he should make the purification complete. *Mahānirvāṇa* V. 93 ff.

Bhūtātmaka-mantra: The alphabet divided into five *bhūtas* or elements. Letters a, ā, e, ka, ca, ṭa, ta, pa, ya and ṣa are called *māruta* or *vāyavya varṇa*; they represent the element of air. Letters i, ī, ai, kha, cha, ṭha, tha, pha, ra, and kṣa are *taijasa* or *āgneya varṇa* since they represent the element of fire. Letters u, ū, o, ga, ja, ḍa, da, ba, la and ḷa are *pārthiva-varṇa* representing earth; ṛ, ṝ, au, gha, jha, ḍha, dha, bha, va and sa are *vāruṇa-varṇa* representing water; and ḷ, ḹ, ṃa, ña, ṅa, ṇa, sa and ha are *vyoma-varṇa* representing space. Com. on *Śāradātilaka* 2.10-11; *Prapañcasāra* III. 70-2.

Bhūtirāja: A teacher of Abhinavagupta, who lived in the tenth century. From Abhinava's *Tantrasāra* and Maheśvarānanda's *Mahārtha-mañjarī* it appears that he was a follower of the Tantric Krama system.

Bhuvana: Planes of existence based on 36 *tattvas* (12 of the Śaiva-Śakti tradition in addition to the 24 of the Sāṅkhya). According to Rāghavabhaṭṭa (on *Śāradātilaka* V. 90) five material elements constitute five *bhuvanas* containing various planes of spiritual exercise from *mūlādhāra* to *unmanī*. According to the general conception there are a number of *bhuvanas* which are *bhuḥ*, *bhuvaḥ*, *svaḥ*, *mahaḥ*, *jana*, *tapas*, *satya*, *atala*, *vitala*, *talātala*, *mahātala*, *rasātala* and *pātāla*. *Prāṇatoṣaṇī* VI. 3.436. Śivatattva has ten *bhuvanas* which are *anāśrita*, *anātha*, *anata*, *vyomarūpiṇī*, *vyāpinī*, *ūrdhvagāminī*, *mocikā*, *rocikā*, *dīpikā* and *indhikā*. Śaktitattva has five which are *śāntātīta*, *śānti*, *vidyā*, *pratiṣṭhā* and *nivṛtti*. See *Tantrāloka* IX. 53.

Bhuvaneśī, Bhuvaneśvarī: Tantric goddess who nourishes the *bhuvanas* (q.v.). Her one-letter *mantra* is *hriṃ*. She is described as resplendent as the rising sun, and the moon is her crown. Her breasts are large and face is smiling. She has four hands; two in *varada* and *abhaya* poses, and in the other two a goad and a noose. *Tantrasāra* 526-7; *Prāṇatoṣaṇī* V. 6, 374; *Śāradātilaka* 9.14. Bhuvaneśvarī is also a goddess of the Bhairavī (q.v.) category who is benign, clad in red garments, and decked with a variety of ornaments. She has three eyes, highly developed breasts, four hands holding a noose and a goad and showing the *varada* and *abhaya* postures. Texts such as *Bhuvaneśvarī-rahasya*, *Bhuvaneśvarī-stotra*, *Bhuvaneśvarī-tantra*, *Bhuvaneśvarī-pārijāta*, *Bhuvaneśvarī-Kalpalatā*, etc., are important works on this goddess. *Puraścaryārṇava* IX. 809 ff.

***Bhuvaneśvarī-rahasya*:** An important work dealing with the cult of Bhuvaneśvarī written by Pṛthvīdhara Ācārya who is claimed to be a direct disciple of Śaṅkara. There is also a *Bhuvaneśvarī-stotra* by Pṛthvīdhara.

Bīja: In Tantric belief it signifies the germ-syllable which takes the form of a deity. It is also a term for semen. It is the microcosm of the universe, deity, doctrine and *mantra*. The *vācaka* entity of a *mantra* is made of words and sounds. The subtle state of sound is *bindu* and subtler is *nāda*. The expression of sound is possible through letters and hence the letter is the *bīja* or seed of the *mantra*. The doctrine remains subtle in a single letter conceived of as *bīja* or seed. For its formation and Śakti-orientation see Nāda and Bindu. It is one of the seven limbs of *mantra*, the others being Ṛṣi, Chandas, Kīlaka, Śakti, Nyāsa and Dhyāna. *Dīpikā* on *Śrīvidyāsūtra* I. As *mantra* it is single-lettered in which the deity is revealed in subtle form. See *Śāradā* 57; *Tantrasāra* 182 ff. For details see Bīja-mantra.

***Bījābhidhāna*:** Comprising 86 metrical verses it gives the names of the Bījas in accordance with the *Bhūtaḍāmara-tantra*.

Bīja-bhūmi: The seed of the universe which is Śakti in Tantric belief. It is described as void (*śūnya*) or great void *(mahāśūnya)* because nothing has manifested itself in this stage. That is why it is called *niṣedha-vyāpārarūpa* or the process of negating. *Paramārthasāra* 13-14.

Bījākṣara: Seed-letters like *hriṃ*, *kriṃ*, etc. These letters or rather sounds have well-defined meanings and are rationally planned.

Bīja-mantra: Abbreviated letters or words, symbolic of the tenets of the creed, which are conveyed by the teacher to the disciple after initiation. These *bīja-mantras* are regarded as microcosms of the actual *mantras* and the meaning suggested by them. Just as a tree with its trunk, branches, leaves, flowers and fruits is basically the development of a seed, so also the entire superstructure of Tantrism is based in the *bījas*. Hrim, krim, aim, srim, klim, etc., are *bījas*, proper intonation in the recitation of which makes the meditation perfect and the deities are forced to appear before the eyes of the aspirant. In the first stage it is known as Devatāsiddhi or god-attainment. But the second stage is more important which is known as Jīvanasiddhi or the fulfilment of life which opens the door of direct knowledge. The analysis of *bīja-mantra* reveals the knowledge of letters. To take the example of the *bīja* Hrim, we find that it is composed of Ha (Śiva), Ra (Śakti), I (Māyā, the material aspect of Śakti) and M (Nāda and Vindu). Every *bīja* consists of two causal elements—gross and subtle—and a third element which is beyond the law of causation.

Bījamudrā: The basic character of Trikoṇa-cakra. *Gandharva-tantra* XVII. 85.

***Bījanighaṇṭu*:** Said to be contained in the *Bhūtaḍāmara-tantra*. The work designates itself as *mantrakoṣa* and explains the meaning and significance of various *bījas* and letters. Printed in *Tantrik Text*, I, 28-9.

Bimba: Reflection of a conception of idea thought of in terms of an image or icon-circle of a deity in Tantric Buddhism. When there is a combination of *prajña* (knowledge) and *upāya* (means), the phenomenal world appears in a contracted form which is to be meditated upon in the *bimba* by the aspirant. *Guhyasamāja* XVIII.

Bindu: The seed which issues from the creative union of Śiva (perfect consciousness at rest) and Śakti (which becomes dynamic or creative activity). It also means the state of infinite concentration and condensation and therefore of potency. It is formed when Śakti, which is the substance or matter, approaches to *cit* or consciousness causing in the former the desire to create (*vicikīrṣā*). In the *Śāradā* II. 6, *bindu* or a single dot stands for solar power, and *visarga* or double dot for lunar. It is an evolute of *nāda* produced from the

Kriyāśakti of Śiva. *Śivapurāṇa,* Vāyavīya, Uttara V. 18 ff. In Kashmir Śaivism it is one of the ten Vidyātattvas. *Tantrāloka* I. 210. It is Anuttara Śakti as also *nada*-oriented sound in every being. Ibid. III. 116 ff., *Prapañcasāra* I. 41. *Bindu,* by which Parāśakti is characterized becomes divided into *bindu, nāda* and *bīja,* the first being Śiva-oriented, the second Śakti-oriented and the third a combination of both. *Śāradātilaka* I. 7 ff. *Nāda* and *bindu* of the second category are known as Apara-nada and Apara-bindu, while their primal forms are prefixed by the term *para. Bindu* has three forms—*prakāśa* (static), *vimarśa* (kinetic) and *prakāśa-vimarśa* (combination of both). *Cidvallī* on *Kāmakalāvilāsa* V-VIII. It is the cause of the origin of letters and elements. Com. on *Śāradā* II. 9, VII. 9. The four *kalās*—*pīta, śveta, aruṇa* and *asita*—emanate from it. *Prapañcasāra* 20-1. It also stands for the male organ while the complementary principle *visarga* stands for the female.

Bindu-cakra: The central point in the Śrīcakra (q.v.), the mystic Tantric diagram, symbolizing the universe and its divine cause by two sets of triangles. This is the point (*bindu* q.v.) in which reside *Kāmeśvara* (Śiva in the form of pure consciousness) and Lalitā (Śakti as dynamic creative activity) in undifferentiated union (*abheda*). *Kāma-kalāvilāsa* XXII. The *bindu* diagrams are also known as Uḍḍīyana-pīṭha and Brahmacakra. *Gandharva* V. 123. Attainment in the exercise of *bindu-cakra* is known as *prāptisiddhi. Nityaṣodaśikārṇava* VIII. 173.

Bindūdbhūtā-kalā: *Kalās* (q.v.) emanating from *bindu* (q.v.). These are four in number—*pīta* (yellow), *śveta* (white), *aruṇa* (red) and *asita* (black). Since *bindu* is symbolic of the supreme being these *kalās* contain elements of the same. *Prapañcasāra* III. 24; *Śāradātilaka* II. 24.

Bindu-dhāraṇa: The process of checking the downward flow of the semen, of holding the breath and of stabilizing the mind for the attainment of the state of neutrality which is required for the spiritual upliftment of an individual. Also known as *pavana-niścala* and *citta-nirodha.*

Binduśakti: Power associated with Śaktyaṇḍa, one of the four divisions of the 36 *tattvas* of Śāktism. *Garland of Letters* 198.

Bodhana: Processing of a *mantra.* The *mantras* are to be written down in the form of letters. These letters are to be purified with the colour of *karavī* flowers. The number of the flowers should equal the sum total of the letters. *Tantrasāra* 54.

Bodhicitta: Enlightenment (*bodhi*) by which mind (*citta*) is characterized. According to the Mahāyāna, *śūnyatā* (q.v.) and *karuṇā* (q.v.), being combined, develop *bodhicitta* (etymologically intellectual and mental faculties) which helps an individual to obtain *bodhi* or the highest knowledge. This *bodhicitta* is achieved through ten stages or *bhūmis.* The highest stage is known as *dharmamegha* where the striving individual becomes a Bodhisattva. In Tantric Buddhism the concept of *bodhicitta* acquired a changed significance. Its function here is to create *mahāsukha* (q.v.) or *nirvāṇa* through the sexual union between a man and a woman. In *Hevajra* X the union of *prajñā* (q.v.) and *upāya* (q.v.) is supposed to produce *bodhicitta* as the embodiment of *śūnyatā* and *karuṇā.* This view is maintained in Vajrayāna (q.v.) and other schools of Tantric Buddhism which hold that *bodhicitta* is a state of supreme realization transcending both *bhava* (existence) and *nirvāṇa* (extinction). It is without beginning or end, quiescent, immutable in existence and also in non-existence; it is the non-duality of *śūnyatā* and *karuṇā. Jñānasiddhi* 72-3.

Bodhinī: A form of Śakti situated on the second point above the *ājñācakra.* It is considered as a seed. Kālicaraṇa on *Ṣaṭcakranirūpaṇa* XL. Bodhinī is also described as one of the five *kalās* or manifestations of *nirodhinī-śakti* (the *sakti* which offers resistance to the upward march of *kuṇḍalinī*).

Bodhisattva: See Bodhicitta. They represent a class of deities in Tantric Buddhism who derive their origin from the five Dhyānī Buddhas representing the five primordial elements. The Bodhisattvas have their consorts, known as Śaktis, and emanations, gods and goddesses. Originally Bodhisattvahood was an ideal as opposed to Arhathood. A Bodhisattva could be a god, a householder, a recluse and even a non-human being. His function is to help man to achieve salvation. One who actively endeavours for the development and upliftment of intellect and mind (*bodhicitta*) with the purpose of the attainment of Buddhahood is a Bodhisattva. Although in the beginning Bodhisattvahood was man-oriented, in a later period a class of gods was created that came to be known as Bodhisattvas. They were powerful deities who could grant desired effects to their worshippers. The Bodhisattvas are twenty-five in number. Their names are Samantabhadra, Akṣayamati, Kṣitigarbha, Ākāśagarbha, Gaganagañja, Ratnapāṇi, Sāgarmati, Vajragarbha, Avalokiteśvara, Mahāsthāmaprāpta, Candraprabha, Jālinīprabha, Amitaprabha, Pratibhānakūṭa, Sarvaśokatamonirghātamati, Sarvanivāraṇaviśkambhi, Maitreya, Mañjuśrī, Gandhahasti, Jñānaketu, Bhadrapāla, Sarvāpāyañjaha, Amoghadarśī, Suraṅgama, and Vajrapāṇi. *Nispanna* 46, 50, 57.

Brahmabīja: The original seed emanating from *praṇava*, the token of *brahman*, which forms the substratum of the seeds of other deities. *Kulārṇava* VI.

Brahmacakra: The *cakra* (q.v.) representing the equilibrium of Śakti in the form *bindu* (q.v.). It has been equated with the *pīṭha* (holy resort of the Mother Goddess) of Uḍḍīyāna. *Gandharvatantra* V. 23; *Nityaṣoḍaśikārṇava* VIII. 171.

Brahmadvāra: The passage through which the *kuṇḍalinī* (q.v.) moves. Viśvanātha's com. on *Ṣaṭcakranirūpaṇa* II.

Brahmagranthi: One of the three knots situated in the *mūlādhāra-cakra* (q.v.). Com. on *Brahmavidyopaniṣat* 70.

Brahmakapāla: Or Brahmaśiraḥ, the severed head of Brahmā who is credited with four faces, grey beard and with a crown of matted hair. This severed head of Brahmā is found carried by the Buddhist gods.

Brahmamayī: The general name of the Supreme Being of the Śāktas.

Brahman: The all pervasive reality in Indian religio-philosophical tradition. In the Tantras various theories have been put forward to explain the relation between the infinite, pure consciousness, eternal and changeless *brahman* and the finite, material and impermanent world; between the universal and individual soul; and also the evolution of the latter from the former in terms of both nondualist and dualist viewpoint. *Brahman* is identified with the supreme deity of every Tantric sect, and also a special term *saṃvit* (q.v.) is used to denote the essence of the concept of *brahman*. According to the nondualist Tantras the material world is caused by the self-expression or manifestation of the pure consciousness of *brahman* which works through its Śakti or inherent power working in two aspects, Vidyā-śakti and Māyā-śakti. Both of these are conscious principles, the difference is that while the former is illuminating consciousness the latter is veiled consciousness, i.e. consciousness appearing as unconsciousness. This Māyā-śakti is not unreal and is the cause of the material world. In the dualistic Tantras both *brahman* and its *śakti*, the static (*prakāśa*) and vibrating (*vimarśa*) aspects of the same reality, are treated as individual conscious principles. *Brahman* is the unity behind all diversity. Śakti is the same but because it acts on different things, it is expressed as the inherent nature of the things themselves on and through which it works.

Brahmanāḍi: A nerve situated within the *citriṇī* nerve, or it may be on the inner side of the *citriṇī*. Some authorities equate it with *susumnā*. *Yogaśikhopaniṣat* V. 17.

Brahmānanda: Disciple of Tripurānanda and spiritual guide of Pūrṇānanda. He flourished in the first half of the sixteenth century. Of his works, the *Śāktānandataraṅginī* is the best known and most popular which deals, in eighteen chapters, with the worship of Śakti. His *Tārārahasya*, in four sections, deals with the rites connected with the worship of Tārā and her various forms. *Śāktānandataraṅgiṇī*, ed. by Panchanan Sastri, with Bengali trans., Calcutta 1942; ed. by Rasik Mohan Chattopadhyaya in *Vividhatantra-saṃgraha*, Calcutta 1876; by R.N. Tripathi in *Yogatantra Granthamālā*, Vol. II, Varanasi; *Tārārahasya*, ed. by J. Vidyasagara, Calcutta 1896; ed. by P.C. Pal et al., Calcutta 1948. *V.S.* by T. Giritirtha, Calcutta 1977.

Brahmāṇḍa: Ordinarily the world or universe, a mythological interpretation of which is supplied by the cosmogonic ideas of Brahmā's Egg, Hiraṇyagarbha, the Golden Germ, etc. In the Tantras the cosmic particles are the worlds, each containing seven *lokas* or regions, seven grounds of Śakti and their presiding deities. These worlds (*brahmāṇḍas*) are innumerable: *brahmaṇḍāstatra jāyante lakṣaṃ lakṣaṃ sulocane*. They belong to a larger universe which is known as *bṛhad-brhmāṇḍa*. The latter is contained in a macrocosmic universe known as *mahā-*

brahmānda: *mahābrahmāṇḍamadhye tu bṛhadbrahmāṇḍameva ca, tanmadhye jantavo devi tanmadhye bhuvanāni ca.*

Brahmānanda Lokeśvara: A form of Avalokiteśvara. He is one-faced and four-armed, sits in the *lalita* attitude on a lotus accompanied by his *śakti* who sits on his lap. His two right hands show the *tridaṇḍī* and *varada* pose, while the two left show the *ratnakalasa* (vessel containing jewels) and a *mudrā* with the index and little fingers pointing outwards. The *śakti* displays the *varada* pose in the right hand and the *abhaya* in the left.

Brahmāṇḍa Maṇḍala: One of the four *aṇḍas* or *maṇḍalas* or spheres constituting the five *kalās* which represent the Śakti aspect of the 36 *tattvas*, others being those of Prakṛti, Māyā and Śakti. It comprises the worlds (*bhuvanas*, q.v.) of the earth (*kṣiti*) category.

Brahmāṇī, Brāhmī: One of the seven or eight Divine Mothers or Mātṛkās who, according to the Puranic legends, appeared from Brahmā, during the war between the gods and the demons endowed with his emblems and characteristics. In the Tantric conception the Mātṛkās represent the 50 letters of the Sanskrit alphabet. As such, according to the *Svacchandatantra*, Brahmāṇī or Kamalodbhavā presides over *Ka-varga*, i.e. the consonants beginning with Ka. Brāhmī is also the name of Gāyatrī, the goddess of knowledge and speech, who is the Śakti of Brahmā.

Brahmapadma: Name of the four-petalled lotus of the *mūlādhāra* (q.v.). *Nirvāṇatantra* IV.

Brahmapura: A conception of the human body as found in the *Chāndogya Upaniṣad* VIII. 1-3. According to this conception the space within the human heart is the same as that outside the body. The earth and heaven, fire and wind, the sun and the moon, the lightning and the stars, are all within the human body. The doctrine of *brahmapura* is thus the precursor of the *Piṇḍa-Brhmāṇḍa* concept of the Tantras.

Brahmarandhra: The space in the central cerebral region which holds the thousand-petalled lotus. It is the breeding spot of Icchā Śakti (q.v.) and Para-Nāda (q.v.). It is part of Visarga-maṇḍala (q.v.) which is the great causal state of *brahman* or *saṃvit* (q.v.) symbolized by Śabdabrahma or Kuṇḍalinī (q.v.). The union of Kuṇḍalinī with its source produces nectar which flows from *brahmarandhra* to *mūlādhāra* flooding the *kṣudrabrahmāṇḍa* or microcosm, i.e. the body of the aspirant. *Brahmarandhra* is also known as Śūnya. *Haṭhayogapradīpikā IV*. 10 ff.

Brahmarekhā: One of the three lines of the Trikoṇa (q.v.) or Kāmakalā (q.v.) drawn by joining three *bindus* (q.v.) each symbolizing the three powers of Vamā, Jyeṣṭhā and Raudrī. These three lines are also known as A, Ka and Tha respectively. The line A which is composed of sixteen letters from A to *visarga* is also known as Brahmarekhā. Com. on *Pādukāpañcaka* II.

***Brahma Saṃhitā*:** Meant for the Vaiṣṇavas and commented upon by Jīva Gosvāmin. Pub. in *Tantrik Texts*. Vol. XV.

Brahmasvarūpiṇī: An attribute of Śakti conceived as the supreme being.

***Brahma Yāmala*:** Palm leaf manuscript dated 172 Nepal Saṃvat (AD 1052) of this text is found in the Nepal Darbar library. *Brahma Yāmala* is extensively quoted in many Tantras and Tantric manuals. It relates how the original knowledge was communicated in 1,25,000 verses to Śrīkaṇṭha who imparted it to others in amplified versions in different countries. Its main emphasis is on *Srotanirṇaya*, i.e. classification of Tantric sects according to the three currents of *dakṣiṇa* (right), *vāma* (left) and *madhyama* (middle), details of which are given in terms of their deities, modes of worship, holy places and sacred texts. A list of gods and sages who divulged the knowledge of Śiva is given. In enumerating the Dakṣiṇa current special importance is given to the Bhairavas of the Vidyāpīṭha and Mantrapīṭha. To the former category belongs Svacchanda, Krodha, Unmatta, Ugra, Kapāli, Jhankāra, Śekhara and Vijaya and to the latter Canda, Guḍaka, Vīra, Mahā and Mahāvireśa.

***Bṛhannīlatantra*:** A modified form of *Nīlatantra*, *Mahānīla-tantra* and *Nīlasarasvatītantra* all of which are dedicated to the worship of Tārā. *Bṛhannīlatantra* gives a detailed list of the Śākta *pīṭhas*.

Buddha: Same as Gautama Buddha. He recognized the *ṛddhis* or supernatural powers and mentioned four *iddhipādas* conducive to the attainment of supernatural powers. He himself practised the āsphānaka-yoga or *yoga* of psychic expansion. In Mahāyāna Buddhism the Buddha was deified and his human character was denied. He was treated as *lokattara* or supermundane and thought of as possessing three *kāyas* (bodies) —*dharmakāya, sambhogakāya* and *nirmāṇakāya*. In Tantric Buddhism the *cakras* or nerve plexuses within the human body are named after the *kāyas* of the Buddha. In Mahāyāna-Vajrayāna, the five *skandhas* as promulgated by the Buddha—*rūpa* (form), *vedanā* (feeling), *saṃjñā* (perception), *saṃskāra* (impression) and *vijñāna* (ego-consciousness)—were conceptualized into five Dhyānī Buddhas (q.v.): Vairocana, Ratna-sambhava, Amitābha, Amoghasiddhi and Akṣobhaya (q.v.) respectively. Subsequently there developed the concept of Ādi Buddha (q.v.). Various schools of Tantric Buddhism emphasize the doctrine of the attainment of Buddhahood as the ultimate goal of the human beings and suggest various ways and means to achieve this end.

Buddhaḍākinī: Śakti of the Tantric Buddhist god Mahāmāyā or Hevajra, an emanation of Akṣobha whose four faces are red, yellow, white and green. She carries in her four hands *kapāla*, arrow, *khatvāṅga* and a bow. *Niṣpanna* 22.

Buddhakapāla: A form of Heruka. This emanation of Akṣobhya has one face and four arms each holding *khatvāṅga, kapāla, kartri* and *damaru* respectively. He is embraced by his Prajñā Citrasenā and remains in *yab-yum. Sādhana* 501-2.

***Buddhakapāla Tantra*:** A text of Mantrayāna which was known to Saraha, a pupil of Haribhadra. It was composed about AD 800. It is found in Tibetan, the original Sanskrit is missing.

Buddhabodhiprabhā: The twelfth and the last goddess in the *vaśitā* series. In the *Dharmadhātuvāgīśvara-maṇḍala* of the *Niṣpannayogāvalī* she is described as having a yellow complexion and holds in her right hand a *vajra* with five thongs on a yellow lotus, and in the left the discus on the Cintāmaṇi banner.

Buddhi: The first product of the evolution of *prakṛti*, also known as Mahat in the Sāṅkhya. Its special functions are ascertainment and decision and it is the ground of all intellectual processes. Being influenced by the three constituents (*guṇas*) of *prakṛti* it is capable of producing different attributes. *Sāṅ Sūt.* I. 71, II. 40-3, *Kārikā* 36-7. In the Śaiva Siddhānta it is conceived as an evolute of *aśuddha-māyā. Mṛgendra Āgama* II, 3.7, III. 1, etc., *Pauṣkara Āgama* II. 17, III. 4, *Śivajñānabodham* II. 5. In Tantra it is a category of quality. *Kaṅkālamālinī* II, Rāghava on *Śāradātilaka* I. 17.

Cc

Caitanya: Pure consciousness, also called *cit* and in Tantric language *saṃvit*. Absolute, all-pervading, perfect and pure-consciousness is *brahman*. In the sense of pure consciousness, resulting from self-illumination achieved through spiritual exercise *caitanya* occurs in all the religio-philosophical systems of India. In the Kashmirian Śaiva Tantras *caitanya* is the *śakti* aspect of reality and is compared to a clear mirror in which reality sees itself. *Caitanya* is sometimes regarded as feminine though reality in itself is neither masculine nor feminine. *Kāmakalāvilāsa* 2, with Puṇyānanda's commentary. Tantric conceptualizations and practices are calculated to effect the transformation of the worshipper, the worshipped and the means and acts of worship into *cit* or *caitanya*. In Tantric internal worship (*antaryāga*) the aspirant has to think that the goddess is enshrined within his body as pure consciousness or the Self. *Guru*, *mantra* and *devatā* are also conceived of as three forms of *caitanya*, *Śaktisaṅgama*, Sundarī, III. 11-13. See *brahman, cit, saṃvit, cit-Śakti*.

Caitanyabhairavī: Tantric goddess, mother of three worlds, whose *mantras* are given in symbolic letters in the *Jñānārṇava*. In the *Merutantra* her resplendance has been compared to a million rising suns. She is decked in all sorts of ornaments. Her robes are red and the moon reflects on her crown. She is ever youthful with enlarged and pointed breasts. She holds a noose and a goad in her left hands and exhibits *varada* and *abhaya* poses with her right hands. *Tantrasāra* 228; *Puraścaryārṇava* IX. 809-10.

Caitanyatritaya: Guru, Mantra and Devatā. According to the *Śaktisaṅgama-tantra*, Sundarī, III. 11-13, it is the creed of the Kashmiri sect to think in terms of unity of the preceptor, the personal deity and the means of worshipping, all of which merges in the *akṣara*, the ultimate world-ground, having the potentiality of containing sunlike energies arising out of pure consciousness.

Caitraratha: Holy resort of the goddess Madotkaṭā mentioned in Matsya XIII. 28; *Devībhāgavata* VII. 30.57, *Skanda* V. 3. 98.66. It is a forest on the bank of the Acchodā (q.v.). *Vāyu* XLVII. 6

Cakra: Plexuses, or lotuses as they are also called. There are six such plexuses, the first of which is *mūlādhāra* or the sacrococcygeal plexus situated between the penis and the anus; the second, *svādhiṣṭhāna*, is the sacral plexus near the root of the penis; the third *maṇipura*, lumbar plexus in the navel region; the fourth, *anāhata*, is the cardiac plexus situated in the heart; the fifth, *viśuddha* in the laryngeal cardiac plexus at the junction of the spinal cord and the medulla oblongata; the sixth is the *ājñā* between the eyebrows. Above all is the *sahasrāra* or the highest cerebral region where the *kuṇḍalinī* or serpent power meets its source after passing through the *cakras*. The Buddhist Tantras refer to four plexuses. The first is *nirmāṇa-cakra*, lumbar plexus, situated in the navel region; the second *dharma-cakra*, the cardiac plexus in the heart region; the third is the *sambhoga-cakra*, the laryngeal plexus at the junction of the spinal cord and the medulla oblongata; and the fourth, *uṣnīṣakamala*, cerebral plexus, which is situated in the head. *Cakra* also means a circle which is of the nature of *maṇḍala* containing mystic figures and diagrams and figures of gods and goddesses. As such they are same as the *yantras* or mystic diagrams which are variously known as *trikoṇa* (three-angled), *aṣṭakoṇa* (eight-angled) and so forth. In its simplest sense it is a wheel or disc, the sun wheel, the characteristic symbol of Viṣṇu and also the *dharmacakra* symbol of Buddhism. It also means a cycle—of time, existence and so forth. *Cakra* symbolizes the endless rotation of Śakti. In Tantric rituals there are different *cakra-sādhanās* in which male and female aspirants assemble and perform the rites of *pañcamakāra*. See Bhairavi-cakra. According to some Tantras *cakras* are of five types—*rāja, mahā, deva, vīra* and *paśu* each symbolizing a grade of spiritual attainment. See Ṣaṭcakra, Padma.

Cakrabhānu: Śaiva-Tantric teacher of the

Krama system who flourished in Kashmir in the eleventh century.

Cakradvīpa: An *upapīṭha* sacred to the goddess Cakradhāriṇī mentioned in the *Śivacarita*. It is one of the several Cakratīrthas which are situated respectively at Āmalakagrāma (on the Sahyādri range), Cakradhara (Chakdhar in Bijbror in Kashmir) Dvaraka, Mathura and on the Godavari and the Sarasvati. *Varāha* CXXXVII. 19, CLXII. 43; *Vāmana* XLII. 5, LVII. 89, LXXXI. 3; *Brahma* LXXXVI. 1; CIX. 1; CXXXIV. 1; *Rājataraṅgiṇī* I. 38.

Cakrapāṇi: Śaiva-Tantric teacher of the Krama system who flourished in Kashmir in eleventh-twelfth century. To him is ascribed the *Bhavopahāra*. Pub. with *Vivaraṇa* of Ramyadeva in Kashmir Sanskrit Series, no. XIV, 1918.

***Cakrasambara*:** Buddhist Tantric text also known as *Dākinījāla*. There is some obscurity about the various Tibetan recensions of this text. One Tibetan version has been partially edited, and part of it translated by Kazi Dawa-Sampup as *Śrīcakrasambhāra-tantra*. It teaches the mantras, the meditations, the pictures of the male and female principles, rituals of different kinds and symbolical significance of the *mantras* connected with *mahāsukha* or great bliss. It appears to belong to an elaboration of the basic text incorporating some later supplements and commentaries, perhaps arranged by some school in Tibet. Published in *Tāntrik Texts,* Calcutta 1919, VII. (Intro and Eng. trans.) and XI (Tibetan text).

Cakrāṣṭaka: A group of eight Bhairava Āgamas (q.v.) represented by *Mantra*, *Varṇa*, *Śakti*, *Kalā*, *Kāla*, *Bindu*, *Nada* and *Guhya*.

Cakravicāra: Examination of various *cakras* such as *tārācakra*, *śivacakra*, *brahmacakra*, *koṣṭhacakra*, *nakṣatracakra*, *rāśicakra*, *ṛṇidhanicakra*, *kulākulacakra*, *akathahacakra*, *akaḍamacakra*, etc., which is required to be done by the *guru* before initiating his disciple. In some cases such examinations are of the nature of astrological calculation. In the *vārāhītantra* it is said that study of *tārācakra* is required for initiating one into the *mantra* of Viṣṇu, *koṣṭhacakra* for that of Śiva, *rāśicakra* for that of Tripurā, *akadamacakra* for that of Gopāla and Rāma, *haracakra* for that of Gaṇeśa, *kulākulacakra* for that of Mahālakṣmī and so on. But this is not essential. *Tantrasāra* 9-19, 52; *Rudrayāmala*, *Uttaratantra* 304; *Puraścaryārṇava* I. 73; *Śaradātilaka* II; *Prāṇatoṣaṇī* II. 3. 104.

Cakreśvarī: The presiding goddesses of the nine *cakras*. Tripurā, Tripureśī, Tripurasundarī, Tripuravāsinī, Tripuraśrī, Tripuramālinī, Tripurasiddhā, Tripurāmbā and Mahātripurasundarī are *cakreśvarīs* respectively of the following cakras: Trilokyamohana, Sarvāśāparipuraka, Sarva-saṃkṣobhaka, Sarvasaubhāgyadāyaka, Sarvārthasādhaka, Sarvarakṣākara, Sarvarogahara, Sarvasiddhipradā and Sarvānandamaya. Cakreśvarī is also the name of a Jain goddess who is the Śāsanadevatā of Ṛṣabhanātha. The Svetambaras and Digambaras concurrently describe her as holding the symbol of disc and riding Garuḍa. In Śvetāmbara conception she has eight hands and in Digambara either twelve or four hands. By her names and symbols she pertains to be the nature of Vaiṣṇavī, the Śakti of Viṣṇu, whose one name is Cakreśvara. *Tantrarājatantra* V. 9-11; *Kāmakalāvilāsa* 36; *Setubandha* on *Nityaṣoḍaśikārṇava* I. 164-5; *Pravacanasāroddhāra* XXVI; *Ādīśvaracarita* I. 1.

Cākṣusī-Dīkṣā: A form of initiation in which the *guru* or preceptor having concentrated his mind on the supreme being converts the disciple with only one glance. It is otherwise called *dṛk-dīkṣā*. *Kulārṇava* XIV; Rāghava on *Śāradātilaka* V. 127-140; *Merutantra* quoted in *Puraścaryārṇava* V. 390.

Cāmuṇḍā: Mythical goddess adopted in Tantrism. She has a three-lettered *mantra*: Kāmabija-dvayaṃ devi dīrgha-huṃkāramevaca, trākṣari sā mahāvidyā Cāmuṇḍā kālikā smṛtā. *Tantrasāra* 319. Elsewhere she is invoked by uttering Hrim Cāmuṇḍāyi namaḥ. This *mantra* is described as all-purposeful. *Puraścaryārṇava* XII. 1136. She is conceived of as being emanated from the forehead of Ambikā, terrible-faced, holding sword and noose, decorated with a garland of human heads, clad in a tiger-skin, and having an emaciated body, wide mouth and red, sunken eyes. *Durgāsaptaśatī* VII. 5-7. The Buddhist Camuṇḍā rides a corpse and is of red colour. In the first pair of hands she holds *kartari* and *kapāla*. With the second she exhibits the *añjali* posture. Cāmuṇḍa is also the name of the Śāsanadevatā of the Jain Tīrthaṃkara Naminātha. According to the *Svacchandatantra*, as a Mātṛkā, Cāmuṇḍā presides over the letters of *Sa-varga*, i.e. the consonants beginning with the letter Sa. She is described in the *Tantrasāra* as having a pleasant face but a terrible appearance because of her fearful teeth. She has a *khatvāṅga* (a long bone with a skull at the top) and a sword in her two right hands and a noose and a human head in the two left hands. She wears a tiger skin and sits on a corpse. She lives in dense darkness.

Caṇḍā: Śāsanadevatā of the Jain Tīrthaṃkara Vāsupūjya. She is also known as Pracaṇḍā. According to the Śvetāmbara tradition she rides a horse and carries the symbols of spear, flower and club, with the fourth hand in *varada* pose. The Digambara form of the same deity is represented as riding on a crocodile and having the hands equipped with a club, two lotuses and the fourth in *varadamudrā*. Caṇḍā is also the name of Durgā. *Mbh* VI. 23.4; *Harivaṃśa* II. 120. The *Agnipurāṇa* Ch. 50 refers to the rules of image making of the goddesses of the Caṇḍa category comprising Caṇḍā, Caṇḍī, Rudra-caṇḍā, Pracaṇḍā, Caṇḍogrā, Caṇḍanāyikā, Caṇḍavatī, Caṇḍarūpā, Aticaṇḍikā and Ugracaṇḍā.

Caṇḍāli: Female energy having the force of fire which resides in the *nirmāṇa-cakra* according to Tantric Buddhism. It has correspondence to the *kulakuṇḍalini-śakti* of the Śākta Tantras. This Caṇḍālī, being accelerated, kindles the *dharma* and *sambhoga-cakras* and ultimately reaches the *uṣṇīṣakamala,* the highest cerebral region, and then returns to its own place. In Vajrayāna we have a solid form of Caṇḍālī who is described in the Pañcaḍāka Maṇḍala of *Niṣpannayogāvalī*. She is blue in colour and holds a fire-pot in her right hand. The left shows the gesture of *tarjani.*

***Caṇḍamāharoṣana Tantra*:** A Buddhist Tantric text, considerable extracts from a Sanskrit manuscript of which were given by H.P. Sastri. It deals on the one hand with one doctrine of dependent origination according to the philosophical view point of the Mahāyāna and, on the other hand, with the cult of the yoginīs such as Mohavajrī, Piśunavajrī, Rājavajrī, etc., along with elaborate sex rites, *Des. Cat. Sans. MSS in ASB* I, 1917, 131 ff.

Candanaparvata: Holy resort of the goddess Mahānandā mentioned in the *Bṛhannīlatantra* V. It is Candanādri identified with the Malaya range (Eastern Ghats) in the *Trikāṇḍaśeṣa.*

Caṇḍanāyika: Goddess belonging to the Kulasundarī category, i.e. having the status of being worshipped accroding to the rules prescribed by Kaulācara (q.v.). *Kulacuḍāmaṇi-tantra* I. 1-2.

Caṇḍapura, Caṇḍipura: Holy resort of the goddess Pracaṇḍā mentioned in the *Bṛhannīlatantra* V. The place-name reminds us of Chandavar in the Honavar Taluka of North Kanara district, Chandur near Alta in Kolhapur and Chandawar near Etawa in Uttar Pradesh. But it seems to be one of the many insignificant Candpura villages in Bengal.

Caṇḍaroṣaṇa: Also known as Mahācaṇḍaroṣaṇa, Caṇḍamahāroṣaṇa and Acala. He is an emanation of Akṣobhya, having a yellow complexion and two arms, one holding a sword and the other raised in *tarjani mudrā*. A Tantric text is dedicated to his name. *Sādhana* 172.

Caṇḍavajrapāṇi: Consort of Vajragandhārī, an emanation of Amoghasiddhi.

Caṇḍeśvarī: A companion of the Vajrayāna deity Mahākāla. Her position is in the north-west corner. She has a yellow complexion, carries a *vajra* and staff and stands in *ālīḍha* attitide of a corpse. *Sādhana* 536.

Caṇḍi (kā): Puranic war-goddess known by various names such as Aparṇā, Pārvatī, Durgā, Mṛḍāṇī, Ambikā, etc. Conceptually she is also associated with Rātri, Kauśikī, Vindyavāsinī, Ekānaṃśā and a host of war-like goddesses whose mission was to slay demons and restore peace and prosperity on earth. In Tantra there is no mythology in which Caṇḍikā is conceived of either as the whole or as a part of the supreme being. The *Gāyatrī-tantra* V refers to sacrifice before her altar. cf. *Kālikāpurāṇa* LV. 1-2. Menstrual blood is required in her worship. *Kāmākhyā-tantra*, paṭala II. Without *pañcatattva* (Five Ms) the worship of Caṇḍikā is not desirable. *Kaulāvalinirṇaya* IV. Apart from Caṇḍī and Caṇḍikā, she is also known as Caṇḍikālikā. *Mahākālasaṃhitā* quoted in *Puraścaryārṇava* I. 16.

Cāndra: A Vāmācārin sect mentioned in the *Śaktisaṅgama-tantra*, Tārā, I. 92-4.

Candrabhāgā: River sacred to the goddess Kalā or Kālā mentioned in *Matsya* XIII. 26 ff; *Ḍevībhāgavata* VII. 30.55 ff; *Bṛhannīla* V, etc. It is the Chenab in Punjab.

Candrakalā: The symbol of crescent moon which exists on the crown of most Tantric goddesses as the source of overflowing nectar. It is also found on the matted locks of Śiva. *Mahānirvāṇa* XIII. 7.

***Candrakalā-Vidyāṣṭaka*:** A Kashmirian Tantra which expounds Śākta philosophy and rituals. It relates to what is compendiously known as Śrīvidyā or Brahmavidyā which is rather the practical course (*sādhanaśāstra*) not only of the monism of the Upaniṣads but also to a large extent of the final liberation expounded in the Śaiva Siddhānta. It is stated here that Śakti is not different from Śiva and they together constitute the ultimate reality. Śiva or Kāmeśvara is *prakāśa* or subjective illumination, while Śakti, known as Kāmeśvarī, Śivakāmā, Kāmakoti, Lalitā and Tripurasundarī is *vimarśa* or Siva's objective experience of himself.

Cāndrakhaṇḍa: One of the three parts of the fifteen *kalās* (q.v.) mentioned in the commentary on *Saundaryalaharī* 32, the other two being Āgneya and Saura. Cāndrakhaṇḍa consists of *āpūryamāna, purayanti, pūrva* and *paurṇamāsī kalās*.

Candranāḍī: Name of the nerve *iḍā* which is conceived of as a feminine entity, white in colour and representing *śakti* in the form of the moon. *Ṣaṭcakranirūpaṇa* I.

Candraprabha: 'Light of the Moon', Bodhisattva, described in the Mañjuvaramaṇḍala of the *Niṣpannayogāvalī* 50, 58, 67. He is white in colour and his recognition symbol is the moon-on-lotus. Candraprabha is also the name of the eighth Jain Tīrthaṃkara. Candraprabha is a name of Avalokiteśvara as well. He is one-faced and two-armed and sits in *vajraparyaṅka* attitude on a lotus. He exhibits the *vitarka-mudrā* with his right hand and holds a lotus by the stem against the chest with his left.

Candrapura: Holy resort of the goddess Sītā or Asitā mentioned in *Jñānārṇava* V. 66-7 and *Bṛhannila* V. It is probably same as Candrapura mentioned in the Siroda copper plate of Bhoja Devarāja identified with Chandor in Goa.

Candratattva: The introvert mind which develops with successful control of the functions of the *iḍā* nerve.

Capeṭadāna: Mudrā or hand-pose found in certain Buddhist icons which shows the right hand menacingly extended upwards, as though ready to slap (capeṭ) someone.

Carcikā: Companion of Vajrayanic Mahākāla. She belongs to south-west corner, is red in colour, carries *kartari* and *kapāla* and stands on a corpse. *Sādhana* 598.

Caramālā: A garland made of *rudrākṣa*, conch, crystal or other objects meant for *japa* or recalling the name of the deity. *Tantrasāra* 29.

Caraliṅga: The dynamic *liṅga* in Vīraśaiva conception. It is connected with *ādyā-śakti*, the primal energy.

Carcikā: Companion of Mahākāla. She stands in his south-west corner. She has a red complexion, carries the *Kartari* and *Kapāla* in her two hands and resembles Kālikā in all other respects. *Sādhana* 598.

Caryā: Means to achieve the end. The term is used especially in connection with Śaiva and Tantric cults. In the Pāśupata system, the *caryās* are divided into two categories; *vratas* (vows) and *dvāra* (door). In Buddhist Dhāraṇī literature the *caryās* are regarded as one of the five main aspects of spiritual realization. The same is said in the Tantras in which it is regarded as a means to become free from material bondage.

***Caryācaryaviniścaya*:** Also known as *Caryāpada* or *Caryāgīti*, the earliest extant work on the languages of eastern India, composed about the tenth century AD by the Buddhist Siddhācāryas, which was discovered in Nepal by M.M. Haraprasad Sastri in 1916. These are mystic songs composed by the followers of Sahajayāna in which Tantric Buddhist imageries are found in abundance.

Caryā-tantra: One of the four classes of the Buddhist Tantras. 'Caryā' means generally 'conduct', but here it means the actions to be performed in the ritual and the whole conduct of the performer. While *kriyā* is ordinary ritual, *caryā* is somewhat esoteric performed only by the initiate after consecration. Among the Caryā-tantras, the *Mahāvairocana* is important because it refers to consecration and postures for meditation as well as the rituals of symbol and diagram. These are meant to lead the aspirant to a realization of his identity with the Buddha as Vairocana.

Caṭṭala: Also mentioned as Caṭṭagrāma in the *Śivacarita* it is a *pīṭha* where the right hand of Satī is said to have fallen. Here the goddess is mentioned as Bhavānī. The *Pīthanirṇaya* refers to the place as Caṭṭala. It is in the Chittagong district of East Bengal.

Caturbhujā-Sitatārā: A form of Tārā. She has four arms and exhibits in the first pair of her hands the *utpala mudrā* and the lotus, and the *varada* pose in the second. She may be recognized by the presence of two goddesses, Mahāmāyūrī and Mārīcī.

Caturdasāra: A mystic Tantric diagram supposed to represent the combined effects of various *cakras* (q.v.). It is made of fourteen triangles, each presided over by a goddess. These goddesses are collectively known as Sampradāya-yoginī. The attainment derived from it is known as *īśitvasiddhi. Nityaṣoḍa-śikārṇava* IV. 149; VI. 17; XI. 179-83; *Gandharvatantra* V. 99, XVII. 49.

Caturviṃsati Tattva: Twenty-four Sāṅkhya fundamentals which are intimately associated with Tantrism. These are five *bhūtas* or gross elements, five *tanmātras* or subtle elements, five *jñānendriyas* or sense-organs, five *karmendriyas* or organs of action, and *manas* or mind, *buddhi* or intellect, *ahaṃkāra* or egoity and *prakṛti* or primordial substance.

Catuṣkūtā: Arrangement of letters peculiar to the cult of Śrīvidyā, *Tantrasāra* 244.

Catuṣpāda: Four steps or subjects dealt with in Śaiva philosophy. These are Vidyā, Kriyā, Yoga and Caryā (q.v.).

Catuṣpīṭha: Four *pīṭhas* or holy resorts of the goddess collectively mentioned in some Tantric texts. These are Jālandhara, Uḍḍiyāna or Oḍiyana, Pūrṇagiri or Pūrṇaśaila and Kāmarūpa. *Prāṇatoṣaṇī* VII. 4. 548. These four *pīṭhas* are also mentioned in the Buddhist *Hevajratantra* VII. In some texts Jālandhara is substituted by Śrīhaṭṭa or Sirihaṭṭa. cf. *Sādhanamālā* 453.

Caurangīnātha: The last of the five Ādhi Siddhas (cardinal saints) of the Nātha faith who was born out of the feet of Ādinātha (q.v.). Influenced by the personal charm of Gaurī Cauraṅgīnātha (also known as Śiśu-pā or Gabhur) was compelled to consort with his step-mother. Cauraṅgīnātha became a great Nātha-siddha and teacher of mankind. In Tibetan Tanjur collection a Sanskrit work entitled *Vāyutattvopadeśa* by one Ācārya Cauraṅgī is mentioned. He appears to be the same as Cauraṅgīnātha.

Chandas: Metre. *Chandāmsi Chādanāt, Chanḍas* is for protective covering. *Nirukta* VII.12. The gods covered themselves with *chandas* for avoiding death. Com. on *Sāradātilaka* I. 5. In Tantric rituals *Chandas* is to be felt as *nyāsa* (q.v.). *Tārābhakti-sudhārṇava* V. 327.

Chatroṣṇīṣa: The eighth and the last deity in the series of eight uṣṇīṣa gods in Tantric Buddhism. He stands in the *īśāna* corner and holds a parasol. He is white in colour. *Niṣpanna* 66.

Chinnamantra: Broken or torn or defective *mantra.* If in any *mantra* the seed *yam* occurs without any logical attachment or detachment with the first, second or third letter for example, or in which the long-sounded *śakti-bīja* (*hrāṃ, hrīṃ, hruṃ, hraiṃ, hrāuṃ)* becomes separated in three, four or five parts, it is called *chinna-mantra.*

Chinnamastā: One of the Mahāvidyā goddesses. Her devotee should imagine the existence of a white lotus on his navel within which the orb of sun appears like a three-line *yonimaṇḍala* suggestive of the sattva, rajas and tamas aspects. There exists Chinnamastā holding her own head in her left hand which is drinking the blood coming out of her severed neck. She has dishevelled hair, is naked, and stands in *pratyālīḍha* posture. She is ever youthful having the breasts of a sixteen-year old maiden. A snake serves as her sacred thread. She is flanked by her two companions Varṇinī and Ḍākinī. Her *mantra* consists of sixteen letters. She is also known as Chinnā, Pracaṇḍacaṇḍikā and Vajravairocanī. Her Buddhist counterpart is Vajrayoginī. She has a sect of her own which is known as Chinna-mastākrama. The followers of Cīnācāra are also associated with her cult. *Śaktisaṅgama*, Sundarī. I. 188-93; *Prāṇatoṣaṇī* V. 6. 578-9; *Puraścaryārṇava* IX. 814-15.

***Cidgaganacandrikā*:** Tantric treatise ascribed to Kālidāsa; ed by Trivikramatirtha in *Tantrik Texts*, Vol. XX. It is connected with the Śrīvidyā-Lalitā cult. The *Pratyabhijña-sūtra* has been freely drawn upon in this text. The Śaiva aspect is elaborated in the *Śivadṛṣṭi*, and the Śākta aspect is developed in the *Cidgaganacandrikā.*

Cīnācāra: The Chinese rituals, mainly connected with the goddess Tārā, supposed to be imported by Vasiṣṭha, which form the substratum of Tantric *vāmācāra* (q.v.). The Taoist rituals which came into the fold of the Tārā cult in China as well as Yinism or Exaltation of the Female Principle in Taoism, which developed in that system as a corollary of the Chinese Buddhist cult of the Female

Principle, were also able to counter-influence the development of the Indian *vāmācāra* rites of both the Buddhist and non-Buddhist Tantras. The qualifications for *cīnācārā,* also known as *cīna-krama* and *cīna-sādhana*, are given in *Tantrasāra* 20, *Śaktisaṅgama*, Sundari, I. 188 ff., *Puraścaryārnava* I. 20.

Cīnakrama: See Cīnācarā. It is also known as Cīna-sādhana. It is the worship of Tārā with *pañcatattva* or five Ms. It is a form of Kaulācāra. In the *Viśvādarśa-tantra*, as quoted in the *Tārātantra*, it is said that Cīnakrama is meant only for those who are free from the fallacy of dualistic knowledge, engaged in welfare of all beings, have given up the *varṇāśrama*, are quiet, sinless, and detached. In the *Merutantra* five kinds of Vāmācāra are mentioned which are Śabara, Siddhānta, Cīna, Vāma and Kaulika. These are compared with the five fingers of a palm and Cīnakrama or Cīna-sādhana is identified with the middle finger. *Puraścaryārṇava* I. 20-2.

Cintā Devī: Tamil equivalent of the Vedic goddess Vāc who later received prominence in the Tantras. She was later called Kalaimagal, the goddess of learning and arts.

Cintāmaṇi: The gem that satisfies all desires. In images it is sometimes represented in the form of a small round object and sometimes in the shape of a flame.

Cintāmaṇi Lokeśvara: A form of Avalokiteśvara. He is one-faced and two-armed and stands on a lotus. He carries a *caitya* in his right hand while the empty left is held near his navel.

Cit: Consciousness, the sentient principle. In all forms of Indian religio-philosophical system, the universe of *cit, jīva* and *acit* has its ultimate source in the *brahman.* The principle of consciousness, *cit*, is real and infinite, while *acit* (also known as *jaḍa*) is the material world and *jīva* is the individual soul. According to some Tantric schools, there are three kinds of *cit*: the disposition (*svarūpa*) of the individual, the quest (*jijñāsā*) and the understanding of the principal object of knowledge (*bimba*). It is said that during dissolution (*pralaya*) the entire universe returns to *brahman* and remains in it in a subtle state as its natural power, but at the beginning of creation it manifests its *cit-śakti* (power of sentience) and *acit-śakti* (power of non-sentience) in the form of souls (*jīva*) and matter (*prakṛti*) (q.v.). From the latter there is a gradual evolution of the material world. There are some extreme non-dualist views in the Tantras which treat *cit* as the only reality and deny the objective existence of all perceived through the gross sense organs. Most Tantras hold that *cit* and *acit* are only different states of one substance but not different substances in themselves. See Caitanya, Māyā-śakti, Saṃvit, Citśakti.

Citi-Śakti: The independent Śakti which is the cause of the creation and manifestation of the universe according to Kashmir śaivism: *Citi svatantrāviśvasiddhihetu.* In the *Pratyābhijñahṛdaya* 2 it is said that the manifestation of the world takes place when this Śakti expands itself and dissolution occurs when this Śakti contracts itself: *asyāṃ hi prasarastyām jagat unmiṣati vyavatiṣṭhate ca, nivṛttaprasarāyām ca nimiṣati.*

Cit-jaḍātmikā: One of the many attributes of Śakti which combines in itself both the conscious (*cit*) and material (*jaḍa*) principles. Bhāskara rāya says that the *cit* aspect of Śakti pertains to all beings in the form of consciousness while the *jaḍa* or *acit* aspect of Śakti is the transformation of the same *cit* in the form of *māyā. Lalitāsahasranāma* 148; *Saubhāgyabhāskara* 108-9. Thus *jaḍa* represents the visible aspect of *māyā*: *jaḍaṃ dṛśyamātramātmā svarūpaṃ yasyā māyāyāḥ sā jaḍātmikā.* Combining these two basic aspects Śakti is at the same time both transcendent and immanent.

Citkalā: Name of *saṃvit* or pure consciousness. It is that which forms the vibration caused by the break of *prakāśavimarśa* equilibrium of the supreme being.

Cit-kaṇa: The position of the individual in the process of *pāra-saṃvit* (q.v.) or the supreme experience. The *jīva* or individual in his inner self is of the same pure essence and is a manifestation of God-power in a certain aspect. He is a 'point' (*kaṇa*) at and through which contact is established with the essence of divinity.

Citrakūṭa: Holy resort of the goddess Sītā mentioned in *Matsya* XIII. 39 *Devībhāgavata* VII. 30.68, etc. It is a hill in the southern division to *Bṛhatsaṃhitā* XIV. 13; XVI. 17. It is modern Chitrakoot or Chatarkot hill or district near Kampta in Bundelkhand. The name occurs in the Sirur inscription of AD 866. Chitor in Rajasthan is also known as

Citrakūṭa. There is also a holy place of the same name on the Mandākinī in central India where Rāma is said to have lived for a short time. *Rām.* II. 54-6; II. 93.8; *Mbh.* III. 85-58; *Raghuvaṃśa* XIII. 47.

Citrasenā: Prajñā or Śakti or consort of Buddhakapāla (q.v.) also known as Heruka or Hevajra. She is youthful, intoxicated, nude and fearless. *Sādhana* 501-2.

Citriṇī: A nerve, which is like the fibre of a lotus stem. Also known as *brahma-nāḍi.* It is very often equated with *susumnā* (q.v.). It is also said that the *susumnā* is constituted by three *nāḍis* (nerves)—*citriṇī* which is of *sattva* quality, *vajra* which is of *rajas* and *brahma* which is of *tamas* quality. *Prāṇatoṣaṇī* I. 4.32.

Cit-Śakti: Power of sentience. The important modes of power (Śakti) are *cit* (intelligence), *ānanda* (bliss), *icchā* (will) *jñāna* (knowledge) and *kriyā* (action). With the opening out of Śakti, the universe appears, and with her closing up, it disappears. Śakti is *citi* or *cidrūpiṇī*, the formative energy of consciousness. *Pratyabhijñāhṛdaya* 2 ff. In the Tantras it is said that if the worship is intelligently done, that is, with understanding and appreciation of the principles, then *mantra*, *yantra* and other parapharnalia of worship are all transformed into forms and expressions of *cit-śakti* and *cit-vilāsa*. The objective is to effect the transformation of the articles and acts of ordinary experience which are material limited and limiting factors, operative in certain narrow spheres of usage and convention into forms of *cit-satta* (being), *cit-śakti* (power) and *cit-vilāsa* (bliss and play). The rituals are all calculated to effect the transformation of the worshipped, and the means and acts of worship into *cit* or *caitanya*, which they all are in essence. They thus culminate in realizing the essential identification in perfect experience of the principle of 'thou' (*tvam*) and the principle of 'that' (*tat*).

Citta: Mind and mental discipline. The concept of *citta* has a special significance in early Buddhism the culture of which is conducive to liberation. In Tantric Buddhism it is one of the three elements by which the holder of the *vajra* is characterized. From the eternal Śūnya evolved three elements—*kāya*, *vāc* and *citta* and from them the five *skandhas* and Dhyānī Buddhas.

Cittabhūmi: The levels of mental life according to yoga. These are *kṣipta* or *mūḍha* (torpid), *vikṣipta* (distracted), *ekāgara* (concentrated) and *niruddha* (restrained). The last two are conducive to *yoga*. When *ekāgra* (the state of concentration) is firmly established it is called *samprajñātayoga* and when the state of *niruddha* is firmly established it is called *asamprajñātayoga*. The followers of Sahajayāna hold that to judge the state of *samarasa* of *sahaja* as a pure state of *yoga*-arrest (*samadhi*) one should first examine the lane of mind *(cittabhūmi)* in which *yoga* is practised.

Cittadhātu Lokeśvara: A form of Avalokiteśvara (q.v.). He is one-faced and two-armed and stands on a lotus. He holds the image of a Jina, probably Amitābha, in his right hand and displays the *abhaya* pose with his left.

Citta-nirodha: Attainment of the state of 'nativity' or 'neutrality'. It is a stalibity of the mind which is the aim of yogic practices. Since existence and extinction are the resultants of man's desire and cogitation, in the same way, his fetters and release are, as it were, his own creation. A true yogin should strive for the state of neutrality where the physical reflexes and mental attributes are removed. This state may be achieved by disciplining the body and mind. *Citta-nirodha* is also technically known as *bindu-dhāraṇa* and *pavana-niścāñcalya.*

Cittasuddhi: Purification of mind. It is twofold, external and internal. External purification of mind is possible by the purification of body (*kāyaśuddhi*) which is to be done by means of bathing and other forms of cleansing of the body. Internal purification is caused by boldness of character and improvement of mental faculties. In some texts there is the concept of the purification of the self (*ātman*). Though *ātman* is always pure one should be aware of the purity of one's soul or self. This awareness is sufficient. *Śāradātilaka* IV. 2 ff.

Cittavaśitā: Tantric Buddhist goddess of the Vaśitā (q.v.) category who is described as white in colour and holding a red *vajra* with five thongs. *Niṣpanna* 56.

Cuḍacakra: A type of spiritual exercise meant only for those who have attained the status of *vīra* (q.v.). The exercise consists of laya-yoga (q.v.). *Śaktisaṅgama*, Sundarī, I. 197-200.

Cundā: Embodiment of *Cundā Dhāriṇī.* Three

sādhanas of the *Sādhanamālā* describe a four-handed form of this goddess which is more frequently seen in sculptures and paintings. The *Ņispannayogāvalī* refers to one which contains as many as twenty-six hands. In her common four-handed form she is one-faced, bearing a pot in the main pair of hands. In the other pair she holds a book-on-lotus in the left and the right is in *varada* pose. As a Dhāriṇī goddess she is white in colour and holds a rosary from which a *kamaṇḍalu* has been suspended. *Niṣpanna* 57. Her *mantra* is *om cāle cule cunde svāhā*. Cundā is mentioned in the *Śikṣāsamuccya* of Śāntideva. There are several images of Cundā with sixteen arms. These can be identified with the help of a miniature painting available in manuscript (no. AD 1643) of Prajñāpāramitā in the Cambridge University Library. The miniature bears a label in old Newari characters which reads as Pattikere Cundā Varabhavane Cundā. The *mudrā* of Cundā is akin to the *dharmacakra-mudrā* (q.v.) displayed by Vairocana.

Dd

Dadhīcī: One of the teachers of the *madhyama* (middle) current of Tantra represented by such texts as *Candrajñāna, Bimba, Prodgīta, Lalitā, Siddha, Santāna, Sarvodgīta, Kiraṇa* and *Parameśvara.*

***Ḍākārṇava*:** A Buddhist Tantra which has come down to us in Apabhraṃśa language. It has also a Tibetan version. The *Ḍākārṇava* was edited by N.N. Chaudhuri, Calcutta 1935.

Ḍākinī: Female deities of a lower order in the pantheon of Tantric Buddhism. They are represented mostly in dancing posture and can be both benign and terrible. In the Śākta-Tantric pantheon Ḍākinī is a subordinate companion of Chinnamastā (q.v.) who, along with Varṇinī, drinks the blood that comes out from the severed head of the former. Ḍākinī is full of effulgence; she has matted dishevelled hair, three eyes, white teeth, developed breasts; she holds a skull vessel in her left hand and a knife in the right. Lākinīs, Rākinīs, Śākinīs and Hākinīs are special forms of parā-Śakti. Ḍākinī is the presiding deity of *mūlādhāra*. *Ṣaṭcakranirūpaṇa* 7. In the *Nāradapāñcarātra* Ḍākinī is described as the companion of Pārvatī. *Prāṇatoṣaṇī* V. 6. 378-9. Regarded as a special form of Parāśakti, the existence of Ḍākinī is to be conceived in the *mūlādhāra* (q.v.). *Tantrasāra* 338. In the Buddhist Tantras there are four deities of the Ḍākinī group. They are Ḍākinī, Lāmā, Khaṇḍarohā and Rūpinī. *Sādhana* 425.

Dakṣiṇa Āmnāya: Tantric geographical region said to have come into existence from the southern face of Śiva. *Kulārṇava* III. 7. This region is efficacious for the *sādhakas* of *paśu* category. *Niruttara* quoted in *Prāṇatoṣaṇī* I. 9.64. The Āgamas known as *Vijaya, Niśvāsa, Svāyambhūva* and *Vīra* were composed in this region. *Kaulamārgarahasya* 92-3. The goddesses of this *āmnāya* are Vagalāmukhī, Vaśinī (Bālabhairavī), Tvaritā, Dhanadā, Mahiṣāghnī and Mahālakṣmī. *Prāṇatoṣaṇī* I. 9.64. The gods are Prasāda-sadāśiva, Vaṭuka, Mañjughoṣa, Bhairava and Mṛtyuñjaya. This *āmnāya* is also characterized by *Mahaprasāda-mantra*; *Dakṣiṇa-mūrti* and *Mṛtasañjivanī-vidyā.*

Dakṣiṇācāra: Way of spiritual attainment without the use of *pañcamakāra* (the Five Ms) and other extreme forms of rituals. Often Vedācāra, Vaiṣnavācāra and Śaivācāra are included in this category. The followers of Dakṣiṇācāra worship the great goddess in the traditional way. They believe in *varṇāśrama* and in the existing Brahmanical methods. Pañcamudrādirahito dakṣiṇācārasaṃjñakaḥ, *Kaulamārgarahasya* II. *Ācāro dvividho devi vāmadakṣiṇabhedataḥ; janmamātraṃ dakṣiṇaṃ hi abhiṣekeṇa vāmakam. Prāṇatoṣaṇī* VI. 4,532.

Dakṣiṇakāli(kā): The first *(ādyā)* among eight or nine common forms of Kālī. *Toḍalatantra* 3; *Puraścaryārṇava* I. 13. The *Mahākālasaṃhitā* identifies Dakṣiṇākālī with Ādyākālī (q.v.) a position which is contested in *Mahānirvāṇa* V. 141. Speculations on this name are found in *Nirvāṇatantra* X and *Kālītantra* IX. According to *Niruttara* II Dakṣiṇākālī is the *saguṇa* (with attributes) form of the Supreme Being who produces the world assuming female form. She is Mahālakṣmī, Viṣṇumāyā, Tārā and Śyāmā. She stands on the chest of Śiva supine as a corpse. She has four hands in two of which she holds a skull and a sword and the other two exhibit *vara* and *abhaya* poses. She has open hair and a lolling tongue pressed by her teeth. But the image worshipped by Tantrics is different. Here Śiva lies on the ground with his penis erect and the goddess is seated naked on him having taken his penis into her sex organ in *viparīta rati.* cf. *Tantrasāra* 310-11; *Niruttara* II. See Śyāmā.

Dakṣiṇamārga: See Dakṣiṇācāra. The term *dakṣiṇa-mārga* is less frequent. In the *Puraścaryārṇava* there is a chapter (*Taraṅga* I) with the title *āmnāyabhedena mārga-bhedanirṇayaḥ* in which *dakṣiṇācāra* or *dakṣinamārga* has been called *dakṣa-mārga* on the authority of a quotation from *Vāḍavānaliya-tantra.*

***Dakṣiṇāmūrti Saṃhitā*:** A text on Śrī-vidyopāsanā is 65 *paṭalas* and about 1,700 verses. Published in Sarasvati Bhavana Series.

Dakṣiṇasrota-tantra: Tantra of the 'southern current' which are said to be pure and of *sattva* quality. These are *Yoginījāla, Yoginīhṛdaya, Mantramālinī, Aghoreśi, Aghoreśvarī, Krīḍāghoreśvarī, Lākinikalpa, Māricī, Mahāmāricī* and *Ugravidyāgaṇa*. Dakṣiṇasrota is characterized by *sattva* elements and is pure in nature; it issued from the right mouth of Śiva. It is classified according to the four *pīṭhas* (modes of *sādhanā*) and also according to the degree of purity. The *pīṭhas* are *vidyā, mantra, mudrā* and *maṇḍala*. The eight Bhairavas, givers of eight *yāmalas*, belong to the *vidyāpīṭha*.

Ḍāmara: A class of Tantric texts traditionally six in number. They are Yoga, Śiva, Durgā, Sārasvata, Brahma and Gandharva. The *Vārāhītantra* ascribes to each of them 23,533, 11,007, 11,503, 9,905, 7,105 and 60,060 *ślokas* respectively. The Ḍāmaras are often referred to as Āgamas of the *tāmasika* category.

Ḍamaru: Small drum, such as is carried by Śiva.

Ḍambara-Kālī: A form of Kālī mentioned in the *Jayadratha-yāmala*

Dānapāramitā: Pāramitā (q.v.) goddess of the Buddhist Tantras described as whitish red in colour holding in her left hand ears of corn and in the right the *cintāmaṇi* banner. *Niṣpanna* 56.

Daṇḍa: The staff or mace carried by Hayagrīva. It cannot be translated as the magic wand as the Khaṭvāṅga serves that purpose. When the staff is surmounted by a *vajra* it is called *vajradaṇḍa*.

Danturā: A form of Cāmuṇḍā revealing the *ghoradaṃṣṭrā* aspect of the goddess. Several images of this goddess have been found from different parts of Bengal. An image showing the two-armed goddess sitting on her haunches, found originally in a Burdwan village, strikingly portrays the weird and uncanny figure with its bare canine teeth, rounded eyes, ghastly smile, emaciated body, lean and pendulous breasts, sunken belly and peculiar sitting posture. It is now in the Vaṅgīya Sāhitya Pariṣat Museum, Calcutta.

Dārita: A kind of defective *mantra* which does not contain either at the beginning or at the end the *dhruva*, that is, *om* (*klim*). Com. of *Śāradātilaka* II. 110-1.

Dārukeśa: A river sacred to the goddess which is probably same as Dvārakeśvara running through the Bankura and Hooghly districts.

Daśabhujasita-Mārīcī: White Mārīcī (q.v.) with ten hands described in the Buddhist Tantras as riding a chariot drawn by seven pigs and trampling Indra, Śiva, Viṣṇu and Brahmā. She bears the effigy of Vairocana on her crown and is accompanied by three junior goddesses.

Daśa-Mahāvidyā: Ten Tantric goddesses—Kālī, Tārā, Ṣoḍaśī, Bhuvaneśvarī, Bhairavī, Chinnamastā, Dhūmāvatī, Vagalā, Mātaṅgī, and Kamalā. *Prāṇatoṣaṇī*.V. 6.374. The names vary in different Tantras. In one list we have Kālī, Tārā, Chinnā, Sundarī, Vagalā, Mātaṅgī, Lakṣmī, Śyāmalā, Siddhavidyābhairavī and Dhūmāvatī. *Śaktisaṅgama*, Tārā VI. 16-17. Another list gives them as Kālī, Tārā, Mahādurgā, Tvaritā, Chinnamastā, Vāgvadinī, Annapūrṇā, Pratyaṅgirā, Kāmākhyāvāsinī, Bālā, and Śailavāsinī Mātaṅgī. *Mālinīvijaya* quoted in *Śāktānandataraṅgiṇī* III. Sometimes thirteen, or more often eighteen, Mahāvidyā goddesses are mentioned. They are Kālī, Tārā, Chinnā, Mātaṅgī, Bhuvaneśvarī, Annapūrṇā, Nityā, Mahiṣamardinī Durgā, Tvaritā, Tripurā, Puṭā, Bhairavī, Vagalā, Dhūmāvatī, Kamalā, Sarasvatī, Jayadurgā and Tripurasundarī. *Niruttaratantra* XV.

Daśa-Mudrāśakti: Ten Tantric goddesses, known as *mudrā-śakti*, who are supposed to reside in the *śiva-rekha* (one of the three lines) of the mystic triangles. *Nityaṣoḍaśikārṇava* I. 199-200.

Daśāṅga-Puraścaraṇa: Puraścaraṇa (q.v.) of ten parts comprising *japa* (muttering the syllables relating to the identity of *guru mantra* and *devatā*), *homa* (offering made to fire), *tarpaṇa* (rememberance of deities, sages and fathers), *abhiṣeka* (consecration), *aghamarṣaṇa* (the rite of driving out sin), *sūryārgha* (offering to sun), *jalapāna* (drinking water), *praṇāma* (salutation) *pūjā* (worship) and *brāhmaṇabhojana* (feeding the Brāhmaṇas). *Kaulavalinirṇaya* XV.

Daśa Saṃskāras: Ten sacraments. These are *garbhādhāna* (causing pregnancy), *puṃsavana* (rite ensuring birth of a male child), *sīmantonnayana* (parting of the hair of the wife by blades of *kuśa* grass), *jātakarman* (performance of *homa* and uttering of *mantras* at the birth of the child), *nāmakaraṇa* (naming of the child), *niṣkramaṇa* (taking the child outside the house), *annaprāśna* (feeding the child cooked food for the first time), *cuḍākaraṇa* (shaving the hair), *upanayana* (intiation into student life) and *udvāha* (marriage).

Daśasiddhi: Ten attainments which are *animā* (atomization) *laghimā* (levitation), *mahimā* (magnification), *prakāmya* (non-obstruction of desire), *vaśitva* (power of charming), *īśitva* (sovereignty over all things), *bhukti* (material success), *icchā* (fulfilment of will), *prāpti* (power of getting anything) and *sarvakāma* (attainment of all desires), *Gandharvatantra* V. 76; *Nityaṣoḍaśikārṇava* I. 169-71.

Daśa-vahni: Ten kinds of fire: *recaka* (purgative), *pācaka* (digestive), *śoṣaka* (absorbing), *dāhaka* (burning) *plāvaka* (flooding), *kṣāraka* (alkaline), *udgāraka* (belching), *jṛmbhaka* (yawning) and *mohaka* (infatuating). Each is presided over by a goddess. They are Sarvajñā, Sarvaśakti, Sarvaiśvaryapradā, Sarvajñānamayī, Sarvavyādhināsinī, Sarvādhārasvarūpā, Sarvapāpaharā, Sarvānandamayī, Sarvarakṣāsvarūpinī and Sarvepsitaphalapradā respectively. *Nityaṣoḍaśikārṇava* I. 187-90, *Tantrarājatantra* XXXV. 10; *Bhāvanopaniṣat* 18-20.

Daśa-vāyu: Ten kinds of vital airs are mentioned in the Tantras. Among them *prāṇa* or life-breath is that without which life becomes lifeless which is why all the vital airs of the body are known by this name. Four other *prāṇa* airs are known as *apāna* situated near the region around the genital organ, *samāna* around the navel region, *udāna* in the throat and *vyāna* which pass through all the nerves. The other five vital airs are *nāga*, *kūrma, kṛkara, devadatta* and *dhanañjaya*. *Nāga* is the wind of belching, *kūrma* is that of opening the eyes, *kṛkara* is that of yawing and *dhanañjaya* is all pervading within the physical frame of a man. These ten vital airs are presided over by ten goddesses known as Sarvasiddipradā, Sarvasampatpradā, Sarvapriyaṃkarī, Sarvamaṅgalakāriṇī, Sarvakāmapradā, Sarvasaubhāgyadāyinī, Sarvamṛtyuprasamanī, Sarvavighnanivāraṇī, Sarvāṅgasundarī and Sarvaduḥkhavimocinī, *Prānatoṣaṇī* I. 5.35; *Śivasaṃhitā* III. 7; *Gheraṇḍasaṃhitā* V. 62-3; *Nityaṣoḍaśikārṇava* I. 184-6; *Bhāvanopaniṣat* 17.

***Dattātreya-tantra*:** A medieval syncretistic Tantra (Deccan College Ms. no. 962 of 1887-91) which claims to be based on the Vedas. Āgamas, Smṛtis and Purāṇas and suggests that there is an easier and quicker way to the final goal of liberation.

Dehalikā: A place sacred to the goddess Ambā mentioned in the *Bṛhannīlatantra* V. It is possibly modern Delhi, Dehalikā resembles Trihalikāgrāma of the *Viṣṇusaṃhitā*.

Dehasādhanā: See Dehayantra, Kāyasādhana. The conception and worship of the body as the microcosm of the universe and the seat of pure consciousness is the basis of *dehasādhanā*. It is also known as the *sādhanā* of *bhūmi* (ground or the base), and is also found among the Sahajiyā Vaiṣṇavas and the Bauls. The primary aim of this *sādhanā* is a transmutation of the biological faculties and thus obtaining a rejuvenated body *dehasiddhi*. See Divya-deha, Divya-tanu. The ultimate aim is *rasasiddhi*, to be revitalized with the elixir of immortality. Union of *puruṣa* and *prakṛti* impersonated by the aspirant and his female partner is conducive to such attainment. This union is for *bindu-sādhanā* (Śiva-Śakti union) in the *sahasrāra* (q.v.) and as such it should not be considered as ordinary male-female union.

Deha-sthairya: Balance of the body made possible by the use of the mercurial drugs according to the Raseśvara-darśana. Mādhavācārya says that a class of Māheśvaras or worshippers of Śiva is tādātmyavādin, who believe in the identity of the individual and universal soul. If the two are the same *jivanmukti* (liberation within the span of life) is a reality. But this reality depends on *piṇḍasthairya* or *dehasthairya* which is a typical balance of the interior. *Saravadarśanasaṃgraha* IX. 1-3.

Dehayantra: The body itself which is the seat of *saṃvit* or pure-consciousness regarded as the subject of worship. According to the *bhāṇḍabrahmāṇḍatattva* of the Tantras, macrocosm is in microcosm and as such the universe is in the human body. Therefore the human body (*deha*) is the *śrīyantra*, to be worshipped according to the rules with all the necessary materials. *Ātmanyeva yajeddevīmupacārairyathāvidhi, nijadehākhyayantraṃ tu sarvayantrāt paraṃ śivam. Gandharvatantra* XXV. 29.

Deśika: A term for teacher or guru used exclusively in the Tantras. The word is prepared by taking the initial letters of *devatā, śiṣya* and *karuṇā*. Etymologically it means one who is proficient in imparting knowledge. In the *Kulārṇava* XVII. 14 it is said that Deśika suggests one who is godlike, benevolent to his disciple and the embodiment of compassion.

Devadāruvana: Holy resort of the goddess Puṣṭi mentioned in *Matsya Purāṇa* XIII. 46.; *Devībhāgavata* VII. 3075. It is located in the region of Badrinath in the Himalayas or modern Aundh in the Deccan.

Devadevatā Lokeśvara: A form of Avalokiteśvara. He is four-faced and eight-armed. His hands carry *vajra*, bow, *triśūla*, sword, bell, arrow, jewel and noose.

Devatā: Deity; divinity or any kind of divine being or entity regarded in Tantras as the subject of the *mantra*. When a deity is invoked with a particular *mantra*, the latter itself assumes the form, character and essence of the deity to whom it is dedicated. Rāghavabhaṭṭa on *Śāradātilaka* I. 5. In the Tantras the aspirant is advised to establish identity with *guru, devatā* and *mantra,* the accomplishment of which is conducive to the attainment of highest knowledge, eternal bliss and final liberation. Often *devatā* is stated to be one of the six constituents of the *mantra*, the others being *ṛṣi, chandas, bīja, śakti* and *kīlaka. Śyāmārahasya* I. Tantric deities, both Hindu and Buddhist, though very often named after Vedic, Epic and Puranic gods and goddesses, have no mythology. They are all mental creations. Their anthropomorphic and iconological forms are also symbolic.

Devatānyāsa: Feeling of the deity in different parts of the body. All the six limbs of Tantric *mantra* require *nyāsa* (q.v.) The place for *devatānyāsa* is the heart region. *Tārābhaktisudhārṇava* V. 169.

Devapratiṣṭhātattva: One of the 28 sections of Raghunandana's (sixteenth century) celebrated *smṛtitattva* which deals with the rules relating to the installation and consecration of images. In this work the rules relating to the *prāṇapratisṭhā* (endowing the lifeless image with life) have been quoted from *Śāradātilaka* XXIII. 71-6 and explained in detail. It also speaks of Mātṛkānyāsa and Tattvanyāsa.

Devatasiddhi: See Bīja-mantra.

Devataśuddhi: Purification of the image of a deity by *mantras* and water. *Puraścaryārṇava* III. 153.

Devī-bīja: A term for mica used in the preparation of chemical drugs for the rejuvenation of the body. See *Divya-deha, Divya-tanu.* The process of the transmutation of the body with the help of chemical drugs is known as Haragaurīsṛṣṭi, according to the *rasa* school. In such chemical preparations mercury and mica are special ingredients. The former is known as Śiva-bīja and the latter as Devī-bīja. *Sarvadarśanasaṃgraha* IX. 18.

Devī-cakra: General name of nerve plexuses.

Devikātaṭa: Holy resort of the goddess Nandinī on the river Devikā, modern Deeg in Rajasthan. *Matsya* XIII. 37. *Devībhāgavata* VII. 30. 66

Devikoṭa, Devikoṭṭa: Holy resort of the goddess Mahābhāgā or Akhileśvarī. *Kālikā* XVIII. 42 ff.; *Jñārṇava* V. 66 ff; *Bṛhannīla* V. It was the headquarters of Koṭṭivarṣa in the Puṇḍrabardhanabhukti. The ruins of the city have been discovered in the village of Bangarh, about eighteen miles south of Dinajpur town, North Bengal. Variant readings: Devakūṭa, Devīkūṭa, Devidaikoṭha.

Devīnaya: A name of Krama-mata (q.v.), a Śākta-oriented form of Kashmiri Śaivism.

Devi-Pīṭhas: Holy resorts of the great goddess. In a restricted sense the *pīṭhas* mean certain specific holy resorts which are associated with the later Puranic versions of the Dakṣayajña legends. According to *Devībhāgavata* VII. 30, *Kālikā Purāṇa* XVIII, etc., Śiva became inconsolable at the death of his beloved wife Satī and after the destruction of Dakṣa's sacrifice, he wandered over the earth in a mad dance with Satī's dead body on his shoulder. The gods became very anxious to free Śiva from his infatuation. Thereupon Brahmā, Viṣṇu and Śani entered the dead body and disposed of it gradually and bit by bit. The places where Satī's dead body fell are said to have become *pīṭhas* or holy seats in all of which she is represented to be constantly living in some form together with a Bhairava, i.e. a form of her husband Śiva. The story of the association of particular limbs of the goddess with the Śākta *tīrthas* which may have some relations with the Tantric ritual called *pīṭhanyāsa* belongs to the latest stage.

Devī-Sūkta: *Ṛgveda* X. 125 which is a famous hymn to Vāc. This is considered to be the first important evidence of the worship of Śakti or Devī or Vāc, later the main theme of the Tantras.

Dhāmatraya: Candra (moon), Sūrya (sun) and Agni (fire) regarded as the abode and expression of *bindu*. *Tantrāloka* III, 120-1.

Dhanadā, Dhanadāyikā: Tantric goddess who bestows wealth and is conceived of as a youthful maiden wearing costly ornaments.

Dhanada-Tārā: One of the four-armed varieties of Tārā. As her name implies, she is the bestower of wealth. She is surrounded by eight goddesses, originating from the eight syllables of the famous *mantra*: Om Tāre Tuttāre Ture Svāhā. *Sādhana* 219.

Dhanakālikā: Also known as Dhanadā and Dhanadakālikā. She is one of the eight or nine forms of Kālī. *Puraścaryārṇava* I. 16.

Dhani-mantra: One of the two classes of *mantras* according to a special point of view. The other class is known as Ṛni-*mantra*. When the number of the letters of the *mantra* exceeds that of the aspirant it is called Ṛni and the reverse is Dhani.

Dhāraṇa, Dhāraṇā: Attention consisting in fixing the mind on the desired object; it is the sixth discipline of yoga. It is the 'holding by', i.e. fixing the mind on a particular object of thought. In Tantric Buddhism it is the meditation of one's own *mantra* on the heart, and the placing of it on the *prāṇabindu* or heart-centre after restraining the jewels of sense organs. When it is done the *nimittas* (q.v.) make their appearance.

Dhāraṇa Yantra: The Yantras (q.v.) generally used as an amulet or talisman. These are drawn on leaves and dedicated to the name of different deities. Their use is regarded as efficacious for warding off evil spirits and the attainment of merit. *Tantrasāra* 585; *Śaktisaṅgama, Tārā*. LI. 2.

Dhāraṇī, Dhāriṇī: A conglomeration of syllables used as a charm or prayer by the followers of Tantric Buddhism. These were composed between the fourth and eighth centuries AD and formed part of the Mahāyāna Buddhist literature. The Dhāraṇis refer to Tantric concepts like *mantra*, *mudrā*, *kriyā*, *caryā*, etc. The *prajñapāramitā Sūtras* in their shortest forms, such as *Alpākṣara-prajñāpāramitā*, etc., were used as Dhāraṇis. The collection of five Dhāraṇis entitled *Pañcarakṣā* is popular in Buddhist countries. The Dhāraṇis often appear as parts of Sūtras. They consist of numerous invocations to female deities as well as to Buddhas and Bodhisattvas and exorcism formulas against snakes, the influence of ill-omened constellations, poison, demons, etc., and spells for healing of diseases the lengthening of life, bringing luck in war, rebirth in Sakhāvatī heaven, release from sin and so forth. There are numerous Dhāraṇis which have come down single and also there are large collections of Dhāraṇis. The word is a synonym for *rakṣā* and the Pali *parittā* (protecting magic formula). According to *Saddharmapuṇḍarīka* 399, the Dhāraṇis are taught 'for the protection, safety and shelter of the preachers'. In the Vajrayāna the Dhāraṇis are deified into twelve goddesses known as Sumati, Ratnolkā, Uṣṇīṣavijayā, Māri, Parṇaśabarī, Jāṅguli, Anantamukhī, Cundā, Prajñāvardhanī, Sarvakarmavaraṇa-viśodhanī, Akṣayajñānakaraṇḍa and Sarva-buddhadharmakośavatī.

Dharmacakra: One of the four nerve-cycles in the Tantric Buddhist conception. It is situated near the region of the heart and is connected with the *dharma-kāya* of Buddha. It is kindled by a female energy having the force of fire known as *caṇḍālī*.

Dharmacakra Lokeśvara: A form of Avalokiteśvara who is one-faced and two-armed and stands on a lotus. He carries a *vajra* in his right hand and an axe in his left.

Dharmacakra-Mudrā: Also known as Vyākhyāna-mudra it is the gesture of hands exhibited by the Buddha while preaching his first sermon at Sarnath. The pose is depicted variously but the most artistic and correct representation of this *mudrā* is to be found in the celebrated Prajñāpāramitā image from Java. The palms are placed near the breast in the mode of explaining something.

Dharmadhātu Lokeśvara: A form of Avalokiteśvara. He is one-faced, two-armed and stands on a lotus. He holds in his two hands a water-pot near his navel.

Dharmadhātu Vāgīśvara: A form of Mañjuśrī (q.v.). When represented he is white in colour with four faces and eight arms, and he bears five jewels in his diadem. He is clad in celestial garments and the leading sentiment displayed by him is one of *śṛṅgāra* (amour). In his hands he carries bow, arrow, noose, goad, book, sword, *ghaṇṭā* and *vajra*. In another form he exhibits the *dharmacakra-mudrā*. *Sādhana* 128.

Dharmakāya: One of the three bodies or *kāyas* of the Buddha, the others being *sambhoga* and *nirmāṇa*. *Dharmakāya* is the spiritual form of the Buddha which, theoretically speaking, pervades the universe. *Sambhoga-kāya* is the divine body which can only be seen by the saints of higher order while *nirmāṇakāya* or *rūpakāya* refers to the human Buddha. In Tantric Buddhism, in accordance with the theory of the identification of macrocosm and microcosm, the three *kāyas* of the Buddha have been identified with the nerve-plexuses (*cakras*) within the human body. Thus the *dharmacakra* (representing the *anāhatacakra* of the Hindu Tantras) situated in the cardiac region represents the *dharmakāya* which is defined in the Buddhist Tantras as the 'principle of non-dual cosmic existence'.

Dharma-meghā: Tantric Buddhist goddess of the *bhūmi* (q.v.) category who holds the *prajñāpāramitā* manuscript composed of the clouds of *dharma. Niṣpanna* 55.

Dharma-mudrā: A stage of *sādhana* which is said in the Buddhist Tantras to be of the nature of *dharma-dhātu* (i.e. the ultimate element of the *dharmas*), non-phenomenal (*nisprapañca*), free from thought-constructions (*nirvikalpa*), natural (*akṛtrima*) uncreated, of the nature of compassion and it produces *paramānanda* (great bliss).

Dharmavaśitā: Goddess of the *vaśitā* (q.v.) category of Tantric Buddhism described as being white in colour and carrying a bowl on a lotus. *Niṣpanna* 57.

Dhātu: Components of Śiva-Śakti triangles. According to the *Kāmikāgama*, from the viewpoint of the macrocosm, the Śakti triangles denote the five *dhātus,* namely *tvac* (skin), *asṛi* (blood), *māṃsa* (flesh), *medas* (fat), and *asthi (bone)*; the Śiva traingles denote *majjā* (marrow), *śukra* (vital fluid), *prāṇa* and *jīva*. From the viewpoint of the macrocosm, the Śakti triangles stand fot the five vital functions, the five senses of knowledge, the five senses of action, the five subtle and the five gross forms of matter, and the mind, while the Śiva triangles represent the four higher *tattvas*, namely *māyā*, *śuddhavidyā*, *māheśvara* and *sadāśiva*.

***Dhāturatnamālā*:** A late-medieval text on alchemy, which is devoted exclusively to the short processes of 'killing' metals and minerals. The use of opium as a drug prescribed here was probably due to foreign influence. Chinese drugs are also mentioned.

Dhātuśakti: Collective name of Ḍākinī, Rākini, Lākinī, Kākinī, Śākinī and Hākinī, presiding goddesses of the *cakraṣ* (q.v.).

***Dhātuvāda*:** One of the Sanskrit treatises on alchemy which was translated into Tibetan. It was recovered from the xylographs of the Tanjur manuscripts of the Narthang edition belonging to the Visva Bharati university. It has been translated into English and published along with original Tibetan in Roman script by Vidhusekhar Sastri.

***Dhātuvādaśāsatra*:** One of the Sanskrit treatises on alchemy which was translated into Tibetan. It was also known as *Dhātuvādaśāstroddhṛti* and formed part of the now lost *Rasasiddhiśāstra*. It is available in the xylographs of the Tanjur manuscript belonging to the libraries of the Asiatic Society of Bengal and Calcutta University.

Dhauti: One of the six actions of the yogic practices denoting washing, internal and external, for making the body pure. Dhauti is of four kinds—*antar*, *danta*, *hṛd* and *mūlaśodhana*. See Śodhana. *Gheraṇḍa* I. 13.

Dhavalāmukhī: Tantric goddess who is described as smoke-coloured, with three eyes and matted locks. She wears a tiger's skin and holds a rosary of bones in one hand and a knife on the other.

Dhenumudrā: Tantric *mudrā* or hand pose. It is a complicated posture made by intertwining the fingers of both hands to show a cow like figure. *Naivedya,* or offering, should be presented in this posture to the life-principle (Parā-Prakṛti).

Dhūmāvatī: Goddess said in the *Svatantratantra* to have been formed of smoke when Satī gave up her life in the sacricifial fire of Dakṣa. According to the *Nāradapāñcarātra* Vagalā and Dhumāvatī are the same goddess. She devoured her own husband which is why she is a widow. In the *Kubjikā* she is described as the destroyer of Dhumrāsura. *Prāṇatoṣaṇī* V. 6, 381-3. Her eight-lettered *mantra* bestows all attainments upon her worshipper. Aṣṭāksarī mahāvidyā bhajatāṃ sarvasiddhidā, *Puraścaryārnava* IX. 821. It can also destroy an enemy. Dhumāvatimanuḥ proktaḥ śatrunigrahakāraka. *Phetkārinī* VII. She is described as being pale, fickle, angry and tall. Her attire is faded and teeth are sparse. She is a widow having loose breasts. The banner of her chariot is a crow. She is always hungry, vindictive and querrelsome. *Tantrasāra* 385.

Both in her Dhumāvatī and Vagalā forms she is known as *Siddhavidyā.*

Dhvajāgrakeyurā: Tantric Buddhist goddess who is an emanation of Akṣobhya. She has both three and four-faced forms. Her colour is blue and appearance terrible. She stands in *pratyālīḍha* pose. *Sādhana* 403.

Dhyāna: Meditation. It refers generally to that portion of *sādhanā* or spiritual exercise in which the practitioner identifies himself with the object of his concentration. Dhyāna is also the name of a *mudrā* and *āsana (samadhi-mudrā* and *vajraparyaṅka* respectively). It is defined as steady contemplation of the object without break which reveals the reality of the contemplated object to the aspirant's mind. It is the seventh discipline of yoga. In Tantric Buddhism *dhyāna* is explained as the conception of five desired objects through the five Dhyānī Buddhas, namely Vairocana, Ratnasambhava, Amitābha, Akṣobhya and Amoghasiddhi. This *dhyāna* is again subdivided into five kinds: *vitarka* (cogitation), *vicāra* (thinking), *prīti* (pleasure), *sukha* (happiness) and *ekāgrata* (concentration). *Guhyasamāja,* XVIII. For Dhyāna as one of the eight limbs of yoga see Dhyāna-yoga.

Dhyanapāramitā: Pāramitā (q.v.) goddess described in the Buddhist Tantras as being of the colour of sky and holding a lotus and the *cintāmaṇi* banner. *Niṣpanna* 56.

Dhyānāsana: See Vajraparyaṅka.

Dhyāna-yoga: Concentration of mind through which it acquires the quality of realization. It is of two kinds—*saguṇa* or meditation on a form, and *nirguṇa* in which the self is its own object. The *Kulārṇava* IX. 3 divides *dhyāna* into *sthūla* (gross) and *sukṣma* (subtle). In *sthūla* meditation the practitioner visualizes the form of his Istadevatā (personal god). The next stage, known as *jyotirdhyāna*, is a conception in the abstract, not of the deity but its energy. The *sūkṣma* or subtle meditation is possible when the *kuṇḍalini* is roused. *Gheraṇḍa* VI.

Dhyāni Buddha: Deification of the five cosmic elements or *skandhas* in Vajrayāna Buddhism. The five Dhyānī Buddhas are Amitābha, Akṣobhya, Amoghasiddhi, Ratnasambha and Vairocana. Each of them is an embodiment of a particular element (*rūpa* or matter, *vedanā* or sensation, *saṃjñā* or perception, *saṃskāra* or impression and *vijñāna* or consciousness). Each belongs to a particular *kula* (tribe), has attendant Boddhisattvas (q.v.), emanated gods and goddesses as also *śakti* (consort).

Digmbara: A class of Avadhutas (q.v.) having the quality of Śiva. *Prāṇatoṣaṇī* VII. 7, 532. The term also applies to a sect following Vāmācara (q.v.). Lakṣmīdhara's com. on *Saundaryalaharī* 32.

Dīksā: Consecration. The word *dīksā* is derived from the root *dā* (to give) and *kṣī* (to destroy). According to the *Viśvasāra-tantra* it is of four types—*kriyāvati*, *kalāvati*, *varṇamayī* and *vedhamayī*. *Prāṇatoṣaṇī* II. 4.118. According to the *Kulārṇava* XIV, it is of seven kinds—*kriyā*, *varṇa*, *kalā*, *sparśa*, *vāk*, *dṛk* and *mānasa*. These are again subdivided into different categories. According to the *Rudrayāmala*, *dīkṣā* is of three types—*anavī*, *śāktī* and *śāmbhavī*. In some Tantras *ānavī* is replaced by *māntrī*. *Prāṇatoṣaṇī* II. 4. There are other types of *dikṣā* like *krama*, *pañcāyatana*, *ekamantra*, etc. Other types of *dikṣā* include *tattva*, *bhuvana*, *pāda*, *varṇa*, *yantra*, *śakti*, *nāda*, *prāṇa*, *jīva*, *cora*, *sparśa*, *vastra*, *ghaṭa*, *nirvāṇa*, *sadyonirvāṇa*, *āloka*, *jñāna*, etc. Ordinary *dīkṣā* is called *kriyā-dīkṣā* and the extraordinary variety is called *vedha-ḍīkṣā*. The *Jayadratha-yāmala* mentions 25 kinds of *dīkṣā*. By means of *dīkṣā* the aspirant receives a kind of rebirth.

Dīkṣāguru: The *guru* or teacher from whom initiation is to be received. There are certain conflicting rules regarding selection of such a *guru.* According to *Kulārṇava* XII. 52, XII. 100, the *guru* who initiates the disciple is never to be abandoned. The view is echoed in other Tantras as well which hold that since knowledge, its bestower and object belong to the same category he who imparts the knowledge, that is *guru*, is no other than Śiva, hence he should always be adhered to, *Kāmākhya*, paṭala IV; *Paraśūrāmakalpa-sūtra* I. 20. This general rule can, however, be ignored under special circumstances. If the *guru* is not sufficiently qualified a better teacher may be resorted to. For the sake of higher knowledge and truth a Kaula can have any number of *gurus*; *Kaulika, guravo' nantāḥ. Setubandha* on *Nityaṣoḍaśikārṇava* VI. 4. Again it is said that the *dīkṣāguru* should belong to the same spiritual clan as the disciple. For a Śākta the *guru* should be Śākta, for a Vaiṣṇava he should be Vaiṣṇava, for a

Gāṇapatya he should be a Gāṇapatya and so forth. But a Kaula *guru* can initiate anyone. *Mahānirvāṇa* X. 200-1. A *guru* ought to be a householder and not an ascetic. It is so because the latter may not always be capable of understanding the wordly problems of his disciple. One should not have initiation from one's father and near relations. A husband should not be the *guru* of his wife, the father of his sons and daughters, or a brother of his brothers. *Tārābhaktisudhārṇava* II. 10; *Tantrasāra* 5.

***Dīkṣāparīkṣā*:** A treatise on Ḍīkṣā (q.v.) as gleaned from various textual sources which was composed by Viṣṇubhaṭṭa, pupil of Satyānandanātha, in Śaka 1719 (AD 1797). Published by Nirṇaya Sāgara press 1935.

***Dīkṣātattva*:** One of the 28 sections of Raghunandana's (sixteenth century) famous *Smṛtitattva.* It gives a lengthy treatment of Dīkṣā (q.v.) at the beginning of which it remarks that in the *Śāradātilaka* and other works numerous topics of Dīkṣā are described, but in course of time those were not followed. The text says that the *guru* giving Dīkṣā should be of the same sect as the disciple, but a Kaula is a good Guru for all.

Dīpā: One of the four Tantric Buddhist goddesses of light who is blue in colour and holds in her hand a light stick. *Niṣpanna* 76.

Dīpana: Processing of *mantra. Tantrasāra* 54.

Dīpanī: The addition of *om* to the original *mantra* and reciting it seven times for the purpose of illuminating (*dīpana*) it. *Mantra dīpanī* is like a dark room without a lamp. *Sarasvatī tantra* quoted in *Prāṇatoṣaṇī* IV. 1, 225. According to the *Śaktānandataraṅgiṇī* XI, by prefixing and suffixing *aim* to the original *mantra* when it is recited seven times, the purpose of *dīpanī* is achieved: *yonimantram manorddatvā cādyante parameśvari, saptavāraṃ japitvā tu dīpanīyaṃ prakīrtitam.*

Dīpaṅkara: An early incarnation of the Buddha. In the *Guhyasamāja Tantra* it is said that when the Buddha came to the world as Dīpaṅkara he did not preach the secret doctrines of the Guhyasamāja school because people in those days were not found fit to receive the instructions. *Guhyasamāja* 144.

Dīpaṅkara Srijñana Atīsa: Indian Buddhist monk who reached Tibet in AD 1042 as a teacher reformer and was referred to by the Tibetans as 'the great lord' and 'super god'. In his younger days he travelled in South East Asia and mastered different branches of Buddhism. His astonishing scholarship is attested to by more than 220 works which he authored. These are in the Tanjur and Kanjur collections. He passed away near Lhasa in AD 1054.

Divya-bhāva: The highest spiritual standard of the Tantric aspirant. This standard is achieved by an individual only when his acquired qualities become part and parcel of himself. It is in this state that a man has some feeling of egoity. But in the Divya state he is as simple as a child. The transformation from the state of Paśu to that of Divya is the aim of all Śākta-Tantric aspirants. It is also called the *mahābhāva* state in which bonds do not exist in substance and so they do not require to be 'burnt', but the semblance or mere form of them is dissolved in the 'Ocean of nectar'.

Divyacakra: A *cakra* (q.v.) ritual, also known as *tattvacakra*, meant only for those who have attained a special stage of spiritual progress. This *cakra* requires the use of the five Ms. *Mahānirvāṇa* VIII. 204-19.

Divya-deha: Rejuvenated body. The Raseśvara (q.v.) Siddhas and the Nātha Siddhas (q.v.) hold that death may either be put off *ad libitum* by a special course of restrengthening and revitalizing the body, so as to put it permanently in rapport with the world of the senses. They hold that by way of transubstantiation of his corporeal substance, one may acquire a new or divine body. It is said that the natural body of man is formed of impure matter (*aśuddha-māyā*) and that by a special method the *aśuddha-māyā* is to be transmuted into one of pure matter (*śuddha-māyā*). When this is achieved the rejuvenated body becomes *praṇava-tanu* and its owner *jīvanmukta* (q.v.), that is, 'liberated within the span of life'. This is to be accomplished through an elaborate process which begins with the purifying cure of the cells, tissues, and organs, by disciplining the body ultimately directed to the dematerialising transmutation of the refined, albeit perishable physical basis of life into a transplysical incorruptible and permanent one. The Rasa school holds that the transmutation is possible by the use of chemical drugs. See Divyatanu, Jīvanmukti. Raseśvara Darśana, Siddha-Cikitsā, Sittar.

Divya-pāna: One of the three forms of

drinking wine before the goddess, others being Paśu and Vīra. *Kulārṇava* VII; *Śaktisaṅgama*, Tārā, XXXIII. 6-8.

Divya-pañcatattva: The higher view pertaining to the pañca-makāras or five Ms, according to which wine (*madya*) is that material which helps to get rid of wordly fetters and achieve salvation by removing the eight kinds of suffering. Flesh (*māṃsa*) is that material which is beneficial, dear to all gods and bestows absolute bliss; fish (*matsya*) is that material which helps to control the senses and fix the mind on the supreme being; cereal (*mudrā*) means eating a plateful of items fried in *brahmāgni* which are the eight evil mental propensities; and sexual intercourse (*maithuna*), the union of Śiva in the form of *bindu* (q.v.) and *kuṇḍalinī-śakti* in the *sahasrāra* (the central cerebral region). *Kulārṇava* V. 107-12, XVII. 64 ff. *Śaktisaṅgama*, Tārā XXXII. 25; *Kaulamārgarahasya* 255; *Rudrayāmala*, Uttara 26; *Yoginītantra*, pūrva VI; *Prāṇatoṣaṇi* VII. 2. 508.

Divyarātri: The time of the appearance of the Mahāvidyā goddess Ṣoḍaśī. It is also one of the names given to this goddess on the event of her appearence.

Divya sādhaka: The aspirant whose spiritual exercise is of the highest level.

Divya-tattva: One of the three categories of *pañcatattva* (q.v.) others being *pratyakṣa* and *anukalpa*.

Divya-tanu: Rejuvenated body. This rejuvenation is possible through certain physical and chemical processes. The transmutation does not outwardly interfere with the relative disposition of the bodily parts. Only their vitality is strengthened by a supply of extra-physical nourishment. The effect of the transmutation of the body into the *mantra-tanu* is indicative of the wiping up of the impure *māyā* from the corrupt material body and changing it to an incorruptible deathless substance. Further changes towards a spiritual objective leads one from the *jīvanmukta* to the *paramukta* stage, and the veritable transformation thus caused creates the body known as *praṇava-tanu* or *vaindava-tanu*. It is a form in which its owner finds himself in the realm of pure spirit in a transfigured body also known as *jñāna-tanu*. Though the spiritually freed man has the capacity to have an indefinitely long life, he does not generally choose to do so. He lives the necessary span of his earthly life and at the right time he disappears openly in the transparency of space. See Divya-deha.

Divyaugha: One of the three lines of the succession of the Tantric *gurus*, others being *siddhaugha* and *manavaugha*. *Bhavacuḍāmaṇi* quoted in *Śyāmārahasya* III.

Ḍombī: 'The Doma girl' which is often a designation of Prajña (q.v.) in the Buddhist Tantras. Ḍombī is also an epithet of the goddess Caṇḍālī who is awakened in the *nirmāṇa-cakra* when the Bodhicitta is produced in the navel region. She is variously known as Yoginī, Sahajasundarī, Nairātmā or Nairāmaṇi. As a specific deity of Tantric Buddhism she is described in the Pañcaḍāka Maṇḍala as an associate of Vajraḍāka in *Niṣpanna* 75. She is of mixed colour and carries in her right hand a banner and her left hand displays the common gesture of *tarjani* against the chest.

Doṣa: Faults. In Tanric belief *doṣa* means defects in regard to *mantras*. Defective *mantras* like *chinna*, *ruddha*, etc., do not produce any result. *Śāradātilaka* II. 64-108.

Dravyaśuddhi: Purification of cultic materials with *mantras* and *dhenumudrā*. *Puraścaryārṇava* III. 153.

Dṛk-dīkṣā: See Cākṣusī-dīkṣā. It is said in the *Kulārṇava* XIV.36 that just as a fish rears its progeny with its eye-sight, so also the teacher may initiate his disciple merely by his enlightened gaze. He should stare at his disciple considering himself to be no other thạn Śiva. This is *dṛk-dīkṣā*. Rāghavabhaṭṭa on *Śāradātilaka* V. 127-40.

Dṛk-śakti: Five kinds of *aiśvaryas* (supernatural powers) which a Siddha-yogī receives from Maheśvara. These are *darśana* (sight) *śravaṇa* (hearing), *manana* (contemplation), *vijñāna* (understanding) and *sarvajñatā* (omniscience). *Sarvadarśanasaṃgraha* VI. 49-51.

Duraṅgamā: Tantric Buddhist goddess of *bhūmi* (q.v.) category who is described as being green in colour. Her symbols are a double thunderbolt and lotus. *Niṣpanna* 55.

Durgā: A river sacred to the goddess of the same name mentioned in *Bṛhannīla* V. It is a tributary of the Śābarmatī in Gujarat.

Durgottāriṇī-tārā: A form of the green Tārā, the saviour of fortresses. In the first pair of hands she holds noose and goad and displays in the second pair a lotus and the *varada* pose.

Duritāri: The Śāsanadevatā of the third Jain Tīrthaṃkara Sambhavanātha according to the Śvetambara tradition. She rides a ram and is four-handed. The hands hold *varada*, rosary, fruit and *abhaya*. The ram symbol implies her connection with the wife of Agni. The symbols of *vara* and rosary support this supposition. The description is found in *Nirvāṇakalikā* and *Pratiṣṭhāsārasaṃgraha.*

Dutī: Female partner of the aspirant.

Dūtiyāga: Ritual union with *dūti*. Her organ is conceived of as the sacrificial fire and the semen of the aspirant as the clarified butter which is to be offered in the fire. *Paraśurāmakalpasūtra* X. 63.

Dvādaśa-dharma: The twelve codes of conduct of one who performs *puraścarana* (q.v.). These are *bhūśayyā* (lying on the ground), *brahmacarya* (celibacy), *mauna* (silence), *anasuyatā* (malice to none), *trisandhyāsnāna* (bathing thrice a day), *nitya-pūjā* (daily worship), *nitya-dāna* (daily offering gifts), *kṣudrakarmā-vivarjana* (shunning useless acts), *devatāstutikīrtana* (singing the glory of god), *naimittika-pūjā* (occasional worship) and faith in *guru*. *Gautamīya-tantra* XIV.

Dvādása-karaṇa: Twelve organs—five of action, five of knowledge plus *manas* and *buddhi*. They are also called Mārtaṇḍa. Being united with *ahaṃkāra* or the principle of egoity they constitute *pūrṇakalpa* or *paramāditya* according to the *krama* doctrine.

Dvādaśānta: A subtle centre in close proximity to the pericarp of the *sahasrāra-kamala* (thousand-petalled lotus in the brain). It is above twelve centres—the three higher centres, namely, *anāhata*, *viśuddha* and *ājñā*, and the nine subtle centres beginning from the middle of the forehead and going up to the *brahmarandhra*. The Dvādaśanta represents *jñāna*, *sahaja-samādhi* and transition from *turīya* to *turīyātīta* state.

Dvaitādvaitavāda: Identity-in-difference. According to this doctrine, *brahman* transforms itself into the world. The process of such transformation is due to its efficient character. During dissolution (*pralaya*) the entire universe returns to and remains in it in a subtle state as its natural power. At the beginning of creation it manifests its *cit-śakti* (power of sentience) and *acit-śakti* (power of non-sentience) in the form of soul and *prakṛti* and from the latter there is a gradual evolution of the material world. The cause-effect relation between the *brahman* and the world is that of identity-in-difference. *Brahman* is different from the universe because it is transcendent to it, and non-different because it is immanent in it. In Vaiṣṇavism Dvaitādvaitavāda is represented by the school of Nimbārka and in Śaivism to a certain extent in Śrīkaṇṭha Śivācārya's and Śrīpati-Paṇḍita's commentaries on the *Brahmasūtra*. In the Śāktyādvayavāda of Kashmir Śaivism and Śaktiviśiṣṭādvaitavāda of Vīra Śaivism we have reflection of this approach which is otherwise called Bhedābhedavāda.

Dvaitavada: Unqualified dualism according to which *brahman* (equated with the Supreme Being of all the theistic systems) is independent and the maker of all. The world of consciousness and matter is real, essentially dependent, having derived its reality from *brahman*. This dualism is represented in Vaiṣṇavism by the school of Madhva. In Śaivism it is represented by the Śaiva Siddhānta doctrine from which Śākta dualism has drawn heavily.

Dvāravatī: Holy resort of the goddess Rukminī mentioned in *Matsya* XIII. 38; *Devībhāgavata* VII. 30. 67; *Bṛhannīla* V, etc. It is modern Dwarka in north-western Kathiawar.

Dveṣa: One of the five *kleśas* (stains) which envelopes the soul. The others are *avidyā* (ignorance), *asmitā* (egoity), antipathy or malice, *rāga* (attachment) and *abhiniveśa* (intentness). These arise from *aśuddha-māyā* and are collectively called *puṃstvamala*.

E e

***Ekādaśamukha*:** Name of a Mantrayāna Buddhist Sūtra associated with the Dhāraṇī trend. Its Sanskrit version has been found in Gilgit. It has a Tibetan version as well. It prescribes the use of incantations to achieve success and avert various kinds of evils. Its central figure is Amitābha. Edited in *Gilgit Manuscripts*, V1. I, Srinagar 1939.

Ekāgratā: Singularity of mind according to the *Yogasūtra* III. 11.12.

Ekajaṭā: Same as Ugratārā and Nīlasarasvatī whose *mantra* is *hrīṃ, strīṃ, hūṃ, phaṭ* which is to be maintained in secret. *Tantrasāra* 329. She is four-armed; her two right hands hold a sword and chopper and her left hand a skull and lotus. She has a single matted lock which accounts for her name and also a miniature figure of Akṣobhya on her head. *Nīlatantra* IV; *Tantrasāra* 334; *Puraścaryārṇava* IX. 794-5; *Tārārahasya* I. In the Buddhist tradition she is an emanation of Akṣobhya whose effigy she bears on her crown. According to the Buddhist tradition Ārya Nāgārjuna recovered the Ekajaṭā cult from Bhoṭadeśa (Tibet). Images of Ekajaṭā are found in almost all Buddhist countries of the North including China. Four *sādhanas* in the *Sādhanamālā* 266 describe her three different forms. She may have one face with two, four or eight arms. She is blue in colour and of terrible appearance and she stands in *pratyālīḍha* attitude. When two-armed she carries a chopper and a skull cup; when four-armed the two extra hands carry a lotus and a sword; and when eight-armed, the extra hands carry a bow, an arrow, an axe and a *vajra*. It is said that if a person listens to her *mantra* but once, he is at once freed from all obstacles and is attended always with good fortune; his enemies are destroyed and he becomes religiously inclined, even attaining the level of a Buddha.

***Ekajaṭā Tantra*:** A late medieval Tantric text dealing with the worship of Tārā.

***Ekākṣara-kośa*:** Attributed to Puruṣottama of the twelfth century AD it explains in 38 verses the meaning of the letters of Tantric alphabet.

Ekāmra: Holy resort of the goddess Kīrtimatī mentioned in *Matya* XIII. 29; *Devibhagavata* VII. 30.58; *Jñānārṇava* V. 66 ff; *Bṛhannīla* V. It is modern Bhuvaneswar in Orissa. Also known as Kṛttivāsa it is described as a holy place in *Brahma Purāṇa* XII. 10-93.

Ekānaṃśā: Tribal goddess later identified with Pārvatī and her changed forms like Kauśikī, Vindhyavāsinī, etc. Historically she may also be identified with Stambheśvarī, the goddess of the Śulkis. In a subsequent stage in the development of her conception she became Subhadrā and began to be depicted as having her place between Jagannātha and Balarāma. In the temple of Purī she is worshipped along with her brothers in Vaisnavite Tantric system with *anukalpas* of the Pañcatattva. In the *Harivaṃśa* Viṣṇu 120, the supreme goddess is invoked as Ekānaṃśā. In *Matsya Purāṇa* CLIV-CLVII the story of her transformation from Rātri or Niśā is vividly described. In the *Skanda Pūrāṇa*, Kumārikā, LXV the hymn addressed to Ekānaṃśā by Yudhiṣṭhira and her greatness are described.

***Ekavīra Tantra*:** A late medieval Tantric text dealing with the worship of Tārā.

Elāpura: Holy resort of the goddess Vīrā mentioned in *Matsya.* XXII. 50, *Jñānārnava* V. 66 ff; *Bṛhannīla* V. It is same as Ellora in the Aurangabad district, Maharashtra.

Evam, Evaṃkāra: Symbolic syllable for the union of Prajñā and upāya in which 'e' stands for the former and 'va' for the latter while the *anusvāra* or *bindu*, 'ṃ' denotes the union itself. According to another interpretation found in the Buddhist Tantras 'e' denotes earth represented by the goddess Locanā (*karma-mudrā*) and 'vaṃ' water represented by Māmakī *(dharma-mudrā*). 'E' and 'vam' also stand respectively for the female and male organs of generation.

G g

Gaganagañja: Bodhisattva described four times in *Niṣpannayogāvalī* 50, 58, 67. In *Sādhanamālā* 49 he is described as *raktavarṇo nīlotpalavarapradaḥ*. An eighth century bronze image of this Bodhisattva from Nalanda is now in Patna Museum. There is also a Gaganagañja Lokeśvara who is a form of Avalokiteśvara. He is one faced and two-armed and sits in the *vajraparyaṅka* attitude on a lotus. He exhibits *vitarka mudrā* in his right hand and holds a book in his left.

Gajakrāntā: A geographical region of Tantric culture; same as Aśvakrāntā.

Gaṇapati: Puranic deity whose worship is conducted before starting the worship of other deities. The worship of Gaṇapati has also a Tantric equivalent. The *Bhaviṣya-Purāṇa*, Brahmaparva, XXIX. 9-15, provides that *gaṁ svāhā* is the *mūla-mantra* of Gaṇapati worship, cites the *mantras* for *hṛdaya*, *śikhā*, *kavaca*, etc., and a Gāyatrī suited to Gaṇapati. This Gāyatrī is: *mahākarṇāya vidmahe vakratuṇḍāya dhīmahi, tanno dantiḥ pracodayāt*. Gaṇapati is also worshipped in Tantric Buddhism. The *Sādhanamālā* 592-3 describes Gaṇapati as having a red complexion, bearing the *jaṭā-mukuṭa*, having twelve arms, a protruding belly and an elephant face. He stands in a dancing attitude, is three-eyed and has one tusk. In the *Niṣpanna* 62 he is described as riding on a mouse and a snake forms his sacred thread. In his two right hands he carries a *triśūla* and a *ladduka* (a round sweetmeat) and in the two left a *paraśu* (axe) and a *mūlaka* (radish).

Gaṇapatihṛdayā: Tantric Buddhist goddess who is not attached to a particular Dhyānī Buddha. But she must have been the *śakti* of the Buddhist Gaṇapati. She is one-faced, two-armed, exhibits in her two hands the *varada* and *abhaya* poses, and shows dancing attitude. Her information is obtained from Amṛtānanda's *Dharmakośa-saṁgraha*.

***Gaṇapatitattva*:** An important sectarian Tantra of the Gāṇapatyas found in an old Javanese collection which refers to the march of *kuṇḍalinī* through the six *cakras* of the body, by means of *kāyasādhana*, to the six *aṅgas* of yoga, to the concepts of *bindu, mantra, bīja* and so on. Critically edited, annotated and translated by Sudarsadevi Singhal, New Delhi 1958.

Gāṇapatya-liṅga: A class of Śiva-liṅga (q.v.) mentioned in the *Kāmikāgama* without any specification.

Gāṇapatyas: Followers of the cult of Gaṇapati or Gaṇeśa. In Ānandagiri's *Śaṅkaradigvijaya* and Dhanpati's *Diṇḍimākhya* commentary on Mādhava Vidyāraṇya's *Śaṅkaradigvijaya*, six sects of Gāṇapatyas are mentioned. Among these sects the followers of Ucchiṣṭa-gaṇapati were Tantrics and followers of *Vāmācara*. The god is conceived of as having four arms, three eyes, a noose, club and *abhaya* posture; the front portion of his trunk smells a scent of intoxicating liquor; his *śakti* is on his left side whom he embraces and kisses and whose genital region he presses with his trunk. The followers of Ucchiṣṭa-gaṇapati did not believe in the caste system. They did not make any distinction between virtue and vice. They approved drinking of wine and wore a red dot on their foreheads. They held Gaṇeśa to be the highest cosmic principle, both efficient and material cause of the world. He was conceived of as the universal soul in the form of consciousness and bliss.

Gaṇḍakī: The river Gandaki, a place on the bank of which having the same name is regarded as a holy resort of the goddess in the *Pīṭhanirṇaya*. The *Śivacarita* refers to it as a *Mahāpīṭha*. The Gandaki is a tributary of the Ganges which it meets near Bakhtyarpur in Patna district, Bihar. In *Bhāgavata* V. 7.70, X. 70.11, it is called Cakranadī because it has pebbles marked with *cakra* (Śālagrāma stone). *Mbh.* I. 170.20-1, II. 20.27; III. 222.22; *Padma* I. 38.36; IV. 20.12; *Varāha* CXLIV. 35.38; *Brahmāṇḍa* II. 16.26.

Gandhahasti: A Bodhisattva who has been described in the texts of Tantric Buddhism as belonging to a group of sixteen Bodhisattvas headed by Maitreya and having two independent forms. In the Mañjuvajra

Maṇḍala of the *Niṣpannayogāvalī* he is described as being green in colour and holding in his left hand the trunk of an elephant on a lotus while right hand exhibits the *varada mudrā*. In the Durgatipariśodhana Maṇḍala of the same text he is described as being whitish green in colour. He holds in his right hand a conch containing sandal paste; the clenched left hand is placed on the hip.

Gandhamādana: Holy resort of the goddess Kamākṣī (variant reading Kāmukī, Kāmukā) mentioned in *Matsya* XIII. 26; *Devībhāgavta* VII. 30. 55; *Visnu* III. 2.18; *Mārkaṇḍeya* LI. 19. It is a Himalayan peak at Badarikāśrama.

Gāndhārī: Śāsanadevatā of the Jain Tīrthaṃkara Vāsupūjya according to the Digambara tradition. She is represented as riding on a crocodile her hands equipped with a club, two lotuses and the fourth in *varada mudrā*.

***Gandharva Tantra*:** A Tantra in 42 chapters which mainly deals with the worship of Devī in her manifold forms. Apart from usual Tantric topics like *guru*, *dīkṣā*, *mantra*, etc., it introduces items like *pañcamī-vidyā*, *haṃsabīja*, *kāmakalā*, etc. The 36 *tattvas* of southern Śaivism and the Sāṅkhya categories are also described. It is of the nature of a manual. Ed. R.C. Kak and H.B. Sastri, Srinagar 1934.

Gandhāṣṭaka: Eight fragrant substances—*candana, agaru, karpura, cora, kumkuma, goracanā, jaṭāmāṃsī* and *kāpi*—combined together and used as a substitute for wine of three kinds, each being associated with Śiva, Śakti and Viṣṇu respectively. *Sāradātilaka* IV. 79-80.

Gaṇeśa: Same as Gaṇapati (q.v.). Gaṇeśa occurs in Tantric Buddhism as well which draws a distinction between Gaṇapati and Gaṇeśa. The Buddhists conceived of a super-Gaṇeśa under the name Vighnāntaka who wards off *vighnas* (troubles and disturbances) and thus appropriates the functions of Gaṇeśa and tramples the latter heavily. But in iconography of Vighnāntaka the trampled Gaṇeśa in order to keep up the dignity of his godhead, exhibits the *abhaya* pose even in his agony. *Sādhana* 358-9. The goddess Parṇaśabarī is also depicted in sculptures as trampling the *vighnas* represented in the form of Gaṇeśa. He is also depicted in sculptures as being trampled upon by the goddess Aparājitā. The Buddhist attributed complete divinity to his functions as 'lord of the host' (Gaṇapati, q.v.), but for warding off calamities and disturbances (*vighnas*) and granting of *siddhi* (attainments) made independent conceptualizations.

Gangādvāra: Holy resort of the goddess Ratipriyā or Haripriyā mentioned in *Matsya* XIII. 37; XXI. 10; *Padma,* sṛṣti XVII. 95 *Agni* IV. 7, *Devībhāgavata* VII. 30.66; *Brhannila* V. It is same as Haridvāra (Hardwar) the place where the Ganges enters the plain from the Himalayas.

Gaṅgāhari: Commentator on *Saundarya-laharī* attributed to Śaṅkara.

Garbha-dhātu: Name of the 'matrix element' or the phenomenal world, corresponding to the *tathāgata-garbha* according to the Buddhist Tantras.

Garbhapurīṣa: A Tamil Siddha belonging to the Suddha-mārga with a Śākta Agamic orientation. He was the head of a mendicant school of spiritual discipline. He was also celebrated for performing miracles. His Tamil name was Karuvīrār.

Gauḍa-sampradāya: A section of vāmācārin Tantrikas belonging to eastern India. This sect depends solely on the rituals of five Ms and believes categorically in the unity of *devatā*, *guru* and *mantra* as manifestation of the energy of the great goddess. *Puraś-caryārṇava* IX. 866; *Śaktisaṅgama*, Sundarī, III. 15-18.

Gauḍīya-Śaṅkara: Tantric teacher who flourished in the sixteenth century as inferred from a manuscript of the *Tārārahsyavārtika* in Maithili script. His full name seems to have been Śaṅkara Āgamavāgīśa as is indicated by the colophon of the *Tārārahasya-vārtika* in the Ms. of the India Office Library. His other works are *Śivārcana-mahāratna, Śaivaratna, Kulamūlāvatāra* and *Kramastava*. *Tārā-rahasyavārtika*, Varendra Research Museum, Rajshahi 1961.

Gaurī: Puranic goddess, same as Umā and Pārvatī. In Tantric Buddhism this goddess has been especially selected and made the head of a group of goddesses known as Gaurī, Caurī, Vetālī, Ghasmarī, Pukkasī, Śabarī, Caṇḍālī and Ḍombī. They occur in the Pañcaḍāka Maṇḍala of the *Niṣpannayogāvalī*. All the deities are violent in character with fearful appearance and ornaments and garlands of skulls. They dance in *pratyālīḍha* and show the raised index finger with clasped fist against the chest as the common gesture. Gaurī herself is white and holds in her right hand a goad. With the left she shows the *tarjani* against the chest.

Gaurīpaṭṭa: The pedestal on which a Śiva-liṅga is erected. It looks like the female organ which it symbolizes. It is also known as *yoni.*

***Gautamīya Tantra*:** Vaisnavite Tantra extolling the *mantra* of Kṛṣṇa in 32 chapters. Apart from the usual Tantric topics it describes Vṛndāvana, ten-fold purification of the Vaiṣṇavas, *pañcagavya*, praise of Śālagrāma, worship of Dikpālas, *mantras* or various syllables relating to Kṛṣṇa, worship of Gaṇeśa and Vāstupuruṣa and so forth. Ed. B. Jha. Varanasi 1977.

Gayā: Holy resort of the goddess Maṅgalā or Gayeśvarī mentioned in *Bṛhannīla* V. It is a celebrated *tīrtha* of all India reputation in Bihar.

Gāyatrī: The *prapañcasāra* devotes a complete chapter to the explanation of the words of Vedic Gāyatrī. But there is a different Tantric Gāyatrī which is: *ādyāyai vidmahe parameśvari dhīmahī, tan naḥ Kālī pracodayāt. Mahānirvāṇa* V. 62-3. The Tantras also refer to a goddess Gāyatrī who is conceived of as presiding over knowledge and speech. She is also known as Brāhmī, the Śakti of Brahmā. In one of her *dhyānas* she is described as resembling the rising sun, wearing the skin of a black antelope and holding a manuscript and rosary in her hands.

Ghaṇṭā: Bell. When the bell is surmounted by a *vajra* it is called *vajraghaṇṭā* and becomes a symbol of Vajrasattva.

Ghaṭa: A pot full of water which is used, either by itself or in addition to other forms, to represent the deity or the formless all-pervading spirit. The word *ghaṭa* or vessel is also used to designate the human body, and the space within it (*ghaṭākāśa*) designates the soul. It is held that as there is no difference between the space inside the *ghaṭa* and that outside it, so also there is no difference between the individual and universal soul. Also known as *kumbha* or *pūrṇakumbha*.

Ghaṇṭāpāṇi: Bodhisattva of the sixth Dhyānī Buddha Vajrasattva. His recognition symbol is *ghaṇṭā* or bell and his complexion is white.

Ghasmari: A goddess mentioned in the Pañcaḍāka Maṇḍala of *Niṣpannayogāvalī* 75.

Ghāṭaśilā: Holy resort of the great goddess where the left leg of Satī fell according to the *Caṇḍīmaṅgala*. It is situated in the Bengal-Bihar border between Kharagpur and Tatanagar on the South-Eastern Railway.

***Gheraṇḍa-saṃhitā*:** An important text on yogic exercises. It deals with as many as 84 *āsanas* or bodily postures. While the yoga of Patañjali concentrates all efforts on the discipline of mind, the *Gheraṇḍa* and similar other works (cf. *Haṭhayogapradīpikā*, *Gorakṣaśataka*, etc.) mainly concern themselves with the body, its health, its purity and freedom from disease. The *āsanas* are conducive to the strength and fitness of the body. The *Gheraṇḍasaṃhitā* also speaks of 25 *mudrās* and describes them in one hundred verses. *Gheraṇḍa-saṃhitā* concerns itself mainly with Haṭha-yoga and Rāja-yoga and is not philosophical in nature. Eng. trans. by S.C. Bose, Bombay 1896.

Ghoracaṇḍī: Goddess associated with the Saptākṣara variety of Hevajra (q.v.) symbolizing one of the spokes of the sun-wheel. Her colour is red, hair dishevelled, appearance fierce and she has three eyes. She is sky-clad. She carries *ḍamaru* (drum) and *ghaṇṭā* (bell) in the first pair of hands and human skin in the second pair. She stands in *ālīḍha* attitude, in the orbit of the sun placed on a corpse. Her head dress is decorated with rows of skulls.

Gītā: Tantric Buddhist goddess of the dancing group described in the *Pañcaḍāka*-maṇḍala of the *Niṣpannayogāvalī* 76. She is described as reddish white in colour. With her two hands she is engaged in playing the gong (kaṃsī).

Gocari: One of the five constituents of the Pañcavāha of the *Krama* doctrine, others being Vyomavāmeśvarī, Khecarī, Dikcarī, and Bhucarī. The five *vāhas* are the five flows or streamlike downward motions of the Supreme Being which constitute a *cakra* signifying five phenomenal realities. See Pañcavāha.

Godavarītīrtha: Also known as Godāśrama, it is a holy resort of the goddess Trisandhyā or Viśveśrī or Rākinī mentioned in the *Kubjikā* XVIII. 42 ff.; *Matsya* XIII. 37; *Devībhāgavata* VII. 30.66; *Brhannīla* V; etc. According to *Śivacarita* it is a *mahāpīṭha* where the left leg of Satī fell and the goddess is known as Viśvamātṛkā. The *Brhannīla* and *Prāṇatoṣaṇī* mention the goddess as Gaveśvarī. It is on the celebrated river Godāvarī in the Deccan.

Gokarṇa: Holy resort of the goddess

Bhadrakarṇikā or Bhadrā or Sarvamaṅgalā or Kālikā mentioned in *Jñānārṇava* V. 66 ff.; *Matsya* XIII. 30; *Devībhāgavata* VII. 30.59; *Bṛhannīla* V, etc. It is modern Gendia about 30 miles from Goa.

Goloka: Abode of Viṣṇu which the followers of Sahajiyā Vaiṣṇavism conceive of as existing near at hand. Man and woman are but physical representations of Kṛṣṇa and Rādhā and *rāsa* (love) and *rati* (the exciting cause of love and the support of love) of Goloka. A similar view centering around the union of Śiva and Devī, of Karuṇā and Śūnyatā, of Upāya and Prajñā is found in the Tantras. Vṛndāvana is thought of as the earthly counterpart of Goloka while in the heavenly Goloka region there is a Vṛndāvana where Kṛṣṇa is engaged in eternal sports with Rādhā.

Gopīcandra: Son of queen Mayanamati of Pāṭikā who at his mother's insistence became a disciple of the Nātha-siddha Jālandharī or Hāḍi-pā leaving his wives Adūna and Padunā. He half-heartedly took initiation from Hāḍi-pā and began to abuse his yogic power. At this Hāḍi-pā reprimanded him and an angry Gopīcandra ordered the Siddha to be buried alive. Learning this Kānu-pa, the chief disciple of Hāḍi-pa, hurried to Paṭikā and by using his occult powers got his guru dug up. Haḍī-pā's wrath against Gopīcandra was removed by the intercession of Kānu. Then Gopīcandra willingly submitted to the will of the Siddha and left home as a yogi mendicant in the company of Hāḍi-pa.

Gorakṣakāriṇī: Holy resort of the goddess of the same name mentioned in the *Kubjikā* XVIII. 42 ff.; variant reading Gorakṣacāriṇī. It is in the Gomanta or Goa where, according to *Matsya* XIII. 26 ff.; *Devībhāgavata* VII. 30.55 ff.; etc., the goddess is Gomati. Another Gorakṣa is the town of Gorkha, 53 miles to the west of Kathmandu in Nepal. Gorakhpur in Uttar Pradesh should also be mentioned in this connection.

Gorakṣanātha: One of the five Ādi-Siddhas of the Nātha faith. In order to put him in family life, Ketakā or Gaurī, wife of Śiva, stooped to despicable tricks, but the Siddha could not be tripped. Śiva, however, arranged Gorakṣa's marriage with an ascetic princess who bore his son Karapaṭinātha. Gorakṣa then rescued his *guru* Mīnanātha or Matsyendranātha from the women of the Kadali country who under their influence had forgotten his own power and attainments. The name Gorakṣanātha does not appear as the author of any early yogic or Tantric work. What has been published as *Gorakṣa Saṃhitā* is a late compilation. Gorakṣa was a true Ādi-Siddha of that strictly celibate and rigidly austere yogic cult which is called the Way of Gorakṣa or Gorah Panthā. It seems to have been in contrast with the esoteric cult patronized by Mīnanātha, Jālandhari and Kānu-pa which allowed yogis to have the companionship of Yoginīs. Gorakṣa's attitude to his infatuated *guru* is reflected in, and probably based on, the teachings of Saraha. The latter's instructions and admonitions, intended possibly for earning disciplehood, form the basis on which the story of Mīnanātha's rescue by Gorakṣanātha was subsequently built up. The sum and substance of Gorakṣas's teachings is that existence and extinction are the resultants of man's desire and cogitation. His fetters and release are his own creation. A true yogī moves beyond the world of thought. To him activity (*karma*) has no appeal, and salvation (*nirvāṇa*) is meaningless. Gorakṣa himself became an object of worship in Nepal. He plays a part in many local traditions of different parts of north and west India between the eighth and the fourteenth century.

***Gorakṣasaṃhitā*:** A late medieval text dealing with some aspects of the doctrines and practices of the Nātha Siddhas. Though it is attributed to Gorakṣanātha (q.v.), the latter does not appear to be the author of any Yogic or Tantric work, either in original or in Tibetan translation.

***Gorakṣa-śataka*:** A late-medieval text on Yogic exercises attributed to Gorakṣanātha, though the latter has nothing to do with its composition. It is a book on Rāja-yoga and Haṭha-yoga. It describes various *āsanas* and *mudrās* or gymnastic postures which are helpful for maintaining health and vigour. It has very little to do with the philosophy of Yoga.

***Gorakṣasiddhāntasaṃgraha*:** An important Tantric text which asserts that the Kaula Tantras were introduced on earth by nine Nātha teachers. Many features of Vajrayāna Buddhism and also the esoteric concepts of the Nātha Siddhas are found in this text. It emphasizes the importance of the Yoga, qualifications of the Avadhūta, characteristics of the Kāpālikas, the *ācāras*, the duties of the house-holders and the requirements of salvation. Published in Sarasvati Bhavana Texts, no. XVIII, 1925.

***Gorakṣavijaya*:** The story of the spiritual awakening of Mīnanātha by his disciple Gorakṣanātha. *Mīnacaitanya*, as it is sometimes called in Middle Bengali literature, deals with the achievement of Gorakṣa. By the curse of Ketakā or Gaurī, wife of Śiva, Mīnanātha became oblivious of his spiritual attainments and was directed to go over to the country of Kadalī women and to rule over them. Determined to rescue his *guru* from leading a life of sensual pleasures in the company of women, Gorakṣa entered the royal court of the Kadalī country in the disguise of a female dancer. In the court he began to dance and spelt out the supreme knowledge to Mīnanātha, who had lost all recollections of his previous life, in the code of his dancing steps and the beating of his drum (*mṛdaṅga*). When the message was completed, Mīnanātha's stupor of ignorance fell away, and all at once the lamp of the supreme knowledge was re-lit in his heart. Led by the disciple he left the palace at once.

Gosāin Bhaṭṭācārya: Also known as Ratnagarbha. He is said to have been the *guru* of Cānda Rāya and Kedāra Raya, two famous Bengali chiefs, who flourished towards the end of the sixteenth century. He attained *siddhi* in the temple of Digambarī at Mayaisar in Dacca District. He was a *vīra sādhaka* and practised a spiritual discipline on the basis of *pañcatattva.* Many stories are told about his supernatural powers.

Govardhana: Holy resort of the goddess Ambikā mentioned in *Kubjikā* XVIII. 42 ff., *Bṛhannīla* V and *Prāṇatoṣaṇī*. It is near Nasik in Maharashtra.

Govindācārya: Commentator on Nāgabhaṭṭa's *Tripurāsārasamuccya.*

Grāhaka-Grāhya: The perceiver and the perceived. According to the idealist approach as found in certain Tantras, in the absolute state there is neither the subject (*grāhaka*) nor the object (*grāhya*). Pure consciousness is absolutely free from the notions of the *grāhya* and the *grāhaka.*

Grahamātṛkā: An emanation of Vairocana. She has three faces—white, yellow and red in colour. Six arms displaying the *dharma cakra mudrā* in the principal pair of hands and carrying the *vajra* and arrow in the two right hands, and in the two left a lotus and a bow.

Grahaṇālambanā: The kind of devotional attachment with which the *sādhaka* depends on God just as an infant depends on its mother, surrendering himself completely to the will of the Supreme Being. *Śaktibhāṣya* on *Brahmasūtra* I. 31.

Grahitrālambanā: That kind of devotional attachment to the Supreme Being in which the *sādhaka* is in undifferentiated relation with the object of his worship just as the baby in the womb is undifferentiated with its mother. *Śaktibhāṣya* on *Brahmasūtra* I. 31.

Grāhyālambanā: That kind of devotional attachment of the *sādhaka* to the Supreme Being which resembles a child's sweet claim to the affection of its mother. *Śaktibhāṣya* on *Brahmasūtra* I. 31.

Granthi: The three 'guardian knots' which bind the soul to the *prākṛta* (natural order) according to the Tantric tradition.

Gṛhāvadhūta: A Tantric *sādhaka* who is a house holder. He who is with clothes and with wife, who is a thinker, an aspirant and a pure entity, who is devoted to his teacher, wise, internally and externally faithful, accustomed to Yogic practices, free from passions and is pure in soul. *Prāṇatoṣaṇī* VII. 7. 532.

Guhyābhiṣeka: Initiation into the secret cult according to the Buddhist Tantras. Here the preceptor explains all the secret processes of the Yogic *sādhanā* by which Bodhicitta should be produced through the union of Prajñā and Upāya, how its downward tendency should be checked, how it should be sent upward to the *uṣṇīṣakamala* and how *mahāsukha* (the highest bliss) is to be attained.

Guhyakālī (Kā): One of the many form of Kālī. *Toḍalatantra* III. In the Anusmṛtiprakarana of *Mahākālasaṃhitā* it is said that of the nine forms of Kali Guhyakālī is the highest Vidyā. *Puraścaryārṇava* IX. 764. She has eighteen *mantras* which are all secret. These are mostly of 14, 21 and 22 letters. *Tantrasāra* 324. She has generally ten faces but these may be increased or decreased. Her colour is like a cloud, dress black, tongue outstretched, teeth fearful-looking though she smiles. Her sacred thread is a snake. Often she is two-armed with a delightful appearance. *Tantrasāra* 326.

Guhya-sādhanā: Observance of secret rituals meant for aspirants at the *vira* stage. The symbolic features are to be understood from the teacher. These rituals are formed in secret *cakra* assembly. Uninitiated persons are not entitled to participate. *Niruttaratantra*, X.

Guhya Samāja: Secret societies in the Buddhist Saṇgha, the members of which believed in Tantrism. They composed their own scriptures and has them sanctioned by the words of Buddha. A Buddhist Tantric text also bears this name as its title.

***Guhyasamāja Tantra*:** One of the earliest extant Buddhist Tantras which was composed about the fourth century AD. It deals mainly with *yoga* and *anuttara-yoga* and incidentally with *maṇḍalas*. Its chief aim is to explain the *tathāgataguhya*, i.e., the unknowable reality, the source of all Tathāgatas as also of the phenomenal world, and how to realize it. According to this text the truth is *vajra*—the oneness of the universe in which there is no distinction between a man and a woman, or even between a wife or sister or mother. *Kāya* (body), *vāc* (speech), and *citta* (mind) are called *trivajra*. It puts forward a quick and short method for realizing Buddhahood and for the attainment of miraculous powers such as killing an enemy with magical rites, causing rainfall in a drought, etc., and methods for the attainment of *siddhi* which is of two kinds—the ordinary (*sāmānya*) and extraordinary (*uttama*). It sets forth the six *aṅgas* of yoga, omitting the first three of Patañjali and adding *anusmṛti*. It knows of six black acts—*śānti* (for averting diseases), *vaśīkaraṇa* (for bewitching), *stambhana* (stopping the movements of others), *vidveṣaṇa* (creating bad blood), *ucāṭana* (driving away persons) and *māraṇa* (killing). It permits the use of several kinds of flesh and also ritual incest. Ed. B.T. Bhattacharyya in GOS, no. LIII, Baroda 1931.

Guṇas: Some unchanging essential characters of a substance, although the word is variously interpreted. In the Sāṅkhya and the Tantras, Prakṛti (q.v.) has been characterized by the equilibrium of three *guṇas*—*sattva, rajas* and *tamas*. These *guṇas* are not qualities in the general sense of the word, but constitute primordial matter. *Sattva* is of the nature of pleasure and is light (*laghu*) and illuminating (*prakāśaka*). *Rajas* is the nature of pain and is mobile (*cala*) and stimulating (*upastambhaka*). *Tamas* is of the nature of inertia and heavy (*guru*) and enveloping (*varṇaka*). In the sense of qualities (existence, enjoyability, substantiveness, knowability, specific characters and capability of possessing forms, etc.) the *guṇas* adhere to specific substances and cannot exist by themselves. In all changes some collection of qualities appears to remain unchanged (*dhruva*), some new qualities are generated (*utpāda*) and some old qualities are destroyed (*vyaya*). In the philosophical tradition *guṇas* are conceived as inherent in the substance and dependent upon it. At the same time they are also conceived as distinct from substance because they can be known by themselves and are thus independent realities.

***Guptasādhana Tantra*:** A late Tantra dealing with Kulācāra in twelve chapters. It describes nine varieties of women known as *nava-kanyās* required in Tantric *sādhanā*. They are also known as Kulāṅgaṇās. In this text Śakti is called Kula and Śiva Akula. Guru is extolled. Details of initiation and *japa* are given. The utility of Five Ms is recognized. The procedure of worshipping different goddesses, through letters, *mantra*, *dhyāna*, *stotra*, *kavaca* and other usual Tantric topics are described.

Guptatarayoginī: Collective name of the goddesses serving as *āvaraṇadevatā* (q.v.) of the mystic diagram known as *aṣṭadala-padma*. *Gandharvatantra* V. 96. The goddesses are Anaṅgakusumā, Anaṅgamekhalā, Anaṅgamadanā, Anaṅgamadanāturā, Anaṅga-rekhā, Anaṅgaveginī, Anaṅgāṅkuśā and Anaṅgamālinī.

Guptayoginī: Āvaraṇadevatā of sixteen Śaktis associated with the sixteen-petalled lotus. *Gandharvatantra* V. 93. These goddesses are known as Kāmākarṣiṇī, Buddhyā-karṣiṇī, Ahaṃkārākarṣiṇī, Śabdākarṣiṇī, Sparśākarṣiṇī, Rūpakarṣiṇī, Rasākarṣiṇī, Gandhākarṣiṇī, Cittākarṣiṇī, Dhairyākarṣiṇī, Smṛtyākarṣiṇī, Nāmākarṣiṇī, Vījākarṣiṇī, Ātmākarṣiṇī, Amṛtakarṣiṇī and Śarīrākarṣiṇī.

Gupti: Term for keeping the *mantras* to be uttered in secret. *Tantrasāra* 54.

Guru: Teacher, who is the pivot of Tantric *sādhanā*, the one who dispels darkness. The characteristics of *guru*, woman-*guru* and false *guru*, are recorded in *Kulārṇava* XIII, XVI, *Rudrayāmala*, uttara II, *Prāṇatoṣaṇī* II. 2, VI. 4; *Tantrasāra* 2; *Gandharva tantra* II,

Tantrarāja I, *Śāradātilaka* II. The methods of securing a *guru*—the testing of competence, his divinity, and the duties of the disciples towards him—are described in *Mahānirvāṇa* XV. 139, Rāghava on *Śāradātilaka* II. 143-5, *Kulārṇava* XI, XIV, *Prāṇatoṣaṇī* II. 2, III. 1. Complete self-surrender to the *guru* is necessary. If he commands the performance of any low work it should be done. Rāmeśvara on *Parasurāmakalpasūtra* X; *Śāktānanda-taraṅgīnī* II. His mere command leads to liberation. *Kaulāvalinirṇaya* X. Hymns for worshipping *guru*, *Gandharvatantra* VI. 19-25. Gifts to be offered to him. *Śāradātilaka* II. The best form of *guru* is *Kaula guru*. *Mahānirvāṇa* X. 200-1.

Guru-catuṣṭaya: Four classes of teachers—*guru*, *paramaguru*, *parāparaguru* and *parameṣṭhiguru*—conceived as identical with śiva. *Nirvāṇa-tantra* III.

Gurudhyāna: Meditation on the *guru* who is to be conceived of as a god of white complexion, with two hands held in the *varada* and *abhaya* postures, and with Śakti on his left side. *Tantrasāra* 78.

Gurupaṅkti: Rows or lines of the Gurus to be worshipped. There are three such rows known as Divyaugha, Siddhaugha and Mānavaugha. According to another tradition, rows of *gurus* are to be determined in terms of Vidyās such as Kālividyā, Tārāvidyā and so forth. Again, there is a hierarchy such as Paramaguru (teacher's teacher), Parāparaguru (teacher of the latter) and Parameṣṭhiguru (teacher of the latter). Again it is stated that *guru* is the Ṛsi of *mantra*, the giver of *mantra* is Paramaguru, Bhairava or Śiva is Parāparaguru, and Bhairavī or Devī is Parameṣṭhiguru. *Śyāmā-rahasya* III, *Puraścaryārṇava* III. 206-7. *Tantrarājatantra* II. 4; *Tārābhaktisudhār-ṇava* V. 196; *Mahānirvāṇa* VI. 98.

Guru-pātra: Pot of wine required in Tantric rites. *Kaulavali-nirṇaya* III.

Guru-praṇāma: Ritual salutation to the *guru* or preceptor. In the early morning after rising and cleansing himself the disciple should utter the *mantra* of salutation which speaks of the *guru* as one who pervades and envelops the world in the form of an unbroken circle and who opens blind eyes of the ignorant with a pin smeared by the collyrium of knowledge. *Tantrasāra* II. 78.

***Guru Tantra*:** A small Tantric treatise consisting of 151 verses which deals with the propitiation of preceptors whose names end in Nātha. Ed. and trans. into Bengali by J. Tarkalankara, Calcuta 1928.

Guruvaktra: A stage in the process of *kuṇḍalinī-yoga*. While rousing the *kuṇḍalinī-śakti*, the letters (*varṇas* or *mātṛikās)* associated with each *cakra* are to be assimilated with the presiding deity of the *cakra*: those of *mūlādhāra* with Brahmā, of *svādhiṣṭhāna* with Viṣṇu, of *maṇipura* with Rudra, of *anāhata* with Īśvara, of *viśuddha* with Sadāśiva, of *ājñā* with Bindu or Śiva. Bindu has to be assimilated with Kalā, the latter with Nāda, the latter with Nādānta, the latter with Unmanī, the latter with Viṣṇuvaktra and the latter with Guruvaktra. Guruvaktra is Para-bindu, the Paramaśiva of *sahasrāra*. *Śāradātilaka* V. 130-7.

Hh

Hādimata, Hādividyā: One of the three Tantric schools, others being Kādi and Kahādi (q.v.). *Śaktisaṅgama*, Tārā LVIII. 81-2. Ha denotes Śiva which is why Hādimata considers Śiva as the primal principle. Hādimata is called Tripurasundarīmata, Tripurasundarī, being the chief deity of this school. It is also known as Haṃsarāja Ibid., *Kālī* VI. 125. Tantras of Kashmir belong to this school. According to this school the great Śakti is called Tripurā in Kashmir, Kālī in Kerala, and Tārā in Gauḍa. Hādividyā is named after the first letter of *Kāmarāja-bīja*. It is said to have been instituted by Lopāmudrā.

Hāḍi-pā: One of the five Ādi Siddhas, also known as Jālandharī, who is believed to have flourished about the eleventh century AD. According to the legends he was born from the bones of Ādinatha. He was directed by Gaurī to go to the kingdom of Pātikā and serve as a stable-sweep of queen Mayanāmatī who was a Siddha Ḍākinī possessing occult power. She recognized the spiritual power of Hāḍi-pā and bade her son Gopīcandra receive initiation from him. Various such legends about Hāḍi-pā are found in Middle Bengali literature. From the Tibetan Tanjur it is known that he was the author of a number of treatises on Tantric Buddhism, the Tibetan versions of which exist. The works are *Vajrayoginīsādhanā*, *Suddhivajrapradīpa* (a gloss on *Hevajrasādhanā*), *Śrīcakra-sambaragarbhatattvavidhi* and *Huṃkāra-cittabindubhāvanā-krama.*

Hakārārdhasvarūpiṇī: A conception of the great goddess impersonating the combined energies of Agni and Candra who for the sake of creation have sexual intercourse with the Male Principle sitting on his penis in inverted posture with the body bent recalling one-half of the letter *ha*. Adaḥkṛtvā tu puruṣaṃ hakārār-ardhasvarūpiṇī; viparītena ramate vahnīndvarkasvarūpiṇī. *Gandharva Tantra* XXXIX. 8-9.

Hākinī: The presiding goddess (Śakti) of the Tantric *ājñacakra* (q.v.). She is six-faced and white in complexion according to the *Ṣaṭcakranirūpaṇa.*

Hālāhala: A form of Avalokiteśvara or Lokeśvara who is generally accompanied by his Śakti (female energy) whom he carries on his lap. He is the great compassionate Bodhisattva originating from the syllable *hriḥ*. His complexion is white, he has three faces and six hands. His companion is Prajñā. *Sādhana* 65-6.

Haṃsa: A symbolic *mantra*, which means the breath of life—haṃsaḥ. It is in the form of inhaling (*haṃ*) and exhaling (*saḥ*) of breath. Haṃ is the symbol of *bindu* (Puruṣa, the male principle of creation) and Saḥ of *Visarga* (Prakṛti, the female principle of creation). Kālicaraṇa on *Ṣaṭcakranirūpaṇa* XLIII. *Om* is but a subtle form of the sacred formula *haṃsaḥ*, also called the *ajapā mantra*, which is the carrier of Brahmā, the creator.

Haṃsakālī: One of the many names of Kālī mentioned in the *Śaktisaṅgamatantra*, Kālī VI. 130.

Haṃsamantra: Name of the *mantra* based on the *haṃ* and *saḥ* and symbolic for the awakening of *kuṇḍalinī* (q.v.). See Haṃsa.

Haṃsanyāsa: One of the several kinds of *nyāsas* (mentally invoking gods or *mantras* or holy texts to come and occupy certain parts of the body in order to make the body pure and a fit receptacle for worship and meditation) mentioned in Rāghava's com. on *Śaradātilaka* IV. 19-41. Here *haṃ* is associated with the essence of Puruṣa (q.v.) and *saḥ* with that of Prakṛti (q.v.) *Haṃsa* is an invocation of both on the body of the aspirant.

Haṃsapāda: See Hārdhakalā.

Haṃsapīṭha: The region of *haṃsa* supposed to exist within the pericarp of the lotus of *sahasrāra* (the highest cerebral region). It is indicated by the letters *a-ka-tha*. In this region the aspirant should meditate on the *guru* as the form of Śiva. Kālicaraṇa on *Pādukāpañcaka* I.

Haṃsarāja: Another name of the Hādimata.

Haṃsatīrtha: Holy resort of the great goddess mentioned in *Bṛhannīla-tantra* V and *Prāṇatoṣaṇī*. It is possibly connected with

Haṃsamārga, probably Haṃsadvāra or the Niti pass in Kumaon. It is identified with modern Hunza and Nagar in the Himalayas.

Haṃsāvatī-ṛk: *Ṛgveda* IV. 40.5: Hrīṃ haṃsaḥ śuciṣad, etc., which is known as Haṃsāvatī-ṛk. Revealed by Vāmadeva this *ṛk* is supposed to be the precursor of the Tantric *haṃsa* or *aja mantra*, cf. *Kaṭhopaniṣad* II. 2.2.

***Haṃsavilāsa*:** A late work named after its author. It has 52 chapters and its subject-matter is in the form of a dialogue. It deals with the knowledge of the self, the existing philosophical systems, *rasa* (sentiment), rhetoric and prosody, music, yoga, initiation, praise of guru and women, the signs of male-female non-duality, *puraścaraṇa, mantras* and allied Tantric topics. The author was born in Gujarat in AD 1738. The work quotes *Kulārṇava*, *Kaularahasya*, *Yoginitantra* and *Śāradātilaka*. Apart from Tantric topics it deals with figures of speech, erotica, etc. Pub. in GOS 1937.

Haragaurīsṛṣṭi: Chemical processing of mercury and mica to make the elixir of immortality.

Harakumāra Ṭhākura: A rich landlord of the Tagore family of Calcutta who compiled several works pertaining to different aspects of Tantra under the titles *Haratattvadīdhiti* and *Puraścaraṇabodhinī*. Published respectively by Harakumāra's sons Saurindra Mohan Tagore, Calcutta 1881 and Jatindra Mohan Tagore, Calcutta 1885.

Harārikusuma: The flower which is enemy of Śiva. It is *karavī* flower which is used for *abhiṣeka*, one of the ten purificatory rites of a *mantra*. *Tantrasāra* 52. According to a Puranic legend this particular flower antagonized Śiva by giving him a false information.

Haratīrtha: Holy resort of the goddess Gavīśvarī mentioned in the *Bṛhannīla-tantra* V and *Prānatoṣaṇī*. It is probably the same as Harakṣetra or Bhuvaneswar.

Hārdhakalā: The sex organ drawn on mystic diagrams. It is also known as *haṃsapāda* or *yoni*. Hārdhakalā is also the name of the wave of bliss arising out of the union of Śiva-Śakti.

Haridrā: Holy resort of the great goddess mentioned in the *Bṛhannīla-tantra* V. It may be same as Haridvāra.

Haridvāra: Also known as Haradvāra and Gaṅgādvāra (the town of Haridwar in Uttar Pradesh). It is described as a *mahāpīṭha* in the *Śivacarita*.

Harihara Lokeśvara: A form of Avalokiteśvara. He is one-faced and two-armed and stands on a lotus. He displays the *vyākhyāna mudrā* or *dharmacakra mudrā* (q.v.) against his chest.

Harihari-harivāhana: A form of Avalokiteśvara. He has white limbs and a crown of matted hair. He cites the Tathāgata as witness with one of his right hands, carries a rosary in the second and instructs deluded people with the third. He carries a staff in one of his left hands, a deer-skin in the second and a *kamaṇḍalu* in the third. He sits on the shoulder of Viṣṇu below whom there are Garuḍa and the lion.

Hariścanrda: Variant reading Harmacandra. Holy resort of the Goddess Candrikā according to the *Matsya Purāṇa* XIII. 39; *Devībhāgavata* VII. 30. 68, etc. In the *Bṛhannīlatantra* V and the *Prāṇatoṣaṇī* the presiding goddess of this place is Śubheśvarī. The site has not been identified.

Hārīta: Holy resort of the goddess Hariṇākṣī mentioned in the *Bṛhannīlatantra* V and *Prāṇatoṣaṇī*. It is probably same as Hārit-āśrama near Udaipur in Rajasthan.

Harivāhana Lokeśvara: A form of Avalokiteśvara. One-faced and two-armed Bodhisattva stands on a lotus and carries a *kamaṇḍalu* (kettle-like pot) in his right hand and a *chowrie* (fly-whisk) in his left.

Hastināpura: Holy resort of the goddess Jayantī mentioned in *Jñānārṇava* V. 66 ff.; *Matsya Purāṇa* XIII. 28; *Devībhāgavata* VII. 30.57, etc. The *Bṛhannīlatantra* V and *Prāṇatoṣaṇī* refer to Rājeśvarī and Mahālakṣmī as presiding goddesses. It is same as the present-day Hastinapur in Meerut district, Uttar Pradesh.

Haṭhayoga: A form of physical exercise for making the body so disciplined as to serve all spiritual purposes. In the *Yogaśikhopaniṣad* I. 133 it is described as the unity of the sun (*ha*) and the moon (*ṭha*). In the *Haṭhayogapradīpikā* I. 10 it is regarded as the source of all forms of yoga. It says that by Haṭhayoga the body becomes healthy, the eyes bright, the semen hardened, the *nāḍis* purified, the internal fire increases and the *nāda* sound heard. It consists of seven practices: cleansing (*śodhana*) by six processes (*ṣaṭkarma*); the attainment of strength (*dṛḍhana*) by bodily postures (*āsana*); of fortitude (*sthiratā*) by bodily position (*mudrā*); of steadiness of mind (*dhairya*) by restraint of senses (*pratihārya*); of lightness by breath-control (*prāṇāyāma*) of realization (*pratyakṣa*) by meditation (*dhyāna*); and of detachment (*nirliptattva*) in *samādhi*.

***Haṭhayogapradīpikā*:** Text on *haṭhayoga* (q.v.). Its original name appears to be *Haṭhapradīpikā*. The technique of *haṭhayoga* claims three kinds of results. They are cure of diseases of body as also disorders of mind; attainment of supernatural powers called *siddhis*; and preparation for Rājayoga and *kaivalya*. The *Haṭhayogapradīpikā* enumerates the names of the same eight *aṅgas* of yoga as Patañjali does, but its *yamas* are ten of which taking a light meal is the principal while *ahiṃsā* is the first among the *niyamas*. Besides the eight *aṅgas*, it deals specially with *mahāmudrā, khecarī, jālandhara, uḍḍīyāna* and *mūlabandha, vajroli, amaroli* and *sahajoli*. It states that *haṭhayoga* started from Ādinātha and then enumerates 35 great Siddhas from Matsyendranātha onwards. It names and describes fifteen *āsanas* (gymnastic postures) required for maintaining health and vigour. The *Haṭhayogapradīpikā* was composed by Svātmārāma Yogin and it has a commentary called *Jyotsnā* by Brahmānanda. Eng. trans. by Srinivasa Iyangar, Madras edition 1949.

Hayagrīva: A companion of Khasarpaṇa, who is a form of Avalokiteśvara. He is the spiritual son of Amitābha and is commonly known as Saptaśatīka Hayagrīva. The special cognizance of this god is the scalp of a horse over his head. In the Buddhist Tantras Hayagrīva is also an emanation of Akṣobhya. He is red in colour, has eight hands and three faces. He sits in *lalita* posture and his appearance is terrible. *Sādhana* 508. The image of Hayagrīva is often found to the right of Parṇaśabarī. Hayagrīva is also a form of Avalokiteśvara and is popularly known as Hayagrīva Lokeśvara. He sits in *vajraparyaṅka* posture on a lotus, has four hands, the principle ones exhibit *vyākhyāna* pose. The second pair holds a rosary and a lotus. He is accompanied by six other gods and a dragon. According to the Brahmanical Purāṇas Hayagrīva was a demon whom Viṣṇu killed assuming the horse-headed form.

***Hayagrīvavidyā*:** Name of a Mantrayāna Buddhist Sūtra associated with the Dhāraṇi trend. Its Sanskrit version has been found from Gilgit. It has a Tibetan version as well. It prescribes the use of incantations for protection against enemies. Hayagrīva is connected with Avalokiteśvara. Edited in *Gilgit Manuscripts*, Vol. I. Srinagar 1939.

Hemakūṭa: Holy resort of the goddess Manmathā mentioned in *Matsya* XIII. 50; *Devībhāgavata* VII. 30.79; *Padma*, Sṛṣti, XVII. 208; *Skanda*, V. 3.98.88; etc. It is the name of the Varṣaparvata lying to the north of Kiṃpuruṣa-varṣa that is situated to the north of Himavat and the Bhāratavarṣa. Apparently it is a part of the northern Himalayas.

Heruka: One of the most popular deities of the Buddhist pantheon whose worship is described in *Heruka Tantra*. He stands on a corpse in *ardhaparyaṅka* attitude, is clad in human skin with *vajra* in his right hand and a *kapāla*, full of blood, in the left. From his left shoulder hangs a *khaṭvāṅga* with a flowing banner. Decked in ornaments of bones, his head is decorated with five skulls. He bears the effigy of Akṣobhya whose emanation he is. Nairātmā is the Śakti or Prajñā of Heruka. When in embrace with this Śakti Heruka is known as Hevajra.

***Heruka Tantra*:** A very important Buddhist Tantra which has received its name from the god Heruka. That the purpose of this text is to assist human beings to attain *nirvāṇa* (the *summum bonum* of life) is stated in the *abhiṣeka-paṭala* with reference to the ritual exercises of the aspirant. In the *bodhicitta-saṅkramaṇa-paṭala* the placing of the *mantras* in the form of letters in different parts of body and their arrangements in the *cakras* (nerve-plexuses) along the spinal cord are discussed. The *Heruka-tantra* deals at length with the conception of Vajrasattva or Vajradhara (q.v.) and his consort variously called Vajra-sattvātmikā, Vajravārāhī, Prajñāpāramitā, etc., and his *bījamantra* is *hum*. It says that the Lord is in the form of seed while the pleasure is called the field which implies the relation between Prajñā and Upāya (q.v.), the female and male principles which are also thought of in terms of Lalanā and Rasanā nerves. Heruka as Lord is filled with erotic emotion (*śṛṅgāra-rasa-samanvitam)* and deeply embraces his consort Vajravairocanī in great joy of compassion (*karuṇā-mahotsava*). In the 31st *paṭala* the lotus of the Mahāsukha-cakra is described; its four petals are the four categories (*catuṣkoṭi*) forming the circle of enlightenment (*bodhimaṇḍala*) as the receptacle (*ādhāra*) and the seed (*bīja*) of all. Inside the letter *ha* of the nature of Bodhicitta and 15 digits of moon as well as the Yoginī of 16 *kalās* are flanked by the Lalanā and Rasanā nerves. These two nerves and the Avadhūtī as their comingling is the goddess Nairātmā or the Sahaja-damsel according to this Tantra which also deals with the *vṛta* and *samvṛta* forms of Bodhicitta and the need to transform pleasure into permanent bliss. The *Heruka-tantra* is also a mine of iconographical information. Ms. 11279 of the Asiatic Society of Bengal.

Heruka-vajra: Same as Nīladaṇḍa. The god of direction in Tantric Buddhism who is described in the Dharmadhātuvāgīśvara-maṇḍala of the *Niṣpannayogāvalī* as Herukavajra. He is blue in colour and has three faces which are blue, white and red in colour. He holds a blue staff, a sword, a jewel and a lotus.

Herukī: Śakti of Heruka, associated with the Saptākṣara form of Heruka-Hevajra. She is blue in colour and has dishevelled hair, a fierce appearence and three eyes. She is sky-clad and four-armed; in two hands she carries a drum and bell and in the other two a piece of human skin. She stands on a corpse in *ālīḍha* attitude.

Hevajra: Heruka-in-union-with-Nairātmā. He is the principal deity of the Hevajra-maṇḍala of *Niṣpannayogāvalī*. He has two-armed, four-armed, six-armed and sixteen-armed forms. Hevajra in *Yuganaddha* form is popular in Tibet. Images of Hevajra is comparatively rare. The *Hevajra Tantra* deals elaborately with his worship.

***Hevajratantra*:** A work of the eighth century AD which has several manuscripts. The Sanskrit manuscripts are divided into two *kalpas* of ten chapters each. In the Chinese translation the chapters are numbered continuous. Hevajra, signifying the non-dual state, is Heruka-in-union-with-his-Śakti in Yuganaddha (q.v.) position. In this tantra the term for Śakti in Prajñā. It describes how its followers have sexual experience with women called *mudrās* and how thereby they attain *siddhi*. It also deals with *Kāyasādhana* and holds that there are 32 *nāḍis* in the body which carry the Bodhicitta upwards and ultimately lead to the place of great bliss (*mahāsukhasthāna*). Three principal *nāḍis* are *lalanā*, *rasanā* and *avadhūtī* which are suggestive respectively of *prajñā*, *upāya*, and their union leading to absolute non-duality conceived of as beyond the reach of the 'taken' and the 'taker' (*grāhya-grāhaka*). *Sandhyābhāṣā* (twilight language used in Buddhist esoteric expressions) here is characterized as the great language and time (*mahāsamaya*) of the yogīs. Among the cult centres the text refers to Jālandhara, Oḍḍiyāna, Pūrṇagiri and Kāmarūpa. Edited and translated by D. Snellgrove in two parts (Oxford 1959). The first part consists of an introduction, English translation, contents, diagrams and glossary. The second contains Sanskrit and Tibetan texts based on a Nepalese manuscript and a commentary called *Yogaratnamālā*, included from an old Bengali manuscript.

Himādri: Holy resort of the goddess Bhīmā mentioned in *Matsya* XIII. 47; *Padma*, Sṛṣti XVII. 205; *Devībhāgavata* VII. 30.76; *Skanda* V. 3.98.85; etc. The name of the goddess reminds one of Bhīmāsthāna of the *Mahābhārata* which was situated near Shahbazgarhi in Peshawar district. Himādri is the Himalaya, also known as Himavat.

Himavat: Same as Himādri and Himālaya mentioned in *Matsya* XIII. 30; and other Purāṇas as the holy resort of the goddess Nandā, cf. *Devībhāgavata* VII. 30. 59; *Padma*, Sṛṣti XVII. 188, *Skanda* V. 3.98.68. The name of the goddess has a variant reading which is Mandā. The *Bṛhannīla-tantra* V refers to the goddess as Pārvatī. The Goddess Nandā reminds us of Nandisthāna which is different from Bhīmāsthana and is no doubt the same as the celebrated Nandādevī peak in the Garhwal district of Uttar Pradesh.

Hiṅgalāja: Mentioned as a *pīṭha* in the *Caṇḍimaṅgala* where the navel of the goddess fell. Variant readings—Hiṅgulā and Hiṅgulāṭā—are found in *Kubjikā* XVIII. 42 ff., *Rudrayāmala* and *Pīṭhanirṇaya*. These texts hold that the *brahmarandhra* of Satī fell here and the goddess was known as Koṭṭarī, Koṭṭavī and Koṭṭareśa. The *Śivacarita* refers to this place as a *mahāpīṭha*. It is modern

Hinglaj in Baluchistan whre the goddess is locally called Bībī Nānī.

Hiraṇyapura: Holy resort of the goddess Suvarṇā mentioned in *Bṛhannīlatantra* V and *Jñānārnava* V. 66 ff. It is modern Herdoun about 70 miles from Agra.

Hlādinī: The blissful Śakti of the Supreme Being. In later Vaiṣṇavism as well as in Vaiṣṇavite Tantras it is symbolized by Rādhā. *Caitanyacaritāmṛta* I. 1.5.

Homa: Creation of sacred fire for sacrificial and ritual offerings. It is of three kinds—*nitya* (permanent), *naimittika* (occasional) and *kāmya* (desirable). *Puraścaryārṇava* VI. 515. Common *homa*, made for achieving certain objects, is known as *sthūla* (gross) *homa* for which a pedestal has to be erected and many articles are needed. In *sūkṣma* (subtle) *homa* external formalities are not needed. The fire which is latent in the *kuṇḍalinī* has to be kindled by yogic exercises by which equilibrium of Śiva-Śakti is possible. Still higher is *para homa* in which the distinction between subject and object is removed and the *sādhaka* identifies himself with the Supreme Being. *Mātṛkābheda* III. 28; XI. 8; *Tantrarājatantra* XXIX-XXX; *Śāradātilaka* III; *Tārābhakti-sudhārṇava* 247; *Tantrasāra* 441. A symbolic interpretation of *homa* has been provided by Umānandanātha in *Nityotsava* I.

Hotrī-dīkṣā: A form of Tantric initiation in which the guru (q.v.) offers *homa* for purifying the six quarters. Rāghava on *Śāradātilaka* V. 127-40.

Hrasvanātha: A teacher of Kashmir Tantrism who flourished in the eleventh century. He was a contributor to the Krama system.

Hṛṣikeśa: Holy resort of the great goddess mentioned in *Kubjikā* XVIII. 42 ff. It is the holy place of the same name—Rishikesh—on the Ganges about 24 miles to the north of Hardwar on the way to Badrinath.

Hṛtpadma: The lotus which is meditated upon in the heart. This lotus is generally identified with *anāhata-cakra* or *anāhata-padma*. There is an eight-petalled lotus within the hollow of the heart-lotus; it is the seat of the *iṣṭadevatā* (the specially chosen deity of the aspirant). *Mānasa-pūjā* or mental worship is to be done on this lotus. Kālīcarṇa in his commentary on *Ṣaṭcarkranirūpaṇa* XXV. In the *Mahānirvāṇa* V. 143 it is said that the seat of the goddess is to be established on the *hṛtpadma* and her feet should be washed with the nectar flowing from the Sahasrāra. The seat of the Guru to be worshipped is also to be located in the *hṛtpadma*.

I i

Iccha-śakti: Will power of the supreme being which is the cause of the generation of the universe, along with two other powers—knowledge (*jñāna*) and action (*krīya*). Com. on *Pāśupata-sūtra* II. 5-6. In Kashmir Śaivism the power of *icchā* is spoken of simultaneously with *anuttara* (power of sentience) and *unmeśa* (power of knowledge) as constituents of *trika*. *Tantrāloka* III. 191. What is known in Tantra as *śāmbhavopāya* (q.v.) is based on the power of *icchā* which is why the latter is also called *icchopāya*. That which instantly springs up from the manifestation of an initial indeterminate knowledge may be termed as *icchā*. *Tantrāloka* I. 184 ff. *Icchāśakti* is threefold: the plain wish (*icchā*) is the purest from though in this form the subject is passive. In the second (*śīghrātmaka*) and the third (*sthairyātmaka*) form the subject becomes more and more enthusiastic. *Tantrāloka* III. 162-3. According to Rāmeśvara the will-power of the supreme being to have numerous manifestations is the basic point of emphasis in Śakti-tattva. *Saubhāgyaśudhodaya* VI. 1.

Icchā-siddhi: The attainment received through performance of the ritual of the *trikoṇacakra*. *Nityaṣoḍaśikārṇava* XVII. 85.

Icchopāya: Same as *śāmbhavopāya*. It is the manifestation of the will power of the supreme being. The way in which this will power dominates is known a *icchopāya* or *śakṣāt-upāya*. Attainment of this power is possible only by one who is under the ecstasy (*śāmbhava-āveśa*) which is possible by the grace of preceptor. It brings a condition which has no substitute, the state of non-duality with the supreme being. *Tantrāloka* I. 146 ff.

Iḍā: One of the fourteen principal nerves. It is a symbol of the moon and is situated on the left side of the spinal cord. The *piṅgalā* is the symbol of the sun, situated on the right. *Ṣaṭcakra-nirūpaṇa* I. Idā is to be conceived of as white in colour and represents *amṛta*, the life-giving power aspect of Śakti.

Idam: The known; the enjoyed; the object; the 'It-ness' of anything. Since creation in the Tantras is regarded as the self-expression of the Supreme Being, the subject views itself as object, I (*aham*) as It (*idam*). It is same as *bindu*, the eternal material entity, the constituent of the objective world. Both *aham* and *idam*, i.e. I-ness and it-ness, exist in a unitary state in Parāsaṃvit (q.v.). *Idam* is also equated with the *vimarśa-śakti*. It is also the expression of *māya-śakti* that unfolds itself in the emergence of multiple objects forming the universe.

Idantā: Objecthood as opposed to *ahantā* or subjecthood. *Pratyabhijñāhṛdaya* 10.

Iddhi, Iddhipāda: Ten kinds of powers, also known as *ṛddhi*, and *abhijñā*, mentioned in the Buddhist texts such as to project a mind-made image of oneself, to become invisible, to pass through solid things, to penetrate solid ground, to walk on water, to fly through the air, to touch the sun and moon, to ascend to the highest heavens, etc. See *iddhi* in Rhys Davids and Stede, *Pali Dictionary*. The Buddha recognized the *iddhis* or supernatural powers and mentioned four *iddhipādas* conducive to the attainment of supernatural power. The four *iddhipādas* are *chando* (will), *viriyam* (effort), *cittam* (thought), and *vivaṃsā* (investigation). But the meanings of these terms as have been suggested by Childers in *Dictionary of Pali Language*, 157, hardly signify supernatural powers. See *Brahmajāla-sutta* I. 26; *Mahāvagga* VI. 24; *Cullavagga* V. 8.

Indīvarakālikā: One of the many forms of Kālī described in the *Jayadratha-yāmala*.

Indra: The first of the eight Hindu gods of directions accepted in Vajrayāna. He is described in *Niṣpanna* 61 as riding on the Airāvata and as yellow in colour. He holds in his two hands the *vajra* and the breast of a woman.

Indrabhūti: Author of *Jñānasiddhi* (see *Two Vajrayana Works* by B.T. Bhattacharyya, GOS, no. 44, Baroda 1929) which is an explanatory treatise on Tantric Buddhism and contains a summary of some chapters of the *Guhyasamāja-tantra* (q.v.). The *Jñānasiddhi* of Indrabhuti is stated in the last colophon as having started from Uḍḍīyana. The Sādhana literature refers to Indrabhūti as a Mahāsiddha. He lived about AD 700 and had a daughter even more illustrious than himself, Lakṣīṃkarā by name, well-versed in the doctrines of both Vajrayāna and Sahajayāna.

Indrāṇī: One of the seven or eight Mātṛkās (Divine Mothers) who, according to the Puranic accounts, appeared with Indra's emblems, attributes and characteristics during the war between the gods and the demons. In the Vedic texts, as also in the Epics and Purāṇas, Indrāṇī, also called Aindrī, Śacī and Paulomī, is the spouse of Indra. In the Tantras, however, her Mātṛkā form predominates. Apart from being the Divine Mothers the Mātṛkās (q.v.) represent the fifty letters of Sankrit alphabet. As such, according to the *Svacchandatantra*, Aindrī or Indrāṇī is *Ya-vargastha*, i.e. presides over the letters beginning with *Ya.*

Indranīla: Holy resort of the goddess Mahākānti mentioned in the *Prāṇatoṣaṇī* and the *Bṛhannīlatantra* V. It is probably the Himalayan peak Indrakīla mentioned in the *Kāvyamīmāṃsā* of Rājaśekhara.

Indrayoni: A nerve-plexus situated between the *viśuddha* and the *ājñā* (q.v.) *cakras.*

Irāvati: River on the banks of which are places sacred to the Devī mentioned in the *Prāṇatoṣaṇī* and *Bṛhannīlatantra* V. It is modern Ravi in the Punjab.

Irṣyārati: Consort of the Dhyānī Buddha Ratnasambhava who was originated from Vajradhara or Ādi Buddha as vibrant sound and was placed in the southern direction. *Guhyasamāja* on the formation of Dhyānī Buddha-maṇḍala.

Īśāna: The fifth in the series of gods of direction in Vajrayāna Buddhism. He is described as staying on the *īśāna* (north east) corner, riding on a bull, having a white complexion holding in his two hands *triśūla* (trident) and *kapāla* (skull cup) on his body is a sacred thread of serpent and his throat is blue. He is no other than Śiva. *Niṣpanna* 61.

Īśānakālikā: One of the forms of Kālī described in the *Jayadratha-yāmala*.

Īśanaśakti: The power of self-manifestation of Parama Śiva in Kashmir Śaivism which, along with the powers respectively of *anuttara, ānanda, icchā, unmeṣa* and *ūrmi*, is symbolized by long vowels. Abhinavagupta, *Tantrasāra* 12-13.

***Īśānaśivagurudevapaddhati*:** A text belonging to the Mattamyūura sect of Śaivism which flourished in central India in the ninth and tenth centuries. It is written by Īśānaśivagurudevamisra about AD 1100. Described as a Tantric work it is in four parts—Sāmānyapāda, Mantrapāda, Kriyāpāda and Yogapāda—and contains 18,000 *ślokas*. It expounds the six categories of Śaiviam—*paśu, pāśa, pati, śakti, vicāra* and *kriyācāra*. Published in Trivandrum Sanskrit Series.

Īśitrī: A terrible form often assumed by the goddess when her will-power (*icchāśakti*) is adversely excited. The symbol of such goddesses is the letter long Ī.

Īśitva-siddhi: The spiritual attainment from the rituals of Caturdasāra (q.v.). *Nityaṣoḍaśikārṇava* VIII. 149.

Iṣṭadevatā: One's own personal chosen deity identified with the supreme being. In the *Sammohana-tantra* it is said that after offering oblation to the sun, the devotee should worship his personal deity, and in the *gāyatrī* verse which is to be recited in that connection the name of the devotee's *iṣṭadevatā* is to be inserted. *Tantrasāra* 80. While meditating on the *iṣṭadevatā* the devotee should conceive of his own heart as an ocean of nectar in which there is an island containing the most beautiful garden in the world with a wish-fulfilling tree (*kalpavṛkṣa*) in the middle, the branches of which are the four Vedas. The worshipper should mentally place himself just below that tree and meditate on the figure and attributes of his own personal deity. *Gheraṇḍa* VI. 2-8.

Iṣṭa-liṅga: The distinctive mark of Vīra-Śaiviam which advocates the wearing of a *liṅga* (phallic symbol) upon the body of each person so that the body shall be a temple fit for god to dwell in. Iṣṭaliṅga is also conceived of as one of the three aspects of the Divine, the others being Prāṇa and Bhava.

***Īśvarapratyabhijñā*:** Text of the Kashmir school of Śaivism composed by Utpaladeva in the first quarter of the tenth century. It is divided into four sections. They are *jñānādhikāra* dealing with cognition and sources of knowledge in eight subdivisions; *Kriyādhikāra* dealing with activities, ritualistic and mental and cause-effect relations in four subdivisions; *āgamādhikāra* dealing with 36 *tattvas* of Śaivism in three subdivisions; and *tattvārtha-saṃgrahādhikāra* dealing with the essential nature of the Supreme Being in two subdivisions. Its commentary is also by Utpaladeva. Another commentary is Abhinavagupta's *Īśvara-pratyabhijñāvimarśinī*, briefly called *Vimarsinī* or *Laghu-Vimarśinī*. Published with *Siddhitraya* in Kashmir Sanskrit Series 34, ed. by M.S. Kaul 1921. Abhinava's com. has been published in *KSS* nos. LX (1938), LXII (194) and LXV (1945).

Itaraliṅga: One of the three forms of *liṅga* (phallus) the symbol of Śiva. Others are *bāṇa* and *svayambhū*. In Tantrism it is connected with the *ājñā-cakra* (q.v.). *Śāradātilaka* IV.

Jj

Jaḍaśakti: One of the two kinds of Śakti, the insentient, material energy, acording to the school of Śrīkaṇṭha Śivācārya. The other kind is known as *cit* which is conscious. Both pertain to Śiva. The *jaḍaśakti* is unconscious (*acit*) though at the same time a phenomenal reality. *Śivārkamaṇidīpikā* on *Brahmasūtra* I. 1-2. According to Bhāskara Rāya *jaḍaśakti* or material energy is the transformation of *māyā Saubhāgyabhāskara* 108-9.

Jāhnavīsaṅgama: Holy resort of the goddess Tṛpti according to *Bṛhannīlatantra* V and of Svadhā according to *Prāṇatoṣaṇi.* The site may denote Prayāga.

Jālandhara: One of the four *pīthas* according to the *Hevajratantra* VII where the breasts of Satī fell. The goddess of this celebrated place in Punjab is mentioned under different names in different texts. According to the *Śivacarita* it is a *mahāpīṭha* where the left breast of Satī fell and the goddess is known as Tripuramālinī. The *Pīṭhanirṇaya* substitutes Tripuranāśinī for Tripuramālinī. The *Rudrayāmala, Jñānārṇava* V. 66 ff.; *Kubjikā* XVIII. 42 ff.; *Matsya* XIII. 46; *Devībhāgavata* VII. 30.75; *Padma,* Sṛṣti, XVII. 204; *Skanda* V. 3. 98.84, refer to the goddess as Viśvamukhī, while the *Bṛhannīla* V as Jvālāmukhī. Abul Fazl has caused confusion by attributing the name of the *pīṭha* to the goddess. The Jālandhara-pīṭha is now located near Jvālāmukhī (q.v.) which place name has been wrongly given in many texts to the goddess.

Jālandharī: Better known as Hāḍi-pa he wrote some treatises in Sanskrit on Tantric cults, such as *Vajrayoginīsādhanā*, *Śuddhivajrapradīpa* (a gloss on *Hevajrasādhanā*), *Śrīcakrasambara-garbhatattva-vidhi* and *Huṃkāra-cittabindu-bhāvanā-krama.* These are mentioned in the Tanjur Catalogue.

Jaleśvara: Holy resort of the great goddess mentioned in *Jñānarṇava* V. 66 ff. It is in Balasore District, Orissa.

Jāliniprabha: Bodhisattva, the name meaning 'light of the sun'. Also known as Sūryaprabha he is described three times in the *Niṣpannayogāvalī.* In the Mañjuvajra-maṇḍala he is described as being red in colour and holding the disc of the sun on a lotus in the left hand while the right displaying the *varada mudrā*. In the Dharmadhātu-vāgīśvara-maṇḍala he is described as whitish red in colour holding a sword and the disc of sun on a lotus in his right and left hands respectively. In the Durgatipariśodhana-maṇḍala he is described as red in colour holding a *vajra*-marked cage in the right hand and resting the clenched left on his lap. Jālinīprabha is also a form of Avalokiteśvara who is one-faced and two-armed, sitting in *vajraparyaṅka* on a lotus. He holds a sword in his right hand and a lotus against his chest with the left.

Jambhala: Corresponding to the Hindu Kubera, Jambhala is regarded as an emanation of Akṣobhya as well as that of Ratnasambhava. He is regarded as the god of wealth. The *Sādhanamālā* has a fairly large number of *sādhanas* describing his forms. Usually he has one face and two-hands, the right holding a citron and the left a mongoose vomitting jewels. Also he is described as three-faced, six-armed carrying in the right hands citron, goad and arrow and embracing his Śakti Vasudhārā with his first left hand, the others carrying a mongoose and an arrow. In *yab-yum* Jambhala has another form with two faces and six eyes embracing Vasudhārā. A variety is known as Ucchusma Jambhala and another as Vasya Jambhala.

Janana: Procreation. The term is also used in the sense of processing a *mantra*, its gradual recovery from the *mātṛkā-yantra. Tantrasāra* 54.

Janārdana: Grandson of Śrīnivāsa Bhaṭṭa Gosvāmin (q.v.), son of Jagannivāsa and brother of Śivānanda Gosvāmin (q.v.). He was the author of *Mantracandrikā.*

Janasthāna: A *mahāpīṭha* according to the *Śivacarita* where the goddess is known as Bhrāmarī. It is on the Godavari in the Nasik district of Maharashtra.

Jangama: A Śaiva sect having affiliation with the Pāśupatas mentioned in Ānandagiri's *Śaṅkaravijaya.*

Jāṅguli: Emanation of Akṣobhya; a goddess who cures snakebite, a Tantric Buddhist counterpart of Manasā. According to a *saṅgīti* in the *Sādhanamālā* she is as old as the Buddha himself. Her secrets and *mantra* are said to have been imparted to Ānanda by Lord Buddha. She has three forms: white, green and yellow. Her basic symbol is a snake. *Sādhana* 248, 253. She is also a goddess of the Dhariṇī series who is described as white in colour and holding the buds of poisonous flowers. *Niṣpanna* 57.

Japa: To internalize and mutter the syllables relating to the identity of *guru, mantra* and *devatā* (q.v.) which is the easiest process of spiritual attainment. It is of three kinds: *vyakta* (manifested), *avyakta* (unmanifested) and *sūkṣma* (subtle) also called *vācika, upāṃsu* and *mānasa* respectively. The first is loud utterance heard by everyone, the second is whispered and to be heard only by the practitioner himself and the third is mental and is heard by none. There are other three categories of *japa: nitya* (to be done everyday), *naimittika* (to be done occasionally) and *kāmya* (to be done for special purpose). *Puraścaryārṇava* VI. 541, *Yoga sūtra* I. 28, *Kulārnava* XV, XVII, *Rudrayāmala,* Uttara XXVI, *Saktisaṅgama*, Tārā, XLVI. 2-3, *Gandharvatantra* XXIX. 9. Rāghava on *Śaradātilaka* IV. 55-6.

Japamālā: Rosary used for muttering name of the chosen deity. Before using the inanimate rosary it has be ritually purified, made animate by uttering *mantras* and worshipped. *Tantrasāra* 33, *Puraścaryārṇava* VI. 446. The Japamālā has to be used with the thumb and the middle finger. *Gautamīyantra* quoted in *Tantrasāra* 34.

Japasamarpaṇa: The last feature of *japayoga,* mental concentration with the help of *japa* (q.v.). After the *japa* is complete its result is to be surrendered to the deity. *Śyāmārahasya* III.

Japyeśvara: Holy resort of the goddess Triśūlinī mentioned in the *Brhannīlatantra* V. It is probably same as Jalpeśvara in the Jalpaiguri district, North Bengal.

Jaṭāmukuṭa: The crown of matted hair. The hair is tied up above the head in such a way as to resemble a crown or a tiara.

Jaṭāmukuṭa Lokeśvara: A form of Avalokiteśvara. He is four-armed and one-faced, carrying the image of Amitābha on his crest. The right hands show rosary and *varada* pose and left hold a waterpot respectively.

Jātasutaka: The born child. Since *mantra* (q.v.) is a living entity, it is conceived of as a new-born child during initiation. *Śaktisaṅgama*, Tārā, XIV. 7.

Jayā: One of the 24 goddesses surrounding Buddhakapāla in three circles. Jayā represents the western direction in the second circle. She is blue in colour and has one face, two arms. She wears ornaments of bones and her brown hair is swept upward. She carries the *kapāla* in her left hand and *kartari* in the right and dances in the *ardhaparyaṅka* attitude.

***Jayadratha Yāmala*:** A very big work, divided into four parts or *ṣaṭkas*, each containing 6,000 verses, found in Nepal Darbar library. The manuscript of the fourth part belongs to the twelfth century AD while the other parts belong to a much later date. The second part is incomplete. Regarded as a supplement to the *Brahmayāmala*, the *Jayadratha* contains much important material for the history of Tantric literature. This is dealt with in chapter 35 of the first part which is known as the Sambandāvatāra. The next chapter called, Sutranirṇya contains an enumeration of the Tantras of various traditions. Chapter 41 deals with Yāmala, Maṅgala, Aṣṭaka and the lineage of the sages who promulgated the Tantras. The second part, divided into 41 chapters (not all have been found) deals with the deities and their rituals. The third and fourth parts have similar contents in which *mantras* and *maṇḍalas, dhyānas,* description of deities and various modes of initiation have been described.

***Jayākhya Saṃhitā*:** A Pāñcarātra text composed about AD 450. Apart from the usual Tantric topics like *mantra*, *nyāsa*, *mudrā*, *varṇa*, *guru*, *puraścaraṇa*, etc., it deals with magical arts like *stambhana*, etc., *homa* for securing desired objects, *yakṣiṇī-sādhanā*, *cakrayantra sādhanā*, etc. It is described as one of the three gems (ratnatraya) of the Pāñcaratra Agamas. Critical edition, Oriental Institute, Baroda 1967.

Jayantī: Also known as Jayanta, Jayantā and Jayantikā, it is regarded as a *mahāpīṭha* in the *Pīṭhanirṇaya* and *Śivacarita* where the left thigh of Satī fell. The goddess is known as Jayantī. The place exists by the same name in Sylhet district, now in Bangladesh.

Jayaratha: The reputed commentator of Abhinavagupta's *Tantrāloka* who flourished in Kashmir in the twelfth century. In his commentary known as *Viveka* Jayaratha has given information on his family and ancestors. He was the son of Śṛṅgāranātha and pupil of Śaṅkhadhara.

Jayinī: One of the eight Śaktis presiding over the *aṣṭakoṇacakra.* She represents the *sattva* quality and serves along with others as Āvaraṇadevatā or Rahasyayoginī. According to the *Vāmakeśvara-tantra*, she is the presiding goddess of the letters beginning with Pa. *Gandharvatantra* XVII.74

Jīvacakra: One of the five cakras associated with five *vīras* mentioned in the *Śakti-saṅgama*, Sundarī I. 197-200. This *cakra* is conducive to *bhāvayoga* or concentration in the sphere of ideas—*bhāvayoga jīvacakre.*

Jīvakālī: One of the many forms of Kālī as described in the *Jayadratha-yāmala.*

Jīvana: One of the ten saṃskāras (processing of *mantras*). *Tantrasāra* 52. Every *mantra* comprising of letters when prefixed by *om* becomes processed , when recited a hundred times it comes to be known as *jīvana*. Ibid. 54.

Jīvanasiddhi: See Bīja-mantra.

Jīvanmukti: Liberation within the span of life. It is possible according to the Sāṅkhya, by the complete destruction of the three fold misery (duḥkhatrayābhighāta). In the Tantric tradition, he who has complete grasp of the knowledge of the Self, who has dispelled from within the darkness of false knowledge by constant practice and meditation and is reaping the fruits of his *karma* may be called a *jīvanmukta.* The term is also used in the sense of immortality which is possible by transforming the material body, through certain chemical processes, into a divine one. In the first chapter of the *Rasārṇava* the aim of Rasāyana is explained in terms of Jīvanmukti. According to the Raseśvara philosophy, as enumerated in Mādhava's *Sarvadarśana-saṃgraha* IX, the attainment of liberation is the highest aim of life. It is possible in one's lifetime if one is able to acquire a divine body with the help of mercurial drugs. See Rasa, Rasāyana, Raseśvara Darśana, Siddha-cikitsā, Sittar.

Jīvaśakti: Name of the *kuṇḍalinī* (q.v.) which works as the energizing force within the human body. *Tantrarājantra* XXX. 34

Jīvatattva: Jīva or inidividual fettered by *niyati* (destiny), *kāla* (time), *rāga* (dissatisfaction), *kalā* (conceit) and *avidyā* (ignorance). Also known as *puruṣatattva.* Rāmeśvara on *Paraśurāmakalpasūtra* I. 4.

Jñāna: Knowledge or cognition, divided into *anubhava* or presentive and *smṛti* or representative, aspects of experience and memory. It is that which eliminates suffering which arises from *avidyā* or false notions. It is basically of two kinds—*bauddha* (intellectual) and *pauruṣa* (intutive). By meritorious practices the latter is developed within the human being and is conducive to *mokṣa* or liberation It should, however, be supplemented by some sort of intellectual attainment; this is possible through the study of the scriptures, deep meditation and so on. *Tantrāloka* I. 41 ff.

Jñānabhūmikā: Seven stages of knowledge, often identified with seven Tantric *ācāras.*

Jñānacatuṣka: The four means of Tantric knowledge: *anupāya* (q.v.), *śāmbhavopāya* (q.v.), *śāktopāya* (q.v.), and *āṇavopāya* (q.v.)

Jñānaḍākinī: Śakti of Yogāmbara, both being emanations of Akṣobhya (q.v.). She has three faces, six hands, and has a blue complexion. In her hands, she carries *khatvāṅga,* axe, *vajra,* bell, cup full of blood and sword. *Niṣpanna* 12.

Jñāṇadhātu Lokeśvara: A form of Avalokiteśvara. He has one face and eight hands two pairs of which are in *añjali* and *kṣepana mudrā.* The others hold a rosary, *tridaṇḍa,* book and noose. He stands on a lotuṣ

Jñāna-homa: The *homa* (q.v.) offered during internal worship or *antarpūjā* (q.v.). *Nitya-tantra* quoted in the *Prāṇatoṣaṇī* VIII. 4.535.

Jñānaketu: One of the sixteen Bodhisattvas under the leadership of Maitreya. In the Mañjuvajra-maṇḍala of the *Niṣpanna-yogāvalī* he is described as yellow in complexion, holding in his right hand a flag marked with *cintāmaṇi* jewel while the left hand displays *varada-mudrā.* In the Durgati-parisódhana-maṇḍala he is described as blue in colour, holding in his right hand the jewel-marked flag and the left rests on the hip.

Jñana-Mudrā: 'The woman of knowledge', a term for the female partner of the aspirant found in the Buddhist Tantras.

Jñānapadma: Two-petalled lotus on the *ājñācakra* (q.v.) in which the symbolic preceptor resides for commanding and processing the spiritual exercise of the aspirant. *Saubhāgyabhāskara* on *Lalitā-sahasranāma* 90. It is situated above the *viśuddhākhyacakra* serving as the *maṇḍala* of the full-moon. *Nirvāṇatantra* IX. When the *kuṇḍalinī* touches the *jñānapadma* all the darkness of ignorance is dispelled. Kālīcaraṇa on *Ṣaṭcakranirūpaṇa* 32.

Jñānapāramitā: Goddess of the Pāramitā category of Tantric Buddhism who has a white complexion, two hands and the *bodhi* tree as symbol. *Niṣpanna*. 56.

***Jñānārṇava Tantra*:** A text containing 26 *paṭalas* and about 2,300 verses. It emphasizes the functioning of the *cakras* (nerve-plexuses) within the body and the wonderful power of the *mantras*. It states that at the time of initiation the aspirant has to learn all about the six *cakras;* the number of petals and three colours, and the letters of the alphabet assigned to them. It names over thirty *mudrās*. It also holds that *maṇḍala* and *cakra* are synonymous and lays down rules for making different kinds of *maṇḍalas*. It mentions eight important Śākta Pīṭhas. The 24th *paṭala* deals elaborately with Dikṣā (q.v.). It was composed evidently before the 16th century AD, since it has been quoted amply by Brahmānanda and Pūrṇānanda. It also throws light on *kumārī-pūjā* or virgin worship. Ed. G.S. Gokhale, Poona 1952.

Jñānaśakti: The power of knowledge often symbolized by an angle of the *trikoṇa* (q.v.). *Setubandha* on *Nityaṣodaśikārṇava* VI. 36-40; Rāmeśvara on *Parasurāmakalpasūtra* V. 11. This power is impersonated by Vāgīśvarī. Vāgīśvarī jñānaśaktirvāgbhave mokṣarūpiṇī. *Nityaṣoḍaśikārṇava* IV. 17.

***Jñānasaṃkalinī Tantra*:** A late small work containing only 110 stanzas dealing with the knowlege of *brahman* which is characterized as the spiritual knowledge (*adhyātma-vidyā*) leading to happiness and salvation. It refers to the philosophical systems and Purāṇas and confuses Sāṅkhya with Vedānta. It refers to *khecharī-mudrā, śāmbhavī-vidyā,* the five kinds of *prāṇas*, ten kinds of wind, nine gateways of the body, 7,200 *nāḍis*, two kinds of body, significance of the syllable *om* and so forth. Text with Bengali translation in *Aruṇodaya*, Calcutta 1894.

Jñānasiddha: A *tattva* (fundamental) of the *krama* doctrine of Kashmir Śaivism. Seventy such *tattvas* are indicated by streams which are known as *bhūcarī, gocarī, dikcarī, khecarī* and *vyomavāmeśvarī*. The first stream is also known as *jñānasiddha*. It consists of sixteen *vikāras* or evolutes of Prakṛti, comprising sense organs and the subtle and gross elements. *Tantrāloka* XXIX.

***Jñāna-siddhi*:** A Buddhist Tantra attributed to Indrabhūti (q.v.), disciple of Anaṅgavajra, who is said to have lived about AD 717. It deals with the doctrines of Vajrayāna. It states that a Yogin's way of life may be different from others. In order to attain *siddhi* one may resort to sexo-yogic practices with women. Women of the lower orders of society have a natural qualification to be the holders of *vajra* and companions of the aspirants in their spiritual exercise. Ed. by B.T. Bhattacharyya under the title *Two Vajrayāna Works* in GOS, no. 44, Baroda 1929.

Jñāna-tanu: The spiritual body. According to the Siddha tradition it is the transfiguration of the material body for those who aspire to *jīvanmukti* (q.v.), liberation within the span of life.

Jñanavaśitā: Tantric Buddhist goddess of the Vaśita (q.v.) category who has a whitish blue complexion, two arms and sword-on-lotus as symbol. *Niṣpanna* 57.

Jñānendriya: Five organs of knowledge. The external organs which correspond to those of smell (*ghrāṇa*), taste (*rasanā*), *sight* (*cakṣu*), touch (*tvak*) and hearing (*śrotra*). Mind (*manas*) is the internal organ which perceives such qualities of soul as desire (*icchā*), aversion (*dveṣa*), striving (*prayatna*), pleasure (*sukha*), pain (*duḥkha*) and cognition (*dhāraṇa*).

Jñānopāya: Same as Śāktopāya, the means by which alternative knowledge turns into absolute knowledge leading the individual self to be identified with the universal self according to the Trika philosophy. *Tantrāloka* 187.

Jvālāmukhī: A *pīṭha* known under the names Jvāla and Jvalanti. The goddess of this *pīṭha* is known as Ambikā and is mentioned in *Kubjikā* XVIII. 42 ff., *Bṛhannīla* V and *Śivacarita*. It is in Kangra district, Himachal Pradesh. The *Ain-i-Akbari* speaks of the goddess of Nagarkot-Kangra as Jālandharī which is the same as Jvālāmukhī. The tongue of Satī fell here.

Jyotirdhyāna: Meditation of the self supposed to reside on the *kuṇḍalinī* coil in the *mulādhāra* (q.v.) in the form of light. It is also known as *tejodhyāna*. *Gheraṇḍa* VI. 17.

K k

Kādimata, Kādividyā: One of the three principal Tantric schools mentioned in the *Śaktisaṅgama-tantra*, Tārā, LVIII, 81-2. Its theoretical doctrines make the letter *ka* as their symbol. Rāghavabhaṭṭa in his commentary on *Śāradātilaka* 1.1. says that this school derived its name from the first letter of the Vāgbhava-bīja (*ka*, *r*, *i*, *la*, *hrān*). This school is also known as Virādanuttara and Kālimata. It was popular in the Gauḍa region. *Śaktisaṅgama*, Kālī, V. 24-6. It is said to have been initiated by Kāma or Manmatha. Madhumatī-mata is synoymous with the views of Kādi school which is found mostly in *Tantrarāja*, *Mātṛkārṇava*, *Yoginīhṛdaya* and *Tripurārṇava* (q.v.). Kādividyā is one of the two main currents of Śrīvidyā, the other being Hādividyā (q.v.).

Kahādimata: One of the three principal Tantric schools mentioned in the *Śakti-saṅgama-tantra,* Tārā, LVIII. 82-9. It is also known as Tāriṇīmata. Ibid. Kālī, VI. 125.

Kailāsa: Holy resort of the goddess Bhuvan-eśvarī mentioned in the *Jñānārṇava* V. 66 ff and *Bṛhannīlatantra* V. It is Kailāsa in the Himalayas.

Kairātī: Goddess named after the Kirāta tribes of the northern and north-eastern hill region. *Harivaṃśa* LVIII; *Varāha-purāṇa* XXVIII. 34. In the Tantric texts she is described as dark-complexioned, her head adorned with a peacock's tail, clad in leaves and decked with a girdle of *guñja* berries. Eight Nāgas, including Vāsuki, serve as her ornaments. She is three-eyed. Her hands show *varada* and *abhaya* postures. *Śāradātilaka* X. 7.

***Kākacaṇḍeśvarīmata Tantra*:** A treatise on alchemy which mainly deals with mercurial preparations, copper and liquefaction of mica. It also gives a method for the transmutation of iron into gold but the process is not clear.

Kārinī: The presiding goddess of the *anāhata-cakra* (q.v.). She is three-eyed, yellow in colour, and has her abode within the pericarp of a twelve-petalled red lotus. *Ṣaṭcakra-nirūpaṇa* XXIV.

Kākinī Mudrā: A bodily posture by which the aspirant inhales *prāṇa-vāyu* and unites it with *apāna-vāyu*, the lips forming a shape to resemble the back of a crow. *Gheraṇḍa* III. 86-7.

Kakkola (Ka): A technical name for *vajra* (the male organ of generation) signifying the principle of Upāya (q.v.) while the female organ, or the lotus symbolizing Prajñā (q.v.), is known as *vola* or *volaka*. In the *Hevajra-tantra* it is said: *vajraṃ volakaṃ khyātaṃ padmaṃ kakkolakaṃ matam*.

Kāla: Time, conceived of as the First Principle in *AV* XIX. 54; *Śvet. Up.* I. 2, VI. 6. *Nīlakaṇṭha* commenting on *Mbh.* XII. 232. 11 says *kāla iti dravyajñānam*. Like space, time is also inferred, though not perceived. Modification or change of states cannot be conceived without time. According to Rāmeśvara's com. on *Paraśurāmkalpa-sūtra* I. 4 it is said that the enternalism of Śiva, owing to the influence of six *bhavavikāras* (conditions), becomes contracted and is known as *kāla*. When the goddess Kālī is described as *Kālagatā-śakti* it is in the sense of time, cf. *Mahanirvāṇa-tantra*, IV. 30-2.

Kalā: Evolutes of *varṇa* (q.v.). In Tantra every letter (*varṇa*) symbolically reflects an aspect of the Great Mother. From the three groups of letters, Saumya, Saura and Āgneya, 38 *kalās* are emanated; 16 from Saumya, 12 from Saura and 10 from Āgneya. *Prapañcasāra* III. 11-12. A *kalā* is identical with the *varṇa* from which it evolves. Rāghava *on Śāradātilaka* III. 111. According to another tradition there are 50 *kalās* which emanate from the five parts of the *praṇava*—A, Va, Ma, Bindu and Nāda. Ibid. II. 17. In the Tantras and other Śaiva-Śākta texts the term *kalā* has also been used in other senses. It denotes Prakṛti, Śakti and Māyā. Ibid. I. 6, I. 15, *Propañcasāra* I. 26. In the com. on *Haṭhayoga-pradīpikā* V. 1. *Kalā* is described as *nādaikadeśaḥ*, i.e. a portion of *nāda*.

Kālabhairava: Name of the Bhairava of Dhuamāvatī, one of the ten Mahāvidyās. *Puraścaryārṇava* I. 13-14. Kālabhairava is the lord of the cremation ground. Ibid. VII. 618-19.

Kālacakra: A minor nerve-cycle; it is situated

above the *viśuddha* and below the *ājña*. It is also known as *lalanā-cakra*. Kālacakra denotes the wheel of time; it is the principal god of the Tantric Buddhist Kālacakrayāna (q.v.). Its Tibetan synonym dus-kyi-kór-lo also means the circle of time.

***Kālacakra Tantra*:** A Buddhist Tantra which introduces the cult of Kālacakra (q.v.) which came into vogue from the 10th century AD onwards. The Sanskrit manuscript of this Tantra is in the Cambridge University Library (Ms. Add. no. 1364). A Tibetan version is also found. From the *Sekoddeśaṭīkā* (ed. M.E. Carelli, Baroda 1941) which is a commentary on the Sekoddeśa section of the text the concept of Kālacakra is clearly understood. There is another commentary on the *Kalācakratantra* known as *Vimalaprabhā* (Asiatic Society Ms. no. 4727) which has been edited and published by Biswanath Bandyopadhyoya. The Tibetan version of the *Kālacakratantra* was worked out by A.I. Vostrikov who rendered it into Russian.

Kālacakrayāna: An offshoot of Vajrayāna (q.v.) Buddhism based on the cult of *kālacakra* (wheel of time) which came into vogue in the tenth century and became popular in Tibet and China. On the basis of the *Kālacakratantra*, *Sekoddesaṭīkā* and *Vimalaprabhā* it may be said that by *kāla* is denoted the ultimate immutable and unchanging reality of all the elements; by *cakra* is meant the unity of the three kinds of existence. As such *Kālacakra* is the same as the unity of *prajñā* (q.v.) and *upāya* (q.v.). In principle there is no difference between Vajrayāna and Kālacakrayāna.

***Kāladahana Tantra*:** See *Kāmikāgama*.

Kāladūti: Companion goddess of Mahākāla who presides over the western direction. According to the *Sādhanamālā* 598 she carries in her four hands *kapāla*, cow's head, *mudgara* and *triśūla* respectively. She stands in the *ālīḍha* attitude on a horse, has a red complexion and dishevelled hair.

Kālāgni: One of the two aspects of reality according to the Nātha tradition. It is the principle of destruction through the process of death and decay represented by the sun, while the moon stands for the principle of immutability.

Kālāgnirudrakālī: One of the twelve Kālīs described by Abhinavagupta. *Tantrāloka* IV, 157 ff. She represents *pāra-saṃvit* and symbolizes the sustainer form of the Supreme Being. Ibid. 182-3.

***Kālajñāna*:** A Tantric text devoted to the cult and conception of Kālī in which the goddess is described as impersonating eternal time. This Tantra belongs to the Kālīkula (q.v.).

Kālakālī: One of the nine forms of Kālī as described in *Mahākālasaṃhitā*. *Puraścaryārṇava* I. 16.

Kālāmukha: An extremist Śaiva sect, akin to the Kāpālikas (q.v.) mentioned by Rāmānuja, Keśava, Kaśmīrī, Haribhadra and others. Epigraphical evidence establishes the existence of this sect at Kanchi, Tiruvariyur, Melpadi, Kodumbalur and other places.

Kalāmūrti: Complete or fragmentary forms of the figure of *śakti* of the deity. In Tantra the *śakti* of a deity is divided into sixteen *kalas*. When the figure is complete in sixteen *kalas* it is known as *purṇa-kala mūrti* and the parts are known as *kalamurti*. Further subdivisions are known as *amśa-mūrti* and *aṃśāmśa-mūrti*.

Kālañjara: Holy resort of the goddess Kālī mentioned in the *Matsya Purāṇa* XIII. 32; *Devībhāgavata* VII. 30. 61; *Padma*, Sṛṣṭi, XVII. 190; *Skanda* V. 3.98.70, *Bṛhannīla* V, etc. Kālañjara is the Banda district, Uttar Pradesh.

Kalānyāsa: Feeling the existence of the deity in different parts of the body of the Śakti (female partner) of the Tantric aspirant. *Tantrasāra* 628.

Kālarātri: Puranic goddess, a form of Caṇḍikā or Kauśikī; an attribute of Caṇḍī and one of the many names of the goddess. In her original form she was the same as Rātri or Niśā who was instrumental, at the command of Brahmā, for blackening the womb of Pārvatī's mother. In Tantric Buddhism there is reference to this goddess who is often depicted as being trampled upon by Sambara and also by Vajravārāhī.

Kalasa: An ordinary water vessel of metal or earth. It is different from *kamaṇḍalu* or *kuṇḍikā* which is smaller in size and is provided with a projecting pipe for discharging water.

Kalasābhiṣeka: One of the four kinds of initiation according to the Buddhist Tantras. It comprises six *abhiṣekas* according to the *Śrīcakrasambhāratantra*: initiation with *udaka* (water), *mukuṭa* (crown), *vajra* (thunder), *ghaṇṭā* (bell), *nāma* (name) and *ācārya* (preceptor). These correspond to the nature of six Tathāgatas: water (ideal knowledge) of Akṣobhya, crown (equalizing knowledge) of Ratnasambhava, thunder (discriminating knowledge) of Amitabha, bell (performance of duties) of Amogha-siddhi, name (knowledge of *dharma-dhātu*) of Vairocana and preceptor (adamantine knowledge) of Vajrasattva. *Advayavajra-saṃgraha* 36-7. In its simpler and most common form it is the rite of initiation by pouring water from a jar.

Kālasaṃkarṣiṇī: A name of Kāli according to one school of *krama* doctrine. This doctrine acknowledges the existence of five *śaktis*, the fifth of which is known as *bhāṣā-sakti* or *pratibhā* identified with this goddess. It is pure consciousness independent of time and space and womb of all which accounts for her name. She belongs to the northern region and is the bestower of *dharma*, *artha*, *kāma* and *mokṣa*. *Puraścaryārṇava* I. 13.

Kāla-tattva: The contracted manifestation of Śiva in individuals. *Tantrāloka* IX. 155.

Kalāvatī-dīkṣā: A form of initiation in which the *ācārya* (teacher, guide) locates the existence of five *kalās* known as *nivṛtti*, *praṭiṣṭhā*, *vidyā*, *śānti* and *śāntyātīta* in different parts of the body of his disciple, and having meditated on them, anoints him. *Śaradātilaka* V. 121-6.

Kālighāṭa: Holy resort of Kālī mentioned as a *mahāpīṭha* in the *Śivacarita* where the toes of Satī's right foot had fallen. The *Pīthanirṇaya* refers to it as Kālipīṭha and to its presiding deity as Jayadurgā. The *Bṛhannīlatantra* refers to it as Kālighaṭṭa and its presiding deity as Guhyakālī. It is in the southern suburb of Calcutta. The *Śivacarita* refers to Kālipīṭha as an *upapīṭha whose* goddess is Caṇḍeśvarī different from Kalīghāṭa.

Kāli(kā): Dark-complexioned deity, originally of some dark-skinned primitive tribe, brought into the traditional pantheon connecting her with the conception of Kāla (time or death). Later she was considered to be the supreme being in Śakta Tantrism. *Devībhāgavata* III. 27.57; *Mahānirvāṇa-tantra* IV. 30-2. She is the controller and destroyer of the universe and bestower of transcendental knowledge. Abhinavagupta, *Tantrasāra* 30. Her association with eternal time is indicated by the phrase kālagata-śakti. *Ahirbudhnya Samhitā* 68. The *Toḍalatantra* III refers to her eight forms—Dakṣiṇakālikā, Siddhakālikā, Guhya-kālikā, Śrīkālikā, Bhadrakālī, Cāmuṇḍa-kālikā, Smasānkālikā and Mahākālī. Nine forms—Dakṣiṇa, Bhadra, Smasāna, Kāla, Guhya, Kāmakalā, Dhana, Siddhi and Caṇḍī—are mentioned in *Mahakāla-saṃhitā*. *Puraścaryārṇava* I. 16. Among other Kālis we have Ḍambara, Rakṣā, Indīvara, Dhanada, Ramaṇi, Īśāna, Jīva, Vīrya, Prajñā, Saptārṇa, Haṃsa and Vaśīkaraṇa. According to Hādimata the Mahāśakti is called Kālī in Kerala, Tripurā in Kashmir and Tārā in Gauḍa, but according to the Kādimata she is Tripurā in Kerala, Tārinī in Kashmir and Kālī in Gauḍa. *Śaktisaṅgama*, Kālī, V. 24-6. The gods are generated from her and she is their destroyer. Nirvāṇatantra X. She is in inverted coital posture and is both with and without attributes. *Viparītaratā Kālī nirguṇā saguṇāpi ca. Niruttara* II. In Kaliyuga Kālī is the only goddess who can assure existence and liberation. *Śyāmārahasya* I.

***Kāli Kalpa*:** A late Tantric text devoted to the worship of Kālī.

Kālī-kula: A Tantric school which lays supreme importance on the cult of Kālī. The scriptures of this school are *Kālajnāna*, *Kālottara*, *Mahākālasaṃhitā*, *Vyoma-keśasaṃhitā*, *Jayadrathayāmala*, *Uttara-tantra* and *Śaktisaṅgamatantra*.

***Kālīkulakramārcanā*:** A Tantric work dealing with the cult and conception of Kālī. It is meant for the worshippers belonging to the Kāli-Kula.

***Kālikuslasarvasva*:** A late Tantric text dealing with the theories and practices of Kālikula (q.v.).

***Kālī Tantra*:** A popular Tantric text, late in origin, and having more than one version. It deals mostly with the doctrine of *brahman* and with different branches of Yoga. Though named after Kālī it has a chapter on Lakṣmī. The upaniṣadic doctrine of *prāṇa* and the Vedantic concept of *avidyā* or *māyā* are also dealt with here. The doctrines of liberation, transmigration, rebirth and metempsychosis are also found. One chapter deals with diseases, their causes and cures and another with six black acts: *mārana*, *ucātana*, *stambhana*, *mohana*, *vidveṣaṇa* and *vaśikaraṇa*. Three kinds of meditation are described—*sthula*, *sūkṣma* and *jyoti*. In a shorter version of the text various concepts of Kālī are described. Published with Sanskrit com. and Bengali trans., Calcutta 1922; different version published by K. Vidyaratna, Calcutta 1892; Bombay edn. 1933.

Kālinī: A Tantric goddess, a derivation of Kālī, who is treated as a Mātṛkā and regarded as the presiding deity of the letters of *Savarga*, i.e. those beginning with the first letters Sa. She is one of the eight Śaktis of the Aṣṭakoṇa-cakra and belongs to the category of Āvaraṇadevatā or Rahasyayoginī. *Gandharvatantra* XVII. In some Tantras, Kālinī is called Kaulinī. *Nityaṣoḍaśikārnava* I. 191-2.

***Kālitattva*:** A treatise on Kālī, which was once widely popular in north India, written by Rāghavabhaṭṭa, the commentator on the *Śāradātilaka*.

***Kālisaparyākramakalpavalli*:** A late Tantric text devoted to the cult of Kālī.

***Kālīvilāsa Tantra*:** A late-medieval Tantra probably composed somewhere in eastern India. It is centred on the goddess Durgā. It deals with the three *bhāvas* (modes of worship in Kaliyuga), sexo-yogic practices giving the semen an upward motion, *pañca-tattvas*, *siddhis*, *prāṇāyama*, *saṅketa*, *vaśī-karaṇa*, *puraścaraṇa*, *abhiṣeka*, *kuṇḍalinī*, various names of Mahāvidyā goddesses, Kṛṣṇakālī relations, made of worship of deities who are associated with Durgā in various capacities, *yantra*, *śtotras*, *kavacas*, *homa*, *tarpaṇa*, etc. One chapter speaks of Rādhā's union with Kṛṣṇa. In X. 20-1 it frankly allows adultery provided the sexual act is not completed. It mentions in X.1 the *Kālikāpurāṇa* and in XV. 12-13 contains a *mantra* in a language resembling Assamese and Bengali. Ed. by A. Avalon, *Tantrik Texts* VI. 1917.

***Kālīyāmala*:** A late Tantric text dealing with the cult of Kālī. Though the term *Yāmala* is used as a suffix to this work it is not a text belonging to the acknowledged Yāmala group.

Kallaṭa: Pupil of Vasugupta (q.v.) who wrote, among other works, *Spandasarvasva* in which he explained the meaning of the *Śiva Sūtras* as taught by his master. He lived in the ninth century AD.

***Kālottara Tantra*:** A late-medieval Tantra dealing with the cult and conception of Kālī. This Tantra belongs to the Kālī-kula (q.v.).

Kalpanā: Divine imagination, as opposed to institutionalized religion, which is the essence of Tantrism. It is to 'turn round' the self so that it may be *en rapport* with divine consciousness. Since the 'whole' is involved at every 'point', be it an individual or a thing, contact and communion can be established with the 'whole' at any point of the universe through this divine imagination.

Kalpataru: Wish-fulfilling tree. In the Tantras the term is used to denote the *anāhata-cakra* (q.v.). Kalpataru gives more than is desired. *Ṣaṭcakranirūpaṇa* XXII.

***Kāmadhenu Tantra*:** A late Tantra in 22 chapters dealing with the significance of the *varṇas*, *mantras*, rules of *japa*, 25 *tattvas*, doctrines of *brahman* and *prakṛti*, upward march of *Kuṇḍalinī* and so forth. Published in *Vividha-tantra-saṃgraha*, Calcutta 1876; ed. by R. Shukla, Calcutta.

Kāmakalā: The sexual art. In Tantra *kāma* is the equilibrium of *prakāśa* (static) and *vimarśa* (dynamic) Śakti of Śiva. *Setubandha* Com. on *Nityaṣoḍaśikārṇava* VI. 10.11. Technically Kāmakalā is conceived of as the combination of the three *vindus* (q.v.) of Ravi, Agni and Soma. Conceived as Mahā-tripurasundarī it is of the nature of consciousness (*cit*), bliss (*ānanda*), will (*icchā*), knowledge (*jñāna*) and action (*kriyā*). Cidvalli com. on *Kāma-kalāvilāsa* VII. In the human body Kāmakalā is said to reside in the form of a pericarp of the inverted white lotus known as *sahasrārapadma* (q.v.) situated in the cerebral region. Kālicaraṇa on *Ṣaṭcakra-nirūpaṇa* XI.

Kāmakalākālī: One of the Vidyās or presiding goddesses of the northern region (*uttara āmnāya*). *Puraścaryārṇava* I.13. According to the Anusmṛtiprakaraṇa of Mahākālasaṃhitā she is one of the nine forms of the supreme being. Ibid. I.16.

***Kāmakalārahasya*:** A treatise on the Śākta-Tantric concept of *Kāmakalā* as the twin aspect of the static and dynamic forms of Śakti composed by Nīlakaṇṭha, the eighteenth-century Tantric scholar from Maharashtra.

***Kāmakalāvilāsa*:** Composed by Puṇyānanda-nātha in 55 verses. Its famous commentary by Naṭanānanda is known as *Cidvallī*. It is a theoretical assessment of the Śākta Tantric concept of Śakti in its *prakāśa* (static) and *vimarśa* (vibrating) aspects, symbolized by the letters A and Ha, white and red bindus, *kāma* and *kalā*. These two aspects are combined is inseparable relation by A and Ha which is *ahaṃkāra*. It also deals with the *mantras*, *mātṛkās*, *vāc*, *cakras*, *mudrās*, *bhūtas*, *ḍhātus*, etc. Details of *cakra* symbolism are given. The male and female principles are thought of in terms of Kāmeśvara and Tripurasundarī. The latter in her subtle form is vidyā transcending herself into 36 *tattvas*. The four aspects of Vāc, namely, *parā*, *paśyantī*, *madhyamā* and *vaikharī*, are demonstrated in the triangles of the *cakra* or *yantra*, several of which are mentioned. Ed. with Eng. trans. and notes and with Naṭanānanda's *Cidvallī* Com. by A. Avalon, third edn., Madras 1961; originally in *Tantrik Texts*, Vol. X.

Kāmākhyā: Name of the Pīṭha of Kāmarūpa as well as its presiding goddess who is worshipped in the form of *yoni* in Nīlācala on the Brahmaputra near Guwahati. Kāmākhyā seems to be called Mahāgaurī in the records of Vanamāla (end of ninth century) and Indrapāla (twelfth century). The name of the goddess is traced to the Austric words *kamoi* (demon), *kamoit* (devil), *komin* (grave), *kamet* (corpse), *kamru* (a god of the Santals), etc. The temple of Kāmākhyā is kept closed for some time in a year because it is believed that for that period she remains unclean because of her menstruation. There is a theory that she was originally the Khasi tribal mother Ka-mekha who later came to the fold of Śākta-Tantric cults. Details on her cult are given in the *Kālikā Purāṇa*, Ch. LXII.

***Kāmākhyā Tantra*:** A Tantra in 12 chapters composed in the late medieval period. It deals with Kāmākhyā in her *yoni* form, Kāmākhyā-*mantra*, by which one will be successful in performing six black acts, rules of worshipping the goddess, consecration, forms of salvation, Kāmākhyā Pīṭha, Kumārī pūjā, *japas* of different goddesses, ten kinds of *mantra-saṃskāras* and so forth. Published in *Vividha-tantra-saṃgraha*, Calcutta 1876.

Kāmākhyā Yoni: The soft and bright Tantric triangle on the *mūlādhāra* (q.v.) lotus. Viśvanātha on *Ṣaṭcakranirūpaṇa* VIII.

Kamalā: One of the Mahavidyā goddesses. She is Lakṣmī in Pātāla and Kamalā in Vaikuṇṭha. *Kubjikā* quoted in *Prāṇatoṣaṇī* V. 6, 374. In *Svatantratantra* she is called Śrībhuvana and Mahālakṣmī. Her origin is attributed to the austerities of Brahmā and she is associated with Tāriṇī, Śivā. Krodharātri, Ramā and Mahāmātaṅgī. Ibid. 382. Her iconic description is as follows. Her body is golden. She is shown as being bathed by four elephants who pour nectar-water on her from golden vessels held in their trunks which look like the Himalayan peaks. Her lower left hand is in *varada* posture and lower right in *abhaya*. The upper left and right hands hold the lotus. She is also seated on a lotus. *Śāradātilaka* VIII. 2-4. Her seed *mantra* is *śrīm* which bestows beauty, wealth and happiness. She is also known as Śrī. *Tantrasāra* 140-2.

Kāmakoṭipīṭha: Kāmākṣī temple of Kāñcī (Kanchipuram) in which Śaṅkara is said to have installed a Śrīcakra. Its replica is worshipped by the Gurus of the Kāñci Advaita monastary later transferred to Kumbakonam.

Kāmakoṭṭam: Name of the Amman shrines of south India mentioned in Tamil inscriptions. The name means Kāmakoṭi's shrine and the term came into vogue from about the eleventh century. Before this time there were temples dedicated to Devī independent of and not related to Śiva shrines, but from about this time the twin shrines of Śiva and Āmmān came to represent the dual aspect of Śiva-Śakti.

Kāmākṣī: See Kāmakoṭipītha. In praise of this goddess worshipped at Kāñci, Mukakavi composed 500 verses. According to local tradition the goddess was extremely blood thirsty but she changed her habit after having been propitiated by the great Śaṅkarācārya. In *Matsya Purāṇa* XIII. 26 Kāmākṣī is described as the presiding goddess of the Gandha-mādana region. cf *Devībhāgavata* VII. 30.55.

Kamalacandra: A form of Avalokiteśvara, who is one-faced and two-armed and stands on a lotus. He displays the *vitarka-mudrā* in his two hands.

Kamalākānta: Saint and author of Śākta lyrics in Bengali who is next in importance to Ramaprasada. He was born at Ambika Kalna in the district of Burdwan in the last quarter of the eighteenth century. Besides occasional songs he also composed a work called *Sādhakarañjana*, which sought to elucidate in simple Bengali verses the basic principles of yoga as elaborated in the Tantras.

Kamaṇḍalu: See Kalasa. It is the symbol of the goddess Bhṛkuṭī. There is a Kamaṇḍalu Lokeśvara, a form of Avalokiteśvara who stands in *samabhaṅga* attitude and is endowed with six hands. His two principal hands draw a bow to its full length, the remaining hands carrying *vajra*, *cakra*, *ghaṇṭā* and *kamaṇḍalu*.

Kāmarāja-bija: Name given to the Tantric letters Ha, Sa, Ka, Hā, La, Hrān, each symbolizing an aspect of Śakti or Vidyā. *Siddheśvarīmata* quoted in the com. of *Śāradātilaka* I.1.

Kāmarājakūṭa: Totality of Tantric Kāmarāja-bīja (q.v.). Kūṭa means total; hence it is the complete recitation of the letters belonging to the said category.

Kāmarūpa: Also known as Kāmagiri and Kāmākhyā it is a *mahapīṭha* where the *mahāmudrā* or *yoni* of Satī had fallen. It is also known as Kubjikā-pīṭha in the *Kālikā Purāṇa*. The *Pīṭhanirṇaya* associates Gauriśikhara with this place, while the *Kālikāpurāṇa* LXII ff. places the seats (*sthānas*) of the Dikkaravāsinī and Lalita-kāntā in the Kāmarūpa country which comprises the Guwahati district of Assam and adjoining regions. The temple of Kāmeśvarī or Kāmākhyā stands on the Nīlakūṭa or Nīlaparvata in the city of Guwahati on the bank of the Brahmaputra, called the Kamarūpa-parvata by Rājaśekhara in the *Kāvyamīmāṃsa*. The blue hill is same as Kāmagiri. Kāmeśvara and Mahāgaurī (Kāmākhya) were tutelary deities of the ancient kings of Assam. *Kāmarūpa-śāsanāvalī*, Intro. 32.

Kāmarūpī: A class of Tantras mentioned in the *Piṅgalāmata,* the other being Uḍḍiyānī.

Kāmatattva: Theoretical interpretation of sex symbolism. According to *Tantrāloka* III. 150 the effect of sexual intercourse brings a mental detachment which is conducive to obtaining pure knowledge.

Kāmeśvara, Kāmeśvarī: The Being and the Power-to-Become, symbolized by the Male and Female Principles in the concrete form of the deities. The first represents the *prakāśa* (static) aspect and the second *vimarśa* (dynamic) aspect in Tantric cults. According to the *Vāmakeśvara Tantra* Kāmeśvarī is the presiding deity of letters beginning with Ka (*Ka-varga*). In the *Tantrasāra* Kāmeśvarī is regarded as one of the eight yoginīs (Aṣṭayoginī q.v.) who is described as having a moon-like face, eyes as fickle as those of the Khañjanā bird, agitated movements and weapon and arrows made of flowers.

Kāmeśvarī Tantra: A late Tantric work dealing with the Kāmeśvarī (q.v.) form of Kālī.

Kāmikā: The seat used when reciting *kāmya-japa*, the *mantra* meant to attain a specific purpose. It is either made of the skin of deer, tiger, ram or of cane. *Puraścaryārṇava* VI. 420.

Kāmikāgama: Agamic text belonging to Śaiva Siddhānta school of southern India. It is a metrical work in two parts, Pūrvabhāga and Uttarabhāga. It enumerates various rituals and a considerable part of it deals with temple architecture. The *Kāladahana Tantra* on which the followers of the Suddhamārga depend for the whole of their disciplinal, sacramental, mystical and dogmatic contents is a part of *Kāmikāgama*.

Kāminī: One of the 24 goddesses surrounding Buddhakapāla in three circles. She belongs to the north-east direction. She is blue in colour, has two arms, one face, ornaments of bones and brown hair swept upwards. She carries *kapāla* and *kartari* and dances in the *ardhaparyaṅka* pose.

Kāmrāj: Holy resort of the goddess Śāradā mentioned in the *Ain-i-Akbari*. It is modern Sardi in Kashmir.

Kāmyapūjā: Worship for the attainment of a specific purpose. *Gandharvatantra* XXII. 12.

Kaṇaka-Prajñāpāramitā: A form of Prajñāpāramitā who has golden complexion. She stands in *vajraparyaṅka* and exhibits the *dharmacakra-mudrā* with her two hands. There are two books on two lotuses rising from under her two armpits. An image of this variety of Prajñāpāramitā is in the Indian Museum. Calcutta.

Kaṇakavati: One of the eight yoginīs described in the *Tantrasāra*. She is conceived of as a fierce-faced but youthful goddess having *bimba* (a kind of fruit) like red lips and wearing red clothes.

Kanakhala: Holy resort of the goddess Śraddhā mentioned in the *Bṛhannīlatantra* V. The *Prāṇatoṣaṇi* refers to the goddess as Śivogrā. It is modern Kankhal near Hardwar.

Kāñcī: Modern Kanchipuram or Conjeevaram in the Chingleput district, Tamilnadu, mentioned in the *Pīṭhanirṇaya* as the seat of the Goddess Devagarbhā. The *Śivacarita* alters the name of the goddess as Vedagarbhā. Kāñcī is also mentioned as a *pīṭha* in the *Rudrayāmala*, *Bṛhannīlatantra* and *Prāṇatoṣaṇī*. Kāñcī is also known as Kāmakoṭipīṭha celebrated for its presiding goddess Kāmākṣī (q.v.).

Kañcuka: The six *tattvas* (fundamentals) known as *māyā*, *kalā*, *vidyā*, *rāga*, *kāla* and *niyati* (q.v.), which are the coverings of true knowledge (*saṃvid*). Sometimes *māyā* is omitted from this list. *Tantrāloka* IX. 204.

Kanda: The root of the *nāḍis* (nerves). According to the *Śivasaṃhitā* V. 79-80 it is situated near the yoni or sex organ. It looks like the egg of a bird. Kālīcaraṇa on *Ṣaṭcakranirūpaṇa*-I.

Kandaḷi: A Tamil attribute of Durgā meaning 'the Divine Principle' beyond form and name transcending all manifestations. This appellation was given to the goddess especially by the Tamil members of a famous medieval trading corporation.

Kanjur: Collection of translations into Tibetan from the Indian texts. Bkah-hgyur as it is also called, it consists of 1,108 texts and is divided into seven parts: Vinaya, Prajñāpāramitā, Buddhāvataṃsaka, Ratnakūṭa, Sūtra, Nirvāṇa and Tantra.

***Kaṅkālāmālinī Tantra*:** A late Tantra in five chapters describing the symbolism of the letters, importance of *yoni-mudrā* and raising of the Kuṇḍalinī, procedure of propitiating the Guru, rules of *puraścarana* and methods of Mahākalī and Durgā worship. This Tantra seems to have been composed in Bengal.

Kāṇha-pā: Also known as Kānhu-pā or Kānu-pā (Sanskrit Kṛṣna-pāda), he was a Siddha who lived about the middle of the eleventh century. In Nātha tradition he is said to have been born from the ears of Ādi Nātha. He was despatched by Gaurī to Dāhukā country but the texts do not record his assignment there. He may be called a major poet in old Bengali literature inasmuch as no less than twelve mystic songs written by him have come down to us. Didactic couplets (*doha*) in Apabhramsa, written by him, are also extant. Several Sanskrit treatises on Tantric rituals and mystic practices are ascribed to him.

Kān-phaṭ: Split-ear Yogī mendicants belonging to the Nātha-Siddha tradition. The esoteric cult professed by them is widely known in northern, central and western India. They practise *haṭhayoga* and wear huge *mudrās* (ear-rings), either flat, called *darśana*, or cylindrical called *kuṇḍala*.

Kānyakubja: Holy resort of the goddess Gaurī mentioned in the *Jñānarṇava* V. 66 ff; *Matsya* XIII. 28; *Devībhāgavata* VII. 30.57; etc. The *Bṛhannīla* V refers to the goddess as Brahmāṇī. It is Kanauj in the Farrukhabad district, Uttar Pradesh.

Kanyākumārī: The Tamil Magna Mater. According to the *Mani-mekalai* priests, garbed as Bhairavas, officiated in her worship chanting Tantric *mantras*. She is the eternal Virgin enshrined in Kanyākumārī, site and shrine named after her, and is mentioned by Pliny and the author of the *Periplus*.

Kanyāśrama: Holy resort of the goddess Sarvāṇī mentioned in the *Pīṭhanīrṇaya*. It is located at Kumārīkuṇḍa near Kumira railway station in Chittagong district, Bangladesh.

Kapāla: Either the severed head of a man, or a cup made of a skull, or a bowl. The skull-cup is of two kinds: when it is filled with blood it is called *asṛkkapāla* and when filled with human flesh it is called *māṃsakapāla*. The deities are supposed to partake of the blood or the flesh carried in these cups. Potsherds for baking sacrificial cakes are also known as Kāpala. It also denotes a type of Bhairava.

Kapālabhāti: One of the *ṣaṭkarmas* (six acts) required for Yogic exercise. The others are *dhauti*, *vasti*, *neti*, *laukikī* and *trāṭaka*. Kapālabhāti is of three kinds—*vāmakrama*, *vyutkrama* and *śītkrama*. These practices prevent various diseases. *Gheraṇḍa* I. 13-60; *Haṭhayogapradīpikā* II. 24-35.

Kapālī: Ramya-Śakti; it is the personification of that aspect of Śakti which becomes sexually passionate on seeing the performance of her rites. *Niruttaratantra* XV. In the *Uttaratantra* such aspects of Śakti are mentioned as Kulanāyikā. *Tantrasāra* 627.

Kāpālika: An extremist Śaiva sect commited to the Tantric cult of Śakti mentioned in Mahendravarman's *Mattavilāsa*, Bhavabhūti's *Mālatīmādhava*, Ānandagiri's *Śaṅkaravijaya* and other works. According to the *Śaṅkaravijaya*, they did not believe in the Vedas. They used to drink wine in human skulls which they considered as the elixir of life resulting from the union of Śiva and Śakti. The *Gorakṣasiddhāntasaṃgraha* 16 ff. connects the Kāpālikas with Nathism.

Reference to a Kāpālika text known as *Kapāla-āgama* is found in *Ṣutasaṃhitā* I. 1.12. The Śākta conception of Kāpalika is recorded in the *Śaktisaṅgama-tantra*, Kālī, VIII. 9-10.

Kapālinī: One of the Vidyās (presiding goddesses) of the northern region (Uttara āmnāya). *Puraścaryārṇava* I. 13. In Tantric Buddhism Kapālinī is one of the 24 goddesses surrounding Buddhakapāla in three circles. She belongs to the first circle and is blue in colour. She is located in the northern direction.

Kapāṭā: One of the four door-goddesses mentioned in the Pañcaḍāka-maṇḍala of the *Niṣpannayogāvalī*. She is red in colour and holds in her two hands the door-planks.

Karālavadanā: 'Grim-faced', an epithet of Kālī which accounts for such names as Karālā, Karālī, Karāla-Cāmuṇḍā and so forth. She is 'grim-faced' because she devours not only the universe but also eternal time. *Mahānirvāṇa-tantra* IV. 30-2.

Karamālā: Small hand-garlands or rosaries made of various seeds or small round wooden pellets for counting the number of times god's name or mantra is muttered. There are certain methods of using them. *Puraścaryārṇava* IV. 447-9.

Karaṇa: A *mudrā* or hand-pose. It shows the hand held palm facing outward with the index and little fingers erect, while the two middle fingers are pressed towards the palm of the hand by the thumb.

Kāraṇa: Tantric term for wine. In the *Kaivalyatantra* it is said that since wine is the cause (*kāraṇa*) of all knowledge of *dharma*, *artha*, *kāma* and *mokṣa*, it is known as *kāraṇa*. *Prāṇatoṣaṇī* VII. 2. 510.

Kāraṇa-deha, Śarīra: A form of subtle body capable of containing the doctrines of Śiva.

***Kāraṇḍvyūha*:** Name of a Mahāyāna text which is deified as a form of Avalokiteśvara in Tantric Buddhism, Kāraṇḍavyūha, Lokeśvara. He is one-faced and two-armed and sits in the vajraparyaṅka attitude on a lotus. He holds *vajra* in his right hand and a book against the chest in the left.

Karanyāsa: Feeling the deity in the palms. The fingers and back of the hand are used to invoke deities in the forms of letters. *Tantrasāra* 88 ff.

Karatoyātaṭa: Holy resort of the goddess Aparṇā mentioned in the *Pīṭhanirṇaya* and *Śivacarita*. It is located at Bhavanipura near the bank of Karatoyā in Bogra district, Bangladesh.

Karavīra: Holy resort of the goddess Mahālakṣmī according to *Matsya* XIII. 40, *Devībhāgavata* VII. 30.69, 1, etc., of Mahiṣamardinī according to *Pīṭhanirṇaya* and of Satī according to *Prāṇatoṣaṇī*. It is modern Karvir in Kolhapur, Maharashtra.

Kariṇī: One of the four companion-goddesses of Buddhakapāla. She belongs to the south-west, is blue in colour, has two arms and one face. She wears ornaments of bones and her brown hair is swept upwards.

Karkoṭa: Variant reading Makoṭa found in *Skanda* V. 3.98.70 and *Devibhagavata* VII. 30.61. The goddess is known as Mukuteśvarī. Karkota is modern Karra, about 40 miles north-west of Allahabad. According to local tradition, Satī's hand fell at this place.

Karmacāṇḍālinī: One of the various kinds of Ramyās or Śaktis serving as the female partner of the Tantric aspirant. She who having seen the articles of Tantric worship leaves her husband of Paśu nature and resorts to the aspirant of the Vīra category is known as Karmacaṇḍālinī or Svapacī. *Niruttara-tantra* XIV.

Karmamala: A kind of impurity according to the Kashmir Tantras whch is responsible for continuing the fetters of embodiment, and it is due to this impurity (*mala*) that the Puruṣa (individual) becomes the subject of good and bad acts and entangled in repeated births and deaths. *Īśvarapratyabhijñā* III. 2.4-6. The Vīraśaivas regard this as impurity of action which gives rise to *jāti* (nature of species), *āyus* (length of life) and *bhoga* (type of enjoyment). Tied by these three bonds, the individual soul is called *paśu*, to be reborn, reshaped and retempered.

Karmamudrā: One of the four *mudrās* (q.v.) according to the Buddhist Tantras. In Catur-mudrā, four stages in the spiritual progress and the resulting realizations are metaphorically described as the four *mudrās* (great women of the aspirant). Karmamudrā is a physical yogic process and its realization is of sensual pleasure (*ānanda*). The knowledge produced in this stage is not perfect. The remaining three *mudrās*—Dharmamudrā, Mahāmudrā and Samayamudrā—reveal higher stages the groundwork for which is done by Karmamudrā.

Karmavaśitā: Tantric Buddhist goddess of Vasitā (q.v.) category who is described as having a green complexion, two hands and a double crossed thunderbolt as symbol. *Niṣpanna* 56.

Karṇamātaṅgī: One of the six Mātaṅgīs mentioned in the *Puraścaryārṇava* IX. 827-32. By uttering her *mantra* the devotee receives mastery over speech.

Karpurādi Stotra: A *kaula* hymn in 22 verses describing the *dhyāna, yantra, sādhana* and characteristics of the goddess Kālī. The name of its author is not known, but it has two commentators, Durgārāma Siddhāntavagīsa and Vimlananda Svami. Eng. trans. by John Woodroffe, *Hymns to Kāli*, Calcutta 1922.

Kartari, Karttari: A small knife which serves as a weapon of god. Sometimes the edge is serrated like the edge of a saw. It is called *vajrakartari* when surmounted with a *vajra* (q.v.) Kartari is also a form of *mantra* containing two letters. *Tantrarāja* XXXV. 28-9.

Kārttikeya: Holy resort of the goddess Yaśaskarī or Śankarī or Atiśaṅkarī mentioned in the *Matsya Purāṇa* XIII. 26 ff. etc. It is possibly modern Baijnath near Almora in Kumaon District, Uttar Pradesh. The Puranic god Kārttikeya has been adopted in Tantric Buddhism and described as riding a peacock, red in colour and having six faces. With his two right hands, he holds *śakti* (javelin) and *vajra,* and with the two left a hen. With the third pair he shows the *añjali* posture. *Niṣpanna* 62.

Karuṇā: A term used basically to denote compassion (of Buddha). Karuṇā gradually came to be counted as one of the four *brahmavihāras* (special meritorious deeds), the others being *maitrī*, *muditā* and *upekṣā*. In Mahāyāna, Śūnyatā and Karuṇā became two basic principles and their combined work is supposed to generate *bodhicitta* (q.v.). In Vajrayāna, Śunyatā has been identified with Prajñā (knowledge) and Karuṇā, the principle of compassion, with Upāya or means to attain perfect knowledge. The *bodhicitta* can become ultimate reality through the principle of Karuṇā. This Karuṇā is symbolized in the form of Avalokiteśvara, the great compassionate Bodhisattva.

Kāryabindu: Bindu (q.v.) in effect. Of the various connotations of *bindu* one is that which is the contracted form of the conscious Śakti when it desires to create. *Prapañcasāra* I. 41. This is causal or *kāraṇabindu*; when it manifests itself into effect it is known as *kāryabindu*. According to Bhāskararāya, *kāryabindu* has three separate definitions in terms of *ādhidaivata*, *ādhibhautika* and *ādhyātmika* forms. In the first form it is *avyaktā*, *śāntā* and *ambikā*; in the second *kāmarūpapīṭha*; and in the third *śaktipiṇḍa*, *kuṇḍalinī*, *parā vāk* and *parāśabda*, *Rāghava* on *Nityaṣodaśikārṇava* VI. 36.

Kāśinātha Bhaṭṭa Bhaḍa: Also known as Śivānanda Nātha of Vārāṇasī. He was the author of a large number of small Tantric treatises. He lived between the second half of the seventeenth and first quarter of the eighteenth centuries. He followed what is called Dakṣiṇācara or 'rightist' form of worship of the usual and orthodox type which he claimed to have established on a firm footing when Vāmācāra or the 'leftist' form of worship, with its apparently 'revolting' practices, was fast becoming the order of the day. He took pains in his works to refute the doctrines of the Vāmācāra and set forth the rites and practices of the Dakṣiṇācāra.

Kāśmīra Sampradāya: Tantrics of Kashmir region whose theories and practices are described in the *Śaktisaṅgama-tantra*. Sundarī, III. 11 ff., and *Puraścaryārṇavā*. IX. 866. They depend also on the texts of Kashmir Śaivism.

Kaṭaka: An *upapīṭha* with the goddess Kaṭakeśvarī mentioned in the *Śivacarita*. It is modern Cuttack in Orissa.

Kātyāyanī: Same as Mahākalī (q.v.) and Mahāraudrī (q.v.).

Kauberī: One of the 24 companion goddesses of Buddhakapāla according to the Tantric Buddhism. She represents the southern direction, is two-armed and blue in colour.

Kaula: See Kaulācāra and Kaulamārga. Kula stands for Śakti and so the Kaula schools were Śākta-Tantric in character. According to the *Kaulajñānanirṇaya* (q.v.), the manuscript of which goes back to the eleventh century, the Kaula class of Tantras was introduced by Matsyendranātha. But he was the founder of only one Kaula school called Yoginī-kaula of Kāmarupa. A number of other Kaula schools are also mentioned. They are Vṛṣaṇottha-kaula, Vahni-kaula, Kaulasadbhāva, Padottiṣtha-kaula, Jñānanīrṇīti-kaula, Mahā-kaula, Siddha-kaula, Siddhāṃrta-kaula, Sṛṣti-kaula,

Candra-kaula, Śaktibheda-kaula, Urmi-kaula and Jñāna-kaula. It is difficult at present to determine the nature of these sects, but it is clear that in the eleventh century the Kaula schools were numerous.

Kaulācāra: The most important form of Vāmācāra (q.v.). According to Abhinavagupta, Kula is the penultimate state of *pūrṇa-saṃvit* (realization of the ultimate reality). In the Tantras the term Kula has been used in a variety of senses. According to the *Rudrayāmala*, Kaulācāra is that form of the Tantric cult in which the worship of Kula-strī, Kula-guru and Kula-devī is essential. The text traces the origin of Kaulācarā to Vasiṣṭha's visit to China. There are two types of Kaulācara, wet and dry. The former includes the five Ms while the latter excludes them. According to Lakṣmīdhara, there are two sects of the Kaulas, Pūrva and Uttara. The former believes in Śiva-Śakti equilibrium while the latter upholds only Śakti. The *Mahānirvāṇa* prescribes Kaulācara for all castes and sects. The Kaula should regard every woman as his mother. 'There is no friend better than a woman, no way better than a woman, no luck better than a woman, no kingdom better than a woman, no *tīrtha* better than a woman, no *yoga* better than a woman and no *japa* better than a woman.' In the *Nityotsava* it is stated that the Kaula system should be accepted only by those who are fit in body and mind, who are selfless and bold, who have controlled their senses and who have firm faith in the creed. There are various Kaula schools like Siddha-kaula, Yoginī-kaula, etc., *Mahānirvāṇa* VII. 97-8. *Prāṇatoṣaṇi* VII. 4, 531; *Gandharva* XXXIV. 9; *Śaktisaṅgama*, Tārā, XII. 43-7; *Nityotsava*, GOS. XXIII, 6-7; *Paraśurāmakalpa-sūtra*, X. 77 ff; etc. See Kaulamārga.

***Kaulajñānanirṇaya*:** An important Tantric work belonging to the Nātha tradition, supposed to have been composed by Matsyendranātha who was the founder of one of the Kaula schools called Yoginī-kaula. The doctrines of this school, as may be gathered from the text, have something in common with the Buddhist Tantras of the Sahajiyā class. H.P. Sastri assigned the manuscript of this work to the ninth century AD, but P.C. Bagchi placed it in the middle of the eleventh century. Ed. P.C. Bagchi in Calcutta Sanskrit Series, 1934.

Kaulamārga: The last of the seven Tantric *ācāras* which is so influential that it is often equated with Tantrism itself. It is the exclusive cult of Śakti as the Female Principle with the rituals of *sāmarasya* (q.v.) of Śiva and Śakti within the self. Śrīvidya and her forms are the principal objects of this cult. In some texts it is regarded as anti-Vedic and imported from China. The Tantric texts distinguish the categories of Kaulamārga. They also describe in detail the qualification and competence of aspirants, nature of spiritual exercise, physical and mental fitness required in this cult, the *kaula* theory of knowledge, its attitude towards women, its secrecy, warn against its misuse and various kindred topics. See *Saubhāgya-bhāskara* on *Lahitāsahasranāma* CXLIV; *Kaulamārgarahasya* 5; *Nirvāṇatantra* XI; *Kulārṇava* II, IX, XI, XVII; *Devībhāgavata* XII. 9. 96; *Kulacudāmaṇi* I. 1-3; *Prāṇatoṣaṇī* VII. 7. 531-2; *Rudrayāmala*, Uttara XIII, XVII, XXII; *Kaulajñānanirṇaya* XIV, XVI, XXI; *Mahānirvāṇa* I. 58-60; IV. 38-43; VII. 94, X. 108; XIV. 184 ff; *Kaulāvalinirṇaya* X, XXI. 189-90; *Gandharvatantra* XXXIV, XXXVI; *Niruttara* XII; Rāmeśvara on *Paraśurāmakalpasūtra* III. 31; VII. 1; *Śaktisaṅgama*, Tārā, XI. 43-47, etc.

***Kaulamārgarahasya*:** Tantric text belonging to the late medieval period. It interprets the way of Kaula as that of one aspiring for the knowledge of non-dualism by performing rites received through the tradition of teachers and experiencing Śiva-Śakti immanence and bliss of *brahman* by visualizing the equilibrium of Śiva and Śakti in his own self. The text holds that there is a subtle difference between vāmācara and kaulācara, the former being of *tāmasika* nature while the latter is purely *sāttvika*. The text deals with details of the Kaula mode of Tantric endeavour and attainments. Ed. by S.C. Vidyabhusan, Sāhitya Pariṣat, Calcutta Series no. LXXVI.

***Kaulāvalinirṇaya*:** Composed by Jñānānandagiri in 21 *ullāsas* it gives a list of Tantric works including the *Yāmalas*, deals with the Kaulamārga, names eight Tantric *gurus*, lays emphasis on the rituals of the Five Ms and offers various substitutes, praises women as manifestations of the Great Mother, insists on drinking wine and sexual union and in giving an upward motion to the semen. It also describes in detail the *mantrasiddhi* or *śava-*

sādhanā in which the aspirant has to perform rituals with a corpse besides the usual topics such as the *bhāvas*, *homa*, *puraścarana*, *antar yāga*, *bahir yāga*, *mantras*, *mudrās* and so forth. It is not a very early work. Ed. A. Avalon in *Tantrik Texts*, Vol. XIV.

Kaulika: Followers of the Kula or Kaula school. For their characteristics see *Nirvāṇa-tantra* XI; *Kulārṇava* II. XVII.

Kaulikī-śakti: Same as Kula-nāyikā, the śakti within the heart which is stainless and independent. It is also known by the name *anuttarā*, *parā*, *pratibhā*, *khecarī*, etc. *Tantrāloka* III. 67; *Parātriṃśikā* 61.

Kauliki-siddhi: Name of *mokṣa* or liberation according to the Kula-mata of Kashmir Śaivism. The experience of Kula or the ultimate reality through body and soul brings this form of liberation. *Parātriṃśikā* 36.

Kaulinī: See Kulayoṣit.

***Kaulopaniṣad*:** A late work containing 45 *sūtras* or aphorisms which deal with knowledge, *brahman* and *ātman*, Śakti, Guru, *sādhanā*, *mantrasiddhi* (success) and liberation.

Kaumārī: One of the seven or eight Mātṛkās (Divine Mothers) who, according to the Puranic accounts, appeared with the emblems and characteristics of Kumāra or Skanda-Kārttikeya during the war between the gods and the demons. In the Tantras the Mātṛkās (q.v.), apart from being Divine Mothers, represent the fifty letters of the Sanskrit alphabet. As such, according to the *Svacchandatantra*, she presides over the letters belonging to the *Ṭa-varga*, i.e. those which begin with *Ṭa*.

Kavaca: That which saves the body from the weapons of the enemy. In Tantra the term is used to denote a special *mantra* which protects the body and soul of the aspirant. This *mantra* is to be recited during worship and its written version is to be carried on the body as a talisman, *Kavacas* are connected with the names of different Tantric deities and they are supposed to be more efficacious than worship, meditation, etc.

Kāya: The body; it is regarded in the Tantras as the microcosm of the universe. The esoteric Tantric-yogic school of Buddhism holds that the body is the abode of truth and the best instrument or medium for realizing it. With this belief it locates four plexuses (lotuses) in different parts of the body along the spinal column. The first is *maṇipura-cakra* or *nirmāṇa-cakra* situated in the navel region, representing the *nirmāṇa-kāya* or the principle of material transformation. The second is the *anāhata-cakra* or the *dharma-cakra* situated in the cardiac region, representing the *dharma-kāya*, or the principle of non-dual cosmic existence. The third is the *sambhoga-cakra* situated near the neck, representing the *sambhoga-kāya* or the principle of the body of bliss.

Kāyasādhanā: Disciplining of the body. See Kulakuṇḍalinī, Ṣaṭcakrabheda, Mantrayoga, Haṭhayoga, Layayoga, Rājayoga, Raseśvara Darśana. In the system of the Siddhācāryas, the attainment of the highest goal means certain perfections in the physical apparatus, hence a good deal of emphasis is placed on *kāya-sādhanā* which invloves attempts to bring about the transubstantiation of the body. Later followers of the Siddhācāryas carried this theory and practice to an extreme, and were thus concerned only with the means of attaining a perfect changeless body. This culture of the body implies its transubstantiation first into a subtle ethereal body and that again, finally, into an immutable divine body having an eternal existence.

Kāyāvarohana: Holy resort of the goddess Mātā mentioned in *Matsya Purāṇa* XIII. 47; *Devībhāgavata* VII. 30.76., etc. Also called Kāyāvatāra, it is associated with the tradition of Nakuleśa. It is Karvan at Dabhoi in Baroda.

Kerala-Sampradāya: Name of a Tantric sect the followers of which are scattered in nineteen countries from Āryavarta to the sea. *Śaktisaṅgama*, IV. 3.6. Their theories and practices are described in the *Siddhānta-saṃgraha*. See *Puraścaryārṇava* IX. 867.

Khaḍga: Sword. The sword in the hand of Mañjuśrī is called the Prajñākhaḍga, 'the sword of wisdom', which is believed to destroy the darkness of ignorance by the luminous rays issuing from it.

Kha-dhātu: 'The void element' which in the *Guhyasiddhi* has been identified with Śūnyatā or Prajñā.

Khadiravanī Tārā: Green Tārā who bears the image of Amoghasiddhi on her crown and shows the *varada mudrā* and the *utpala* with her right and left hands respectively. She is flanked by Aśokakāntā Mārīcī and Ekajaṭā. She is commonly known as Śyāma Tārā. *Sādhana* 176.

Khagarbha: Same as Ākāśagarbha (q.v.).

Khaṇḍarohā: One of the four Ḍakinī goddesses of Tantric Buddhism. The others are Ḍakinī, Lāmā and Rūpinī. Khaṇḍarohā is red in colour, one-faced and four-armed. She carries *khatvāṅga*, *kapāla*, *damaru* and *kartari*. *Sādhana* 425.

Kha-puṣpa: Menstrual blood required in Tantric worship. The blood of a virgin is known as *sayambhūkusuma* or *raktacandana* that of a married woman is known as *kuṇḍodbhava* while that of a widow is known as *golodbhava*.

Khasarpaṇa: A form of Avalokiteśvara (q.v.) who is accompanied by Tārā with Suddhanakumāra to his right and Bhṛkuṭi and Hayagrīva to the left. According to *Sādhana* 39-41, he is of white colour, wears jaṭāmukuṭa (q.v.), holds the image of Amitābha (q.v.) on his head and sits in *ardhaparyaṅka* or *lalita* attitude on a double lotus. His right hand exhibits *varada* pose and the left holds a stem of lotus. Named after a village of eastern Bengal, the popularity of Khasarpaṇa is proved by a number of images of this god discovered in different parts of Bihar and Bengal.

Khaṭvāṅga: Magic wand which has skulls. The stick is generally surmounted either by *vajra* or *kapāla* or *triśūla* or banner, occasionally all of them.

Khecarī-mudrā: A yogic posture which bestows spiritual attainment and enables one to overcome disease and death. The stages of contraction and extension of the muscles of the body required in this *mudrā* are thought of as having symbolic spiritual significance. See Khecari Śakti. *Gheraṇḍa* III. 1-3, *Haṭhayogapradīpikā* III. 67. It is required for the meditation of Tripurasundarī. *Mudrānighaṇṭu* 14-16.

Khecarī-śakti: Same as Kaulikī-śakti (q.v.). *Kha* denotes *brahman*, and *cara* that power which moves. The kinetic energy of *brahman* is known as *khecarī*. Though one and undifferentiated it is manifested in numerous forms.

Khecarī Samatā: Identity with Khecarī śakti (q.v.) which is the cause of *Jīvanmukti* (q.v.).

Kīlaka: A Tantric *nyāsa* (q.v.).

Kirīṭa, Kirīṭakoṇā: Holy resort of the goddess Bhuvaneśī according to the *Pīṭhanirṇaya* and *Śiva carita*. She is also known as Vimalā and Kirīṭeśvarī. The *tīrtha* is located at Vatanagara near Lalbag in Murshidabad district, West Bengal.

Kiskindhyāparvata: Holy resort of the goddess Tārā mentioned in *Matsya* XIII. 46. etc. It is modern Kekind in Jodhpur, Rajasthan.

Kokāmukhā: A *mahāpīṭha* according to the *Śivacarīta* with Kokeśvarī as the presiding deity. It is modern Barahchatra on the Kausiki in Nepal.

Kolvagiri: Holy resort of the goddess mentioned in the *Jñānārṇava* V. 66 ff. It has been identified with Kolhapur in Maharashtra.

Kramadīkṣā: A form of Śākta *dikṣā* (q.v.) in the *mantras* of Kālī, Tārā and Tripurasundarī. It is not for all. *Prāṇatoṣaṇī* II. 5.143.

***Kramadīpikā*:** A Vaiṣṇava Tantra in eight *paṭalas*. It is meant for the worship of Kṛṣṇa though contains *mantras* and various rites of Tantric character. It is said to have been composed by Nimbārka's spiritual successor Keśava. Published in Chowkhamba Sanskrit Series no. CCXXXIII, ed. with com. by D.P. Sukla, Varanasi 1967.

Krama-mata: A corollary of monastic Śaivism of Kashmir, the Krama system lays greater stress on the Śakti aspect of the supreme being and is called *bhedābhedupāya* because it seeks to discover identity in phenomenal difference and considers immanence to be an essential expression of transcendence. It is more mystical and less metaphysical than Pratyabhijñā and Spanda schools. Instead of instantaneous and immediate self-revelation it believes in a progressive step-by-step approach towards the spiritual goal. There are two phases of Krama Tantrism. In the earlier phase there was a penchant for philosophical and intuitional issues, but later the ritualistic aspect became predominant. Of its two schools the Sāhasa is represented by the *Vātulanātha-sūtra* which holds that realization takes place through divine grace and that no previous preparation is necessary. The other school is known as Chumnā Sampradāya which endeavours to preserve the esoteric nature of the system. Among the Krama Āgamas mention may be made of *Pañcaśatika*, *Sārdhaśatika*, *Kramarahasya*, *Kramasadbhāva*, *Kālikākrama*, *Kramasiddhi*, etc. The system has been popular since the ninth century AD in different parts of India. *Tantrāloka* IV. 157 ff.

Krāntā: Tantric division of Bhāratavarṣa according to the zone of influence of the cult. There are three divisions: Viṣṇu-krāntā, Ratha-krāntā and Aśva-krāntā.

Kriyā-dīkṣā: One of the three forms of Dikṣā (q.v.) others being Mantra and Vedha. It is an ordinary form of Dīkṣā which is attended with a proper ceremonial form. In all Indian systems Kriyā-dīkṣā is prevalent. During this occasion, among the Vīraśaivas, the *guru* invests the novice with *liṅga.*

Kriyā Śakti: That aspect of Śakti which pertains to action. Three forms of occult power—*manojavitva* (doing any act at any time), *kāmarūpītva* (assuming any form at will) and *vikiraṇadharmitva* (infinite material power to consume and transmit)—are often understood by this term. *Sarvadarśana-saṃgraha* VI. 56-7.

***Kriyāsaṃgrahapañjikā*:** A Buddhist text written by Kuladatta in which detailed prescriptions are given for the creation of vihāras and images and for other rituals. H.P. Sastri, *Descriptive Catalogue of the Sanskrit Manuscripts in ASB*, I. 119 ff.

Kriyā Tantra: One of the four classes of the Buddhist Tantras having a lower position than those belonging to the Caryā, Yoga and Anuttara categories. The Kriyā-tantras insist on rituals, constructions and performances. Texts like the *Mañjuśrīmūla* supply us with a great deal of information on ritual (*kriyā*) in its most tangible forms, with symbols and diagrams and also instruction for painting. Much of the ritual is designed simply to honour the compassionate Bodhisattvas and other beings.

Kriyāvatī-dīkṣā: One of the forms of Tantric dīkṣā (q.v.) in which the *guru* (q.v.) purifies the six *adhvas* (see under *adhvaśodhana*) of the disciple's body, infuses him with his own consciousness and anoints him with different rites. *Prāṇatoṣaṇī* II. 5, 140-2.

Kriyāyoga: A form of Yogic exercise prescribed for those who have attained the status of Puṣpacakra-vīra, a special heroic status in the Tantric cult. *Śaktisaṅgama*, Sundarī I. 197-200.

***Kriyoḍḍīśa Tantra*:** A late Tantric text in 22 chapters dealing with the performance of six black acts, amulets for protection and averting diseases, charms for success in love, making a barren woman fruitful, birth of a son, destruction of enemy, various kinds of seats, hymns to and worship of Śiva, consecration, worship of Kriyādevī and Lakṣmī, description of Maṅgalacaṇḍī and so forth.

Kriyopāya: Same as Āṇavopāya (q.v.).

Krodha-Bhairava: One of the eight Bhairavas of Śiva, others being Svacchanda, Unmatta, Ugra, Kapālin, Jhaṅkāra, Śekhara and Vijaya. He was the recipient of the *Kanda* and *Skanda Yāmala*. The *Brahma Yāmala* says that one of the disciples of Krodha Bhairava worshipped the goddess Bṛhodarī on the outskirts of the village of the same name. This obviously indicates the process of assimilation of the local cults.

Kṛṣṇamohana: The celebrated compiler of the *Āgamacandrikā.*

Kṛṣṇānanda Āgamavāgīśa: The celebrated author of *Tantrasāra* often described as *Bṛhat-Tantrasāra* to distinguish it from the *Tantrasāra* (q.v.) of Abhinavagupta (q.v.) who flourished about the 16th-17th century AD. Kṛṣṇānanda's work is a compilation of the subject matter of all Tantras. It is the most comprehensive and popular of the numerous digests that are known in Bengal. It has no sectarian bias and the views of Vaiṣṇava, Śaiva, Gāṇapatya and other sects are given. Though a compilation the work is not devoid of poetical qualities as is attested to by the beautiful hymns addressed to various deities. It quotes long extracts from many original Tantras. Kṛṣṇānanda is supposed to have introduced the worship of Kālī in Bengal and the iconological conception of Dakṣiṇa-Kālikā. The authorship of *Śrītattvacintāmaṇi* is often attributed to him.

Kṛṣṇayamāri: A form of Yamāntaka, the killer of Yama, the Brahmanical god of death. His worship is mostly performed with a view to enchanting men and women. Kṛṣṇayamāri is represented singly as well as in union with his Prajñā or Bhagavatī. His colour is blue and he has four varieties. Another form of Yamāntaka is known as Raktayamāri. *Sādhana* 530, 544, 547.

Kṛtāñjali: A form of Avalokiteśvara described as two-armed and one faced, standing on a lotus. He exhibits the *añjali* pose against his chest with his two hands.

Kṣāntipāramitā: Tantric Buddhist goddess of

the *Pāramitā* (q.v.) category who has a yellow complexion, two arms and a white lotus as her recognition symbol. *Niṣpanna* 56.

Kṣemānanda: A disciple of Mādhavānanda he was the author of *Saubhāgyakalpalatikā*.

Kṣemarāja: Commentator on Vasugupta's *Śiva-sūtras*, the primary source of Kashmir Saivism and the Saiva Tantras of that region. His commentary on the *Spandakārikā* is known as *Spandasandoha*. Ed. M.R. Shastri, Kashmir Sanskrit Series, no. XVI, 1917. In his *Uddyota* commentary on *Netra Tantra* he refers to Krama as a distinct system. Ed. M.S. Kaul, Bombay 1926, 1939, by V. Dvivedi, rpt. Delhi 1985. He also wrote a commentary on verses 1-23 of Vijñānabhairava.

Kṣepaṇa: The *mudrā* (q.v.) of sprinkling exhibited by the Buddhist Nāmasaṅgati. The two hands are joined, palm to palm, with fingers extended and pointed downwards to enter a vessel containing nectar.

Kṣīragrāma: Modern Khirgram near Katwa in Burdwan district, West Bengal, which is the holy resort of the goddess Yogādyā or Yugādyā according to *Kubjikā* XVIII. 42 ff,. *Candimaṅgala*, *Pīṭhanirṇaya* and *Śivacarita*.

Kṣitigarbha: 'Matrix of the earth', the third Bodhisattva. In one description he has been made identical with his sire Vairocana using the *cakra* symbol. In another description he shows the earth-touching *mudrā* with his right hand and holds a lotus with a symbolic wish-fulfilling tree in the left. *Niṣpanna* 58, *Sādhana* 49.

Kṣiti-tattva: The conception of earth as one of the five traditional elements which constitute matter. This element is said to reside in the *mūlādhāra* (q.v.) within the human body according to Tantric ideas. *Ṣaṭcakranirūpaṇa* XI.

Kubjāmraka: Holy resort of the goddess near Hṛṣikeśa (modern Rishikesh) in the Himalayas, the same as Kanakhala. *Matsya* XIII. 37.

Kubjikā: One of the presiding goddesses of the western direction (*paścima-āmnāya*). *Puraścaryārṇava* I. 13.

***Kubjikāmata*:** An early Tantra, a manuscript of which in Gupta characters is preserved in the Asiatic Society of Bengal. It deals with the concept of Śakti, worship of virgin girls as her manifestations, Mahāvidyā goddesses, customs originating from Mahācīna, *puraścaraṇa* and allied rituals, *mantracaitanya* (consciousness of *mantras*), *yonimudrā*, raising of *kuṇḍalinī* and various attainments. H.P. Sastri has shown that the *Kubjikāmata* belonged to a distinct school in which were also included different branches like the Kulālikāmnāya, Śrīmata, Kādimata, Vidyāpīṭha, etc. It has a few supplements such as *Śrīmatottara* or *Manthanabhairava*, *Kubjikāmahottara*, etc. The original Kubjikā literature consisted of four *ṣaṭkas* each comprising 6,000 verses. Abhinavagupta in his *Triṃśikā* refers to *Kubjikāmata*.

Kula: Clan or family. In the *Saubhāgyabhāskara* com. of the *Lalitāsahasranāma* the term is used in the sense of a spiritual lineage from Paramaśiva to one's own *guru*. This lineage is equated with *gotra* in *Kulārṇava* XVII. *Kaulamārga* or *Kulācāra* is thus a way of *sādhanā* restricted to the spiritual lineage of a particular group of Tantric teachers. The concept of Kula is also current in Tantric Buddhism. Each Dhyānī Buddha belongs to a particular *Kula* to which also belong his Bodhisattva and gods and goddesses who are conceived of as his emanations.

Kulācāra: See Kaulācāra and Kaulamārga. In Buddhism the process of worshipping the Dhyānī Buddhas is also known as Kulācāra. The *Niruttaratantra* refers to Kulācāra as the fifth *āśrama*. Kulācāra is equated with *kuladharma* in the *Kulārṇavatantra* (II. 140-1) which says that it is based on and inspired by the Vedas. Historically, however, the rites involved in the Kulācāra are of heterodox origin and basically non-Vedic in their contents. Abhinavagupta's *Tantrāloka* is concerned with the systematic presentation of the teachings of the Kula and Trika systems. It is from the Kula system that he seems to have attained perfection. Presumably, it is on account of this that he paid a more glowing tribute to Śambhunātha, his Kaulika teacher, than to anyone else.

***Kulacuḍāmaṇi Tantra*:** An early Tantra, though the present form belongs to the late medieval period. It begins with the description of various goddesses known as Kulasundarīs. It describes the efficacy of *kulācāra* in the form of answers by Devī to questions asked by Śiva and is in seven *paṭalas* or chapters. A Devī-oriented cosmogony is also found in this text. Ed. by G.C. Vedantatirtha, Calcutta 1917; *Tantrik Texts* Vol. IV, 1915.

Kula Dravya: Same as Kulatattva (q.v.) or Pañcatattva (q.v.). *Kaulāvalinirṇaya* VIII.

Kulajñāna: The knowledge of *Kaulamārga*, admission to which is highly restricted. Rāmeśvara on *Paraśurāmakalpasūtra* III. 31.

Kulakaulayoginī: Presiding deities of the Cakras (q.v.) belonging to the *bahirdasāra* (q.v.) class. *Gandharvatantra* V. 102.

Kulālikā: One of the presiding goddesses of the western region (*paścimāmnāya*). *Puraścaryārṇava* I. 12.

Kulamārga: See Kaulamārga. The word Kaula is a derivative of Kula with *sna* suffix.

Kulakuṇḍalinī: See Kuṇḍalinī.

Kulamata: See Kaulamārga. In Kashmir Saivism it is regarded as a left-handed way in which the rituals of five Ms are excluded.

Kulāmṛta: The nectar which flows from the cerebral *candramaṇḍala* (lunar orb) down the inner body of the aspirant when the Kuṇḍalinī (q.v.) pierces the *ṣaṭcakra* (q.v.).

Kulanāyikā: The Śakti within the heart conceived in the form of the heroine of the clan. *Parātriṃśikā* 61.

Kulapatha: The way through which Kuṇḍalinī (q.v.) pierces the *ṣaṭcakra*. See *Saundaryalaharī* X.

Kulapadma: A six-petalled lotus within the *Sahasrāra* (q.v.).

***Kulārṇava Tantra*:** Said to be Tantra of *ūrdhva-āmnāya* and part of a lost work of 25,000 verses; probably composed about AD 1,000. The present form contains seventeen *ullāsas* (chapters) and over two thousand verses. Quoted in numerous Tantric digests and commentaries it establishes superiority of Kauladharma. Śiva is called Akula and Śakti Kula. It maintains that *mokṣa* is to be attained through an understanding of these two principles; considers every woman to be born in the *kula* of the Great Mother; that to follow the path of *kula* is more difficult than walking on the edge of a sword. Two chapters are devoted to the qualifications and greatness of the Guru. It recommends the five *makāras* and endeavours to give their esoteric meaning and symbolic significance. It lays down rules of *puraścaraṇa*, *dīkṣā*, *nyāsa*, *yantra*, etc., explains various terms and concepts and refers to eighteen Śākta *pīṭhas*. Published in *Tantrik Texts*, Vol. V, 1917; ed. and trans. by R.K. Rai, Varanasi 1983.

Kula Saṅketa: Technical mysteries of the Kaulamārga (q.v.). These relate to the practices in connection with *karma* (initiation) *pūjā* (worship), *mantra* (spell), *tantra* (way), *mantrayantralikhana* (drawing of diagrams) and so on. *Niruttara* XII; *Kulārṇava* II; Rāmeśvara on *Paraśurāmakalpasūtra* VII. 1.

Kulastrī: Worshipped by the followers of Vāmācāra in different ways. Kulastrī does not mean any housewife; but rather a woman specially chosen who functions as the female principle, in whose worship the rites of the Five Ms and the use of *khapuṣpa* (menstrual blood) are essential. All women symbolize Śakti, but since their *kumārī* (virgin) form is the most attractive, the great goddess is always pleased with virgin-worship.

Kulasundarī: Goddesses like Tripurā, Kālikā, Vāgiśvarī, Vimalā, Mātaṅgini, Purṇā, Caṇḍnāyikā, Ekajaṭā, Durgā, etc., who are worshipped according to Kulācāra or Kaulācāra. *Kulacuḍāmaṇitantra* I. 1-2.

Kulatattva: Another name for Pañcattava or Pañcamakāra (q.v.). *Yoginītantra* Pūrva VI.

Kulayoṣit: The Kuṇḍalinī-Śakti (q.v.) situated in the *mūlādhāra* (q.v.) also known as Kaulinī (q.v.). Lakṣmīdhara on *Saundarya-laharī* VIII, XLL.

Kulīśeśvarī: Companion goddess of Mahākāla according to Tantric Buddhism. She remains in the north-east corner, has a white complexion, carries *vajra* and staff and stands in the *ālīḍha* attitude on a corpse. She is nude and looks terrible with bare fangs, three eyes and dishevelled hair.

Kullukā: A kind of secret *mantra* meant for the *kula* worship of the Vidyās. These are capable of removing faults and defects in worship. *Puraścaryārṇava* VI. 529; *Prāṇatoṣaṇī* IV. 1, 223-4; *Nīlatantra* V.

Kumāra, Kumāradhāma: Holy resort of the goddess Kaumārī mentioned in *Bṛhannīlatantra* V. It is same as Cape Comorin.

Kumārīpūja: Worship of a virgin as a symbol of the great goddess. See Kulastrī.

***Kumārī Tantra*:** A late Tantra in nine chapters dealing with *mantras*, mental worship, *kālikā-yantra* and external worship, worship of Kālī, *puraścaraṇa* and sexo-yogic Kaula practices, *kulācāra* with different classes of women, places of Devī worship, various forms of Kālī, etc. Published in Devananda's *Śāktapramoda* 1890; ed. by A.K. Kalia, by Krishnamacharya with Hindi com.

Kumbhaka: Breath-control. *Tantrasāra* 85 ff.

Eight types of Kumbhaka are mentioned in the *Gheraṇḍasaṃhitā* V. 46. These are *sahita*, *sūryabheda*, *śitalī*, *bhastrikā*, *bhrāmarī*, *murcchā* and *kevalī*. The *Haṭhayoga-pradīpikā* II. 44 adds two more types, *śitkārī* and *plāvinī*.

Kuñci: One of the four door goddesses of Tantric Buddhism mentioned in the Pañcaḍāka-maṇḍala of the *Niṣpannayogāvalī*. She is described as being yellow in colour and she holds keys in her two hands. She is also known as Kuñcikādhārā.

Kunda-golodbhava: Menstrual blood sacred to any Tantric goddess. *Kuṇḍodbhava* is the blood of a married woman and *golodbhava* that of a widow.

Kuṇḍalinī: Śakti which as serpent power remains latent in the *mūlādhara-cakra* (q.v.); as the source of all energy it reveals itself when roused by Yogic exercises. Through different nerve-channels it takes up an upward motion and eventually reaches the *sahasrāra* (highest cerebral region) and then comes down to its original place. The rousing and stirring up of Kuṇḍalinī is a form of the merging of the individual with the universal consciousness. The whole process is very complex and depends entirely on the mental and intellectual faculties of the aspirant. It has two forms—dynamic or kinetic and static or potential. The *āsanas*, *kumbhakas*, *mudrās*, etc., are used to rouse *kuṇḍalinī* so that the life force withdrawn from the *iḍā* and *piṅgalā* may enter the *susumnā* and then go upwards towards the *brahmarandhra*. Prāṇa which exists in the form of vital air, generates heat which causes *kuṇḍalinī* to be aroused which then hisses and straightens itself and pierces the *cakras*. This is possible through repeated efforts and by a gradual process. The uncoiled *kuṇḍalinī* first enters the *citriṇī-nāḍi* and then pierces each of the lotuses. Thus the *kuṇḍalinī* absorbs 23 *tattvas* and then meets its source in the *sahasrāra*. This union is known as *sāmarasya*. The Sādhaka (aspirant) thinking of himself as Śakti experiences union with Śiva and enjoys infinite pleasure through the flow of nectar which runs from *brahma-randhra* to *mūlādhāra*, flooding the *kṣudra-brahmāṇḍa* or microcosm, i.e. the body of the aspirant. Forgetful of all in this world the aspirant is immersed in ineffable bliss. For various interpretaions of *kuṇḍalinī*, its awakening and functions, see Lakṣmīdhara on *Saundaryalaharī* X; *Rudrayāmala*, Uttara XXI; *Siddha-siddhantāsaṃgraha* IV. 20 ff., *Prāṇatoṣaṇī* I. 6.41 ff.; *Tantrarāja* XXX, *Mātṛkābheda* XIV; *Ṣaṭcakranirūpaṇa* XI; *Śāradātilaka* XXX. 27; etc.

Kuṇḍika: Same as *kamaṇḍalu*. See Kalasa.

Kūrmāsana: A Yogic *āsana* in which the heels are placed cross-wise under the gluteals.

Kurukṣetra: Same as modern Kurukṣetra near Thanesar in Haryana mentioned as a *pīṭha* in *Kubjikā* VII, *Bṛhannīla* V, *Pīṭhanirṇaya* and other texts. It is here that the heel of the right leg of Satī is said to have fallen.

Kurukullā: A form of Tārā (q.v.) who is the emanation of Amitābha. She has many varieties. Śukla or white Kurukullā is two-armed with the symbols of rosary and a bowl of lotus. Tārodbhava Kurukullā is four-armed, the left hands showing *abhaya-mudrā* and holding an arrow, while in the right hands are a bow and lotus. Uḍḍīyāna Kurukullā is red in colour, four-armed and sits on a corpse. She has five skulls on her head, protruding teeth and tongue and wears a garment of tiger skin. Among other forms of Kurukullā we have eight-armed Aṣṭabhujā and six-armed Māyājālakrama. Both are of red complexion. *Sādhana* 351-3.

Kūṭa: Means collection. It is suffixed to such terms as Vāgbhava, Kāmarāja, Śakti, etc. More precisely, the letters of a Vidyā, which are to be uttered simultaneously, jointly form a *kūṭa*. In *Śrītattvacintāmaṇi* X. 26-8 Śrīvidyā is described as *pañcakūṭā*. Often one-lettered *bīja-mantras* are called *kūṭa*. *Tantrasāra* 241.

L

Laghimā: One of the ten *siddhis* or miraculous attainments. *Nityaṣoḍaśikārṇava* I. 166-8. The word *laghiman* means lightness, buoyancy levity, absence of weight, etc. As a *siddhi* it denotes a super-natural faculty of assuming excessive lightness at will.

Lākinī: The presiding goddess of the *maṇipura cakra* (q.v.). She and other goddesses presiding over the Ṣaṭcakra owe their origin to the Buddhist Tantras. The *Ṣaṭcakranirūpaṇa* says that Lakinī is to be meditated upon in the form of flames on the pericarp of the lotus in inseparable company of Rudra who represents the element of fire.

Lakṣaṇa: Auspicious marks. Their number varies in Brahmanism, Buddhism and Jainism. Minor marks are known as *anuvyañjanās*.

Lakṣmaṇa Deśikendra: Author of the celebrated Tantric work *Śāradātilaka* which has been commented upon by various scholars from time to time. It deals with the details of the worship of various deities and also discusses certain aspects of Śākta philosophy. Among his other works is *Tārāpradīpa* which appears to have enjoyed popularity in Bengal; it is a metrical work dealing with the details of Tārā worship. Lakṣmaṇa Deśikendra flourished in the eleventh century. Rāghavabhaṭṭa's commentary on the *Śāradātilaka* is dated about AD 1393-4.

Lakṣmī: Puranic deity, consort of Viṣṇu, later brought into the Tantric fold and identified with Śakti regarded as the supreme being. So elevated is her position, as described and analysed in the *Lakṣmītantra*, a Tantric text which bears her name, that this particular text is regarded as highly authoritative even by the Śāktas themselves. She is identified with Śrī and Kamalā. Her *mantra* is the single-lettered *śrīm* which offers beauty, grace and luck. She has a golden complexion. She sits on a lotus. Her hands depict the *varada* (boon-giving) and *abhaya* (protection) pose. She has also other *mantras* and *dhyānas*. In the Tantras we also come across her Mahālakṣmī (q.v.) and Sāmrājyalakṣmī (q.v.) forms. *Śāradātilaka* VIII. 1-4; *Prāṇatoṣaṇī*.

Laksmīdhara: Author of the commentary on the *Saundaryalaharī* attributed to Śaṅkara. He is probably different form his namesake, the author of the well-known Smṛti digest *Kṛtyakalpataru*.

Lakṣmīṅkarā: Regarded as one of the founders of Sahajayāna, Lakṣmīṅkarā Devī was the sister of Indrabhūti, the king of Uḍḍīyāna and a Sādhaka. Lakṣmīṅkarā preached that when truth is known, there is no restriction of any kind for the worshipper. She declared also that no suffering, fasting, rites, bathing, purification or obedience to the rules of society, image worship were necessary for the purpose of obtaining liberation. The worshipper should, with concentration, offer worship only to his own body where all the gods reside. Like her brother Indrabhūti she did not believe in restrictions regarding food and drink and advocated Śakti worship. She flourished in the eighth century AD.

***Lakṣmītantra*:** A Pāñcarātra text with definite Śākta orientation. Because of its exclusive treatment of Lakṣmī as Śakti of Viṣṇu, later Śākta philosophers and commentators like Bhāskara Rāya, Nāgeśa Bhaṭṭa, Appaya Dikṣita and others have not only mentioned it, but cited it as an authoritative work for the understanding of Śāktism. It was composed between ninth and twelfth centuries AD. It deals mainly with the Pāñcarātra philosophy and cosmogony and alludes to the peculiar *sādhanā* of the left-handed Tantras that requires a female partner. Here the *vyuha* doctrine is explained in terms of Lakṣmī as the supreme being. *Lakṣmītantra* is divided into 49 chapters which deal with emanations of Mahāśrī, Mahāvidyā and Mahāmāyā from Mahālakṣmī, evolution of material world from Prakṛti, the *avatāras* of Lakṣmī in six sheaths, her exclusive incarnations and true nature, *mantras* and their characters, the origin of letters, the *mātṛkās*, method of initiation and practice of meditation, Tārā and Anutārā *mantras*, elucidation of seven Vidyās, Tārikā in the three stages of existence, hand postures, purification of the body, images, *puraścaraṇa*, revelation of

Lakṣmī's various manifestations, etc., Sanskrit edition, V. Krishnamacharya, Adyar Library Series, no. 87; Eng. edn. with trans. with intro. and notes, by Sanjukta Gupta, Leiden 1972.

Lakulīśa: One of the main exponents of the Pāśupata system. The *Mahābharata* says that the Pāśupata doctrines were first preached by Śiva Śrīkaṇṭha who might have been a human teacher. A Tantric text called *Piṅgalāmata* composed in AD 1174, speaks of Bhagavat Śrīkaṇṭhanātha as its author. Lakulīśa was probably his disciple. According to an inscription of the Gupta king Candragupta II Lakulīśa had four disciples—Kuśika, Gārga, Mitra and Kāruṣya; variants of the last three names are found in the Purāṇas. They lived about ten generations before the time of Candragupta II. This would place Lakulīśa almost in the time of Patañjali who first speaks of Śivabhāgavatas in his *Mahābhaṣya*. Pāśupatism is based on a literature known as Āgamas and as such it may be regarded as an incipient north Indian form of Āgamanta Śaivism. The Āgamas are eighteen in number according to one tradition and 28 according to another. In the Purāṇas Lakulīśa is often mentioned as Lakulin and his seat is located at Kāyārohana, modern Karavan in Dabhoi Taluka. The variant readings of his name are Nakulīśa, Nakulin and Nakula. The last name is regarded as that of the Bhairava of the goddess presiding over the Upapīṭha of Kālighāṭa in Calcutta.

Lalanā: Name of a nerve found in the Buddhist Tantras. It is same as the Iḍā of the Hindu Tantras which is situated to the left of Susumnā or Avadhūtī. The one on the right is known as Rasanā (q.v.) which corresponds to Piṅgalā (q.v.). Lalanā is of the nature of Prajñā and Rasanā of Upāya. Lalanā is also conceived of as the moon, the Female Principle, and is said to be the container of seed. Besides Prajñā she is known as Āli, Gaṅgā and by various other names.

Lalanā-cakra: See Kālacakra, Lambikāgra.

Lalitā: One of the presiding goddesses of the northern direction. *Puraścaryārṇava* I, 12-13. She is very often described as the supreme being, the anthropomorphized primordial energy. The *Lalitāsahasranāma* section of the *Brahmāṇḍa-purāṇa*, which has been commented upon by Bhāskara-rāya, is an important text for the followers of Śrīvidyā. Lalitāsundarī or Tripurasundarī is another name of Śrividyā Ṣoḍaśī. The commentary by Bhāskara, son of Gambhīrarāya, is known as *Saubhāgyabhāskara*. It was composed in 1729. Published by Nirnaya Sagar Press 1935. Lalitapura, possibly Lalitpur in the Jhansi district, Uttar Pradesh, is the holy resort of the goddess Lalīta according to *Bṛhannīlatantra* V.

***Lalitārcanacandrikā*:** A late medieval text for the followers of Śrividyā, also known as Lalitā or Ṣoḍaśī or Tripurasundarī.

***Lalitāsahasranāma*:** See Lalitā.

Lalitāsundarī: Another name of Ṣoḍaśī or Tripurasundarī whose *mantra* is known as Śrividyā and who is worshipped in Śrīyantra or Śrīcakra.

***Lalitā-triśatī*:** One of the two components of the *Lalitopākhyāna* which is said to form the Rahasyakāṇḍa (the 'Book of Secret Doctrines') of the *Brahmāṇḍa Purāṇa*.

***Lalitopākhyāna*:** A section of the *Brahmāṇḍa Purāṇa* of which the *Lalitāsahasranāma* (q.v.) and *Lalitātriśatī* are components. Most verses in Chapter 42 are same as in *Mudrānighaṇṭu*.

Lāmā: One of the four goddesses of the Dākinī group mentioned in the Buddhist Tantras; the others are Dākinī, Khaṇḍārohā and Rūpinī. She is green in colour, one-faced and four-armed. The hands hold *khatvāṅga*, *kapāla*, *ḍamaru* and *kartari*. *Sādhanamālā* 425. In the enumeration of the various female energies (yoginī) in the Brahmanical Tantras we find a type called Lāmā (Rūpikā, Cumbikā Lāmā). The corresponding god is called Lāmeśvara. The word Lāmā, like a few others such as Dākinī, Śākinī, Lākinī and Hākinī, in spite of their later explanations, seems to be exotic. Lāmā is certainly the Tibetan word 'Lha-mo' which means Devī or Śakti.

Lāmāvarga: A group of Tantric aspirants mentioned in the *Jayadratha Yāmala*. It constitutes 24 varieties of Lāmās—Yoginī, Rūpinī, Lāmā, Śākinī, Nalinī, Khāgī, Culī, Bilā, Trikhagagā, Peśinī, Dehinī, Jalā, Klevati, Budhani, Luki, Padabhi, Raktinī, Hisā, Karothi, Kalusi, Bhadrā, Dundubhi, Mukharā and Āturā.

Lambikāgra: A minor nerve-cycle situated above the *viśuddha* (q.v.) and below the *ājñā* (q.v.). It is also known as *lalanā* and *kālacakra*.

Laṅkā: Holy resort of the goddess Śaṅkarī or

Indrākṣī mentioned in the *Pīthanirṇaya*. The *Śivacarita* refers to it as an Upapīṭha. It appears to be Ceylon or modern Srilanka, but the *Aṣṭādaśapīṭha* makes a separate mention of Laṅkā and Siṃhaladvīpa. The word *laṅkā* means an island in the sea or a river.

Lāsyā: One of the four dancing goddesses in Tantric Buddhism; the others are Mālā, Gītā and Nṛtyā. She is red in colour and with pride she arranges her two hands in a rhythmic act. *Nispanna* 76.

Latā: The female partner of the Tantric aspirant. Also known as Dūtī. See Latā-sādhanā.

Latā Sādhanā: *Pañcamakāra* (q.v.) rituals with female partners. *Mahānirvāṇa* I. 52. *Maithuna* is regarded as *pañcamatattva*. The woman with whom sexual intercourse is to be had or who is associated with a male in Tantra worship is called Śakti or Prakṛti or Latā, and this special ritual is called Latāsādhanā. *Kulārṇava* VII. 39-43; *Mahānirvāṇa* VI. 18-20.

Laukika Tantra: Tantras of the popular category which are not burdened with sophisticated superimpositions. They reflect the liberal attitude of the simpler peoples towards religion and society. This attitude is marked by the negation of all external formalities and doctrinal intricacies in regard to the spiritual quest and by the affirmation of the beliefs and practices which are regarded as the heritage of the primitive and unsophisticated way of life. In the case of society this attitude is marked by the rejection of the caste system and patriarchy as upheld in the Brahmanical Smārta-Pauranic tradition and by its insistence on regulating the practical aspects of life like manual and technical labour, chemical sciences, medicine, metallurgy and so on. The Laukika Tantras were accepted in principle by the Atimārgikas (q.v.) and the Vedhabāhyas (q.v.), the radicals and reformists belonging to the major religious systems as well as by the followers both of the non-conformist and popular religious ideas and practices and the followers of the medieval saints and their teachings.

Laulikī: Also known as Nauli it is one of the six acts (*saṭ-karma*) of Haṭhayoga. It is creation of certain movements within the body by which diseases may be cured and the heat of the body increased. See Śodhana. *Gheraṇḍa* I. 13-60; *Haṭhayoga-pradīpikā* II. 24-35.

Laya: A practical demonstration of how the outwardly directed evolving process is reversed until the whole *prapañca* (universe) is resolved into unitary consciousness and perfect bliss. Also known as Kuṇḍalinī-yoga (q.v.) in the Tantric tradition.

Laya Bhogāṇgavidhāna: The method of separating three fetters—*āṇava* (caused by material ingredients), *karma* (caused by the effects of deeds) and *māyīya* (caused by false knowledge)—from the body of an individual. It is part of Smārtī Dīkṣā, Rāghava on *Śāradātilaka* V. 127-40; *Puraścaryārṇava* V. 395.

Layasiddhiyoga: The state of absolute bliss according to the Tantras. The aspirant through yoni-mudrā acquires spiritual power and experiences sexual pleasure leading to realization of a sense or non-duality with the supreme being. *Gheraṇḍa* VII. 12-3.

Laya-yoga: One of the four general divisions of yoga (q.v.). It is a physical process—an exercise of supersensible forces and functions of the inner body. Laya-yoga is a higher form of Haṭha-yoga (q.v.). It is specially connected with the functioning of *kuṇḍalinī* which is why the Tantras lay the greatest emphasis on this form of yoga. It destroys all forms of mundane desires. It is an experience of eternal bliss in which the mind totally merges in the supreme being. *Haṭhayogapradīpikā* IV. 31-4.

Līlāśakti: A form of *acit-sakti* (non-sentient energy) also known as *parigraha-śakti* or *upādāna-śakti*.

Liṅga-deha, Śarīra: The subtle body. The human body is identified in the Tantras with Śrīcakra or Śrīyantra. *Setubandha* com. on *Nityaṣoḍaśikārṇava* VI. 25-7. In the subtle body of an individual there are 32 lotuses on the *suṣumnā* cord. A human being has three form of body—gross (*sthūla*) subtle (*sūkṣma*) and causal (*kāraṇa*).

Liṅgadhāriṇī: Also known as Prajñā. She is the presiding goddess of Naimiṣāraṇya, modern Nimsar or Nimkhar in Sitapur district, Uttar Pradesh *Matsya* XIII. 26; *Devībhāgavata* VII. 30.55.

Liṅga-puṣpa: The Raktakaravī flower. It is used as a substitute for *maithuna* (q.v.), the other item being *yonipuṣpa* which is blue Aparajitā flower. Com. on *Paraśurāma-kalpasūtra* X. 63.

Liṅga-sāyatta-dīkṣā: Initiation in the Vīraśaiva system; it is marked by carrying a small *śivaliṅga* on the body irrespective of sex.

Liṅgatraya: Three types of Śiva liṅgas (Śiva-phallus). They are known as Itara, Svayambhū and Bāṇa and are symbolically connected in Tantrism with the nerve plexuses within the human body.

Lipinyāsa: See Mātṛkānyāsa.

Locanā: The Śakti or female consort of the Dhyānī Buddha Vairocana. She belongs to the Tathāgata family. She comes into existence from the white germ syllable *lom*. She is white in colour. Her recognition symbol is the discus. She is the embodiment of the cosmic element of earth. *Advayavajrasaṃgraha* 42.

Lokanātha: A common form of Avalokiteśvara. Many standing images of this god with four or six hands have been found in different parts of India. A seated variety is also found. The four-armed figures show *vara* (boon-giving pose), *akṣamālā* (rosary), *bhṛṅgāra* (drinking pot) and *padma* (lotus) respectively. Sucīmukha and Hayagrīva to the right and left respectively are the usual attendents of this god. The six-armed figures have *vara*, *mātuluṅga*(pomegranate) and *akṣamālā* in the right hands and *bhṛṅgāra*, *pāśa* (noose) and *padma* in the left ones. Here both the attendant figures are females, Tārā and Bhṛkuṭī.

Lokeśvara: A common name of Avalokiteśvara used as suffix of his 108 forms. Lokeśvara stays on the left side of the Buddha. He is described as white in complexion, carrying in his right hand a fly-whisk and a lotus in the left.

Lokāyata: A culture-complex of the common people. An aspect of this culture-complex is primitive Tantrism. The Tantric concept of *dehavāda* equating the human body with the universe and the cosmogony of the Tantras are but elaborations of the corollaries of a most primitive belief. The Sāṅkhya philosophy was originally a development of the primitive proto-materialism which formed the substratum of Tantrism itself. The primitive empirical and analogical belief in the equation of earth and woman, of natural and human fertility, formed the infrastructure of numerous agricultural rites. The mode of securing the material means of subsistence, invariably connects the mystery of nature with that of human body. Carrying the analogy further it transpires that the birth of the universe is the result of the same or a similar process as the birth of the human being. Apart from cosmogony many Tantric ideal and rituals are directly adopted from the Lokāyata or popular tradition which is manifested in numerous non-Brahmanical and heterodox systems, scientific and technological treatises, regional, tribal, proletarian and popular cults, beliefs and practices and in the broad background of the history of Indian thought generally.

Lopāmudrā: The *mantras* of Śrīvidyā consisting of fifteen symbolic letters. *Tantrasāra* 242-3.

Lu(yi) i-pāda: A name of Matsyendranātha (q.v.) who is honoured by the Buddhist mystic as the first of Siddhas under the name Lui-pāda. The fundamental doctrine of his teachings is that of Sahaja. The songs composed by him are preserved in the collection called *Caryāscaryaviniścaya* or *Caryāgītikoṣa*. He is described in the Tantric Buddhist texts as a Mahāsiddha.

Mm

Mādhavānandanātha: Author of the *Saubhāgyakalpadruma* who lived in Varanasi in the first half of the nineteenth century.

Mādhavavana: Also known as Mādhavīvana it is the holy resort of the goddess Sugandhā mentioned in *Matsya* XIII. 36; *Devībhāgavata* VII. 30.65, etc. It is same as Madhuvana or Mathura.

Madhumatī: One of the eight Yoginīs (Aṣṭayoginī q.v.) described in the *Tantrasāra*. She has the colour of white crystal. She is decked with various jewels and ornaments such as anklets, necklace, armlets and ear-rings.

Madhupurī: Name of a symbolic *pīṭha* which is situated on the neck of a human being. During *nyāsa* this region is to be touched upon by the aspirant. *Tantrasāra* 339. There is also a real Madhupurī, Mathura in Uttar Pradesh, which is a place sacred to the goddess. *Kubjikā* VII, *Rudrayāmala* quoted in *Tantrasāra* 521-2.

Madhyamā: A special type of sound; it lies between *paśyantī* (q.v.) and *vaikharī* (q.v.) and forms the third stage of its development. It is within and connected with the intellect. Com. on *Prapañcasāra* II. 43. It is also called as a state of equilibrium of *parā* (q.v.) and *paśyantī* (q.v.), *Cidvallī* on *Kāmakalāvilāsa* XXVI. According to Bhāskara Rāya, *brahman*, having manifested itself as sound becomes specially articulated with the help of wind in the heart regions as *nāda* (q.v.). This state is known as *madhyamā*. *Saubhāgya-bhāskara* on *Lalitāsahasranāma* 99. It is a cognitive aspect of mental movement.

Madhyamasrota Tantra: Tantric works belonging to the middle current of the tradition. These are *Vijaya*, *Niśvāsa*, *Svāyambhūva*, *Vātula*, *Vīrabhadra*, *Raurava*, *Makuṭa*, and *Vireśa*.

Madreśvara: Probably a variant reading of Bhadreśvara in Hooghly district regarded as a holy resort of the goddess. It may also be Madra in the Sialkot region of Punjab.

Madya: The first of the Five Ms; it is wine of various types. *Paraśurāmakalpasūtra* X. 62. Paiṣṭī, Gauḍī and Mādhvī are the three best types. *Kulārṇava* V, *Mahānirvāṇa* VI. 2-3. Thirteen types of wine were used by the Gauḍa-sampradāya, *Śaktisaṅgama,* Kālī, IX. 46. Any type of wine purified by *mantra* is fit for *sādhanā*. *Mahānirvāṇa* IV. 4. Milk, honey and sugar syrup are regarded as substitutes for wine. Ibid. VIII. 170-1. Symbolically *madya* is described as the nectar-essence of the union of Śiva-Śakti which flows from the highest cerebral region, *Kulārṇava* V. Madya is called *tīrthavāri* in some texts.

Madyaśodhana: Purification of wine, one of the five *makāras,* with *mantras*. Such purification makes wine turn into ambrosia. *Gandharva-tantra* XXXIV. 86-9; *Mātṛkā-bheda* III. 13. According to *Kaulamārga-rahasya* 32, the *sattva* or pleasant and blissful element (*ānanda*) of wine remains covered by the intoxicating *tamas* and deluding element (*moha*) which is why purification is necessary. Five methods are employed for this purpose. These are *vīkṣaṇa* (looking through), *prokṣaṇa* (sanctification by sprinkling holy water), *dhyāna* (meditation), *mantra* (incantation) and *mudrā* (various postures). *Kulārṇava* VI. 35.

Magadha: Modern Gaya-Patna region in South Bihar. An unspecified site in this vast region is mentioned as a holy resort of the goddess Sarvānandamayī in the *Pīṭha-nirṇaya*. It is said that the right thigh of Satī fell here.

Mahā-abhayakarī: A form of Lokeśvara (q.v.), three-faced and six-armed. He holds a book against his chest with his two principal hands, *vajra* and rosary in the other right hands and *ghaṇṭā* and *tridaṇḍī* in the left.

Mahā-abhayaphalada: A form of three-faced and six-armed Lokeśvara (q.v.) who holds *vajra*, sword and lotus in his three right hands and two bells and a book in his three left hands.

Mahābala: An emanation of the Dhyānī Buddha Amitābha who is described in *Sādhanamālā* 507 as having one face, four arms and a red complexion. His brown hair rises upwards and is tied by a snake. His face looks terrible with bare fangs and he is bright like the orb of the sun.

Mahābhāva: The *divya* and *vīra* stages of Tantric attainment. The *paśu* stage belongs to *adhama* (low category). Divyovīrau mahābhāvādhamaḥ paśubhāvakaḥ. *Prāṇatoṣaṇī* VII. 1. 488.

Mahābīja: See Bīja.

Mahābindu: See Bindu.

Mahācakra: One of the five Tantric *cakra* rituals; the others are *rāja*, *devī*, *vīra* and *paśu*. In *mahācakra* mother, sister, daughter, daughter-in-law of the aspirant are to be worshipped as *pañca-śakti or Śakti* in her form with five aspects. *Niruttara* X. See *cakra* and *bhairavī-cakra*. I

Mahacandrabimba: One of the three-faced and six-armed forms of Avalokiteśvara who holds an arrow, a lotus and a fruit in his three right hands and a bow, a bolt and a wheel in the three left.

Mahācīnācāra: See Cīnācāra and Cīnakrama.

***Mahācīnacārakrama*:** A medieval Tantra dealing with the cult of Mahācīnatārā. It is stated in this Tantra that the sage Vasiṣṭha was instrumental in bringing the cult of Tārā from Mahācīna and the rituals associated with her worship which are known as *cīnācāra* (q.v.). This *cīnācāra* is regarded as a form of *vāmācāra*.

***Mahācīnākhyātantra*:** A text dealing with *cīnācāra* or *cīnakrama* which is frequently quoted in later Tantras, such as *Tārātantra*, etc.

Mahācīnatāra: Also known as Ugratāra and Ekajaṭā (q.v.). The description of this goddess, as given in *Sādhanamālā* 210, has her standing on a corpse in *pratyālīḍha* attitude. Her complexion is like that of a blue lotus, and she is three-eyed and one-faced. She is most terrible, appears fierce, with bare canine fangs; she carries a sword and *kartari* in two right hands and *utpala* and *kapāla* in the two left. Her *jaṭāmukuṭa* of one coil is brown and fiery and bears the image of Akṣobhya on it. Almost the same description is found in Brahmānanda's *Tārārahasya* and Kṛṣṇānanda's *Tantrasāra.* On the basis of *Brahma* and *Rudra Yāmalas*, *Mahācīnārakrama* and other Tantras it has been suggested that her cult was brought to India from China by the sage Vasiṣṭha. See Mahā-Nīlasarasvatī.

Mahāgaṅgā: A river sacred to the goddess mentioned in *Bhṛannīlatantra* V. It is Alakanandā in the Himalayas.

Mahākāla: Personification of eternal time. In Brahmanical Purāṇas Śiva is often identified with Mahākāla. The god also occurs in as many as four fierce forms in the Buddhist Tantras.

Mahākāla: Holy resort of the goddess Mahākālī mentioned in *Matsya Purāṇa* XIII. 41, *Devībhāgavata* VII. 30.70, etc. It Probably refers to the temple of Mahākala in Ujjayini.

Mahakālahṛdaya: A special efficacious *mantra,* mentioned in *Harṣacarita* III, by means of which the Śaiva ascetic Bhairavācārya subdued a *vetāla* and ultimately attained the position of a Vidyādhara.

***Mahākāla Saṃhitā*:** A Tantric text dealing mostly with the conception, forms, cult and rituals of Kālī. Passages from this text have been quoted in Tantric manuals. The text is not available in its entirety but some portions of this work have been secured from Nepal.

Mahākālī: That form of Kālī which is associated with Mahākāla (eternal time). Nīlakaṇṭha in his com. on *Mbh.* VII. 23.5, describes her as *mahatī cāsau kālī ca kālayitrī saṃhantrī kālarūpā mahākālī.* Here *mahatī* signifies her greatness while *kālarūpā* suggests that she is one's inevitable destiny. Besides she is described as *saṃhantrī* or destroyer. She is described as having ten faces, ten hands and ten legs. Every face contains three eyes. Her colour is blue. According to another description she has five faces. She is frequently identified with Yoganidrā. *Puraścaryārṇava* IX. 754; XI. 956.

Mahākāraṇa-deha, Śarīra: The subtle body an individual acquires by means of Tantric Sādhanā.

Mahālakṣmī: One of the names of the supreme being found in the Tantras. She is different from her Puranic counterpart. Very often she is a form of Kamalā, and as such a Mahāvidyā goddess. In the *Śāradātilaka* VIII. 74-88 the brightness of her body has been compared to that of the rising sun. Slightly bent owing to the weight of her breasts, her body is adorned with elaborate jewellery. In hands she holds a rice-plant, two lotuses and the *kaustubha* jewel. She is three-eyed and extremely beautiful. She is the darling of

Viṣṇu. Her twelve-lettered *mantra* bestows all success. Ibid. VIII. 45-6. In the *Svacchanda-tantra* it is stated that the letters (*varṇas*) of the *A-varga* (the vowels beginning with A) are presided over by Mahālakṣmī. Her physical features and figures are perfect; they radiate the highest degree of eroticism.

Mahālakṣmī: Holy resort of the goddess Ambikā mentioned in *Jñānārṇava* V. 66-7 and *Bṛhannīlatantra* V. It is possibly same as Kolhapur where the great shrine of the goddess Mahālakṣmī. But the *Jñānārṇava* makes a distinction between Kolvāgiri and Mahālakṣmī.

Mahālaya: Holy resort of the goddess Mahābhāgā or Mahāpadmā mentioned in the *Prāṇatoṣaṇī* and *Bṛhannilatantra* V. It is same as Oṃkāranātha or Amarakaṇṭaka.

Mahā-māṃsa: The flesh of eight animals—cow, man, ram, horse, buffalo, boar, goat and deer—regarded as sacred to the deity. *Śyāmārahasya* III; *Tantrasāra* 630.

Mahāmānasī: Śāsanadevatā of Jain Tīrthaṃkara Śāntinātha according to the Digambara tradition. Her vehicle is the peacock and she holds a disc, a fruit, a sword and displays *varada-mudrā*. Her name shows her association with learning which is why she is mentioned also as a Vidyādevī. Her vehicle, the peacock, also indicates the same.

Mahāmañjubhūta: One of the three-faced and six-armed forms of Lokeśvara (q.v.) who carries a sword, a *vajra*, and a *kamaṇḍalu* in his three right hands and a rosary, a lotus and a bell in the three left.

Mahāmañjudatta: One of the three-faced and six-armed forms of Lokeśvara who carries a bell, a sword, and a *ratnapallava* in his three right hands and the *vajra*, a bell and a lotus in the three left.

Mahāmantrānusāriṇī: A *pañcarakṣā* goddess described in the Buddhist Tantras as an emanation of Akṣobhya. She is four-armed and one-faced. She originates from the syllable *hum*. *Sādhana* 401.

Mahāmātṛkāsundarī: A name of *kuṇḍalinī* which personifies the fifty letters (*mātṛkās*) of the Sanskrit alphabet. The 51 coils of *kuṇḍalinī* are also known as *mātṛkās* or subtle forms of the gross letters or *varṇas*.

Mahāmāyā: The body of glory and power; it is the transfiguration of the ordinary body caused by purging all the impurities by the several ways and means prescribed in the Siddha tradition. Mahāmāyā is also an epithet of the Female Principle conceived of as the supreme being owing to her impersonation of the forces of Prakṛti or Māyā.

Mahāmāyūrī: A goddess of the Pañcarakṣā group and an emanation of Amoghasiddhi. The three-faced and six-armed form of Mahāmāyūrī is described in *Sādhanamālā* 400. Her complexion is green. In another form she is three-faced and eight-armed, her symbol being the 'mendicant bowl'. *Niṣpanna* 42.

Mahāmudrā: A form of bodily posture intended to maintain physical fitness and mental alertness. In this the fingers of both hands are specially utilized in forming different poses. *Gheraṇḍa* III. 1-3. Mahāmudrā also stands for woman and the female organ. In Tantric Buddhism, when the *bodhicitta* (q.v.) moves upward, a transcendental knowledge and realization is produced and it is called the *mahāmudrā*. In the *Śrīsaṃpūṭa* four *cakras* are associated with four *mudrās*, viz., *karmamudrā*, *dharmamudrā*, *mahā-mudrā* and *samayamudrā*. *Mahāmudra* is also associated with the goddess Pāṇḍarā.

Mahanāda: Same as *śabda-brahman* (*brahman* in the form of sound) and its constituent *anāhata-nāda* (so called because this sound has a spontaneous origin and is not produced by friction or percussion). *Mahānada* is also different from that form of *nāda* (q.v.) which is produced from the union of *kāraṇa-vindu* and *bīja* (q.v.). It is caused by the unmanifested sound of the letters which is conveyed by the *kuṇḍalinī*. It serves as a link between the Para and Apara Nādas, between conscious and non-conscious elements.

Mahānāda: Holy resort of the goddess Māheśvarī mentioned in the *Bṛhannīlatantra* V. It is same as modern Mahanād in Hooghly district, West Bengal.

Mahānadī: River sacred to the goddess Mahodayā mentioned in the *Bṛhannīlatantra* V. It runs through Orissa.

Mahā-Nīlasarasvatī: A form of Mahācīnatārā (q.v.). According to a legend recorded in the *Sammohatantra*, Nīla Sarasvatī or Ugratārā was born in a lake called Cola on the western side of mount Meru. The name Cola is probably connected with *kul*, *kol*, the common word for lake in the west and north of the T'ien-shan in the pure Mongolian zone.

The cult of this goddess is said to have been discovered by Siddha Nāgārjuna in Tibet (*ārya-nāgār junapādaiḥ bhoṭeṣu uddhṛtam*).

Mahānirvāṇa Tantra: Regarded by scholars as a 'refined' work; the present form is not much earlier than eighteenth century. It is burdened with Vedantic elements; the earlier form was probably Buddhist. It discusses the doctrine of *brahman*; upholds also a Śākta monotheism with Durgā as the highest Prakṛti; explains the Sāṅkhya *tattvas* as well; emphasizes *kula* practices and the rituals of the five Ms; says that wife may also act as Śakti in the case of the householders. It refers to *bhairavī-cakra* and *tattva-cakra*; deals with duties of *varṇas* and *āśramas* and king and his officers; is against caste restrictions in the case of those who have undertaken Tantric initiation; describes ten sacraments and Śaiva marriage; deals with *śrāddhas*, *prāyaścittas* and *vyavahāra* apart from the usual *dīkṣā*, *nyāsa*, *puraścaraṇa*, *mantras* and so forth. It has an element of progressiveness and modernism. Published by Ādi Brahmasamāj Calcutta 1876; Eng. trans. by M.N. Dutt, Calcutta 1900; by A. Avalon, London 1913. The Ādi Brahmasamāj edition was prepared from three manuscripts—one belonging to the library of the Samāj, the second supplied by Durgadas Chaudhuri and the third taken from the library of Raja Rammohun Roy. The *Mahanirvāṇa* represents the best of the sophisticated Tantric tradition.

Mahāpaśu: The uninitiated individual. *Niruttara* XII.

Mahāpātāla: A three-faced and six-armed form of Avalokiteśvara holding in the three right hands *vajra*, *viśvavajra* and *utpala* and in the three left a banner, a bell and *kamaṇḍalu*.

Mahāprakāśa: Saiva-Tantric teacher of the Krama system who flourished in Kashmir in the twelfth century. He is mentioned in the *Parimala* commentary on the *Mahārtha-mañjari* as author of several *stotras*.

Mahāpratisarā: A goddess of the Pañcarakṣā group who has a yellowish red halo and is three faced. She is twelve-armed. Her left hands hold jewel, discus, thunderbolt, arrow, sword and protection pose and the right thunderbolt, noose, trident, bow, axe and conch. *Niṣpanna* 42. Elsewhere she is an emanation of the Ratnasambhava; either three-faced and ten-armed or four-faced and eight-armed. *Sādhana* 401-2.

Mahāpratyaṅgirā: Tantric Buddhist goddess, an emanation of Akṣobhya whose origination is from the syllable *hum*. She is blue in colour, six-armed and one-faced. *Sādhana* 402.

Mahārāga: Intense emotion or attachment. In the *Kriyāsaṃgraha* it is said that the nectar-like *bodhicitta* (q.v.) is to be meditated upon as melting through *mahārāga*. The bliss produced from it is called *mahārāga-sukha*. The intensity of the bliss through which the mind attains a transcendental stage where all the principles of phenomenalism vanish is also *mahārāga*.

Mahārasa: Nātha concept of great juice which—as Soma or moon-power—resides below the *sahasrāra* (central cerebral region). The yogī, by the culture of the body (*kāya-sādhana*) consumes it through the *vakra-nālā*, the curved duct or nerve channel connecting the spinal cord with the brain and thus receives an immutable divine body.

Mahāratnakīrti: Three-faced and six-armed form of Avalokiteśvara holding a fruit, a lotus and a conch in his three right hands and a bow, a whip and displaying the *namaskāra-mudrā* in the three left.

Mahāratnakula: Three-faced and six-armed form of Avalokiteśvara carrying a sword, a lotus and a rosary in his three right hands and a book and two lotuses in his three left.

Mahāraudrī: Same as Mahākālī (q.v.) and Kātyāyanī (q.v.) who is described in the *Tantrasāra* as having five faces, each containing three eyes, and in each pair of hands she holds in the left and right a spear and a trident, a bow and arrow, a sword and shield, and exhibits the *vara* and *abhaya* poses. This description is also given in the *Merutantra*. She has also a ten-faced form. *Puraścaryārṇava* IX, 754; XI. 956.

Mahārthadarśana: Another name of the Krama view of Kashmir Śaivism expounded by Abhinavagupta in his *Tantrāloka* and other works.

Mahāsahasrapramardinī: Goddess of Pañcarakṣā (q.v.) category who is an emanation of Vairocana. White in colour she has six arms. She holds a sword, arrow, and shows the *varada* pose on one side and a bow, noose and *paraśu* on the other. *Sādhana* 400.

Mahāsahasrasūrya: A form of Avalokiteśvara having eleven faces and eight hands. The two principal hands exhibit *abhaya* pose. Other hands in the right show rosary, *cakra* and *varada* pose and in the left bow, arrow and lotus. This form of Lokeśvara is very popular in Tibet.

Mahāsāmrājyā Dīkṣā: A form of initiation which is a precondition of Kaula-*sādhanā*.

Mahāśaṅkhamālā: Rosary made of the bones of a human skull. This is effective in muttering the *mantra* of Tārā. The bones situated between the ears and the eyes are knowns as *mahāśaṅkha*. *Tantrasāra* 30.

Mahāsaṅkhanātha: Three-faced and six-armed form of Avalokiteśvara showing *namaskāra-mudrā* and two *vajras* in his three right hands and a noose, an arrow and a bell in his three left hands.

***Mahāsannipāta*:** A collection of Sūtras belonging to the fourth century AD. The *Ratnaketudhāraṇī* (q.v.) of Tantric affiliation is a part of it. *Mahāsannipāta-Ratnaketu-dhāraṇīsūtra*, edited by N. Dutt and S.N. Sharma in *Gilgit Manuscripts*, Vol. IV, Calcutta 1959, 114 ff.

Mahāsarasvatī: A variety of Buddhist Sarasvatī who is white in colour, youthful and good-looking. She shows the *varada mudrā* with the right hand and holds a lotus in the left. Thus she is similar to Tārā. The only distinguishing feature is that she is surrounded by four goddesses, identical in form with herself. They are Prajñā, Medhā, Śruti and Mati. *Sādhana* 329.

Mahāsetu: 'The great bridge', to cross the great ocean of knowledge (*mahāvidyārṇava*), a technical means to attain the goal of liberation. It is of the nature of *mantra* and has to be muttered. The *mahāsetu* of Tripurasundarī is *hrim*, of Kālī *krim*, of Tārā *hum* and of others *strīm*. *Śaktānanda-taraṅginī* X; *Puraścaryārṇava* VI. 529.

Mahāsiddhas: Great Siddhas (q.v.) who can fulfil their desires by mere thought and are able to conquer death, commune with gods, enter unperceived into dead bodies, move through the air, understand all terrestrial truths, bewitch people, perform miracles and cultivate good qualities. It is the honorific title given to certain Buddhist saints of Tantric connection such as Saraha, Nāgārjuna, Śabarī-pa, Anaṅgavajra, Indrabhūti, etc.

Mahāśitavatī: Rakṣā or protection-goddess who is red in complexion, has three faces and eight arms and is symbolized by the lotus. *Niṣpanna* 42. Elsewhere she is described as an emanation of Amitābha and having four hands. *Sādhana* 401.

Mahāśrī Tārā: 'Tara of great beauty'. An emanation of Amoghasiddhi (q.v.) this two-armed green-coloured youthful goddess exhibits *vyākhyanā mudrā* and is accompanied by Ekajaṭā, Aśoka-kāntā Mārīcī, Jāṅguli and Mahāmāyūrī (q.v.). *Sādhana* 244-5.

Mahāsthāmaprāpta: A Bodhisattva, white or yellow in complexion, having six lotuses or sword as his recognition symbol. *Niṣpanna* 50, 58.

Mahāsukha: Literally the highest pleasure (*nirvāṇa*), the *summun bonum* and the real manifestation of Bodhicitta (q.v.) according to Tantric Buddhism. In order to have this experience woman and man should first realize that they embody Prajña (q.v.) and Upāya (q.v.) respectively and that only their physical, mental and intellectual union can bring the experience of the highest truth (see Samarasa and Yuganaddha). The union of man and woman, of Upāya and Prajñā, brings the maximum pleasure in which all mental action is abdicated and the world around forgotten. A blissful experience of non-duality pervails.

Mahāsukhacakra: A name for the Buddhist Uṣṇīṣakamala and Hindu Sahasrāra (q.v.). It is the seat of great bliss and also called *mahāsukhakamala*. Samaya-mudrā refers to the Bodhicitta in the *Mahāsukhacakra*.

Mahāsukhakāya: The fourth *kāya* (body) of the Buddha invented by the followers of Vajrayāna and Sahajayāna.

Mahāsukha-samādhi: A self-absorbed spiritual meditation during which the meditator loses his identity in great bliss, the doctrine of which was expounded by Lord Buddha to the goddess Vārāhī in *Ḍākārṇava* 135.

Mahāsukhasthāna: The place of great bliss. According to the Buddhist Siddhācaryas it is the topmost station, or the central cerebral region, as the storehouse of psychic energy carried through 32 nerve channels; the female generative organ in certain Hindu and Buddhist Tantric texts.

Mahāsukhayāna: 'Vehicle of great bliss', a designation for esoteric Buddhism mentioned in *Kriyāsaṃgraha*.

Mahāśūnya: Kashmir Śaiva concept of the *bīja-bhūmi* (seed-ground) of all ideas or *bhāvas* in the consciousness of Śiva. It is described as void (*śūnya*) or great void (*mahāśūnya*), because nothing has manifested itself at this stage. *Paramārthasāra* 14. In Nāgārjuna's *Pañcakrama*, *mahāśūnya* is regarded as one of the four gradations in the Śūnyatā doctrine. It proceeds from the union of Prajñā and Upāya or *āloka* and *ālokābhāsa* or Śūnya and Atiśūnya and it is called the intuition of light (*ālokopalabdhi*) and is of absolute nature (*pariniṣpanna*).

Mahāśvetā: A Tantric *mantra*, the muttering of which on Sunday while fasting is deemed to yield all desires.

Mahattarī Tārā: A form of Śyāma (green Tārā) who is distinguished by the *vajra-paryaṅka* attitude in which she sits and also by the fact of her being represented without any companion whatsoever.

***Mahāvairocana*:** A Mantrayāna Buddhist Sūtra, belonging to the category of the Caryā-tantra, which invloves a consecration and postures for meditation as well as the rituals of symbol diagram. It was translated into Chinese in the eighth century by Śubhākara Siṃha who hailed from Kaliṅga and studied at Nālandā. There is a Tibetan version though the original Sanskrit is missing. It purports to lead the aspirant to a realization of identity with the Dhyānī Buddha Vairocana who is the Great Illumination and attended by the Bodhisattva Samantabhadra. The means for the communion with Vairocana include incantation (*mantra*), diagrams (*maṇḍala*), symbols (*mudrā*) and concentration (*yoga*). Partial translation by Tajima in *Etude sur le Mahāvairocana-sūtra*, Paris, Maison-neuve 1936.

Mahāvana: Holy resort of the goddess Bhadrā, Bhadrakālī or Bhadreśvarī. It is identified with Purāṇa-Gokula, six miles from Mathura. *Bṛhannīla* V.

Mahāvidyā: See Daśa Mahāvidyā. The ten Mahāvidyā goddesses of the Purāṇas are connected with the Dakṣayajña legend, but in the Tantras they have nothing to do with the story of Dakṣa's sacrifice. The names of ten Mahāvidyās vary in different Tantras. Sometimes thirteen, or more often eighteen, Mahāvidyā goddesses are mentioned. In the *Nāradapāñcarātra* it is stated that there are seven crore Mahāvidyās and seven crore Upavidyās (*saptakotirmahāvidyā upa-vidyāśva tādṛśa*). *Prāṇatoṣaṇī* V. 6, 376.

***Mahāvidyā Tantra*:** A work dealing with the Mahāvidyās (q.v.). It is a compilation of 249 passages meant for Tantric practitioners. It refers to a number of Tantras and has a list of Tantric *gurus*. It also deals with alchemy. Though P.C. Ray assigns this Tantra to a period earlier than the fourth century AD, the present form of the text seems to be of a much later date.

Mahāyoni: Female sex organ. It is the supposed triangle of the *sahasrāra* (q.v.). *Kaulajñānanirṇaya* 256.

Mahendra, Mahendrapura: Holy resort of the goddess Mahāntaka or Jagadīśvarī identified with the celebrated peak of the same name in Ganjam district, Orissa. *Jñānārṇava* V. 66-7; *Bṛhannīla* V.

Maheśvarānanda: Śaiva-Tāntric teacher and a prolific writer. He flourished in the twelfth-thirteenth century AD and was widely acclaimed as the celebrated author of *Mahārthamañjarī* with its commentary, *Parimala*. Ed. by T. Ganapati Sastri. Travancore Sanskrit Series, no. LXVI, 1919.

Maheśvarapura: Same as Māhismatī, holy resort of the goddess Svāhā, consort of Agni, which is modern Maheśvara in Indore in Madhya Pradesh or less probably, Mandhata in Nimar district, *Matsya* XIII. 42, *Devī-bhāgavata* VII. 30.71.

Māheśvara Siddha: See under Sittar, Siddhacikitsā, Rasa, Raseśvara Darśana.

***Maheśvara Tantra*:** A late Tantric text with Śākti affiliation. It was probably compsed in Bengal. It is in 51 *paṭalas* with 3,060 verses. It (I. 15; XXVLII) mentions that there are 64 Tantras and refers specially to 25 Vaiṣṇava Tantras (XXVI. 16-20). It holds that the Buddhist Tantras are misleading and meant for cruel rites (XXVI. 21-2). Published in Chowkhamba Sanskrit Series, Benares.

Maheśvarī, Māheśvarī: One of the *tattvas* (fundamentals) of Śaiva Siddhānta doctrine. From the *śuddha-māyā* sent by Śiva-Śakti originate Nāda, Bindu, Sādākhya, Māheśvarī and Śuddhavidyā, the five fundamentals. Maheśvarī is associated with the subtle *vaikharī* sound. According to the Puranic accounts, Maheśvarī or Māheśvarī is also the name of one of the seven or eight Mātṛkās who came into existence, with the elements of Śiva during the fight between the gods and the demons. Māṭṛkās (q.v.) represent the Sanskrit alphabet in Tantric tradition. According to the *Svacchandatantra*, the letters of *Ca-varga* (consonants beginning with *Ca*) are presided over by Maheśvarī, also described as Maheśānī and Śivānī.

Mahīdhara: Author of the Naukā commentary on the *Mantramahodadhi* who hailed from Ahicchatra and settled at Varanasi in the sixteenth century.

Mahimāsiddhi: A kind of miraculous attainment acquired through the rituals of *aṣṭadala-padma* (q.v.). *Nityaṣoḍaśikārṇava* VIII. 143.

Māhismatī: Holy resort of the great goddess mentioned in *Kubjikā* VII. See Maheśvara-pura.

Maināka: A holy mountain associated with the goddess Akhilavardhanī. There are many mountain-peaks of this name.

Maithuna: Sexual intercourse which is regarded as one of the *pañcamakāras* (five Ms); alternately called Yuganaddha (q.v.). For its procedure and reasons see *Mahānirvāṇa* VI. 10 ff., *Prāṇatoṣaṇī* VII. 4.548. For its substitutes see com. on *Paraśurāmakalpasūtra* X. 63; *Mahānirvāṇa* VIII. 172-3. For spiritual interpretation see *Kaulamārgarahasya* 256-7; *Yoginītantra Pūrva*, VI; *Kulārṇava* V.

Maitreya: The future Buddha who also figures in Tantric Buddhism. It is said that he will come to the earth 4,000 years after the disappearance of Gautama Buddha for the deliverence of all sentient beings. Asaṅga is said to have visited Maitreya in Tuṣita heaven and to have been initiated by him into the mysteries of Tantra. He is golden in colour. His hands exhibit *vyākhyāna mudrā* and his recognition symbol is a *nāgakeśara* flower in full bloom. Maitreya heads the list of Bodhisattvas in the Mañjuvara Maṇḍala of the *Niṣpannayogāvalī*.

Makāra: See Pañcamakāra.

Mala: Fetters which cover knowledge and actions of the individual; it is a term used by different Śaiva schools. It is same as *pāśa*, the cause of wordly existence and suffering. It is of three types—*āṇava, kārma* and *māya*. Āṇavamala is the impurity of the bound self which is responsible for non-intuition. *Karmamala* is responsible for contuining the fetters of embodiment and *māyāmala* covers the individual soul entirely.

Mālā: Garland of flowers, seeds of fruits like *rudrākṣa* and beads. Kālī wears a garland of severed human heads. Rosary is *akṣamālā*.

Malaśakti: Power of that nescience which covers and fetters the *jīva* (individual). Śrīkumāra's com. on *Tattvaprakāsa* I. 9.

Mālava: Modern Malwa. The eastern part is known as Ākara or Daśārna with its capital at Vidiśā, and the western part as Avantī or Apara-Malava with its capital at Ujjayinī. Some unspecified site of this region is regarded as the holy resort of the goddess Mālinī or Raṅginī. *Jñānārṇava* V. 66-7; *Bṛhannīla* V.

Malaya: Southern part of the Western ghats to the south of the Nilgiris which is said to be the holy resort of the goddess Rambhā or Kalyāṇī. Variant reading Mānasa. *Matsya* XIII. 28, *Devībhāgavata* VII. 30.57.

Mālinī: A class of female partner (ramyāśakti) of the Tantric aspirant. *Niruttara* XIV. Mālinī is also the name by which the *māṭṛkā* (q.v.) letters are known.

***Mālinīvijaya-Vārtika*:** A commentary written by Abhinavagupta on some of the obscure verses of the *Mālinīvijaya Tantra* also called Śrīpūrva Śāstra. Aspects of Krama philosophy have occasionally been dealt with in this work. The portion, discovered hitherto, is philosophical in nature aimed at a criticism of some Nyāya-Vaiśeṣika formulations. See *Mālinīvijayottara*. Ed. by M.S. Kaul, Kashmir Sanskrit Series XXXI, 1911.

***Mālinīvijayottara*:** A Tantra of Kashmir Saivism regarded by Abhinavagupta as the essence of the Trika system. It is dedicated to the goddess Mālinī who is often equated with Māṭṛkā or Mātā signifying the letters of the alphabet. The text consists of 23 chapters called adhikāras. It deals with the infinite, omniscient, all-doing and all-sustaining supreme controller of the universe; the self manifested in Śiva, Mantramaheśa, Mantreśa and Mantra; Guru and stages like Śākta, Śāmbhava, etc.; *tattvas* in four heads—earthly, material, pertaining to Māyā and pertaining to Śakti;—three chief forms of Śakti—*aparā* (*ghoratarā*), *parāparā* (*ghorā*) and *parā* (*aghorā*); four stages on the path of yoga; acceptable and avoidable categories of knowledge; and duties of the initiated. Ed. by M.S. Kaul, Kashmir Sanskrit Series XXXI, 1911; rpt. Delhi 1984.

Māmakī: Spiritual consort of the Dhyānī

Buddha Akṣobhya. She belongs to the *vajra* family and originates from the germ syllable *mam*. She is blue in colour and embodiment of the element of water. *Advayavajra-saṃgraha* 43.

Māṃsa: Flesh; it is one of the *pañcamakāras* (five Ms). It is supposed to be the body of Śiva. Ginger, garlic, etc., can be used as its substitute.

Mānasa: Lake, popularly known as Mānasa-sarovara, which is the source of the river Śatadru (Sutlej) in the Himalayas. It is the holy resort of the goddess Kumudā or Gaurī. *Matsya* XIII. 27; *Bṛhannīla* V. In the *Pīṭha-nirṇaya* it is described as a *pīṭha* where the right hand of Śati fell. The *Śivacarita* refers to it as a Mahāpīṭha.

Mānasa-dīkṣā: See Manodikṣā.

Mānasī: Śāsanadevatā of the Jain Tīrthaṃkara Dharmanātha according to the Digambara tradition. She rides a tiger and holds in her six hands a lotus, bow, *varada* pose, goad, arrow and another lotus.

Mānavaugha: One of the three classes of *gurus*, the two others being *divyaugha* and *siddhaugha*. While the two latter classes have divine and supramundane affiliations respectively, *gurus* of the *manavaugha* class are associated with human beings. The hierarchy of the *manavaugha* gurus comprises *parameṣṭhi-guru*, *parāpara-guru*, *parama-guru* and *guru*. These four also constitute *svaguru* category. *Śyāmārahasya* VI; *Tantrarāja-tantra* II. 4; *Tārābhakti-sudhārṇava* V. 196; *Mahānirvāṇa* VI. 98; *Tārātantra* IV. 3; *Puraścaryārṇava* III. 206-7.

Mānavī: Name of the Śāsanadevatās of the Tīrthaṃkaras Śītalanātha and Śreyāṃśanātha found in the Digambara tradition. Her warlike attributes—goad, noose, bow, etc.—are symbols befitting her characteristic of a Yakṣiṇī (guardian angel). The benign symbols such as *varada*, fruit, lotus, etc., indicate her Vidyādevī form.

Maṇḍala: A gathering of aspirants who perform collectively the rituals of the Five Ms. They sit in a circle (*cakra*) along with their female partners, with the *nāyaka* or *adhīśvara*, the central figure of the ritual and his consort in the middle. *Kaulāvalinirṇaya* VIII, *Mahānirvāṇa* VIII. 154-9. Maṇḍala also denotes Tantric diagrams of which there are many varieties such as, *sarvatobhadra*, etc. In the Buddhist Tantras *maṇḍala* is the magic circle—mystic figures and diagrams and figures of the gods and goddesses constitute the *maṇḍalà*. In the *Niṣpannayogāvalī*, *Kriyāsamuccaya* and *Vajrāvalināma-maṇḍalopāyikā* there are descriptions of a great number of deities constituting the circle. Maṇḍalas for ordinary Tantric worship are geometrical diagrams drawn on the ground with powder using five colour. Several maṇḍalas are described in *Śāradātilaka* III. 106-9. It specially deals at length with the construction of *sarvatobhadra-maṇḍala* which is regarded as common to all forms of worship. The *Jñānārṇava* XXIV. 8-10, XXVI. 15-17 equates *maṇḍala* and *cakra* emphasizes the nine angles to be drawn on an altar which represent the abodes of the deities.

Maṇḍalapīṭha: One of the four zonal *pīṭhas* according to which the provenance of the Tantras and Āgamas is determined, the other three being Vidyā, Mantra and Mudrā *pīṭhas*. *Mudrāmaṇḍalapīṭham tu mantrapīṭhaṃ tathaiva ca; vidyāpīṭham tathaiveha catuṣ-pīṭha tu saṃhitā*.

Mandara: Mandar hill in Bhagalpur district, Bihar, described as the holy resort of the goddess Kāmacāriṇī or Bhuvaneśvarī. *Matsya* XIII. 27, *Devībhāgavata* VII. 30.56.

Māṇḍavya: Same as Māṇḍavyapura, modern Mandor in Jodhpur, Rajasthan, which is regarded as the holy resort of the goddess Māṇḍavī or Māṇḍukī. *Matsya* XIII. 42; *Devībhāgavata* VII.30.71.

Maṅgalakoṭa: Holy resort of the goddess Maṅgalā. It is at the junction of the Ajay and Kunur rivers in the Burdwan district, West Bengal. *Prānatoṣaṇī*, *Bṛhannila* V.

Maṅgalāṣṭaka: A group of eight Bhairava Āgamas (q.v.) represented by *Bhairavī*, *Picu*, *Samudbhava*, *Brāhmīkalā*, *Candrākhyā*, *Maṅgalā*, *Vijayā* and *Sarvamaṅgalā*.

Mani: Jewel. In most cases *Cintāmaṇī*, the one that satisfies all desires, is meant.

Maṇipura: A Tantric *cakra* (nerve plexus) located near the navel region. It is also known as *nābhicakra*. It looks like a ten-petalled blue lotus, each petal containing a letter. Within the lotus there is a triangle the colour of the rising sun. On the three outer sides of the triangle are represented three *svastikā* symbols. The goddess Lākinī presides over this *cakra*. On the ten petals are the letter Ḍa, Ḍha, Ṇa, Ta, Tha, Da, Dha, Na, Pa, and Pha. *Ṣaṭcakranirūpaṇa* XIX-XXI.

Mañjughoṣa: A variety of Mañjuśrī (q.v.) that closely resembles Mañjuvajra (q.v.). He is golden in colour with the lion as his vehicle. He shows the *vyākhyāna mudrā* (q.v.) with his hands and his symbol is the lotus held in the left hand.

Mañjuśrī: Most important Bodhisattva, equal to Avalokiteśvara in status. The *Āryamañjuśrī-mūlakalpa* contains the earliest iconographical description of Mañjuśrī. Forty-one *sādhanas* are attributed to him in *Sādhanamālā*. According to *Niṣpanna* 48 he is three-faced and six-armed. In the three right hands he has sword, *varada mudrā* and arrow, and in three left hands he has the *prajñāpāramitā* manuscript, blue lotus and bow. In sculptural representations, which are numerous, he is generally one-faced and carries a sword in his right hand for destroying ignorance, and a manuscript in his left hand indicating transcendental wisdom. These symbols are often placed on lotuses.

***Mañjusrīmūlakalpa*:** See *Ārya-Mañjuśrī-mūlakalpa*.

***Mañjuśrīnāmasaṅgīti*:** A Tibetan Tantric text, closely allied with *Ārya-Mañjuśrī-mūlakalpa* (q.v.), which was edited by Minayeff in his Russian work on Buddhism as early as 1887. It was formerly a Yogatantra but later became attached with Kālacakra (q.v.). A Sanskrit manuscript of this text is in Salu.

Mañjuvajra: A form of Mañjuśrī who is golden yellow in colour and shows the images of five Dhyānī Buddhas on the head crest. His hands display the *dharmacakra mudrā* (q.v.). A blue lotus bears the *prajñāpāramitā* manuscript. Mañjuvajra images are fairly common, often two female figures of Keśini and Upakeśinī are depicted on either side.

Manobhavā: Name of Tripurasundarī mentioned in the *Siddhayāmala* in connection with the *kavaca* of Śrividyā or Ṣoḍaśī in which form she protects the sex organ of the amulet-holder. *Tantrasāra* 526-7.

Manodīkṣā: Also known as *mānasa* or *vedhamayī dīkṣā*, it is a form of initiation performed only by the Guru's thought and mental action. *Kulārṇava* XIV.

Manoharā: One of the eight Yoginīs (Aṣṭa-yoginī, q.v.) described in the *Tantrasāra*. As her name implies, she has deer-eyes, an autumnal-moon-like face, red lips like the *bimba* fruit and her body is smeared with sandaī paste. Though dark-complexioned, she has a pleasing appearance and full breasts. She wears *cīnāṃśuka*, i.e. dress made of China silk.

Manonmanī: A state of transcendental bliss which comes about as a result of *bhaktiyoga-samādhi* (loss of identity through deep meditation in a spirit of absolute devotion). *Gheraṇḍa* VII. 14-5. Mononmanī is also the name of the *śakti* of Sadāśiva in south Indian Śaivism.

Mantra: Śakti (power) in the form of sound, words, and letters. It is a cultivation (*man, manana*) of true knowledge necessary to get rid of wordly fetters. Rāghava on *Śāradātilaka* VIII. 1. *Mantra* is *brahman* or ultimate reality in the form of sound. Letters, words and sentences are its different forms through which *Śakti* appears in the individual. *Gandharvatantra* XL. 10; com. on *Tantrārajatantra* XXVI. 36-43, *Śāradātilaka* I. 55, II. 57. The *mantras* constitute the backbone of Tantric Buddhism. The Vajrayānists maintain that the *mantras* are endowed with great powers, and can confer Buddhahood or omniscience. The *mantra* is powerful when it comes from a preceptor who is pure, and has repeated it continuously and is able to visualize the *mantra* -person or the deity sacred to the *mantra*. When the *mantra* becomes powerful, the vibrations let loose by the worshipper react on the universal *śūnya*. *Mantras* are of illimitable varieties. The power of *mantra* is two-fold—*vācaka* and *vācya* (q.v.). There are two grades of sound, the more subtle state is known as *bindu* and the most subtle as *nāda*. The expression of sound is possible through letters, and hence the letter is the *bīja* (seed) of *mantra*. The mystery of *mantra* is equated also with the principle of creation.

Mantra-Adhva: Blood, to be purified for Tantric sādhanā. *Adhva* means contituents of the body. These are of six types—*bhuvana* (cerebral organs), *mantra* (blood and flesh), *pada* (muscles), *varṇa* (veins), *dhātu* (bones) and *rīta* (fluid substance). Rāghava on *Śāradātilaka* V. 95-6.

***Mantrābhidhāna*:** A collection of 35 verses in which the meanings of the letters of the alphabet are given.

Mantra-Caitanya: Consciousness latent in *mantra* which must be roused by efforts. *Prāṇatosaṇī* IV. 1, 222; *Puraścaryārṇava* VI. 528; *Gandharvatantra* XXIX. 24-25.

Mantrādya: *Praṇava* or *Om*. According to Bhāskara-rāya *mantrādya* is that which precedes the utterance of *mantra*. *Oṃkāra vartulastāro mantrādyaḥ praṇavo dhruvaḥ*. *Saubhāgyabhāskara* on *Lalitasahasrānama* 24.

***Mantramāharṇava*:** A medieval Tantric text which deals especially with the Yantras besides the usual Tantric topics.

***Mantramahodadhi*:** A Tantric manual, a very popular work which gives *mantra* of various deities, composed by Mahīdhara in 1589. Published by Rasikmohan Chatterjee in his *Vividhatantrasaṃgraha*, Calcutta 1876; ed. J. Vidyasagara, Calcutta 1893; Venkateswar Steam Press, Bombay 1910. About Mahīdhara and his works see *ABORI*, XXI, 248-61.

Mantra-naya: Also known as *mantrāyāna* it is one of the two subdivisions of the Mahāyāna in which great importance is attached to *mantra*. Naropā and Advayavajra were inclined to use the term *mantra-naya* to designate Tantric Buddhism. *Sekoddésaṭīkā* 2-5, *Advayavajrasaṃgraha* 14. According to this school, if the *mantras* are applied in a proper way anything can be performed. Their power and effiicacy are beyond dispute; they offer the possiblility of attaining Buddhahood to the aspirant. *Sādhanamālā* I, 87, 270, 332, II. 575, 606; *Guhyasamāja* 27 ff.; *Hevajra* I. 50 ff. The *mantra-naya* or *mantra-yāna* is the precursor of Vajrayāna (q.v.) and its offshoots are Kālacakrayāna (q.v) and Sahajayāna (q.v.).

Mantranyāsa: One of the many kinds of *nyāsa* which means mentally invoking a god or gods, *mantras* and holy texts to come to occupy certain parts of the body in order to render the body a pure and fit receptacle for worship and meditation. The *Brahmapurāṇa* (LX. 35-9) deals with the *nyāsa* of the *mantra* '*om namo nārāyaṇāya*' on the fingers and on other parts of the body.

Mantrāṅga: Limbs of a *mantra* which consists of *ṛṣi* (seer) *chandas* (metre), *devatā* (god), *bīja* (seed), *śakti* (power) and *kīlaka* (locking), *Śyāmārahasya* I; *Kālītantra* I. 8-9. In *Tripurasiddhānta devata* is omitted and in its place *nyāsa* (feeling the deity in different parts of the body) and *dhyāna* (meditation) are added. *Dīpikā* on *Śrividyāsutra* I. According to *Gāyatrītantra* II, a *mantra* has five limbs: *āvāhana* (invocation), *dhyāna* (meditation), *smaraṇa* (recollection), *samarpaṇa* (offering over) and *visarjana* (immersion). The *Gautamīya-tantra* II insists on *ṛṣi*, *chandas*, *devatā* and *viniyoga* (application).

Mantrapuruṣa: A term for deity in the Tantric Buddhist tradition. The deity is supposed to be the embodiment of a cluster of letters which are dynamized by intense concentration and repetition. The second set of letters set up strong vibrations and ultimately condense themselves in the form of deities. This is called the *mantrapuruṣa* or *mantra* person.

Mantrārtha: Understanding the significance of *mantra*; it is the sense of identity of the preceptor, deity and *mantra*, a belief that every letter of it is the manifestation of the real nature of Śakti, and the merger of the aspirant is the essence of the object of his exercise. *Puraścaryārṇava* VI. 526; *Tantrarāja* XXXV. 64-6.

***Mantrārthābhidhāna*:** Said to be a part of *Varadātantra*, this work comprising 49 metrical lines explains various *bījas* in terms of their corresponding deities.

Mantra-śakti: The power *mantra*; it is beyond thinking and reasoning. *Paraśuramakalpasutra* I.8. It is neither good nor bad. It is determined only by the purpose of its application.

Mantrasaṃskāra: Ten ways of purifying *mantras*. They are *janana*, *jīvana*, *tāḍana*, *bodhana*, *abhiṣeka*, *vimalīkaraṇa*, *āpyāyana*, *tarpaṇa*, *dīpana* and *gupti*. *Tantrasāra* 52.

Mantraśikhā: A purificatory flame aroused in the body during the march of *kuṇḍalinī* (q.v.). *Puraścaryārṇava* VI. 527-8; *Haṭhayogapradīpikā*, IV. 10.

Mantrasiddhi: Spiritual attainment through *mantras*. Those who have attained it acquire a special brightness of the body and an ever peaceful state of mind. *Puraścaryārṇava* VI. 557-8.

Mantra-snāna: Symbolic or partial bathing by means of *mantra*. The *bāhya* (external) *mantrasnāna* is required in cold countries or seasons, when there is scarcity of water, in inaccessible regions, in old age and during illness. It is done by washing certain parts of the body and performing *nyāsa* (q.v.) on different parts of the body. *Āntara* (internal) *mantrasnāna* is purely symbolic. It is by the awakening of *kuṇḍalinī* (q.v.) and pushing it to the *sahasrāra* (q.v.) region that one may have bath in the supposed ocean of ambrosia. Rāghava on *Śāradātilaka* IV. 2; *Tārābhakti-sudhārṇava* V. 131; *Puraścaryārṇava* 499.

Mantraśodhana: Purification of *mantra* with *prāṇayāma* (breath-control) according to the Yonimudrā process (q.v.) and reciting it one thousand and eight times. Rāghava on *Śāradātilaka* II, III.

Mantra-śuddhi: Purification of *mantra* by reciting the letters from left to right and right to left. *Kulārṇava* VI.

Mantra-tanu: Transformed state of the body achieved either by Yogic exercise or by the use of drugs. The body of God is also called *mantratanu.*

Mantra-yāna: A form of Tantric Buddhism. See Mantra-naya.

Mantra-yoga: The *haṃsa* (q.v.) practice of yoga by inhaling (*haṃ*) and exhaling *(saḥ)* of breath. *Yogāśikhopaniṣat* I. 130-2. Mantra-yoga is one of the four divisions of the science of yoga. It comprises all those forms of *sādhanā* in which the mind is controlled by means of its subject. In Mantra-yoga the aspirant is selective about the object of his contemplation. This is called *sthūla* or *saguna dhyāna* of the gods in images, emblems, pictures, markings, maṇḍalas, *yantras*, *mudrās*, etc. It is the simplest form of yoga.

Māntrī-dīkṣā: Initiation in which the guru by *mantra* and rituals gathers into himself spiritual strength and then consecrates the disciple. Rāghava on *Sárādātilaka* V. 127-40. It requires *kumbha, maṇḍala* and other objects. *Prānatoṣaṇī* II. 4.11.

Mantroddhāra: Identification of the letter functioning as seed (*bīja*) *mantra* of a particular deity from an apparently unintelligible phrase. *Tantrasāra* 182.

Māraṇa: The black act of killing through rites and spells.

Māri: The fourth deity in the Dhāriṇī series of goddesses who is reddish-white in colour and holds in her left hand a needle and thread. Her right hand holds the *viśvavajra*. *Niṣpanna* 57

Mārīcī: Emanation of Vairocana. She is invoked by the Lamas of Tibet at the time of sunrise which shows her connection with the sun. Her chariot is drawn by seven pigs. Sixteen *sādhanās* of the *Sādhanamālā* describe six distinct forms of Mārīcī—Aśokakāntā, Āryā, Māricipicuva, Ubhaya-varāhanana, Daśabhujaśita and Vajra-dhātvīśvarī. She may have one, three, five or six faces and two, eight, ten or twelve arms. She is generally accompanied by four attendants—Varttali, Vadali, Varāli, and Varāhamukhī. She is generally recognized by the sow face and the seven pigs that pull her chariot.

Mārīcīpicuva: Also known as Aṣṭabhujaita-Mārīcī or Saṃksipta-Mārīcī. These two names denote two distinct varities of Mārīcī although both are endowed with three faces and eight arms and carry similar weapons in their hands. Mārīcīpicuva holds a needle and thread in the first pair of hands, *aṅkuśa* and noose in another pair, bow abd arrow in the third pair, and *vajra* and *aśoka* flower in the fourth. She has three faces, each displaying a mixture of three different sentiments (*rasa*) —*śṛṅgāra* (erotic), *vīra* (heroic) and *harṣa* (pleasure). Surprisingly she tramples Prajñā and Upāya. She is surrounded by four attendant goddesses Varttali, Vadali, Varāli and Varahāmukhī.

Mārtaṇḍakālī: One of the twelve forms of Kālī mentioned by Abhinavagupta. *Tantrāloka* IV. 157 ff. Mārtaṇḍa means the sun. There are twelve such Mārtaṇḍas who represent the five organs of action. The five organs of knowledge, mind and intelligence are identified with the egoity of the supreme being which accounts for the name Mārtaṇḍa-Kālī.

Maruta Varṇa: One of the five divisions of the *varṇas* (letters) according to the *bhūtātmaka* or elemental division. A, ā, e, ka, ca, ṭa, ta, pa, ya, and ṣa belong to this division which belong to the element of air, Com. on *Śāradātilaka* II. 10-11.

Matākhyāṣṭaka: A group of eight Bhairava Āgamas (q.v.) represented by Raktākhya, Lampaṭākhya, Lakṣmi, Matta, Cālikā, Piṅgala, Utphullaka and Viśvādyā.

Mataṅga: Holy resort of the goddess Mātaṅgī. It is same as Mātaṅgavāpī, modern Mātaṅgāśrama at Bakraur on the Phalgu, opposite Bodhgaya, Bihar. *Prāṇatoṣaṇī*, *Bṛhannīla* V.

***Mataṅgaparameśvarāgama*:** Āgama belonging to the Śaiva Siddhānta school which is divided into four sections—Vidyā, Kriyā, Yoga and Caryā. The Vidyāpāda, containing 26 *Paṭalas*, has a commentary by Rāmakaṇṭha. It deals with various metaphysical doctrines from the Siddhānta point of view. The three other sections deal with the practical aspects of *sādhanā*. *Vidyāpāda* with com. of Ramakaṇṭha, ed. by N.R. Bhatta, Pondicherry, 1977.

Mātaṅgi: Slayer of Mataṅgāsura who protects from all danger according to the *Kubjikā-tantra*; born in the hermitage of Mataṅga as incarnation of Kālī; has various forms such as Mātaṅgiṇī, Ucchiṣṭa-Mātaṅgī, Rāja-Mātaṅgī, Sumukhi-Mātaṅgī, Vaśya-Mātaṅgī and Karma-Mātaṅgī. Her *mantra* is *Om hriṃ kliṃ huṃ mātaṅgaī phaṭ svāhā*. She is dark, three-eyed, has a crescent on the forehead, is seated on golden throne, decked in ornaments, and heavy breasted. Her four hands contain goad, sword, noose and club. *Prāṇatoṣaṇī* V. 6, 374; *Puraścaryārṇava* IX. 827-32; *Tantrasāra* 361. *Mātaṅgī-krama* by Kulamaṇi Gupta and *Mātaṅgīpaddhati* by Ramabhaṭṭa give details about the worship of this form of Śakti.

Mātrā: A means of prāṇayāma (q.v.). *Puraścaryārṇava* III. 161.

Mātṛkā: Divine Mother. It is also the name of mystic letters. The *vācaka* entity of a *mantra* is composed of a sentence which itself is made of words as the words are of sound. The more subtle state is *nāda*. The expression of sound is possible through letters, hence the letter is the *bīja* (seed) of the *mantra*. Hṛm, Krṃ, Aim, Srim, Klim, etc., are thus *bījas*. Just as a big banyan tree remains in subtle form in the banyan seed, so also all the doctrines remain subtle in a single letter conceived of as *bīja* (seed). That is why the alphabet is thought of as Mātṛkā or divine mother. The fifty letters of the alphabet are regarded as *mātṛkāvarṇa*. They are equated with the rosary of Sarasvatī and the garland of ṣkulls of the goddess Kālī. Mātṛkā-varṇas (letters) are Mātṛkā-Śakti and they are of two types—those having *bindu* or *anusvāra* (*ṃ*) and visarga (ḥ) suffixes, and those without them. They are felt in different parts of the body through the process of *nyāsa*. The traditional Mātṛkās or Divine Mothers such as Mahālakṣmī, Brāhmī, Māheśvarī, Kaumārī, Vaiṣṇavī, Vārāhī, Cāmuṇḍā, etc., are conceived in the Tantras as presiding deities of different groups of Mātṛkā-varṇas.

***Mātṛkācakraviveka*:** A Tantric treatise composed by Svatantrānandanātha. Its commentary is written by Śivānanda. Published in Sarasvati Bhavana Series, Benares 1934.

***Mātṛkānighaṇṭu*:** Attributed to Mahīdāsa, this text lays down the meanings of the letters of the alphabet in 59 verses starting with the significance of *om*.

Mātṛkānyāsa: Feeling the Mātṛkās or *śakti* manifested in the form of letters in different parts of the body. It is of two kinds—*antarmātṛkānyāsa* and *bahirmātṛkānyāsa*. *Tantrasāra* 88 ff. See Mātṛkā.

***Mātṛkārṇava*:** A Tantric text belonging to the Kādi (q.v.) school. It is devoted to the cult of Tripurā or Ṣoḍaśī. The form of her worship is known as Śrīvidyā which has come down in two main currents—Kādividyā and Hādividyā.

Mātṛkāvarṇa: The letters from A to Kṣa, each symbolizing one aspect of Śakti or the Great Mother. They are equated with Sarasvatī and Mālinī. These letters constitute ideas and images and from them the knowledge of the *bījamantras* is derived. They are of two types—those having *bindu* or *anusvāra* (ṃ) and *visarga* (ḥ) suffixes, and those without them. Letters of the former category are generally used for the *mantras*. See Mātṛkā, Mātṛkānyāsa.

Mātṛ-sadbhāva: A philosophical conception of Kālī when she is described as the manifestation of *parā-saṃvit*, the ultimate reality. She is conceived in this connection in twelve forms—Sthitināsa, Yama, Saṃhāra, Mṛtyu, Rudra, Mārtaṇḍa, Paramārka, Kālāgnirudra, Mahākāla, Sṛṣṭi, Rakta and Mahābhairava. *Tantrāloka* IV. 157 ff.

Matsya: Fish. It is one of the Five Ms. Three types of fish—*Uttama*, *madhyama* and *adhama*—are described in *Śyāmārahasya* III, *Mahānirvāṇa* IV. 8. Substitutes for *matsya* are cakes made of pulses and other articles. Com. on *Paraśurāmakalpasūtra* X. 63. Symbolically *matsya* is described as that which destroys the fetters and leads to the way of salvation. *Prānatoṣaṇī* VII. 2. 508.

Matsyaśodhana: Purification of fish, one of the five *makāras*, with *mantras*. Com. on *Paraśurāmakalpasūtra* X. 63.

***Matsyasūkta*:** A large work in 64 chapters attributed to Halāyudha, court scholar of king Lakṣmaṇasena (1185-1205). Passages from this Tantra are abundantly quoted in later works.

Matsyendranātha: Founder of Yoginī-kaula according to the *Kaulajñānanirṇaya*. The doctrine of this school agrees with the Buddhist Sahajayāna in many respects.

According to the Nātha Siddha tradition, Matsyendranātha, also known as Mīnanātha, sprang from the navel of Ādinātha and learnt the supreme knowledge (*mahājñāna*) from Śiva through deception which is why he was cursed to forget it at the time of need. In Nepalese and Tibetan tradition he is identified with Avalokiteśvara. On his refusal to marry and settle down, Gaurī, by means of her personal charms deflected him which resulted in his banishment to the country of Kadalī women. He began to rule over the Kadalī women forgetting his identity and attainments. Eventually he was rescued by Gorakṣanātha. He came back to his senses and started his spiritual career once again. In Nepal he is regarded as the guardian deity. In the Buddhist tradition he has been identified with Lui-pā. Among the Bengali Muslims he turned into a Pir called Manchandalī or Mochrā. The historical Matsyendranātha probably belonged to the beginning of the tenth century AD.

Māyā: Also known as Avidyā and Prakṛti (q.v.) the term is used in many senses. In Advaita Vedānta it is regarded as the energy of Īśvara which becomes transformed into *upādhi* (limitation), the unmanifested matter (*avyaktaprakṛti*) from which all existence issues. The Tantras use various non-dualist and dualist interpretations of *māyā* promulgated by different Vaiṣṇava and Śaiva schools. In the Tantras the passive subjective aspect of the ultimate reality is conceived as male, whereas the active counterpart has always been conceived as female. In Vedānta *brahman* is devoid of qualities and indeterminate, while the world-illusion is ascribed wholly to the activity of *māyā*, and this *māyā* in popular Vedantic literature bears an air of femininity. As an active creative principle *māyā* could easily become an epithet of the supreme goddess who is popularly known as Mahāmāyā. Māyā in the form of impure and pure matter is regarded as one of the *tattvas* or fundamentals of Śaivism and Śāktism. In the Tantras Māyā or Māyā-śakti, composed of three *guṇas*, is the material cause of the world. See Avidyā-śakti, Māyā-śakti.

Māyājālakrama: A form of Avalokiteśvara after whom the *Māyājālatantra* was composed. He is five-faced, three-eyed, twelve-armed. Two of the right faces are white and red in colour and the two left are of yellow and green colour. *Sādhana* 86.

Māyāmala: One of the three impurities (malas) according to the Śaiva schools. It covers or conceals the individual soul as a result of which it begins to experience objects as distinct from the self.

Māyāpura: Also known as Māyāpurī and Māyāvatī, it is a holy resort of the goddess Māyā which has been located in the Hardwar region. *Kubjikā* XVIII. 42 ff.; *Bṛhannīla* V. *Matsya* XIII. 33.

Māyā-śakti: Also known as Avidyā-śakti and Triguṇā-śakti (q.v.). It is the material cause of the universe. According to the Tantric cosmogony Māyā-śakti is a conscious principle, but it is veliled consciousness, i.e. consciousness appearing as unconscious. Thus it is that particular aspect of *cit* (consciousness) which it assumes as the material cause (*upādāna-kāraṇa*) in creation. An analogy of a *caṇaka* (grain) may be cited in order to show the functioning of Māyā-śakti. A *caṇaka* has two seeds which are so close to each other that they seem one; they are surrounded by a simple sheath. The seeds are Śiva and Śakti within the sheath of *Māyā*. When the sheath is unpeeled, Māyā-śakti operates, and the two seeds come apart. The sheath unrolls when the seeds begin to germinate and in this process we come across the emergence of multiple selves and objects forming the universe. It is also said that the will-power (*icchā-śakti*) of the supreme being has its first manifestation in the Māyā-śakti. The *para-brahman* appears to be many due to its own Māyā-śakti. *Mahānirvāṇa* IV. 34. Due to the effervescence of Māyā the universe is produced: *sā māyā kṣobhamāpannā viśvaṃ sute samantataḥ*. *Tantrāloka* II. 164-5. Māyā-śakti is single, all-pervading, subtle, without any beginning, infinite and permanent. Ibid. IX. 149 ff. It is *tirodhāna-śakti* which covers the real nature of things which is why it is *mala* or *ajñāna*. *Īśvarapratyābhijñā* III. 1.7 ff. See Avidyā-śakti.

***Māyātantra*:** A late work in fourteen chapters. It deals with the *mantras*, *yantras*, *kavacas*, etc., of Mahāmayā symbolized by Durgā and other goddesses. The mode of their worship is also described along with the method of creating fire-altars for *homa*, etc. Apart from the usual Tantric topics such as *Puraścaraṇa*, *nyāsa*, etc., it refers to the efficacy of yoga and to rituals for progress and prosperity in wordly life. Some chapters of the *Māyātantra* deal with the worship of Durgā and Jagaddhātrī. Here Durgā is said to be Navadurgā having nine forms such as Kālī, Kātyāyanī, Īśānī, Muṇḍamardinī, Cāmuṇḍā, Bhadrakālī, Bhadrā, Tvaritā and Vaiṣṇavī.

Māyiamala: See *māyāmala*. According to Kashmir Śaivism it represents the whole series of categories of existence, beginning from the covers or *kañcukas*. These *kañcukas*, like *māyā* of the Vedantic tradition, are somehow associated with *brahman* or Śiva as creative energy with the potentiality of yielding the material principles. As such they are the cause of the physical organism on the subjective side. These evolve into the physical world constituted by the gross elements which is a reflection on the objective side.

Mayūra: Peacock. Mayūrapiccha signifies feathers of a peacock.

Mekhalā: Holy resort of the goddess mentioned in the *Rudrayā-mala*. It is Mekala, capital of Mekaladeśa in the Amarkantak region or Mekaliganj in Cooch Bihar, North Bengal.

***Merutantra*:** A Tantra of recent origin. It is an extensive work in 35 chapters and 16,000 verses. It refers to the English people and the city of London. Published by Venkatesvar Steam Press, Bombay 1908.

Mīnākṣī: Great goddess of the South, especially of Madurai which represents the *dvādaśānta* or the cerebral hemisphere. She manifests herself in different forms of Bālā, Bhuvaneśvarī, Gaurī, Mātaṅgī, Śyāmā, Pañcadaśākṣarī and Mahāṣoḍaśī.

Mīnanātha: See Matsyendranātha.

Miśrabindu: The *bindu* produced from the equilibrium of *prakāśa* (static) and *vimarśa* (dynamic) aspects of Śakti. *Cidvallī* on *Kāmakalāvilāsa* 6-7.

Miśrācāra: One of the three-fold classifications of the traditional seven stages of the Tantric spiritual progress, the other two being Samayācāra and Kaulācāra according to Lakṣmīdhara, the commentator on the *Saundaryalaharī*. According to Bhāskararāya, there are three schools in the cult of Śrividyā—Samaya, Kaula and Miśra: *samayamataṃ kaulamataṃ ceti vidyopastau matatrayam. Saubhāgyabhāskara* com. on *Lalitāsahasranāma* 144.

Miśramata: See Miśrācāra.

Mitra-varṇa: Friendly letters. Letters are called Mātṛkās and all of them are potential *śaktis*. Letters are sometimes arranged in accordance with the political *maṇḍala* theory, in which besides the friendly (*mitra*) letters there are *ari* (enemy) and *udāsīna* (indifferent) besides *madhyama* (intermediate) and other classes of letters. Com. on *Śāradātilaka* II. 10-1.

Modinī: Also known as Mohinī, she is the presiding goddess of the third angle of *aṣṭakoṇacakra*. Her status is that of Rahasyayoginī. According to the *Vāmakeśvara-tantra* she is the presiding deity of the letters beginning with Ca. *Nityaṣoḍaśikārṇava* I. 191-2; *Bhavanopaniṣat* 21; *Gandharvatantra* XVII. 74.

Mokṣa: Liberation, *summum bonum* of Tantric *sādhanā*. There are various processes for attaining *mokṣa*. But first of all initiation under a competent guru is required. *Kulārṇava* XIV. 3. After initiation the aspirant has to perform five-fold or ten-fold *puraścaraṇa* (q.v.). *Śaktisaṅgama*, Sundarī, III. 155-6; *Purascaryārṇava* VI. 413-14. Not all the ways are easy, nor are they meant for all. For example, the *sādhanā* with Five Ms—in which the underlying principle is that the elements of downfall may also be successfully used for upliftment (*yaireva patanaṃ dravyyrmukti-staireva coditā*)—requires persons who have proved their competence in other ways. *Kulārṇava* V. 106-113. But at the same time it is said that while in other systems the attainment of liberation is a great time-consuming process, in Kauladharma it is much easier to achieve. Ibid. II. 10-13, 22. *Kauladharmāt paro dharma nāsti jñāna tu māmaka*; *yasyānuṣṭhāna-mātreṇa brahmajñānī naro bhavet. Mahānirvāṇa* IV. 43.

***Mṛgendra Tantra*:** Tantra of Raudra class of Kashmir Saivism which contains two sections *vidyāpītha* and *yogapītha*. The first section is divided into 13 *paṭalas* (chapters) which describe three basic categories of Śaivism, namely, Paśu, Pāśa and Pati. It also deals with *māyā* (fetters). Since it refers to surgical instruments the text must be later than the seventh century AD. On circumstantial evidence it may be placed in the tenth century AD. The work is said to be an abridgement of the *Kāmikā Tantra*. Ed. with com. of Bhaṭṭa Nārāyaṇakaṇṭha by M.S. Kaul, Kashmir Sanskrit Series, 1930.

***Mṛtyunāsaka Tantra*:** Part of *Vijayāgama* on which the followers of the Suddhamārga depend. It deals with liberation by monadic transformation of the body.

Mṛtyuñjaya-mantra: Also called *mṛta-sañjivanī-mantra*, it is prescribed for purifying the mind (*cittaśuddhi*) in *Mahānirvāṇa* VIII. 243. It is the same as *tryambaka-mantra* of *Ṛgveda* VII. 59.12.

Mṛtyuvañcana Tārā: A form of white Tārā the distinctive feature of which is that the goddess bears a wheel on her chest. She is unattended and sits in *vajraparyaṅka* (q.v.) attitude.

Mudgara: Hammer. It may also mean a staff or a mace.

Mudrā: Posture of the body, especially of hands, needed for Yogic exercise and spiritual attainment. According to the *haṭhayoga-pradīpikā* IV. 37 *mudra* is so called because it removes pain and sorrow. *Gherenḍasaṃhitā* III. 1-3 records such *mudrās* as Mahā, Nabho, Uḍḍīyāna, Jālandhara, Mulabandha, Mahābodha, Khecarī, Viparītakarī, Yoni, Vajroli, Śakticālanī, Tadagī, Māṇḍuki, Śāmbhavī, Pañcadhāriṇī, Aśvinī, Pāsinī, Kākī, Mātaṅgī and Bhujaṅginī. See also *Haṭhayoga pradīpikā* III. 128. Mudrās like Varada, Abhaya, Namaskāra, Añjali, Dharmacakra (q.v.) etc., are commonly found in iconic representation symbolizing the quality associated with the deity. The common Tantric *mudrās* are *āvāhanī*, *sthāpanī*, *sannidhāpana*, *sunnirodhanī*, *sammukhi-karaṇī*, *sahalikṛti*, *avaguṇṭhana*, *dhenu* and *mahāmudrā* (q.v.). Yoni, Khecarī, Kākinī, Aśvinī and Śakticālana are meant for arousing the sleeping *kuṇḍalinī*.

Mudrā: The fourth *tattva* or fundamental of Tantric *pañcatattva* or *pañcamakāra*. Mudrā denotes cereals which are to be fried and consumed by the aspirant. Pulses, puffed rice or wheat, gram, chick-pea, etc., serve the purpose of *mudrā*. *Mahānirvāṇa* VI. 10. By consuming *mudrā* the practitioner symbolically digests hope, thirst, scorn, fear, hatred, conceit, shame and attachment. Destruction of all these makes an individual almost equal to Śiva.

***Mudrālakṣaṇa*:** A work on *mudrās* appropriate to Viṣṇu and other gods, a manuscript of which is in the Deccan college (Ms. 291 of 1887-91). Some of these *mudrās* in connection with the worship of individual gods occur in *Viṣṇusaṃhitā* VII and *Jñānārṇava* IV.

***Mudrānighaṇṭu*:** Said to be a part of *Vāmakeśvara-tantra* it purports to present in 145 stanzas the significance of various *mudrās* and articles carried by the deities. It names and defines nine *mudrās* (*avāhanī* and others) that may be employed in the worship of any god. Then it enumerates 19 *mudrās* appropriate for Viṣṇu worship, 10 for Śiva worship, 7 for Gaṇeśa worship and 1 for the Sun (called Padma) and *mudrās* pertaining to Śakti, Agni, Tripurā and other deities. It also refers to other *mudrās* mentioned in other texts as well. It says that the *mudrās* should be practised secretly under the cover of a garment and not in presence of many people.

Mudrā-*pīṭhas*: One of the four symbolic *pīṭhas* (sects) of Tantric *sādhanā*. The others are *vidyā*, *mantra* and *maṇḍala*.

Mudrāśodhana: Mudrā (cereals) are purified by uttering certain verses—*ṚV* I. 22.20-1. *Prānatoṣaṇī* VII. 2.

***Mudrāvidhi*:** A Jain work dealing with 114 *mudrās*. Another Jain work which lists 73 *mudrās* is known as *Mudrāvicāra*.

***Muhūrtakalpadruma*:** Composed by Viṭṭhala Dikṣita in 1628 it is an astronomical-cum-astrological work dealing with *muhūrta*, the auspicious time for undertaking anything. It especially deals with the times and places for various kinds of *dīkṣā* (q.v.).

Mūkamantra: A class of defective *mantras*. Rāghava or *Śāradātilaka*. II. 111

Mukhaśodhana: Purification of the tongue by *mantras*. *Prāṇatoṣaṇī*, VI. 1. 215.

Mukundā: Kettledrum goddess of Tantric Buddhism who is described as being white in colour, having two arms and plying on the drum with her fingers. *Niṣpanna* 76.

Mūlādhāra: The first of the six nerve-plexuses, situated in the lowest extremity of the spinal cord where the *kuṇḍalinī* is coiled. It is said that the earth with all its spheres is situated on the *mūlādhāra-cakra*, otherwise called *brahmapadma*. It is symbolically viewed as a crimson lotus with four petals representing four forms of bliss—*parama*, *sahaja*, *yoga*, and *vīra*, and four letters—Va,

Śa, Ṣa and Sa. In the pericarp is the square *dharā-maṇḍala* (the supposed earth) within which is *dharā-bīja* (seed of earth symbolized by the letter La). The presiding deity of this *cakra* is Ḍākinī. In the pericarp there is also the *yoni* triangle (female organ), *kāma-vāyu* (vital wind of passion) and *kāma-bīja* (vital fluid symbolized by the letter *klim*). Above this Svayambhū-liṅga round which the *kuṇḍalinī* is coiled. *Ṣaṭcakranirūpaṇa* II-XIII; *Mantramahodadhi* IV. 19-25; *Jñānārṇava* XXIV. 45-54; *Nirvāṇatantra* X, *Mahānirvāṇa* V; *Devībhāgavata* XI. 1.43.

Mūlakarma: The technique of bringing under one's control a person or a woman by herbs and *mantras*.

Muṇḍamālā: The garland of severed heads which Kālī wears. The heads are fifty in number and they represent fifty *mātṛkās* or letters (*varṇas*). It symbolizes the *śabda-brama* concept.

Muṣala: Pestle.

N n

Nābhipadma: Another name of *maṇipura-cakra* (q.v.). *Ṣaṭcakra-nirūpaṇa* XIX.

Nāda: Sound. There are two grades of sound, the subtle is known as *bindu* and subtler as *nāda*. The expressed aspect of *bindu* and *nāda* which constitutes sound is *bīja* (q.v.). In Tantrism, the supreme being (Para Śiva or Parā Śakti) is soundless without any vibration. When Parā Śakti begins to express itself in creation, its first vibration is known as *nāda*. It is the manifestation of the consciousness of the supreme being revealed as sound. This manifestation is thought of in terms of the union of Śiva and Śakti (the static and kinetic aspects, also known as *prākāśa* and *vimarśa*, of the same ultimate reality). The thrill of the pleasure of this union (*maithuna*) is also known as *nāda*. The condensed form of *nāda* is *bindu*. *Śāradātilaka* I. 6 ff; Kālicaraṇa on *Ṣatcakranirūpaṇa* XXXIX; *Prapañcasāra* I. 41. For other aspects and interpretation see *bindu* and *bīja*.

Nādabrahma: Nāda conceived as *brahman* in the form of primordial sound expressed in *pāra, paśyanti, madhyamā* and *vaikharī* (q.v.). *Cidvallī* on *Kāmakalāvilāsa* IX; Lakṣmīdhara on *Saundaryalaharī* XLI.

Nāḍa-pāda: See Nāro-pā.

Nādaśakti: The energy or *śakti* of *nāda* (q.v.). It has four *kalās* known as *indhikā, dīpikā, rocikā* and *mocikā*.

Nāda-Udbhūtā: Sixteen *kalās* or śaktis which are said to have been derived from *nāda* (q.v.). These are Nivṛtti, Pratiṣthā, Vidyā, Śānti, Indhikā, Dīpikā, Rocikā, Mocikā, Parā, Parāparāyanā, Sukṣmā, Amṛtā, Āpyāyinī, Vyāpinī, Vyomarūpā and Ānandā. *Prapañcasāra* III. 25-7: *Śāradātilaka* II. 26.

Nādayogasamādhi: A yogic attainment which is to be achieved by means of Khecarī-mudrā. (q.v.) *Gheraṇḍasaṃhitā* VII.9.

Nāḍī: Nerves of the human body. These are supposed to be 72,000 in number. There are 72 major nerves; the most important 14 are *iḍā, piṅgalā, suṣumnā, gandhārī, hastijihvā, yaśasvinī, alambuṣā, kuhū, śaṅkhiṇī, sarasvatī, vāruṇī, puṣā, viśvodarā* and *payasvinī*, *Prāṇatoṣaṇī*, I. 4.32-3. See Upanāḍī.

Nāḍīśuddhi: Purification of nerves. When done by *mantras* it is known as *samāna* and then by physical exercises like *dhauti*, etc., it is known as *nirvāna, gheraṇda* V. 36.

Nāgabodhi: South Indian Tantric Ācarya who was the teacher of Vajrabodhi, the celebrated monk of Vajrayāna sect. He flourished about the beginning of the eighth century.

Nāgakeśara: Flower, symbol of Maitreya.

Nagarakoṭa: A *pīṭha*, holy resort of the goddess Jālandharī or Jvālāmukhī, mentioned in the *Ain-i-Akbari*. According to the *Caṇḍīmaṅgala*, the head of Satī fell here. It is in the Kangra district of Himachal Pradesh.

Nāgārjuna: Author of *Rasaratnākara*, *Kakṣapuṭatantra* and *Ārogyamañjarī*, and redactor of the *Suśrutasaṃhitā*, who flourished in the eighth century. Two other treatises of Nāgārjuna—*Yogasāra* and *Yogāṣṭaka*—are recorded in the Nepal collection of manuscripts. He was different from the Nagarjuna I, the famous exponent of the Mādhyamika system, though he was also a Buddhist and his *Rasaratnākara* bears the stamp of Mahāyāna Buddhism.

Nāgas: Serpents. They have the character of water spirits and the power to bring or withhold rains. The Tantric deities are fond of ornaments of snakes, especially those of their eight lords.

Naimiṣa: Same as Naimiṣāraṇya, the holy resort of the goddess Liṅgadhāriṇī. *Matsya Purāṇa* XIII. 26; *Devibhagavata* VII. 30. 55, *Bṛhannīla* V. According to *Prāṇatoṣaṇī* it is the holy resort of the goddess Prajñā. Naimiṣa is modern Nimkhar or Nimsar and Misrikh regions in Sitapur district, Uttar Pradesh.

Nairātmā: The Śakti or Prajñā of Heruka. Nairātmā is in union with Heruka when the latter is known as Hevajra. When represented singly, Nairātmā is two-handed, conceived as dancing in *ardhaparyaṅka* on a corpse, the right hand holding *kartari* and the left *kapāla* with *khatvāṅga*. She is blue in complexion. *Sādhana* 451.

Naivedya: Food offering to the deity. It is to be offered with *dhenu-mudrā* (sign of cow) and the *prāṇāhuti* or offering to the *prāṇas* or 'life-breaths'. When material food is offered, it denotes the offerings of life-principle or the Parā Prakṛti. The *amṛta* (ambrosia, deathlessness) in the *naivedya-mantra* (*amṛte amṛtodbhave amṛtavarṣiṇī amṛtaṃ srāvaya srāvaya svāhā*) denotes the immotal factor of 'spirit' offered in Tantric worship.

Nakulī: Mongoose, the characteristic animal of Jambhala. The mongoose is believed to be the receptacle of all gems and when the god of wealth presses the animal, it vomits forth all the riches.

Nakulīśa: See Lakulīśa.

Nalahati: Holy resort of the goddess Śephālikā which is an *upa-pīṭha* according to the *Śivacarita*. Here the head-channel of Satī fell. In the *Pīṭhanirṇaya* the goddess is Kālī. In both the texts the Bhairava is Yogeśa or Yogīśa. In *Śivacarita* another *upa-pīṭha* named Nalasthāna is mentioned with Bhrāmarī as the presiding deity. Both the sites refer to Nalhati in Birbhum district, West Bengal.

Nalinī: One of the eight yoginīs (Aṣṭayoginī, q.v.) described in the *Tantrasāra*. She charms the three worlds. She is fair-complexioned, wears beautiful clothes and ornaments and has the appearance of a pleasant dancing girl.

Nāmasaṅgīti: An emanation of Vairocana mentioned in the *Dharmakośasaṃgraha* of Amṛtānanda. He is one-faced, has twelve hands, is white in colour, has eyes half-closed in meditation and a smiling countenance. A form of Mañjuśrī is also known as Nāmasaṅgīti.

Namaskāra: The *mudrā* assumed by the Bodhisattvas when paying homage to the Buddhas or Tathāgatas, or by the minor deities to the principal ones. The hands, slightly bent, are raised in a line with the shoulder, fingers extended or slightly bent, with the palm turned upwards.

Nandipura: Holy resort of the *pīṭha* category of the goddess Nandinī mentioned in the *Pīṭhanirṇaya*. The *Śivacarita* refers to it as an *upa-pīṭha*. Nandipura is near Sainthia in the Birbhum district, West Bengal.

Napuṃsaka-mantra: Mantras which are neither for the male deities (*puruṣa-mantra*) nor those intended for female deities (*strī-mantra* or *vidyā*). *Śāradātilaka* II. 57-8.

Napuṃsaka-varṇa: Letters which are neither male nor female. To this category belong long *ṛ* and long *ḷ*. Rāghava or *Śāradātilaka* II. 5-7.

***Nārada Tantra*:** A Tantric text quoted in *Varṣakriyākaumudī* which deals with *mudrās* specially appropriate in the worship of Viṣṇu, such as Śaṅkha, Cakra, Gadā, Padma, Kaustubha, Śrīvatsa. Vanamālā, Veṇu, etc.

Naradattā: Śāsanadevatā of the Jain Tīrthaṃkara Muni Suvrata. She is represented as seated in *bhadrāsana* posture (sitting posture in which both legs are pendant) showing her four hands which hold *varada*, rosary, citron and trident.

Nārasiṃhī: Name of a Mātṛkā. She represents the female form of the man-lion (*narasiṃha*) incarnation of Viṣṇu.

Naratattva: One of the three sections of the thirty-six *tattvas* or fundamentals of Śaivism others being Śaktitattva and Śivatattva. Nara-śakti-śivātmakatvana traividhyam. *Tantrāloka* IX, 244. While Śivatattva is monistic and Śakti-tattva dualistic, Naratattva is pluralistic according to the Kashmir school of thought.

Nārāyaṇakaṇṭha: A Kashmirian author, son of Vidyākaṇṭha who wrote a commentary on the *Mṛgendratantra*.

Narmadā: River, sacred to the goddess of the same name who is her presiding deity. Some unspecified sites on this river are mentioned as *pīṭhas* and *upa-pīṭhas* in texts like the *Pīṭhanirṇaya*, *Bṛhannīlatantra*, *Prāṇatoṣaṇī* and so forth. It is the celebrated river rising from Amarkantak which flows into the Gulf of Cambay.

Nāro-pā: A great Siddha, an historical personality who flourished in the eleventh century and author of a whole series of works on the special modes of *sādhanā* preserved in the Tibetan tradition. His real name was Nāḍapāda and he was a disciple of Tilo-pā. Among his works specially important is his commentary on the *Kālacakra-tantra* (Sanskrit Ms. in Cambridge University Library, Add. no. 1364) known as *Sekoddeśaṭīkā* (ed. by M.E. Carelli, Baroda 1941), which purports to explain *kāla* as denoting the ultimate immutable and unchanging reality remaining in all the elements and *cakra* as the unity of three kinds of existence. Image of Nāro-pā is found in Bodhnath in Nepal. Nāro-pā was a teacher of Atīśa Dīpaṅkara (q.v.) in philosophical matters and before the latter's departure for Tibet he paid a visit to Vikramaśīlā Vihāra and encouraged him to go. Nāro-pā was the *dvāra-paṇḍita* of the northern gate of the Vikramaśilā monastery.

Nartakī: 'The dancing girl', an epithet ascribed to Prajñā in the *Hevajratantra*. She is so called because beginners cannot grasp her steadily.

Naṭanānandanātha: Author of the *Cidvallī* commentary on Puṇyānanda's *Kāmakalā-vilāsa*.

Nātha-Panthā: A non-Brahmanical cult having a complicated texture, heterodox rituals and ingredients from Tantra, Śaivism, Śāktism, Buddhism and local cults as well as from Islam. The aim of the esoteric practices of this cult is the attainment of the state of 'nativity', i.e. neutrality (*sahaja*) where there is no birth and death as such. Existence and extinction are resultants of man's desire and cognition. His fetters and his release are of his own creation, according to this system.

Nātha-Siddha: The Nātha Yogīs; they are supposed to have attained *siddhi*, i.e. psychic and supernatural power. These Siddhas include 84 Buddhist Siddhas mentioned in the Tibetan tradition, as well as the Raśesvara and Māheśvara Siddhas (q.v.) well-known for their knowledge of alchemy. Specially prominent are those who are traditionally associated with the foundation of *Natha-panthā* and who are credited with composing the texts expounding the system. They are Matsyendra or Mīnanātha, Gorakṣanātha, Jālandharī or Hāḍi-pā, Kṛṣnapāda or Kānha, queen Mayanāmatī, Cauraṅgīnātha, etc. See Siddhas.

Nāthayoga: Yogic practices for the attainment of the state of neutrality as prescribed in Nathism. A Natha Yogī, following the guru's instruction, has to check the downward flow of the semen, hold his breath and stabilize the mind. These processes are technically known as *bindudhāraṇa*, *pavana-niścāñcalya* and *cittanirodha*.

Naṭī: Female dancer. The term applies to Śakti when the goddess dances out of delight at the performance of her rituals. *Niruttara* XV.

Navacakra: The nine *cakras* or circles (actually these are triangular) of which Śrīyantra is constituted. According to the *Bhairavayāmala* five of these belong to Śakti and the remaining four to Śiva; thus the Śrīyantra consisting of nine *cakras* is the combined body of Śiva and Śakti. The five Śakti triangles are pointed upwards and the four Śiva triangles downwards. Lakṣmīdhara on *Saundaryalaharī* IX. Navacakra has three parts which deal symbolically with creation. Preservation and destruction. *Setubandha* com. on *Nityaṣoḍaśikārṇava* I. 47. It is also known as Āvaraṇacakra and is said to exist even in the human body. Ibid. on VI. 25-7.

Navadurgā: Durgā of nine forms worshipped especially in south India as the auspicious mother who transcends time and causation—in the lustrous flame, in a *yantra* (mystic diagram), or in figures drawn with rice-flour, turmeric powder and saffron. The worship includes all the Tantric rituals beginning with self purification (*bhūtaśuddhi*, *ātmaśuddhi*) and ending with oblations (*bali*, homa). Along with the *bīja mantras* the *durgā-sukta* is often chanted.

Navamīsiṃha: The minister of king Bupālendra of Nepal (1689-94); also known as Ādyānandana. He composed two extensive Tantric digests, the *Tantracintāmaṇi* and *Kulamuktikallolinī*. See *Descriptive Cat. of Sans. Mss. RASB*, VIII.

Navanāda: Nine Nādas, or special forms of sound, supposed to denote the nature of Kuṇḍalinī. These are known as *cinī, ghaṇṭā, śaṅkha, tantrī, karatāla, veṇu, bherī, mṛdaṅga* and *megha*. *Cidvallī* on *Kāma-kalāvilāsa* XXVII. The letters A, Ka, Ca, Ṭa, Ta, Pa, Ya, Sa and Kṣa are also known as Navanāda, Lakṣmīdhara on *Saundaryalaharī* XXXX.

Navarasa: Nine sentiments which are *śṛṇgāra* (erotic), *bhayānaka* (terrible), *raudra* (rage), *vībhatsa* (repulsive), *hāsya* (humorous) *vīra* (valorous), *karuṇa* (compassion), *adbhuta* (odd) and *śānta* (tranquil). Bhāskararāya's com. on *Bhāvanopaniṣat* XI.

Navavarga: Nine groups of letters beginning with A, Ka, Ca, Ṭa, Ta, Pa, Ya, Sa, and La. *Cidvallī* on *Kāmakalāvilāsa* XXVII.

Navayonicakra: Cakra or diagram consisting of nine triangles or *yonis*. It is also known as *navatrikoṇa*.

Nepāla: Also known as Naipāla it is country of Nepal. When the texts on the holy resorts of the goddess describe Nepāla as a *pītha* or *upa-pīṭha*, evidently some unspecified sites in this country are meant though the entire country in itself is the patron of Śākti-Tantric cults. In the *Kubjikā* XVIII. 42 ff, *Jñānārṇava* V.66 ff., *Bṛhannīla* V and *Prāṇatoṣaṇi* the presiding deity of Nepal is Punyadā. The *Pīthanirṇaya* calls it a *mahāpīṭha* where the knee of Satī fell. The goddess is known as

Mahāmāyā. The *Śivacarita* says that the right thigh of Satī fell here and the presiding deity is Mahāmāyā or Navadurgā.

Neti: See Śodhana.

***Netra Tantra*:** A Kashmirian Tantra written on the model of *Svacchandatantra*. It is of the nature of a manual dealing with the mode of initiation to the worship of Śiva. The work, commented upon by Kṣemarāja, consists of 22 chapters. Here Śiva is worshipped in the name and form of Amṛteśvara and Mṛtyujinnātha. It deals elaborately with the mystic significance of Amṛteśvara-*mantra*, purificatory rites, the yoginīs and their function and the gross and subtle forms of divine meditation. In his *Uddyota* commentary on *Netra-tantra*, Kṣemarāja (AD 975-1125) refers to Krama as a distinct system. Ed. by M.S. Kaul in Kashmir Sanskrit Series.

Nididhyāsana: Roughly translated as meditation. Actually the term means meditation of a higher order in which there is no sense of exertion of will, no conscious employment of the thinking process, in fact, no intellection whatsoever. According to Sureśvara it is a form of *aparokṣānubhūti* or direct realization of the Self. It is one of the three ways of Jñānayoga, the others being śravaṇa and manana—listening to the scripture and reflecting on that.

Nigama: Pure Vedic tradition, while Āgama stands as the general name of the texts of Tantra and those of theistic sectarian systems like Vaiṣṇavism or Śaivism. The second part of the *Nirukta* (IV-VI) is called Naigamakāṇḍa which includes the etymologies of a large number of *nigama* words, i.e. words extracted from Vedic passages. The Vedānta is known as Naigamānta Vidyā. The Smṛtis or Dharma Śāstras also belong to the category of *nigama*. But in Tantric tradition *Nigama* is stated by the goddess, heard by Śiva and established by Vāsudeva: *nirgato girijāvaktrāt gataśca giriśaśrutim, mataśca Vāsudevasya nigamaḥ parikathyate*. According to Bhāskararāya Vedic Āgamas are Nigamas since they are expressed at the command of the supreme being. *Saubhāgyabhāskara* on *Lalitāsahasranāma* 118.

Nigarbhā: Āvaraṇadevatā or Yoginī of Sarvarakṣākaracakra presided over by Tripuramālinī. *Setubandha* com. on *Nityaśoḍaśikārṇava* I. 164-5.

Nigarbhayoginī: Collective name of the goddesses, of the *navayonicakra* (q.v.). They are Sarvajñā, Sarvaśakti, Sarvaiśvaryapradā, Sarvajñānamayī, Sarvavyādhināśinī, Sarvādhārasvarūpā, Sarvapāpaharā, Sarvānandamayī, Sarvarakṣāsvarūpiṇī and Sarvepsitaphalapradā. *Nityaśoḍaśikārṇava* I. 187-90. They preside over ten fires which burn within human body. *Tantrarājatantra* XXXV. 10. They have the status of Āvaraṇa-devatā. *Gandharvatantra* V. 105.

Niḥśreyasa: The supreme good, the achievement of which, along with *abhyudaya* or upliftment in the physical, vital and mental planes, is the aim of the Tantras. It is to be achieved through the coordination of *karma, yoga, jñāna* and *bhakti*.

Nīlācala: Also known as Nīlaparvata it is the holy resort of the goddess Vimala according to the *Bṛhannīlatantra* and *Prāṇatoṣaṇī*. The *Śivacarita* refers to it as an *upa-pīṭha* and its presiding deity Vimalā as consort of Janannātha. See Virajā. This refers to the Puri temple said to be on the Nīla mountain in Orissa. But there is another Nīlācala in Kāmarūpa within the jurisdiction of the city of Guwahati which is the seat of the great goddess Kāmākhyā. The latter is also called Nīlapārvatī.

Niladaṇḍa: Presiding deity of the *nairṛta* corner according to the Buddhist Tantras. He is blue in colour, has three faces and holds staff, sword, jewel and lotus.

Nīlakaṇṭha: A form of Avalokiteśvra. This god has been modelled on Śiva. The *jaṭāmukuta* of Nīlakaṇṭha is adorned with the crescent and the effigy of Amitābha. He wears a tiger-skin and his throat is blue. Nīlakaṇta Lokeśvara is one-faced and two-armed and sits on a lotus in *vajraparyaṅka* attitude. He carries a bowl of gems.

Nīlakaṇṭha Caturdhara: The celebrated Maharashtrian commentator on the *Mahābhārata* who also wrote *Anūparāṇu*, a commentary on the Tantric work *Śivatāṇḍava*. He was an inhabitant of Pratiṣṭhānapura or Paithan and flourished in the seventeenth century. Another Maharashtrian Nīlakaṇṭha who flourished in the middle of the eighteenth century was the commentator on the *Devībhāgavata*. His other works are *Kātyāyanītantra*. *Śaktitattva-vimarśinī* and *Kāmakalārahasya*.

***Nīlapaṭadarśana*:** A spurious Tantric text. A story is narrated of a *guru* of the Sāmmitiya

Buddhist sect who went dressed in a blue dress to a courtesan. When asked in the morning by his disciples why he put a blue dress, he explained the great spiritual merit of the blue-coloured dress. Since then his followers began to wear blue and in their book called, *Nīlapaṭadarśana*, they popularized the view that *triratna* (three jewels) comprised Kāmadeva, courtesan and wine and not the commonly believed Buddha Saṅgha and Dharma. *Ind. Ant.* CCXXV, 1934, 216.

Nīlasarasvatī: One of the presiding goddesses of northern region (*uttarāmnāya*) often identified with Ugratārā and Ekajaṭā. She is invoked for granting good luck and prosperity. She is described as standing on a corpse in *pratyālīḍha* posture, short statured, having three eyes, wearing a tiger-skin and she holds chopper, skull, lotus and sword in four hands. Her *mantra* is *hriṃ strīṃ huṃ phaṭ*. The *Nīlatantra* propitiates her in eight stanzas reading which one is gifted with knowledge in all scriptures and poetic abilities. *Tantrasāra* 539-40. The colour of the goddess is blue. She has her origin from *cola* lake situated to the north of Meru: *mero paścimakule tu colanākhya hrado mahān, tatra jajñe svayam devī mātā nīlasarasvatī.* See Ekajaṭā, Ugratārā, Mahācīnatāra.

***Nīlatantra*:** An important Tantra consisting of 22 chapters composed probably in Bengal about the middle of the fifteenth century AD. It is referred to in many Tantric works indicating its popularity and authenticity. It is written in the form of questions asked by the Devī and answers given by Lord Bhairava. It deals with the worship and ritual of the primordial energy (*ādyāśakti*) in the form of Nīla, the importance of Guru, usual Tantric topics like *Puraścaraṇa*, etc., Mahācīnācāra, Kumārī-pūjā or Virgin worship, *śavasādhanā* or meditation on a deadbody, high praise of women, various *bīja-mantras* of Nīlasarasvatī and allied deities, *miśrācāra* meant for householders, Tārā-*mantra*, eight Bhairavas, Ugratārā and Śākta Pīṭhas.

Nimeṣa Śakti: The power of will by which the concept of Sadā-śiva in Kashmir Śaivism is characterized. *Īśvarapratyābhijñā* III 1.3, Nimeṣa technically means the latent condition of 'itness' within 'I-ness'.

Nimittakāraṇa: Efficient cause, as the potter is who makes the jar.

Nimittas: Signs, which make their appearance after meditation on one's own *mantra* according to Tantric Buddhism. The *nimittas* are of five kinds and appear in succession. The first is the sign of a mirage, the second that of smoke, the third is of fire-flies, the fourth is of light and the fifth of constant light like a cloudless sky. *Guhyasamāja* XVIII.

Nirmāṇa-cakra: One of the four nerve cycles in Buddhist conception. It is situated near the region of the navel and is connected with the *nirmāṇa* or *rūpa-kāya* (the material or created body) of Buddha. Like the Kuṇḍalinī Śakti (q.v.) of the Śākta Tantras, the Buddhist Tantras speak of a female energy having the force of fire, known as Caṇḍālī (q.v.) which resides in this *cakra*. *Nirmāṇa-cakra* stands for the element of earth represented by the syllable 'e' and presided over by the goddess Locanā who is associated with *karma-mudrā*.

Nirmāṇa-kāya: Historical personage of the Buddha. The historical Buddha is regarded as an incarnation of the eternal Tathāgata or the manifestation in condescension of the Dharmatathatā. In Tantric Buddhism *nirmāṇa-kāya* is the 'transformation body' which is the same as consciousness deified and individualized.

Nirodhinī: One of the five aspects of Śakti. *Śāradātilaka* V.79.

Nirukti: Goddess of the *prasaṃvit* (acknowledged branches of logical analysis) category symbolizing etymological analysis in Tantric Buddhism. She is described as having a red complexion and holds a chain in her hands from which a lotus is suspended.

***Niruttara Tantra*:** A medieval Tantric text presented in the form of dialogue between Devī and Śiva. It refers to the nature of Siddhavidyās and contemplation on them, details of the worship of Dakṣiṇakālī and of Rajanīdevī, various *cakras* and related Śaktis, *puraścaraṇa*, *abhiṣeka* and allied rituals, the Yogins, female devotees, *rahasya-pūjā*, different kinds of *veśyās*, women in *kulārcaṇa*, sexo-yogic practices, consecration of wine, the Mahavidyās and so forth. Edited and published by R.M. Chatterjee, Calcutta, 1876; edited with Bengali translation by N. Smrititirtha, Calcutta 1978.

Nirvāṇa: Buddhist term for liberation which is used indiscriminately also by non-Buddhist sects in the same sense (*mokṣa*, *mukti*, *apavarga*, etc.). In Tantra *nirvāṇa* also means liberation which is defined as amalgamation of the devotee with the deity which is to be achieved by performing faultlessly the rituals of *pañcatattva* or *pañcamakāra*. *Nirvāṇa-tantra* XI.

Nirvāṇa Dikṣā: The highest form of initiation in Āgamanta Śaivism. It is meant for those who are entitled to depend on the way of *jñāna* (knowledge) and who aspire for the *sāyujya* stage of spiritual progress in which they feel themselves as identical with god.

Nirvāṇa-kalā: An aspect of Śakti. It is said to be the essence of Amākalā; is conceived of as the seventeenth *kalā* and also as a goddess. *Ṣaṭcakranirūpaṇa* XLVII; *Kaṅkālamālinī* II.

***Nirvāṇa Tantra*:** A late-medieval work in 14 *paṭalas* presented in the form of a dialogue between Caṇḍikā and Śiva. Its subject matter includes the concept of *brahman*, creation of the world, concept of Prakṛti, nature of Gāyatrī, cosmic egg, yoga, characteristics of guru, Sannyasin, Avadhūta, Gṛhastha Brahmacārin, description of Brahmā, Viṣṇu and Rudra and their abodes, Bhuvaneśvarī, Sadāśiva, Mahāgaurī, *jñānapadma, sahasradalapadma* on the summit of Sumeru, Śiva's imparting of metaphysical knowledge, fivefold *tattvas* of the Vaiṣṇavas, *dasārṇamantra*, and *pañcattava*, etc. Edited and published by R.M. Chatterjee, Calcutta; ed. with Bengali trans. by N. Smrititirtha, Calcutta 1978.

Nirvāṇī: Śāsanadevatā of the Jain Tīrthaṃkara Śāntinātha according to the Śvetāmbara tradition. She is represented as seated on a lotus and four-armed, the attributes being a book, flower, a vessel and a bud.

Nirvikalpa samādhi: That blissful state of mind (*samādhī*) in which the distinction between the knower, knowledge and what is to be known vanishes absolutely.

Niṣkriyānandanātha: Śaiva-Tanric author of the eighth century whose *Chumna Sampradāya* deals with a sect of the followers of the Tantric Krama doctrine which banks on esoteric rituals.

***Niṣpannayogāvalī*:** Written by Abhayākara Gupta of the Vikramaśilā monastery who flourished during the reign of the Pāla king Rāmapala (AD 1084-1130). It is a work on *maṇḍalas*, 26 in all, describing the numerous deities of Tantric Buddhism. Many of the deities described in this work are not mentioned elsewhere and as such a large number of its descriptions are absolutely original. Ed. B.T. Bhattacharyya, GOS, CIX, Baroda 1949.

***Niśvāsatattva Saṃhitā*:** A Śaiva Āgama manuscript, written in Gupta characters, which was found by H.P. Sastri in the Nepal Darbar library. The manuscript consists of 114 palm-leaves and belongs to the eighth century AD. The text consists of five *sūtras*—Laukikadharma, Mūlasutra, Uttarasūtra, Nayasūtra and Guhyasūtra. The first chapter deals with initiation and the initiated, the second with sacrifice and mode of worshipping Śiva, the third with *muktimaṇḍalam*, the fourth with *muktidīkṣā* and the fifth with the nature of the *mantras*. The subject matter of the last three chapters is not well arranged. It is second section (*uttarasūtra*) there are five chapters, the first two dealing with *sivalaya-sthāpana* (erection of Śiva temples), *mātṛkās* (letters) and *homa*, the third and fourth with *abhiṣeka* and *dikṣā* and the fifth with *jñānayoga*. Holy places, different kinds of *liṅgas* and a description of the Śivatantras are also met with. There are reasons to hold that among the four *sūtras* of the *Niśvāsatattva Saṃhitā* the Uttara and Naya *sutras* formed part of the Cambodian Tantric text, *Nayottara*.

Nityā: Same as Annapūrṇā (q.v.). The term is also used in the Tantric texts to denote the eternal character of Prakṛti, or the quality of Kāla, or Mahākāla, or Mahākālī, or the attribute to the supreme goddess herself. Nityā is Śakti that is non-different from Śiva. *Nityaṣoḍaśikārṇava* I. 138 ff.

Nitya-āsana: One of the two kinds of seats required for performing *japa* or muttering the *mantra* or name of the deity. The other kind is known as *Kāmika*. While the former is for daily use, the latter is used for achieving desired specific purpose. *Puraścaryārṇava* VI. 426.

Nityānandanātha: Author of *Tripura-sundarīmahimnaḥstotraṭīkā, Lalitāstavaratna, Śāktasūtra Agastya, Śrīvidyābhasya Agastya*, etc.

Nityanatha Lokeśvara: A form of one-faced and two-armed Avalokiteśvara holding a rosary in his right hand and a book in his left.

Nitya-sāmarasya: The inseparable equilibrium of Śiva and Śakti. This has been compared to a gram seed. Just as in the gram seed, the original seed, of two equal parts joined to each other, remain under the cover of an outer skin so Śiva and Śakti in their equilibrium stay under the cover of *māyā*. *Kaulamārgarahasya* 55.

***Nityaṣoḍaśikārṇava*:** An authoritative Tantra which is a part of now-lost original *Vāmakeśvara-tantra*. Its commentary, known as *Setubandha*, was written by Bhāskararāya. The last three chapters of the *Nityaṣoḍaśikārṇava* form a different Tantra known as *Yoginīhṛdaya*. The *Dīpikā* commentary on the latter was composed by Amṛtānandanātha, disciple of Puṇyānandanātha. Published in Anandasrama Sanskrit Series; LVI, 1948; ed. by Vraj Vallabh Dvivedi in Sanskrit Yogatantra Series, IX, Varanasi 1968; *Dīpikā* ed. by Gopinath Kaviraj in Sarasvati Bhavana Texts, VII, Varanasi 1923, Anandasrama, Poona 1944.

***Nityotsava*:** Composed by Umānandanātha in AD 1745. It is regarded as a supplement to the *Paraśurāmakalpasūtra*. It contains seven *ullāsas* (q.v.) or chapters conceived and named after the seven stages of Tantric *sādhanā-ārambha*, *taruṇa*, *yauvana*, *prauḍha*, *tadanta*, *unmana* and *aṇavastha*. These seven *Ullasas* deal respectively with Dīkṣākrama, Gaṇapatikrama, Śrīkrama, Śyāmākrama, Daṇḍinīkrama, Parapaddhatī and Sādhāraṇakrama. All the Tantric exercises from initiation to salvation are described under these seven headings. Published in GOS XXIII, 1923.

Nivṛttikalā: One of the five Kalās or aspects of Śakti. *Śāradātilaka* V. 79. Other Kalās are Pratiṣṭhā, Vidyā, Śānti and Śantyātītā. From these five Kalās the five *mahābhūtas* or 'great elements' are produced. Com. on *Śārada* I. 25. Nivṛttikalā is the energy of the *kṣiti* (earth element) and as such she is a form of Kuṇḍalinī. She is the creator of the outer surface of the earth. In the human body Nivṛttikalā represents the region between the abdomen and the knees.

Niyama: Niyama is commitment to certain moral values by which the mind is elevated and conditioned for some higher attainment. It is the second discipline of Yoga consisting of *śauca* (purification of body and mind); *santoṣa* (contentment), *tapas* (observation of austere vows), *svādhyāya* (habit of study) and *īsvarapraṇidhāna* (resignation to god).

Niyati: Term for fate or destiny, which has been regarded as the only truth of human existence according to the Ājīvika school of thought. The concept of *niyati* has been advanced in some Upaniṣads as the First Principle. In Tantra, *niyati*, denotes the condition in which the all-independence of Śiva is limited or contracted in the *jīva* (individual) by means of *avidyā* or false knowledge. Rāmeśvara on *Paraśurāmakalpasūtra* I.4. The doctrine of *niyati* envisages two worlds—Samvarta and Krodha.

Nṛtyā: Dancing goddess mentioned in the Buddhist Tantras belonging to the Lāsyā group. She is of variegated colour and dances holding in her hands a *vajra*. *Niṣpanna* 76.

Nupura: Anklet. Small bells are attached to the ornament so that when the leg moves, it chimes melodiously.

Nyāsa: Feeling the deity in different parts of the body. *Saubhāgyabhāskara* on *Lalitāsahasranāma* I. 4. It is an exercise for the aspirant to become god. *Gandharva* IX. 2. It also serves as a protection against evil. *Tantrasāra* 93. Without proper *nyāsa* worship is meaningless. *Tārātantra* II. 3. There are many types of *nyāsas* such as Mātṛkānyāsa, Ṣoḍanyāsa, Tārakanyāsa, Ṛṣyādinyāsa, Ṣaḍaṅganyāsa, Karaṅganyāsa, Vidyānyāsa, Tattvanyāsa, etc., each of which produces a special result. *Śāradātilaka* VII. In Mātṛkānyāsa, which is divided into Antaḥ and Bahiḥ, the Śakti of letters (Mātṛkās) is to be felt consecutively in the head (*ṛṣi*), face (*chandas*), rectum (*bīja*), legs (*śakti*) and the whole body (*kīlaka*). *Tārābhaktisudhārṇava* V. 169. In Ṣoḍanyāsa six kinds of *nyāsas* are used to experience the Vidyās like Kālī, Tārā, etc. *Puraścaryārṇava* XII. 1165. There are other types of Nyāsas besides those found in the classified lists. For example, in Pīṭhanyāsa, *pīṭhas* or holy resorts of Śakti are to be felt in different parts of the body like Kāmarūpa in heart, Jālandhara in the forehead and so on. *Tantrasāra* 339.

Oo

Oḍḍiyāna Lokeśvara: Same as Trailokyavaśaṅkara, a form of Avalokiteśvara, who was worshipped at Oḍḍiāna, a great centre of Tantric learning. His limbs are reddened by the intense sentiment of passion. He is one-faced, two-armed and three-eyed. He is seated on a red lotus in the *vajraparyaṅka* attitude and is decked in celestial garments and ornaments. *Sādhana* 80.

Oghavatī: River, sacred to the goddess Mahāvidyā as mentioned in the *Prāṇatoṣaṇī*. cf. *Bṛhannīla* V. It is the river Apagā, a branch of the Chittang, running by Thanesar near Pehoa in Haryana.

Om: A sacred syllable, the symbol of *brahman*, it may be called a *bīja* in Tantric language. cf. *Taittirīya Upaniṣad* I. 8. 'Om is the bow, the soul is the arrow and *brahman* is the target.' *Praśna Upaniṣad* V. 5. According to the *Yogasūtra* I. 23 ff. this mystic syllable is expressive of God, the *japa* of which leads to one-pointedness of mind. *Om* is called Tārā in Tantric works. As the mystic syllable *par excellence* it has been attractive because repetition of it has effect of inducing concentration. Thus it has been made the subject of meditation while it is also regarded as the most natural expression of the Absolute. The Buddhist place Om as the beginning of their mystical formulary.

Oṃkāra: Same as *Om*. It also means a prosperous and auspicious beginning. In feminine form Oṃkāra denotes a Buddhist Śakti (the female personification of divine energy).

Oṃkāra: Holy resort of the goddess Gāyatrī. *Bṛhannīla* V; cf. *Jñānārṇava* V. 66 ff. It is modern Oṃkāreśvara or Oṃkāranātha, the island of Mandhata on the Narmada, 32 miles north-west of Khandwa, in Nimar district, Madhya Pradesh.

Ostārakī: Goddess belonging to the outermost circle surrounding Buddhakapāla. She representes the southern region. She is blue in colour, has two arms, one face, ornaments of bone and brown hair rising upwards. She holds *kapāla* and *kartari* and dances in *ardhaparyaṅka* attitude.

Pp

Padma: Lotus. The blue lotus is designated by the word *utpala* or *nīlotpala*. *Padma* is the day lotus. When the lotus shows petals in both the upper and lower directions it is called *viśvapadma* or the double lotus. *Padma* also indicated purity of descent. The six nerve-plexuses (*ṣaṭcakra*) are also described as six *padmas*. From an historical point of view it may be suggested that the *padma* or *cakras* were originally conceived of in terms of human anatomy. They were identified with the sacral, prostatic, epigastric, cardiac, laryngral and cavernous plexuses respectively and the *sahasrāra* or the Buddhist *Uṣṇīṣakamala* with the central cerebral region. See Cakra, Ṣaṭcakra.

Padmaḍākinī: Goddess associated with the Buddhist Tantric Mahāmāyā who represents the west. She is reddish white, has four faces—red, yellow, blue and green in colour—and carries a bow and a skull in her two left hands and arrow and double lotus in the two right.

Padmakaraghoṣa: Buddhist Tantric scholar and a Vajrācārya from Kashmir who flourished about the eighth century AD.

Padmākaragupta: Scholar and translator of the Buddhist Tantras who flourished in the tenth century. Rin-chen-bzaṅ-po of Tibet invited him along with Buddhaśrīśānta, Śradhākaravarman, Buddhapāla and Kamalagupta and got the philosophical part of the four divisions of Tantra translated by them into Tibetan. He belonged to the *Guhyasamāja* school.

Padmakula: Name of a *kula* or clan which according to the Indo-Tibetan literature is headed by Bhagavan Śākyamuni. Avalokiteśvara is the *kulādhipati* (head of the clan) while Tārā is the protecting deity (*mātṛkā*). Hayagrīva and Parṇaśabarī are the deities who safeguard the family. Pratyaṅgirā and Mahālakṣmī are members of this *kula*.

Padmanartteśvara: A form of Bodhisattva Avalokiteśvara (q.v.) dancing with yoginīs in *ardhaparyaṅka* style. He has three varieties. The eighteen-armed variety is one-faced, and all his hands hold a double lotus. The two-armed variety shows *suci-mudra* (q.v.) and the lotus. He bears the effigy of Amitābha on the crown and is embraced by Pāṇḍaravāsinī in the left. The third variety is eight-armed; the dancing god is surrounded by eight goddesses. *Sādhana* 65-6, 75-6.

Padmāntaka: Lord of the Western quarter described in *Niṣpannayogāvalī* 2, as red in colour. He has three faces—red, blue and white; he holds a red lotus, sword, jewel and discus. His two principal hands hold his Śakti in embrace. In the Vajrahuṅkāra Maṇḍala he is known by the name of Vajroṣṇīṣa.

Padmapāda: Celebrated author of the *Prapañcasāra* attributed to Śaṅkara.

Padmapāṇi: The most common form of Bodhisattva Avalokiteśvara (q.v.). Padmapāṇi is most widely represented in sculpture. He belongs to the lotus family presided over by the Dhyānī Buddha Amitābha. In iconography Padmapāṇi is red in colour and a full-blown lotus is his symbol.

Padmasambhava: Tantric Buddhist Ācārya who flourished about the eighth century. It is believed that he descended as a representative incarnate of all the Buddhas to bestow grace and improve the conditions of the living. He is said to have subdued all the terrible beings in Tibet but prescribed the worship of eight particular terrific deities appointed by *dharmapālas*. According to the records of Sikkim, Padmasambhava came northward and convinced the Lamas of Tibet that he was sent to Tibet as an incarnation of Buddha. To the people of Ladakh he represents a second Buddha, an enlightened Bodhisattva. He personifies the totality of the secret doctrines of Mahāyāna and is conceived of as having three *kāyas* or bodies like those of the Buddha. In the Tibetan tradition he is credited with founding the bsam-Yas monastery along with Śāntarakṣita who brought him to Ṭibet. Numerous biographies of him are extant, all of which give different accounts of his life. He is said to be the son of king Indrabhūti of Udyāna. He has many wives one of whom was Śāntrakṣita's sister Mandaravā. From infancy he exhibited all sorts of miraculous feats. He was greatly addicted to drinking. Specially grotesque are the stories of the way in which he subdued the devils and demi-gods of Tibet. He is said to have authored a good number of Tantric texts.

Padmavajra: Author of *guhyasiddhi* who not only advocated the cause of Tantric Buddhism but also gave a succinct digest of a work which he called *Śrīsamāja*, 'the venerable *samāja*'. He wrote a detailed commentary on Buddhaguhya's *Tantrārthāvatāra*. The Tibetan tradition speaks of two lines of Vajrācāryas, one commencing with Padmavajra and the other with Saraha. Padmavajra was also connected with the *Hevajra-tantra* according to Lāmā Tāranātha. Apart from *Guhyasiddhi* he wrote *Utpattikramasādhana* and a few other works.

Padmavāsinī: Companion goddess of Padmantteśvara (q.v.) whose position is in the north-west. She is yellow in colour and holds a red lotus.

Padmāvatī: Śāsanadevatā of the Jain Tīrthaṃkara Pārśvanātha according to both Śvetāmbara and Digambara tradition. Her association with snake connects her with the nether regions as well as with the Hindu goddess Manasā also known as Padmāvatī. In her four-handed form she holds a lotus, noose, fruit and goad. There are also six-handed, eight-handed and twenty-four-handed types of this goddess.

Padminī: One of the eight yoginīs (Aṣṭayoginī q.v.) described in the *Tantrasāra*. She is dark-complexioned; she has exaggerated breasts, soft limbs, a smiling face and eyes like the petals of a red lotus.

Padmoṣṇīṣa: The third deity in the series of eight *uṣṇīṣa* gods of Tantric Buddhism. He resides on the western spoke, is red in colour and shows the *dhyāna-mudrā*. *Niṣpanna* 66.

***Pādukapañcaka*:** A short Tantric text dealing mostly with the ritualistic aspects. Ed. by A. Avalon in *Tantrik Texts*, Vol. II, 1913.

Palāśī: Eater or enjoyer of *pala* or flesh. The *Kulārṇava* recommends the drinking of wine and eating of flesh to the followers of the Kaula doctrine. At the same time it endeavours to give esoteric meaning to the *makāras* in V. 107-12. It is said that *pala* (flesh) stands for *para* (highest) as *r* and *l* are often interchangeable in Sanskrit and the root '*as*' may mean 'to reach' as well as 'to eat'.

Pampāsaras: Holy resort of the goddess Sāraṅgā mentioned in the *Bṛhannīlatantra* and *Prāṇatoṣaṇī*. It is near modern Hampi in Bellary district, Karnataka.

Pañcabhūta: The five material elements—earth, water, fire, air and space—which have a place in Tantric rituals. Earth (*pṛthvī*) is represented in a diagram by a square or a cube, water (*ap*) by a circle, fire (*tejas*) by triangles, air (*vāyu*) by flying bodies and space (*ākāśa*) by heavenly bodies. In iconography also, whether Tantric or non-Tantric, these symbols prevail.

Pancadaśa-kalā: See Kalā. Laksmīdhara in his com. on *Saundaryalaharī* 32 refers to fifteen Kalās—Darśā, Dṛṣṭā, Darśatā, Viśvarūpā, Sudarśanā, two Āpyāyamānās, Āpyāyā, Sunṛtā, Irā, two Apūryamāṇās, Purayantī, Pūrṇa and Paurṇamāsī—grouped into three *khaṇḍas*—Āgneya, Saura and Cāndra.

Pañcadsākṣarī: Mantra in fifteen letters; it is supposed to be the subtle form of Lalitā according to the Tantric tradition. The votary of this *mantra* rouses the power (*cit-śakti*) latent in him, which represents the Jīva and is known as the *kuṇḍalinī*.

Pañca-dhyeya: Five objects of meditation according to the Krama doctrine (q.v) which are Śrīpīṭha, Pañcavāha, Netratraya, Vṛndacakra and Gurupaṅkti.

Pañca-kalā: Five aspects of Śakti. They are Nivṛtti, Pratiṣṭhā, Vidyā, Śāntī and Śāntyatītā. *Śarādātilaka* V. 79.

Pañcakleśa: Five afflictions which are *asmitā* (egoity), *avidyā* (ignorance), *rāga* (attachment), *dveṣa* (hatred) and *abhiniveśa* (absorption). These are also called *puṃstvamala* and *pāśa* (q.v.). They are *tama* (gloom), *moha* (illusion), *mahāmoha* (great mental obsession), *tamisra* (dark elements of human nature) and *andhatamisra* (overcast with the above elements) end are known as Pañcakleśa. *Saubhāgyabhāskara* on *Lalitāsahasranāma*, 129.

Pañca-kañcuka: According to the Śaiva Āgamas, Sadāśiva, by virtue of his own energy, creates from Aśuddha Māyā three *tattvas* (fundamentals) called Kāla, Niyati and Kalā (q.v.) and from Kalā Vidyā and Rāga (q.v.). These five fundamentals are called *pañcakañcuka* or covers.

Pañcakośa: Five sheaths by which the concept

of the relative position of the individual and pure blissful soul is explained. The grossest is *annamaya* which is nourished by material food. Others in ascending order are *prāṇamaya* (nourished by vital force), *manomaya* (by mind), *vijñānamaya* (by intellect) and *ānandamaya* (by pure bliss-consciousness).

***Pañcakrama*:** An extract of the *Guhyasamāja* (q.v.) which is an Anuttarayoga-tantra (q.v.); it deals more with Yoga than with the actual Tantric usages. It is a presentation of the 'five stages' to be attained by magic formulas, mysterious syllables and the worshipping of the Mahayanist and Tantric deities. The text belongs to the commentarial literature of the Mantrayāna and was edited by Vallee Poussin in 1896.

Pañca-kriyā: Five active expressions of Śakti—*sṛṣṭi* (creation) *sthiti* (maintenance), *saṃhāra* (destruction), *tirodhāna* (disappearance) and *anugraha* (favour). *Tantrāloka* I. 121.

Pañcakṛtya: Five works of Śiva carried out respectively through five Śaktis or *mantras*. These are *sṛṣṭi* or creation (by means of Īśāna *mantra*), *sthiti* or preservation (Tatpuruṣa), *saṃhāra* or destruction (Aghora), *tirobhāva* or covering of self (Vamādeva) and *anugraha* or grace (Sadyojāta), *Sarvadarśanasaṃgraha* VII. 66-78.

Panca-kula: The five *kulas* (clans) of Tantric Buddhism. According to the *Hevajra*, these are (1) Tathāgata, adherent to the knowing of the intrinsic nature of phenomena in the same way as it is and becoming in the same way as the former Buddhas came into the past; (2) Padma, governed by Avalokiteśvara who sees all beings with an eye of compassion; (3) Vajra, led by Samantabhadra with his adamantine *vajra* (knowledge) protecting the sayings of Buddha; (4) Karma, generating a specified power through actions to reach Buddhahood; and (5) Ratna, leading to mundane prosperity together with spiritual progress by generating potential efficiency.

***Pañcamakāra*:** See Pañcatattva.

***Pancamakāraśodhanavidhi*:** Name of the text which describes the sanctification of *makāras* (the five Ms of Tantric ritual) with Vedic *mantras*.

Pañcamatattva: Same as *maithuna* (q.v.).

Pañcāmnāya: Five *āmnāyas* (zones) celebrated in Tantric culture.

Pañcamudrā: See Pañcatattva.

Pañcamuṇḍi: Seat for Tantric *sādhanā* prepared from the severed heads of two Caṇḍālas, a jackal, a monkey and a snake.

Pañcānga-nyāsa: Feeling the deity in the heart, head, central cerebral region, protective amulet (*kavaca*) and intestine.

Pañcāṇga-puraścarana: *Japa* (to internalize and mutter the syllables relating to the identity of *guru*, *mantra* and *devatā*), *homa* (offering made to fire in the name of different deities), *tarpaṇa* (rememberance of deities, sages and fathers), *abhiṣeka* (consecration of the aspirant) and *viprabhojana* (feeding of the Brāhmaṇas). *Tantrasāra* 48.

Pañcaparvan: Eighth and fourteenth day of the dark-half of the moon, new and full moon day and the last day of the month on which the preceptor is to be saluted. Rāmeśvara on *Paraśurāmakalpasūtra* X. 67.

Pañca-preta: Five gods who hold the throne of the great goddess. They are Brahmā, Viṣṇu, Rudra, Īśā and Sadāśiva. *Puraścaryārṇava* IX. 801.

Pañcarakṣā: Five protectresses or *rakṣā* deities as they are called in Tantric works. They are Mahapratisarā, Mahasahasrapramardinī, Mahamantrānusāriṇī, Mahāsitavatī and Mahāmāyūrī, all popular and well-known amongst the Mahāyāna Buddhists. A manuscript copy of the *Pañcarakṣā*, describing the five *rakṣā* deities, their worship on different occasions and their powers, is to be found in almost every Buddhist house in Nepal. Such manuscripts are often very artistically written and they bear miniature pictures of not only the five *rakṣā* deities but also of other Buddhist deities and their Śaktis.

Pāñcarātra Āgamas: Also known occasionally as Tantras and Kāṇḍas, the Pāñcarātra texts comprise, according to tradition, a set of 108 works. Actually they number at least 215 works. Otto Schrader refers to as many as 224 works. The earliest of the series are the *Pauṣkara*, *Vārāha* and *Brāhma*. These are followed by the *Sātvata*, *Jaya* and *Ahirbudhnya* Saṃhitās. Then there is a succession of Saṃhitās—*Parameśvara*, *Sanatkumāra*, *Parama*, *Padmodbhava*, *Māhendra*, *Kānva*, *Pādma* and *Īśvara* Saṃhitā.

Pañca-śakti: Mother, sister, daughter, daughter-in-law and preceptor's wife, collectively known and worshipped as five great śaktis. *Niruttara* X.

Pañca-śuddhi: Purification of the self, place, *mantra*, articles of worship and deity. *Kulārṇava* VI.

Pañcatattva: Tantric esoteric ritualism which consists in the use of *pañcamakāras* (five Ms). These are *madya* (wine), *māṃsa* (flesh), *maithuna* (sexual intercourse), *mudrā* (cereals) and *matsya* (fish). Also known as Pañcamakāra, Pancamudrā, Kuladravya, Kulatattva, etc. We do not find any direct mention of these *pañcamakāras* in the Buddhist Tantras though we find sporadic mention of wine, fish and meat, etc., and more often of the *pañcakāmaguṇas* or the five objects of enjoyment.

Pañcavāha: Five streams of the supreme being according to the Krama doctrine as Vyomavāmesvarī, Khecarī, Dikcarī, Gocarī and Bhucarī. They represent the five means of valid knowledge and collectively form a cakra. *Tantrāloka* XXIX, 76.

Pañcavāk: Five substrata of sound according to the Krama school. These are Parā, Sūkṣmā, Paśyantī, Madhyamā and Vaikharī.

Pañcavaṭī: Holy resort of the goddess Tapasvinī mentioned in the *Bṛhannīlatantra* and *Prānatoṣaṇī*. It lay in Janasthāna in the Nasik region, on the Godavari, in Maharashtra.

Pañcāyatanī-dīkṣā: Initiation to the cults of Śiva, Śakti, Viṣṇu, Sūrya and Gaṇeśa. *Tantrasāra* 70-2.

Pañcopacāra: Five *upacāras* (materials) which are offered in worship. These are *pādya* (water as the symbol of element *ap*) *gandha* (sandal, etc., as symbol of the element *pṛthvī), puṣpa* flower as the symbol of the element *ākāśa*), *dhūpa* (incense as symbol *vāyu*) and *dīpa* (light as symbol of *tejas*). The seed-*mantras* of these *upacāras* connected with the five elements are *vam, lam, ham, yam* and *ram* respectively. This *pañcopacāra* was later elaborated into ten (*daśopacāra*), sixteen (*ṣoḍaśopacāra*) and at times to sixty-four. *Puraścaryārṇava* III. 224.

Pāṇḍarā: Also called Pāṇḍaravāsinī she is the spiritual consort of Amitābha (q.v.). She belongs to the lotus family and originated from the germ syllable *paṃ*. Her colour is red and her symbol, the lotus. She is the embodiment of the element of fire. *Advayavajrasaṃgraha* 43.

Paṇḍita Kānha: Name of the commentator on the *Hevajratantra*.

Parā: *Sabda-brahma*, i.e. *brahman* in the form of sound, unmanifest (*avyakta*), the spread of pure *nāda* (q.v.) experienced in deep sleep. According to the Tantric tradition, the *kriyā-śakti* or the power of the action of Śiva remains dominant in it. The *parā* rises from the *mūlādhāra* and is produced by air (*prāṇa*). It is the motionless causal sound conceived as existing in the *kuṇḍalinī* in the *mūlādhāra-cakra* in a dreamless state of deep sleep (*suṣupti*). See under Parā-śabda, Parā-vāc, Paśyantī, Madhyamā and Vaikharī.

Para-bindu: One of the categories to which the evolution of the material world is traced. In the course of this evolution the appearance of Śakti causes an unmanifested sound called Para-nāda (q.v.) which eventually concentrates itself on a point or centre. This point or centre is called Para-bindu; it is subdivided into three parts known respectively as Apara-bindu, Bīja and Aparanāda. The sound caused by the subdivision of Para-bindu is often called Śabdabrahma. *Śāradātilaka* I. 7 ff.; *Prapañcasāra* I.44. See Bindu.

Parabrahmasvarūpiṇī: An epithet of the great goddess in the Tantras. Parabrahma denotes the supreme being, the absolute, the ultimate reality in the form of pure-consciousness.

Pārada: Mercury. It is regarded as the essence of Śiva's body and is conducive to *mokṣa* or liberation. *Sarvadarśanasaṃgraha* IX. 5-9.

Parakīyā: A female partner of the spiritual aspirant other than his own wife.

Paraliṅga: Imaginary phallus in terms of which the *bindu* or vacuity within the *sahasrāra* triangle is conceived.

Paramahaṃsa: The Tantric aspirant who has attained success in Haṃ-sa (q.v.). Paramahaṃsas are of two kinds: *vidvat* (those who have already realized *brahman*) and *vividiṣu* (those who are eager seekers after realization). The *Jabālopaniṣat* 6 and the *Sutasaṃhitā* II. 6. describe the state of Parama-haṃsa at length.

Paramānanda: One of the four kinds of bliss mentioned in the Buddhist Tantras. The others are Ānanda, Virāmānanda and Sahajānanda. It pertains to the Dharmacakra. It is more intense than Ānanda or ordinary transient pleasure. It is called *bhava* or existence in the world of life and death. It acts as the provisional world. *Sekoddeśaṭīkā* 54-5.

***Paramānanda-tantra*:** Also known as *Pārānanda-tantra*, it is an important work on Śrīvidyā.

***Paramārthasāra*:** A very important work of Abhinavagupta which is an adaptation of an earlier Advaita work of the same name by Ādi Śeṣa (ed. by S.S. Suryanarayana Sastri, Adyar 1941). It deals with the essential principles of the Trika system which primarily refers to the triple principles of Śiva-Śakti-Anu or Pati-Pāśa-Paśu. Ed. with Eng. trans. and notes by L.D. Barnett, *JRAS*, 707-47; ed. with com. of Yogarāja by J.C. Chatterji, Kashmir Sanskrit Series, VII. 1916.

Paramaśiva: Ultimate reality in Kashmir Śaivism, it is also known as Anuttara, Cit, Caitanya, Pūrṇa or Para Saṃvid, Parameśvara and Ātman. This state can be attained by an individual. It is the realization of perfect and supreme *sivatva*—the condition of the equilibrium of Śiva and Śakti. The attainment of the state of Paramaśiva is also to become the lord of *śakti-cakra*, the circle of powers. *Spandanirṇaya*, I. 1.

Paramāśva: Tantric Buddhist deity, an emanation of Akṣobhya who is also a form of Hayagrīva, 'horse-neck' as his name indicates. He is described as being red in colour, he has four faces, eight arms and four legs. He stands in *pratyālīḍha* attitude and tramples Indrāṇī and Śrī, Rati and Prīti, Indra and Madhukara, and Jayakara and Vasanta. *Sādhana* 510-1.

Parameṣṭhi-guru: The fourth spiritual ancestor of the guru. *Mahānirvāṇa* VI. 98.

Parameśvarī: An epithet of the supreme being conceived of as the Female Principle which is the source and spring as well as the controller of the universe. In Buddhist Tantras Paramaśvarī is sometimes mentioned as Avadhutikā or the Suṣumnā nerve on both sides of which are *lalanā* and *rasanā* (q.v.).

Paramīkaraṇa: Anointing of the deity with the help of *mahāmudrā*. *Puraścaryārṇava* V. 346.

Pāramitā-nayą: One of the two subdivisions of Mahāyāna according to the *Tattvaratnāvali* collected in the *Advayavajra-saṃgraha*; also known as Pāramitā-yāna. The followers of this school based their religious practices on the cultivation of the *pāramitās* and derived the main impulses of their doctrine from the *Prajñāpāramitā* texts. The conception of the goddess Prajñāpāramitā as the embodiment of spiritual knowledge may also owe something to this school.

Pāramitās: Twelve Pāramitās (perfections) are cardinal human virtues deified in Tantric Buddhism as goddesses. They are Ratna, Dāna, Śīla, Kṣānti, Vīrya, Dhyāna, Prajñā, Upāya, Praṇidhāna, Bala, Jñāna and Vajrakarma.

Paramudrā: Subtle form of *mudrā*. *Tantrarāja* IV. 55.

Parā-nāda: See Parā-śabda. It is one of the categories to which the evolution of the material world has been traced. Parameśvara is the supreme being with whom śakti is in inseparable relation. The appearance of Śakti causes an unmanifested sound. This is Parā-nāda that fills up the vacuum and eventually concentrates itself on a point or centre called Para-bindu (q.v.). *Brahmarandhra* (q.v.) (the space in the central cerebral region) is the breeding spot of Parā-nāda. It is the causal state of pure consciousness which is symbolized by Śabdabrahma (q.v.).

***Pārānandasūtra*:** Composed about AD 900, it is a work on Kauladharma which is described as the cream of the Vedas. It holds that the supreme being is one and refers to seven sectarian deities—Brahmā, Viṣṇu, Śiva, Gaṇeśa, Sūrya, Śakti and Bhairava. According to this text Dakṣiṇa-mārga, one of the three ways of *sādhanā*, is sanctioned by the Vedas, the Smṛtis and Purāṇas; the Vamamārga by the Vedas and the Āgamas and the Uttaramārga only by the words of the Guru. Vāmamarga is of two kinds; that which insists on the *pañca-tattva* (q.v.) is the better one. The preceptor should collect the materials of the five *makāras* and give the disciple a bowl for drinking wine, *mudrā* (fried cereal), and a woman (generally a courtesan). It is stated that any woman, even a courtesan, is *brahman*. Details of Kauladharma are given in this text. It also describes the procedure of Tantric festivals, the efficacies of *mantras* and *mudrās*, names of teachers ending in Ānanda, and details of sexual techniques. Published in GOS, 1931.

Parāpara Guru: Third spiritual ancestor of the Guru. *Mahānirvāṇa* VI. 98.

Parā-pratibhā: Same as Kaulikī Śakti (q.v.). *Parātriṃsikā* 102, *Tantrāloka* III. 24.

Parā-śabda: One of the four constituents of

the sound-producing energy conceived as identical with Kuṇḍalinī (q.v.). Parā is the motionless causal sound which produces on the one hand, *nāda* or articulated sound-particle and, on the other, *vāk*, the uttered speech. The subtle forms of these two are, therefore, known as *parā-nāda* and *parā-vāk* (q.v.) and their combination is supposed to be *parā-śakti* (q.v.), the source of everything. This *parā-śakti* is the same as the Kuṇḍalinī residing in the Mūlādhāra.

Paraśakti: The primordial energy in the abstract, conceived of as the Female Principle. Paraśakti also means the female partner of the Tantric aspirant. Female partners are of three types—*svakīyā* (one's own wife), *parakīyā* (wife of another person or any woman who is not one's own wife) and *sādhāraṇī* (common woman). In most cases Paraśakti is one's own wife by the special Śaiva form of marriage.

Parā Śakti: A term variously used to denote different aspects of Śakti; it is also that power which denotes the Śivaness of Śiva. *Śivārkamaṇidīpikā* on *Brahmasūtra* II. 2.38. Parā Śakti is therefore the energy of Śiva, often regarded as the instrumental cause of creation. The term is also used to denote the power of independence of the supreme being. It is that power, undifferentiated from Saṃvit (pure-consciousness) by which the supreme being expresses itself. *Pratyabhijñāhṛdaya*. 68. In *Tantrāloka* III. 103-4 it is regarded as Visarga-śakti which is by nature extrovert. Ibid. III. 141-2. In Śaiva and Śākta outlook Parā Śakti is the Vimarśa, that is, the vibrating energy of the supreme being. Parā Śakti is conceived in different names and forms. When it manifests itself in creating the vibration caused thereby it is called Nāda. Com. on *Śāradā* I.7. It is revealed in the form of Vāk, etc. *Nityaṣoḍaśikārṇava* VI. 36. All the goddesses are its forms, *Mahānirvāṇa*. V.2. Conceived as Female Principle Parā Śakti is said to be in union with the other part of herself, that is Para Śiva, within the body of the aspirant, and this forms the *mithunatattva* of Tantra. *Kulārṇava* V. Ḍakinī, Rākinī, etc. are special forms of Parā Śakti. It is the force behind the formation of Parāvāk, Paśyantī, Madhyamā and Vaikharī, the ingredients of Śabdabrahma. *Kāmakalāvilāsa* XXII-XXIII. It is equated with Kuṇḍalinī and its functioning. Parā-Śakti is also a term for the female partner of the aspirant, *Śāradā* I. 51-4; Kālīcaraṇa on *Ṣaṭcakranirūpaṇa* LI.

Parā-saṃvit: Pure-consciousness, the realization of which is achieved only when the mind transcends the limit of worldly existence and becomes one with the subject of its contemplation. It is the state of complete *samādhi*, the ecstacy resulting from the equation of the individual soul with the ultimate reality. Pure consciousness or Parā-saṃvit is universal in nature. There is nothing to limit or cover it and the material world is contained in it. In the Tantras the evolution of the material world from pure-consciousness has been conceived of in three stages. The first is the seed stage, regarded as pure, in which matter does not express its existence and appear as an entity different from consciousness. Thus in the second stage, regarded as the mixed state, there is a marked difference between consciousness and matter, both of which are subject to subtle manifestations. In the third stage the categories of the mixed state have gross manifestations. In this stage we have the evolution of Prakṛti (primordial matter), in the shaping of the material world. The evolution of the material world is traced to the following categories: Parameśvara, Śakti, Para-nāda, Para-bindu, subdivided into Apara-bindu and bīja, and Apara-nāda (q.v.). Thus Parā-Saṃvit or the ultimate reality seems to be self-expressive both inwardly and outwardly. See Saṃvit. *Tripurārahasya*, Jñānakhaṇḍa XIV ff.; *Śāradātilaka* I. 7 ff.; *Prapañcasāra* I. 44.

Paraśu: Axe.

***Paraśurāmakalpasūtra*:** Composed about AD 1300; commentary known as *Saubhāgyodaya* written by Rāmeśvara. The special features of this work are the *āmnāya* classifications, insistence on the secrecy of knowledge, concept of the five *makāras*, thirty-six *tattvas* including those of the *Sāṅkhya system,* āsana, maṇḍapa, kuṇḍa, maṇḍala, dīkṣā, etc. It provides that after initiation the preceptor is to give a name to the disciple ending in Ānandanātha. The efficacy of *mantras* is greatly stressed and it is held that the *sādhaka* should come to feel that the *guru*, *mantra*, deity and his own self are all one. Published in *GOS*, 1923.

Pārātaṭa: Holy resort of the goddess Mātā mentioned in *Matsya Purana* XIII. 43, etc.

Its variant reading is Pārāvāratīra and Pārāvaratața. It is same as the Parvati in Malwa.

Parātriṃśikā-vivṛti: A commentary written by Abhinavagupta on *Parātriṃśikā*, the text of which constitutes the concluding portion of the *Rudrayāmala*. In this work, aspects of the Krama doctrine are occasionally discussed. It is also known as *Parātriṃśikavivaraṇa*. Ed. with notes by M.R. Sastri, Kashmir Sanskrit Series, no. XVIII, 1918.

Parāvāk: See Parā-śabda. It is the first stage of sound expressing itself only in the Mūlādhara. It is without any vibration. It is like a flame of light, unmanifested yet indestrutive. *Cidvallī* on *Kāmakalāvilāsa* XX. It is not only connected with Kuṇḍalinī but also serves as the middle point of the triangle representing Kāmakalā. Ibid. XXIII.

Parigraha-śakti: Same as *Upādāna-śakti* (material energy). It has two forms—*śuddha* (pure) and *aśuddha* (impure). Pure non-sentient energy is the material for pure world, which is beyond *māyā* (illusion). This is called *śuddhasattva* by the Vaiṣṇavas and *bindu* or *mahāmāyā* by the Tāntrikas. Impure non-sentient energy creates the world of illusion, the phenomenal world.

Pariṣkāra: The third in the series of *vaśitā* goddesses who is described in the Dharma-dhātuvāgīśvara Maṇḍala of the *Niṣpanna-yogāvalī* as yellow in colour; she holds in her left hand the *cintāmaṇi* banner and in her right hand a lotus.

Parivrājakācārya: His proper name is not known; he is usually prefixed by the title Mahāmahopādhyaya. His only work that has come down is the *Kāmyayantroddhāra*. A manuscript of the work described by M.M. Haraprasad Sastri was copied in Śaka 1297 (AD 1375). Therefore, Parivrājakācārya must have lived before this date.

Parṇaśabarī: Goddess of epidemics who is regarded as an emanation of Akṣobhya and or of Amoghasiddhi. In one conception she is described as three-faced, the frontal face being yellow in complexion. She has six hands. She holds *vajra*, *paraśu*, and arrow in the right hands and, in the left, noose, cluster of leaves and bow. Her *jaṭāmukuṭa* is decorated with flowers and an image of Akṣobhya. She stands in *pratyālīḍha* trampling the *vighnas* (i.e. Gaṇeśa). In another conception she has a green complexion, three faces, three eyes and six hands. The attributes of the six hands are the same as above. Here she tramples various diseases and pestilences and bears the image of Amoghasiddhi on the crown.

Pārthiva varṇa: Letters (*varṇa*) are thought of as originating from the five *bhūtas* (material elements). Those sprung from the earth are known as Pārthiva-varṇa. In this category are included u, ū, o, ga, ja, ḍa, da, ba, la and ḷa; com. on *Śāradātilaka* II. 10-1.

Paryaṅka: Āsana or sitting posture. It is akin to *Dhyānāsana* or *Vajraparyaṅkāsana* or *vajrāsana*, the meditative pose in which the two legs are firmly locked with both the soles apparent, the characteristic sitting attitude of the Dhyānī Buddhas. This should be distinguished from the reverse posture in which case the legs are placed one upon the other with both the soles invisible.

Pāśa: A noose or lasso. When a *vajra* (q.v.) is attached to the end of it, it is called *vajrapāśa* (adamantine noose). It is a weapon of Varuṇa. Certain Buddhist deities also have *pāśa* as an attribute. *Paśa* also denotes fetters, generally considered to be eight in number. *Paraśurāmakalpasūtra* X. 70. A list of 62 fetters is also found in different texts. See *Saubhāgya-bhāskara* on *Lalitāsahasranāma* 129.

Paścimāmnāya: The western Tantric region presided over by such goddesses as Kubjikā, Kulālikā, Mātaṅgī and Amṛtalakṣmī. *Puraścaryārnava* I, 12.

Paśu: Fettered individual. To this category belong men, animals and even gods. *Kauṇḍinya-bhāṣya* on *Pāsupatasūtra* I. 1; V. 7. In Tantra Paśu is divided into two classes; Sabhāva (when influenced by knowledge) and Vibhāva (when knowledge leaves a mark on it). *Kaulāvalinirṇaya* XI. 187. It is also divided into *dikṣita* (initiated) and *adīkṣita* (uninitiated) categories. *Niruttara* XII.

Paśu Bhāva: The ordinary human state. Certain spiritual exercises and cultivation of virtues are prescribed for individuals belonging to this state. Through the performance of these they are able to reach the higher level known as Vīra. *Rudrayāmala*, Uttara VI. 50-1; XI. 28-9. Paśu denotes individual soul (*jīva* or *jīvātman*). An individual aspiring for upliftment in the Vīra stage should follow the way of justice and truth, work for social welfare, control his senses, feel equality and respect towards women and fight for the right cause. He does not need to become a Śākta or Tantric, or to have initiation into a particular creed; he may continue to be a Vedist, a Vaiṣṇava, or a Śaiva.

Paśu-cakra: One of the five *cakra* (q.v.) rituals, other being Rāja, Mahā, Deva and Vīra. *Niruttara* X.

Pāśupata: One of the earlier forms of the Śaiva system; the ultimate cause is believed to be Śiva (Pati or Lord) who is omniscient, omnipotent and almighty. The world or individual (Paśu) fails to recognize him owing to *pāśa* (q.v.) or fetters. All the problems and conditions of wordly existence can be solved by a proper comprehension of the five main tenets of this system—*kārya* (effect, all the problems and conditions of worldly existence), *kāraṇa* (cause, the supreme being who creates), *yoga* (concentration), *vidhi* (the way to achieve the end) and *caryā* (culture, practice). The *caryās* are again subdivided into *vratas* (vows) and *dvāra* (door) and *duḥkhānta* (extermination of suffering).

Paśu Śāstra: The Tantric texts belonging to the non-Kaula groups. *Kulārṇava* II.

Paśvācara: A term by which Vedācara, Vaiṣṇavācara, Śaivacara and Dakṣiṇācāra are characterized. *Prānatoṣaṇī* II. 1, 149; *Kaulamārgarahasya* 9.

Paśyantī: One of the constituents of sound, regarded as the second stage of its development. This form of sound belongs to the region around the navel. It has little vibration and is connected with Nādatattva. Paśyantī represents a non-particularized motion (*sāmanya-spanda*) Com. on *Prapañcasāra*.

Paṭadhāriṇī: Goddess of the Dhāriṇī series of Tantric Buddhism who is described in the Pañcaḍāka Maṇḍala of *Niṣpannayogāvalī* as blue in colour and holding in her two hands a curtain (*kāṇḍapaṭa*).

Pātāla: Holy resort of the goddess Parameśvarī mentioned in the *Matsya Purana* XIII. 38, etc. Pātāla means the nether region. But the name is reminiscent of the region of Patalene, the ancient city and district, located by classical writers about the mouths of the Indus. In the *Bṛhannīla* and *Prānatoṣaṇī* Pāṭala is mentioned as the holy resort of Pātāleśvarī. This Pāṭala is probably Pāṭaliputra.

Pati: Term denoting God or Supreme Soul which is one of the three entities of most forms of Śaivism; the others are *pāśa* (fetters), and *paśu* (*jiva* or soul, i.e. individual). Pati means one who protects or controls *paśu* by five-fold activity: creation, preservation, destruction, dispensation and emancipation.

Pātra: Bowl generally found in the images of the five Dhyānī Buddhas. Sometimes *kapāla* (q.v.) is used to denote a bowl.

Pavana-niścāñcalya: Process of holding the breath which is a feature of yogic exercise.

Payoṣṇī: A river sacred to the goddess Piṅgaleśvarī mentioned in *Matsya Purāṇa* XIII. 44, *Devībhāgavata* VII. 30.73, etc. It is the river Paisuni, a tributary of the Yamuna, between the Ken and the Tons.

Piṇḍa: Name of a one-lettered *mantra*. *Tantrarājatantra* XXXV. 28-9.

Piṇḍabrahmāṇḍamārga: The route taken in the upward march of Kuṇḍalinī (q.v.). It is also known as Ṣaṭcakramārga.

Piṇḍapātra Lokeśvara: A form of Avalokiteśvara who is one-faced and two-armed and stands on a lotus holding a *piṇḍapātra* (bowl) near his navel.

Piṇḍāraka: Holy resort of the goddess Dhṛti mentioned in *Matsya Purāṇa* XIII. 48; *Devībhāgavata* VII. 30.77, etc. The *Bṛhannīla* and *Prāṇatoṣaṇī* refer to the goddess as Dhanyā and the site as Piṇḍārakavana. It is sixteen miles to the east of Dvārakā in Kathaiwar.

Piṅgalā: One of the major nerves. Together with its sister nerve Iḍā, it rises from Mūlādhāra and ends in the right nostril. *Prānatoṣaṇī* I. 4, 33. It is also known as Sūrya-nāḍi and has the masculine characteristics of the sun. *Sanmohana* quoted by Kālīcaraṇa in the com. on *Ṣaṭcakra-nirūpaṇa* I. It symbolizes the waking state and leads individuals to violent actions. Rāghava on *Śāradātilaka* XXV. 38. In the Buddhist Tantras it is known as Rasanā (q.v.).

***Piṅgalāmata*:** Palm-leaf manuscript found in Nepal Darbar Library of this text is dated 294 Nepal Saṃvat (AD 1174). It is narrated in the form of a conversation between the goddess Piṅgalā and Bhairava. It begins with explanation of such words as Āgama, Śāstra, Jñāna, Tantra, etc., and the purpose of the communication of Tantric knowledge to others. The *Piṅgalāmata* belongs to the Kalpārtha sub-division of the *Kriyāsūtra* which is described in the text as one of the seven classes of Tantras. It claims that it belongs to the uncommon (*asādhāraṇa*) type of Tantra, seeks to explain the denomination (*abhidhāna*), cause (*nimitta*), maker (*kartā*) and extent (*pariṇāma*) by which things are conditioned. It claims to be a supplement to *Jayadratha-yāmala* (q.v.).

Piśācasiddhi: A form of *siddhi* (attainment) by which one is supposed to maintain control over departed souls and other subtle-bodied beings through different types of mental practices.

Pīṭha: Holy resorts of Śakti, traditionally 51 in number. Their origin is associated with the Purānic Dakṣayajña legend. Each *piṭha* is supposed to contain a limb of Sati, the Śakti of Śiva, a presiding goddess and her Bhairava. There are also minor *piṭhas* known as *upapīṭhas*.

***Pīṭhamālā Mahātantra*:** A late work of encyclopaedic nature and has little to do with Tantra, except the seventeenth and eighteenth chapters entitled *yoga-niyamādi* and *śāmbhavī-siddhi* respectively. Occasional references to six black acts are found here and there in the text.

***Pīthanirṇaya*:** Also known as *Mahāpīṭhanirūpaṇa* it is a chapter of the *Tantracuḍāmaṇi* describing fifty-one pilgrim spots associated with the great goddess under some of her various names. Each one of the Pīthas is mentioned along with a particular form of the goddess and that of Śiva associated with it. There are many manuscripts of this text—three in the Library of the Asiatic Society of Bengal (nos. 196, 3400 and 5363), the Indian Museum (no. 10863), and the Vaṅgīya Sāhitya Pariṣad (no. 402). The text itself with variant readings in regard to the holy resorts and the deities occurs in a few Tantras and Purāṇas. A critical edition presenting a Probable Original Text of the Pīthanirṇaya and providing a Modified Text was prepared by D.C. Sircar in his *The Śākta Pīṭhas* in *JRASB* (L) 1948, a new edition of which was published in 1971 with a detailed index by N.N. Bhattacharyya.

Pīṭhanyāsa: See Nyāsa.

Pīṭha Śakti: Collective name for the goddesses Icchā, Jñāna, Kriyā, Kāmadā, Kāmadāyinī, Rati, Ratipriyā, Nandā and Mānonmānī; Each representing an aspect of Śakti. *Śyāmārahasya* III.

Potapāda Lokeśvara: A form of Avalokiteśvara who sits in *vajraparyaṅka* attitude. He has four hands, the principal ones exhibiting the *añjali* pose against the chest, while the other pair holds a rosary in the right and a noose in the left.

Prabhākarakīrti: A Buddhist Tantric author who is said to have compared the *dhyāna* or Candaroṣaṇa which is included in the *Sādhanamālā*.

Prabhāsa: Holy resort of the goddess Puṣkarāvatī according to the *Matsya Purāṇa* XIII. 43, *Devībhāgavata* VII. 30.72, *Padma* I. 17.201, *Skanda*, Reva V. 3.81, etc. In *Bṛhannīla* and *Prāṇatoṣaṇī* the goddess variously is Īśvarī, Surapūjitā and Puṣkarekṣaṇā. The *Pīṭhanirṇaya* says that the belly of Satī fell here and the goddess is Candrabhāgā. The same goddess is mentioned in the *Śivacarita* which refers to it as a Mahāpīṭha. The latter text also refers to Prabhāsakhaṇḍa with Siddheśvarī as the guardian deity. Prabhāsa is modern Somnath in Kathiawar. There are two other Prabhāsas near Kurukṣetra and Kauśambī.

Pracaṇḍacaṇḍikā: Same as Chinnamastā (q.v.). Of her numerous *dhyāna* the one quoted in the *Tantrasāra* is the most widely known. She holds her own severed head in her left hand and drinks the blood flowing from her severed throat with her dreadful tongue. Her hair is dishevelled. She holds a skull-vessel in the left hand and a knife in the right. Fierce and naked, she stands in *pratyālīḍha* attitude on Rati and Kāma who are engaged in *viparīta-rati* (inverted sexual intercourse). Ḍākini (q.v.) stands to her left and Varninī (q.v.) to her right, both of them drinking the blood which flows from her severed throat. The concept of Pracaṇḍacaṇḍikā or Chinnamastā, often described as Chinnā, recalls that of Buddhist Vajrayoginī. *Puraścaryārṇava* IX. 816-17.

***Pracaṇḍacaṇḍikā Tantra*:** A late work also known as *Chinnamastā Tantra*. It has 196 stanzas containing the *mantras* and mode of worship of Chinnamastā and her 100 and 1,000 names at two places respectively.

Pradyumna Bhaṭṭa: Śaiva-Tantric author of the ninth century whose *Tattvagarbha Stotra* appears to have some bearing on the Krama doctrine.

Prajñā: The female principle in Tantric Buddhism, the union of which with Upāya, the male principle, produces great bliss (*mahāsukha*) which is the non-dual quintessence of all entities. The Mahayanic concept of *śūnyata* and *karuṇā* are substituted by Prajñā and Upāya in Tantric Buddhism. In *Hevajratantra* X Prajñā is conceived as *mudrā* (woman) and Upāya as the Yogin; their union is supposed to produce *bodhicitta* (q.v.) as the embodiment of *śūnyata* and *karuṇā*. cf. *Prajñopāya* 5; *Advayavajra-samgraha* 2, 26, 55. Prajñā is variously designated as a goddess (*bhagavatī*), a woman to be adopted for *sādhanā* (*mudrā, mahāmudrā, vajrakanyā*), a young woman (*yuvati*) and sometimes the female organ. *Advayavajrasaṃgraha* 62, *Sādhanamālā* 321, 329 ff., *Guhyasamāja* 19, 153; *Śrī-cakrasambhāra* 28, etc. She is also called *jananī* (mother), *bhaginī* (sister), *rajakī* (washer-woman) and *nartakī* (dancing girl). Prajñā and Upāya are also called *lalanā* and *rasanā* which are also names of the two nerves *idā* and *piṅgalā* said to carry seed and ovum and to be associated with the moon and the sun respectively. In certain Buddhist Tantras, such as the *Nirṇāda* and *Ucchuṣma*, Prajñā and Upāya have been identified respectively with Śakti and Śiva. The common meaning of Prajñā is wisdom.

Prajñābhadra: The teacher of Atīśa. His name occurs in the list of fourteen teachers found in various Tibetan Tantras whose fame spread far and wide in the land of snow. We have no historical information on many of them.

Prajñābhiṣeka: Initiation of the disciple into *prajñā* or *śakti* according to the *Guhyasamāja* 161. The preceptor takes the hand of a beautiful woman, known by the term *vidyā* or *śakti*, and placing it on the hand of the disciple says that as Buddhahood is impossible to attain by any other means this *vidyā* should be accepted and never abandoned in life.

Prajñāgupta: A red-robed Indian Tantric who is said to have primarily been responsible for popularizing corrupt practices in Tibet before the coming of Atisa Dīpaṅkara. He is said to have been a *paṇḍita* from Oḍḍīyana and a disciple of the Kashmirian Ratnavajra. His eighteen important Tibetan disciples are known as robber-monks (ar-tsho-ban-de-s).

Prajñā-Kālī: One of the many forms of Kālī as described in the *Jayadratha-yāmala*.

Prajñākaramati: One of the six *dvāra-paṇḍitas* of the Vikramaśīlā monastery who was in charge of the southern gate. He flourished in the tenth century and was well-versed in Buddhist Tantras.

Prajñāntaka: Tantric Buddhist god who presides over the southern direction. He is described in the Vajrahuṅkāra Maṇḍala of the *Niṣpanna* as having a white complexion, three faces and four arms. He holds a white staff marked with *vajra*, sword, jewel and lotus.

Prajñāpāramitā: The goddess regarded as the personified form of the Mahāyāna treatise *Prajñāpāramitā* which is said to have been recovered by Nāgārjuna. She is usually recognized by *vyākhyāna mudrā* and the manuscript *Prajñāpāramitā* on a lotus. She is of three types—*sita* (white), *pīta* (yellow) and *kaṇaka* (golden). She has the image of Akṣobhya on her crown, is two-armed, one-faced, and is generally represented in *vajra-paryaṅka*, carrying a lotus in her right hand and the manuscript in the left. In another form her two hands display *vyākhyāna mudrā*. On a lotus to her left rests the manuscript. In some cases there are two manuscripts on two lotuses rising from under her arm-pits. One of the finest images of this goddess, originally from Java, is now in the Leiden Museum.

Prajñapti: Śāsanadevatā of the third Jain Tīrthaṃkara Sambhavanātha according to the Digambara tradition. Her vehicle is a bird and her six hands are adorned with an axe, crescent, fruit, sword and *varada mudrā*.

Prajñāvardhanī: Tantric Buddhist goddess of the *dhāriṇī* category who is described as being white in colour, holding in her left hand a sword on a blue lotus and in her right hand *viśvavajra*. *Niṣpanna* 57.

***Prajñopāya*:** A text on Vajrayāna which was composed about AD 705 by Anaṅgavajra, one of the eighty-four Siddhas. Its complete name being *Prajñopāya-viniścayasiddhi* it deals mainly with the concepts of Prajñā and Upāya, the two basic entities conceived as the Female and Male Principles. The state of perfection, accroding to this text is neither duality nor non-duality. Wisdom, conceived as the Female Principle, and the means of its attainment through the Male, are to be combined in one's own self for the purpose of liberation which is perfect enlightenment through the practical experience of the Female Principle. Prajñā (wisdom) is linked with a state of intense emotion called *sukha* or *mahāsukha* (great bliss) which is conducive to complete enlightenment. Prajñā is often definitely identified with flesh-and-blood woman, and the concept of *mahāsukha* (great bliss) is sought to be explained in terms of sexual symbolism which is in general agreement with the common Tantric tradition. Ed. B.T. Bhattacharyya, GOS, XLIV, Baroda 1929.

Prākāmyasiddhi: A type of *siddhi* (attainment of miraculous power) which may be obtained through the rites of Antardasāra. *Nityaṣoḍaśikārṇava* VIII. 159.

***Prakārāntara Mantrābhidhāna*:** This work comprising 173 verses purports to give the meanings of the letters of the alphabet starting with various meanings of *oṃkāra*. Traditionally believed to be a part of the *Rudrayāmala*.

***Prakārāntara Mātṛkānighaṇṭu*:** Attributed to one Mādhavācārya, described as *deśika-maṇḍali-mukuṭa-māṇikyopama-paramahaṃsa*, it lays down the meanings of the letters of the Tantric alphabet in 52 couplets starting with the significance of *om*.

***Prakārāntara Varṇanighaṇṭu*:** Said to be a part of *Rudrayāmala*, it enumerates the meanings of the letters grouped into five classes after the name of the five gross elements.

Prakāśa: The static aspect of the ultimate reality. According to the Śaiva and Śākta schools, *śakti* is *prakāśa-vimarśamaya*. In the background is *prakāśa* (illumination) and in the foreground is *vimarśa* (vibration) of *prakāśa* which is the subjective awareness of the static and latent power. *Prakāśa* is like the manifestation of all the qualities of an individual and *vimarśa* is his awareness of having those qualities. Prior to creation the *prakāśa-śakti* remains latent in the supreme being. Śiva or Maheśa is pure illumination (*prakāśamātra-tanu*) or the abstract self-shining thought with all the principles of activity contracted within him (*antarlīna vimarśaḥ*). Śakti is the principle of activity or the inherent activity of thought (*vimarśa* or *kriyāśakti*) and she contains the seed of the future worlds (*bhāvicarācarā-bījaṃ*). Śiva realizes himself through Śakti, and therefore it is said that he is the form which is to be reflected in the clear looking-glass of *vimarśa*. *Kāmakalāvilāsa* 1 ff.

Prakāśānanda Deśika: Disciple of Subhagānanda (q.v.) who completed the *Manoramā* commentary on the *Tantrarājatantra*. The first 22 chapters were written by his teacher.

Prakaṭayoginī: Āvaraṇadevatā of ten *mudrā-śaktis*: Sarvasaṃskobhinī, Sarvavidrāvinī, Sarvākarṣaṇī, Sarvaveśakārīṇī, Sarvonmādinī, Mahāṅkuśā, Khecarī, Vījamudrā, Yonimudrā and Trikhaṇḍā. *Nityaṣoḍaśikārṇava* I, 199-200. *Gandharvatantra* V. 87-8.

Prakṛti: Ultimate cause of the world of objects which is an unintelligent and unconscious principle, uncaused, eternal and all-pervading, very fine and always ready to produce the world of objects. It is the primordial matter or substance, often conceived as a Female Principle and known by different names like Pradhāna, Avyakta, etc. It is constituted by three *guṇas—sattva, rajas* and *tamas* (q.v.). The whole of the cosmos exists in a subtle form in Prakṛti and becomes manifest in creation through the union with the conscious principle, *puruṣa*, conceived as the male element. The evolutes of *prakṛti* are *mahān* or *buddhi*, *ahaṃkāra*, *manas*, *tanmātras* and *mahābhūtas*.

Prakṛti-doṣa: Impure mental states of defilement such as forgetfulness, illusion, stupor, laziness, etc., associated with the *svādhiṣṭhāna-citta*. The absorption of mind on the *cakra* is a matter of great achievement of the aspirant, but this stage is not free from *avidyā* or ignorance and kindred impurities.

Pralayākala: One of the three classes of fettered beings (Paśus) according to the Śaiva Āgamas. Other two classes are Vijñānākala and Sakala. Pralayākala beings are fettered by *karma* and *mala* (q.v). *Tattvaprakāśa* I. 11.

Pramuditā: Tantric Buddhist goddess of the *bhūmi* (q.v.) category described as having a red complexion, two arms and a jewel as recognition symbol. *Niṣpanna* 55.

Prāṇamañjarī: Commentator on the *Tantrarājatantra*. She was the wife of Premanidhi Pantha and lived in the eighteenth century.

***Prānatoṣaṇī Tantra*:** A Tantric manual composed by Rāmatoṣana Vidyālaṅkāra in 1820. Also spelt as *Prāṇatoṣiṇī* it is modelled on Kṛṣṇānanda's *Tantrasāra*. It is named after Prāṇakṛṣṇa Viśvāsa of Khardaha, the patron of the author. Rāmatoṣaṇa himself belonged to the dynasty of Kṛṣṇānanda Āgamavāgīśa. It is a very large modern work having more than 1,000 pages. The author has mentioned his sources and carefully classified the usual Tantric topics with a view to catering to the requirements of the practitioners. Certain special topics such as praise of the life of householders, description of the ācāras, special magical rites, means of understanding the language of birds and beasts and so forth are also dealt with. Though Durgā Pūjā and other Śākta rituals are described, it appears that the author has a Vaiṣṇavite bias. Published by Vasumati Sahitya Mandir, Calcutta.

Praṇava: *Om*, the first seed-syllable (*bijā-mantra*) signifying *brahman*, the Absolute. Belief in a syllable representing any god or supreme being is very old. The equation of *praṇava* or *oṃ* with *brahman* is found in the Upanisads. Even Patañjali in his yoga philosophy accepts the *praṇava* (i.e. *om*) to be representative of Īśvara.

Praṇava Tanu: Also known as *baindava-śarīra* it is the transubstantiated body which a Siddha (q.v.) attains by disciplining his body and through various other processes. The followers of Siddha-mārga believe that by using the ceaseless supply of unseen extraphysical nourishment it is possible to revitalize the body. When the transmutation of *aśuddha-māyā* into *śuddha-māyā* is accomplished the body becomes incorruptible and freed from the thraldom of impure matter. It becomes known as *praṇava-tanu*; the man with *praṇava-tanu* is called *jīvanmukta*.

Prāṇayāma: Regulation of breath which is the fourth discipline of Yoga. It consists in *recaka* (exhalation), *puraka* (inhalation) and *kumbhaka* (retention) during the breathing process. There are also other processes of *prāṇāyama*. The theory is that the vital air (*prāṇa*) should enter the *susumnā* and stay there until it gathers sufficient momentum to pierce the *cakras* and reach the *brahma-randhra*. Prāṇāyāma becomes successful only when the *nāḍis* are purified. *Prāṇatoṣaṇī* VI. 1. 408. Breath in Tantric Buddhism is of the nature of five *bhūtas* (elements) and the five kinds of knowledge. It is like a bright gem drawn from inside and placed like a lump on the tip of the nose and is then meditated upon. *Guhyasamāja* XVIII.

Praṇidhāna: Tantric Buddhist goddess of the Pāramitā (q.v.) and Vaśitā (q.v.) category. Under the former she is blue in complexion, with two arms and the sword-on-lotus is her symbol while under the latter she is yellow in colour and the blue lotus is her symbol. *Niṣpanna* 56-7.

Prapañcasāra: A very important Tantra ascribed to Śaṅkarācārya. It has 36 *paṭalas* (chapters) supposed to represent the 36 *tattvas* of Śakti. It deals with creation, embryology, *kuṇḍalinī*, alphabet (*varṇas*), herbs, *bīja* (q.v.), initiation; worship of Vāc, Sarasvatī, Tripurā, Mulāprakrti, Ambikā, Tvaritā, Lakṣmī, etc., with their *yantra*, *gāyatrī*, *bīja*, *dhyāna*, *japa*, *homa* and other requirements; worship of Durga, Sun, Moon, Mahāgaṇeśa, Manmatha; Yoga, Siddhi, Yantras, Viṣṇu and Nārāyaṇa; *mantras* called Trailokyamohana; *mantras* pertaining to Varāha, Nṛsiṃha, Viṣṇupañjara, Prasāda, Ardhanārīśvara, Gāyatrī, Triṣṭubḥ, Havana, Anuṣṭbh, etc., and drawing of *yantras*; avatāras of Viṣṇu and so forth. This Tantra has a commentary known as *Prapañcasāra-vivaraṇa* and the latter has a gloss called *Prayogakramadīpikā*. Other commentaries are *Vijñānacandrikā*, *Sambandhadīpikā*, *Ṣaṭsampradāyarahasya*, *Prapañcasāravyākhyā*, *Prapañcasāradīpa*, *Prapañcasāragūḍārthadīpikā*, *Vijñāna-dyotinī*, *Prapañcasāravivṛti*, *Prapañça-sāraprayogavidhi*, *Prapañcasārasambandha-ṭīkā* and *Prapañcasāravṛtti*. Published in *Tantrik Texts*, Vol. III, new ed. Vols. XVIII-XIX, 1939; ed. by A. Sarasvati, Delhi 1981.

Prasanna Tārā: An emanation of Ratna-sambha. Mentioned twice in *Sādhanamālā* 241, once as a companion of Aṣṭabhujā Kuru-kullā and once again as a principal deity. She has eight faces and sixteen arms. Except for the face on the top all her seven faces are represented as having a charming, sweet expression though she is not benign and peaceful.

Praśāntamitra: Tantric Ācārya who was a disciple of Jñānapāda. He studied the *Prajñāpāramitā* and some sections of the Kriyā and Yoga Tantras and attained Yamāntaka-*siddhi*. He built a monastery called Amṛtakara to the south of Nālandā, Bihar.

Pratibhānakūṭa: Bodhisattva described thrice in *Niṣpanna* as having a green, yellow, and red complexion and a whip as his symbol. He is affiliated with the families of Amogha-siddhi, Amitābha and Ratnasambhava. Pratibhānakūṭa is also a form of Avalok-iteśvara or Lokeśvara, described as one-faced and two-armed and sitting in *vajraparyaṅka* pose on a lotus holding a noose against his chest with his right hand and a bowl of gems in his left. There is another Pratibhāna who is a goddess of *Pratisaṃvit* category. In the Dharmadhātuvāgīśvara Maṇḍala of the *Niṣpanna* she is described as being of northern direction; her complexion is emerald, and she holds a bell in her two hands.

Pratibhāsa: Term for revelation in Tantric Buddhism which takes place through a psychic exercise in the form of constant meditation on an object, conceptual or otherwise, which appears in a contracted form before the aspirant. *Guhyasamāja* XVIII.

Pratihārya: One of the eight limbs of Yoga (q.v.); it is the restraint and subjugation of the senses to the mind.

Pratīka: A symbol through which the deity is worshipped. The aim is to recognize in the limited the presence of the all-pervading spirit which transcends all limitations of time and space. The *pratīka* may be internal—like the mind, intellect or soul of the worshipper, or it may be external—any token object which serves as a substitute or symbol of the real object of worship or meditation.

Pratisaṃvits: Acknowledged branches of logical analysis which have been deified in Tantric Buddhism as goddesses. The four goddesses of this category are Dharma (nature), Artha (analysis), Nirukti (etymological analysis) and Prabhāna (context). *Niṣpanna* 57-8.

Pratyāhāra: Withdrawal of the senses from their respective external objects and keeping them under the control of the mind. It is the fifth discipline of Yoga. In the Buddhist *Guhyasamāja* XVIII it is described as the process by which the sense organs are controlled.

Pratyālīḍha: A posture of sitting in which the left leg is outstretched while the right is slightly bent and placed under it. It is the opposite of Ālīḍha.

Prauḍha, Prauḍhānta: The fourth and fifth stages (*ullāsas*) of spiritual attainment. In both the stages worldly fetters do not cease though the joy of spiritual upliftment leads the aspirants to an ecstatic state. *Kulārṇava* VII. 56 ff.; *Paraśurāmakalpasūtra* X. 68; *Kaulamārgarahasya* 41-2. These stages are for persons who have reached the Vīra (q.v.) state. In these stages the aspirant learns the essentials and tries to concentrate his mind. The Prauḍha stage belongs to the Samayācāra category and the Prauḍhānta to the Svairācāra. *Vṛtti* on *Paraśurāmakalpasūtra* VII. 1; X. 68; X. 80.

Prayāga: Holy resort of the goddess variously known as Lalitā, Mādhaveśvarī and Kamalā which is the confluence of the Gaṅgā and Yamunā in Allahabad. *Matsya Purāṇa* XIII. 26; *Devībhāgavata* VII. 30.55; *Kubjikā* XVIII. 42 ff.; *Jñānārṇava* V. 66 ff.; etc.

Pretasantarpita: A form of Avalokiteśvara (q.v.) who bears *jaṭāmukuṭa* (q.v.), is six-armed, and exhibits in his first pair of hands the *varada* pose, in the second pair a jewel and a book, and in the third a rosary and *tridaṇḍī*. He is white in colour. *Sādhana* 89.

Pṛthudaka: Holy resort of the goddess Mahāvegā mentioned in the *Bṛhannīla* and *Prāṇatoṣaṇī*. It is modern Pehoa in Karnal district, Haryana.

Pṛthvībīja: The later *laṃ* which is regarded as the seed of earth. In the womb of the *mūlādhārapadma* exists the square-shaped Pṛthivīmaṇḍala yellow in colour. *Māyātantra* quoted in *Ṣaṭcakravivṛti*. In its centre is the seed *laṃ* which is also described as Indrabīja and conceived of as being seated on an elephant. On the *bindu* just above this *bīja* resides Brahmā with his Śakti Vedamātā or Sāvitrī. Kālīcaraṇa on *Ṣaṭcakranirūpaṇa* 5; *Nirvāṇatantra* IV.

Pūjā: Worship, the ultimate purpose of which is unification with the deity. *Mahānirvāṇa* XIV. 123-4. It is of two kinds: Bāhya (external) and Abhayantra (internal). It may be Sādhāra (with object) or Nirādhāra (without object). It is often classified into Vedic, Tantric and Miśra. Among other classifications we have Nitya, Naimittika and Kāmya; Sāttvika, Rājasika and Tāmasika; and Uttama, Madhyama and Adhama. *Gandharva* XXII, 10-2; XXIV. 22-3; *Mahānirvāṇa* XIV. 122.

Puṃ-mantra: The *mantras* by which male gods are invoked. Those meant for goddesses are *strī-mantras* or *vidyās*. Others are of neuter gender (*napuṃsaka*). A *puṃ-mantra* ends with *huṃ phaṭ*; *strīmantra* with *svāhā*; and *napuṃsaka-mantra* with *namaḥ*. *Śāradātilaka* II. 58-60.

Puṃstvamala: See Pañcakleśa.

Puṇḍravardhana: Also known as Pauṇḍravardhana and Puṇyavardhana it is the holy resort of the goddess Pāṭalā. It is identified with modern Mahasthan in Bogra district, Bangladesh. *Matsya Purana* XIII. 35; *Devībhāgavata* VII. 30.64; etc.

Puraścaraṇa: Repeated recitation of a *mantra* without which it cannot be effective. *Śaktisaṅgama*, Sundarī, III. 155-6; XVI. 45-6; *Gandharva* XXVIII, 7-8. It is regarded as the first step of Sādhanā. *Puraścaryārṇava* VI. 413 lists have five steps—Japa, Homa, Tarpaṇa, Abhiṣeka and Viprabhojana. *Tantrasāra* 48. In some texts another five steps are added. There are different degrees to this rite which apply to aspirants accroding to whether they belong to Paśu, Vīra or Divya categories. In this age—Kali Yuga—proper Puraścaraṇa is not possible. *Kālivilāsatantra* IV. 6-7. Japa or muttering the *mantra* is the main feature. *Kriyāsāra* quoted in *Tantrasāra* 48. There are elaborate rules and taboos regarding food habits, behaviour, time and space. The purpose of Puraścaraṇa is to attain *mantrasiddhi*.

Purṇābhiṣeka: The highest form of initiation.

Pūrṇagiri: Holy resort of the goddess variously known as Kālikā, Pūrṇeśvarī, etc., mentioned in *Hevajra* VII, *Jñānārṇava* V. 66 ff. etc. Same as Pūrṇa and Pūrṇaśaila it has been mentioned in the *Ain-i-Akbari* as located in the Bijapur region. The name may not be unconnected with that of the Pūrṇa, modern Paira, a branch of the Godavari. The *Ānandārṇava* gives the name of the *pīṭha* as Pūrṇabhudhara.

Pūrṇāhamtā: Attainment of perfect subjecthood, which takes the form of complete identification of the subject and the object. This concept finds its best expression in Kashmir Śaivism. *Paramārthasāra* 13-14. *Īśvarapratyabhijñāvimarśinī* II. 192-3.

Pūrṇakalā: The first among the four Kalās (q.v.) of Śakti; the others are *kalā*, *aṃśa* and *aṃśāṃśa*. The Śakti (energy) of any deity consists of sixteen *kalās*. Together they form perfection and are collectively known as Pūrṇakalā. The other three are concerned with parts, portions and parts of those portions. *Ṣaṭcakraviveka* 131-2.

Purnānanda: Compiled the Tantric text *Śyāmārahasya* (ed. with Bengali trans. by S. Tirthanath, Calcutta 1982). His other works are *Tattvānandataraṅgiṇī*, *Ṣaṭkarmollāsa*, *Śāktakrama* and *Śrītattvacintāmaṇi*, Calcutta Sanskrit Series XIX. Often suffixed by the epithets Paramahaṃsa and Parivrājaka. He flourished in the village Katiholi in Netrakona, Mymensingh district of East Bengal, in the sixteenth century.

Purṇatākhyāti: Attaining the highest goal in Tantric aspiration.

Puruṣa: Cosmic principle first mentioned in the Puruṣasukta portion of the *Ṛgveda* (X. 90). In later Vedas it is the male principle of creation *AV*. X. 2; *VS* XXXI. 18, XXXII. 2. In *ŚB* XIII. 6.1.1 and *Nirukta* II. 3 it is equated with the universe. In the Upanisads it is identified with *ātman*, *Bṛhadāraṇyaka* I. 4, *Kaṭha* III. 10-1, *Muṇḍaka* II. 10-1, etc. In *Śvetāśvatra* I. 2, it is the First Principle. In the *Sāṅkhya*, Puruṣa is the Male Principle, the contact of which with Prakṛti causes the evolution of the world. It is indifferent and inactive but not devoid of intelligence and as such a conscious principle. Just as a blind and a lame man cooperate in order to go out of a forest so also material and unintelligent Prakṛti in cooperation with the inactive, indifferent but intelligent Puruṣa, enables the evolution of the world. The Tantras accept the Sāṅkhya concept but not the position. There it is stated that Śakti herself assumes the form of Puruṣa in order to perform the function of creation. It is for her sport, which is why the inactive and passive Puruṣa is shown lying under the feet of dancing Prakṛti. According to another version Mahāśakti combines both Puruṣa and Prakṛti, the former being the cause of bondage and the latter of liberation. Puruṣa has also been ragarded as one of the *tattvas* (fundamentals). It has six worlds—Ekavīra, Īśāna, Bhaveśa, Ugra, Bhīma and Vāma. Also known as Ātma-tattva Puruṣattva is of four kinds—Sakala, Pralayākala, Vijñānākala and Śuddha. *Tantrāloka* I, 126.

Puruṣadattā: Śāsanadevatā of the Jain Tīrthaṃakara Sumatinātha according to the Digambara tradition. She rides an elephant and holds in her hands a disc, *vajra*, fruit, and displays the *varada-mudrā*.

Pūrva-Kaula: A sect of the Kaulas (q.v.) mentioned by Lakṣmīdhara in his commentary on *Saundaryalaharī* XXXIII. They believe in Śiva-Śakti equilibrium. The Uttarakaulas worship the symbolic triangle of the *Śrīcakra* (q.v.).

Puryaṣṭaka: The eight subtle and gross

elements of which the body of the goddess as represented in the *aṣṭakoṇa-cakra* is composed. *Kāmakalāvilāsa* XI.

Pustaka: Book in the form of a manuscript which represents the *Prajñāpāramitā* or 'the book of transcendental knowledge'. The book is carried by certain Buddhist deities, notably, Prajñāpāramitā, Mañjuśrī, Sarasvatī and Cundā.

Putraka: Those who have been initiated into *viśeṣa-dīkṣā* of Āgamanta Śaivism. They are so called because they belong to the *sāmīpya* stage of spiritual progress in which they feel themselves to be the sons of god.

Rr

Rāḍha: Some unspecified sites of the Rāḍha region comprising Burdwan, Hooghly, Howrah, Birbhum, Bankura, Midnapore, parts of Murshidabad and Purulia districts of West Bengal, regarded as the holy resorts of the goddess Maṅgalacaṇḍī are mentioned in the *Rudrayāmala*, *Bṛhannīla* and *Prānatoṣaṇī* Tantras. More precisely these sites seem to be on the land watered by the Ajay and its affluents and tributaries in the Birbhum and Burdwan districts. The Birbhum district is celebrated for Śākta-Tāntric activities.

Rāga: Attachment. It belongs to the *cit-acit* category of thirty-six principles of cosmic evolution. In its negative aspect *rāga* is the attachment towards worldly life and pleasure. *Jīva*, the individual, is like pure white cloth. *Rāga* emanating from Kalātattva (q.v.) colours it with attachment by which human beings are caught in worldly fetters. *Tantrāloka* IX. 210. Elsewhere it is said that when the permanent satisfaction of Śiva is contracted it resorts as rāga, to imperfect Jīvas. Ibid., IX, 199. The number of the worlds of *rāga-tattva* is five—Ekaśiva, Ananta, Aja, Umāpati and Pracaṇḍa. In esoteric Buddhism too *rāga* is attachment. The term is also used for *karuṇā* and *kṛpā* signifying compassion. But gradually the word acquired the meaning of intense and transcendental bliss, the means or expedient (*upāya)* for attaining the Bodhicitta and so forth.

Rāgarati: Queen of the Dhyānī Buddha Amitābha. In *Guhyasamāja* I it is stated that she came into existence owing to the meditation of the Lord Bodhicittavajra and was placed in the western direction.

Rāghavabhaṭṭa: Author of *Padārthādarśa*, the celebrated commentary of *Śāradātilaka* who flourished in Maharashtra. He was a man of encyclopaedic learning who had interpreted Kālidāsa and Bhavabhūti. The authorship of *Uttaracampu* based on the *Rāmāyaṇa* is attributed to him. He had written elaborate notes on *mudrā* and *puraścaraṇa* and held that the *Prapañcasāra* was Śaṅkarācārya's own work. He quoted elaborately from the Śulvasūtras which referred to numerous passages on *nyāsa*. He held that the Tantras were based upon the Upaniṣads like the *Rāmapūrvatāpanīya*, etc.

Raghunātha Tarkavāgīśa: Tantric teacher who composed, in Śaka 1609 (AD 1687), the *Āgamatattvavilāsa*, ed. P. Sastri, Calcutta 1985. He was a scion of the family of the renowned scholar-devotee Sarvānanda (q.v.).

Rahasya: Āvaraṇadevatā or Yoginī of Sarvarogaharacakra, the presiding goddess of the *cakra* being Tripurasiddhā. *Setubandha* on *Nityaṣoḍaśikārṇava* I, 164-5.

Rahasya-Āmnāya: Mysterious area of Pañcarātra knowledge comprising letters and formulae, meditation on them, and special modes of worship by means of *mantras* of various kinds.

***Rahasyakāṇḍa*:** 'Book of Secret Doctrines', a section of the *Brahmāṇḍa Purāṇa* which contains the teachings of Hayagrīva to Agastya which are said to have been imparted at Kanci. The *Lalitopākhyana*, together with the two exquisite hymns, *Lalitāsahasranāma* and *Lalitātriśati*, is said to be a part of this Rahasyakāṇḍa.

Rahasyamālā: A rosary for muttering *tāriṇīmantra*. It is made of mahaśaṅkha (bone of human forehead) and fifty pearls. *Tantrasāra* 30.

Rahasya-Sampradāya: The followers of the Trika doctrine of Kashmir Śaivism.

Rahasyayoginī: The eight presiding goddesses of the *aṣṭakoṇa-cakra*. *Gandharva* XVII. 74.

Rāhulabhadra: Buddhist Tantric scholar and Vajrācārya who flourished in the eighth-ninth century.

Rājabalahāṭa: Holy resort of the goddess Viśālalocanī mentioned in the *Caṇḍimaṅgala*. It is modern Rajbalhat in the Serampore subdividion of Hooghly district, West Bengal.

Rājacakra: One of the five forms of *cakra* worship in which mother, sister, daughter, daughter-in-law and preceptor's wife are regarded as Śaktis. *Niruttara* X.

Rajakī: Woman of the washerman caste who serves as a female partner of the Tantric aspirant. The term is also used to denote Śakti as Kulanāyikā. *Niruttara* XV; *Tantrasāra* 627. In Buddhist Tantras Rajakī is the name of Prajñā (q.v.). In the *Hevajratantra* it is said that Prajñā is so called because she pleases all beings. (*rañjanāt*).

Rājamātaṅgī: One of the six forms of Mātaṅgī. She is described as having the colour of the rising sun; she has a smiling face, two hands and attractive breasts. She looks like a girl of sixteen years, and her eyes seem to be of one who is intoxicated having drunk wine. She is adorned with various ornaments. Her *mantra* is given in the *Merutantra*. She is conceived of as residing within a triangle inside the pericarp of a lotus. She has long hair, wears a garland of *kadamba* around her neck, the moon on her head and a *tilaka* mark on her forehead. The region below her navel is marked by *trivali* or three lines under which is the pubic hair. Śuka and Sārī are her com-panions. She is the embodiment of 64 arts.

Rājarājeśvarī: Name of Śakti when she represents the *rajoguṇa*—the quality that affects the senses. She represents knowledge in its abstract sense and is known as Śrīvidyā (q.v.). Her attributes and iconological features are explained in the *Kāmikāgama*.

Rajas: That constituent of Prakṛti (q.v.) which is of the nature of pain and is mobile (*cala*) and stimulating (*upastambhaka*). It gives rise to wrath, greed, egotism, worldly activity and boastfulness. *Rajas* also denotes energy and as such it is active in the nerve known as *vajra* (q.v.).

Rājayoga: A form of Yoga in which the mind automatically merges in *brahman* just as air merges in the sky. *Prāṇatoṣaṇī* VI. 3.433. It is free from all dualism. *Śivasaṃhitā* V. 17. It leads to *nirvikalpa-samādhi* in which there is absolute unity of knower, knowledge and the source of knowledge. It is also possible by a special *kumbhaka* process of breath-control known as *manomurchā* which connects the mind with the supreme being. *Gheraṇḍa* VII. 16.

Rākinī: One of the six presiding goddesses of the *cakras*. Rākinī resides on the inner lotus of the Svādhiṣṭhāna-cakra. *Ṣaṭcakra-nirūpaṇa* 17.

Rakṣākālī: A form of Kālī (q.v.) variously depicted in Tantric literature. She has a white complexion, three faces, six arms, nine eyes, and matted locks of hair. Her garment is red. She is generally invoked as a protectress from calamities.

Rakṣās: Five protectress deities of Tantric Buddhism. They are Mahāpatisarā, Mahāsāhasrapramardinī, Mahāmantrānusāriṇī, Mahāsitavatī and Mahāmāyurī. A manuscript copy of the *Pañcarakṣā* describing these five rakṣā deities, their worship on different occasions and their powers, is to be found in almost every Buddhist household in Nepal. Such manuscripts contain miniature pictures of the Buddhist deities. According to the *Sādhanamālā*, the *rakṣā* deities, when worshipped grant long life, protect kingdoms, villages and meadows, destroy evil spirits, save mankind from diseases and famines, dangers and difficulties, illness, adversities, loss of wealth, cattle, etc. These five deities are worshipped either singly or collectively in a *maṇḍala*. In the *maṇḍala* Mahāpratisarā is the central deity while the four others occupy the four cardinal directions.

Rakta-Lokeśvara: A form of Avalokiteśvara. This Bodhisattva is flanked by Tārā to his right and on his left is Bhṛkuṭī. He is red in colour and carries in his four hands noose, goad, bow and arrow. He stands under an Aśoka tree. *Sādhana* 83.

Raktayamāri: A form of Yamāntaka, slayer of Yama, the god of death. When red in colour he is known as Rakta-Yamāri and when he is blue he is Kṛṣṇa-Yamāri (q.v.). He is one-faced and two-armed. He is an emanation of Akṣobhya whose image he bears on the crown.

***Raktayamāri Tantra*:** A text of Mantrayāna which belongs to the eighth century AD. It was known to Virūpa who flourished about AD 750. It is in Tibetan but there is a Sanskrit manuscript of it in Salu.

Rāmagiri: Holy resort of the goddess Trisandhyā or Śivanī mentioned in *Kubjikā* XVIII. 42 ff., *Matsya* XIII. 26 ff., *Devībhāgavata* VII. 30-55 ff., *Pīṭhanirṇaya*, etc. It is regarded as an important *pīṭha* where the right breast of Satī fell. The place is celebrated in Kālidāsa's *Meghadūta* and is identified with modern Ramtek near Nagpur in Maharashtra. Some scholars identify Rāmagiri with Citrakūṭa in the Banda district Uttar Pradesh. It may also be identified with Rāmatīrtha (q.v.).

***Rāmapūrvatāpanīya Upaniṣad*:** An important work in the field of Tantric studies according to Rāghavabhaṭṭa. The text is however, of late origin. It deals elaborately with the purpose and symbolism of the *yantras*. It also deals with the importance of the *mantras* stating that it is derived from the root *man* and is so called because it saves from all dangers, as the aspirant is thereby led to ponder over the subject of immeasurable refulgence which is the only principle in the world.

Rāmaśaṅkara: A Tantric teacher, most probably of Bengal, who composed the *Gurutantra* in Śaka 1416 (AD 1494) which lays down the means of attaining *mantrasiddhi*.

Rāmatīrtha: Holy resort of the goddess Ramaṇā mentioned in *Matsya Purāṇa* XIII. 40; *Devībhāgavata* VII. 30.69; *Padma Purāṇa*, Sṛṣṭi XVII. 198; *Skanda* V. 3. 98. 78. The *Bṛhannīla* and *Prāṇatoṣaṇī* refer to the goddess as Mahadhṛti. Rāmatīrtha is the same as Śurpāraka, modern Sopara in Thane district, Maharashtra. In this case, however, Rāmagiri (q.v.) may be indicated.

Rāmatoṣaṇa Vidyālaṅkāra: Seventh in descent from Kṛṣṇānanda Āgamavāgīśa, the compiler of *Tantrasāra* who had composed in 1820 the *Prāṇatoṣaṇī-tantra* named after his patron Prāṇakṛṣṇa Viśvāsa of Khardaha. Ed. J. Vidyasagara, Calcutta 1898; ed. and published by Vasumatī Sahītya Mandira, Calcutta.

Rāmeśvara: The commentator on the *Pararśurāmakalpasūtra*. His views seem to be rather conservative because he insists on the question of the competence of the aspirant, *adhikāra*, who wants to receive initiation into the *Kaulamārga*. He has given a list of conditions after the fulfilment of which one becomes eligible for undertaking Kaula initiation. This attitude is in direct conflict with what the *Mahānirvāṇa* and some other Tantras say—that all men from the Brāhmaṇas to the untouchables have eligibility for Kaula practices.

Rāmeśvara: Holy resort of the goddess Prabhā mentioned in the *Bṛhannilatantra* V. The *Prāṇatoṣaṇī* refers to the goddess as Mahāsiddhi. It is the celebrated Setubandha Rāmeśvara in Ramnad district, Tamil Nadu. Another Rāmeśvara lies at the confluence of the Banas and the Chambal in Madhya Pradesh.

Ramyadeva: Śaiva-Tantric teacher of the Krama system who flourished in the twelfth century. His commentary on *Bhāvopahāra* is known as *Vivaraṇa*. Pub. in Kashmir Sanskrit Series, no. XIV, 1918.

Rasa: Sap; elixir; sentiment. Accroding to Raseśvara-darśana (q.v.) the use of chemical drugs, especially those prepared from mercury, makes possible the renovation of the body and is conducive to *Jīvanmukti* (q.v.), *Sarvadarśanasaṃgraha* IX. 1 ff. *Rasa* is also conceived in terms of intense emotional attachment between the male and female principles symbolizing two aspects of Śakti, embodied by the aspirant and his partner. *Lalitāsahasranāma* 106. See Jīvanmukti, Rasāyana, Raseśvara, Darsana, Siddhacikitsā.

***Rasacintāmaṇi*:** A treatise on alchemy written by Madanāntadeva which describes the process of the preparation of calomel, the fabrication of gold and silver, extraction of zinc from calamine, copper from vitriol, etc.

***Rasahṛdaya*:** A treatise on alchemy composed by Bhikṣu Govinda. It is a text of Buddhist origin composed between the eleventh and thirteenth century AD. It is based on Nāgārjuna's *Rasaratnākara* (q.v.).

Rasanā: Name of a nerve. In the Buddhist Tantras it stands for Upāya. Prajñā and Upāya are called Lalanā and Rasanā respectively which are the names for the two nerves Īḍā and Piṅgalā well known in the Hindu Tantric nervous system. It is on the right side of the middle nerve Avadhutī or Suṣumnā and is also known as Yamunā, Kālī, Sūrya, Camana, Grāhaka and Vam. It also symbolizes the *nirmāṇa-kāya* of the Buddha.

***Rasanakṣatramālikā*:** Treatise on alchemy written by the medieval author Mathanasiṃha.

Rasānanda-yoga Samādhi: A state of yogic bliss achieved through breath-control *Gheraṇḍa* VII. 10-1.

***Rasapradīpa*:** Treatise on medicinal alchemy of the late-medieval period which refer to veneral diseases as *phiraṅgaroga* and their treatment with *rasakarpura* (calomel), *chobcini* (smilex-china), etc.

***Rasaprakāśasudhākara*:** A treatise on alchemy composed by Yaśodhara. It is a text of Buddhist origin composed between eleventh and thirteenth centuries AD. It is based on Nāgārjuna's *Rasaratnākara*, but Yaśodhara has made a substantial contribution to the metallurgy of zinc.

***Rasarājalakṣmī*:** Treatise on alchemy written by the medieval author Viṣṇudeva which gives an account of common *rasas* and *uparasas*, mainly on the basis of the *Rasaratnasamuccaya*.

***Rasaratnākara*:** Tantric treatise on alchemy written by Nāgārjuna in the eighth century. It contains methods for the purification of important minerals—crude copper by means of 'poling', extraction of the essence of minerals, liquifaction of mica, fixation of mercury, a recipe for Aethiops mineral, 'killing' of mercury. It also describes the nature of the apparatuses used. There is another work of the same name composed by Siddha Nityanātha which deals mainly with the tests for 'killing' mercury.

***Rasaratnasamuccaya*:** One of the most important works on medicinal chemistry which deals with minerals having medical properties and classes them under the four categories of *rasa*, *uparasa*, *ratna* and *loha*. Rasa was almost exclusively applied to the employment of mercury and metals in medicine. *Abhra* (mica), *vaikrānta*, *mikṣika* (pyrites), *vimala*, *adrija* (bitumen), *sasyaka*, *capala*, and *rasaka* were the eight principal *rasas*. Sulphur, red-ochre, vitriol, alum, orpiment, realgar, *añjana* and *kamkuṣṭha* were the eight *uparasas*, useful in the operation of mercury. *Ratna* (gems) were also regarded as agencies which would help the fixation or coagulation of mercury. So also were *lohāni*—metals like gold, silver, iron, tin, brass, bell-metal, etc. Elaborate rules are laid down in this text for initiation through Tantric rites into the secrets of mercurial lore. The text also deals with the practical questions of laboratory, technical terms, apparatus, etc. Emphasis is laid upon the ingredients for crucibles and the purification, fixation and incineration of mercury and so on.

***Rasārṇava*:** A Śaiva Tantric work of the twelfth century. It is mainly based upon Nāgārjuna's *Rasaratnākara* (q.v.). It gives a list of the apparatuses used for chemical purposes and treats of the crucibles and the colour of flames. It also deals with the alkalis, colouring and 'killing' of metals, purification of quick-silver, extraction of zinc and copper and a variety of other chemical subjects. Here mercury is said to have been composed of five elements representing Śiva himself.

***Rasasāra*:** A medieval treatise on alchemy written by Govindācārya which deals with eighteen operations of mercury. The author has described his indebtedness to the Buddhists of Tibet for the knowledge of certain processes.

***Rasasiddhiśāstra*:** One of the Sanskrit treatises on alchemy which was translated into Tibetan. It is lost, only its name occurs in the Tibetan catalogue. It was composed by Vyādhipāda and was translated into Tibetan by Narendrabhadra and Ratnaśrī.

Rasatattva-sādhana: A Vaiṣnavite aspiration in which the realization of the experience of the union of Rādhā and Krṣna is aimed at. But the procedure of this *sādhana* is Tantric because its basis is the concept of the union of Puruṣa and Prakṛti. It may be in the form of the experience arising out of the physical union of the aspirant and his female partner or it may be a mental experience.

Rasāyana: The science of alchemy, meant for revitalization of the body with the help of *rasa* or chemical preparations. Patañjali in the Kaivalya-pāda of his *Yogasūtra* says that *siddhi* (q.v.) can be attained even by the application of herbs or medicines (*janmauṣadhi-mantra-tapaḥ-samādhijāḥ siddhayaḥ*). His commentators hold that this *auṣadhi* refers to the school of the Yogīs who attained perfection with the help of Rasāyana. In Mādhava's *Sarvadarśanasaṃgraha* the Rasāyana school is recognized as a school of Indian philosophy. The school is styled here as Raseśvara Darśana (q.v.) and the doctrines of this school are explained with reference to well-known texts on alchemy. The Rasāyana school is fundamentally based on the ideal of *jīvanmukti* (q.v.) (liberation within the span of life), and the method advocated is that of transubstantiation with the help of *rasa* or chemical preparations, generally of mercury, thus making the body immutable. *Rasahṛdaya-tantra* XIX. 63-4.

***Rasāyanaśāstroddhṛti*:** Tibetan version of a medieval treatise on alchemy which has been edited and translated by S.K. Pathak.

***Rasendracintāmaṇi*:** Treatise on alchemy of unknown authorship. It is a late-medieval text based on the *Rasaratnasamuccaya*.

Rasendracuḍāmaṇi: A late medieval treatise on alchemy composed between the eleventh and thirteenth centuries AD. It is based on Nāgarjuna's *Rasaratnākara* (q.v.). There is also another text of the same name which refers to *phiraṅga-roga*, or veneral disease, and its treatment with calomel, china-root, etc.

Raseśvara-darśana: Also known as *kāya-tattva* this philosophy is based on the idea of rendering, by varied physio-chemical processes, the human body deathless and also the spiritual liberation of man by his monadic transfiguration. It is believed that the preservation of the body can be achieved by the use of mercury, medicaments and breathing exercises. In this philosophy vibrating, cleansing, stimulating and projecting the body with the help of a special *elixir vitae* are considered to be essential preconditions for emancipation within the span of life. Mādhava's *Sarvadarśana-saṃgraha* describes Raseśvara Darśana as one of the schools of Indian philosophy and presents the arguments of its advocates against those of their opponents. It cites passages from Govindabhāgavata, Sarvajña-rāmeśvara and others and also from the celebrated chemical texts like the *Rasārṇava*, *Rasasiddhānta*, *Sākārasiddhi*, *Rasahṛdaya*, etc. See Jīvanmukti, Rasa, Rasāyana, Siddha-cikitsā.

Rathakrānta: A zone of Tantric culture extending from the Vindhyas to Mahācīna. According to the *Mahāsiddhasāratantra* this region has 64 Tantras. Among the principal Tantras of Rathakrāntā are: *Mahākāla*, *Kālabhairava*, *Kaivalya*, *Kulasadbhāva*, *Mahālakṣmī*, *Cīnācāra*, *Sammohinī*, *Śakti-saṅgama*, *Śāradā*, *Sarasvatī*, *Yakṣadāmara*, *Kaṅkāmālinī*, *Yogasāra*, *Nāradīya*, *Parameśvara*, *Prapañcasāra*, *Puraścaraṇa-candrikā*, *Ekajaṭā*, *Mahānirvāṇa*, *Meru*, *Mahanīla*, etc.

Ratisundarī: One of the eight yoginīs (Aṣṭayoginī, q.v.) described in the *Tantra-sāra*. She is of pleasing appearance with a complexion like gold. Her eyes resemble the lotus and she is adorned with all kind of ornaments like anklets, armlets and necklace.

Ratnaḍākinī: Goddess of the Dākinī category associated with the Tantric Buddhist Mahāmāyā. She belongs to the south, has a yellow complexion, four faces which are of blue, yellow, white and green colour, and four arms. She carries *khaṭvāṅga* and *ghaṇṭa* in two left hands and *vajra* and *kapāla* in the two right.

Ratnadala: A form of Avalokiteśvara, one-faced and two-armed, who stands on a lotus. He displays the *varada* pose in his right hand while his empty left touches his left shoulder.

Ratnākaragupta: Tantric Buddhist scholar who flourished about AD 100. He composed a number of *sādhanas* or meditative descriptions pertaining to the deities of Vajrayāna.

Ratnākaraśānti: One of the six *dvāra-paṇḍitas* of Vikramaśilā who flourished in the tenth century. He was a Buddhist Tantric scholar and was in charge of the eastern gate.

Ratnaketu Dhāraṇī: Sūtra in the collection entitled *Mahāsannipāta* (q.v.) which was translated into Chinese in the fifth century. In this text the Buddha preaches the doctrine of incantation. The *Ratnaketudhāraṇī* is a fairly long Sūtra containing a great deal of Tantric elements. *Mahāsannipāta-Ratnaketu-dhāraṇīsūtra*, edited by N. Dutt and S.N. Sharma in *Gilgit Manuscripts*, Vol. IV, Calcutta 1959, 114 ff.

Ratnapāṇi: Bodhisattva of the Dhyanī Buddha Ratnasambhava. He is of the nature of his sire and when represented he either stands erect or sits in different postures. He holds the stalk of a lotus on which appears the *kula* symbol which is a jewel. In *Niṣpanna* 58 he is described as being green in colour, holds the jewel in the right hand and the disc of the moon on a lotus in the left hand. Ratnapāṇi Lokeśvara holds a sword in his left hand and displays the *varada mudrā* with his right.

Ratnapāramitā: Tantric Buddhist goddess of Pāramitā (q.v.) category who is described as holding the *cintāmaṇi* flag in her right hand and the moon's disc on a lotus in the left. *Niṣpanna* 56.

Ratnas: Three permanent categories—Śiva, Śakti and Bindu. Śiva and Śakti represents the static (*prakāśa*) and kinetic (*vimarśa*) aspects of the same reality. Bindu is an eternal material entity outside the realm of Śakti but dependent on the latter's functioning.

Ratnasambhava: One of the five Dhyānī Buddhas. He is yellow in colour. His recognition symbol is a jewel. He exhibits *varada mudrā*. He originates from the syllable *tram* placed on the orb of sun. He represents the cosmic element *vedanā* (sensation). He possesses the knowledge of equality and presides over the spring season, saline taste and dental group of letters. *Advayavajrasaṃgraha* 41.

Ratnavajra: One of the six *dvāra-paṇḍitas* of Vikramaśilā who flourished in the tenth century. He was well-versed in Buddhist Tantras. He was from Kashmir and held as well the post of the first *mahāstambha*.

Ratnavali: Holy resort of the goddess Kumārī according to the *Pīṭhanirṇaya* where the right shoulder of Satī fell. The *Śivacarita* refers to the goddess as Śivā and describes the site as a *mahāpīṭha*. Possibly it is the same as the city of Ratnavati mentioned in the *Kāvya-mīmāṃsā*, but may also be a locality in Bengal. Ratnavali is also the name of a sacred tributary of the Vagmati in Nepal.

Ratnolkā: Tantric Buddhist goddess of light described in the Pañcaḍāka Maṇḍala of the *Niṣpannayogāvalī* as being yellow in colour and holding a jewel in her hand. *Ratnolkā pītā ratnadharā*. There is also a Dhariṇī goddess of the same name who is red in colour and holds the *cintāmaṇi* banner. *Ratnolkā raktā cintāmaṇi-dhvajadharā*.

Ratnoṣṇīṣā: Tantric Buddhist goddess of the Uṣṇīṣa (q.v.) category who is described as staying on the southern spoke; she is blue in colour and shows the *varada* pose: *dakṣiṇāre ratnoṣṇiṣo nīlo varadamudrayānvitaḥ*.

Rātri-sūkta: Hymn to Night; Night is conceived as a female deity like Dawn (Uṣas). *Ṛgveda* X. 127. Rātri or Niśā has a vital role to play in the Puranic literature from an historical point of view according to which her conception and functions were essentially needed to bring the tribal and non-vedic goddesses like Kauśikī, Vindyavāsinī, etc., in to the main stream of the Devī cult and to associate them with the developing concept of the Female Principle of creation. The influence of Rātri on the development of the concept of Kālī cannot be ignored—the Rātri-sūkta itself bears testimony to it.

Raudra Āgamas: A group of eighteen Śaiva Āgamas comprising *Vijaya*, *Niśvāsa*, *Madgīta*, *Parameśvara*, *Mukhavimba*, *Siddha*, *Santāna*, *Narasiṃha*, *Candrāṃśu*, *Vīrabhadra*, *Āgneya*, *Svayambhū*, *Visara*, *Raurava*, *Vimala*, *Kiraṇa*, *Lalita*, and *Saumeya*. The *Kiraṇāgama* substitutes *Prodgīta* for *Madgīta*, *Candrahāsa* for *Candrāṃśu*, *Bhadra* for *Virabhadra*, *Virakta* for *Visara*, *Kauravya* for *Raurava*, *Mukuṭa* for *Vimala* and *Para* for *Saumeya*.

***Raurava Āgama*:** An ancient Agamic text of which the aphorisms of the *Śivajñānabodham* form a part according to Śiva-jñāna-munivar, the commentator on the Sūtras.

Ṛddhi: Supernatural powers. The Buddhist texts speak of ten kinds of powers (*ṛddhi*, *iddhi*, *abhijñā*); they are to protect a mind-made image of oneself, to become invisible, to pass through solid things, to penetrate solid ground, to walk on water, to fly and so forth. The Brahmanical works speak of eight *siddhis* (q.v.) such as *animā*, *laghimā*, *mahimā*, *prakāmya*, *prāpti*, *vaśitva*, *iśitva* and *kāmavasāitva* (q.v.). They signify more or less the same powers as mentioned in the Buddhist texts in more general terms.

Ṛddhivaśitā: Tantric Buddhist goddess of the *vasitā* (q.v.) category who is described as being green as the sky *nabhaśyāmā* and holding in her left hand the discs of the sun and the moon on a lotus. *Niṣpanna* 57.

Ṛṇi-mantra: A kind of *mantra* so called when the number of the letters of the *mantra* exceeds those of the name of the aspirant. The reverse is *dhani mantra*. *Tantrasāra* 17-18.

Rohinī: Śāsanadevatā of the Tīrthaṃkara Ajitanātha according to the Digambara Jain tradition. She has an iron seat (*lohāsana*) and her hands depict the *varada* and *abhaya* poses, and hold a conch and a disc.

Ṛṣi: One of the six or seven limbs of a *mantra* others being Chandas, Devatā, Bīja, Śakti and Kīlaka. In some texts Aṅganayāsa and Dhyāna are added. *Śyāmārahasya* XII; *Kālītantra* I. 8-9; *Dīpikā* on *Śrīvidyāratnasūtra* 2.

Ruddha-mantra: Defective Tantric *mantra*; it contains *lam* in the beginning, middle or end. *Śāradātilaka* II. 72.

Rudrabhairavī: One of the forms of the Mahāvidyā goddess Bhairavī. She is described as having ten hands in which she holds a trident, drum, sword, shield, horn, arrow, noose, goad, book and rosary. She is seated on Śiva's throne, dressed in a red garment with a garland of severed heads around her neck. She is three-eyed and has a crescent on her head, and is resplendent like a thousand rising suns. In the *Jñāārṇava* her *mantra* is given. *Puraścaryārṇava* IX, 813.

Rudra-granthi: A knot in the *ājñācakra* (q.v.) obstructing the upward march of Kuṇḍalinī (q.v.). Com. on *Yogaśikhopaniṣad* I. 87; *Saubhāgyabhāskara* on *Lalitāsahasranāma* 85.

Rudrakālī: One of the twelve Kālīs mentioned by Abhinavagupta *Tantrāloka* IV, 157 ff. Identified with Para Saṃvit or ultimate reality. She is so called because she stops the influx of false notions (*rodhana*) and purges off the remnants of ignorance (*dravana*). She is also known as Bhadrakālī. Ibid. IV. 171-3.

Rudrakoṭi: Holy resort of the goddess Rudrāṇī or Kalyāṇī. *Matsya* XIII. 32; *Devībhāgavata* VII. 30. 61; *Padma*, Sṛṣṭi, XVII. 190; *Skanda* V. 3. 98.70. It is either the *tīrtha* of this name in Kuruksetra or that near the source of the Narmadā.

***Rudra Yāmala*:** An extensive work in 66 chapters and 6,000 verses; contains a panegyric of *Atharvaveda* and deals with the mysterious *kuṇḍalinī*, yogic practices and six *cakras* in the body. It prescribes sexual union and use of wine. The woman may be the aspirant's own wife or another's. The guru or preceptor is regarded as the source of all spiritual efforts. It mentions a number of Śākta Pīṭhas and states that the goddess appeared to the sage Vasiṣṭha and asked him to go to Cīnadeśa where he was initiated into the doctrines of the five Ms by the Buddha himself. It belongs to the Kashmirian Āgama Śāstra. In some manuscripts of the *Dhanda-puraścaraṇa-vidhi* it is stated in the colophon to be a part of *Rudrayāmala*. Ed. R.M. Chatterjee, Calcutta. *Uttaratantra* by Jivananda Vidyasagar, Asiatic Society, third ed. 1937; by R.K. Pai, Varanasi 1996; with Hindi com., Bombay 1983.

Rūpiṇī: One of the four Ḍākiṇī goddesses mentioned in the Buddhist Tantras. She is white in colour, has one face and four arms. Her hands hold *khaṭvāṅga*, *kapāla*, *damaru* and *kartari*. *Sādhana* 425.

S

Śabara-mārga: A branch of Tantric Śakti worship outlined in *Merutantra.* In this Tantra five branches of the Vāmā-mārga—Kaulika, Vāma, Cīnakrama, Siddhāntīya and Śabara—have been compared to the five fingers of the hand. This particular way must have been an adaptation of the cults and rituals of the tribes of central and coastal India bearing the generic name of the Śabaras. That the Śabaras had a position in the Vajrayāna Buddhism can be proved with reference of the Caryā songs. Śabara females are conceived of in terms of Sahajasundarī, Nairāmaṇi, Nairātmā, etc. There is a Tantric text known as *Śabaratantra.*

Śabaratantra**:** A Tantric text dealing with Śabaramārga (q.v.). It does not seem to be very old but it is highly interesting for the study of the tribal cults and rituals which have survived through the ages as an alternative tradition and which form the substratum of Tantrism itself. It is also important for the study of Indian folklore. One of the most interesting features of this text is that it contains mystic and ritualistic formulae in Arabic and refers to a Mohammedan Siddha called Ismail Pir or Ismail Yogin.

Śabarī: Tantric Buddhist goddess described in the *pañcaḍāka maṇḍala* of *Niṣpannayogāvalī* 75 as being white in colour and holding in her right hand Meru mountain. Her left hand exhibits the *tarjani mudrā*. Śabari, in the sense of a Śabara woman, has an important symbolism in the Caryā songs: 'High is the mountain there; on it sits Śabari decked with coloured feathers of a peacock.' The mountain is the spinal column, the *mahāsukha-cakra* and the Śabarī is Sahajasundarī. She is also conceived of as Nairātmā and union with her is thought of in terms of the eternal bliss arising out of the realization of non-dualism.

Śabarī-pā: One of the 84 Siddhas mentioned in *Caturasīti-siddhapravṛtti*. According to the Tibetan tradition he was the author of five texts of Vajrayāna. These works mainly pertain to the Sādhanā literature.

Śabda: Sound, which is the quality of *ākāśa* or space. When unlettered it is known as *dhvanyātmaka* and when lettered as *varṇātmaka*. Śabda has four states (*bhāvas*) called Parā, Paśyantī Madhyamā and Vaikharī (q.v.). It is said that consciousness moves as Śakti, at first in the subtle form of mind which is in itself the motionless causal sound (*parā-śabda*), then assumes a general undifferentiated movement (*paśyantī: sāmānya-spanda*), then a differentiated movement (*madhyamā: viśeṣa-spanda*) and finally in clearly articulated speech (*vaikharī: spaṣṭatara-spanda*) in the gross form of language as the expression of ideas and of physical objects (*artha*). In Ṫantrism, all *mantras* are in the body as unmanifest (*avyakta*) power of Śabda. Every *mantra* is a particular sound form. *Nāda*, the articulated sound-particle in the form of *bindu* (point without space), is eventually expressed as Śiva-Śakti equilibrium endowed with all consciousness. *Nāda*, *bindu* and *bija* (q.v.) form the *yoni* or *trikoṇa*, the seat of kāmạkalā (q.v.). With the help of *mantra*, the *kuṇḍalinī-śakti* may thus be awakened and made to pass through the states of sound-mechanism like Parā, Paśyantī, Madhyamā and Vaikharī. *Śaradātilaka* I. 108-11. See Gopinath Kaviraj in *Journal of Ganganath Jha Research Institute*, III. 97-108.

Śabdabrahma: Sound thought of as the highest cosmic principle. There are two grades of sound, the subtler is known as *bindu* and the subtlest as *nāda.* The expressed aspect of the *bindu* (q.v.) and *nāda* (q.v.) constituting sound is *bīja* (q.v.), and these three in conjuction constitute Śabdabrahma, which is consciousness inherent in matter. In special Tantric language it is the all-pervading serpent power or serpent-like *kāmakalā.* Bindu is the symbol of Siva, Bījā of Śakti and Nāda of their union. The great causal state of *brahman* or *Saṃvit* is symbolized by Śabdabrahma. *Śāradātilaka* II. 108-11.

Sādākhya-tattva: The expression in which 'I' or *aham* (subject) and 'this' or *idam* (object) are held in unity.

Ṣaḍakṣari Lokeśvara: A form of Avalokiteśvara, four-armed—the front ones in *namaskāra-mudrā* and back ones holding a rosary and a lotus which is flanked by his male and female attendants—Maṇibhadra and Saḍakṣarī Mahāvidyā.

Saḍakṣarī Mahāvidyā: Goddess associated with Sāḍakṣarī Lokeśvara. She has a yellow complexion. She sits in *vajrāsana* with her left hand holding a jewel and the right remaining empty.

Saḍaṅga Nyāsa: *Nyāsa* for feeling the deity in six parts of the body—heart, head, top of the head, protective amulet, eyes and intestines. It is exemplified by *Dharmasindhu* which declares that *nyāsa* of any kind has no Vedic background.

Saḍaṅga Yoga: Six limbs of yoga which are Prāṇāyāma, Dhyāna, Pratyāhāra, Dhārana, Tarka and Samādhi. *Tantrāloka* IV. 15. This list does not contain Yama, Niyama and Āsana of Patañjali's Aṣṭāṅga-yoga. The Ṣaḍaṅga is accepted by the Vaiṣnava Āgamas and Buddhist Tantras. The latter, however, substitutes Anusmṛti for Tarka.

Sadasadāgama: The Āgamas (q.v.) have a two-fold classification-*sat* and *asat*. According to *Śaktānandataraṅgiṇī*, Sad-āgamas are Āgamas *par excellence* (*sad-āgama eva āgamaśabdasya mukhyatvāt*) while the Asadāgamas are meant for deluding people. Ullāsa II.

Sadāśivatattva: One of the fundamentals of the Śaiva-Śākta philosophy. Also known as Sādākhyatattva, its insistence is on *icchā* (the power of will) though Somānanda and his followers of the Kashmir school hold that it has also much to do with the power of *jñāna* (knowledge) and *karma* (action). This *tattva* is explained as *nimeṣo'anta sadāśivaḥ* which means merger of *aham* (I-ness) and *idam* (Itness). Abhinavagupta also suggests the same: *evaṃ nimeṣonmesaśakti eva sad-āśiveśvarau.* The presiding deity of this *tattva,* which also accounts for the dissolution of the universe, has the same name. *Śivadṛṣṭi* 36-7; *Īśvarapratyabhijñā* III. 1.3.

Ṣaḍbhujā Sitatārā: Three-faced and six-armed Tārā of white complexion. Her right face is yellow, left is blue; the three right hands show *varada mudra*, rosary and arrow, and left hands carry *utpala*, lotus and bow. She sits in ardhaparyaṅka attitude and bears the effigy of Amoghasiddhi on her crown of matted hair. *Sādhana* 216.

***Saddharmapuṇḍarīka*:** The lotus Sutra, basic text of Mahāyāna. Chapter 21 of this book contains a number of Dhāraṇis indicating that Tantrism had influenced Mahāyānism since its very inception. Other elements of Mantrayāna are contained in it which show that Tantric Buddhism was already in vogue in the second century AD.

Sādhaka, Sādhanā: Sādhanā is religious endeavour with which the Tantras are primarily concerned. Sādhaka is the spiritual aspirant who is engaged in *sādhanā.* The main object of the Tantra is to indicate and explain the practical method for realizing the truth. Tantric knowledge has always been transmitted from the preceptor to the disciple in the most secret manner. But there are some visible elements in *sādhanā* such as the chanting and muttering of *mantras*, drawing various mystic diagrams, making of postures and gestures, worshipping various types of gods and goddesses including a host of demi-gods and other such beings, meditation and salutation of various types and Yogic practices, sometimes involving sex relation. It is, however, a matter of great offence on the part of the *sādhakā* to divulge the secrets of his *sādhanā* to the uninitiated.

Sādhanas: The process prescribed for receiving different attainments. Thousands of *sādhanas* were written, both in prose and in verse, in Sanskrit, and thousands were translated into Tibetan. The Buddhists had a special literature called the *sādhanas* which were written by many of the well known Tantric authors. Some collections of such *sādhanas* are still extant. These collections were given the names of *Sādhanamālā* and *Sādhanasamuccaya.* A critical edition of all available *sādhanas* in these two collections has been published in two volumes in GOS, nos. XXVI and XLI.

Sādhanadeha: Conditioned body which an aspirant should acquire by means of *haṃsa-mantra. Gautamīyatantra* IX; *Mahānirvāṇa* V. 102-5.

***Sādhanamālā*:** A collection of *sādhanas* or conceptual descriptions, meditative forms and ritualistic aspects of Buddhist deities intended for the attainment of *siddhi* which is miraculous power or self-realization. The present edition comprises 312 such *sādhanas* which not only give valuable details regarding the deities but a study of them reveals much information on the Tantric tradition, its philosophy and psychic exercises, and also of the

Tantric authors, Siddhas, *mantras*, *maṇḍalas* and various other matters of historical and cultural interest. A *sādhana* is prescribed for the realization of a particular god or goddess according to a fixed procedure laid down therein. The gods have no independent, real existence apart from that of the mind of the worshipper and the manner of worship. They possess no external form but represent purely the mental conditions of the aspirant. Ed. B.T. Bhattacharyya, 2 vols. GOS, XXVI, XLI, Baroda 1925-8.

Sādhana-śāstra: Practical sciences of realization. The *Kulārṇava-tantra* lays down as many as seven paths *(ācāras)*, starting with *vedācāra* and ending with *kaula*. The denotation of the word *tantra* is as wide as it is varied, embracing not only the Śākta, but the Śaiva, Vaiṣṇava, Saura and Gāṇapatya forms within the fold of orthodox Hinduism itself. Besides there are well-developed Buddhists and other Tantras outside this fold. In their spiritual endeavour aspirants have to carve out their own suitable paths or lines of approach.

Sādhya-mantra: *Mantras* which become efficacious by performing *homa* and allied rituals. *Puraścaryārṇava* I. 59.

Sādi-vidyā: A branch of knowledge designated after the symbolic first letter of the śakti-bīja.

Sādividyā: Equilibrium of the senses of *aham* (I-ness) and *idam* (It-ness). *Īśvara-pratyabhijñā* II, 196. Beginning from *śuddha* or *sad-vidyā* up to *śiva-tattva*, the endeavour of the aspirant should be to overcome the sense of separation between *aham* and *idam*. The process of creating this equilibrium is known as *ātmasāt* i.e., making the other one's own. Among the Vīra-Saivas *sad-vidyā* is the *vidyā* or knowledge of the fifth category which is marked by the predominance of the power of action.

Sāgarmatī: Bodhisattva who is mentioned in the Mañjuvajra Maṇḍala of *Niṣpanna-yogāvalī* 50 as being white in colour with both hands outstretched and the fingers displaying sea-waves. Elsewhere, in *Niṣpanna* 58, he is described as holding a conch and a sword marked with *vajra*.

Sāgarasaṅgama: Holy resort of the goddess Svāhā mentioned in the *Bṛhannīla* and *Prāṇatoṣaṇī*. It is same as Gaṅgāsāgara.

Sahaja: The *mārga* (way of spiritual exercise) which is the easiest and most natural. It is also the term for ultimate reality among the Sahajiyas, i.e. those who believe in this *mārga*.

Sahaja-kāya: A fourth body of the Buddha, supposed to have been a transformation of Vajra-kāya (q.v.). Sahaja-kāya is located in the Uṣṇīsakamala, which is same as the Sahaṣrāra (q.v.) of the Hindu tradition, it is also called Mahāsukha-cakra or Mahāsukha-kamala being the seat of great bliss.

Sahaja-Mahāsukha: The peaceful, blissful, radiant and waveless experience of *sahaja*. This *mahāsukha* (intense bliss) is thought to be the ultimate nature and perfect knowledge and is often spoken of as Yoginī whose Yogin is Bodhisattva.

Sahajānanda: One of the four kinds of bliss explained in the *Hevajratantra*. It is absolute bliss, neither *bhāva* (existent) nor *nirvāṇa*, but transcends both.

Sahajasundarī: Female principle, also known as Caṇḍālī, Ḍombī, Yoginī, Nairātmā, Nairamaṇi, etc. She resides in the Nirmāṇa-cakra when the Boddhicitta is produced in the navel region. When she is awakened the moon situated in the forehead begins to pour nectar which rejuvenates and transubstantiates the body of the aspirant.

Sahaja-tanu: Same as Sahaja-kāya (q.v.). It is said in the *Kālacakratantra* that the *sahaja*-body *(sahaja-tanu)*, or the *dharma-kāya*, is neither *prajñā* nor *upāya*, it is of the nature of them both. *Na prajñā nā' py upāyaḥ sahaja-tanur iyaṃ dharma-kāyo vabhuvā*.

Sahajayāna: Offshoot of Vajrayāna (q.v.) which holds that truth is something which can never be found through the prescribed codes of study, discipline, conduct, worship and ritual. What is natural *(sahaja)* is easiest, and hence there is no need for religious formalities, austere practices of discipline, reading, philosophising, fasting, constructing temples and images and so on. The followers of this school lay greater emphasis on the imperative necessity of making the body sufficiently strong and fit before starting yogic processes and believe in the existence of an internal female-force in the *nirmāṇ-cakra* (q.v.). Sahajayāna considers the human body itself as the seat of all human experience including that of *sahaja-mahāsukha* (q.v.).

Sahajayoginī Cintā: Female ascetic who was a contemporary of Lakṣmīṃkarā (q.v.). Her remarkable literary work is *Vyaktabhāva-nugatatattvasiddhi* in which she has described the *mahāsukha* theory of the mind for the attainment of Buddhahood. She lived in the eighth century.

Sahajoli: A *mudrā* for the contraction and expansion of the muscles and nerves associated with the root of the penis. It is mentioned in the *Haṭhayogapradīpikā.*

Sahamarga: The path of yoga.

Sahasradalapadma: Same as Sahasrāra (q.v.).

Sahasrāra: The highest cerebral region above all the *cakras* (nerve plexuses) where Kuṇḍalinī meets its source. For a description of it see *Ṣaṭcakranirūpaṇa* XLI-XLIII. It is designated to be the abode of Śiva while the lowest region—*mūlādhāra* is the seat of Śakti in the form of an electric force, generally known as *kulakuṇḍalinī.* The *mūlādhara* is the region of *pravṛtti* (attachment) while the *sahasrāra* is that of *nivṛtti* (detachment). The *sahasrāra cakra* or *padma* is of a thousand petals which have the fifty letters placed in twenty rounds. In the *sahasrāra* there is the union of Śiva and Śakti. See also *Śiva Saṃhitā* V. On the pericarp is Haṃsa and above it is Parama-Śiva himself. Above these are the *sūrya* and *candra-maṇḍalas.* In the latter is a lightning-like triangle within which is the sixteenth *kalā* of the moon. Its subtle aspect is known as *nirvāṇa-kalā*, the *para-bindu* symbolizing Śiva and Śakti.

Sāhib Kaula: A Tantric ecclesiastical designation in Kashmir. It was a highly dignified position as is indicated by the way in which it has been referred to in a number of Śākta-Tantric works. The epithets Mahā-maheśvarācārya and Sāhib Kulānandanātha are used either singly or jointly to refer to spiritual persons belonging to this exalted position. See *Descriptive Catalogue of Sans. Mss. RASB*, VIII.

Śaivācāra: A form of *dakṣiṇācāra* which insists on the cult of Śiva-Śakti, the Vedic way, eight-fold yogic practices and animal sacrifices. A follower of this Ācāra should go up to the extent of *dhyāna* and *samādhi* and think about the world in terms of the immanence of Śiva. He may resort to the path of knowledge. *Prāṇatoṣaṇī* VII. 1, 499.

Śaivāgama: Traditionally 28 in number which are also regarded as authoritative by the Śaktas. These are *Kāmika*, *Yogaja*, *Cintya*, *Mukuṭa*, *Aṃśumān*, *Dīpta*, *Ajita*, *Sukṣma*, *Sahasra*, *Suprabheda*, *Vijaya*, *Niśvāsa*, *Madgīta*, *Parameśvara*, *Mukhavimba*, *Siddha*, *Santāna*, *Narasiṃha*, *Candrāṃsu*, *Vīrabhadra*, *Āgneya*, *Svayambhū*, *Visara*, *Raurava*, *Vimala*, *Kiraṇa*, *Lalita* and *Saumeya*. The *Kiraṇāgama* substitutes *Kāraṇa* for *Mukuṭa*, *Prodgīta* for *Madgīta*, *Candrahāsa* for *Candrāṃśu*, *Bhadra* for *Vīrabhadra*, *Virakta* for *Visara*, *Kauravya* for *Raurava*, *Mukuṭa* for *Vimala* and *Para* for *Saumeya*.

Sakala: A being (*paśu,* ordinary human being) fettered by *mala* (stains caused by ignorance), *karma* (action) and *māyā* (false notions). *Sakala* is of two kinds—*pakvakaluṣa* (mature) and *apakvakaluṣa* (immature). *Tattvaprakāśa* I. 9.

Sakalikṛti: Tantric *mudrā* (pose) showing bodily positions in terms of *nyāsa* (q.v.).

Śākinī: The presiding goddess of viśuddha-cakra (q.v.). Kālīcaraṇa on *Saṭcakranirūpaṇa* XXX.

Śākṣādupāya: Same as Śāmbhavopāya (q.v.).

Śāktas: Those who worship the supreme being exclusively as a female principle. They hold that the unmanifested Prakṛti (q.v.) alone existed before creation. She wished to create and having assumed the form of the Great Mother she created Brahmā, Viṣṇu and Śiva out of her own body. The *Devīmahātmya* is one of their chief religious texts. Devī or the Great Goddess has been eulogized in the Purāṇas such as the *Vāmana* (XVIII-XIX), *Devībhāgavata* (III. 27), Brahmāṇḍa (containing the *Lalitāsahasranāma* in 44 chapters). *Matsya* (XIII. 24-54), etc. In *Kūrma* (I.12) Devī is called Mahiṣamardinī, Anāhata, Kuṇḍalinī, Durgā, Kātyāyanī, Caṇḍī and Bhadrakālī. The Tantras and Śākta works have much in common, the main point of difference being that in the Śakta cult the Devī or Śakti is worshipped as the highest principle, while the Tantras, which may be Buddhist, Jain, Vaiṣṇava, Śaiva, etc., in character and contents, are not restricted to the worship of the Devī but may be agnostic,Vedantic or Sāṅkhya in their philosophical outlook. The *Vāyu Purāṇa* (CIV. 16) enumerates Śāktism among the six *darśanas.* The Śāktas hold all women to be manifestations of Śakti and as such pure in all conditions. Like the Vaiṣṇavas and the Śaivas, the Śāktas also lay emphasis on *bhakti* (devotion), but many of them prefer to perform the Tantric *pañcamakāra* rites. Their aim is to realize their identity with *yantra, mantra, guru* and *devī*. Their supreme aim is to achieve liberation which is possible through the grace of the Devī. Śāktavidyās are known as Kādi, Hādi and Sādi. Though in its present form Śaktism is a medieval religion its roots are to be traced to the primitive Mother Goddess cult. An incipient form of the Śakta religion is found in the pre-Vedic Harappa civilization.

***Śaktānandataraṅgiṇī*:** A Tantric digest composed by Brahmānandagiri (q.v.) in the sixteenth century. It deals with embryology, doctrines of *karma,* transmigration of soul and rebirth, ignorance as the cause of worldly fetters, meditation on the great goddess as the true form of knowledge and the means of salvation, man's ultimate destiny, initiation and preceptor, *saguṇa* and *nirguṇa* forms of *brahman,* efficacy of concentration, worship of Śakti with specific ends and the usual Tantric features like *cakra, yoga, antaryoga, japa, pūjā, kulācāra, homa, maṇḍapa,* etc. Ed. and published by Rasik Mohan Chattopadhyaya in *Vividha-tantra-samgraha,* Calcutta 1876; by P. Sastri with Bengali trans. Calcutta 1942.

Śāktasiddha: An offshoot of *Vṛndacakra* according to the Krama doctrine. It comprises five *tanmātras, manas, buddhi* and *ahaṃkāra.* It belongs to the valid sources of pure knowledge.

Śākta Sūtras: Some works of Sūtra type pertaining to Śāktism and Tantra. One such work is *Śaktisūtra,* the date and authorship of which is not known. There is another work *Śrīvidyāratnasūtra* attributed to Gauḍapāda. A third work of this category is *Pārānandasutra* (q.v.). There is also a reference to *Agastyasūtra* belonging to Kādimata.

Śākta Upanisads: As many as ten works, all obviously of a later date and specifically śākta in character. They are *Tripuropaniṣad, Tripurā-tāpanī-upaniṣad, Bahvṛcopaniṣad, Bhāvaopaniṣad, Sarasvatīrahasyopaniṣad, Sītopaniṣad, Saubhagyālakṣmi-upaniṣad, Sumukhiupaniṣad, Guhyakāli-upaniṣad* and *Devī-upaniṣad.* They resemble the Tantras in which the secret doctrines and esoteric methods of worship and meditation are unfolded. Some of them deal with the glory of a particular goddess, like Sītā or Sarasvatī, while others go deeper into the methods of Śākta worship.

Śakta Upapurāṇas: A class of Upapurāṇas devoted exclusively to the Devī or Sakti. They are *Devī, Kālikā, Mahābhāgavata, Devībhāgavata, Bhagavatī, Caṇḍī, Devīrahasya* and *Satī* or *Kālī;* some of them claim to be of Mahāpurāṇa category. There are also some other Śakta Upapurāṇas which are lost and are known only by their names—*Bṛhannandikeśvara, Kālikā, Nandikeśvara, Nandi* and *Śāradā.*

Śakti: Primordial energy, the source of all divine and cosmic evolution. From a religious point of view, this Śakti is identified with the supreme being conceived of as the source and spring, as well as the controller, of all the forces and potentialities of nature. According to the Śākta-Tantric world-view, at the time of the dissolution of the universe pure consciousness (*saṃvit*) remains absolutely free from material contamination as pure *cit-śakti* or *parā-prakṛti.* Just as oil is expressed from oil-seed so also in the beginning of creation Śakti appears, like the reappearance of the memory of a person who rises from deep sleep. Śakti first appears as *icchā-sakti* (will-power), and then it works in its two aspects—*vidyā-sakti* and *avidyā-śakti* or *māyā-śakti.* Both of these are conscious principles with the difference that while the former is illuminating consciousness, the latter is veiled consciousness, i.e. consciousness appearing as unconsciousness. Creation is thus the self-expression of Śakti, the subject viewing itself as object, I (*aham*) as It (*idam*). *Māyā-śakti* is, therefore, that particular aspect of *cit* (consciousness) which it assumes as the material cause (*upādāna-kāraṇa*) in creation. There are two aspects of Śakti—*prakāśa* (static represented by Śiva) and *vimarśa* (dynamic); the latter in its subtle state is *cidrūpiṇī* (in the form of consciousness) and in its gross state *viśvarūpiṇī* (in the form of universe). The *vimarśa-śakti* contracts itself in succession into gross or more gross entities until it assumes physical form. It works as the life-principle of all things. At the end of this process, in dissolution, it again returns to its source and remains there in undifferentiated state with the other part, the *prakāsa* aspect. As the universe in dissolution sinks into a memory which is lost, so it is born again from the germ of recalled memory which is also the work of Śakti whose special function is to negate its fulness and remake it in the cyclical process of dissolution and erection. Śakti in its functional aspect works by negation, contraction and finitization. As a Mother power she unfolds herself as the world and again withdraws the world into herself.

Śakti: Power of the supreme being conceived as the Female Principle through which the manifestation of the universe is effected. The important modes of this power are *cit* (intelligence), *ānanda* (bliss), *icchā* (will), *jñana* (knowledge) and *kriya* (action). *Cit* is the power of consciousness, the sentient principle, by which *jīvas* or individuals are characterized. This *śakti* is absolute all pervading, perfect and pure. *Ānanda* is the power of bliss-consciousness in which the distinction of subject and object ceases to exist. *Icchā* is one of the main aspects of Śakti. It is the power of will conceived of as inherent energy of the supreme being, the perceptive modification of which is *jñāna-śakti* (power of knowledge). *Icchā, jñāna* and *kriyā* are respectively the affective, cognitive and conative-cum-functional aspects of Śakti.

Śakti: Female partner of the aspirant. She may be of three kinds—*svakīyā* (the aspirant's wife), *parakīyā* (wife of another), *sādhāraṇī* (common woman). Her qualifications are described in *Kulārṇava* VII. Women of lower castes and despised professions are regarded as excellent partners. *Niruttara* XIV, *Tantra-sāra* 627, *Gandharva* XXIII, *Prāṇatoṣanī* VII. 4. 548.

Śakti: One of the six limbs of *mantras*. The others are Ṛṣi, Chandas, Devatā, Bīja and Kīlaka. *Dīpikā* on *Śrīvidyāratnasāra* I. According to another tradition there are seven limbs, Nyāsa and Dhyāna are added and Devatā dropped.

Śaktibhūmi: Seven regions of Śakti which are supposed to exist in every individual being conceived of as a microcosm of the universe. *Nirvāṇatantra* 10.

Śaktibīja: A seed-*mantra* comprising the letters *sa*, *ka*, *la* and *hrim*. Com. on *Śāra-dātilaka* I. 10.

Śakti cakra: 'Circle of powers', a concept found in the Kashmirian Tantras. The attainment of the state of Paramaśiva makes one the lord of Śakti-cakra. Though it is described in terms of knowledge, it is the realization of perfect and supreme *śivatva*—the condition of equilibrium, also called *yāmala*, of Śiva and Śakti. It is the state in which neither *prakāśa* (q.v.) nor *vimarśa* (q.v.) is predominant over the other; it is timeless eternity holding in itself endless succession. *Spandanirṇaya* I. 1. Śakticakra also denotes the five Śakti triangles in Śri-yantra. *Bhairavayāmala* quoted by Lakṣmī-dhara on *Saundaryalaharī* IX.

Śakticālanī: A *mudrā* which bestows great success. *Haṭhayogapradīpikā* III. 6-7; *Gheraṇḍa* III. 1-3. The process is as follows: The aspirant has to sit in *siddhāsana* posture. Through both his nostrils he inhales air and sends it to the spinal cord. Until it reaches there he contracts his anus and stops exhaling by the *kumbhaka* process. The confined wind will then push the *kuṇḍalinī* upwards.

Śākti-dīkṣā: Initiation which does not require any external rite; it depends on pure knowledge. In the Śakti-dīkṣā the preceptor infuses his own energy into the heart of his disciple. Rāghava on *Śāradātilaka* IV. 1; *Prāṇatoṣaṇī* II. 4. 118.

Śaktikāraṇavāda: The conception of 'Śakti as the material and efficient cause of the universe'. *Nityaṣoḍaśikārṇava* IV. 5; *Kaula-mārgarahasya* 196; *Lalitāsahasranāma* 112 ff.; *Saundaryalaharī* I; *Śaktisaṅgama*, Tārā, VIII.38; *Devībhāgavata* I. 8-39; III. 6.19.

Śaktipāta: Grace of the Great Goddess with which the novice must be favoured before he can be initiated into the creed of Āgamānta Śaivism.

***Śaktipramoda*:** A recent work compiled by Śrīrājadevanandana Siṃha, Chief of Sivahara. It contains 16 Tantras: *Kālī*, *Ṣoḍaśi*, *Bhuvaneśvarī*, *Chinnamastā*, *Tripura-bhairavī*, *Dhumāvatī*, *Vagalāmukhi*, *Mātaṅgī*, *Kamalātmikā*, *Kumārikā*, *Balidānakrama*, *Durgā*, *Śiva*, *Gaṇeśa*, *Sūrya* and *Visṇu*. Pub. by Venkateswar Press 1951.

Śakti-pīṭhas: Holy resorts of the goddess associated with different parts of her body. Their traditional number is 51 though in reality the *pīṭhas* are many more and there is no uniformity in the Purāṇas, Tantras and regional literature with regard to their names and locations. The *pīṭhas* are divided into great (*mahā*) and small (*upa*) categories. It appears that with the universalization of the concept of the all-powerful Devī or Śakti when the need was felt to identify the powerful local goddesses with her—the legend of Dakṣayajña, the death of Satī, the dismemberment of her body, the falling of her limbs at different places—the *pīṭhas* were invented. Every *pīṭha* has a special goddess specially the legend about which particular limb of Satī is said to have fallen there, and the Bhairava representing the consort of the goddess. See *Pīthanirṇaya*.

***Śaktisaṅgama Tantra*:** Composed between AD 1525 and 1660, it is divided into four parts—Kālī, Tārā, Sundarī and Chinnamastā. It holds that Kaulācāra is a cult of Śakti in any of her forms but it is done with the five *tattvas* or *makāras* and the knowledge derived from it must be kept secret. It states that the Devi manifests herself for the destruction of Buddhist and other heretical sects, for the removal of the confusing admixture of different cults and for the establishment of true religion. Symbolic interpretation of the five Ms has been given according to which *madya, mudrā, maithuna*, etc., are not to be used in the ordinary popular sense. The text regards an eclipse of the sun on the moon as the best time for undergoing initiation. It refers to the Tantric sects and treatises of the Vaiṣṇavas, Gāṇapatyas, Śaivas, Svāyambhūvas, Candras, Pāśupatas, Cīnas, Jainas, Kālāmukhas and Vaidikas. Ed. by B.T. Bhattacharyya, Vols. I-III. GOS, nos. LXI, XCI, CIV, Baroda, 1932-47; *Sundarīkhaṇḍa* and *Chinnamastākhaṇḍa* published separately.

Śaktiśodhana: Purification of Śakti, the female partner of the Tantric aspirant, by means of anointing, *mātṛkānyāsa*, and so forth. *Prāṇatoṣaṇī* VII. 2, 512.

Śakti Sūtras: Sūtras of unknown authorship, attributed to Agastya by the commentary. They mention Jaimini and Vyāsa. 113 sutras and com. on 19 Sutras are published in Sarasvatī Bhavana Studies, Vol. X.

Śakti Tattva: The doctrine of Śakti (q.v.) in a general sense. In Kashmir Saivism, however, the term Saktitattva is used in a special sense. There are five *tattvas* (categories) of *śuddhamāyā* of which *śakti* is one. In these *tattvas*, 'I-ness' (*aham*) and 'It-ness' (*idam*) have a common substratum (*samānādhī-karaṇa*) In the *śaktitattva* which represents the fourth stage or category there is only the idea or experience of being what may be expressed as 'I am'. In this stage the object (*idam*) has little or no appearance. Śaktitattva is described as the seed of the universe, the *bīja-bhūmi* of all ideas (*bhāvas*) in the consciousness of Śiva. It is also described as void (*śunya*) or great void (*mahāśūnya*), because nothing manifests in this stage. It denotes a process of negating which is why it is called *niṣedhavyāpārarūpa*. While *cid-śakti* (power of consciousness, awareness of himself as 'I') is said to be predominant in the Śiva-tattva, the *ānanda-śakti* (power of bliss, when there is experience of 'I am', there is bliss) predominates in the *śaktitattva*. *Īśvarapratyabhijñāvimarśinī* II. 192-3; *Paramārthasāra* 13-14.

Śakti Trikoṇa: Śakti triangles supposed to exist in different parts of the body. They are depicted in diagrams and carved on stone, wood or other objects for cultic purposes. The three lines symbolize any set of three-fold theories and the angles are said to be presided over by different goddesses.

Śakti-varṇa: The vowels. Com. on *Śāradā-tilaka* VI. 2.

Śakti-Viśiṣṭādvaitavāda: Vīra Śaiva doctrine according to which *brahman*, or Śiva, is of eternal existence, consciousness and bliss and it is only through his *vimarśa-śakti* that he is aware of these. The real nature of Śiva is like the luminescence of a gem which the gem itself cannot realise. The relation between Śiva and Śakti is that of identity (*tādātmya* or *sāmarasya*) like that between heat and fire, or light and sun, in which there is no difference between the quality and nature of the substance.

Śāktopāya: Also known as Jñānopāya, it demonstrates the means of attaining absolute knowledge experimenting through alternatives by which identification of one's self with the supreme being is possible. *Tantrāloka* I. 187. It is one of the four means of liberation according to the Trika doctrine. The others are Anupāya, Śāmbhavopaya and Āṇavopaya. The four are interrelated, one being the resting place of the other. Ibid. I, 182, 255, 258. While Śāmbhavopāya (q.v.) stands for an absolute monistic approach Śāktopāya insists on various alternative means for the understanding of the former. *Vikalpa hi krameṇa akhaṇḍavastvavabhāso bhavati*. Ibid. I. 234. While the former exclusively belongs to Kula doctrine, Śāktopāya is the *summum bonum* for the followers of Krama.

Śāktyadvayavāda: A theory of the Kashmir Śaivas according to which Śakti is not different from Śiva and as such the material world is the *pariṇama* (consequence) of Śakti.

Śaktyaṇḍamaṇḍala: A sphere comprising the worlds of nine of the 36 *tattvas* or fundamentals from *śuddhavidyā* to *śakti*. The function of *śakti* is often mentioned as *kalā* in which sense *śāntikalā* is the *kalā* of Śaktyaṇḍa.

Śālagrāma: Holy resort of the goddess Mahādevī mentioned in *Matsya* XIII. 33, *Devībhāgavata* VII. 30.62; *Padma*, Sṛṣti, XVII. 191; *Skanda* V. 3.98.71. It is at the source of the river Gaṇḍakī.

Samādhi: The *summum bonum* of meditation, *Yogasūtra* III. 3. It is limb of Yoga but is often equated with the entire Yoga itself. It is the ecstacy resulting from the equation of the individual soul with the ultimate reality. The state of complete *samādhi* is called Parā-saṃvit (pure consciousness). There are two degrees of *samādhi—svavikalpa* in which the mind is yet to transgress the limit of worldly existence, and *nirvikalpa* in which this has been achieved with the effect that it becomes one with the subject of its contemplation. It is that condition when mind dissociates with the body and associates with the universal soul; when there is equilibrium in individual and cosmic self and in which stage one transcends the limit of one's sense-organs. *Vyāsabhāṣya* on *Yogasūtra* I. 1; *Gheraṇḍa* VII. 2; *Haṭhayogapradīpikā* IV. 5-7; *Gandharvatantra* VI. 66-7; *Kulārṇava* IX. 13-14. In the Buddhist Tantras *samādhi* is described as the accumulation of all meditation of existence in the form of a circular mass (bimba) produced through *prajñā* and *upāya* and the quick attainment of that knowledge through that meditation. *Guhyasamāja* XVIII. 163. There are six types of *samādhi*: Dhyanayoga by which the Yogin realizes *brahman* by means of *śāmbhavi-mudra*; Nādayoga by means of *khecarī-mudrā*; Rasānandayoga by means of *bhrāmarikumbhaka*; Layasiddhiyoga by means of *yonimudrā*; Bhaktiyoga by means of tearful emotional meditation; and Rājayoga by means of a *kumbhaka* called *manomurcchā*. *Gheraṇḍa* VII. 5-16; *Haṭhayogapradīpika* IV. 3-4.

Samādhi-mudrā: Also known as *dhyānamudrā*, it is the position of hands while in meditation—the hands with fingers stretched, lie one upon the other on the lap.

Samanā-Śakti: Also known as Samanī it belongs to Śiva as the primal energy of bliss and consciousness. Endowed with the energy Śiva becomes the ultimate cause. Kālīcaraṇa in his com. on *Ṣaṭcakranirūpaṇa* describes it as the intermediate (*avāntara*) form of *parāśakti*. It is the highest level of the world of mind; in the hierarchy of grades the position of *samanā-śakti* is just below that of *unmanī*. *Samanā* or *samanī śakti* has seven *kalās* known as Sarvajñā, Sarvagā, Durgā, Savarṇā, Spṛhaṇā, Dhṛti and Samanā.

Samantabhadra: Leader of the tribe of sixteen Bodhisattvas who is described in the Dharmadhātuvāgīśvara Durgati-pariśodhana and Kālacakra Maṇḍalas of *Niṣpannayogāvalī* 58, 67, 85. He is yellow and/or blue in colour and his symbol is a jewel. Often he is six-handed. His three right hands hold *vajra*, *kartari* and *paraśu* and left hands hold *ghaṇṭā*, *kapāla* and *utpala* or the severed head of Brahmā. His consort is Dharmavajrā. *Sādhana* 49.

Samarasa: The union of the female (prajñā) and male (upāya) principles, same as Yuganaddha (q.v.). One who can unite these two principles in oneself can have the highest knowledge and supreme bliss and become free from the fetters of birth and death. In the Hindu tradition it is Sāmarasya and is regarded as the equilibrium of Śiva and Śakti. Very often this equilibrium is conceived of in sexual terms. See Mahāsukha. Complete understanding of this equilibrium leads to the sense of non-duality.

Sāmarasya: See Samarasa.

Samayācāra: A *mārga* (way) of the Śrividyā cult. For details see Lakṣmīdhara's com. on *Saundaryalaharī* 31 ff.; *Saubhāgyabhāskara* on *Lalitāsahasranāma* 144; Rameśvara on *Paraśurāmakalpasūtra* VII. 1; X. 80. According to Bhāskararāya there are three schools in the cult of Śrīvidya—Samaya, Kaula and Miśra. The Samayācārins worship the goddess Samayā as Śakti and the god Samaya as Śiva, and their relation is conceived as that of perfect equilibrium. They lay special emphasis on the cult of Sahasradalakamala and on *antaryāga*. Rameśvara defines Samaya as the creed established by the Kulaśāstras; it is a secret system. The first four of the seven states of Sādhanā —*arambha*, *taruna*, *yauvana* and *praudha*— are described as Samayācāra.

Samaya-dīkṣā: Initiation into Āgamānta Śaivism for ordinary people. Those who take *samaya-dīkṣā* have to worship the preceptor and Śivāgni (fire dedicated to Śiva). They have to consider themselves as the servants of god.

Samaya-mudrā: One of the four *mudrās* mentioned in *Śrisamputika* and other Tantric Buddhist texts. It is the *mudrā* of knowledge and of perfect bliss.

Samayasattva: An epithet of Vijrasattva who is always engaged in the right method of religious observances (samaya).

Sambara: Tantric Buddhist god who is not very different from Hevajra since he is also Heruka in *yuganaddha*, i.e. in union with his *śakti* Vajravārāhī. Representations of this deity are well known in Nepal and Tibet but they are extremely rare in India.

Śāmbhavas: A tantric sect performing *vāmācāra* rites. *Śaktisaṅgama*, Tārā, I. 90-4. From a spiritual viewpoint they should be residents of the world of Śivatattva. *Tantrāloka* IX. 52-3. Often they are mentioned with the suffix *gaṇa* (tribe) which denotes *pramatā* (experiencer) according to the monist Śaivas, Ibid. IX. 53-4. They belong to one of the five *siddha* groups emanating from Binducakra according to the Krama doctrine.

Śāmbhavī-dīkṣā: A higher form of initiation which is conducted by the mere touch, or a glance, or the will of the guru. It is connected with the secret cult of Kāmeśvarī. Śambhavīdīkṣā is not for ordinary persons. It is also beyond the ability of ordinary preceptors. It is the initiation into Śrividyā or Lalitā or Kāmeśvarī doctrine. The Male Principle or Bhairava of Śrīvidyā is known as Kāmeśvara. In this system, the person initiated has to perform secret rites for the realization of the *sāmarasya* (equilibrium of Śiva-Śakti within his own self). *Nityotsava* 9.

Śāmbhavopāya: One of the four means of salvation according to the trika doctrine. The others are Anupāya, Śāktopaya and Āṇavopaya. The four are mutually connected. Śāmbhavopaya pertains to will-power (*icchāśakti*) that which expresses itself from elementary non-dualistic knowledge. *Tantrāloka* I. 146. Śāmbhavopaya is also known as *sākṣāt-upāya* because it is the means of direct experience (*sākṣāt*). Ibid. I. 234-5. It is also called Śāmbhava-āveśa, *āvesa* being ecstasy which one receives through non-dual experience of the absolute (*saṃvit*). Ibid. I. 210. It belongs exclusively to the Kula doctrine while Śāktopāya (q.v.) belongs to the Krama doctrine.

Sambhoga-cakra: One of the four nerve-cycles in the Buddhist conception. It is situated near the neck and is connected with the *sambhoga-kāya* of Buddha. It is kindled by the female energy having the force of fire known as Caṇḍālī, just as the Kuṇḍalinī-śakti of the Śakta Tantras.

Sambhoga-kāya: Refulgent body of the Buddha. It is a very subtle body from every pore of which stream forth countless brilliant rays of light illuminating the *lokadhātus*. This body again displays thousands of Tathāgata-vigrahas preaching to Boddhisattvas, Gṛhasthas, Pravrajitas and other persons the *dharma* consisting of six *pāramitās*. *Sambhoga* means enjoyment of the six *rasas*. The *sambhogakāya* is of the nature of all existence as pure delight. When the concept applies to individual human beings it is supposed to be symbolically situated near the neck.

Saṃhāra-cakra: One of the constituents of *navacakra*. *Nityaṣoḍaśikārṇava* I.

Saṃhāra-kalā: The art of destruction which emanates from the letter M symbolizing Rudra. There are ten Saṃhāra-kalās—*tīkṣṇa*, *raudrī*, *bhaya*, *nidrā*, *tandrā*, *kṣut*, *krodhinī*, *kriyā*, *utkāri* and *mṛtyu*. *Prapañcasāra* III. 23-4.

Saṃhārakālī: One of the twelve forms of Kālī described by Abhinavagupta. *Tantraloka* IV. 157 ff.

Saṃhitā: General term for denoting religious texts. The terms Tantra, Āgama and Saṃhitā are very often used in the same sense. The Vaiṣṇavite texts particularly are known as Saṃhitās or Āgamas. They are Ahirbudhnya, Bhāradvaja, Brāhma, Īśvara, Jaya, Kānva, Mahendra, Pādma, Padmodbhava Parama, Parameśvara, Pauṣkara, Puruṣottama, Sanatkumāra, Sātvata, Varāha, Viṣṇu, etc. Śaivite texts such as Niśvāsatattva, Mahākāla, Śiva, Vāyavīya, etc., Yogic texts like Gorakṣa, Gheraṇḍa, etc., even law-books like that of Manu, carry the suffix Saṃhitā. Originally the term Saṃhitā was used to denote the four Vedas.

Saṃketa: Clue to the esoteric rituals. Such clues are known as *kramasaṃketa*, *mantrasaṃketa*, *pūjāsaṃketa*, etc., which the Tantric aspirant should know from his preceptor. *Niruttara* X.

Sammelana-cakra: A combination of Śiva-cakra and Śrīcakra required in the Śrīvidyā cult.

***Sammoha(na) Tantra*:** Manuscript in Newari character found in the Darbar Library of Nepal. Quotations from this text are frequently found in various Tantric manuals. The *Sammohatantra* begins with the enumeration of the nine traditions of *mantras* according to the *Kālikāmata* and the 20 divisions of the Śambhavas in terms of their holy places, literary traditions, and script and language used. In the fifth chapter there is an enumeration of various Tantric sects, their distribution and the account of Tantric literature prevalent in various countries. The followers of the Kādi (q.v.) and Hādi (q.v.) modes are distributed into nine *āmnāyas* (divisions). The four general divisions—Kerala, Kāśmīra, Gauḍa and Vilāsa; three main types of rites—Divya, Kaula and Vāma, are mentioned along with the number of principal and subsidiary Tantras in different countries. The sixth chapter is a detailed enumeration of the literature of various sects, while in chapter seven there is a six-fold classification of Tantric *sādhanā* from various points of view. It knows the existence of 462 Śaiva Tantras, 339 Vaiṣṇava Tantras, 180 Saura Tantras, 122 Gāṇapatya Tantras and 39 Bauddha Tantras and states that Chīna possesses 100 principal Tantras and 7 subsidiary ones, Dravida 20 principal end 20 subsidiary ones and Gauḍa 27 principal and 16 subsidiary ones.

Sammukhīkaraṇī: Tantric *mudrā* (handpose) in which the closed fist is held upwards.

Sampatpradā: Bhairavī, same as Tripurabhairavī according to *Jñānārṇava*: *yatheyaṃ tripurā bālā tathā tripurabhairavī, sampatpradā nāma tasyāḥ śṛṇu nirmalamānase. Tantrasāra* 227. She is red in colour, resplendent like a thousand suns; has a crescent on her matted locks and her body is adorned with elaborate jewellery. She wears a garland of severed heads. Her left hands hold a book and display the *abhaya* pose while in the right hands is a rosary and *varada. Puraścaryārṇava* 811-2.

Sampradāyayoginī: Common name of the Āvaraṇadevatā (q.v.) or the presiding goddesses of the fourteen triangles of the mystic Caturdasāra (q.v.) diagram. *Gandharvatantra* V. 99.

Sāmrājya dīkṣā: Higher form of initiation. An ordinary individual should first receive initiation from a competent *guru* in Vedic, Vaiṣṇava and Śaiva ācāras and live a pious householder's life. In case he has more spiritual aspiration he should then have Śakta *dīkṣa* and practise Dakṣiṇācāra. The next higher initiation is *pūrṇābhiṣeka* which qualifies him to become a *gṛhāvadhūta* and perform Vāmācāra in the capacity of a *sādhaka* of *vīra* level. Thereafter he may have *sāmrājya-dīkṣā* and be initiated into Siddhāntācara. Subsequent initiations meant for the *divya* stage are *mahāsāmrājya-dīkṣā* and *pūrna-dīkṣā.*

Sāmrājyalakṣmī: A form of Kamalā. Her complexion is like that of the *atasī* flower and she is adorned with ornaments made of pearls. She has eight hands—holding conch, wheel, club, lotus, bow and arrow and showing *varada* and *abhaya* poses respectively. *Puraścaryārṇava* IX. 840.

***Sāmrājyalakṣmipīṭhikā*:** Said to be a part of the great Śaiva Tantra *Ākāśabhairava.* It has 139 chapters; the first 30 deal with *mantra, japa, homa,* etc. The remaining part is *Akāśabhairava Mahātantra.* Published in Tanjore Sarasvati Mahal Series.

Saṃvit: The ultimate reality which is pure consciousness. In Vedānta, especially according to its non-dualistic interpretation, it is not limited by time, space and cause. The Śakta-Tantric Āgamas recognize its power to create motion, although owing to the influence of Vedānta some texts hold the world to be simply an illusion. In most Tantras, however, Saṃvit is both immanent and transcendent; the former condition prevails when Śakti in its static state assumes the form of matter (*anaham*) and the latter condition when Śakti in its dynamic (*vimarśa*) state assumes the form of consciousness (*aham*). At the time of the dissolution of the universe pure consciousness or *saṃvit* remains absolutely free from material contamination. It remains as pure *cit-śakti* or *parā-prakṛti.* But when the alternatives or material entities develop owing to the self-contraction of *saṃvit, śakti* manifests itself as *avidyā* or material Prakṛti. Pure consciousness works through its *śakti* (inherent power). This *śakti* first appears as *icchā-śakti* (will-power), the desire to be manifested. Subsequently it works in its two aspects—*vidyā-śakti* and *avidyā-śakti* or *māyā-śakti*. Both of these are conscious principles with the difference that while the former is the illuminating consciousness, the latter is veiled consciousness, i.e. consciousness appearing as unconsciousness. This *māyā-śakti* is composed of three *gunas*—Sattva, Rajas and Tamas—and known as *triguṇa-śakti* or Kāmakalā symbolized by the triangle. Hence this *māyā-śakti* is not unreal; it is the cause of the material world. Thus the concept of Tantric *saṃvit* instead of subscribing to the Advaita Vedantic view that there is no ultimate reality apart from pure consciousness, insists that the inward self-expression of the ultimate reality has an outward content as well which works through its Śakti or inherent power. *Tripurārahasya*, Jñānakhaṇḍa XIV ff; *Śaradātilaka* I. 7. ff; *Prapañcasāra* I. 44 ff. See Parā-Saṃvit.

Samvṛta: The restless aspect of the Bodhicitta. Its motionless and blissful form is called *vivṛta* or *paramārthika*. According to the *Hevajratantra*, *samvṛta* is like a *kunda* flower while in its physical form. It should be remembered in this connection that according to the Mādhyamikas *samvṛtī-satya* is the phenomenal or provisional truth and *paramārthika* is the ultimate truth, corresponding to the *vyavahārika* and *paramārthika* of the Vedantists.

***Sanatkumāra Tantra*:** A Vaiṣṇava Tantra in eleven *paṭalas* (chapters) dealing with the procedure of Kṛṣṇa worship with sixteen items. It is a dialogue between Sanatkumāra and Pulastya in 375 verses while it lays down the rules of initiation and principles of Yoga, it also explains Tantric techniques and inculcates Kṛṣṇa worship in Tantric *bījas*. Published by Jyestharam Mukundji, Bombay 1905.

Śaṅkarācārya: The famous Advaita teacher of the eighth century. Tradition ascribes to him the authorship of *Saundaryalaharī*, hymns addressed to the goddess, and the *Prapañcasāra-tantra*. Some other works which do not seem to be composed by him also go by his name. These are *Ānandalaharī*, *Bhujañgaprayātastotra*, *Brahmanāmāvalimālā*, *Dakṣiṇamūrtistotra*, *Nirvāṇāṣṭaka*, *Ṣaṭpadīstotra* and *Viṣṇupādādikeśāntavarṇanastotra*.

***Śaṅkaradigvijaya*:** Composed by Mādhava Vidyāraṇya for glorifying Śaṇkarācārya (q.v.). Its Diṇḍimākhya commentary by Dhanapati describes various sects of the Gāṇapatyas. A few of these sects are exclusively Tantric in character and composition.

Śaṅkarānandanātha: Author of *Sundarīmahodaya* a treatise on Śrividyā cult who lived in the beginning of the eighteenth century. His original name was Sambhubhaṭṭa.

Śaṅkha: Conch-shell. It is specially given as a symbol to the gods because sound vibrated through a shell penetrates far and wide.

Śaṅkhanātha Lokeśvara: A one-faced and two-armed form of Avalokiteśvara who is described as holding a conch against his chest with his right hand and a lotus in his left. This Boddhisattva has a few sculptural representations.

Śaṅkhinī: Name of cerebral nerve. *Prāṇatoṣaṇī* I. 4.33.

Śaṅkhoddhāra: Holy resort of the goddess Dhvani mentioned in *Matsya* XIII. 48, *Devībhāgavata* VII. 30.77; *Pādma*, Sṛṣṭi XVII. 206; *Skanda* V. 3.98.86. It is the island of Bati or Beyt at the southwestern extremity of the Gulf of Kutch.

Sāṅkhya: The earlier substratum of the sophisticated Tantra with its doctrine of Prakṛti and its evolutes. Later, however, the Vedantic concept of non-dualism took the lead. The available philosophical texts on Sāṅkhya cannot claim much antiquity, but the philosophy itself, with its traditional name and topics like the evolutes of Pradhāna or Prakṛti, the concepts of Puruṣa, the three *guṇas* and their equilibrium, the twenty four Tattvas, etc., are dealt with in detail in the *Mahābhārata* and other earlier works. The Sāṅkhya categories by themselves form part not only of the theoretical structure of Śaivism and Śaktism, but underly the Vaiṣṇava *vyūha* doctrine as well. The Purāṇas—*Viṣṇu* and *Kūrma*—describe Sāṅkhya in detail, and the Chinese sources refer to its eighteen schools. Sāṅkhya is referred to as *Sāṅkhyatantra* by Śaṅkarācārya who characterized the Sāṅkhya system as anti-Vedic. He considered the Sāṅkhya as his chief adversary (*pradhānamalla*) and tried to refute the doctrine by pointing out to its inner contradictions. The Sāṅkhya cosmogony has been enumerated in the *Yājñavalkya-smṛti*. The doctrine is said to have been expounded by Kapila to Āsuri. Among the Sāṅkhya texts the most important is Īśvara Kṛṣṇa's *Sāṅkhya-kārikā* which was translated into Chinese in AD 546 by Paramārtha. It has several commentaries such as *Māṭharavṛtti*, *Yukti-dīpīka*, the one by Gauḍapāda and Vācaspati-miśra's *Sāṅkhyatattvakaumudī*. The *Sāṅkhya-sūtra* or *Sāṅkhyapravacanasūtra* (*bhāṣya* by Vijñānabhikṣu) attributed to Kapila is a late work composed about AD 1400. It has been published with two commentaries, viz., that of Aniruddha and parts of the *Ṭīkā* of Vedāntin Mahādeva, edited by R. Garbe BI Series, Calcutta 1881. There is also an edition of 23 sūtras called *Tattvasamāsa* with a commentary *Krama-dīpikā*. Though these works deal mainly with philosophical topics, their cosmogonical sections have some bearing on the Tantras. Moreover the Sāṅkhya categories also form the infrastructure of the yoga philosophy, the practical aspects of which are also related to Tantrism in which Prakṛti is looked upon as the substance of Śakti under whose direction it evolves into material elements and the physical and psychical portions of all sentient beings.

Ṣaṇmudrā: The torque, the bracelet, the jewel, the girdle, the ashes and the sacred thread which represent the six *pāramitās*. When one of the six is absent they are called Pañcamudrā.

Sannidhāpana: Tantric *mudrā* or hand pose in which two hands form a closed fist with the thumbs raised up.

Śāntā: Śāsanadevatā of the Jain Tīrthaṃkara Supārśvanātha according to the Śvetāmbara tradition. She is described as riding an elephant, and in her hands she holds a *varada*, rosary, lance and shows *abhāya* mudra.

Śāntarakṣita: Philosopher and dialectician who, at the invitation of the Tibetan king Khri-sron-lde-tsan, went to Tibet and stayed there upto AD 762. There he was called Paṇḍita Bodhisattva Dharmaśāntighoṣa. He came of a royal family of Bengal and became a distinguished Ācarya of Nālandā. He wrote a commentary on Dharmakīrti's *Vādanyāya* but his masterpiece was the voluminous *Tattvasaṃgraha* (GOS, XXX-XXXI). He made Buddhism the state religion of Tibet in place of Bon and introduced a heirarchical system which is now known as Lamaism. He was helped in this onerous task of reorganizing the religious system by another Indian monk named Padmasambhava. The Tantric tradition set up in Tibet by Śāntarakṣita was enriched by a number of Indian scholars among whom may be mentioned Dharmakīrti, Vimalamitra, Buddhaguhya and Śāntigarbha.

Śāntaśakti: That power which appears in the combined form of will, knowledge and action. Rāmeśvara on *Paraśurāmakalpasūtra* I. 4.

Śāntikalā: One of the five main *kalās* (q.v.) from the view point of 36 *tattvas* (fundamentals) of Śākta philosophy; the others are Nivṛtti, Pratiṣṭhā, Vidyā and Śāntyatīta. It is situated between the *tattvas* of Suddhavidyā and Sadāśiva.

Śāntyatīta: One of the five main *kalās* (q.v.) from the view-point of 36 *tattvas* (fundamentals) of Śakta philosophy; the others are Nivṛtti, Pratiṣṭhā, Vidyā and Śānti is situated between the *tattvas* of Śakti and Śiva. It is also called Avakāśadā.

Śāpamocana: Removal of curses by which some *mantras* are afflicted through certain prescribed rituals. *Puraścaryārṇava* II. 85-90.

Sapta bhūmi: Seven grounds of cosmic power which are known as *bindu*, *bodhinī*, *nāda*, *mahānāda*, *vyāpikā*, *samanī*, or *samanā*, and *unmanī* or *unmanā*.

Sapta-bhūmikā: Seven stages of Tantric perfection—Veda, Vaiṣṇava, Śaiva, Dakṣiṇa, Vāma, Siddhānta and Kaula.

Sapta bhuvana: Seven centres of cosmic power. Satyaloka presided over by Parama Śiva or Mahāviṣṇu and Mahākālī; Tapaloka by Śambhu and Siddhakālī; Janaloka by Sadāśiva and Mahāgaurī; Maharloka by Īśa and Bhuvaneśvarī; Svarloka by Adhīśvara and Adhiśvarī; Bhuvarloka by Viṣṇu and Rādhā; and Bhurloka by Brahmā and Ṣāvitrī.

Saptagodāvara: Holy resort of the goddess Śrī or Akhileśvarī mentioned in the *Bṛhannīla* and *Prāṇatoṣaṇī*. It is modern Solangipur, 16 miles from Piṭhapuram in Godavari district, Andhra Pradesh.

Saptamātṛkās: Group of Seven Mothers. They are Brāhmī (Bhrhmāṇī), Māheśvarī, Kaumārī, Vaiṣṇavī, Vārāhī, Mahendrī (Aindrī, Indrāṇī) and Cāmuṇḍā (often substituted by Śivadūtī and other goddesses). The Saptamātṛkā sculptures abound in India, but they are specially favoured in south India in the larger temples of the Pallava and early

Cola periods. The group is represented in sculptures with the images of Gaṇeśa and Vīrabhadra on either side.

Saptārṇa Kālī: One of the many forms of Kālī described in the *Jayadratha yāmala*.

Saptākṣara: A variety of Heruka (q.v.), called Saptakṣara because his *mantra* consists of seven syllables. He is embraced by Vajravārāhī. He tramples upon Kālarātri, holds *viśvavajra* on his crown and crescent on his head, and is endowed with six auspicious symbols. He is attended by six goddesses, namely Herukī, Vajravārāhī, Ghoracaṇḍī, Vajrabhāskarī, Vajraraudrī and Vajraḍākinī.

Saptaśatika Hayagrīva: A form of Hayagrīva (q.v.), spiritual son of Amitābha. He has a red complexion, terribly awe-inspiring, is three-eyed and brown-bearded. He has a protruding belly and his second face is like that of a horse. He tramples the top of the world with one leg and the bottom with the other. *Sādhana* 509.

***Śāradātilaka*:** Composed about eleventh century AD by Lakṣmaṇa Deśikendra. It has several commentaries, the most important being Rāghava-bhaṭṭa's *Padārthādarśa* (AD 1393-4). Divided into 25 *paṭalas*, more than 4500 verses, it deals with the concepts of *nāda*, *bīja*, *bindu*, *parā-śakti*, *parā-devatā*, *śabdabrahma*, *ādhāra-cakra*, *kulakuṇḍalinī*, *dīkṣā*, *nyāsa*, *puraścaraṇa*, *mantras yantras*, etc. It contains *mantras* of such deities as Durgā, Tripurā, Gaṇapati, Candramas, Sarasvatī, Lakṣmī, Bhuvaneśvarī, Tvaritā and others and those for magical purposes such as bringing women under control, bringing about destruction of enemy, and so forth; divides *mantras* into masculine, feminine and neuter; *mantras* for infusing life found in this text are quoted in the late medieval digests on the Dharmaśāstras. Here Śiva is both *nirguṇa* and *saguna*, the two aspects being conceived in terms of difference from and identity with Prakṛti. When Śiva is identical with Śakti or Prakṛti, he is *saguṇa*. In this connection the Sāṅkhya categories are also explained. The all-pervading and at the same time most subtle Śakti remains coiled like a serpent in her *kuṇḍalinī* form and becomes manifest in the form of the fifty letters of the Sanskrit alpha-bet. Ed. A. Avalon, *Tantrik Texts*, Vols. XVI-XVII, 1933, rpt. Delhi 1982.

***Sārańgadhara-saṃgraha*:** A treatise on medicinal alchemy based upon the *Caraka-saṃhitā* on the one hand and Tantric chemical treatises on the other. The author dates this work in Saṃvat 1420 or AD 1363.

Sarasvatī: Goddess of knowledge whose rosary is equated with the mātṛkāvarṇa (q.v.)—the fifty letters of the Sanskrit alphabet. She is known by various names such as Vāgdevatā, Vāgdevī, Vāgīśvarī, Bhāratī, Vāṇī, etc., and is regarded as the goddess of the eastern region (*āmnāya* q.v.). Her Nīlasarasvatī form is equated with Ugratārā and Ekajaṭā. Sarasvatī, or Bhāratī, is referred to as Parā-Śakti in *Śāktānanda-taraṅgiṇī* III. Her *bījamantra* (q.v.) is *aim*. *yantrābhidhāna* 65-7. As the name of a holy river sacred is to the goddess Devamātā, running by Pehoa, Sarasvatī is mentioned in the Purāṇas. Again as a goddess, staying in the mouth of Brahmā, Sarasvatī is mentioned in the Āgamic and Puranic literature, especially in *Matsya* XIII. 51, *Devībhāgavata* VII.30.80; *Padma*, Sṛṣti XVII, 209; *Skanda* V. 3.98.89.

***Sarasvatī Tantra*:** A late work which in six chapters deals with the significance of the *mantras*, meditation on *mūlavidyā* or *Kulakuṇḍalinī* to be raised in the *sahasrāra* region, and *setu* and *mahāsetu* connected with *japa* and *homa*.

Sarasvatītīrtha: Also known as Paramhaṃsa Parivrājakācārya he was a teacher of Indian philosophical systems and a commentator on *Prapañcasāra*. He hailed from south India.

Sarayu: River, sacred to the goddess Śāradā according to the *Bṛhannīla* and *Prāṇatoṣaṇī*, which runs through Oudh. Now called Ghagra or Gogra.

Sarkarāra: Modern Sukkur in Sindh which is regarded as a *mahāpīṭha* in the *Śivacarita* where the presiding goddess is Mahiṣamardinī. The *Pīṭhanirṇaya* has a variant reading—Karavīra.

Sārthavaha: A form of Avalokiteśvara or Lokeśvara who is described as one-faced and two-armed displaying *varada mudrā* with the right hand and carrying *piṇḍapātra* (bowl) in the left.

***Sarvadurgati Pariśodhana*:** A Buddhist work belonging to the yoga tantra category. There are two distinct versions of this work, both available in Tibetan translations. The Sanskrit original of one version is available. It is presented in the form of discourses either by Śākyamuni or Vajrapāṇi and deal with the *maṇḍalas*, initiation and rituals. Ed. by T. Skorupski, Delhi 1983.

Sarvajñadeva: Tantric Buddhist scholar who, according to Lāmā Tāranātha, went to Tibet at the time of Ral-pa-can to translate Buddhist texts. He lived in the ninth century and was one of the translators of *Dul-va* or Vinaya.

Sarvānanda: Author of *Sarvollāsa* which deals with Tantric *sādhāna* in general and Vīra *sādhanā* in particular. He lived in the fifteenth century at Mehar in Tippera district, East Bengal. The Kālī temple established by him at Mehar later became a place of pilgrimage.

Sarvānandamaya: One of the nine *cakras* with Mahātripurasundarī as presiding deity and Parāpararahasya or Parāparātirahasya as yoginī or Āvaraṇadevatā. *Setubandha* on *Nityaṣoḍaśikārṇava* I. 164-5.

Sarvarakṣākara: One of the nine *cakras* with Tripuramālinī as presiding deity and Nigarbha as yoginī or Āvaraṇadevatā. *Setubandha* on *Nityaṣoḍaśikārṇava* I. 164.65.

Sarvarogahara: One of the nine *cakras* with Tripurasiddhā as presiding deity and Rahasya as yoginī or Āvaraṇadevatā. *Setubandha* on *Nityaṣoḍaśikārṇava* I. 164-5.

Sarvārthasādhaka: One of the nine *cakras* with Tripurāśrī as presiding deity and Kulakaulā as Āvaraṇadevatā or yoginī. *Setubandha* on *Nityaṣoḍaśikārṇava* I. 164-5.

Sarvasaṃksobhaka: One of the nine *cakras* with Tripurasundarī as presiding deity and Guptatarā as yoginī or Āvaraṇadevatā (q.v.). *Setubandha* on *Nityaṣoḍaśikārṇava* I. 164-5.

Sarvāśāparipuraka: One of the nine *cakras* with Tripureśī as presiding deity and Guptā as yoginī or Āvaraṇadevatā (q.v.). *Setubandha* on *Nityaṣoḍaśikārṇava* I. 164-5.

Sarvasiddhiprada: One of the nine *cakras* with Tripurambā as presiding deity and Atirahasyā or Parāpararahasyā as yoginī or Āvaraṇadevatā. *Setubandha* on *Nityaṣoḍa-śikārṇava* I. 164-5.

Sarvaśūnya: The fourth state of the doctrine of vacuity (śūnyata) as described in the *Pañcakrama* of Nāgārjuna. It is all-void and perfect-void, free from the three-fold impurities. It is purified knowledge, the supreme omniscience without change, appearance and verbal expression. In the *Abhisambodhikrama* of the *Pañcakrama* it is said that perfect void may be with or without beginning, middle or end. It is free from the categories of being and non-being, nor is it a combination of both.

***Sarvatathāgatādhiṣṭhānavyūha*:** Name of Mantrayāna Buddhist Sūtra associated with the Dhāraṇī trend. Its Sanskrit version has been found from Gilgit; it has a Tibetan version as well. It prescribes the use of incantations to achieve success and avert various kinds of evils. Its central figure is Avalokiteśvara who is given an abode on Mt. Potalaka in Andhra. Edited in *Gilgit Manuscripts*, Vol. I, Srinagar 1939.

***Sarvatathāgatatattvasaṃgraha*:** A Buddhist Yoga-tantra belonging to the school of Mantrayāna said to have been imparted by the Buddha himself in his *dharma-kāyu*. It was translated in the eighth century into Chinese by Amoghavajra (q.v.). It is found also in its Tibetan version. A Sanskrit manuscript of this text has been found in Nepal. It is a root Tantra of the 24 *vajradhātumaṇḍalas* which contain Tantric Buddhist approaches to the goddesses of the Pāramitā, Dhāraṇī, Karma-vajreśvarī, Lāsyā and other categories along with their consorts and characteristics.

Sarvatobhadra-maṇḍala: A geometrical diagram on which the *pūrṇakumba* (vessel filled with water) is placed during Durgā worship. The *Sāradātilaka* III. 106-30 deals at length with it and remarks that it is common to all worship. The text (III. 122-4) further provides that the *maṇḍala* should be drawn with five coloured powders—yellow with turmeric powder, white produced from husked grains of rice, red with *kusumbha* powder, black with powder of half-burnt inferior cereals and green with powder of the leaves of *bilva*, cf. *Prapañcasāra* 64-5; *Jñānārṇava* XXVI. 16-17; *Agni Purāṇa* CCCXX, etc.

***Sarveśvararasāyana*:** One of the Sanskrit treatises on alchemy which was translated into Tibetan. It was recovered from the xylographs of the Tanjur manuscripts of Narthang edition belonging to Visva-bharati University. It has been translated into English and published along with original Tibetan in Roman script by Vidhusekhar Sastri.

Sarveśvarī: Presiding goddess of the letters beginning with Ya according to the *Vām-akeśvara-tantra*. She is one of the Śaktis of Aṣṭakoṇacakra and belongs to the category of Āvaraṇadevatā and Rahasyayoginī (q.v.).

***Ṣaṣṭhītantra*:** Name of a work on the Sāṅkhya

system. The *Sāṅkhya-kārikā* LXX. 72 refers to Pañcaśikha as the author of *Ṣaṣṭhītantra*. It was so called because it expounded 60 topics.

Śāsvatavajra: Tantric Buddhist author who composed many Sādhanas. His description of Mahācīnatārā, as found in the *Sādhanamālā*, tallies totally with the *dhyāna* of Tārā as found in the *Tantrasāra* (q.v.) of Kṛṣṇānanda Āgamavāgīśa.

Śatadru: Modern Sutlej running through the Punjab which is regarded as especially sacred to the goddess Śatarūpā according to the *Bṛhannīla* and the *Prāṇatoṣaṇī*.

***Śataratnasaṃgraha*:** Compiled with a commentary of Umāpati Śivācaryā of 13th-14th century which attempts to harmonize the different ideals of self-realization. It is a Śaiva work in which the three essential categories—Pati (lord of beings), Paśu (individual in bondage) and Pāśa (fetters)—are explained. The authority of Śruti, Smṛti and Āgamas has been implicitly accepted. Vimukti or liberation is treated in terms of Parā (realization) of the self independent of any concept of God and Aparā (identification of individual self with gods known to be directly caused by Śiva).

Ṣaṭcakra-bheda: Piercing of the six nerve-cycles. According to the Tantric scheme there are six nerve cycles in the human body—in the rectal region (*muladhara*), in the region around the generative organ (*svādhiṣṭhāna*), around the navel (*maṇipura*), around the heart (*anāhata*), in the region connecting the spinal cord and the lower portion of the medulla oblongata (*viśuddha*) and between the brows (*ājñā*). The highest cerebral region is known as *sahasrāra*. The Kuṇḍalini Śakti, i.e. Śakti as serpent power, remains latent in the *mūlādhāra*. By yogic exercises this Śakti has to be pushed up through the two main nerves, *idā* and *piṅgalā*, so that it may reach the *sahasrāra* (the highest cerebral region), where it should meet its source. The head and trunk of the body is one unit and the lower body is the other. The centre of the body is in between these two, at the base of the spine. The spinal cord is the axis of the body just as Mount Meru is that of the earth. The body below this centre is conceived of as being comprised of the seven lower or nether worlds and from the centre upwards constitutes the seven upper regions marked by six nerve-plexuses and the highest cerebral region. In a general way it may be said that these nerve-plexuses (*cakra* or *padma* q.v.) are related in a particular way to a special mechanism of the body through intermediate conductor-nerves (*nāḍis*).

***Ṣaṭcakranirūpaṇa vivṛti*:** Sixth chapter of the *Śrītattvacintāmaṇi* or Pūrṇānanda composed in AD 1577. In 85 verses it deals with the six nerve-plexuses within the body. Ed. Y.N. Vidyaratna, in *Tantrik Texts*, Vol. II, Calcutta 1913; Eng. trans. *The Serpent Power* by A. Avalon, seventh ed., Madras 1972.

Ṣaṭkañcuka: Six veils which are the causes of human bondage. *Tantrāloka* IX. 164, 204.

Ṣaṭkarma: Six purificatory acts of Haṭha-yoga: *dhauti*, *vasti*, *neti*, *laukīkī*, *trātaka* and *kapālabhāti*. *Gheraṇḍa* I. 13-60; *Haṭha-yogapradīpikā* II. 24-35. The term also denotes six black acts—*śānti*, *vaśya*, *stambhana*, *vidvesaṇa*, *ucāṭana* and *māraṇa*, *Yogīni-tantra*, IV, *Śāradātilaka* XXIII. 123 ff.

Satkaula: The genuine *sādhaka*, who finds *brahman* in everything and everything in *brahman*, is liberated in his physical existence and free from all ignorance. *Sarvaṃ brahmaṇi sarvatra brahmaiva paripaśyati, jñeyah sa eva satkaulo jīvanmukto na saṃśayaḥ*. *Mahānirvāṇa Tantra* X. 212.

Ṣaṭkuṭabhairavī: A goddess of the Bhairavī (q.v.) category who has the complexion of the rising sun. She is adorned with necklaces made of severed human heads. Her breasts are developed and look like golden jars. She holds in her four hands noose, goad, manuscript and rosary. *Puraścaryārṇava*, IX. 809 ff.

Ṣaṭ-tṛmśa tattva: The 36 fundamentals of Śaivism and Śāktism which comprise Śiva, Śakti, Sadāśiva, Īśvara, Śuddhavidyā, Māyā, Kāla, Niyati, Kalā, Vidyā, Rāga, Puruṣa, Avyakta, or Prakṛti, Buddhi, Ahaṃkāra, Manas, Karṇa, Tvak, Cakṣu, Jihvā, Nāsikā, Vāk, Pāṇi, Pada, Pāyu, Upastha, Śabda, Sparśa, Rūpa, Rasa, Gandha, Vyoma, Marut, Tejaḥ, Ap and Kṣiti. *Tattvaprakāśa* II. 1-3.

Sattva: That constituent of Prakṛti (q.v.) which is of the nature of pleasure and light (*laghu*) and illuminating (*prakāśaka*). It gives rise to happiness and love, tranquility and modesty, health and lightness of body, patience and forgiveness, courage, magnanimity, self-restraint and illumination of knowledge.

***Sātvata Tantra*:** A Vaiṣṇavite Tantra, also known as *Tantra-bhāgavata*, a late-medieval composition. In this Tantra Viṣṇu identified with Kṛṣṇa is described as the highest cosmic principle to whom the Vedic gods are subordinate. The process of cosmic evolution is described in terms of the Sāṅkhya categories with the goddess Prakṛti as its fountain-head. Viṣṇu as supreme being is described as Puruṣa and identified with Kāla, Karman and Svabhāva. The categories are *mahat*, *ahaṃkāra*, and the five organs of perception—*śabda*, *sparśa*, *rūpa*, *rasa* and *gandha*—and these are both *kāraṇa* (cause) and *kārya* (effect) under different circumstances. It also deals with incarnations of Viṣṇu, different kinds of *bhakti* and the thousand names of *Kṛṣṇa*. Ed. by P.B. Ananthachariar, Kanchipuram 1902.

***Saubhāgyabhāskara*:** Commentary on the *Lalitāsahasranāma* of the *Brahmāṇḍa Purāṇa* composed by Bhāskararāya, one of the greatest Tantric scholars of the eighteenth century.

***Saubhāgyakalapadruma*:** An important work on Śrīvidyā written by Mādhavā-nandanātha.

***Saubhāgyasubhagodaya*:** A philosophical treatise on Tantra composed by Amṛtānanda, a disciple of Puṇyānanda. He was also the author of the *Yoginīhṛdayadīpikā* (q.v.).

Saumya-Kalā: Expressions of the power of the sixteen Saumya-varṇas (vowels) which are *amṛtā*, *mānadā*, *puṣā*, *tuṣṭi*, *puṣṭi*, *rati*, *dhṛti*, *śaśinī*, *candrikā*, *kānti*, *jyotsnā*, *śrī*, *prīti*, *aṅgadā*, *pūrṇā* and *pūrṇāmṛtā*. They are conceived of in terms of goddesses who fulfill all human desire. *Prapañcasāra* III. 15-16. There is also a different list of the Saumya-kalās. *Śrītattvacintāmaṇi* XVIII. 16-17.

***Saundarya Laharī*:** A Tantric poetical work comprising 100 (103 and 104 in some versions) verses attributed to Śaṅkarācārya. It begins with the statement that without Śakti Śiva is unable even to move. Then it describes creation and dissolution, the beauty of the Divine Mother surpassing even Urvaśī and Rambhā, the nerve-plexuses and rise of *kuṇḍalinī*, oneness of Śiva and Śakti and so forth. Notwithstanding poetic exaggeration in describing the physical beauty of the goddess from tip to toe the work does not lack sublimity and depth. In some manuscripts the first 40 verses of *Saundaryalaharī* is entitled *Ānandalaharī* which is why the two works are taken to be the same. *Saundaryalaharī* has many commentaries of which the most well-known are *Sudhāvidyotinī* and *Lakṣmīdharā*. It also refers to the existence of 64 Tantras. Ed. with com. and Eng. trans. by J. Woodroffe, Adyar 1937; ed. N. Brown with Eng. trans., Cambridge Mass 1958; ed. with Eng. trans. and notes by R.A. Sastri and R.K. Guru, Madras 1957; ed. with nine expositions and trans. etc. by Kuppusvami, Delhi 1976.

Saura-kalā: Expressions of the power of twelve Saura-varṇas (pairs of 24 *sparśa varṇas*—25 letters from *ka* to *ma* with the exclusion of the last letter). which are *tapanī*, *tāpani*, *dhumrā*, *māricī*, *jvālinī*, *ruci*, *susumnā*, *bhogadā*, *viśvā*, *bodhinī*, *dharaṇī* and *kṣamā*. They are conceived of in terms of goddesses who bestow wealth on their devotees. *Prapañcasāra* III. 17. For a different list see *Śrītattvacintāmaṇi* XVIII. 10-11.

Saurakhaṇḍa: One of the three parts of the fifteen kalās (q.v.) mentioned in the commentary on *Saundaryalaharī* 32, the other two being Āgneya and Cāndra. Saurakhaṇḍa consists of *āpyāyamānā*, *āpyāyā*, *sunṛtā*, *irā* and *āpūryamānā kalās*.

Śavasādhanā: Tantric ritual with a corpse. For details see *Kaulāvalinirṇaya* XIV; *Śyāmārahasya* XIV; *Tārābhaktisudhārṇava* IX, *Puraścaryārṇava* IX.

Savikalpa Samādhi: A state of *samādhi* (q.v.) in which the mind is yet to transcend the limit of wordly existence. This is the first degree of *samādhi* on the way to its final culmination in which the distinction between the subject and the object does not remain.

***Sekoddeśaṭīkā*:** A Buddhist work of Śrī Nāḍapāda. Text edited by Mario E. Carelli in GOS with introduction in English. See *Kālacakra-tantra*.

Setu: Bridge made of knowledge to cross the ocean of suffering. Crystallized as a form of *mantra* which is to be muttered. The higher form is known as Mahāsetu. *Puraścaryārṇava* VI. 532-3.

***Setubandha*:** Commentary of Bhāskararāya on *Vāmakeśvara-tantra*. It deals exclusively with Śrīcakra. It emphasizes that the worship of Tripurasundarī is of the nature of *upāsanā* and not of the nature of *bhakti* and that this *upāsanā* is of two sorts, one consisting of the recitation of the *mantra* of the Devī and the other consisting of the worship of the *yantra* or *cakra*.

Sevā: Worship, which is one of the four ingredients of Upāya (q.v.) in Tantric Buddhism. Sevā is again subdivided into two categories—*sāmānya* (ordinary) and *uttama* (excellent). The former consists of four Vajras, namely, the concept of Śūnyatā; its transformation into germ-syllable; its evolution in the form of a deity; and the external representation of the deity. In the *uttama* category *yoga* with its six limbs are employed. When they combine in the state of highest meditation and concentration, an artificial cognition akin to deep sleep is brought about, and the deity appears in the mind in flashes and sparks. The infinite energy is Sūnya which is invoked by the worshippers of different classes with different desires and different degrees of mental development. In the realization of the deity, there are thus three elements, the worshipper, the deity and their connection or identity. *Guhyasamāja*, XVIII. ff.

Siddha: Persons who have attained *siddhi* (perfection) and have acquired supernatural powers. Apart from such individual Siddhas, two other groups are generally recognized. The first consists of nine and the second of 84 whose names are mentioned in the Tibetan tradition. Most of them hailed from the East and belonged to lower castes. There are Siddha sects also in the South like the Māheśvara Siddhas of the Śuddhamārga. See Sittar. The Nāthas also belong to the Siddha tradition. In Tantric Buddhism, the Siddhas who attain super-normal powers are considered to be of three distinct varieties—Best, Middling and Mild. Siddhas of the first group can fulfill all their desires by mere thought; Siddhas of the second group have supernatural powers and access both in spiritual and temporal affairs; and the Siddha of the third group has temporal attainment. Siddhas belonging to the first and second groups are called Mahāsiddhas (q.v.).

Siddha-cikitsā: Method of treatment by mercurial drugs practised by the Siddha sect of the South. Also known as Māheśvara Siddhas of the Śuddhamarga. The founder of one of their seven subsects was a Chinese Taoist named Bhoga who possessed wonderful knowledge of alchemy. The Nātha Siddhas were closely associated with Raseśvara Siddhas. Each of the nine Nātha Siddhas was generally held to stand at the head of a community of expert alchemists who were masters in preparation of antidotes against old age, disease, and poison. See Jīvanmukti, Rasa, Rasāyana, Raseśvara Darsana, Sittar.

Siddhācāryas: See Siddhas. The names of the 84 Siddhas are known from the Tibetan sources are as follows: Luipā, Lilāpā, Virupā, Ḍombipā, Śabaripā, Sarahapā, Kankaripā, Mīnapā, Gorakṣa, Cauraṅgī, Vinapā, Śāntipā, Tāntipā, Camaripā, Khaḍgapā, Nāgārjuna, Kānhapā, Kārnaripā or Āryadeva, Thaganpā, Naropā, Salipā, Tillopā, Catrapā, Bhadrapā, Dokhandi, Ajogī, Kalapā, Dhobipā, Kamkana, Kambalapā, Dinkpā or Dhenkipā, Bhandapā, Tandhipā, Kukkuripā, Kusulipā, Kucipā, Dampā, Mahipā, Acinta, Babhai, Nalin, Bhusuku, Indrabhūti, Mekopā, Kotolipā or Kodālipā, Kamaripā, Jālandhara, Rāhula, Dharmapā, Dhokari, Medinī, Pankaja, Ghanṭapā, Yogipā, Celukapā, Gorua, Lucika, Naguni, Jayānanda, Pacaripā, Campakapā, Bhikṣaṇapā, Telipā, Kumaripā, Caparipā, Maṇibhadrā or Yoginī, Bahudi, Mekhḷalī, Kankhalā, Kalkala or Kolāhala, Udhali, Kapāla, Kirpāla, Sakar, Sarabhakṣya, Nāgabohi, Dārika, Putalīpā, Panaha, Kokalipa, Anaṅga, Lakṣmīṅkarā, Samuda and Vyalipā or Vyadipā.

Siddhaikavīra: Form of Mañjuśrī (q.v.) Four *sādhanas* in the *Sādhanamālā* 140 describe him. He bears the image of Akṣobhya on the crown, is two-armed, one-faced and white in colour. He sits in *vajraparyaṅka* attitude with *utpala* in his left hand and displays *varada-mudrā* with the right. He is accompanied by four subsidiary deities—Jāliniprabha, Candraprabha, Keśinī and Upakeśinī. If represented without companions and without the figure of the paternal Dhyānī Buddha on the crown, a confusion is likely to arise between the forms of Lokanātha and Siddhaikavīra, because both of them have the same symbol and same *mudrā*. It is only by the ornaments and the treatment of hair that the two forms may be distinguished.

Siddhakālī: One of the many forms of Kālī described in the *Toḍalatantra* III and *Mahākālasaṃhitā*. *Puraścaryārṇava* I. 16.

Also known as Siddhikālī, she is a form of Dakṣiṇākālī. Her *mantra*, known as Kālihṛdaya, is *Om hrīṃ krīṃ me svāhā*. She is three-eyed with dishevelled hair; has a crown on her head; her colour is blue. The sun and moon are her ear-rings. She is the greatest protectress. *Kālītantra* X. 33 ff.

Siddha-mantra: The *mantra* which becomes effective at once. Very few possess such *mantras*. If the occasion arises, such *mantras* may be accepted even by disregarding scriptural rules. *Rudrayāmala*, Uttara III; *Tantrasāra* 6; *Puraścaryārṇava* I. 59.

Siddhāntācara: One of the seven Tantric *ācāras* or *mārgas* (ways). In particular it is described as a form of *vāmācara* and is meant for aspirants of the *vīra* (q.v.) state. It insists more on *antaryāga* (internal worship) than on external. One of the interesting characteristics of Siddhāntācāra is that its followers worship Viṣṇu in the day time, while at night they practise the rites of Pañcamakāra (q.v.). *Puraścaryārṇava* I. 22; *Kaulamārgarahasya* 10.

***Siddhāntaśikhāmaṇi*:** Vīraśaiva text which speaks of Śakti as *brahmaniṣṭhā-sanātanī* suggesting that it is intrinsic and ever abiding in Śiva. Śakti as the attribute is not different in nature from the substance. By way of comparison the expressions heat of fire, the light of sun, etc. are used. So it cannot be said that *bheda*, in being the attribute of a thing, and *abheda*, in being the nature of a thing, are always opposite. Between the substance and attribute there is an inseparable union which points to a reality that continues to remain in the character of an undivided organic whole. This Śaktiviśiṣṭādvaita theory is discussed in this text.

Siddhapura: Also known as Siddhavana and Siddhavaṭa, it is the holy resort of the goddess Mātā Lakṣmī or Umā Lakṣmī mentioned in *Matsya* XIII. 45; *Devībhāgavata* VII. 30. 74, *Padma*, Sṛṣṭi, XVII. 202; *Skanda* V. 3.98.83. It is either Siddhaur, near Barbanki in Uttar Pradesh or Sidpur, about 64 miles from Ahmedabad.

***Siddhasiddhāntasaṃgraha*:** An authentic text on the Nāthasiddhas and their yogic practices which has been edited by M.M. Gopinath Kaviraj in Sarasvati Bhavana Texts, no. 15.

Siddhavidyā: Another epithet for Mahavidyā goddesses. *Prāṇatoṣaṇī* V. 6. 314. Among the Mahāvidyā goddesses Vagalā is specially invoked under this name. Ibid. In *Niruttara* II it is said that among the Siddhavidyās, Dakṣiṇākālī, is both Puruṣa and Prakṛti.

Siddhāyikā: Śāsanadevatā of the last Jain Tīrthaṃkara Mahāvīra who is described as riding a lion and who holds in her four hands a book, a citrus, a lute, and displays the *abhaya* pose.

Siddhi: Eight miraculous powers. These are *animā* (atomization), *laghimā* (levitation), *mahimā* (magnification), *garimā* (greatness), *prāpti* (power of getting anything), *prākāmya* (non-obstruction of desire), *vaśitva* (power of charming) and *iśitva* (sovereignty over all things). *Prapañcasāra* XIX. 62-3. Those who gained such Siddhis were called Siddhas and the process through which they obtained Siddhis was called Sādhanā. The *Yogasūtra* which is recognized to be the earliest work in Sanskrit on the subject of phychic exercises enumerates the eight Siddhis mentioned above. Later works mention more while the *Brahmavaivarta Purāṇa* mentions 34 kind of Siddhis.

Siddhibhairavi: Vidyā or goddess of Uttarāmnāya, i.e. of the northern region. *Puraścaryārṇava* I. 12.

Śikhāṣṭaka: A group of eight Bhairava Āgamas (q.v.) represented by *Bhairavī*, *Viṇā*, *Viṇāmaṇi*, *Sammoha*. *Ḍamaru*, *Ātharvaka*, *Kavandha* and *Śiraścheda*.

Śīlapāramitā: Tantric Buddhist goddess of pāramitā (q.v.) category described as being white in colour and holding in her hands a discus and the *cintāmaṇi* banner. *Niṣpanna* 56.

Siṃhanāda Lokeśvara: A form of Avalokiteśvara who has a white complexion, three eyes, and *jaṭāmukuṭa*. He is without ornaments; clad in a tiger skin he sits on a lion in *mahārājalīlā* pose. His symbols are a sword-on-lotus and a *triśūla* entwined by a snake. Images of Siṃhanāda Lokeśvara are fairly common.

Simhāsyā: Lion-faced goddess described in the Nairātma Maṇḍala of *Niṣpannayogāvalī*. She is also described in the Havajra Maṇḍala of the same text as four-faced and four-armed and as similar in appearance to Vajraghaṇṭā.

Śiraścheda: A special mode of *sādhanā* described in the *Jayadrathayāmala* which says that this was introduced in Kambuja (Cambodia). From the epigraphical evidence it is known that Tantrism was very much in vogue in Cambodia in the early ninth century. It may be inferred that this special mode of *sādhanā* must have existed in India much earlier.

Śiṣya: Disciple. His method of selecting a teacher is described in *Kulārṇava* XI. XIV; *Rudrayāmala*, Uttara II, *Prapañcasāra* XXXVI. 50; his test before initiation in *Tantrasāra* 3; *Śāradātilaka* II. 153; characteristics of a good disciple in *Śārada* II. 145-50; *Tantrarāja* I. 23-4 of a bad disciple in *Rudrayāmala*, Uttara II. His duties in *Kulārṇava* XII; *Kaulāvalīnirṇaya* X; *Paraśurāmakalpa-sūtra* X. 74.

Sitaprajñāpāramitā: White Prajñapāramitā with Akṣobhya on the crown. She is two-armed, one-faced and sits in *vajraparyaṅka* attitude on a white lotus. She carries a red lotus in her right hand and the *prajñā-pāramitā* book in the left. *Sādhana* 310-11.

Sitātapatrā: A form of Tantric Buddhist goddess Aparājitā, an emanation of Vairocana. She has three faces and six hands. *Sādhana* 395.

Sitatārā: Tārā of the white variety with one face and four arms. She is accompanied by two goddesses, Mārīcī and Mahāmāyūrī, and she bears the images of five Dhyānī Buddhas on her crown. Decked in ornaments, she exhibits the *utpala mudrā* with the first pair of hands, displays *varada* with *cintāmaṇi* jewel in the right hand and *utpala* in her left. *Sādhana* 215.

Sittar: South Indian Tantric Siddhas (q.v.) who were zealous adepts in alchemy. Their works deal with alchemy by itself, alchemy and Yoga, alchemy and medicine or medicine pure and simple. They are written in verse, using easy colloquial and ungrammatical words and often hiding the names of the herbs or minerals in big phrases and metaphors. There are many *nigaṇṭus* or lexicons of these works. Many recipes containing minerals, metals, herbs and salts are mentioned in these works. They recognize Śiva as their god and reveal a strong antagonism to Śaṅkara's doctrine of pure illusion. Although according to Tamil tradition the origin of the Sittars is traced to the mythical Agastya, they actually belonged to the tenth century AD and after. One Chinese Taoist, Bhoga or Bogar, became the founder of one of the seven subsects of the Sittars. Quite a large number of works were left by the Tamil Sittars but only a few are now in print. See Raseśvara Darśana, Siddha Cikitsā.

Śiva-bīja: Name of *pārada* or mercury.

Śivacakra: The four Śiva triangles as constituents of Śrīyantra, Binducakra, Aṣṭadala-padma, Bhūpura (q.v), etc. Lakṣmīdhara on *Saundaryalaharī* IX.

Śivahasta: The hand of the preceptor which is purified by *mantras* when it is used to initiate some one in sparśa-dīkṣā (q.v.) Rāghava on *Śāradātilaka* V. 127-40.

***Sivajñānadīpa*:** Written by Rāvaṇāradhya it is a useful supplement to Kumāradeva's *Śuddhasādhaka* which deals with the doctrines of Śuddhamārga.

Śivānanda: Author of the *Ṛjuvimarśinī* commentary on the *Nityaṣoḍaśikārṇava*.

Śivānanda: Śaiva-Tantric teacher of the Krama system who flourished in Kashmir in the twelfth century. Authorship of *Krama-vāsana, Mahānayaprakāśa*, etc. had been attributed to him.

Śivānanda: Commentator on *Mātṛkācakra-viveka* of Svatantrānandanātha.

Śivānanda Gosvāmin: Grandson of Śrīnivāsa Bhaṭṭa Gosvāmin (q.v.) and son of Jagan-nivāsa. He was a Tantric scholar and composed the *Siṃhasiddhāntasindhu* at the request of his patron, Devisiṃha of Bundel.

Śivanātha: Son of the celebrated Tantric *sādhaka* Sarvānanda who flourished at Mehar in Tippera district in the sixteenth century. Śivanātha wrote a biography of his illustrious father under the title *Sarvānandataraṅgiṇī*.

***Śivaṣamhitā*:** A work of Śaivism which, besides the doctrinal and ritualistic topics, deals with ten kinds of *mudrās* (IV.15.31) and 84 kinds of *āsanas*. The text also emphasizes the importance of *guru* and *dīkṣā*. It is said that the disciple should possess certain qualifications, such as implicit faith in the *guru*, respect for matters spiritual, some knowledge of the units and the basic scriptures and readiness to devote time and energy to the study and practice of the teachings of the *guru* III. 10-19.

Śivayuvati: Name of *śakti* triangle *Saundarya-lahari* IX.

Śivopādhyāya: Śaiva-Tantric scholar who flourished in the eighteenth century. His commentary, *Viviṛti* on *Vijñānabhairava* deserves special mention.

Smārtī dīkṣā: Initiation when the candidate is

absent. The teacher by mental recall frees him from the three fetters known as *āṇava, karma* and *māyia* (q.v.) and by his power elevates the soul of his disciple for union with the supreme being. Rāghava on *Śāradātilaka* V. 127-40.

Śmaśānakāli(kā): One of the many forms of Kālī mentioned in the *Toḍalatantra* and *Mahākālasaṃhitā*. *Puraścaryārṇava* I. 16. She has four, eleven and twenty-one lettered mantras. *Tantrasāra* 373. She is described as being black in complexion, three-eyed and untied hair, and has a smiling face. Her left hand holds a skull filled with wine and the right hand a severed head. She is in the habit of dancing wildly having become intoxicated by drinking wine. She has also a four-armed form. She is surrounded by jackals and Yoginīs. Other forms of her *dhyāna* are quoted in the *Śyāmārahasya* IV and *Prāṇatoṣaṇī* V. 6, 389.

Ṣoḍaśadala-padma: Tantric concept of sixteen-petalled lotus, each petal has a vowel symbolizing a Mātṛkā. *Kāmakalāvilāsa* XXXIII. It is also conceived as existing in the *cakra*.

Ṣoḍaśādhāra: Sixteen containers of the human body. They are Mūlādhāra, Svādhiṣṭhāna, Maṇipura, Anāhata, Viśuddha, Ājñā, Vindu, Kalā, Pāda, Nivodhika, Ardhendu, Nāda, Nādānta, Unmanī, Viṣṇuvaktra and Dhruvamaṇḍalikā. *Prāṇatoṣaṇī* II. 2.93.

Ṣoḍaśī: Mahāvidyā goddess identified with Śrīvidya (q.v.), Tripurā and Mahātripurasundarī. She has three forms, her *maṇḍala* has three angles, *mantra* three letters, *bhūpura* three lines. She appears like a maiden of sixteen which accounts for her name. She is also known as Lalitā. She has many *mantras* among which the fifteen-lettered one is most efficacious. *Prāṇatoṣaṇī* V. 6.374-8; *Setubandha* on *Nityaṣodaśikārṇava* I. 118-19. Her physical description as found in the *Tantrasāra* 282-3 is that of a sexually attractive lady having no terrible or fearful element. Apart from her physical beauty details of her abode and throne are furnished in the *Mahākālasaṃhitā* and *Siddhāntasaṃgraha*, *Puraścaryārṇava* IX. 799. Many hymns extolling her beauty and benevolence have been composed. *Tantrasāra* 523-4.

Ṣoḍaśopacāra: Sixteen articles required for worship. They are *āsana, svāgata, pādya, arghya, ācamanīya, madhuparka, punarācamanīya, snānīya, bhuṣaṇa, gandha, puṣpa, dhūpa, dīpa, naivedya* and *vandanā*. *Mahānirvāṇa* XIII. 203-4.

Śodhana: Cleansing which is effected by six processes known as *ṣaṭkarma*. They are *dhauti* (inner-washing), the clearance of wind, phlegm, and bile, in a variety of ways, the most important being, filling the stomach with sufficient water and evacuating it by vomiting; *vasti* or contraction and expansion of the anus in water; *neti* or cleaning the nostrils; *laulikī* or whirling of the belly from side to side; *trāṭaka* or clearing the eyes; and *vyutkrama* or removal of phlegm by inhalation and exhalation or by water drawn through the nostrils and ejected through the mouth or reverse. *Gheraṇḍasaṃhitā* III. 8 ff.; *Haṭhayoga-pradīpikā* II. 21 ff.

Ṣoḍhanyāsa: A form of *nyāsa* in which the deities are singly felt in the body. It has six processes. See *Tārābhaktisudhārṇava* XII, 1165; *Tantrasāra* 272, 309 ff.

Somacakra: A minor nerve cycle within the body.

Somānanda: A pupil of Vasugupta (q.v.) who was the author of *Śivadṛṣṭi* and a *vṛtti* thereon. He lived in the ninth century AD. *Śivadṛṣṭi*, a work on Kashmir Śaivism and Śaiva Tantra, has been commented on by Utpaladeva. Ed. M.S. Kaul, Kashmir Sanskrit Series, LIV, 1934. Chapter I. trans. and com. by R. Gnoli in *East and West*, NS, VIII, 1957.

Somaputra: Śaiva-Tantric teacher of Krama system who lived in Kashmir in the twelfth century. He is eulogized in the *Cidgaganacandrikā*.

Soma Siddhānta: A branch of Śaivism which served as a bridge between Pāśupata and Śākta cults. *Prabodhacandrodaya*, Act. III.

Someśvara: Holy resort of the goddess Varārohā mentioned in *Matsya* XIII. 43, *Devībhāgavata* VII. 30, 72; *Padma*, Sṛṣṭi XVII. 201; *Skanda* V. 3.98.80. It is same as Somanātha or Prabhāsa in Kathiawar.

Sonasaṅgama: Holy resort of the goddess Subhadrā mentioned in *Matsya* XIII. 45; Devībhāgavata VII. 30, 75; *Padma*, Sṛṣṭi XVII. 203; *Skanda* V. 3-98.83. It is Sona-Gaṅgāsaṅgama near Patna.

***Spandakārikā*:** Text of Kashmir Śaivism which consists of 52 *kārikās* divided into three *niṣyandas* (sections) called *svarūpaspanda, sahajavidyodaya* and *vibhutispanda* respectively. It holds that Śiva possessed of Śakti creates the world by opening his eyes (*unmeṣa*) and dissolves it by closing them (*nimeṣa*); that the effects (*kārya*) are perishable but the efficience (*kartṛtva*) which is of the nature of *cit* (consciousness) is not; that the *cit* is felt by one who is *saprabuddha*, i.e. fully possessed of knowledge (*jñāna*) of what is to be known (*jñeya*) in the waking state (*jāgrat*), deep sleep (*suṣupti*) and dream (*svapna*); that the qualities, *sattva, rajas* and *tamas*, do not envelope the original nature of the Yogin; that a devotee by means of *mantras* becomes one with the deity that the Śakti inherent in *mantras* makes the devotee's mind free from the taints of *māyā*; and that when one's ego disappears one attains the supreme state. Ed. with Kallaṭa's *Vṛtti* and *Śivasūtra-Vārtika* of Bhāskara by J.C. Chatterjee, Kashmir Series, 1916; *Spandakārikā-Vivṛti* of Rāmakaṇṭha, ed. J.C. Chatterjee, KSS VII, 1913.

***Spandapradīpikā*:** Bhaṭṭa Utpala's (tenth century AD) commentary on *Spandakārikā*. In certain places this commentary appears to be familiar with the Krama system. The author has tried to interpret Spanda and Yoga concepts in the light of Tantric Krama philosophy. Ed. V. Islampurkar, 1898.

Sparśa (Sparśinī)-dīkṣā: Initiation by touch. *Kulārṇava* XIV; *Puraścaryārṇava* V. 391; Rāghava on *Śāradātilaka* V. 127-40.

Śrīcakra: Same as Śrīyantra (q.v.). It consists of nine *yonis* or sex organs in triangles, five of which have their apex pointing downwards; these represent Śakti. The remaining four, with apex pointing upwards, represent Śiva. The *bindu* is situated in the smallest triangle pointing downwards. There are two sets of ten triangles, another set of fourteen triangles, two lotuses—eight and petalled—three circles and three boundary lines with four gates. The *Nityaṣoḍaśikārṇava* 126-204 gives details of different items in the worship of the Śrīcakra.

***Śrīcakrasambhāra Tantra*:** A Buddhist work. Tibetan text and English translation by Lama Kazi Dawa Samdup and edited in *Tantrik Texts,* Vol. VII by A. Avalon 1919.

Śrīhaṭṭa: A *mahāpīṭha* according to the *Śivacarita* where the neck of Sati is said to have fallen. The presiding deity is Mahālakṣmī. The *Sādhanamālā* refers to this *pīṭha* as Sirihaṭṭa. It is a holy place in modern Sylhet.

Śrikaṇṭha: Name of Śiva-triangle of the Śrīyantra. *Saundaryalaharī* XI.

Śrīkula: A major Tantric school. Texts like *Tripurārahasya, Subhagodayastuti, Prapañcasāra, Saundaryalaharī, Prayogakramadīpikā, Śarādātilaka*, etc., belong to this school.

***Śrīmahātripurasundarī-varivasyā*:** A late medieval compilation by Karapātrisvāmin dealing with such Tantric topics as *puraścaraṇa, nyāsa, maṇḍala, yantra, dīkṣā*, etc. It refers to gods like Sūrya, Viṣṇu, Śiva, etc., and goddess like Suvasīnī, Ṣoḍaśī, Cakradevī, etc.

Śrīnivāsa: Author of the *Tātparyadīpikā* commentary on the *Tripurarahasya* of Haritāyana.

Śrinivāsa Bhaṭṭa Gosvāmin: A Brāhmaṇa Tantric scholar of the late-medieval period from Kanci who was a disciple of Sundarācārya of Jālandhara and author of the *Śivārcanacandrikā*. His post-initiation name appears to have been Vidyānandanātha. He settled at Vārāṇasī. See *Des. Cat. of Sans. Mss. RASB,* VIII.

Śrīpura: Holy resort of the goddess Śriramā mentioned in the *Bṛhannīlatantra* V. It is Sripur in Raipur district, Madhya Pradesh.

***Śrītattvacintāmaṇi*:** Tantric treatise composed by Pūrnānanda (q.v.) in Śaka 1499 (AD 1577) which is basically metaphysical in nature. It also deals with the cult of Śrīvidyā and the classifications of yoginīs. The sixth chapter has the self-explanatory title *Ṣaṭcakranirūpaṇa*. Pub. in Calcutta Sanskrit Series, no. XIX.

Śrīvidyā: Primordial energy (Ādyā Śakti) called by this name by the followers of Śrīkula. Śrī Vidyā is also called Tripurā or Tripurasundarī as well as Ṣoḍaśi and Lalitā. *Setubandha* com. on *Nityasoḍaśikārṇava* IV. 18; *Kubjika* quoted in *Prāṇatoṣanī* 6.374. Her *mantras* in symbolic letters are known as Catuṣkūṭā, Pañcakūṭa, etc. *Śrītattvacintāmaṇi* X. 26-8, XI. 7-10, etc.; *Śāradātilaka* XII. 5. Her *mantra* of sixteen letters merits the most exaggerated praise in the Tantras. cf. *Jñānārṇava* XXIV. 74-6. Śrividyā is the subject in various poetic hymns. She is sometimes referred to as Śrividyā-tripurā. *Puraścaryārṇava* IX. 799-801; *Tantrasāra* 523-4.

The text of her Kavaca is given in *Tantrasāra* 526-7.

***Śrīvidyāratnasūtra*:** A Tantric text attributed to Gauḍapāda which is said to have been commented upon by Śankarācārya. It is in 101 Sūtras. Ed. by Gopinath Kaviraj, Sarasvati Bhavana, Benares 1924.

Śrīyantra: The most important Tantric diagram connected with the cult of Śrividyā. It is also known as Śrīcakra and Tripurā-cakra. This diagram symbolizes the body of the goddess. It consists of nine triangles (*yonis*), five in the name of Śakti and four in that of Śiva. The Śakti triangles are pointed downwards and Śiva triangles upwards. Laksmīdhara on *Saundaryalaharī* IX. *Nityaṣodaśikārṇava* VI. 24; *Kāmakalāvilāsa* XXXVI.

Srota: Three currents of the Tantric tradition: *dakṣiṇa* (right), *vāma* (left) and *madhyama* (middle). They represent the three *śaktis* of Śiva. Each of these is again subdivided into two classes, inner (*hārdya*) and outer (*bāhya*). This division is also made in terms of *divya*, *kaula* and *vāma*. A classification of Tantric texts on the basis of these currents is found. Tantras of the right current comprise *Yoginijāla*, *Yoginīhṛdaya*, *Mantramālinī*, *Aghoreśī*, *Aghoreśvarī*, *Kriḍāghoreśvarī*, *Lākinīkalpa*, *Mārīcī*, *Mahāmārīcī* and *Ugravidyāgaṇa* while those of the middle comprise *Vijaya*, *Niśvāsa*, *Svāyambhūva*, *Vātula*, *Vīrabhadra*, *Raurava*, *Mukuṭa* and *Dhīreśa*. There is no reference to Tantras belonging to the left current.

Sṛṣṭicakra: The three triangles of the Śrīyantra (q.v.) representing the creative aspect of Śakti.

Sṛṣṭi-kalā: Expressions of the power of creation beginning from the symbolic letter 'A' denoting Brahmā. These are ten in number—*sṛṣṭi*, *ṛddhi*, *smṛti*, *medhā*, *kānti*, *lakṣmī*, *dhṛti*, *sthirā*, *sthiti*, and *siddhi*. *Prapañcasāra* III. 20-1.

Sṛṣṭikāntā: A form of Avalokiteśvara or Lokeśvara. He is one-faced and two-armed and displays *varada* pose with his right hand while his empty left hand rests near his navel. A large number of four-armed gods issue from various parts of his body while Amitābha appears on his head.

Sṛṣṭikramanyāsa: Nyāsa or feeling the deity in different parts of the body. The deity should be conceived in terms of letters from A to Kṣa and felt in different spots between the forehead and the heart. *Puraścaryārṇava* V. 328-9; *Tantrasāra* 90.

Stambhana: One of the *Ṣaṭkarmas* (q.v.) by which the efforts of the opponents can be arrested. Śarādā XXIII. 124.

Sthala; Vīra Śaiva concept of the source and support of all phenomenal existence. *Stha* means *sthiti* or existence and *la* means *laya* or dissolution. It represents the absolute and eternal self-consciousness. The potential and material movement of the absolute is called Śiva while its actual and formal movement is called Śakti. Creation is the result of the *vimarśa-śakti* of Śiva that has the power to do anything and everything. Śiva as *brahman* through his Śakti is the material cause and in his own nature the efficient cause of the world. The relation is relative and is not indicative of real difference, for there is identity between Śakti and Śaktimat as between attribute and substance.

Sthāna-śuddhi: Purification of the place of worship. *Kulārṇava* VI.

Sthānvīśvara: Modern Thanesar in the Kurukshetra district Haryana described as the holy resort of the goddess Bhavānī in *Matsya* XIII. 30, *Devībhāgavata* VII. 30. 59; *Padma*, Srṣṭi, XVII. 188; *Skanda* V. 3.98.68.

Sthāpanī: Tantric *mudrā* or hand-pose in which the folded hands are held upside down.

Sthiracakra: A rare form of Mañjuśrī (q.v.). In the iconographical texts he is described as being white in colour, seated with his own Śakti; the right hand is in *varada mudrā* and the left holds a sword. Often he is viewed as having a sword and a manuscript in his two hands.

Sthiticakra: One-third of the triangles of Śrīyantra representing the preserving aspect of Śakti. *Setubandha* on *Nityaṣoḍaśikārṇava* I. 42.

Sthiti-kalā: Expressions of the power of preservation beginning from the symbolic letter 'U' denoting Viṣṇu. These are ten in number—*jarā*, *pālinī*, *śānti*, *aiśvarī*, *rati*, *kāmikā*, *varadā*, *hlādinī*, *prīti* and *dīrghā*. *Prapañcasāra* III. 21-2.

Sthitikramanyāsa: Nyāsa (q.v.) in which deities are to be conceived in terms of letters from Da to Kṣa and felt in different spots from the heart to the knee. *Puraścaryārṇava* V. 322.

Sthūla dhyāna: Meditation on some specified objects like the image of the deity, etc. It is regarded as very helpful in spiritual quest. *Mahānirvāṇa* V. 139; *Śaktisaṅgama* Sundarī, II.126.

Strī guru: Female preceptor. For her characteristics see *Rudrayāmala* Uttara II. The *Yoginītantra* describes the efficacy of getting initiated under a female teacher. *Tantrasāra* 3; see also *Śaktisaṅgama*, Tārā LVIII. 7-8. The *Mātṛkābheda* VII gives the verses of her worship. The process of the mediation on her form is given in *Prāṇatoṣaṇī* III. 1, 155.

Strī-mantra: *Mantras* attributed to female deities. Com. of *Śāradātilaka* II. 57 ff.

Strī-varṇa: The long vowels are known by this name. Com. on *Śāradātilaka* II. 5-7.

***Subhāgamapañcaka*:** Five Tantric texts, each said to be propounded respectively by Vasiṣṭha, Sanaka, Śuka, Sanandana and Sanat Kumāra, which were intended for the followers of the Vedic way.

Subhagānanda: Author of the *Manoramā* commentary on the *Tantrarājatantra*. He belonged to the Kashmir school and his real name was Śrīkaṇṭha.

***Subhagodaya-stuti*:** A hymn believed to have been written by Gauḍapāda in 52 verses. Śaṅkara is said to have written a commentary on it.

Subhākarasiṃha: Buddhist monk who hailed from Kaliṅga and studied at Nālandā. He went to China in the eighth century and translated the Mantrayāna Sutra entitled *Mahāvairocana* (q.v.) belonging to the category of the Caryā-tantra (q.v.) and dealing with the means of communion with the Dhyānī Buddha Vairocana.

Sucimudrā: Pose used generally in the act of dancing, though it is to be seen in other cases also. All the fingers are stretched with the tips joining at the end, so as to resemble a needle (*sucī*).

Sudarśana-yantra: A form of Tantric *cakra* or *yantra* described in the *Ahirbudhnya Saṃhitā* (XXXVI. 6-66) used for worship to attain wealth and prosperity.

Śuddha-mārga: Theoretical viewpoint of the Māheśvara Siddhas who based their doctrine of the process of overcoming death by revitalizing the body with extra-physical nourishment on the lines laid down in Āgamanta Śaivism and Śāktism. It is said that the Chinese Taoist Bhoga taught the *suddhamārga* of the siddhas.

Śuddha-māyā: The pure aspect of *māyā*, the material cause of the world, according to different Śaiva schools. It represents the stages of progressive unification of the self with the whole universe. From *śuddha-māyā* is produced *nāda* (cognitive energy), from *nāda bindu* (conative energy), from *bindu sādākhya* (cognitive and conative energies held in equipoise), from *sādākhya maheśvari* (cognitive energy subordinated to the conative), and from *maheśvari śuddhavidyā* (conative energy subordinated to the cognitive). *Mṛgendra Āgama* II. 3-7; III. 1; VII. 11; VIII. 1-5; IX. 2-4; *Pauṣkara Āgama* II. 17, III. 4, V. 9; *Śivajñānabodham* II. 5; XII. 3.

***Śuddhasādhaka*:** A treatise meant for the followers of the Sudhamārga which was composed by Kumāradeva. It contains the mystical and dogmatic contents of Śuddhamārga along with the concept of liberation by monadic transformation of the body.

Śuddha vidyā: See Śuddha-māyā. It is also known as Sad Vidyā. It is that stage of knowledge in which the difference between subject and object is not completely wiped out.

Sudurjayā: Tantric Buddhist goddess of the Bhūmī (q.v.) category. She is yellow in colour and carries an emerald on her open palm which rests on the lap. Her right hands holds *vajra*. *Niṣpanna* 55.

Sugandhā: Modern Sikarpur on the Sondha near Barisal, Bangladesh, which is described as a holy resort of the goddess Sunandā. The *Pīṭhanirṇaya* refers to it as a *pīṭha* where the nose of Satī is said to have fallen. The *Śivacarita* mentions it as a *mahāpīṭha*.

Sugatisandarśana: A form of Avalokiteśvara which has been described in *Sādhanamālā* 88 as being white in complexion; he has six hands-showing *varada*, *abhaya* poses and an *akṣamālā* in the right hands and *padma*, *kuṇḍī* and *tridaṇḍī* in the left. In images of this Bodhisattva Tārā and Bhṛkuṭī are often found as companions, and Sucimukha on the pedestal.

Sukhāvati Lokeśvara: A form of Avalokiteśvara described in the *Dharmakośasaṅgraha* of Amṛtānanda. He is white in complexion, three-faced and six-armed. The hands show the arrow-throwing and boon-giving poses, hold a rosary, bow and lotus, and one is placed on the thigh of Tārā. He sits on *latitāsana* and is surrounded by goddesses belonging to the Tārā group. Nepal abounds in images of this Sakhāvatī Lokeśvara.

Sumati: Tantric Buddhist goddess of Dhāriṇī (q.v.) category. She is yellow in colour and holds in her left hand ears of corn. *Viśvajra* is held in her right hand. *Niṣpanna* 57.

Sumukhī: A form of Mātaṅgī, also known as Ucchiṣṭa-Caṇḍālinī, who removes all sins and bestows all desirables. Her *mantra* is *Ucchiṣṭa-caṇḍalinī sumukhī devī mahā-piśācinī hriṃ ṭhaḥ ṭhaḥ ṭhaḥ*. She looks like a young lady of sixteen years with elevated breasts and carries in her hands a skull and a chopper. *Puraścaryārṇava* IX. 830.

***Sumukhīpūjāpaddhati*:** A well-known manual on the forms and methodologies of the worship of Sumukhī (q.v.), a form of Mātaṅgī (q.v.). Its author, Śaṅkara, who was a disciple of Sundarānanda, belongs to the line of the great Vedantist, Vidyāraṇya.

Sundarācārya: Also known as Saccidānandanātha he was a medieval Tantric teacher who was the preceptor of Śrīnivāsa Bhaṭṭa Gosvāmin and presumably the author of *Lalitārcanacandrikā* and the *Laghucandrikā*. He hailed from Jālandhara.

Sundarī: A Mahavidyā goddess mentioned in *Śaktisaṅgama*, Tārā VI. 16-7. She is often identified with Tripurasundarī (q.v.). Rājamātaṅginī was born from the rays of her eyes. *Prāṇatoṣaṇī* V. 6.874.

Sunnirodhanī: Tantric *mudrā* or hand-pose in which two hands form a closed fist with the thumbs hidden within.

Śūnya, Śūnyatā: Translated as 'void' in the absence of a suitable and more expressive word. It signifies a state of mind after *nirvāṇa*, about which neither existence, nor non-existence, nor a combination of the two can be predicated. This Sūnya in Vajrayāna is identified with knowledge which transforms itself, in the form of divinities of the nature of Sūnya, for the welfare and happiness of man. Śūnyatā or vacuity is conceived in terms of the Female Principle which is the prime cause of all manifestation. It is also known as Prajñā (q.v.). The complementary Male Principle is Karuṇā or Upāya (q.v.).

Surāśodhana: Purification of wine. For the procedure see *Prāṇatoṣaṇī* VII. 2; *Kulārṇava* VI; *Gandharva* XXXIV. 86-9; *Mātṛkā-bheda* III. 13; *Tārārahasya* III, *Mahānirvāṇa* V., etc.

Surasundarī: One of the eight Yoginīs (Aṣṭa-yogini, q.v.) described in the *Tantrasāra*. She is fair-complexioned having a charming face resembling the full moon and highly developed breasts. She wears beautiful clothes.

Sūrya-nāḍi: Another name for the Piṅgalā nerve.

Susiddha-mantra: Mantras which are instantly efficacious. *Puraścaryārṇava* I. 59.

Susumnā: The most important nerve, also known as *brahmanāḍi*. It is said that the universe itself is contained in this nerve. *Yogaśikhopaniṣat* VI. 13. It extends from *mūlādhāra* to *Brahmarandhra*, and is the route by which Kuṇḍalinī marches upwards. *Ṣaṭcakranirūpaṇa* I. 1 ff. According to the *Sāṇḍilyopaniṣat* I. 410 ff. if the *prāṇa* is pushed through this nerve by means of yogic exercise the aspirant will be liberated. That is why it is also called *mokṣamārga*.

Svābhā Prajñā: Also known as Svābhā Vidyā, it is the female counterpart of a Bodhisattva. All goddesses are regarded as female counterparts of one or another of the Bodhisattvas (the emanations of the Dhyānī Buddhas). Svābhā Prajñā or Svābhā Vidyā is same as Śakti. She is either represented singly or in *yab-yum*, i.e. in the actual embrace of the god to whom she is affiliated as a Śakti. Svābhā is *sva abhā*, 'one's own light'.

***Svacchanda Tantra*:** One of the leading Tantras of Dakṣiṇācāra belonging to the Trika schools of Kashmir Śaivism. It has a commentary called *Uddyota* by Kṣemarāja of the eleventh century. It has fifteen chapters dealing with the doctrines, *mantras*, initiation, yogic fixation of mind, aspiring for *siddhis*, internal worship, *mudrās* and so forth. It is mainly ritualistic. It does not deal with black acts but lays emphasis on meditation. According to Kṣemarāja the work is called *Svacchanda* or 'free-going' as it eulogizes and initiates into the secret worship of Aghora, the right mouth of Svacchanda Bhairava. Ed. with Kṣemarāja's com. by V.V. Dvivedi, Kashmir Sanskrit Series.

Svādhiṣṭhāna: The nerve plexus situated above the *mūlādhāra*. *Svādhiṣṭhāna-cakra* (the sacral plexus) is near the root of the penis; it is represented by the letters ba, bha, ma, ya, ra and la. It is like a six-petalled lotus. This *cakra* is presided over by the goddess Rākinī. Just as *mūlādhāra* is associated with earth so *Svādhiṣṭhāna* is associated with water, as is indicated by the octagonal pericarp with a half-moon in the centre. Inside the *bindu* is Viṣṇu seated on Garuḍa with his usual symbols. *Ṣaṭcakranirūpaṇa* XV-XVII; Lakṣmīdhara on *Saundaryalaharī* XI.

Svairācāra: One of the forms of Vāmācara (q.v.) in which the Sādhaka possesses the right to do anything, even ignoring the norms laid down in the sacred texts. Among the seven stages of *sādhanā*, the first four—*ārambha*, *taruṇa*, *yauvana* and *prauḍha* (q.v.)—belong to Samayācāra, and the last three-*prauḍhānta*, *unmanā* and *anavasthā* (q.v.)—belong to the Svairācara. By crossing the first four stages the aspirant reaches a higher stage which is why he may choose his way independently.

Svakula varṇa: Letters belonging to one's own group. There are three other categories of letters—Mitra (friendly), Udāsīna (neutral), and Śatru (inimical). *Prapañcasāra* III. 70-2.

Svapuṣpa: The first menstrual blood of a newly married woman sacred to Devi.

Svarūpa-śakti: Special *śakti* (power) of *brahman* (conceived of in terms of Kṛṣṇa whose *līlā* or sport is possible through its agency) which has three aspects known as *sandhinī, saṃvit* and *hlādini* corresponding respectively to *sat* (reality), *cit* (consciousness) and *ānanda* (bliss). A combination of these three is technically called *śuddhasattva*.

Svātantrya Śakti: Independent power of the supreme being which is identical with *vimarśa* (q.v.) *Svātantryaṃ hi vimarśa ityucyate*, *Tantrāloka* III. 73. It is the power of dominance which it spreads all around. *Īśvarapratyābhijñā* I. 214 ff. Māyā is also *svatantrya-śakti* of Śiva which is not different from him. *Tantrāloka* IX. 149. The concept of *svātantrya-śakti* has been widely utilized in Kashmir Śaivism.

Svayambhūkusuma: Menstrual blood of a maiden.

***Svayambhū Purāṇa*:** Medieval Nepalese Purāṇa which is an important source for the study of the development of Tantric Buddhism in that country. Tantric Buddhist deities like Mañjuśrī and Avalokiteśvara, especially the latter's local manifestations, and various other Buddhist deities as also their Hindu counterparts have been dealt with in detail in this Purāṇa. It is said in this Purāṇa that Ādi Buddha first manifested himself in Nepal in the form of a flame of fire and Mañjuśri erected a temple in order to preserve the flame. This temple is known as Svayambhū-caitya.

Śyāmā (Kālī): Same as Dakṣiṇākālī (q.v.). In the *Tantrasāra* she is described as having a terrible appearance—a fierce face, four hands, untied hair and she wears a garland of severed heads around her neck. In her lower and upper left hands she holds a freshly severed head and a sword, and in the lower and upper right hands she exhibits *abhaya* and *varada* poses. Naked, dark as dense cloud in complexion, her body is streaked with blood. Terrible in face and teeth she has well-developed breasts; her girdle is made of hands cut off fron the bodies of corpses. She lives in the cremation ground. She has three eyes resembling the orb of the rising sun. Her untied hair hangs to the right. She stands on the chest of Śiva lying as a corpse. Often she is engaged in *viparitarati* (inverted sexual intercourse also called *puruṣāyita*) with Mahākāla (Śiva). The *Niruttaratantra*, Paṭala II, gives a slightly different version of this *dhyāna*. Śyāmā is also the name of the Śāsanadevatā of the Jain Tīrthaṃkara Padmaprabha according to the Svetambara tradition.

***Śyāmārahasya*:** Tantric treatise of sixteen chapters composed by Pūrṇānanda (q.v.) in the middle of the sixteenth century which deals with the practices of Kāli worshippers and usual Tantric topics like *mantroddhāra*, *puraścaraṇa*, *dyāna*, *kulācāra*, *dūtiyāga*, etc. Ed. by P.C. Pal and Bros., Calcutta 1948 vs, by J. Vidyasagara, Calcutta 1896; with Bengali trans. by S. Tirthanath, Calcutta 1982.

***Śyāmāsaparyāvidhi*:** A late text on Kālī worship by Kāśīnathā Bhaṭṭācārya Tarkālaṃkāra in seven chapters. It refers to the practice of Kālī worship in Bengal during the Dīpāvalī festival.

Śyāma Tārā: Tārās of the green group. They comprise Khadiravanī Tārā, Vaśya Tārā, Ārya Tārā, Mahattarī Tārā, Varada Tārā, Durgottāriṇī Tārā, Dhanada Tārā, Jāṅguli and Parṇaśabarī.

T t

Tāḍaṇa: Processing of *mantras*. Each letter of the *mantra* concerned should be recited either ten times or a hundred times. Tāḍaṇa is also done by writing the letters and sprinkling sandal wood water on them. *Tantrasāra* 54.

Taḍitkarā: Tantric Buddhist goddess whose name means 'lightning bearer'. She is described as being green in colour and she holds in her hands creeper-like lightning: *taḍitkāra haritā vidyullatādharā*.

Taijasa Varṇa: Same as Āgneya-varṇa—the letters I, Ī, Ai, Kha, Cha, Ṭha, Pha, Ra and Kṣa, said to have sprung from heat or *tejas*. Ten letters from *ya* to *kṣa* are also sometimes supposed to belong to this category. *Prapañcasāra* III. 70-2; com. on *Śārada* II. 1 ff.

Tailaṅga: Holy resort of the goddess Caṇḍanāyikā, an *upapīṭha* with Caṇḍeśa as Bhairava, mentioned in the *Śivacarita*. It is a site in the Telengana region of Andhra Pradesh. The region as Trilinga is mentioned in Rājaśekhara's *Viddhasālabhañjikā*.

Takkirāja: Tantric Buddhist god presiding over the south-western direction. He is described in *Niṣpanna* 2 as blue in colour, having three faces, and holding with two principal hands Śakti, and in the other four a blue staff, a sword, a jewel and a lotus. In the Vajrahuṅkāra Maṇḍala his name is Vajrayakṣa and in Dharmadhātuvāgīśvara Maṇḍala it is Vajrāvālānalārka. His consort is Cundā.

Tālikā: Tantric Buddhist goddess associated with lock and key; also known as Dvāratālakadharā. She is described as being white in colour and holds a lock in her hands. *Niṣpanna* 77.

Tamas: The constituent of Prakṛti (q.v.) which is of the nature of indifference and is heavy (*guru*) and enveloping (*varṇaka*). It gives rise to drowsiness, sloth, stupidity, ignorance and carelessness.

Tamolipta: Holy resort of the goddess Tamoghnī mentioned in the *Bṛhannīla* and *Prāṇatoṣaṇī*. It is modern Tamluk in Midnapore district, West Bengal. Other old forms of the name were Tāmralipta, Tāmralipti, Damalipta, etc.

Tanjur: Collection of translations into Tibetan from the Indian texts. Bstan-hgyur as it is also called, it consists of 3, 458 texts divided into two parts—Tantra and Sūtra.

Tanmātra: Five potential elements of sound, touch, colour, taste and smell, giving rise to the *mahābhūtas* (gross elements). From the essence of sound is produced *ākāśa* or space, from that of touch air, from that of colour light or fire, from that of taste water, and from that of smell earth.

Tantra: A general term for any system serving as the guiding principle of work. In the religious sense Tantra first came to mean 'the scripture by which knowledge is spread'. In the next stage it was defined as a class of texts which promulgates profound matters concerning *tattva* (theory, which came to mean 'pure knowledge') and *mantra* (practical means, which later came to denote 'mystic sound') and was, therefore, looked upon as a technical branch of pure knowledge. Thus Tantra came to mean the essentials of every religious system and subsequently, special doctrines and rituals found only in certain forms of various religious systems.

***Tantrābhidhāna*:** Tantric lexicon comprising *Bījanighaṇṭu* and *Mudrānighaṇṭu*. Ed. by A. Avalon in *Tantrik Texts*, Vol. I, 1913.

***Tantrakaumudī*:** A late medieval Tantric work composed by Devanātha Tarka-pañcānana of Kamatapur. It is mainly a collection of *mantras* from various texts mostly dedicated to the Mahāvidyā goddesses as well as Gaṇeśa and Mañjughoṣa (of Buddhist affiliation). The six black acts and subjects like *dīkṣā*, *mantrasaṃskāra*, *yoni-mudrā*, *puraścaraṇa*, *vīrasādhana*, *japamālāvidhi* and *yantra* are also explained. Ed. by R. Jha, Darbhanga 1969.

***Tantrāloka*:** Work of the great polymath Abhinavagupta (AD 950-1020) which is commented upon by Jayaratha in his *Tantrāloka-viveka*. The work, which mainly follows the *Mālinīvijaya Tantra*, is divided into 37 chapters called Āhnikas and deals with the philosophy and ritual of Kashmir Śaivism. It also systematically presents the views of various Tantric schools and sects. It states that there are three groups of ten, eighteen and sixty-four Śaiva Tantras. The doctrines of the Kaulas and the Krama system have been reviewed. Like any philosophical treatise, it treats the nature of *cit* (pure-consciousness) and the problems of knowledge. The only reality, according to this text is *saṃvit* which has no division. Besides the most sophisticated and abstruse philosophical discussions, the *Tantrāloka* also contains various theories and practices which enable individuals of diverse mentality to satisfy their spiritual urge. Abhinavagupta states that critical analysis of the comparative effectiveness of various practices will lead to true knowledge making one a Mahāsiddha or Yogīśvara, but one can also visualize the supreme reality by meditating on pure consciousness (*nirmala-saṃvid*) without any formal training. The supreme being is termed Śiva who is both immanent (*sarvākṛti*) and transcendent (*nirākṛti*) and Śakti is inseparable from him. All the Tantric topics for practical purposes—like *guru*, *dīksā*, *mantra*, *maṇḍala* and so forth—are elaborately described in this volume though the purpose of the author is to prove *śiva-śāktya-vinābhāvān-nityaikā mula-kāraṇam*. Published in Kashmir Series of Texts and Studies nos. XXIII (I. 1918), XXXIII (II. 1921), XXIX (VI. 1921), XXX (III. 1921), LII (X. 1933), LVII (XI. 1836), ed. by L. Shastri, intro. by A. Avalon, rpt. Delhi 1981.

Tantrarāja Tantra: A very important medieval Tantra which deals with the views of the Kādi, Hādi and Kahādi schools in three sections. The published Kādi portion has 36 chapters of hundred verses each. It deals with the meaning of Kādi, characteristics of guru and selection of *mantras*, *maṇḍalas* of nine Nāthas, *pādukā-mantra*, modes of *pratiṣṭhā* (installation of Devī), *mantras* of 16 Nityās, worship of Lalitā, Kameśvarī and others of the Nityā class, *mātṛkās* or letters, concepts of *kāla*, *prāṇa*, *cakra*, *yantra*, etc., making of *maṇḍapas* etc., *sthula-homa* rites of astonishing nature (*loka-camatkārakara*), and theoretical subjects such as form of the universe, merit and demerit, rebirth, worldly existence, bondage, liberation, time, intelligence, senses, animate and inanimate beings and so forth. It is probably associated with the earlier forms of *Yoginī* and *Mṛḍāṇī* Tantras. It has a few well known commentaries of which *Manoramā* by Subhagānanda deserves mention. Another was written by Prāṇamañjarī, wife of the famous Tantric author Premanidhi Pantha. Published in '*Tantrik Texts*', Vols. VIII, XII. An edition of the first chapter of Prāṇamañjarī's commentary was published by J.B. Chaudhuri, Calcutta 1940.

Tantrārthāvatāra: Buddhist Tantric text composed by Buddhaguhya and commented upon by Padmavajra.

Tantrasamuccaya: A collection compiled about AD 1426 from a number of Tantras. Besides the usual topics it deals especially with architecture and masonry.

Tantrasāra: An abridged version of *Tantrāloka* of Abhinavagupta. It upholds the doctrine that Śiva who is the self of all beings is the ultimate reality, immutable and ever perfect and the manifestation of the universe is effected through the Śakti and Śiva which is not different from him. Regarding the practical aspects of *sādhanā* it deals with *dīkṣā* (initiation), *guru* (preceptor), *kriyā* (action), *upāya* (means), *sthaṇḍita* (place of sacrifice), *dhyāna* (meditation), *dhāraṇa* (concentration), yoga, *japa, abhiṣeka* (consecration), *mudrā*, etc., as also the concepts of *mātṛkās* or *varṇas*, *bindu*, *bīja*, *nāda* and so forth. Published in Kashmir Series of Texts and Studies, No. XVII, 1918, ed. with notes by M.R. Sastri; Italian trans. by P. Baringhieri with intro. by R. Gnoli, Turin 1960.

Tantrasāra: See under Kṛṣṇānanda Āgamavāgīśa.

Tantravaṭadhānika: A very abridged form of *Tantrāloka* and *Tantrasāra* made by Abhinavagupta himself. The name has especially been chosen by him because he holds that the dynamic aspect of Śiva is Śakti, that power which manifests itself in the world, as a banian tree manifests itself from a seed (*vaṭadhānikāvat*). Ed. by M.R. Shastri, Kashmir Sanskrit Series, XXIV, 1918.

Tantrayukti: Term denoting the main canons, or propositions or principles, of exposition of a Śāstra.

Tārā: Most important goddess of the Tantric Buddhist pantheon. She is equally an important deity in the Brahmanical Tantras. She appears to be a very ancient protectress deity (derived from the root *tār* which means 'to save' or 'to protect') who was adopted in both the Brahmanical and Buddhist pantheon in the early centuries of the Christian era. In some Tantras it is said that her cult was brought by Vasiṣṭha from Mahācīna. It, however, appears that several goddesses, Indian and non-Indian, merged to become Tārā in course of time. She was introduced in Buddhism as the Śakti of Amoghasiddhi but became more famous as the consort of Avalokiteśvara. As the supreme female principle of Tantric Buddhism she was elevated to such a position that all other Buddhist goddesses came to be regarded as her manifestations which is why Tārā became the common name of all Buddhist goddesses. In Tantric works there are so many varieties of Tārā that it is very difficult to classify them correctly. A classification, however, has been made on the basis of colour. Thus Green Tārā comprises Vaśya, Khadiravanī, Ārya, Mahattarī, Varada, Durgottāriṇī, Dhanada, Jāṅguli, and Parṇaśabarī. White Tārā comprises Aṣṭamahābhaya, Mṛtyuvañcana, Caturbhuja-Sita, Ṣaḍbhuja-Sita, Viśvamātā, Kurukullā and Jāṅguli. Yellow Tārā comprises Vajra, Jāṅguli, Parṇaśabarī and Bhṛkuṭī. Ekajaṭā and Mahācīnatārā constitute the Blue Tārā group, while the Red Tara is represented by Kurukullā. Besides there are Mahāśrī Tārā, Sita Tārā, Prasanna Tārā, etc. *Om Tāre Tuttāre Ture Svāhā* is her *mantra*. In the Brahmanical Tantras Tārā is a Mahāvidyā goddess. She is also known as Ugratārā, Ekajaṭā and Nīlasarasvatī.

Tārā: Holy resort of the goddess Tāriṇī, a *mahāpiṭha* with Unmatta as Bhairava where part of an eye of Satī is said to have fallen, according to the *Śivacarita*. It has been identified with Tarapur near Nalhati in Birbhum district, West Bengal.

***Tārābhaktisudhārṇava*:** Composed, by Narasiṃha Ṭhakkura about AD 1680. It describes, in eleven *taraṅgas*, details about the worship of Tārā. It also deals with *kulācāra* and qualification of the *guru*. Published in *Tantrik Texts*, Vol. XXI, 1940.

***Tārābhaktitaraṅgiṇī*:** Name of three late-medieval compendiums on the Tārā cult written respectively by Prakāśānanda, Vimalānanda and Kāśinātha.

***Tārākalpalatāpaddhati*:** A late-medieval Tantric compendium of Tārā cult written by Nityānanda.

Tārākavaca: A charm or incantation extolling the greatness and seeking the protection of Tārā, the complete text of which in forty verses is given in the *Rudrayāmala*. Its sage is Akṣobhya, metre *tristubh*, goddess Tārā and *viniyoga* or application is for all success. *Tantrasāra* 540-2.

Taranātha: Also known as Lāmā Tāranātha (Tāranāth) he was born in 1573 or 1575. He wrote in Tibetan a history of Buddhism in India in 1608. Though he has given a confused account, when judged from a purely historical point of view, yet his work is very important for the study of Tantric Buddhism. It was first translated into Russian by V.P. Vasilev (1866). In 1868 A. Schiefner brought out an edition of its Tibetan text and a German translation in 1869. Vasilev's Russian and Schiefner's German apart, the only complete translation of Tāranātha's *History* exists in Japanese done by Enga Taramoto (1928). A few pages of Harinath De's English translation appeared in *The Herald* (1911). Schiefner's German version was translated into English by U.N. Ghoshal and N. Dutt which was serialized in *Indian Historical Quarterly*. In 1970 a fresh English translation of Tāranātha's *History* directly from Tibetan was done by Lama Chima and Alaka Chattopadhyaya. It was edited by Debiprasad Chattopadhyaya and published by the Indian Institute of Advanced Studies, Simla.

***Tārāpradīpa*:** Late-medieval compendium on Tārā written by Lakṣmaṇa Bhaṭṭa. There is a doubt among scholars whether this Lakṣmaṇa Bhaṭṭa is same as the famous Lakṣmaṇa Deśikendra. The *Tārāpradīpa* appears to have enjoyed popularity in Bengal. It is a metrical work dealing with the details of the worship of Tārā. It may have been planned to supplement the *Śāradātilaka*.

***Tārārahasya*:** Composed by Brahmānandagiri (q.v.) in the sixteenth century. It deals, besides the usual Tantric topics, with the cult of Tārā, Ekajaṭā, Ugratārā and Nīlasarasvatī. It also deals with creation and the daily duties of the Tantric aspirants. Ed. by Jīvananda Vidyāsāgara, Calcutta 1896; by P.C. Pal et al., Calcutta 1948 vs; by T. Giritirtha with Bengali trans. Calcutta 1977.

***Tārārahasyavṛtti*:** Composed by Gauḍīya Śaṅkara or Śaṅkara Āgamavāgīśa, it deals with usual Tantric topics such as *dīkṣā*, *puraścaraṇa*, etc. Pub. by Varendra Research Museum, Rajshahi 1961.

***Tārārṇava*:** A late Tantric work devoted to the worship of Tārā (q.v.).

***Tārāsahasranāma*:** A treatise on the thousand

names of Tārā which has been commented upon by Lakṣmīdhara.

Tāratāntra: A medieval Tantra in six chapters and 150 verses which describes the worship of Tārā in detail saying that the Tārā cult with *pañcamakāra* was brought by the sage Visiṣṭha from Mahācīna at the command of the goddess which is why the Tārā rituals are also known as *cīnācāra*. The text is also known as *Tāriṇī-tantra*. Ed. by A.K. Maitra, Varendra Research Society, Gaudagranthamala no. 1, Rajshahi 1913, reprint, New Delhi 1983.

Tāriṇī: Name of Tārā (q.v.) according to a *dhyāna* found in the Pañcākarā section of *Advayavajrasaṃgraha* 43. She originates from the germ syllable *tam*. Tāriṇī is also the name of Tārā in Brahmanical Tantras.

Tāriṇī-mata: Same as Kahadimata. *Śakti-saṅgama*, Tārā, LVIII. 81.

Tāriṇī-pārijāta: A late-medieval Tantric compendium of the Tārā cult written by Śrivīdvad Upādhyāya.

Tārīṇi-tantra: A Tantric text dealing with the cult of Tārā quotations from which are found in various manuals. A very attractive description of the goddess is quoted from this text in *Puraścaryārṇava* IX.

Tarjani-mudrā: A hand-pose in which the index finger is raised in a menacing attitude while the other fingers are clenched in the fist. If a pāśa (noose) appears round the index-finger it is called *tarjanipāśa*. This *mudra* is characteristic of certain Buddhist icons.

Tārodbhava Kurukullā: A form of Kurukullā who has sprung from Tārā. Her colour, ornaments, garments and lotus seat all are red. Her two left hands show *abhaya-mudrā* and arrow, and the right hands holds a bow and a lotus. She sits in *vajraparyaṅka* attitude, and under the seat appear Kāmadeva and his wife riding on demon Rāhu.

Tarpaṇa-mudrā: Mudrā of doing homage to the departed fathers. It is the *mudrā* of Nāmasaṅgīti. In this *mudrā* the arm is bent and raised upward in line with the shoulder, the palm of the hand is turned inward with fingers slightly bent pointing towards the shoulder.

Taruṇollāsa: A stage of spiritual progress in Tantric discipline, when the aspirant receives initiation from a *guru* and begins to study the scriptures. It is one of the seven *ullāsas* of *sadhanā*. This stage, like the preceding *ārambha* is intended for persons belonging to the Paśu or ordinary class. According to Rameśvara this stage belongs to the Samayācāra category. *Paraśurāma-kalpasūtra* I. 68; *Kulārṇava* VIII; *Tārābhaktisudhārṇava* VI. 255.

Taṭasthaśakti: A concept of *jīva-śakti* as marginal power typical of Caitanya Vaiṣṇavism. All *jīvas* (living beings, human or otherwise), are in essence this special power of the supreme being.

Tathāgatas: The Buddhas who have attained the highest state of perfection according to the Buddhists. In the *Sadhanamālā* the word is invariably used in the plural with reference to the five Dhyānī Buddhas, but does not even signify Vajrasattva or Vajradhara. The Buddhas are innumerable and have a hierarchy among them, the different orders being Pratyeka, Śrāvaka, Samyak-Sambuddha, Jina, Arhat, Tathāgata and the like.

Tathatā-garbha: Same as *garbha-dhātu*, the 'matrix element' or the phenomenal world, which is one of the two counterparts of the ultimate reality according to Tantric Buddhism. The other is *vajra-dhātu* which is of immutable nature. They are the two parts of the *maṇḍala*, the circle with Buddha Mahāvairocana in the centre with various manifestations of his body. Their *yoga* consists in the mystic union of the immutable essence, the 'thatness' (*tathatā*) of the *dharmas* (elements) with the active elements of the material world.

Tathatāvaśitā: Tantric Buddhist goddess of Vasitā (q.v.) category who is described as being white in colour, holding in her right hand a white lotus and in the left a bunch of jewels. *Niṣpanna* 57.

Tātparyadīpikā: Commentary on the *Tripurā-rahasya* (q.v.) of Haritāyana composed by Śrīnivāsa.

Tattva: Fundamentals. That which reveals its real nature behind all appearances is *tattva*. The term is derived from the root *tat* meaning 'that' which is an epithet of *brahman*, the ultimate reality. A *tattva* contains elements of universality and permanence in space and time. *Tantrāloka* IX. 161-2. Śaiva-Śākta philosophy has 36 *tattvas* grouped under various categories according to diverse viewpoints. *Śāradātilaka* V. 77-84; *Nityaṣoḍaśikārṇava* VII. 45-6. Com. on *Paraśurāmakalpasūtra* I. 4.

Tattvabhāvanā: Meditation on ultimate truth according to *Prajñopāya* IV. 10-16 which says that truth is both *prajñā* and *upāya* combined together.

Tattvacakra: Also known as Cakrarāja and Divyacakra. The performance of this *cakra* is restricted to those who have attained a certain stage of spiritual development. No external rites are required. The aspirants sit together under the leadership of Cakreśvara and meditate with *haṃsa-mantra*. *Mahānirvāṇa* VIII. 204 ff.

Tattvanyāsa: Feeling of 36 *tattvas* (threefold knowledge: Ātmā, Vidyā and Śiva) in different parts of the body through a variety of methods. *Tantrasāra* 271, 310.

***Tattvasaṃgraha*:** The *magnum opus* of Śāntarakṣita (AD 705-62), the commentary of which was written by Kamalaśīla. The *Tattva-saṃgraha* openly says that the Tantric rituals were directly introduced by the Buddha. Ed. with the com. of Kamalaśīla by E. Krishnamacharya with a Foreword by B. Bhattacharyya, GOS, XXX-XXXI, Baroda 1926, Eng. trans. by G. Jha, GOS, LXXX, LXXXIII, Baroda 1937, 1939.

Tejas-tattva: Theories pertaining to the *mahābhūta* (great element) of fire. Tejas has eight worlds for its manifestation—Bhairava, Kedāra, Mahākāla, Madhyameśa, Āmrataka, Jalpeśa, Śrīśaila and Hariścandra. These are also well known names of *tirthas*.

Tejodhyāṇa: Same as Jyotirdhyāna. In the *mūlādhāra* where *kuṇḍalinī* remains as the serpent power also remains the individual soul (*jīvātman*) shining like the flame of a lamp. This flame has to be conceived of as *brahman* and meditated upon. This meditation is known as *tejodhyāna*.

Tejoṣṇīṣa: Tantric Buddhist deity of *uṣṇīṣa* (q.v.) category. He is described as belonging to the south-western direction and being whitish red in colour. In his right hand he holds the disc of the sun while the left rests on his hip. *Niṣpanna* 66.

Tilo-pā: A contemporary of King Mahīpala I of Bengal (AD 988-1038) and teacher of Nāro-pa (q.v.). A good number of *Caryās* and *dohās* are attributed to his authorship. In the Tibetan tradition he is regarded as one of the 84 Mahāsiddhas. His bronze images have been found in Tibet. A gilt copper image of Tilopā belonging to the seventeenth century, is in the collection of the Linden Museum, Stutt gart. This image shows the Mahāsiddhas as if rising from his seat. In his right hand he holds a fish symbolizing the power of saving sentient beings, while in his upraised left hand he holds a skull cup, full of blood, symbolic of his ability to confer occult power pertaining to the mundane world.

Tirodhāna-śakti: A kind of power of energy which characterizes *māyā*. Tirodhānakarī māyābhidhā punaḥ. *Iśvarapratyābhijñā* III. 1.7. Tirodhāna ordinarily means extinction. But in a special sense it means a veneer or cover which hides one's own self (ignorance). Māyā veils both knower and knowledge. *Tirodhāna-śakti* has thus a negative role.

***Toḍala Tantra*:** A late-medieval Tantra in ten chapters dealing with the concept of Bhairava, *jñānayoga*, seven heavens and seven nether worlds, body as the microcosm of the universe, the nerve-plexuses, the ten incarnations, efficacy of *japa, mudrās, mantras* and *dhyānas* of Kālī, Tārā and Bhūtakātyāyanī.

Trailokyamohana: A *mantra* for accomplishing six magic acts (*ṣaṭkarmāni*) such as *śānti* (rite for averting disease or black magic), *vaśīkaraṇa* (bewitching men and women), *stambhana* (stopping the movements and actions of others), *vidveṣaṇa* (creating enmity between two persons), *uccātana* (driving a person from the village or country) and *māraṇa* (killing or causing permanent injury to living beings) given in the *Prapañcasāra* (XXXIV. 33).

Trailokyavaśāṅkara: A form of Avalokiteśvara. He is described as being one-faced, two-armed and three-eyed. He wears a crown of matted hair and carries in his hands a noose and a goad. *Śādhana* 80.

Trailokyavijaya: An emanation of Akṣobhya (q.v.) who is blue in colour and terrible in appearance. His six arms contains various weapons. He stands in the *pratyālīḍha* attitude, tramples upon the head of Maheśvara with his left leg while the right presses upon the bosom of Gaurī. *Sādhana* 511.

Trailokyavijayavidyā: The *mantras* meant for success. *Agni Purāṇa*. CXXV. 51-5.

Traipura: A triangle within the quadrangular Pṛthivīmaṇḍala which is situated within the pericarp of the container lotus, that is, the nerve-plexus, near the mouth of *vajranāḍi*. It is also called *yoni* or Kāmarūpa Pīṭha in human body. *Ṣaṭcakranirūpaṇa* VIII.

Trāṭaka: A form of Yogic Ṣaṭkarma. The aspirant has to focus his eyes on a point until they begin to water. It makes possible the attainment of Śāmbhavī Śakti. It is supposed to cure eye-diseases and give divine eyesight. See Śodhana. *Gheraṇḍa* I. 54-5.

Tribīja: The seed of the *mantras* of Tripurasundarī which are known as Vāgbhava, Kāmarāja and Śakti. *Cidvallī* on *Kāmakalāvilāsa* XXIII.

Tridhāma: Collective designation of Soma, Sūrya and Agni. *Kāmakalāvilāsa* XIII-XIV.

Triguṇa śakti: See *avidyā-śakti*, *māyā-śakti*.

Trihūta: Holy resort of the goddess Amarī, described in the *Śivacarita* as a *mahāpīṭha* with Amara as Bhairava where the left leg of Satī is said to have fallen. It is in Tirhut (Sanskrit Tīrabhukti) in North Bihar.

Trika: The world view of the Kashmir Śaiva Tantras, the followers of which are also known as Rahasya and Trambaka Sampradāya. The system has two main branches—Spanda and Pratyabhijñā—often referred as distinct schools. Apart from Spanda, Svātantryavāda or Svātantrya is also synonymous and so is Ābhāsavāda (q.v.). Trika is so called because of its emphasis on such triads as *Siddha*, *Nāmaka* and *Mālinī* Tantras; Śiva, Śakti and Anu; Parā, Aparā and Parātparā; *abheda*, *bhedābheda*, and *bheda*, etc. According to the Trika doctrine, reality conceived as transcendent is Śiva and as immanent is Śakti. Śakti is always in the state of perfect identity with Śiva, like fire and its burning power. There is perfect equilibrium, *sāmarasya*, between these two aspects of the same reality. *Cit* or *caitanya*, i.e. pure consciousness, is the Śakti aspect of reality and is compared to a clear mirror in which reality sees itself. Śakti is also known as *svātantrya* (independence or freedom) because her essence does not depend on anything extraneous to herself. She is also *vimarśa* (vibration). Siva's awareness of himself is the integral and all-comprehensive ego. The universe in the Trika conception is a system of subjects and objects, *grāhakas* and *grāhyas*. Śakti is characterised as *prakāśa-vimarśamaya*. *Prakāśa* may be taken to be Śiva, placid and transcendent, *vimarśa* or Śakti is dynamic and immanent. Śakti in its five-fold aspect is the principle of universal manifestation. *Cit* is the power of self-awareness; *ānanda* is the power of absolute bliss, or self-enjoying, without having to depend on anything extraneous; *icchā* is Śiva's power of absolute will to manifest the universe out of himself; *jñāna* is the power of knowing the inherent relations of all manifested or manifestable things among themselves and with his own self; and *kriyā* is the power to assume any form. See Abhāsavāda.

Trikoṇa: Triangle, also known as Yoni. It is said to be due to the elevation of *bindu*. *Kāmakalāvilāsa* XXII. In the drawn triangle which is required for Tantric worship, Parā Śakti or Parāvāk serves as the middle point while the three lines forming the three angles symbolize the three other forms of sound (Paśyantī, Madhyāma and Vaikharī). The three *bījas* (Vāgbhava, Kāmarāja, Śakti), the three *śaktis* (Vāma-Jyestha-Raudrī or Icchā-Jñana-kriyā), the three goddess (Kāmeśvarī, Vajreśvarī and Bhagamālinī), the three *tattvas* (Prakṛti, Mahat, Ahaṃkarā), the three *pīṭhas* (Kāmarūpa, Jālandhara, Pūrṇagiri) and all other three-fold concepts. Ibid. XXIII; *Setubandha* on *Nityaṣoḍaśikārṇava* VI. 26-40; Rameśvara on *Paraśurāmakalpasūtra* V. 11, *Gandharvatantra* V. 112-13; *Tantrarājatantra* XXXV. 12-13.

Trikoṇākāra-yantra: Yoni (female sex-organ) from which the world comes into existence according to the Buddhist Tantras. In the middle of the *yantra* or *trikoṇa* is a *bindu*. From this bindu Ādi Prajñā reveals herself at her own will. From one side of the triangle Ādi Prajñā produced Buddha and from another side *dharma* and from the third side *saṃgha*, cf. *trikoṇākāra-sambhūta dharmodaya iti smṛtaḥ*. Prajñā being first the mother and then the wife of Buddha recalls the Śākta cosmogonical tradition of the Ādi-Śakti who is the mother of Śiva and again his wife in creating the world.

Trikūṭa: Holy resort of the goddess Bhadrasundarī or Rudrasundarī mentioned in *Matsya* XIII. 35; *Devibhāgavata* VII. 30.64, *Padma*, Sṛṣṭi XVII. 93; *Skanda* V. 3.98.73. It is a mythical peak of Śrilaṅkā on which the city of Laṅkā was supposed to have been situated. There was another Trikūṭa in the northern Konkan.

Trilokasandarśana: A form of Avalokiteśvara or Lokeśvara who is one-faced and two-armed and sits on a lotus in *vajraparyaṅka* attitude. His hands are raised, held against the chest, with outstretched fingers and palms turned inwards.

Trilokyamohana cakra: A form of Śrīcakra or Śrīyantra.

Tripīṭha: Collective name of Kāmarūpa, Pūrṇagiri and Jālandhara Pīṭhas. *Kāmakalāvilāsa* XII, XIV.

Tripuṇḍra: Sect mark of both Śaivas and Śāktas. It consists of three parallel lines of holy ashes on the forehead from one eye to the other, drawn with three fingers other than the thumb and small finger. *Devībhāgavata*.

Tripurā: Udayapura or Rangamati, modern Radhakisorpur in Tripurā, described as a holy resort of the goddess Tripurā in *Kubjikā* XVIII. 42 ff. The *Pīṭhanirṇaya* holds that the right leg of Satī fell here; the presiding goddess is Tripurasundarī and the Bhairava Tripureśa of Tripurākṣa. The *Śivacarita* calls it a *mahāpīṭha* and mentions Tripurā as the name of the presiding goddess.

Tripurā: She whose body is the city of three *śaktis*—Brāhmī, Raudrī and Vaiṣṇavī—is known as Tripurā. *Puraścaryārṇava* I, 20. She is so called because the emergence of Brahmā, Viṣṇu and Śiva, is from her own entity. She represents Trayi or the three Vedas. She covers the three worlds before dissolution. *Prapañcasāra* IX. 2. Her *maṇḍala* is a triangle, *bhūpura* three-lined, *mantra* three-letters, and forms three—*mātā*, *māna*, and *meya*. Her three *bindus* are red, white and mixed; three abodes Soma, Sūrya and Agni; three *pīṭhas* Kāmarūpa, Pūrṇagiri and Jālandhara; three *śaktis* Jñana, Kriyā and Icchā; three liṅgas Bāṇa, Itara and Para; and three *mātṛkās* A, Ka and Ṭha. *Kāmakalāvilāsa* 13-14. Her derivatives are *Tripurabhairavī, Tripuramālinī*, *Trīpurasundarī*, etc. Hādimata (q.v.) is known as Tripurasundarī Mata. All these forms are very often identified with Ṣoḍaśī.

Tripurabhairavī: A goddess of the Bhairavī category. Her lustre resembles that of a thousand rising suns. Her three eyes resemble red lotuses and the moon is fixed on her bejewelled crown. Her garment is red. She has a garland round her neck. Her breasts are covered with blood. She holds a rosary and manuscript in two hands and shows *varada* and *abhaya* poses with the other two. *Śāradātilaka* XII. 31.

Tripuracakra: Same as Śrīcakra or Śrīyantra.

Tripurānanda: Preceptor of Brahmānanda Giri, author of the *Śāktānandataraṅgiṇī*. He flourished in the sixteenth century.

***Tripurārahasya*:** Tantric treatise dealing with the mysteries of the cult of Tripurā. It was composed by Haritāyana and has a commentary called *Tātparyadīpikā* by Śrīnivāsa. Published in Sarasvati Bhavana Series, Benares.

***Tripurārṇava*:** One of the important treatises of the Kādividyā (q.v.). It is a Tantric work devoted to the cult of Tripurā or Ṣoḍaśī, the form of their worship being known as Śrīvidyā (q.v.).

***Tripurāsāra Samuccaya*:** A late medieval work attributed to Nāgabhaṭṭa dealing with *bhūtaśuddhi*, *mantrasvarūpa*, *prāṇāyāma*, *yonimudrā*, *ṣaṭcakra*, *yoga*, *yantras*, *bāhyapūjā*, *liṅgas*, *homa*, etc. Ed. by J. Vidyasagara, Calcutta 1897.

Tripurasundarī: Mahavidyā goddess identified with Ṣoḍaśī (q.v.) and Śrīvidyā-tripurā. The name Tripurā has been used to explain all the three-fold Tantric abstractions. This goddess is also known by the name of Lalitā. *Kāmakalāvilāsa* 13-14. See Śrīvidyā.

Tripurasundarī Mata: Name of Hādimata. *Śaktisaṅgama*, Kālī, VI. 125.

***Tripurasundarī Stotra*:** A hymn attributed to Śaṅkara which is a prayer to the Tantric goddess Tripurasundarī. The eighth verse contains some Vaiṣṇava elements.

Triputā: Also known as Ādyaśakti, she is a Tantric goddess. She is described as seated under a *kalpa* tree, holding a bow, a noose, two lotuses, a goad and an arrow made of flowers. She has three eyes, a golden-lotus-like complexion, highly developed breasts and a variety of ornaments. She is worshipped along with six companion deities—Lakṣmī, Hari, Gaurī, Hara, Rati and Smara or Madana.

Triśakti: Jñāna (knowledge), Icchā (will) and Kriyā (action). *Kāmakalāvilāsa* XIII-XIV.

Trisrotā: River sacred to the great goddess mentioned in the *Jñānārṇava* V. 66 ff. It is the river Tistā running through northern Bengal. In the *Pīṭhanirṇaya* some sites are regarded as a *pīṭha*—where the right knee of Satī fell. The name of the presiding deity is Bhrāmarī or Amarī and the Bhairava is Amara. The *Śivacarita* refers to it both are *māhāpīṭha* and as an *upapīṭha*, the presiding goddesses being Caṇḍikā and Pārvatī respectively.

Triśūla: Trident. Siva is believed to carry the trident, hence it is popular among the Tantra symbols as most of the Tantras are in the form of a dialogue between Śiva and Pārvatī.

Tvaritā: Mahāvidyā goddess, supposed to belong to Kālikula. *Niruttara* I. She is described as the goddess who bestows all the desirable in full in the kali age. *Śāktānandataraṅgiṇī* III.

Uu

Ubhayavarāhānana: A form of Mārīcī. She has been given this name because both her right and left faces are like that of a sow. She is clad in a tiger-skin, has a red complexion, a jewelled head-dress and a red scarf. In her six left hands she shows the *tarjanī* pose against the chest, holds an *aśoka* bough, *vajrāṅkuśa*, *kapāla*, head of Brahmā and a vessel; in the six right hands she holds a needle, goad, spear, sword, *kartari* and a staff stamped with *vajra*. She bears the image of Vairocana on the crown and tramples under her feet gods such as Viṣṇu, Siva, Brahmā and others.

Uccāṭana: One of the *Ṣatkarmas* (six black acts) by which one can drive away a rival from the land. *Śāradātilaka* XXIII. 125.

Ucchiṣṭa-Cāṇḍālinī: An epithet of Ucchiṣṭa and Sumukha Mātaṅgīs. Both the goddesses destroy all sins and bestow heaven, liberation and luck in everything. Both are very youthful having well-developed breasts. *Puraścaryārṇava* IX. 828-30; *Tantrasāra* 363.

Ucchiṣṭa-Mātaṅgī: Also known as Ucchiṣṭa-Cāṇḍalinī (q.v.) this goddess is a form of Mātaṅgī. She is conceived of as wearing black robes. Her feet are graced with red slip or wash; she has developed breasts, garlands of pearls and corals around her neck and ear-rings made of conch. *Puraścaryārṇava*, IX, 827 ff.

Ucchuṣma Jambhala: Jambhala (q.v.) in his fierce form. His left leg stretches forward on the forehead of Kubera while the right tramples his legs. He has protruding belly and bare fangs. The left hand as usual holds a mongoose.

***Uḍḍīśa Tantra*:** A late medieval hand book for those who practise Tantric rites to benefit themselves and cause harm to others. Its *paṭalas* (chapters) are *māraṇa-prayoga*, *mālā-nirṇaya*, *dhānyādināsa*, *mohana-prayoga*, *stambhana*, *vidveṣaṇa*, *uccāṭana*, *vaśīkaraṇa*, *dravaṇa*, *ākarṣaṇa*, *vidyā-dharasiddhi*, *bhūtakaraṇa* and *vandhyātva-nirvāraṇī*. It was translated into Bengali in the late eighteenth century by Raja Nṛsimha Devarāya of Bansberia. Its Hindi translation was published from Moradabad in 1898.

Uḍḍīyana: Holy resort of the goddess Kālikā or Kātyāyanī mentioned in *Hevajra* VII, *Jñānārṇava* V. 66 ff., etc. It is the land watered by the Swat in north-western India but sometimes confused with Odra.

Uḍḍīyāna-Kurukullā: The form of Kurukullā (q.v.) worshipped in Uḍḍīyāna. She looks fierce with a garland of heads, five skulls on the head, protruding teeth and tongue, garments of tiger-skin and brown hair rising above her head in the shape of a flame. She is four-armed, red in colour and sits in the *ardhaparyaṅka* attitude on a corpse.

Uḍḍīyāna Lokeśvara: A form of Avalokiteśvara, same as Trailokya-vaśaṅkara (q.v.) and Rakta Lokeśvara.

Uḍḍīyāna Mārīcī: A form of Mārīcī; her other names are Vajravatālī and Vajradhātvīśvarī. She holds a *cakra* in one of her right hands and *khaṭvāṅga-kapāla* in one of the left hands. She has six faces and twelve arms.

***Uddyota*:** Commentary by Kṣemārāja (10th-11th century) on *Netra-tantra* which refers to Krama as a distinct system. Ed. V. Dvivedi, Delhi 1985.

Udvāsana: Establishment and withdrawal. By *udvāsana* the devotee is to withdraw his own deity of worship from the external image and install it in his own heart. *Puraścaryārṇava* VI. 513.

Ugra: One of the eight Tārās (*aṣṭa-tārinī*), others being Tārā, Mahogrā, Vajrā, Kālī, Sarasvatī, Kāmeśvarī and Bhadrakālī. *Tantrasāra* 347.

Ugratāra: Same as Ekajaṭā and Nīlasarasvatī (q.v.), she saves her devotee from all forms of distress. *Tārārahasya* I. Her *mantra* is *om hriṃ striṃ huṃ phaṭ*. If *pranava* or *oṃ* is omitted the *mantra* pertains to Ekajaṭā. When *om* and *phat* are both omitted it pertains to Nīlasarasvatī. *Tantrasāra* 328. Her iconic description is given elaborately in *Nīlatantra* IV. She is described in the *Tantrasāra* as standing in *pratyālīḍha* pose with her right foot on a corpse; she holds a sword, blue lotus, knife and vessel in her hands. She is short-statured with brown matted locks and fierce snakes on her body. She destroys the inactivity of the whole world having put it in a skull-cup.

Ujānī: Holy resort, a great *pīṭha*, of the goddess Ujjayinī or Maṅgalacaṇḍī, mentioned in the *Pīṭhanirṇaya* and the *Śivacarita*. It is modern Kogram on the Ajaya in Burdwan district, West Bengal.

Ujjayinī: Modern Ujjain in Madhya Pradesh regarded as the *pīṭha* or holy resort of the goddess Mahākālī or Maṅgalacaṇḍī mentioned in *Jñānārṇava* V. 66 ff., *Bṛhannīla* V and *Pīṭhanirṇaya*. This Ujjayinī may also stand for Ujānī. (q.v.).

Ullāsa: Stages of Tantric *sādhanā* or spiritual exercises—Ārambha, Taruṇa, Yauvana, Prauḍha, Prauḍhānta, Unmanā and Anavasthā. *Paraśurāmakalpasūtra* X. 68.

Umānandanātha: Disciple of the celebrated Bhāskara Rāya (q.v.). He lived in the eighteenth century and is the author of *Nityotsavapaddhati* which is based upon the *Paraśurāmakalpasūtra* (q.v.).

Umāpati Śivam: An exponent of Śaiva Siddhānta. Of the fourteen authoritative philosophical treatises in Tamil on the Śaiva Siddhānta eight are by him. He has also written a short biography of the 63 Śaiva saints.

Unmanā, Unmanī: The sixth stage in spiritual exercise. The aspirant in this stage has a feeling of great joy and his sense-organs apparently cease to function. *Kulārṇava* VIII; *Tārābhakti-sudhārṇava* VI. 255. In this stage the aspirant has the realization of non-attachment and does not require the aid of any preceptor. It is meant for persons striving for Divya (q.v.) rank who are able to meditate successfully. Rāmeśvara in his commentary on the *Paraśurāmakalpasūtra* X. 68 places this stage in the Śvairācara (q.v.) category.

Unmeṣa-śakti: Same as *jñānaśakti* (power of knowledge) just as *nimeṣa-śakti* is *icchāśakti* (power of will). The word *unmeśa* means 'expression' of *idam* (it-ness, the world) and as such it denotes its *sphūṭva* or externalness. This *śakti* is closely associated with various concepts of the Śaiva-Śākta *tattvas*. *Tantrāloka* IX. 53; *Īśvarapratyabhijñā* II. 193-5. The letters U and Ū symbolize the *unmeṣa śakti*. *Tantrāloka* III. 154-7.

Upacāra: Articles of worship. They may consist of five, ten, twelve, sixteen, eighteen, thirty-six and even sixty-four items. *Puraścaryārṇava* III. 224-5; Rāghava on *Śāradātilaka* IX. 92; *Tantrasāra* 551-2; *Mahānirvāṇa* VI. 78-9, XIII. 203 ff. Among the *upacāras*, *pādya* represents the watery element (*bījamantra vaṃ*) standing for *sneha*, 'acquaintance relationship' to the deity; *gandha* (scent), the earthy element (*bīja: laṃ*) standing for *viśvāsa*, relationship of trust; *puspa* (flower), the space element (*bīja: haṃ*) standing for *sammāna* (honour); *dhūpa* (incense), the airy element (*bīja: yaṃ*) standing for *bhakti* or devotion; *dīpa* or light, the fire element (*bīja: raṃ*), standing for *jñāna* (knowledge); and *naivedya* (food-offering), the life element (*bīja: vaṃ*) standing for *tādātmyabodha* or realization of the identity of the worshipper with the worshipped.

Upa-nāḍi: Smaller nerves which are numerous. The important ones are rasanā, piṅgalā, sūryā, ravi, agni, prāṇa, camana, kāli, bindu, upāya, yamunā, rakta, palita, sukṣma, reta, dharma, sthira, para, dyau, bheda, citta, vidyā, rajas, bhāva, puruṣa, śiva, nirmāṇa-kāya, grāhya, lalanā, iḍā, candrā, śaśin, soma, āpana, dhamana, āli, nāda, prajñā, gaṅgā, sukra, bali, sthūla, rajas, adharma, asthira, apara, pṛithvī, abhāva, prakṛti, śakti, sambhoga-kāya and grāhaka.

Upapatti: Tantric Buddhist goddess of the Vaśita (q.v.) category who is of variegated colour and holds in her left hand creepers of various kinds. In her right hand is a lotus. *Niṣpanna* 56.

Upāsanā: Worship, the act by which one can stay near god. *Kaulamārgarahasya* 113-14. It is the surrendering of one's own self to the supreme being. Rāmeśvara on *Paraśurāmakalpasūtra* I.1. It may be internal or external. See Antaryāga and Bahiryāga.

Upāya: See Prajñā. Originally *upāya* was called *karuṇā* (the principle of compassion); subsequently it came to denote the Male Principle. At a still later stage the original meaning of the term *upāya* (the way or means) became more popular. The ultimate reality of Tantric Buddhism came to be regarded as the unity of *prajñā* (wisdom) and *upāya* (means). In the *Guhyasamāja*, *upāya* is described as *vajrayoga* (the way of obtaining *bodhi* or enlightenment). It is recognized to be of four kinds—Sevā, Upasādhana, Sādhana and Mahāsādhana (q.v.). Though the term *upāya* is widely used for *karuṇā* (cf. Nagarjuna in *Mādhyamikavṛtti*) the use seems to be somewhat technical. In *Hevajratantra* X Upāya and Prajñā have been described under the imagery of the yogin and the Mudrā (the woman to be adopted in *sādhanā*) vis-a-vis the Bodhicitta. In *Prajñopāya, upāya* is compared to a boat which brings all beings to the favourable shore. In some Buddhist Tantras Prajñā and Upāya are expressly identified with Śakti and Śiva, cf. *Nirṇāda-tantra* quoted in *Advayavajrasaṃgraha* 26.

Upāyapāramitā: Tantric Buddhist goddess of Pāramitā (q.v.) category described as being green in colour and holding a *vajra* on a yellow lotus and the *cintāmaṇi* banner. *Ṇispanna* 16.

Ūrdhvāmnāya: The Tantric upper region. *Prāṇatoṣaṇī* I. 9, 64. Deities of this region are Kāmeśī, Lalitā, Vālā, Mahātripurasundarī and Bhairavī. *Puraścaryārṇava* I. 13.

Uśanas: One of the promulgators of the 'tantras of middle current'.

Uṣṇīṣa: A class of deities mentioned in Buddhist Tantras. Though *Uṣṇīṣa* means crown, the deities under this category are associated with the directions. They are eight in number—Vajra, Ratna, Padma, Viśva, Teja, Dhvaja, Tīkṣna and Chatra. They seem to be an extension of the four Dhyānī Buddhas and they show their characteristic symbols and *mudrās*. They are specially described in the Durgatipariśodhana Maṇḍala of the *Niṣpannayogāvalī*.

Uṣṇīṣakamala: One of the four nerve-cycles of the Buddhist conception which is analogous to that of Sahasrāra (q.v.) of the Śākta Tantras. It is in the central cerebral region and is connected with the *vajra* or *sahaja* body of the Buddha. It is the place where the female energy having the force of fire and known as *caṇḍālī* (q.v.) meets its source through the nerves known as *upāya* and *prajñā*. It possesses four petals according to *Sekoddeśāṭikā* 27.

Uṣṇīṣavijayā: Defined form of the Dhāriṇī of the same name included in the group of twelve Dhāriṇī goddesses. Regarded as an emanation of Vairocana she is described as having a white complexion, three faces and eight arms. One of her hands displays the Buddha on lotus. She resides in the womb of a Caitya. *Sādhana* 394.

Utpala: Pupil of Somānanda and author of the *Īśvarapratyabhijñā* or *Pratyabhijñā Sūtra*, a very popular work on Kashmir Śaivism.

Utpalāvartaka: Holy resort of the goddess Lolā mentioned in the *Matsya* XIII. 44, *Devībhāgavata* VII. 30.73; *Padma*, Sṛṣṭi XVII. 202; *Skanda* V. 3. 98.82. The name recalls the river Utpalāvatī, modern Vyapar in the Tinnavelly district, and that of Utpalāvata or Utpalāraṇya, modern Bithoor, near Kanpur, Uttar Pradesh.

Uttarā: River saced to the goddess Uttariṇī, mentioned as an *upapīṭha* in the *Śivacarita*. It is possibly the Uttaragā or Ramagaṅgā iń Ayodhya, Uttar Pradesh.

Uttarakaula: A sect of Kaula worshippers mentioned by Lakṣmīdhara in his com. on *Saundaryalaharī* XXXIII according to which there is no Śiva-*tattva* apart from Śakti-*tattva*. While the Pūrva-Kaulas (q.v.) worship the symbolic triangle of the *Śrīcakra* the Uttarakaulas actual female organ.

Uttarakuru: Holy resort of the goddess Auṣadhī or Oṣadhi mentioned in *Matsya* XIII. 49, *Devībhāgavata* VII. 30.78; *Padma,* Sṛṣṭi, XVII. 208, *Skanda* V. 3.98.87. It is a Himalayan tract, supposed to have included the northern part of Garhwal.

Uttaramānasa: Lake sacred to the goddess Nīlā mentioned in the *Bṛhannīla* and *Prāṇatoṣaṇi*. It is Gaṅgā lake at the foot of the Harmuk peak in Kashmir.

Uttarāmnāya: The northern zone of Tantric culture.

Uttarasādhaka, Sādhikā: Partner of the Tantric aspirant whose qualifications are mentioned in *Kaulāvalinirṇaya*.

V

Vāc: A word which expresses stages of voice. Its substratum is *śabda* or sound which indicates a slight stir, throb or vibration, in reality the self-expression of which is called *parā-vāc* (the supreme word). The other aspect is *artha* or meaning. Vāc has four forms—*parā*, *paśyantī*, *madhyamā* and *vaikharī* (q.v.). The stages preceding *parā* are *śūnya, saṃvit* and *sūkṣma*. The first is the vibrational stage, the next is that when the sound is about to form, and the third is that when it is forming.

Vācaka, Vācya: Śakti or power of *mantra*. The former is the denoting or signifying aspect, while the latter is the basic. Vācya is contained in the Vācaka and formally there is no distinction between them. *Janyajanakayorbhedābhāvād vācasya vācakenāpi*. Vācaka reveals the nature of the Vācya. The later is what is to be known while the former is the method of knowing. *Varivasyārahasya* II. 81.

Vācikī, Vākdīkṣā: The common form of initiation with *mantras*. Rāghava on *Śāradātilaka* V. 127-40; *Puraścaryārṇava* V. 391.

Vagalā, Vagalāmukhī: Mahavidyā goddess, the story of whose origin is described in the *Svatantratantra*. *Prāṇatoṣaṇī* V. 6.382. In the *Sammohana-tantra* we have an account of the incarnation of Vagalā who manifested herself in Saurāṣṭra. Visnu undertook severe penances to please and propitiate her. It is in response to his entreaties that she manifested herself. In the *Merutantra* she is known as Stambhanī. Her *mantra* is of 36 letters. Her colour is golden, she is four-armed and three-eyed. She sits on a lotus. Her right hands hold a club and a noose. Her upper left hand has a thunderbolt while with her lower left hand she pulls the tongue of the enemy. The goddess is very youthful. The *Nārada-pāñcarātra* equates Dhumāvatī with Vagalāmukhī, but the former is an old widow while the latter is youthful and has a golden complexion. *Puraścaryārṇava* IX. 825-6.

***Vagalāmukhī Tantra*:** A short work giving 100 and 1,000 names of Vagalā and the procedure of her worship with Tantric rites. On Vagalā we have also the *Śāṅkhāyanatantra* alias *Ṣaḍvidyāgama* and *Vagalākramakalpavalli*.

Vāgīśāṣṭaka: A group of eight Bhairava Āgamas (q.v.) represented by *Bhairavī*, *Cihikā*, *Haṃsākhya*, *Kādambīka*, *Hṛllekhā*, *Candralekhā*, *Viddyullekhā* and *Vidyunmālā*.

Vāgīśvara: A form of Mañjuśrī which is more than one. His head contains the images of the five Dhyānī Buddhas. He is decked in all ornaments and looks like a prince. His vehicle is the lion. He holds a *nīlotpala* in his left hand while the right is displayed artistically. Another form of Vāgīśvara is Dharmadhātu who is four-faced and eight-handed. The yellow variety of Vāgīśvara is known as Mahārājalīlā Mañjuśrī.

Vāgmatī: River sacred to the goddess mentioned in the *Kubjikā* XVIII. 42 ff. It is a river in Nepal; the confluence with the Maradārikā, Maṇisrohīnī, Rājasmañjarī, Ratnavalī, Cārumatī, Prabhāvatī and Trivenī form respectively the Śānta, Śaṅkara, Rājamañjarī, Pramodā, Sulakṣaṇa, Jaya and Gokarṇa *tīrthas*.

Vāgvādinī: Mahāvidyā goddess. *Śāktānandataraṅgiṇī* III. She is the goddess of Pūrvāmnāya or eastern region.

Vāhana: The vehicle or the mount of gods. It may be any animal, man, demon, or even a corpse. Sometimes gods of an alien faith serve as *vāhana*.

Vaidyanātha: Modern Deoghar-Vaidyanathdham in Bihar, mentioned as a holy resort of the great goddess in *Kubjikā* XVIII. 42 ff. The name of the goddess is mentioned as Ārogā or Ārogyā in *Matsya* XIII. 41, *Devībhāgavata* VII. 30.70; *Padma* Sṛṣṭi, XVII. 199, *Skanda* V. 3.98.79. The *Pīṭhanirṇaya* and *Śivacarita* refer to it as a Mahāpīṭha where the heart of Satī is said to have fallen.

Vaikharī: One of the four ingredients of sound, others being *parā*, *paśyantī* and *madhyamā*. It is said that sound is carried by wind inside the body and becomes articulated in the throat. Gross sound is the uttered speech by which the ideas are expressed. It is clearly articulated in the gross form of language as the expression of ideas and of physical objects (*artha*). According to Rāghava (on *Śāradātilaka* I.1.) *parā* is unmanifested sound, *paśyantī* reveals letters, *madhyamā* words and *vaikharī* sentences. *Setubandha* on *Nityaṣoḍaśikārṇava* VI. 10-11.

Vairocana: One of the five Dhyānī Buddhas. He originates from the white syllable *om*. His colour is white. His recognition symbol is a white discus. He exhibits *bodhyāngi mudrā* and represents the cosmic element of *rūpa* (form), the *ādarśa* (ideal) knowledge, *hemanta* (late autumn), season, sweet taste, guttural group of letters and mornings and evenings of the day. In *Niṣpannayogāvalī* 44 his four-faced and eight-armed form is described. His place is in the sanctum of the Stūpa. His consort is Locanā and Bodhisattva Samantabhadra. *Advayavajrasaṃgraha* 41-2.

Vairoti: Śāsanadevatā of Jain Tīrthaṃkara Vimala according to the Digambara tradition. She is also a Vidyādevī. Her vehicle is a lion and the Śvetāmbara counterpart is Viditā or Vijayā.

Vaiṣṇavācāra: Cult of *bhakti* (devotion) which is regarded as one of the seven Tantric *ācāras* meant for ordinary people. Tantra acknowledges various forms of spiritual quest and exercises and holds that rituals and practices should vary in time and space. Hence following of the Vaiṣṇava way has been prescribed as a necessary step for achieving spiritual salvation. *Nānācāraṇa bhāvena deśakālādhikārinām. Mahānirvāṇa* IV. 36-7. The followers of Vaiṣṇavācāra believe in the Vedas and abstain from sexual intercourse, use of abusive language, enmity and jealousy, meat-eating, *japa* at night with rosary, and touch of *yantra*. They should worship Viṣṇu and feel his existence everywhere. *Prāṇatoṣaṇī* VII .1, 499.

Vaiṣṇavī: One of the seven or eight Mātṛkās (Divine Mothers) who, according to the Puranic accounts, appeared with the emblems and attributes of Viṣṇu during the war between the gods and the demons. In the Tantras, apart from being the Divine Mothers, the Mātṛkās (q.v.) represents the fifty letters of Sanskrit alphabet. As such, according to the *Svacchandatantra*, Vaiṣṇavī is the presiding goddess of the letters belonging to *Ta-varga*, i.e. those beginning with Ta.

Vajra: Thunderbolt shaped in the form of a weapon; it serves as an emblem of certain Buddhist deities. When such weapons are crossed it is called *viśva-vajra* or double-*vajra*. In Buddhist Tantra *vajra* designates Śūnya or Void. The Mahayanic idea of Śūnyatā (q.v.) has been transformed into that of *vajra* meaning the real nature of things. This principle has been crystallized in the form of a supreme being, Lord Vajrasattva or Vajradhara, regarded as the essence of Śūnyatā. The same idea underlines the conception of Vajra-kāya (q.v.) of Buddha. *Advayavajrasaṃgraha* 24.37; *Prajñopāya* III 9, V. 45. Vajra is also name of a nerve situated within the *susumnā* (q.v.).

Vajrā: Name of a nerve. it is encased by Suṣumnā (q.v.) and in its turn encases within it the *citriṇī*, which again has an aperture called the *brahmarandhra* running up to the *sahasrāra*. Viśvanātha on *Ṣaṭcakranirūpaṇa* 2; *Prāṇatoṣaṇī* I. 4.32. This nerve is also known as Vajriṇī.

Vajrābhiṣeka: 'Initiation to the adamantine truth', one of the four kinds of initiation or consecration (*abhiṣeka*). Others are Kalasa, Guhya and Prajñā. The *abhiseka* in the secret cult is generally known as *Vajrābhiṣeka*. *Prajñopāya* V, *Jñānasiddhi* XVII.

Vajrabodhi: Son of Īśānavarman, king of a central Indian state, Vajrabodhi was a famous scholar at Nalanda and the teacher of the Pallava king Narasiṃhavarman II. He went to China in AD 720 and propagated the doctrines of Tantric Buddhism. He translated a number of texts belonging to Matrayāna into Chinese. The *Vajraśikhara* (q.v.) is one of them. He died in AD 732.

Vajracarcikā: An emanation of Akṣobhya described in *Sādhanamālā* 395 as being red in complexion having an emaciated body, and six arms. She dances in *ardhaparyaṅka* attitude on a corpse.

Vajradhara: Also called Ādi-Buddha who is an embodiment of Śūnya. He is the supreme being of Vajrayāna and the Dhyānī Buddhas owe their origin to him. He is conceived in two forms, single and *yuganaddha*. In individual conception he is bedecked in jewels and ornaments, sitting in *vajrāsana* carrying *vajra* in the right hand and *ghaṇṭā* in the left. In *yuganaddha* form he is locked in close embrace with his Śakti who appears to be Prajñāpāramitā representing karuṇā or compassion. *Niṣpanna* 8 describes him as being reddish white in colour, three-faced and six-armed, standing in *ardhaparyaṅka*. With two principal hands he embraces Prajñā.

Vajradharma: A form of Avalokiteśvara (q.v.) who is described as being reddish white in colour; the peacock is his vehicle. He holds a lotus with sixteen petals in his left hand and with the right causes it to blossom against his chest. *Sādhana* 33.

Vajra-dhātu: The 'thunderbolt-element' which denotes the spiritual world in Tantric Buddhism as complementary to *garbha-dhātu* (material world). It is *tathatā*, or 'thatness', and is by nature immutable.

Vajradhātvīśvarī: Goddess surrounded by four Buddhaśaktis—Locanā, Tārā, Pāṇḍarā and Māmakī. She is the embodiment of highest truth named differently as Tathatā, Śūnyatā, Prajñāpāramitā and so forth. She is the spiritual consort of Ratnasambhava, is yellow in colour and has a jewel as her symbol. *Advayavajrasaṃgraha* 41.

Vajragarbha: Bodhisattva described in the *Niṣpannayogāvalī* 58, 67 as being of the colour of the petal of a blue lotus. According to one description he holds *vajra* and a book called *Dasabhūmika* and, according to another, his left hand rests on the hip while the right holds a blue lotus.

Vajraghaṇṭā: Tanric Buddhist goddess of northern direction described as having a green complexion, one face, two arms and the bell as the recognition symbol. *Niṣpanna* 38.

Vajrahuṅkāra: An iconic *mudrā*. The wrists are crossed at the chest with the two hands holding the *vajra* (q.v.) and the bell, both of which are turned inwards. If the two symbols and the hands are turned outward the *mudrā* is called *trailokyavijaya-mudrā*. There is a Tantric Buddhist god of the same name who is an emanation of Akṣobhya. *Sādhana* 506.

Vajra-jñāna: Adamantine knowledge which is *śūnyatā* in which all perceptions of phenomenalization are contradicted. It is the realization of the void (*nairātmyadarśana*). Āryadeva's *Citta-viśuddhiprakaraṇa* 67 ff.

Vajra-jāpa: *Prāṇāyāma* associated with the *mantra* for the control of the vital wind. The *Pañcakramaṭippanī* makes it clear that *vajra-jāpa* is nothing but the process of controlling the same.

Vajrajvālānarka: Tantric Buddhist deity, an emanation of Akṣobhya, blue-coloured, four-faced and eight-armed, who is described as trampling upon Viṣṇu and his wife. *Sādhana* 512.

Vajra-kanyā: 'Thunder' or 'Void' girl; women to be adopted for yogic practices in Vajrayāna. Vajrakanyā also refers to Prajñā in Tantric Buddhism.

Vajra-kāya: The fourth body (*kāya*) of Buddha as conceived in Tantric Buddhism; also known as Sahaja-kāya. Vajra denotes the real nature of things, otherwise known as Sahaja, which is Śūnyatā or vacuity, the essence of Mahayanic teachings.

Vajrāmṛta: An emanation of Amoghasiddhi described as being green in complexion, three-faced and six-armed. *Niṣpanna* 18.

Vajrānaṅga: A form of Mañjuśrī, yellow in colour and with four or six hands. As the name implies he is the Buddhist god of love, the prototype of the Puranic Madana. The flowery bow and the arrow of flowers are strikingly common to both. *Sādhana* 124.

Vajrapāṇi: Boddhisattva with the *vajra* symbol who is the spiritual son of the Dhyānī Buddha Akṣobhya. His spiritual mother is Māmakī. Vajrapāṇi, when represented, either stands or sits and carries usually a lotus on which is placed the symbol of *vajra*. Sometimes he holds the *vajra* against the chest in one of his hands. According to another conception he is related to Amogha-siddhi and Tārā and belongs to the *karma-kula*.

Vajraparyaṅka: Also known as Dhyānāsana, it is the meditative pose. Two legs are firmly locked in a seated posture with both soles apparent, the characteristic sitting attitude of the Dhyānī Buddhas. Sometimes a small thunderbolt is shown on the seat of the god; it indicates the meditative attitude. Dhyānāsana should be distinguished from the *paryaṅka* attitude in which case the legs are also crossed but the feet are tucked under and both the soles are invisible.

Vajrarāga: A form of Mañjuśrī also known as Vāk or Amitābha Mañjuśrī who is characterized by one-face and two arms in *samādhi-mudrā*. He is described as the lord of speech. With the effigy of Amitābha on the crown, he is decked in ornaments on his hands and breast.

Vajrasattva: Sometimes regarded as the sixth Dhyānī Buddha and sometimes as their priest. His Śakti is Vajrasattvātmikā and his

Bodhisattva is Ghaṇṭāpāni. His worship is performed in secret and like Vajradhara he is represented in two forms—single and *yuganaddha*. The conception of Vajradhara and Vajrasattva are sometimes inextricably mixed up. *Advayavajrasaṃgraha* 41.

Vajrasattvātmikā: Spiritual consort or Śakti of Vajrasattva (q.v.). Her *dhyāna* is rarely found in Tantric literature, but her form can be seen in the images when she is in close embrace with Vajrasattva in *yab-yum*.

***Vajraśikhara*:** A text of Mantrayāna, 'Diamond-pinnacle' containing the utterances of the Buddha in his *dharma-kāya*, which was translated into Chinese by Vajrabodhi (q.v.). It is found in Tibetan text.

Vajraśrṅkhalā: Tantric Buddhist goddess who is an emanation of Amoghasiddhi. Her complexion is green and her symbol a chain. She has three faces and eight arms. She sits in *lalita* posture. *Sādhana* 414. Vajraśrṅkhala is also the name of the Śāsanadevatā of the Jain Tīrthaṃkara Abhinandana. The Digambaras represent her as riding on a swan and holding in her four hands a snake, a noose, a rosary and a fruit.

Vajratārā: A very popular form of Tārā. Her colour is golden yellow. She is four-faced and eight-armed. Her *maṇḍala* comprises ten attendant deities known as Puṣpatārā, Dhūpatārā, Dīpatārā, Gandhatārā, Vajraṅkuśī, Vajrapāśī, Vajrasphoṭī, Vajraghaṇṭā, Uṣṇīṣavijayā and Sumbhā. Her spiritual sire is Ratnasambhava.

Vajravārāhī: The Śakti of Heruka. Her union with the latter is the cult of the celebrated *Cakrasambhāra Tantra*. She is called Herukadevasyāgramahiṣī and also Ḍākinī. The latter epithet has brought her in relation to four other deities of the Ḍākinī group. She has a natural excrescence just near her right ear. She is represented as nude. She has two extra forms—Vaśya and Ārya. *Sādhana* 425.

Vajravidāraṇi: Tantric goddess, an emanation of Akṣobhya, described in *Dharmakośasaṃgraha* as five-faced and ten-armed.

Vajrayāna: A form of Tantric Buddhism. It is the cult of five Kulas or families of the Bodhisattvas, each representing a distinct mental state of the aspirant. *Guhyasamāja* 154. It is the path of transcendental perfect enlightenment to be achieved through different rites and ceremonies, *mantras* and meditations. *Sādhanamālā* I. 225, II. 421. It is compared to a raft on which one can cross the ocean of existence. *Jñānasiddhi* 31. Vajrayāna considers Śūnya or Vajra, i.e. vacuity, as the ultimate reality and innumerable gods and goddesses as its manifestations. The gods have no real existence; they are born of the mind from the *bīja-mantras* uttered by the worshippers. In practice Vajrayāna introduces the theory of five Dhyānī Buddhas as the embodiment of five *skandhas* or cosmic elements comprising *rūpa* (form), *vedanā* (sensation), *saṃjña* (perception), *saṃskāra* (impression) and *vijñāna* (consciousness). It also introduces the cult of Prajñā or Śakti. Vajrayāna may be divided into six states: (1) Kriyatantrayāna, (2) Caryā or Upatantra-yāna, (3) Yogatantrayāna, (4) Mahayogatantra-yāna, (5) Anuttarayogatantra-yāna and (6) Atiyogatantra-yāna.

Vajrayoginī: Buddhist counterpart of Puranic Chinnamastā. Four *sadhanas* in *Sādhanamālā* 452-3 describe her forms, from which two types emerge. In one type, she has no head on her shoulder but carries it in her hand, and in another she has her head intact. She is always accompanied by two yoginīs on either side who are called Vajravairocanī and Vajravarṇinī.

***Vajrayoginī sādhanā*:** Name of a Tantric text, said to have been composed by Jālandharī, better known as Hāḍi-pā, mentioned in the Tibetan catalogues.

Vajreśvarī: Presiding deity of the southern angle of Trikoṇacakra. *Nityaṣoḍaśikārṇava* I. 197-8.

Vajroli-mudrā: A method for prolonging the duration of sexual intercourse for Tantric purposes. It is supposed to confer a long life to the yogin even after indulgence in sexual orgies. *Haṭhayogapradīpikā* II. 82-96.

Vajropama: A kind of meditation based on the principle of *yuganaddha* (q.v.) by which the aspirant becomes a Vajrasattva—omniscient, the seer of truth and the perfectly enlightened.

Vāk: See Vajrarāga.

Vakranātha, Vakreśvara: Holy resort of the goddess Mahiṣamardinī or Vakreśvarī mentioned as a great *pīṭha* in the *Śivacarita* where the right arm of Satī fell. It is modern Bakreswar near Dubrajpur in Birbhum district, West Bengal.

Vāmācara, Vāmamārga: One of the seven traditional Tantric Ācāras, but the term is used in a wider sense. The *Merutantra* describes five types of Vāmācāra—Śabara, Siddhānta, Cīna, Vāma and Kaulika. The *Śaktisaṅgama* (Tārā I, 92-4) refers to the Vāmācara system as current among the worshippers of Gaṇeśa, Rudra, Viṣṇu, Śiva, Svayambhū, Veda, Bhairava, Kṣetrapāla, Cīna, Kāpālika, Pāśupata, Bauddha, Kerala, Vīra-Vaiṣṇava, Śāmbhava, Cāndra, Aghora, etc. The followers of Vāmācāra are expected to worship the goddess in the traditional way during the daytime, and at night in the special Tantric way with the help of the five Ms. According to the *Rudrayāmala*, a Vāmācāra aspirant should keep a woman, expert in sexual arts, on his left side and a pot of wine on the right and should have a musical environment for his training under a *guru*. Tantras like *Vāḍavānalīya* categorically say that Dakṣiṇācāra is meant for the Dvijas and Vāmācāra for the lower varṇas. The same is said in *Mahākālasaṃhitā* and *Siddhāntasāra*. In the *Vāmakeśvara* it is said that one is a follower of Dakṣiṇācāra by birth and that of Vāmācāra by consecration; *janmamātram dakṣinaṃ hi abhiṣekena vāmakam*. In the *Ācārabheda* it is stated that in Vāmācāra one should worship the supreme being by transforming oneself into a female: *vāmācaro bhavat tatra vāmā bhūtvā yajet paraṃ*. *Puraścaryārṇava* I. 20 ff; *Prāṇatoṣaṇī* VII. 1, 499; *Tantrik Texts* IX. 7.

***Vāmakeśvara Tantra*:** An early Tantra, passages from which have been frequently quoted in various Tantric manuals. The Nityaṣoḍaśikārṇava (Ānandasrama Sanskrit Series, LVI, 1944) is a part of it. Bhāskara Rāya's *Setubandha* is a commentary on it.

Varada: An iconic *mudrā*, depicting the hand of the god conferring boons. The hand showing this gesture is pendant with its palm outward and fingers stretched. Sometimes a jewel is seen stamped on the hand showing the *mudrā*; in this case it is known as the *ratnasaṃyukta-varada*, that is, the gift-bestowing attitude together with a jewel.

Varadarāja: Also known as Kṛṣṇadāsa he lived in the eleventh century and was an exponent of the Krama doctrine. His commentary on the *Śiva-sūtras* is known as *Śivasūtravārtika*. Ed. by M.S. Kaul, Kashmir Sanskrit Series, no. XLIIII, 1925.

Varada Tārā: A form of Śyama, or green Tārā, who may be recognized by the presence of her companion deities—Aśokākāntā Mārīcī, Mahāmāyūrī, Ekajaṭā and Jāṅgulī.

Varāhaparvata, Śaila: Holy resort of the goddess Jayā mentioned in *Matsya* XIII. 31, *Devībhāgavata* VII. 30-60, *Padma*, Sṛṣṭi XVII. 189, *Skanda* V. 3.98.69. The *Bṛhannīla* and *Prāṇatoṣaṇī* refer to the goddess as Vārāhī. It is either Baramula in Kashmir or Barahachatra in Nepal.

Vārāhī: One of the seven or eight Mātṛkās (Divine Mothers) who, according to the Puranic accounts, appeared with the emblems and attributes of Varāha, the third incarnation of Viṣṇu, during the war between the gods and the demons. In the Tantras the Mātṛkās are representatives of the fifty letters of Sanskrit alphabet. As such, according to *Svacchandatantra*, she is the presiding deity of the letters belonging to the *Pa-varga*, i.e. those beginning with Pa. Vārāhī is also an important goddess in Tantric Buddhism.

***Vārāhi Tantra*:** An authoritative Tantra extracts from which are quoted in various Tantric compendiums and manuals. It refers to twenty Śākta Tantric texts: *Nīlapatākā*, *Vāmakeśvara*, *Mṛtyuñjaya*, *Yogārṇava*, *Māyā or Mahā*, *Daksiṇamūrti*, *Kālikā*, *Kāmeśvarī*, *Haragaurī*, *Kubjikā*, *Kātyāyanī*, *Pratyaṅgirā*, *Mahālakṣmī*, *Tripurarṇava*, *Sarasvatī*, *Yoginī*, *Vārāhī*, *Gavākṣī*, *Nārāyaṇīya* and *Mṛḍāṇī*. It also refers to various Upa-tantras or minor Tantras composed by Jaimini, Vasiṣṭha, Kapila, Nārada, Garga, Pulastya, Bhārgava, etc.

Vārāṇasī: Modern Varanasi in Uttar Pradesh mentioned as the holy resort of the goddess Viśālākṣi in *Matsya* XIII. 26, *Devībhāgavata* VII. 30, 55; *Padma*, Sṛṣṭi XVII. 184; *Skanda* V. 3. 98. 64.

***Varivasyāprakāśa*:** A late-medieval text on Śrīvidyātattva.

***Varivasyā Rahasya*:** Composed by the celebrated Bhāskara Rāya (AD 1700-50) it is a theoretical exposition of the 36 *tattvas* pertaining to Śakti. The text has a commentary called *Prakāśa* composed by the author himself. Ed. by S.C. Sastri with Eng. trans. and notes, Adyar, Madras 1934, 2nd ed. 1948.

Varṇa: Letters, also called *mātṛkās* (q.v.), symbolizing different manifestations of Śakti. In the matter of letters transforming into *mantras*, the Buddhist Tantras agree fully with Hindu Tantras. The Tantras accept the

Mīmāṃsaka view of the eternal nature of the *śabda* (sound, eternal and in the form of letters constituting words) and hold that the movement that produced the world shows itself, or is represented in miniature, in the production of the sound, the process of which is the epitome of the notion, as it were, of the cosmic process of creation. This creative power, which is viewed as the mother of the universe in its aspect as identified with the *varṇas* is called the *mātṛkās*. The different *varṇas* represent different functions of the *mātṛkās* being parts of the creative forces and are associated with particular conative, cognitive and emotional tendencies.

***Varṇabījakoṣa*:** A dictionary in the form of a vocabulary or glossary of words. It gives the meaning of nearly 5,000 Tantric words arranged alphabetically.

Varnamālā: Alphabet endowed with mystic significance. In Kashmir Saivism the alphabet of Śāradā script has been philosophically explained from A to Kṣa in terms of the Kula doctrine *Tantrāloka* III, 81 ff. The beads of the rosary also symbolize the alphabet from A to Kṣa which is why the rosary is called Akṣamālā. *Tantrarājatantra* I. 63; *Mahānirvāṇa* V. 153-4; *Tantrasāra* 28. The vowels from A to U are called *mūla* or root: *svarāṇaṃ ṣaṭkamevehamūlam syādvarṇasantatau*. Among the vowels A denotes *ānanda-śakti*, I *icchā-śakti*, and U *unmeṣa-śakti*. Other letters have also similar denotations. See Mātṛkāvarṇa.

Varṇamayī-dīkṣā: Initiation by infusing the spirit of letters in different parts of the candidate's body. *Śāradātilaka* V. 116-21.

Varṇinī: Companion deity of Chinnamastā (q.v.), who drinks, together with Ḍākinī (q.v.) the blood which flows from the severed throat of her patron goddess. Varṇinī is red complexioned, having matted locks, three eyes, white teeth, developed breasts, dishevelled hair; she holds the skull-vessel in her left hand and knife in the right.

Vaśīkaraṇa: One of the six black acts; it is to hypnotize someone. *Śāradātilaka* XXIII. 123.

Vaśinī: Presiding goddess of one of the angles of the *aṣṭakoṇacakra*. She belongs to the status of Rahasyayoginī or Āvaraṇadevatā. According to the *Vāmakeśvara-tantra* she is the presiding deity of the letters of *A-varga*, the vowels. *Gandharvatantra* XVII. 74.

Vasiṣṭhatīrtha: Holy resort of the goddess Arundhatī mentioned in the *Bṛhannīla* and *Prāṇatoṣaṇī*. It is either on Mount Abu in Sirohi district, Rajasthan, or on Mount Sandhyachal near Gauhati in Assam.

Vaśitā: Various controls and disciplines leading to spiritual progress conceptualized as goddesses. Twelve such goddess are collectively taken to be the spiritual daughters of the Dhyānī Buddha Amitābha. They are Āyu, Citta, Pariṣkāra, Karma, Upapatti, Ṛddhi, Adhimukti, Praṇidhāna, Jñana, Dharma, Tathatā, and Buddhabodhiprabhā.

Vasti: See Śodhana.

Vastrapada: Holy resort of the goddess Bhuvanesvarī mentioned in the *Bṛhannīla* and *Prāṇatoṣaṇī*. The name is possibly a mistake for Vastrapatha, modern Girnar in Kathiawar, although the Vastrapā or Vastrapāda country seems to be located in the *Mahabhārata* (II. 48.14; III. 80.108) in the north-west.

Vasudhārā: Consort of Jambhala; she bears the image of either Akṣobhya or Ratnasambhava on her crown. Her Brahmanical counterpart is Śrī-Lakṣmī. Her symbol is the ears of corn which she holds in her left hand. Her right hand is in *varada mudrā*. Vasudhārā is yellow in colour. She is sometimes represented as one-faced and six-armed and as sitting in *lalita* attitude. In the three right hands she exhibits *namaskāra* and *varada mudrās* and ears of corn. In three left hands she has a book, ears of corn and a vessel containing jewels.

Vasugupta: Author of the *Śivasūtras*, said to have been revealed to him by Śiva himself, which is the source of Kashmir Śaivism and Śaiva Tantras of the same region. He lived towards the end of the eighth or the beginning of the ninth century AD. Ed. with five commentaries and Eng. trans. by K. Sagar, Kashmir Sanskrit Series.

Vaśya-Mātaṅgī: One of the forms of Mātaṅgī whose *mantra* is given in *Puraścaryārṇava* IX. 831-2. In *Merutantra* it is said that her worship should be modelled after that of Rāja-Mātaṅgī: *vijñeyam rājamātaṅgītulyam pūjājapādikam.*

Vaśya Tārā: Also known by the name Āryatāra. She seems to be same as Khadiravanī Tārā. Her colour is green. She sits in *bhadrāsana* (both legs dangling holding a lotus in the left hand and showing the *varada* pose with the right.

Vaṭaparvatikā: Holy resort of the goddess Pañcavargā mentioned in the *Bṛhannīla* and *Prāṇatoṣaṇī*. The name is mentioned in a

Pāla record and in Vijayarāma Sena's *Tīrtha-maṅgala* composed in the second half of the eighteenth century. It is identified with the Valeśvaraparvata, situated near Patharghata in the Patna district, Bihar.

Vātulanātha: An exponent of Krama Tantrism to whom the *Vātulanāthatantra* is traditionally attributed. He is supposed to have flourished in the seventh-eighth century of the Christian era though his historical personality is doubtful.

***Vāyutattvopadeśa*:** A Tantric-yogic text said to have been composed by Ācārya Cauraṅgīnātha. It is mentioned in the Tanjur Catalogue.

Vedabāhya: Those who preferred to base their doctrines on anti-Vedic and anti-Brahmanical ideas. In the *Devībhāgavata* it is stated that the scriptures which are opposed to the Śruti (Veda) and Smṛti (Brahmanical legal texts) belong to the *tāmasa* category. In the same Purāṇa (XII. 9-56 ff) it is said that Gautama cursed a group of Brāhmaṇas as a result of which they left the way of the Vedas and became followers of Pāñcaratra, Pāśupata, Kāmaśāstra, Kāpālikism, Buddhism, etc. (cf. *Kūrma* I. 16.115-19, III. 12). In the *Sūta-saṃhitā* (IV. 1.32, 39.41) the Pāñcarātaras, Pāśupatas, Śāktas, Kāpālikas, Kālāmukhas, Arhats, Bauddhas and Śāmbhavas are described as belonging to non-Vedic (*aśrauta*) Pāṣaṇḍa doctrines. In the *Maheśvaratantra* (18th paṭala), the followers of Advaita Vedānta are cursed with the following words: 'owing to your deeds you all will become fallen from the Vedic way and ungrateful. In the Kali age you all will become fools by denouncing the Veda, Brāhmaṇa, Go (cow) and Mantra and by accepting the Brahma-vāda. Wicked at heart and apparently clean in appearance, you will give up works of religious merit, because of the arrogance caused by the study of *hetuvidyā* (logic) and the knowledge of *brahman*, *Brahman* is true; world is false. When the world is false what is the need of doing meritorious acts?' It has to be admitted that religious systems like Pāñcaratra, Pāśupata, Śākta, Gāṇapatya, etc., had originally nothing to do with the Vedas. But these systems had become extremely popular among the masses; so followers of the Vedic tradition had to give them Vedic sanction. As a result, slowly but steadily, Vedic elements were infused into these systems. Originally Vedabāhyas, these systems later came to be regarded as Vadānusārī.

Vedācāra: One of the seven-fold Tantric Ācāras. It is for ordinary persons belonging to the Paśu (q.v.) grade; it is also called Paśvācāra. The Sādhaka may be a traditional Hindu who believes in the Vedic and Smārta-Pauranic norms. He should rise early in the morning, worship his *guru* and Iṣṭadevatā (personal god) and meditate on the *bījamantra*. He should develop clean habits. *Kaulamārgarahasya* 9; *Prānatoṣaṇī* II. 1, 149.

Vedeśa: Holy resort of the goddess Vedadā mentioned in the *Bṛhannīla* and *Prāṇatoṣaṇī*. It is probably Vaidisa or Vidisa, modern Besnagar in Gwalior.

Vedhamayī-dīkṣā: A form of initiation in which the mental faculties of the candidate are determined by the contemplation of the Guru. See Manodīkṣā and Mānasadīkṣā. *Kulārṇava* XIV.

Vetāla-siddha: Kinds of psycho-physical attainments through which the adepts are supposed to be able to maintain a certain amount of control over departed souls and other subtle-bodied beings using different types of mental practices.

Vibhāsa: Holy resort of the goddess Bhīmarūpā and a pīṭha, where a part of Satī's left leg is said to have fallen, mentioned in the *Pīthanirṇaya* and the *Śivacarita*. It is situated near Tamluk in Midnapur district, West Bengal.

Vibhuti: Miraculous power which is acquired by a Yogin in the course of his progress towards concentration. While to the novice these powers prove intoxicating, the adept is advised to treat them as mere signs of spiritual progress and not as the real attainment. *Yogāmṛta* III. 46; *Haṭhayogapradīpikā* II. 78.

Vicitra: One of the four moments according to the *Hevajratantra*, others being Vipāka, Vimarda and Vilakṣaṇa (q.v.). It is the moment when the realization of pleasure is attended with various kinds of emotions resulting from physical union.

Viditā: Śāsanadevatā of the Jain Tīrthaṃkara Vimala according to the Śvetāmbara tradition. She is also known as Vijayā; she is described as being seated on a lotus and having four hands which hold an arrow, noose, bow and snake. Vidita means 'learned one'.

Vidyā: See also Prajñābhiṣeka. It denotes knowledge; female deities and their *mantras*; the female partner of the aspirant; certain forms of *tattvas* and *kalās*; *vimarśa-śakti* expressed in the idea of I-ness; the name of school and sects and so on. As knowledge, Vidyā is of two kinds—*parā-vidyā* (spiritual knowledge) and *aparā-vidyā* (material knowledge).

Vidyānagara, Pura: Holy resort of the goddess Vidyā mentioned in the *Bṛhannīla* and *Prāṇatoṣaṇī*. It is probably Vijayanagara, modern Hampi in the Bellary district. Vidyanagara was also the name of Rajahmundry, or a place near it, in Godavari district. Another Vidyanagara is supposed to be modern Bijaynagar at the confluence of the Sindh and the Pārā, twenty miles below Narwar.

Vidyās: Tantric goddesses. The following list is given in the *Sammoha-tantra*: Aindrī, Gāyatrī, Brahmavidyā, Ardhanārīśvarī, Tripurabhairavī, Caitanyabhairavī, Rudraśakti, Kāmeśvarī, Śrutidharī, Mātṛkā, Sarasvatī, Śāmbhavī, Śrīparāparā, Kāmarajeśvarī, Mahatripurabhairavī, Aghorabhairavī, Tripurānikṛntabhairavī, Annapūrṇā, Kukkuṭā, Śivā, Bhogavatī, Kubjikā, Saṅkarṣaṇī, Kriyāsaṅkarṣaṇī, Kālasaṅkarṣaṇī, Mahāvidyā, Śūlinī, Mādhavī, Caṇḍayogeśvarī, Cāmuṇḍā, Ratnavidyā, Siddhavidyā, Māyā, Māyāvatī, Ramā, Dhanadā, Śabarī, Durgā, Reṇukā, Siddhi, Sāmrājyasundarī, Rājarājeśvarī, Mahāsāmrājyavidyā, Yakṣiṇī, Putanā, Kavacā, Kuṣmāṇḍinī, Agastyavidyā, Vāgavādinī, Caṇḍalī, Susukhī, Mātaṅginī, Māheśvarī, Rājamātaṅginī, Laghuvārahī, Sutiraṣkārinī, Svapnavārāhī, Padukā, Vārāhīpādukā, Jambukīkkikā, Śukā, Vāgeśī, Śukatuṇḍā, Mohinī, Kirādinī, Ksemankarī, Sumūrti, Śrīmahātimiravatī, Kālamāyā, Ṣoḍaśī, Śriparāvidyā, Caraṇarūpiṇī, Śrīvidyā, Balatripurā, Vagalā, Mahiṣaghnā, Mahalakṣmī, Mahāsarasvatī, Pratyaṅgirā, Bhavānī, Kālikā, Tārā, Chinnamastā, Dhumāvatī, etc.

Vidveṣaṇa: Rite for creating bad blood. *Śāradātilaka* XXIII. 124.

Vidyānandanātha: Author of the *Artharatnāvali* commentary on the *Nityaṣoḍaśikārṇava*. He hailed from Kanchi, had Tantric initiation under Sundarācārya and settled at Vārāṇasī. He lived in the sixteenth century.

Vidyāśakti: An aspect of the *icchā-śakti* (q.v.), or will-power of Śakti, the desire to be manifested. The other aspect is Avidyā or Māyā-śakti (q.v.). Both of these are conscious principles. Vidyā-śakti is illuminating consciousness. It is that aspect of the supreme being which is the efficient cause of the world. It is theoretically immutable and without any transformation, but in its functional aspect it is *pariṇāmī*, i.e. subject to transformation. On this point, however, there is no agreement in the Tantric texts.

Vidyujjvālakarāli: A variety of Ekajaṭā and an emanation of Akṣobhya. She has twelve faces and twenty-four arms. She is blue in colour and tramples upon four Māras represented by Brahmā, Viṣṇu, Śiva and Indra. *Sadhana* 257.

Vighnātaka: An enemy of the *vighnas* (obstacles) represented by the Brahmanical Gaṇeśa which is why he tramples upon the latter as an emanation of Akṣobhya. His colour is blue and symbols are *tarjanipāśa* and *vajra*. *Sādhana* 558-9.

Vighnāpasāraṅa: The removal of evil elements with the help of *mantras*. *Puraścaryārṇava* III. 154; Rāghava on *Śāradātilaka*. IV. 10. Also known as Bhūtāpasarana.

Vigraha: Image or idol. The Āgamas state that idols are a mere aid, though a very necessary one, for the *sādhaka* to conceive and meditate upon the supreme being. According to the *Viṣṇu Saṃhitā* XXIX 55-7, where there is nothing for the mind to attach itself to, it will slip away from meditation. Therefore the aspirant should meditate on some form keeping in mind however, that the form is a superimposition and not the reality. Elsewhere it says that idols are for those who are of poor intellect; *pratimā svalpabuddhīnām*.

Vijñana: Consciousness which is one of the five *skandhas* (aggregates of existence) according to all forms of Buddhism. The specialized Vijñānavāda or Yogācāra school of thought has given a sophisticated metaphysical dimension to this elementary concept. In Vajrayāna, the Dhyānī Buddha Akṣobhya represents this particular *skandha*. In *Śrīcakrasambhāra-tantra* the representative of the element of consciousness in Vajrasattva.

***Vijñāna-Bhairava*:** A late-medieval work in 162 *kārikās* composed in the form of a dialogue; it deals with *bhakti* in the philosophy of non-duality, characteristics of *sādhanā*, means of liberation, awakening of *kuṇḍalinī*, penetration of six *cakras* and so forth. Ed. with notes by M.R. Sastri, KSS no. IX. 1918; Eng. trans. by J. Singh; text and com. trans. with notes into French by L. Silburn, Paris, 1961, Bengali trans. by R.C. Adhikari, Burdwan 1980.

Vijñānākala: The first part (*vijñāna*) of the term means the knowledge of the real nature of the supreme being while the second (*akala*) means that which has no *kalā* or speciality. It is a category of *paśu* or individual. Vijñānākala applies to those beings who are fettered only by *mala* (ignorance). Among the other categories *pralayākala* applies to those who are fettered by *mala* and *karma* (result of action) and *sakala* to those who are fettered by *mala, karma* and *māyā*. *Vijñānākala* is of the two kinds—*samāptakaluṣa* (whose defilement has been purified) and *asamāptakaluṣa* (whose defilements are yet to be purified). Com. on *Sarvadarśanasaṃgraha* VII. 106-23; *Tattvaprakāśa* I. 9.

Vijñanamātrātmaka: A Buddhist Tantric term denoting pure consciousness. The aspirant should realize this pure consciousness within himself on the components of the universe in terms of various colour and shade condensed in the form of syllables.

Vilakṣana: One of the four moments according to the *Hevajratantra*. The others are Vicitra, Vipāka and Vimarda (q.v.). It is the moment when the realization of bliss transcends that of the other three moments and realization is in itself free from any emotion of attachment or detachment.

Vilāsa: One of the four principal Tantric schools. The others are Kerala, Kāsmīra and Gauḍa.

Vimalā: Presiding goddess of one of the eight angles of the *aṣṭakoṇacakra*. She belongs to the status of Rahasyayoginī or Avaraṇadevatā. According to the *Vāmakeśvara-tantra* she is the presiding goddess of the letters beginning with Ṭa (Ṭa-varga).

***Vimalaprabhā*:** Commentary on *Kālacakratantra*. According to this commentary Kālacakra is a deity and an embodiment of *śūnyatā* and *karuṇā* (q.v.) embraced by the goddess Prajñā and represents the philosophical conception on *advaya* or nonduality. He is the Ādi-Buddha and progenitor of the Dhyānī Buddhas. The theory that the human body is the microcosm of the universe finds expression in this book which also contains topics pertaining to stars and planets as well as the circle of time.

Vimalīkaraṇa: Processing of *mantra*. *Tantrasāra* 54.

Vimarda: One of the four moments according to the *Hevajratantra*. The others are Vicitra, Vipāka and Vilakṣaṇa (q.v.). It is the moment when the realization of bliss is attended with the consciousness of the ego as its realizer.

Vimarśa: The vibrating, dynamic or kinetic aspect of the power (*śakti*) of the Absolute, the static aspect is known as Prakāśa (q.v.). These two forms of *śakti* are also inseparable from Śiva. *Nāda* (subtle sound) is produced when Śiva assumes the form of *bindu* while entering as *jyoti* (illumination) or Prakāśa into *śakti* existing in the form of Vimarśa. Without Vimarśa Prakāśa has no special value, just as without Prakṛti Puruṣa is quite inactive, which is why it is stated that without Śakti Śiva is no better than a corpse. *Tantrāloka* III 2 ff. Vimarśa-śakti has two forms. In the subtle state it is the form of consciousness (*cidrūpiṇī*) and in the gross state it is in form of the universe (*viśvarūpiṇī*). The relation between Prakāśa and Vimarśa is one of inseparable connection or inherence. Vimarśa contains the potentialities of the universe within it. It begins to function leaving the Prakāśa standing alone as 'I' without a 'This'. At every stage of the evolution of the māyā-śakti (q.v.) (the material principle of creation), the Vimarśa-śakti contracts itself into gross and more gross entities until it assumes physical form and works as the life-principle of all things. At the end of this process, in dissolution, it again returns to its source and remains there in undifferentiated state with its other part the Prakāśa aspect of the supreme being.

Vināyaka: Holy resort of the goddess Umā or the Rūpā mentioned in *Matsya* XIII, 40, *Devībhāgavata* VII. 30.69, *Padma*, Sṛṣṭi, XVII, 198, *Skanda* V. 3.79.78. It is one of the eight Vināyaka *tīrthas* in Maharashtra. These are Ranjangaon, Margaon, Theur, Leṇadri, Ojhar, Pali, Madh and Siddhatek.

Vindhya, Vindhyakandara: Holy resort of the goddess Vindhyavāsiṇī mentioned in the *Kubjikā* XVIII. 42 ff. In the Purāṇas Vindhya and Vindhyakandara are separately stated to be the abodes of Vindhyavāsinī and Amṛtā respectively. *Matsya* XIII. 39, 41; *Devī-*

bhāgavata VII. 30.68.70; *Padma*, Sṛṣṭi XVII. 197, 199; *Skanda* V. 3. 98, 77, 79. The temple of Vindhyavāsinī lies at Vindhyacal near Mirzapur in Uttar Pradesh. The same site with the same goddess is mentioned as Vindhya-gaṅgāsaṅgama in *Bṛhannīlatantra* V and *Prāṇatoṣaṇī*. The *Jñānārṇava* V. 66 ff. and the *Śivacarita* refer to this place as a *pīṭha* where one of the toes of Satī's left foot is said to have fallen. Vindhyakandara may denote another holy place in the Vindhyan range.

Vipāka: One of the four moments according to the *Hevajratantra*. The others are Vicitra, Vimada and Vilakṣaṇa (q.v.). It is the moment when the bliss is matured to knowledge.

Vīra, Vīrācāra: Tantric aspirant of the second grade whose mental faculties are advanced. For an interpretation of the word *vīra* see *Kulārṇava* XVII; *Rudrayāmala*, Uttara I. 136; characteristics are mentioned in com. on *Paraśurāmakalpasūtra* VI. 39; *Nirvāṇa-tantra* XIV; *Kāmākhyātantra* IV; *Niruttara* XI, *Rudrayāmala Uttara*, LI. 20-1. Classifications: *Śaktisaṅgama*, Sundarī, I. 197-200, Tārā XLIII 204; *Puraścaryārṇava* IX. 863; *Prāṇatoṣaṇī* VIII. 1. 495 ff. The spiritual exercises of a *vīra* are known as *vīracakra*. The characteristics of a Vīra, as enumerated in the *Kāmākhyātantra* are that he should be fearless, of inspiring personality, and be resolute to achieve his purpose. He should be polite in language, attentive, courageous, intelligent and active. Only a man of this stage is eligible for initiation to Dakṣiṇācara; he must follow the path of devotion (*bhakti*) and knowledge (*jñāna*). If he takes up Vāmācara he has to be initiated in *śakti-mantra* and *pañcatattva*.

Vīra cakra: One of the five *cakra* rituals mentioned in the *Niruttaratantra* X. In this *cakra* five *śaktis* are to be worshipped in the form of mother (Bhūmīndrakanyā), daughter (Rajakīsutā), sister (Śvapacī), daughter-in-law (Kapālī) and wife (Yoginī).

Virajā, Virajāpura: The celebrated Virajākṣetra in Utkala mentioned in *Kubjikā* XVIII. 42 ff., *Jñanārṇava* V. 66 ff., *Bṛhannīla* V. It is modern Jajpur on the Vaitaraṇī. The *Pīṭha-nirṇaya* mentions it as a *pīṭha* where the navel of Satī had fallen. The presiding deity is Vimalā and her Bhairava is Jagannātha.

Vīramāheśvara: A sect of the Maheśvara Siddhas which aimed at rendering, by varied physico-chemical processes, the human body deathless, perpetually alive to the light and shade of the sense-world, and capable of weilding the eight supernatural powers of a perfected thaumaturge.

Vīrāmānanda: One of the four kinds of bliss mentioned in the Buddhist Tantras. The others are Ānanda, Paramānanda and Sahajānanda. This bliss is produced when the Bodhicitta is in the Sambhogacakra. It requires detachment from worldly pleasures and represents Nirvāṇa though the aspirant retains his consciousness of egohood. Realization of this bliss, according to the *Sekoddeśaṭīkā* 26-7, is associated with some sort of consciousness of the Self.

Virāṭa: Holy resort of the goddess Ambikā which has been regarded as a *pīṭha* in the *Pīṭhanirṇaya*. The ancient Virāṭa country lay in the Jaipur-Alwar-Bharatpur region of Rajasthan. But another country of this name has been placed in northern Bengal by late medieval writers.

Viśāla: Holy resort of the goddess Viśālā mentioned in the *Bṛhannīla* and *Prāṇatoṣaṇī* Tantras. It is possibly Visāla Badari or Badarikāśrama in the Himalayas.

Visarga: Alphabetical sign of the double dot which is symbolically regarded as the complementary Śakti of Bindu (q.v.). It signifies both the *parā* and *aparā* aspects of Śakti. *Tantrāloka* III. 120 ff. It is also known as Kaulikī Śakti. *Ibid* III. 143. It is the Female Principle (*saḥ*) as complementary to the Male Principle (*haṃ*). *Prapañcasāra* quoted by Kālīcaraṇa in his com. on *Ṣaṭcakranirūpaṇa* XLIII. See also Bindu.

Viśeṣa-dīkṣā: Special initiation into Āgamānta Śaivism in which the candidate is entitled to follow the way of *kriyā* (rites) and *yoga* (concentration) so as to reach the *sāmīpya* (feeling like the son of god) and *sārūpa* (feeling an association of god) stages.

Viṣṇugranthi: A knot on the *anāhata-cakra* (q.v.) which the *kuṇḍalinī* (q.v.) has to pierce during its upward march.

Viṣṇukrāntā: A zone of Tantric culture extending from the Vindhyan range to Caṭṭala. According to the *Mahāsiddhasāra-tantra* this region has yielded 64 Tantras. Among the important Tantras of the Viṣṇukrāntā mention may be made of *Kālītantra*, *Kulārṇava*, *Jñārṇava*, *Nīla*, *Phetkāriṇī*, *Siddhiyamāla*, *Matsyasukta*, *Vārāhī*, *Yoginī*, *Cāmuṇḍā*, *Muṇḍamālā*,

Tantrarāja, Mālinī, Rudrayāmala, Malinī-vijaya, Samayācara, Bhairava, Yogini-hṛdaya, Kulacuḍāmaṇi, Kāmākhyā, Bhūtaḍā-mara, Brahmayāmala, Viśvasāra, Mahākāla, Kubjikā, Kālivilāsa, Māyā, Kuloḍḍīśa, etc.

Viṣṇupāda: Holy resort of the goddess Viṣṇupriyā mentioned in the *Bṛhannīla* and *Prāṇatoṣaṇī* Tantras. It is probably the hill of the same name at Gaya in Bihar.

***Viṣṇu-Saṃhitā*:** Vaiṣṇava Tantra in 30 *paṭalas*. Published in Trivandrum Sanskrit Series 1925.

Viśuddha: The nerve plexus above the *anāhata* (q.v.) in the neck region. It looks like a sixteen-petalled lotus of a smoky purple hue. Its presiding deity is the goddess Śākinī. Its filaments are ruddy, and the sixteen vowels which are red and have the *bindu* above them are on the petals. Inside it is the *candra-maṇḍala* and above it is the *bīja* Ha. On the *bīja* is Sadāśiva in his Ardhanārīśvara aspect. *Ṣaṭcakranirūpaṇa* XXVIII-XXX.

Viśvamātā: A form of Sita or white Tārā. She carries a white lotus in her left hand and exhibits the *abhaya* pose with the right.

Viśvapadma: The heart of the *dharma-cakra* according to the Buddhist Tantras. It is a double lotus with eight petals, one facing upwards and the other facing downwards. Within it there is a syllable *hum*.

Viśvāsa: Faith. The *kuṇḍalinī-yoga* is not a mysterious or esoteric doctrine and ritual peculiar to the Tantras. There are different forms of effort (*sādhanā*) by which the magazine of latent power can be acted upon, and power 'stored' can be lifted as by a lever. Viśvāsa or faith acts as this lever.

***Viśvasāra Tantra*:** A medieval Tantra dealing especially with the cult of Kālī besides the usual Tantric topics. Quotations from this text are found in the later Tantric manuals.

Viśvavajra: The double conventional *vajra*. See Vajra.

Viśvavarṇakamala: A contemplation on the part of the spiritual aspirant mentioned in *Sādhanamālā* I. 18 ff. The aspirant should realize himself as pure consciousness and then think of 'a lotus of the colour of the universe' transformed as the syllable *pam* and on that a clear lunar disc emanating from the letter A.

Vitarka: *Mudrā* assumed in discussion. This *mudrā* is represented with the right arm bent, all fingers erect except either the index or the ring finger which touches the thumb so far as to resemble a ring. The hand is extended forward with the palm outward.

Vivṛta: Also known as *paramārthika* it is the motionless aspect of intense bliss according to the *Hevajratantra*. As opposed to *saṃvṛta*, the phenomenal or provisional truth, it is the ultimate reality in the form of an incorporeal all pervading great bliss (*mahāsukha*).

Vṛndāvana: Holy resort of goddess Rādhā mentioned in *Matsya* XIII. 38, *Devī-bhāgavata* VII. 30.67; *Padma*, Sṛṣṭi XVII. 196, *Skanda* V. 3.98.76. The Pīṭhanirṇaya refers to it as a *pīṭha* with Umā as the presiding goddess. It is modern Brindaban near Mathura in Uttar Pradesh.

Vyākhyāna: Hand pose as if explaining something with palms near the breast. It is that gesture exhibited by Buddha while preaching his first sermon at Sarnath. The pose is depicted variously. See Dharmacakra.

Vyāpakanyāsa: Massaging of the body from head to foot with the palms while continuously uttering the *mantras*. It is a form of Ṣoḍhanyāsa (q.v.) in which the deity is to be felt over the entire body. *Kālītantra* I. 17-18.

Vyāpakaśakti kuṇḍalinī: The sound-element which is the nature of consciousness of all beings. The motionless causal sound assumes a general undifferentiated movement, then a differentiated vibration and finally clearly articulated speech. The *kuṇḍalinī-śakti* may be made to pass through the states of sound mechanism like Parā, Paśyantī, Madhyamā, Vaikharī. *Śāradātilaka* I. 108-11.

Vyutkrama: See Śodhana.

Y y

Yab-Yum: Goddess-in union-with-god. It is a characteristic feature of Tibetan Buddhist iconography. *Yab* means father and *Yum* mother; hence the combined word means 'the father in the embrace of the mother'. Often the god holds the *yum* (the female) on his knee in the archaic manner of Śiva holding Pārvatī or Umā. Avalokiteśvara is depicted as holding his Śakti on the knee. For the spiritual significance of the conception of Yab-yum see Yuganaddha.

Yāgapurī: Holy resort of the goddess Virajā mentioned in the *Bṛhannīla* and *Prāṇatoṣaṇī* Tantras. It is same as Virajākṣetra, Yajapura and Nābhigayā.

Yājapura: Same as Virajākṣetra (q.v.) mentioned as a *pīṭha* in the *Caṇḍimaṅgala.* The Assia range about a mile to the south of Jajpur in Orissa is said to have borne the name Catuṣpīṭha-parvata.

Yakṣas: Ancient vegetation spirits held in high esteem in Buddhism and Jainism. In the epics and Purāṇas they are described both as benevolent and as malevolent beings with Kubera as their overlord. In Tantric Buddhism eight Yakṣas are celebrated. They are known as Pūrṇabhadra, Maṇibhadra, Dhanada, Vaiśravaṇa, Civikuṇḍalī, Kelimali, Sukhendra and Calendra. They hold in their hands citron and mongoose, the natural symbols of Jambhala, the Buddhist god of wealth. Each Yakṣa is accompanied by a Śakti with whom he remains in Yab-yum in the same way as Jambhala remains with Vasudhārā. In Jainism the Yakṣas have an extensive cult. The Buddha and Jina images were originally modelled after the Yakṣa images.

Yakṣiṇīs: Female counterparts of the Yakṣas. In Tantric Buddhism they are eight in number: Citrakālī, Dattā, Sudattā, Āryā, Subhadrā, Guptā, Devī and Sarasvatī. They are in Yab-yum (in union) with their male partners and identical in form with Vasudhārā who is yellow in complexion, carries ears of corn and shows *varadamudrā*. In Jainism the Yakṣiṇīs serve as Śasanadevatās or attending deities of the Tīrthaṃkaras.

Yama: One of the eight limbs of Yoga (q.v.) which is abstinence from evil propensities by which the mind is disturbed. The observance of *yamas* by all men may be called *vrata*. There may be some exceptions for men, but in case of Yogins rigorous observance without exceptions—*mahāvrata* is stipulated. Five *yamas* of the *Yoga Sūtra* are *ahiṃsā* (non-injury to all creatures and at all times), *satya* (truthfulness), *asteya* (non-stealing), *brahmacarya* (control of sexual passion) and *aparigraha* (non-possession).

Yamadaṇḍa: A form of Avalokiteśvara or Lokeśvara. He is one-faced and six-armed and sits in *lalita* attitude on a lotus. His three right hands hold a sword, lotus and *vajra* while his three left display fruit, a bowl of gems and an unspecified *mudrā*.

Yamadūtī: Tantric Buddhist goddess, companion of Mahākāla. She is blue in complexion and has four arms. She carries in her two right hands a lotus and *kartari* and in her left hands a bowl of blood and a fly-whisk.

Yamakālī: One of the twelve forms of Kālī mentioned by Abhinavagupta. *Tantrāloka* IV,157 ff. The prefix *yama* is indicative of yama, one of the limbs of yoga. It is so called because Kālī is the cause of expansion and contraction and regulates (*yama*) the *parā-saṃvit*, or pure-consciousness, by this method.

Yāmala: A class of Tantric literature sub-divided into eight groups: Rudra, Skanda, Brahma, Viṣṇu, Yama, Vāyu, Kubera and Indra. The Yāmalas not only define various Tantric traditions but also introduce a variety of cults of new gods and goddesses. They assimilate a large number of local cults as well and open up the field of Tantric culture to people belonging to the lower castes. According to *Brahmayāmala* the above eight yamalas were communicated by eight Bhairavas. Two other texts—*Piṅgalāmata* and *Jayadrathayamāla*—belong to the Yāmala group.

Yāmalāṣṭaka: Group of Tantric texts of the Yāmala category belonging to the

64 Bhairava Āgamas (q.v.) comprising *Brahma*, *Viṣṇu*, *Rudra*, *Atharvan*, *Ruru*, *Vetāla*, *Indra* and *Svacchanda*.

Yamāntaka: See Kṛṣṇa Yamāri and Rakta-Yamāri. He is also a god of direction. As a guardian of the eastern quarter Yamāntaka is described in the Mañjuvajra Maṇḍala of the *Niṣpanna* as having a blue complexion, three faces—blue, white and red in colour—and a hammer marked with a blue *vajra*, a sword, a jewel and a lotus. In the Vajrahuṅkara Maṇḍala of the same text his second name is given as Vajradaṇḍa.

Yamārī: Same as Yamāntaka (q.v.). He has two forms, black (Kṛṣṇa) and red (Rakta), both being emanations of Akṣobhya, one of the five Dhyānī Buddhas of the Buddhist Tantric pantheon. This god has been conceived of as the killer of Yama. Yamārī is also a god of direction presiding over the eastern quarter.

Yamunā: Name of a nerve, that of Piṅgalā, situated on the right side of the spinal cord. The one on the left, the Iḍā, is known as Gaṅgā, while the one in the centre, running in close correspondence with the spinal cord, is Susumnā.

Yamunā: Principal tributary of the Ganges mentioned as a river sacred to the goddess Mṛgāvatī in *Matsya* XIII. 40, *Devībhāgavata* VII. 30. 69, *Padma*, Sṛṣṭi XVII. 198, *Skanda* 5.3.98.78. It is also mentioned in the *Bṛhannīla-tantra* V. The *Prāṇatoṣaṇī* refers to the goddess as Kālindī which is another name of the Yamunā.

Yantra: Symbol of deity. It is generally in the form of a diagram or geometrical pattern serving as a chart for revealing the characteristics of the deity. For the efficacy of *Yantra* in Tantric worship see *Gandharva* V.1; *Mātṛkābheda* XII. 6 ff. *Yantra* is variously interpreted as an instrument, the body and abode of deity, amulet mental faculties, pure consciousness, doctrinal intricacies, microcosm of human body and so on. *Kulārṇava* VI, XVII; *Gandharva* V. 39-40; *Saundaryalaharī* XI. *Śaktisaṅgama*, Tārā, XII. 203; LI. 2; *Puraścaryārṇava* VI. 518 ff; *Tantrasāra* 312 ff. Yantras are drawn or engraved on cloth, paper, leaves, stone and metal. *Yantra* is often considered as the deity itself. There is a *yantra-gayātrī:Yantrarājāya vidmahe, varapradāya dhīmahi, tanno yantram pracodayāt*. One of the most popular forms of the *yantras* is *śricakra* (q.v.). The worship of *yantra* is called *bahiryāga* or the external worship of Śakti. For *yantras* in general see *Prapañcasāra* XXI, XXXIV; *Śāradātilaka* VII. 53-63; *Kāmakalāvilāsa* 22 ff; *Tantrarāja* II. 44-51. *Mantramahodadhi* XX; *Kaulajñānanirṇaya* X; *Kaulāvalīnirṇaya* III. 105-35; etc.

Yaśora: Holy resort of the goddess Yasoreśvarī according to the *Pīṭhanirṇaya*. The *Śivacarita* refers it as an Upapīṭha. It is located at Īśvarīpura in Khulna district, Bangladesh, not far from Hasanabad in 24-Paraganas district, West Bengal.

Yaugi-dīkṣa: Initiation in which the *guru* enters the body of his disciple in subtle form and impresses his own self on that of the latter. Rāghava on *Śāradātilaka* V. 127-40.

Yauvanollāsa: The third stage of spiritual exercise in which the Tantric aspirant becomes well-versed in scriptures. Rāghava's com. on *Parasurāmakalpasūtra* X. 68. This stage like the preceding *ārambha* and *taruṇa* stages is intended for persons belonging to Paśu (q.v.) or ordinary category. At this stage the aspirant is capable of reading the texts but requires the aid of a preceptor. According to Rāmeśvara, this stage belongs to Samayācāra (q.v.) category.

Yoga: In the classical definition it is *citta-vṛttinirodha*—the control of mental desires and inclinations. *Pātañjala Yogasūtra* I. 2. In the Tantras it is defined as the equation of the individual soul with the universal soul. *Śāradātilaka* XXV. 1; *Kulārṇava* IX. 30; *Mahānirvāṇa* XIV. 123; *Prapañcasāra* XIX. 14. According to *Dattātreya Saṃhita,* Yoga has many varieties such as Mantrayoga, Layayoga, Haṭhayoga, Rājayoga, etc. *Prāṇatoṣaṇī* VI. 3. 439. Among these Haṭhayoga is practical while the others are by nature psychical. Haṭhayoga derives its name from *ha* (sun) and *ṭha* (moon) *Yoga-śikhopaniṣat* I. 133. By the performance of yoga *kuṇḍalinī* (q.v.) is awakened. *Gheraṇḍa* III. 46. Earlier sources refer to eight types of Haṭhayoga which are *yama* (restraint), *niyama* (cultivation of good habits), *āsana* (right placement of the limbs), *prāṇāyāma* (control of breath), *pratyāhāra* (abstraction), *dhāraṇa* (attention), *dhyāna* (meditation) and *samādhi* (absorption). Later and Buddhist sources refer to six limbs; they drop *yama, niyama* and *āsana* but add *anusmṛti* (remembrance). *Yogatattvopaniṣat* 24-5; *Guhyasamāja* XVIII. 163. In some places *anusmṛti* is replaced by *tarka* or *vitarka* (self-examination). The *Gheraṇḍa* I. 10-1 refers to seven limbs. The seventh is *ṣaṭkarma* by which are denoted six acts: *dhauti*, *vasti*, *neti*, *laulikī*, *trāṭaka* and *kapālabhāti*—the physical cleansing and exercises by which the body becomes strong and free from disease.

Yogabhāṣya: Commentary on the *Yoga Sūtra*. It is not later than the fourth century AD. Its author Vyāsa is different from the celebrated author of the *Mahābharata*. It is the most authentic interpretation which has also many sub-commentaries. See Yoga Sūtra.

Yogāmbara: Principal deity of the Yogāmbra Maṇḍala of the *Niṣpannayogāvalī* 32. He is blue in colour, has three faces and six arms. His Prajña or Śakti is Jñānadākinī with whom he is in *yuganaddha* union for ever.

Yoga-nāḍī: A nerve which carries the vital air.

Yoganidrā: A form of the supreme goddess whose form has been extolled by Viṣṇu in the *Harivaṃsa*. She is described as the sister of Indra and also as a virgin who performed austerities for attaining perfection.

Yogaratnamālā: Commentary on *Hevajra-tantra* by Kṛṣṇācarya I of the early ninth century. According to him the special Yoga system as outlined in the Tantra leads to enlightenment. It excels even the *pāramitā* scheme, the way of six perfections. It explains the course of studies prescribed for the aspirant seeking entrance to Mantrayāna. Edited by D. Snellgrove with the text of *Hevajra*, 2 vols. London 1959.

Yogasāra: A treatise composed by Nāgārjuna in the eighth century which contains recipes for cosmetics and for the cure of diseases of hair.

Yoga Sūtra: The celebrated work of Patañjali on the philosophy of Yoga. It is divided into four *pādas*—Samādhi (concentration), Sādhanā (means of attainment), Vibhuti (supernormal powers) and Kaivalya (liberation). There are only 195 *sūtras* in all the *pādas* together. Many editions of the *Yoga Sūtra* with the *bhāṣya* of Vyāsa and the commentary called *Tattvavaiśāradī* (q.v.) of Vācaspati have been published. Among other commentaries the *Rājamartaṇḍa* by king Bhoja, the *Pradīpikā* by Bhāva Gaṇeśa, *Vṛtti* by Nāgoji-bhaṭṭa, the *Maṇiprabha* by Rāmānandayati, the *Candrika* by Anantadeva and the *Yogasudhākara* by Sadāsivendra Sarasvatī deserve special mention.

Yogatantra: One of the four classes of Buddhist Tantras. As the name implies, the Yogatantras deal with the practice of Yoga. This class of Buddhist Tantras is represented by the *Vajrasikhara* and *Sarvatathāgata-tattvasaṃgraha* in which all forms of rituals or performances, whether ordinary or esoteric, are subordinated to meditation, concentration and discipline of the body.

Yogatārāvalī: A hymn attributed to Śaṅkara which is a prayer to the goddess Tārā. It refers to the nerve-plexuses, the serpent-power and some resorts sacred to the goddess.

Yogin: A person who is physically, mentally and spiritually disciplined. According to the *Gītā* VI. 46 a Yogin is superior to *tapasvin*, *jñānin* and *karmin* (those engaged respectively in austerity, knowledge and action). A Yogin may develop certain supernormal powers, but he is advised to ignore them as they are hindrances in his way to his goal. *Yogasūtra* III. 36.

Yoginī: A class of goddess, generally 64 in number, supposed to be multiples of eight Mātṛkās. The term is also used to denote the female partner of the aspirant; the goddesses presiding over the nerve plexuses from *mūlādhāra* to *sahasrāra*; different manifestations of Śakti; a Tantric school; a class of female ascetics imparting Tantric knowledge to the masses; medicine-women; women possessed by goddess; and so on. The *Tantrasāra* quotes the *dhyānas* of eight special Yoginīs from *Bhūtadāmara-tantra*. They are Kaṇakāvatī, Kāmeśvarī, Nalinī, Madhumatī, Manoharā, Ratisundarī, Padminī and Sura-sundarī (q.v.). The Buddhist goddess Prajñā, often addressed as Nairātmā, is called Yoginī or Sahaja-damsel in the esoteric yoga of Sahajayāna. In some places intense bliss (*mahāsukha*) as the ultimate nature and perfect knowledge has been spoken of as the Yoginī and bodhi-mind as the yogin. This Yoginī is variously called the Jñāna-mudrā (the woman of knowledge) or the Mahāmudrā (the great woman), the Sahaja-damsel. In the *Caryāpadas* we find many songs about the transcendental love and union of the yogin and yoginī often garbed in the metaphor of ordinary love and sex-union of man and woman.

Yoginīhṛdaya: The last three chapters of

Vāmakeśvara Tantra are known by this name. It is Chapters VI-VIII of the *Nityaṣoḍaśikārṇava*. They deal with *cakra, mantra* and *pūjā*. Among various *cakras* the spiritual significance of *navayonicakra* is specially described. Six *mantrasaṅketas* (indicative symbols) of the presiding deities of *navayonicakra* are also interpreted. The third section deals with three kinds of Devī worship—*parā, parāparā* and *aparā*. The work has a commentary called *Setubandha* by Bhāskara Rāya. Its *Dīpikā* is by Amṛtānanda. Ed. by Gopinath Kaviraj, Varanasi 1963.

Yoginikaula: A school founded by Matsyendranātha which was popular in the Kāmarupa region. The doctrine of this school, as may be gathered from the *Kaulajñāna-nirṇaya* has something in common with Buddhist Tantras of the Sahaja class.

Yoginipātra: One of the nine special cups of wine required in Tantric worship. *Kaulāvalīnirṇaya* VI.

***Yoginītantra*:** A late medieval Tantric work associated with Assam and North Bengal. It has 19 chapters. It is on the Tantric worship of Kālī. Kulācāra, Yoga and six black acts have been treated here. The goddess Kāmākhyā of Kāmarūpa is glorified. It describes Śiva's relation with Koch peoples. Many Śākta Pīṭhas are described. Ed. by J. Vidyasagara, Calcuttta 1897; by B.N. Sastri 1982; with Hindi trans. by K. Misra, Bombay 1983.

Yoni: Female organ of generation. In the earliest phases of social evolution, it was maternity or production of life that held the field, the life-producing mother being the central figure of religion. This primitive empirical and analogical belief in the equation of earth and woman, of natural and human fertility, connected the mystery of nature with that of the human body in Tantrism which holds that the birth of the universe is the result of the same, or a similar process as the birth of the human beings.

Yoni-mudrā: A seated posture of the body in which the aspirant should fix his anus on the left heel, tongue on the palate and eyes on the tip of the nose. The posture helps to awaken the kuṇḍalinī. *Prāṇatoṣaṇī* I. 10, 70 ff; *Bhūtaśuddhitantravacana* quoted in *Śāradātilaka* IX.

Yoni-puṣpa: Black *aparājitā* flower serving as *maithuna* (sexual intercourse) symbol. *Paraśurāmakalpasūtra* X. 63.

***Yoni tantra*:** Late-medieval work in eight chapters dealing with 64 Tantras, women fit for Tantric worship, animals to be slaughtered, the goddess and ten parts of *yoni* (female organ), efficacy of *japa*, taboos in establishing sex relations, worship of *yoni* and sexual intercourse as an indispensable part of Tantric rites. It also mentions *Cīnācāra*. Ed. by J.A. Schoterman, New Delhi 1980.

Yuganaddha: Iconic representation of god Heruka-in-union-with-goddess Nairātmā, symbolizing the union of Karuṇā and Śūnyatā, or Upāya and Prajñā, in Tantric Buddhism. It is conceived in terms of male and female principles respectively. The Yuganaddha symbolizes unique harmony and interpretation of masculinity and femininity. For a man, woman is the material object of concentration, a goddess for meditation and a symbolic truth for comprehension. See Prajñā, Upāya, Śūnyatā and Karuṇā, Yab-yum.

Yuvatī: 'Young woman'; a name attributed to Prajñā (q.v.) in the Buddhist Tantras.

Bibliography

The entries of the present volume contain names, contents and bibliographical details of the important Tantric texts. Still for the convenience of the readers the major texts are listed below. For a detailed bibliography of the original texts and of important secondary works the readers are also requested to see P.V. Kane's *History of Dharmaśāstra*, Vol. V, Part II, Poona 1962, App. to Sec.VI, pp. 1140-51; M. Eliade's *Yoga, Immortality and Freedom*, New York 1958, special notes, pp. 399-424, bibliography, pp. 435-80; and A. Bharati's *The Tantric Tradition*, London 1965, pp. 302-36, rev. ed. New York 1975. The present bibliography is an updated one containing list of works published till 1999.

Advayasiddhi of the Lakṣmīṅkarādevī, ed. by M.J. Shendge, M.S. Oriental Series No. 8, Baroda 1964.

Advayavajrasaṃgraha, ed. by Haraprasad Sastri, Gaekwad's Oriental Series, XL, Baroda 1927.

Agrawala, P.K., *Goddesses in Ancient India*, Atlantic Highlands N.J., Humanities Press 1983; *Mithuna: The Male-Female Symbol in Indian Art and Thought*, New Delhi 1983.

Allen, Michael, *The Cult of Kumārī: Virgin Worship in Nepal*, Tribhuvan University, Kathmandu 1975.

Alper, H.P. *Understanding Mantras*, Albany State University of New York Press 1989.

Ānandalaharī, Eng. trans. *Wave of Bliss* with notes and comments by Arthur Avalon (John Woodroffe), London 1917, 5th ed. Ganesh and Co., Madras 1961.

Anand, Mulk Raj, *Kāmakalā: Some Notes on the Philosophical Basis of Hindu Erotic Sculpture*, New York 1958; *Tantric Magic* (in collaboration with A. Mookherjee), New Delhi 1977.

Anuruddha, R.P., *Introduction to Lamaism*, Hoshiarpur 1959.

Ārya-Mañjuśrīmūlakalpa, ed. by T. Ganapati Sastri in three parts, Trivandrum Sanskrit Series, Trivandrum 1920-5.

Atre, Subhangana, *The Archetypal Mother*, Pune 1986.

Avalon, Arthur (John Woodroffe), *Principles of Tantra*, Calcutta 1914, 1916; *Introduction to Tantraśāstra*, 1st ed. Madras 1913; *Tantra of the Great Liberation*, Eng. trans. with intro. first ed. 1913, Dover Publications, New York 1972; *The Serpent Power*, Calcutta 1914; General Editor: *Tantrik Texts*, Vols. I-XXI, London and Calcutta 1913 ff.

Ayyangar, T.R.S., *Haṭhayogapradīkā,* Eng. trans. Adyar Library, Madras 1933

Bagchi, Prabodh Chandra, *Studies in the Tantras*, Calcutta University 1939; *Kaulajñānanirṇaya*, Calcutta Sanskrit Series 1934; 'Primitive Elements in Jainism' in *Journal of the Department of Letters*, Calcutta University, V, 1921, 349-64; 'Sandhyābhāṣā' in *Visva-Bharati Quarterly* 1924; 'On some Tantric texts studied in Ancient Kambuja' in *Indian Historical Quarterly*, V, 1928, 754-69; VI, 1930, 97-107.

Bagchi, Subhendu Gopal, *Eminent Śākta Centres in Eastern India*, Punthi Pustak, Calcutta 1980.

Bakshi, D.N., *Hindu Divinities in Javanese Buddhist Pantheon*, Benten Publishers 1979.

Banerjea, Jitendra Nath, *Development of Hindu Iconography*, Calcutta University 1956; *Pauranic and Tantric Religion*, Calcutta University 1966; *Pañcopāsana*, Firma KLM, Calcutta 1960.

Banerji, S.C., *A Brief History of Tantric Literature*, Calcutta 1988; *Tantra in Bengal: A Study in Its Origin, Development and Influence*, Naya Prakash, Calcutta 1978.

Barnett, L.D., *Paramārthasāra of Abhinavagupta with Yogarāja's Commentary*, translated in *Journal of the Royal Asiatic Society*, 1910.

Barrow, H.W., 'On Aghorīs and Aghorapanthīs' in *Journal of the Anthropological Society of Bombay*, III, 1893, 197-251.

Basu, M., *Tantras: A General Study*, Calcutta 1976; *Fundamentals of Tantric Philosophy*, Calcutta 1986.

Bauddha-stotra-saṃgraha, Vol. I comprising *Sragdharā-stotra* of Sarvajñamitra, ed. by S.C. Vidyabhusan, Bibliotheca Indica, Calcutta 1908.

Baumer, Bettina, 'Unmanifest and Manifest Forms according to the Śaivāgamas' in *Shastric Traditions in Indian Arts*, Stainer Verlag Wiesbaden GMBH, Stuttgart 1989.

Beane, Wendell Charles, *Myth, Cult and Symbols in Śākta Hinduism: A Study of the Indian Mother Goddess*, E.J. Brill, Leiden 1977.

Benard, Elisabeth, *Chinnamastā: The Buddhist and Hindu Tantric Goddess*, Motilal Banarsidass, Delhi 1996.

Bernard, T., *Haṭhayoga: Report of a Personal Experience*, New York 1944, London 1958.

Beyer, Stephen, *The Cult of Tārā: Magic and Rituals in Tibet*, University of California Press, Berkley 1973.

Bharati, Agehananda, *The Tantric Tradition*, Garden City, Doubledey 1965, rev. ed. Samuel Weiser, New York 1975; The *Ochre Robe*, London 1961; 'Metaphysics of Tantrism' in *Quest* XXV, 1962.

Bhattacharyya, Benoytosh, *Buddhist Esoterism*, Oxford University Press, London 1924; *An Introduction to Buddhist Esoterism*, London 1932, repr. Delhi 1980; *Indian Buddhist Iconography*, Firma KLM, Calcutta, 1958, repr. Calcutta 1968; *Sādhanamālā*, Gaekwad's Oriental Series (GOS) CCVI, XLI, Baroda 1925, 1928; *Niṣpannayogāvalī*, GOS, CIX, Baroda 1949; *Śaktisaṅgama-tantra* GOS, LXI, XCI, CIV, Baroda 1932, 1941, 1947; *Two Vajrayāna Works*, GOS, XLIV, Baroda 1929. *Guhyasamāja-tantra*, GOS, LIII, Baroda 1931; 'Glimpses of Vajrayana' in *Proceedings and Transactions of the Third Oriental Conference 1924*, Madras 1925, 'The Cult of Bhūtaḍāmara' in ibid of sixth conference 1930, Patna 1933, 349-70; The Date of Bauddha Gān of Dohā' in *Journal of Bihar and Orissa Research Society* XIV, 1928, 341-57; 'A Peep into Vajrayana' in *Annals of the Bhandarkar Oriental Research Institute*, X, 1930; 'The Home of Tantric Buddhism' in *B.C. Law Volume I*, Poona 1945, 254-61; 'Origin and Development of Vajrāyana' in *Indian Historical Quarterly*, III, 1927, 733-46.

Bhattacharyya, Brajamadhaba, *The World of Tantra*, Munshiram Manoharlal, New Delhi 1988.

Bhattacharyya, D., *The Mirror of the Sky: Songs from the Bauls of Bengal*, London 1969.

Bhattacharyya, D.C., *Tantric Buddhist Iconographic Sources*, Manohar, New Delhi 1974; *Studies in Buddhist Iconography*, New Delhi 1978.

Bhattacharyya, Narendra Nath, *Indian Mother Goddess*, third revd. ed., Manohar, New Delhi 1999; *History of Researches on Indian Buddhism*, Munshiram Manoharlal, New Delhi 1982; *History of the Śakta Religion*, Munshiram Manoharlal, New Delhi, 2nd ed. 1996; *Indian Religious Historiography*, Munshiram Manoharlal, New Delhi 1996; *History of Tantric Religion*, 2nd ed., Manohar, New Delhi 1999; *Tantric Buddhism: Centennial Tribute to Dr. Benoytosh Bhattacharyya*, Manohar, New Delhi 1999.

Bhattacharyya-Sastri, Sukhamay, *Tantra Paricaya* (in Bengali), Visva-Bharati, Santiniketan 1952.

Bhattasali, N.K., *Iconography of Buddhist and Brahmanical Sculptures in the Dacca Museum*, Dacca 1929.

Bhāvanopaniṣad, published in *Tantrik Texts* XI, ed. by A. Avalon, London and Calcutta 1922.

Blofeld, J., *The Way to Power: A Practical Guide to the Tantric Mysticism of Tibet*, London 1970.

Bose, D.N. and H.L. Haldar, *Tantras: Their Philosophy and Occult Secrets*, Oriental Publishing Co., Calcutta 1956.

Bose, Manindra Mohan, *The Post-Caitanya Sahajiyā Cult*, Calcutta University, Calcutta 1930.

Brahmasaṃhitā with com. of Jīva Gosvamin, published in *Tantrik Texts* XV, Eng. trans. by Bhaktisiddhānta Sarasvatī, Gauḍiya Math, Madras 1931.

Briggs, George Weston, *Gorakhnath and the Kanphata Yogīs*, Calcutta, YMCA Publishing House 1938; repr., Motilal Banarasidass, Delhi 1989.

Bromage, B., *Tibetan Yoga*, London 1959.

Brooks, Douglas Renfrew, *The Secret of Three Cities: An Introduction to Hindu Śakta Tantrism.* Chicago University Press, Chicago 1990; *Wisdom: the Texts and Traditions of Śrīvidyā Śakta Tantrism in South India*, Albany State University of New York Press 1992.

Brown, C. Makenzie, *God as Mother: A Feminine Theology in India: A Historical and Theological Study of the Brahma-vaivarta Purāṇa*, Hartford Vt. Claude Stark and Co. 1974; *The Triumph of the Goddess: the Canonical Models and Theological Visions of the Devībhagavata Purāṇa*, Albany State University of New York Press 1990.

Brown, G.W., 'Prāṇa and Apāna' in *Journal of the American Oriental Society*, XXXIX, 1919, 104-12.

Cabeźon, José Ignacio (ed), *Buddhism, Sexuality and Gender*, Delhi 1992.

Caṇḍamahāroṣaṇatantra, George Christopher, New Haven 1974.

Carelli, Mario E. *Sekoddeśaṭīkā*, Gaekawad Oriental Series, XC, Baroda 1941.

Catuṣpītha-tantra, Haraprasad Sastri, *Catalogue of Palm-leaf and Selected Paper Manuscripts belonging to the Durban Library of Nepal*, Calcutta 1905.

Chakravarti, Chintaharan, *Tantras: Studies on the Religion and Literature*, Punthi Pustak, Calcutta 1963; 'Antiquity of Tantrism' in *Indian Historical Quarterly* VI, 1930, 114-26; 'The Soma and Saumya Sect of the Śaivas' in *I.H.Q.* VIII 1932, 221-3.

Chakravarti, Prabhat Chandra, *Doctrine of Śakti in Indian Literature*, General Printers and Publishers, Calcutta 1940.

Chandra, Lokesh, *Buddhist Iconography*, Compact ed., Aditya Prakashan, New Delhi 1987; *Maṇḍalas of the Tantrasamuccaya*, Delhi 1969.

Chandra, Pramod, 'The Kaula-Kāpālika Cult at Khajuraho' in *Lalit kalā*, I-II, 1955-6, 98-107.

Chang, C.Y., 'An Introduction to Taoist Yoga' in *Review of Religion*, XXI, New York 1956, 131-48.

Chang, Garma C.C., *Teachings of Tibetan Yoga*, New Hyde Park: University Books 1963; *Esoteric Teachings of Tibetan Tantra*, New York 1968.

Chatterjee, J.C., *Kashmir Saivism*, The Research Dept., Kashmir State, Srinagar 1914.

Chattopadhyaya, Alaka, *Atīśa and Tibet*, Calcutta 1967, repr., Motilal Banarasidass, Delhi 1981; *Catalogue of Tanjur and Kanjur*, Vol. I, Calcutta 1972; *Curāśi Siddher Kāhinī* (in Bengali), Calcutta 1988.

Chattopadhyaya, Debiprasad, *Lokāyata*, Peoples Publishing House, Delhi 1959; ed. *Tāranatha's History of Buddhism in India*, Eng. trans. by Lama Chimpa and Alaka Chattopadhyaya, Simla 1970, 2nd ed. Atlantic Highlands N.J., Humanities Press 1981.

Chattopadhyaya, Rasikmohan, *Vividha Tantra samgraha*, Collection of Tantric Texts (in Bengali), Calcutta 1874 ff., repr. by Nava Bharat Publishers, Calcutta 1978 ff.

Chou-yi-liang, 'Tantrism in China' *Harvard Journal of Asiatic Studies*, VIII, 1945, 241-332.

Cidgaganacandrikā, ascribed to Kālidāsa, ed. by Trivikrama Tirtha, in *Tantrik Texts* XX.

Cittaviśuddhiprakaraṇa, Sanskrit and Tibetan editions by Prabhubhai Bhikhabhai Patel, N.P. Visvabharati 1949.

Clark, W.E., *Two Lamaistic Pantheon*, 2 vols., Harvard Oriental Series, Cambridge Mass 1937; also New York Paragon Book Reprint Corporation 1965.

Coburn, Thomas C, *Devīmāhātmya: The Crystallization of the Goddess Tradition*, Motilal Banarasidass, Delhi 1985; *Encountering the Goddess*, State University of New York Press, Allany 1991.

Coomaraswamy, A.K., 'The Tantric Doctrine of Divine Biunity' in *Annals of the Bhandarkar Oriental Research Institute* XIX, 1938, 173-83.

Courtright, P.B., *Gaṇeśa*, New York 1986.

Dakṣiṇāmūrtisaṃhitā on *Śrīvidyopāsanā*, published in Sarasvati Bhavana Series, Varanasi.

Danielou, A., *Yoga: The Method of Reintegration*, London 1949.

Dargyay, Eva, *The Rise of Esoteric Buddhism in Tibet*, 1977, rev. ed., Motilal Banarasidass, Delhi 1979.

Das, H.C., *Tantrism: Cult of Yoginīs*, New Delhi 1980.

Das, Sukhendu Kumar, *Śakti or Divine Power*, Calcutta University Publication, Calcutta 1934.

Das, Upendra Kumar, *Śāstramūlak Bhāratīya Śaktisádhanā*, 2 vols. (in Bengali), Visva Bharati, Santiniketan 1966.

Dasgupta, Shashi Bhusan, *Obscure Religious Cults as Background of Bengali Literature*,

Calcutta University Publication, Calcutta 1946; subsequently reprinted as *Obscure Religious Cults*, Calcutta, Firma KLM 1962, repr. 1969, 1976; *An Introduction to Tantric Buddhism*, Calcutta University 1950, repr. 1958, 1974; *Bhārater Śakti Sādhanā O Śākta Sāhitya*, Sahitya Samsad, Calcutta 1960; 'Vajra and Vajrasattva' in *Indian Culture* VIII, 23-32.

Dasgupta, Surendra Nath, *Yoga as Philosophy and Religion*, Kegan Paul, London 1924, repr. Motilal Banarasidass, Delhi 1978; *Yoga Philosophy in Relation to other Systems of Indian Thought*, Calcutta University, Calcutta 1930; 'A General Introduction to Tantric Philosophy' in *Philosophical Essays*, Calcutta University 1951.

Dutta, Bhupendra Nath, *Mystic Tales of Lāmā Tāranātha: A Religio-Sociological History of Mahāyāna Buddhism*, Ramakrishna Mission Vedanta Math, Calcutta 1944.

David, Neel A., *With Mystics and Magicians in Tibet*, London 1931.

De, S.K., 'The Buddhist Tantric Sanskrit Literature of Bengal' in *New Indian Antiquary*, I, 1938, 1-23.

Dehejia, Vidya, *Yoginī Cult and Temples: A Tantric Tradition*, National Museum, New Delhi 1986.

Desai, Devangana, *Erotic Sculpture in India: A Socio-Cultural Study*, New Delhi, Tata Mcgrew Hill 1975; *The Religious Imagery of Khajuraho*, Project for Indian Cultural Publication IV, Mumbai 1996.

Dhargeye, Geshe Ngwang, *A Commentary on the Kālacakra Tantra*, trans. by Gelong Jhampa Kelsang (Allen Wallace), Library of Tibetan Books and Archives, Dharmasala 1985.

Dikshit, S.K., *The Mother Goddess*, Poona 1942.

Dikshitar, V.R.R., *The Lalitā Cult*, Madras University Publication, Madras 1942.

Dimock, Edward, *Place of the Hidden Moon: Erotic Mysticism in the Vaiṣṇava Sahajiyā Cult of Bengal*, Chicago University Press, Chicago 1966.

Douglas, N., *Tantra-Yoga*, Munshiram Manoharlal, New Delhi 1971.

Dowman Keith, *Masters of Mahāmudrā: Songs and Histories of Eighty four Buddhist Siddhas*, State University of New York Press, Albany 1985.

Dunuwila, Rohan A., *Śaiva Siddhānta Theology*, Delhi 1985.

Dvivedi, Hazari Prasad, *Nātha Sampradāya* (in Hindi), 3rd ed. Allahabad 1981.

Dyczkowski, Mark S.G., *The Canon of the Śaivāgama and the the Kubjikā Tantras of the Western Kaula Tradition*, Delhi 1989.

Eliade, Mircea, *Le Yoga; Immortalité et Liberté*, Paris 1954; Eng. trans. *Yoga: Immortality and Freedom*, Eng. tr. by W.R. Trusk, Bollingen Series LVI, New York 1958, 2nd ed. Princeton University Press 1969, *Metallurgy, Magic and Alchemy*, Paris 1938; (ed) *The Encyclopaedia of Religion*, Macmillian, New York 1986.

Erndl, Kathleen M., *Victory to the Mother: The Hindu Goddess of Northwest India in Myth, Ritual and Symbol*, Oxford University Press, New York 1993.

Evans-Wentz, W.Y. *Tibet's Great Yogi Milerapa*, Oxford 1928; *The Tibetan Book of the Dead*, London 1935; *Tibetan Yoga and Secret Doctrines*, Oxford 1935, 1958.

Ewing, A.H. 'The Śāradātilaka Tantra' in *Journal of the American Oriental Society*, VI, 1902, 65-76.

Farquhar, J.N., *An Outline of Religious Literature of India*, Oxford University Press, Oxford 1920; repr. Motilal Banarasidass, Delhi 1967.

Farrow, G.W. and I. Menon, *The Concealed Essence of the Hevajra Tantra with the Commentary of Yogaratnamālā*, Motilal Banarasidass, Delhi 1992.

Filliozat, J., *The Classical Doctrine of Indian Medicine*, Eng. trans. by D.R. Chanana, Munshiram Manoharlal, New Delhi 1964.

Gaṇapatitattva, Old Javanese Text, edited, annotated and translated by Sudarsadevi Singhal, International Academy of Sciences, New Delhi 1958.

Gandharva-tantra, ed. by Ramchandra Kak and Haribhadra Sastri, Srinagar 1934.

Garrison, O.V., *Tantra: The Yoga of Sex*, New York 1964.

Gautamīya-tantra, published in Rasikmohan's *Vividha Tantra Saṃgraha*, Calcutta 1876.

Gayatrī-tantra, published in Rasikmohan's *Vividha Tantra Saṃgraha*, Calcutta 1876.

Getty, Alice, *The Gods of Northern Buddhism,* Oxford 1914.

Gheraṇḍa Saṃhitā, The Panini Office, Allahabad 1914; Venkateswar Press, Bombay 1956; Eng. trans. by S.C. Vasu, Adyar Library, Madras 1895.

Ghosh, Atal Behari, *Śiva and Śakti*, Rajshahi 1935.

Glassenapp, A.V., 'Tantrismus und Śaktimus' in *Ostasiatesche Zeitschrift* XII (N.S.) Berlin 1936, 120-33; 'Die Entestehung des Vajrayāna' in *Zeitschrift der Deutschen Morgenländische Gesellchaft,* XC, 1936, 546-72.

Gorakṣasiddhāntasaṃgraha, ed. by Gopinath Kaviraj, Prince of Wales Sarasvati Bhavana Texts, no. XVIII, Varanasi 1925.

Gordon, Antoinette K., *The Iconography of Tibetan Lamaism,* New York 1939, Tokyo 1959, *Foundation of Tibetan Mysticism*, York Beach 1969.

Goudriaan, Teun, ed., *Ritual and Speculation in Early Tantrism*, Studies in Honour of Andre Padoux, State University of New York Press, Albany 1992.

Goudriaan, Teun and Sanjukta Gupta, *Hindu Tantric and Śākta Literature, A History of Indian Literature* II, 2, ed. by Jan Gonda, Otto Harrassowitz, Weisbaden 1981.

Guenther, Harbert, *The Jewel Ornament of Liberation*, London 1959; *Yuganaddha: The Tantric View of Life*, Oxford 1963, 1969, paperback ed. Boulder, Shambhala 1976; *Life and Teachings of Naropā* 1963, repr. Oxford University Press 1975; 'The Concept of Mind in Buddhist Tantrism' in *Journal of Oriental Studies* , Hong Kong, July 1956.

Guha, A., 'Rasa Cult in Caitanya Caritāmṛta' in *Sir Asutosh Mukherjee Silver Jubilee Vol.*, III 1926-7, 368-88.

Guhyasamāja-tantra or *Tathāgataguhyaka*, ed. by Benoytosh Bhattacharyya, Gaekwad's Oriental Series, LIII, Baroda 1931.

Guleri, Vidyadhar Sharma, *Female Deities in Vedic and Epic Literature*, Nag Publishers, Delhi 1990.

Gupta, Sanjukta, *Lakṣmītantra: A Pāñcarātra Text*, E.J. Brill, Leiden 1972.

Gupta, Sanjukta, Jan Hoens Dirk and Goudriaan Teun, *Hindu Tantrism*, E.J. Brill, Leiden 1979.

Gyatso, Geshe Kelsang, *Clear Light of Bliss: Mahāmudrā in Vajrayāna Buddhism*, trans. Tenzin Norbu, Wisdom, London 1982; *Guide to Dākinīland: A Commentary to the Highest Yoga-Tantra Practice of Vajrayoginī*, Tharpa, London 1991.

Haṃsavilāsa, published in Gaekwad's Oriental Series, Baroda 1937.

Harding, Elisabeth U., *Kālī: The Black Goddess of Dakshineswar*, Nicolas-Hays, York Beach 1993.

Harman, William P., *The Sacred Marriage of a Hindu Goddess*, Indiana University Press, Bloomington 1989.

Haṭhayogapradīpikā, Sri Venkateswar Press 1952; Eng. trans. by P. Singh, Allahabad 1945, by T.R.S. Ayyangar, Adyar Library 1933.

Hawley, John Stratton and Donna Marie Wulff (eds.), *Devī: Goddesses of India*, University of California, Berkeley, Los Angles 1996; *The Divine Consort: Rādhā and the Goddesses of India*, Berkeley and Motilal Banarasidass, Delhi 1982.

Hazra, R.C., *Studies in the Puranic Records on Rites and Customs*, Dacca 1940; *Studies in the Upapurāṇas*, Vol. II *Śākta and Non-Sectarian Upapurāṇs*, Govt. Sanskrit College, Calcutta 1963; 'Influence of Tantra on the Tattava of Raghunandana' *Indian Historical Quarterly* IX. 1933, 678-704; 'Influence of Tantra on Smṛtinibandhas' in *Annals of Bhandarkar Oriental Research Institute*, XV, 220-35, XVI, 203-11.

Hevajra-tantra, ed. and trans. by D.L. Snellgrove, 2 vols., Oxford University Press 1959.

Hopkins, Jeffery (ed), *Kālacakratantra: Exposition of Dalai Lama XIV*, Dharmasala 1985.

Ironbiter, Suzanne, *Devī*, Yuganta Press, Stamford, Conn. 1987.

Īśānaśivagurudevapaddhati, ed. in Trivandrum Sanskrit Series by T. Ganapati Sastri 1920; with intro. by N.P. Unni, 4 vols., Bharatiya Vidya Pakashan, Varanasi 1988.

Īśvarapratyabhijñāvimarśinī, pt. I, Kashmir Series of Texts and Studies, no. XXII, 1918, pt. II, no. XXXIII, 1922.

Jackson, Roger, *Wheel of Time: The Kālacakra Context*, New York 1991.

James, E.O., *Cult of the Mother Goddess*, New York 1959.

Jayakar, Pupul, *The Earth Mother: Legends, Ritual Arts and Goddesses of India*, Harper and Row, San Francisco 1990.

Jayākhya Saṃhitā, ed. with intro. by E. Krishnamacharya, Gaekwad's Oriental Series, LIV, Baroda 1931, 2nd ed. GOS, Baroda 1967.

Jhaveri, M.B., *Comparative and Critical Study of the Mantra-śāstra* (with special treatment of Jaina Mantraśāstra), Sarabhai Manilal Nawal, Ahmedabad 1944.

Jikido, Takasaki, *A Study of the Ratnagotravibhāga*, Rome 1966.

Jñānārṇava-tantra, pub. by Anandasrama Press, Poona.

Jñānasiddhi of Indrabhūti, ed. by B.T. Bhattarcharyya, Gaekwad's Oriental Series, XLIV, Baroda 1929.

Jung, C.J. *Maṇḍala Symbolism*, trans. by R.F.C. Hull, Princeton 1972.

Kālacakra-tantra, Cambridge University Library. Ms. Add. No. 1364; Critical ed. by Biswanath Banerjee, Calcutta 1985.

Kālī-tantra, Saṃskṛta Sāhitya Pariṣad Granthāvali Series No. 2, Calcutta 1922; ed. by Pandit Nityananda Smrititirtha, Sans. text with Bengali translation, Nava Bharat, Calcutta 1981.

Kālivilāsa-tantra, ed. by Arthur Avalon in *Tantrik Texts*, Vol. VI, Calcutta 1917.

Kāmakalāvilāsa of Puṇyanandanātha with *Cidvallī* com. by Natanānandanātha, Arthur Avalon *Tantrik Texts X*, repr. Ganesh and Co., Madras 1953.

Kāmākhyātantra, published in Rasikmohan's *Vividha Tantra Saṃgraha*, Calcutta 1876, ed. by Jyotirlal Dasa, Sans. text with Bengali translation and commentary, Nava Bharat, Calcutta 1978.

Kandaswamy, S.N., *Buddhism as Expounded in the Maṇimekalai*, Annamalainagar 1978.

Kane, P.V., *History of Dharmaśāstra*, Vol. V, Bhahdarkar Oriental Research Institute, Poona 1962.

Kapali, Sastry T.V., *The Veda and the Tantra*, Madras 1951.

Karambelkar, V.W, 'Matsyendranatha and His Yoginī Cult' in *Indian Historical Quarterly*, XXXI, 1955.

Kaulajñānanirṇaya, ed. by P.C. Bagchi, Calcutta Sanskrit Series III, Calcutta 1934; Eng. trans. by Michael Magee, Varanasi 1986.

Kaulamārgarahasya, ed. with expository notes by Sastis Chandra Siddhantabhuṣana, Sāhitya Pariṣad Granthāvalī, No. 76, Calcutta.

Kaulāvalinirṇaya of Jñānānandagiri, ed. by Arthur Avalon, *Tantrik Texts* XIV, Madras 1925.

Kaulāvalitantra, published in Rasikmohan's *Vividha Tantra Saṃgraha*, Calcutta 1876.

Kaviraj Gopinath, *Āgam āur Tantraśāstra* (in Hindi), Delhi 1984; *Tantrik Vāṅmaya mein Śākta Ḍṛṣṭi* (in Hindi), Patna 1963; *Tantric Sādhanā O Siddhānta*, Burdwan University, Calcutta 1963; 'Exposition of the Śākta Belief' in *History of Philosophy: Eastern and Western*, ed. S. Radhakrishnan, Vol. I, Delhi 1953, 401-28; 'Philosophy of Tripurā Tantra', Saraswati Bhavana Studies, 1934, IX, 85-8; 'Some Aspects of the Philosophy of Śākta Tantras' in ibid 1938, X, 21-7.

Khanna, Madhu, *Tantra*, London 1979.

Kinsley, David, *Hindu Goddesses: Visions of the Divine Feminine in the Hindu Religious Tradition*, Berkeley, University of California Press, Los Angeles 1986; *The Sword and the Flute: Kālī and Kṛṣṇa*, University of California Press, Berkeley 1975.

Kooij, K.R. Van, *Worship of the Goddess according to the Kālikā Purāṇa*, E.J. Brill, Leiden 1972.

Kramadīpikā with Exposition by Govinda Bhattacharyya, Chowkhamba Sanskrit Series, Varanasi, No. 233; ed. R.C. Kak and H. Sastri, Srinagar 1929.

Kubjikāmata, Manuscript No. 3174 of the Asiatic Society of Bengal.

Kulacuḍāmaṇi-tantra, ed. in Avalon's *Tantrik Texts* by G.C. Vedantatirtha, Vol. IX, Calcutta 1915.

Kulārṇava-tantra, published version in Rasikmohan's *Vividha Tantra Saṃgraha* re-edited by U.K. Das, Nava Bharat, Calcutta 1979; ed. in Avalon's *Tantrik Texts* by Taranath Vidyaratna, Calcutta 1916; repr. Motilal Banarasidass, Delhi 1975.

Kumar, Pushpendra, *Śakti Cult in Ancient India with Special Reference to the Puranic Literature*, Bharatiya Publishing House, Varanasi 1974.

Lakṣmī-tantra, text ed. by V. Krishnamacharya, Adyar, Madras 1959; trans. in English by Sanjukta Gupta, E.J. Brill, Leiden 1972.

Lalitāsahasranāma with Bhāskara Rāya's *Saubhāgyabhāskara*, com. Nirnaya Sagar Press, Bombay 1935; ed. Suryanarayana Murthy, Bharatiya Vidya Bhawan, Bombay 1975.

Lalye, P.G., *Studies in the Devībhāgavata*, Popular Prakashan, Bombay 1973.

Leadbreath, C.W., The *Cakras*, Madras 1927, repr. Madras 1966; repr. London 1972.

Leonard, G.S., 'Notes on Kanphaṭa Yogis' in *Indian Antiquary*, VII 298 ff.

Lessing, F.D. and Alex Wayman, *Mkhas grub rje's Fundamentals of the Buddhist Tantras*, trans. from the Tibetan, The Hague 1968.

Levi Sylvain, 'On a Tantric Fragment from Kucha' in *Indian Historical Quarterly* XII, 1936, 197-274.

Lopez, Donald S. (Jr), *Religions of India in Practice*, Princeton Readings in Religious, Princeton University Press, Princeton, New Jersey 1995.

Lorenzen, David N., *The Kāpālikas and Kālāmukhas: Two Lost Saivite Sects*, Thomson (India) Press, New Delhi 1972.

Mahākala Saṃhitā, pub. by G.N. Jha, Kendriya Saṃskṛta Vidyapitha, Allahabad 1971.

Mahākala-tantra, ed. by Stablein William George, Columbia University 1976.

Mahānirvāṇa-tantra, with com. of Hariharānanda Bhāratī, ed. by Arthur Avalon in *Tantrik Texts* XIII, Ganesh and Co., Madras 1929; 3rd ed. 1953 slightly different, Eng. trans. by Avalon, *The Great Liberation*, Calcutta 1913, 1929, repr. Dover Publications, New York 1972.

Mahāpīṭhanirūpaṇa, Asiatic Society of Bengal, Manuscript Nos. 3400, 5303.

Maheśvara-tantra, pub. in Chowkhamba Sanskrit Series, Varanasi.

Maity Pradyot Kumar, *Historical Studies in the Cult of the Goddess Mānasā*, Punthi Pustak, Calcutta 1966.

Mallmann, Marie T. de, *Introduction le Iconographique du Tantrism Buddhique*, Paris 1975.

Mallik Kalyani, *Nath Sampradāyer Itihās*, in Bengali, Calcutta 1950.

Mantramahodadhi of Mahīdhara with his own commentary, pub. by Venkateswar Press, Bombay 1908.

Māṭrkābheda-tantra, ed. by Chintamani Bhattacharya, Calcutta Sanskrit Series, Vol. VII, Calcutta.

Māṭrkācakraviveka of Svatantrānandanātha with com. on Śivānanda, pub. in Sarasvati Bhavana Series, Varanasi 1934.

Māyātantra, ed. from Rasikmohan's Collection by Jyotirlal Das, Nava Bharat, Calcutta 1988.

McDaniel, June, *The Madness of the Saints: Ecstatic Religion in Bengal*, Chicago University Press, Chicago and London 1989.

Merutantra, published by Venkateswar Press, Bombay 1908.

Mishra, Ramprasad, *Sahajayāna*, Calcutta 1991.

Mitra, Debala, *Buddhist Monuments*, Sāhitya Samsad, Calcutta 1969.

Mitra, K.P., 'Magic and Miracle in Jaina Literature' in *Indian Historical Quarterly*, XV, 1939.

Mitra, S.C., 'On the Cult of Gorakṣanātha in Eastern Bengal' in *Journal of the Dept. of Letters*, Calcutta University XIV, 1927, 1-14; 'On the cult of Gorakṣanātha in the District of Rangpur in Northern Bengal' in *Journal of the Asiatic Society of Bengal* XIV, 1927-8, 1-5.

Mitra, S.K. (ed), *East Indian Bronzes*, Calcutta University, Calcutta 1979.

Mojumdar, Atindra, *The Caryāpadas*, 2nd ed., Naya Prokash, Calcutta 1973.

Mookerjee, Ajit, *Kali: The Feminine Force*, London, Thames and Hudson 1998; *Tantra Art*, Delhi 1966; *Tantra Āsana*, Basil 1971; *The Tantric Way* (with M. Khanna), New York 1977; *Yoga Art*, London 1975.

Mookherjee, R.K., *Rasajalanidhi or Ocean of Indian Chemistry and Alchemy*, 5 vols., Calcutta 1926-38.

Mullin, Glenz H., *Meditations on the Lower Tantras, etc.*, Dharmasala 1983.

Nagaswamy, R., *Tantric Cult of South India*, Delhi 1982.

Nallaswami, Pillai J.M., *Studies in Śaiva Siddhānta*, Madras 1911.

Nath, Radhagovinda, *The Yogis of Bengal*, Mani Bhusan Nath, Calcutta 1909.

Neumann, Erich, *The Great Mother: An Analysis of the Archetype*, trans. by Ralph Manheim 1955, 2nd ed. Pantheon, New York 1969.

Niruttara-tantra, pub. in Rasikmohan's *Vividha Tantra Saṃgraha*, Calcutta 1876.

Nirvāna-tantra, published in Rasikmohan's *Vividha Tantra Saṃgraha*, Calcutta 1876.

Niṣpannayogāvalī of Abhayākaragupta, ed. by Benoytosh Bhattacharyya, Gaekwad's Oriental Series CIX, Baroda 1949, iconological passages quoted in Roman characters and translated into English in *Indian Buddhist Iconography*, Calcutta 1958.

Nityaṣoḍaśikārṇava, part of *Vāmakeśvara* with com. *Setubandha* by Bhāskara Rāya, Anandasrama, Poona 1944; ed. by Vraj Vallabh Dvivedi, S.S. University Yogaratna Granthamālā, Varanasi 1968.

Nityotsava of Umānandanātha, pt. II of *Parasurāmakalpasūtra* pub. in Gaekwad's Oriental Series, XXII, 1923.

Obermiller, E., *History of Buddhism in India and Tibet* by *Bu-ston,* trans., London 1931-2.

Obeyesekere Gananath, *The Cult of the Goddess Pattinī*, Chicago University Press, Chicago 1984.

O'Flaherty, W.D., *Asceticism and Eroticism in the Mythology of Śiva*, Oxford University Press, London 1973.

Olson, Carl (ed.), *The Book of the Goddess Past and Present: An Introduction to Her Religion*, Crossroad, New York 1987; *The Mysterious Play of Kālī: An Interpretative Study of Ramakrishna*, Scholars Press, Atalanta 1990.

Oman, J.C., *The Mystics, Ascetics and Saints of India*, London 1913.

Padma-saṃhitā, ed. by S. Padmanabhan and R.N. Sampath, Pancaratra Pariśodhana Parishad, Madras 1974, 1982.

Padma-tantra, pub. by Śrīvidyā Press, Mysore 1888.

Padukāpañcaka, ed. in Avalon's *Tantrik Texts*, Vol. II by Taranath Vidyaratna, Calcutta 1913.

Pal, D.N., *Śiva and Śakti: An Elaborate Discourse on Hindu Religion and Mythology*, 2 vols. Calcutta 1910.

Pal Pratapaditya, *Hindu Religion and Iconology according to the Tantrasāra*, Los Angeles 1981.

Pañcakrama, ed. by Louis de la Vallée Poussin, Grand 1896.

Pande, K.C., *Abhinavagupta: An Historical and Philosophical Study*, Chowkhamba Sanskrit Series, Varanasi 1968.

Pandit, M.P., *Gems from the Tantras*, Madras 1967; *Studies on the Tantras and Veda*, Madras 1967; *Light on Tantra*, Madras 1957.

Panigrahi, K.C., 'Obscene Sculptures in Orissan Temples' in *Proceedings of the Indian History Congress*, VII. 94 ff.

Paramārthasāra of Abhinavagupta ed. with Yogirāja's Com. in Kashmir Series of Texts and Studies, Srinagar 1916; Eng. trans. by L.D. Barnett in *Journal of the Royal Asiatic Society* 1910, 707-47.

Parama-saṃhitā, ed. and Eng. trans. by S. Krishnaswami Aiyanagar, Gaekwad's Oriental Series, LXXXVII, Baroda 1940.

Pārānanda-sutra, pub. in Gaekwad's Oriental Series, Baroda 1931.

Parasurāmakalpasūtra with com. *Saubhāgyodaya* of Rameśvara, pt. I, pub. in Gaekwad's Oriental Series, XXLL-XXIII, Baroda 1923.

Parātriṃśikā, pub. in Kashmir Sanskrit Series XVIII, Srinagar 1918.

Pāśupata Sūtras, ed. with Kauṇḍinya's *pañcārthabhāṣya* by R. Ananthakrishna Sastri, Trivandrum Sanskrit Series No. CXLIII, Trivandrum 1940; trans. Haripada Chakraborti, Academic Publishers, Calcutta 1970.

Patavardhan, R.V., 'Rasavidyā or Alchemy in Ancient India' in *Proc. and Transactions of the First Oriental Conference 1919,* Poona 1920.

Pauṣkara-saṃhitā, ed. by Y.S. Sampathkumara Ramanuja Muni, Melkota 1934.

Pawate, S.D., *Viraśaiva Philosophy of the Śaivāgamas*, Hubli 1927.

Payne, Ernest A., *The Śāktas: An Introductory and Comparative Study*, Oxford University Press, London 1933.

Pillai, G.S., *Introduction to the History of Śaiva Siddhānta*, Annamalainagar 1948.

Pīthanirṇaya, Manuscript No. 196 of the Asiatic Society of Bengal.

Pott, P.H., *Yoga and Yantra: Their Interrelation and Their Significance for Indian Archaeology*, Martiners Nijhoff, The Hague 1966.

Prajñopāyaviniścayasiddhi of Anaṅgavajra, ed. by Benoytosh Bhattacharyya, Gaekwad's Oriental Series, LXIV, Baroda 1929.

Prāṇatoṣaṇī-tantra, compiled in 1820 by Ramatosana Bhattacharyya under the patronage of Babu Pranakrishna Biswas of Khardaha. Published in Bengali characters by Vasumati Sahitya Mandir, Calcutta.

Pranjoti, V., *Śaiva Siddhānta in the Meykanda Śāstra*, London 1938.

Prapañcasāra, ascribed to Śaṅkarācārya, with Com. *Vivaraṇa* by Padmapāda, pub. in Avalon's *Tantrik Texts* III and later in a new ed. in Vols. XVIII-XIX, 1929.

Pratyabhijñāhṛdaya, pub. in Kashmir Series of Texts and Studies III, 1911; Eng. trans. *Secret of Recognition* with notes by K.F. Leidecker, Adyar Library, Madras 1938.

Preston James J. (ed.), *Mother Worship: Theme and Variations*, University of North Carolina Press, Chapel Hill 1982.

Przylusky, J., 'Mudrā' in *Indian Culture*, II, 1934, 715-19.

Puraścaryārṇava, compiled by Nepalādhirāja Pratāpacandra Shah Bahadur Varma, pt. I, Calcutta 1901; pt. II, 1902; pt. III, 1904.

Rājamārtaṇḍa of King Bhoja, ed. and Eng. trans. by R. Mitra, Bib. Ind. Calcutta 1883; ed. by Jadavji Tricumji Acharya, Ayurveda Granthamala No. 4; 2nd ed. Bombay 1924.

Rasārṇava, ed. by P.C. Ray and H.C. Kabiratna, Bib. Ind. Calcutta 1910.

Ratnaketudhāraṇī, Sanskrit ed. N. Dutta, *Gilgit Manuscripts* I, Srinagar 1939.

Rawson, Philip, *The Art of Tantra*, London 1978.

Ray, Prafulla Chandra, *History of Indian Chemistry*, Vol. I, 1902; Vol. II, 1908, now incorporated in the *History of Chemistry in Ancient and Medieval India*, ed. by Priyadaranjan Ray, Calcutta 1956.

Rele, G., *Mysterious Kulakuṇḍalinī*, Bombay 1927.

Rendel, P., *Introduction to the Cakra*, Northamptonshire 1974.

Rhie, Marylin M. and Robert A.F. Thurman, *Wisdom and Compassion: The Sacred Art of Tibet*, New York 1991.

Rieker, H.V., *The Yoga of Light: Haṭhayogapradīpikā*, New York 1972.

Robinson, J.B., *Buddha's Lions: Liver of Eighty Four Siddhas*, Berkeley 1979.

Roerich, G.W., *The Blue Annals*, 1949, 2nd ed., Motilal Banarasidass, Delhi 1976.

Roerich, G.W. and A.S. Altekar, *Biography of Dharmasvāmin*, Patna 1959.

Rudrayāmala, Uttaratantra, ed. by Jivananda Vidyasagar, Bib. Ind., 2nd ed. Calcutta 1892; ed. by Bhagiratha Prasad Tripathi, Vagesvari Yogitantra Granthamala No. 7, S.S. University, Varanasi 1980.

Rūpamaṇḍana, pub. in Calcutta Sanskrit Series, No. XII; ed. by Balaram Srivastava with Hindi trans., Motilal Banarasidass, Varanasi 1964.

Sādhanamālā, ed. Benoytosh Bhattacharyya, Gaekwad's Oriental Series, XXVI, XLI, Baroda 1925, 1928. Many *sadhanas* are published in Roman character and with English trans. in *Indian Buddhist Iconography*, Calcutta 1958.

Śāktānandataraṅgiṇī, pub. in Rasikmohan's *Vividha Tantra Samgraha*, Calcutta 1876; ed. with Bengali trans. by Panchanan Sastri, Tattvaprakas Granthamālā I, Calcutta 1943.

Śāktapramoda, compiled by Sri Rajadevananda Simha, pub. by Venkateswar Press, Bombay 1951.

Śatisaṅgama-tantra, ed. by B.T. Bhattacharyya, Gaekwad's Oriental Series LXI, XCI, CIV, Baroda 1932-47.

Śaktisūtra attributed to Agastya, pub. in Sarasvati Bhavana Studies, X.

Sāmrājyalakṣmīpīṭhikā, pub. in Tanjore Sarasvati Mahal Series.

Sanatkumāra-tantra, pub. by Jyestharam Mukundji, Bombay 1905.

Śaṅkaravijaya, ed. J. Tarkapanchanan, Bib. Ind. Nos. 46, 137-8, Calcutta 1868.

Śāṅkhyakārikā, ed. with notes and Eng. trans. by S.S. Suryanarayana Sastri, Madras 1948.

Śāradātilaka of Lakṣmana Deśikendra with com. *Padārthādarśa* of Rāghavabhaṭṭa, text and intro. by Arthur Avalon, *Tantrik Texts* XVI-XVII, 1933; repr. Motilal Banarasidass, Delhi 1982.

Saraswati, S.K., *Tantrayāna Art*: *An Album*, Asiatic Society, Calcutta 1977.

Sastri, D.R., 'The Lokāyatas and Kāpālikas' in *Indian Historical Quarterly*, VII, 1931, 152-7.

Sastri, Haraprasad, *Advayavajrasaṃgraha*, Gaekwad's Oriental Series, XI, Baroda 1927; *Bauddha Gān O Dohā*, Calcutta 1916; *Catalogue of Palm-leaf and Selected Paper Manuscripts in the Durbar Library of Nepal*, Calcutta 1905.

Sastri, Hirananda, *Origin and Cult of Tārā*, MASI, XX, Calcutta 1912.

Sastri, M.R., *The Tantrasāra of Abhinavagupta*, Bombay 1918.

Sastri, R. Ananthakrishna, *Lalitāsahasranāma-stotra*, trans. Adyar Library, Madras 1925, *Śakti Sūtra* with notes, Adyar Library, Madras 1896.

Sastri, Vidhusekhar, 'Sandhyābhasa' in *Indian Historical Quarterly*, IX, 1928, 287-96.

Ṣaṭcakranirūpaṇa of Pūrṇānanda, *Tantrik Texts* II, Calcutta 1913; with Kālīcaraṇa's com. and Eng. trans. by J. Woodroffe, *The Serpent Power*, 7th ed. Madras 1964.

Ṣaṭcakravivṛti, Tantrik Texts II, Calcutta 1913.

Saubhāgyabhāskara, com. on Lalitāsahasranāma by Bhāskara Rāya, Nirnaya Sagar Press, Bombay 1935.

Saundaryalaharī ascribed to Śaṅkarācārya, ed. by J. Woodroffe, Madras, Adyar Library 1937; with three coms. and Eng. trans. by Woodroffe, Ganesh and Co., Madras 1953; trans. *The Ocean of Divine Beauty*, by V.K. Subramanian, Motilal Banarasidass, Delhi 1977; ed. with Eng. trans. by W. Norman Brown, Cambridge Mass, Harvard University Press 1958.

Saunders, E.D., *Mudrā*, London 1966.

Sekoddeśaṭīkā of Nāḍapāda, ed. by Marie E. Carelli, Gaekwad's Oriental Series 1941.

Sen, Sukumar, *The Great Goddess in Indic Tradition*, Papyrus, Calcutta 1983.

Shah, U.P., 'A Peep in the Early History of Tantra' in *Bharata-kaumudī* II, Allahabad 1947.

Sharma, R.S., 'Material Milieu of Tantricism' in *Indian Society*: *Historical Probings*, in Memory of D.D. Kosambi, New Delhi 1977.

Shaw, Miranda, *Passionate Enlightenment*: *Women in Tantric Buddhism*, Princeton University Press, Princeton 1994.

Shendge, Malati J., *Advayasiddhi*: *A Study*, M.S. University Oriental Series, No. 8. Baroda Oriental Institute, 1964.

Siddhasiddhāntasārasaṃgraha, ed. by Gopinath Kaviraj, Sarasvati Bhavana Texts, No. XIII, Varanasi 1925.

Śikṣāsamuccaya of Śāntideva, ed. by C. Bendall, in Bibliotheca Buddhica Series, St. Petersburg 1897.

Silburn, Lilian, *Kuṇḍalinī*: *The Energy of the Depths*, trans. Jacques Gontier, State University of New York Press, Albany 1988.

Singh, Mohan, *Gorakhnath and Medieval Hindu Mysticism*, Lahore 1937.

Sircar, D.C., 'The Śākta Pithas' in *Journal of the Asiatic of Bengal* (Letters) 1948, repr. with Index by N.N. Bhattacharyya, Motilal Banarasidass, Delhi 1973; (ed.) *The Śakti Cult and Tārā*, Calcutta University, Calcutta 1969.

Śivadṛṣṭi, Kashmir Sanskrit Series, No. 54, Srinagar 1934.

Śivādvaitanirṇaya of Appaya Dikṣita, ed. with intro. and notes by S.S. Suryanarayana Sastri, Madras 1930.

Sivananda Svami, *Kuṇḍalinī Yoga*, Divine Life Society 1971.

Śivaprakāśam by Umāpati, Eng. trans. by H.R. Hoisington in *Journal of American Oriental Society* IV, 125-244.

Śivasūtravārtikam, pub. in Kashmir Series of Texts and Studies, IV-V, Srinagar 1897.

Snellgrove, D.L., *Hevajratantra*, ed. and trans., 2 vols., Oxford University Press, 1959; *Buddhist Himalaya*, Bruno Cassirer, Oxford 1957.

Snellgrove, D.L. and Skorupski Tadeusz, *The Cultural Heritage of Ladakh*, Prajna Press, Boulder 1977.

Somaśambhupaddhati, ed. with French trans. by Hélène Brunner-Lachaux, Institute Français d'Indologie, No. XXV, Pondicherry, in three parts, 1963, 1968, 1977.

Sragdharāstotra of Sarvajña, ed. by S.C. Vidyabhusan, Bib. Ind. Calcutta 1908.

Śrīcakrasambhāra-tantra, Tibetan text and Eng. trans. by Lama Kazi Dawa Samdup and in Avalon's *Tantrik Texts* VII, Calcutta 1919.

Śrī Kālisahasranāma, trans. Premalata Paliwal, Nilima Harjal, Delhi 1979.

Śrīkarabhāsya, ed. by G.C. Hayavadan Rao, Bangalore 1936.

Śrīsahajasiddhi, Shendge Malati J., *Indo-Iranian Journal* X, 2-3, 1967, 126-49.

Śrītattvacintāmaṇi, ed. by Narendra Candra Vedantatirtha, Metropolitan Printing and Publishing House, Calcutta 1936.

Srivasta, M.C.P., *Mother Goddess in Indian Art, Archaeology and Literature*, Agam Kala Prakasan, Delhi 1979.

Śrividyāratnasūtra, attributed to Gauḍapāda with com. of Śaṅkara, ed. by Gopinath Kaviraj in Sarasvati Bhavana Text Series, No. XI, Varanasi 1924.

Suryanarayana Sastri, S.S., *The Śivādvaita of Śrīkaṇṭha*, Madras 1930.

Śyāmārahasya of Pūrṇānanda, pub. in Rasikmohan's *Vividha Tantra Saṃgraha*, Calcutta 1976.

Tajima, R., *The Enlightenment of Vairocana*, Motilal Banarasidass, Delhi 1992.

Tantrābhidhāna, with *Bījanighaṇṭu* and *Mudrānighaṇṭu*, ed. by Arthur Avalon, *Tantric Texts* I, Calcutta 1913.

Tantrāloka of Abhinavagupta with com. of Jayaratha, pub. in Kashmir Series of Texts and Studies, Vols. I-XI, Series Vols. XXIII, XXVIII-XXX, LII, LVII, Srinagar 1918-36.

Tantrarājatantra with com. *Manoramā* by Subhagānanda, pub. in Avalon's *Tantrik Texts*, VIII, repr. Ganesh and Co., Madras 1954.

Tantrasāra of Abhinavagupta, Kashmir Sanskrit Series, No. XVII, Srinagar 1918.

Tantrasāra of Kṛṣṇānanda, pub. by Vasumati Sahitya Mandir, Calcutta, ed. by Prasanna Kumar Sastri; also by Chowkhamba, Varanasi, 10th ed. 1934.

Tārābhaktisudhārṇava of Narasiṃha Ṭhakkura, ed. by Panchanan Bhattacharyya in Avalon's *Tantrik Texts*, XXI, 1940.

Tārārahasya of Brahmānanda, pub. in Rasikmohan's *Vividha Tantra Saṃgraha*, Calcutta 1876.

Tārā-tantra, ed. by Girish Chandra Vedāntaratna in Gaudagranthamāla I, general editor, A.K. Maitra, Varendra Research Society 1913.

Tattvasaṃgraha of Śāntarakṣita with com. of Kamalaśīla, ed. by E. Krishnamacarya with a Foreward by B.T. Bhattacharyya, Gaekwad's Oriental Series XXX-XXXI, Baroda 1926; Eng. trans. by G. Jha, GOS, LXX, LXXXIII, Baroda 1937, 1939.

Templeman, David, *Tāranatha's Life of Kṛṣṇācārya* (Kanha), trans. Library of Tibetan Works and Archives, Dharmasala 1989.

Thomas, P., *Kāmakālā: Hindu Ritual or Love*, Bombay 1960.

Thompson, Edward J. and Marshman Splender Arthur, trans. *Bengal Religious Lyrics, Śākta*, Association Press, Calcutta 1923.

Tiwari, J.N., *Goddess Cults in Ancient India*, Sundeep Prakashan, Delhi 1985.

Tripurārahasya of Haritāyana, with com. called *Tātparyaṭīkā* of Śrīnivāsa, Sarasvati Bhavana Series No. XV, pt. I, Varanasi 1925.

Tripurāsārasamuccaya of Nāgabhaṭṭa with com. of Govindācarya ed. by Jīvananda Vidyāsagar, Bib. Ind., Calcutta 1897.

Tucci, Giuseppe, *The Theory and Practice of the Maṇḍala*, London 1961; *Tibetan Painted Scrolls*, 2 vols. Rome 1949; 'Apropos the Legend of Naropā' in *Journal of the Royal Asiatic Society*, 1935, 677-88; 'Some Glosses upon the Guhyasamāja' in *Melanges Chinois et Bouddhiques* III 339-53; Brussels 1934-5; *Ratilīlā: An Interpretation of the Tantric Imagery of Temples of Nepal*, Geneva 1969; *The Religion of Tibet* Berkeley 1980.

Valee, Poussin Louis de la, 'Tantric Buddhism' in Encyclopae*dia of Religion and Ethics*, ed. J. Hastings, Edinburgh 1902.

Van Lysebath, Andre, *Tantra, le Culte de la Féminité*, Flammarion, Paris 1988.

Varivasyārahasya of Bhāskara Rāya, ed. by Pandit Sibnarayana Sastri, Adyar Library, 1934, 1941.

Vimalaprabhā, pub. in three parts by the Central Institute of Higher Tibetan Studies, Sarnath 1986, 1994, eds.: Jagannath Upadhyaya, Vraj Ballabh Dvivedi and Janardar Sastri Pandey.

Vira, Raghu and Lokesh Chandra, *A New Tibeto-Mongol Pantheon*, New Delhi 1967.

Vira, Raghu and Q. Taki, *A Dictionary of Tantric Syllabic Code*, Lahore 1938.

Visnu saṃhitā, ed. by T. Ganapati Sastri, Trivandrum Sanskrit Series, No. 85, Trivandrum 1925.

Waddel, L. Austine, 'Lamaism in Sikkim' in *Sikkim Gazetter*, Calcutta 1884, 241-392; *Buddhism in Tibet or Lamaism*, W.H. Allen and Co., London 1895, repr., Dover Publication, New York 1972, 'Dhāraṇī or Indian Buddhist Protective Spells' in *Indian Antiquary*, XLIII, 1914, 37 ff; 'The Dhāraṇī cult of Buddhism: Its Origin Deified Literature and Images' in *Ostasiatasche Zeitschrift* I, 1921, 155-95; 'The Indian Buddhist Cult of Avalokita and His Consort Tārā' in *Journal of the Royal Asiatic Soceity*, 1894, 51-89.

Warrier, A.G. Krishna, trans, *The Śākta Upaniṣads*, Adyar Library and Research Centre, Madras 1967.

Wayman, Alex, *The Buddhist Tantras: Light on Indo-Tibetan Esoterism*, New York 1973; *Yoga of the Guhyasamāja Tantra*, Motilal Banarasidass, Delhi 1977; *Calming the Mind and Discerning the Real: Buddhist Meditation and the Middle View*, New York 1978; *The Enlightenment of Vairocana*, Book one, Motilal Banarasidass, Delhi 1992.

White, John (ed.), *Kuṇḍalinī: Evolution and Enlightenment*, Anchor Books, Garden City, New York 1979.

Wilson, Martin, *In Praise of Tārā: Songs to the Saviouress*, Wisdom, London 1986.

Woodroffe, John, *Shakti and Shakta*, Calcutta 1919, 8th ed., Ganesh and Co., Madras 1975; *Principles of Tantra*, Calcutta 1914, 1916, 5th ed., Ganesh and Co., Madras 1978; *Hymns to the Goddess*, Calcutta 1913; repr. Ganesh and Co., Madras 1964, *Karpurādi Stotra* 1922, repr. Ganesh and Co., Madras 1965. See Arthur Avalon.

Yeshe, Lama, *Introduction of Tantra: A Vision of Totality*, compiled and ed. by Jonathan Landaw, Wisdom, London 1987.

Yoginīhṛdayadīpikā of Amṛtānandanātha, ed. by Gopinath Kaviraj in Sarasvati Bhavana Series No. 7, Varanasi 1923.

Yoginītantra, published in Rasikmohan's *Vividha Tantra Saṃgraha*, Calcutta 1876.

Zimmer, H., 'Zur Bedeutung des Indischen Tantra' in *Eranos Jahrbuch* I, Zurich 1933, 9-94.